DIRECTING

FILM TECHNIQUES AND AESTHETICS

Third Edition

DIRECTING

FILM TECHNIQUES AND AESTHETICS

Third Edition

Michael Rabiger

Focal Press

An Imprint of Elsevier

AMSTERDAM BOSTON LONDON NEW YORK OXFORD PARIS
SAN DIEGO SAN FRANCISCO SINGAPORE SYDNEY TOKYO

Focal Press is an imprint of Elsevier.

Recognizing the importance of preserving what has been written, Elsevier prints its books on acid-free paper whenever possible.

Library of Congress Cataloging-in-Publication Data
Rabiger, Michael.
Directing : film techniques and aesthetics / Michael Rabiger.—3rd ed.
p. cm.
Includes bibliographical references and index.
ISBN 0-240-80517-8 (pbk. : alk. paper)
1. Motion pictures—Production and direction. 2. Motion pictures—Aesthetics. I. Title.

PN1995.9.P7R26 2003
791.43′0233′092—dc21

2003040846

British Library Cataloguing-in-Publication Data
A catalogue record for this book is available from the British Library.

The publisher offers special discounts on bulk orders of this book. For information, please contact:

Manager of Special Sales
Elsevier
200 Wheeler Road
Burlington, MA 01803
Tel: 781-313-4786
Fax: 781-313-4880

For information on all Focal Press publications available, contact our World Wide Web home page at: http://www.focalpress.com

10 9 8 7 6 5 4 3

Printed in the United States of America

In fond memory of my teacher and mentor
Peter Snape (1925–1997).
His recognition nearly half a century ago
made this book possible.

CONTENTS

PART 5: PREPRODUCTION

PART 6: PRODUCTION

PART 7: POSTPRODUCTION

PART 8: CAREER TRACK

INTRODUCTION

Here is a practical, comprehensive directing manual that speaks directly to those who like to learn by doing. No matter what genre or screen medium you work in, and whether you are learning inside an educational institution or out of one, this new edition will occupy your head, heart, and hands with meaningful work.

Happily, new digital technology is making ever more practical the flexible and personal approaches this book has always championed, and a formidable body of work by modern masters shows the artistic gains available from improvisatory approaches and smaller equipment. As Samira Makhmalbaf, the youngest director ever to present a work at Cannes, has said: "Three modes of external control have historically stifled the creative process for the filmmaker: political, financial, and technological. Today with the digital revolution, the camera will bypass all such controls and be placed squarely at the disposal of the artist." Now, she says, cinema has become simple again and accessible to all. And she is right.

WHAT CONCERNS THE DIRECTOR

With so many changes in technology, what should most concern a new director? No single book can attempt to cover everything. It seems clear from the plethora of unwatchable indie films that the conceptual and creative processes remain the toughest challenge, so these are this book's priority.

WHAT'S NEW IN THIS EDITION

This third edition is extensively revised and expanded in content. Naturally the creative implications of the new digital technology are much in evidence, but there are also new sections on the much-misunderstood subject of dramatic beats, dramatic units, and the three-act structure. There is an expanded screen grammar specifically for directors and more explicit information on the difference between neutrally recording a fictional story and telling it instead as a spirited screen storyteller. There are also new sections on the significance of the entrepreneurial producer; the fruitful triangular relationship possible between screenwriter, director, and producer; the significance of lines of tension in a scene and the potent but invisible axes a director must respect; the positive value of any documentary training to fiction makers; the increasingly valuable art of *pitching*, or orally proposing a story; the Dogme Group manifesto and the importance of setting creative limitations; the dangers of embedded values in filmmaking and the ethics of screen representation; sound design in screenwriting and beyond; and the prospectus and sample reel as tools of communication in fundraising. Also new is a section on right and wrong ways to subtitle.

There are entire new chapters on production design, breaking down the script, procedures and etiquette on the set, shooting location sound, script continuity, preproduction meetings, and working with a composer.

A NEW AGE

Today's films are more likely to thrust us into characters' subjective, inner lives using elliptical and impressionistic storytelling techniques. They are more inherently akin to music, employ a less linear narrative development, have more subjective points of view, and are more often driven by their characters' streams of consciousness. More fluid editing, sound design, and intelligently used music draw the audience into the visceral lives of the characters, as do the advances in picture and sound reproduction in people's homes. High-definition television and high-fidelity sound promise a cinema-quality experience from the couch.

The long-dominant mode of Hollywood objective realism is in decline, like the Hollywood studio system itself. But realism still dominates public taste and presents a huge challenge to a new director, so it remains more central to this book's educational purposes than I would prefer.

LEARNING METHODS AND OUTCOMES ASSESSMENT

Learning to make films is like learning a musical instrument. You can't do it with either hands or intellect alone. You need an informed heart, a feel for the other arts, and plenty of practice to internalize what you discover. For this reason the book urges voluminous practical work. Because the *why* of filmmaking is as important as the *how*, practice and self-development are integrated by a common sense film grammar based on everyday perceptual experience.

The projects and exercises, so important to actualizing and reinforcing learning, have brief conceptual instructions, technical and artistic goals, and outcomes assessment criteria to alert young directors and their teachers to their strengths and weaknesses. Modern education looks not just at what the teacher puts into the student but focuses now on defining and assessing the student's expected output. Students like the outcomes assessment method because it supplies an explicit inventory of what to aim for. Circling scores for each criterion produces a bar graph that reveals at a glance where the general areas of strength and weakness lie. Teachers and students can use these levels of success as the basis for a critical and constructive dialogue.

The assessment forms, formerly attached somewhat invisibly to the relevant projects, are now gathered together in Appendix 1 (and can also be found at this book's companion web site, *www.focalpress.com/companions/0240805178*).

This makes the way outcomes assessment methods work more evident and shows by example how they can be written to cover any kind of project or exercise. Also, Appendix 2 contains the Form and Aesthetics Questionnaire, which will yield a useful overview of any project—past, present, or future.

PREPARATION VERSUS EXECUTION

You may wonder why a production manual devotes 16 chapters to the thought and activities prior to preproduction. The answer comes from decades of teaching and will be reiterated by anyone of similar immersion: most of the time, when fiction screen works fail they do so not because they are badly filmed but because the conceptual infrastructure to every aspect of the work is weak or nonexistent:

- The story's world and its characters are not credible or compelling (which requires lots of work to understand the processes of human perception, story structure, dramaturgy, actors, and acting).
- There is no unity, individuality, or force of story concept (which means developing energy and originality in the writing, something worthwhile and deeply felt to say, and a strong awareness of whatever in form, dramaturgy, or sound and visual design can effectively launch a given idea in a fresh and fitting cinematic form).

New students dive into learning screen techniques and technology in the belief that only the mastery of hardware separates them from directing. But this is to confuse learning a language with storytelling. Language *facilitates* telling stories, but learning Russian, for example, won't qualify you to captivate an audience. Narrative skill in the dense and deceptive medium of film is a rare and little-understood accomplishment. If it comes, it's the result of completing a quantity and variety of creative and analytic work (all represented in this book) and from learning to think as a committed screen artist. Aspiring directors will advance only if they come to grips with the notion that their artistic identity as a filmmaker is part of a lifelong endeavor that reaches into every aspect of their lives. To the fun of practicing production crafts, then, you must add the pain and effort it takes to assimilate the purposes and limitations of screenwriting; aesthetics and their association with authorship; textual structure and interpretation; acting and actors; and wise leadership of an ensemble, beginning with thorough, purposeful, and demanding rehearsals.

Many beginners view all this reluctantly or impatiently, finding it unfamiliar, fuzzy, and threatening to the ego. This, however, is the hidden four-fifths of the iceberg and requires more explanation than do shooting and editing, which today's young people accomplish so easily and well. Hence, those 16 chapters.

FILM'S ARTISTIC PROCESS ENHANCED

The organization of this book suggests a rather idealized, linear process for film production, but this is to help you find information in a hurry. In practice, the process is organic, messy, and circular. Everything is connected to everything else and nothing done early ever seems finished or foreclosed. The director must be ready to improvise, solve problems collaboratively with cast and crew, and see crises not as mortal blows to the master plan but as opportunities in heavy disguise. This guerilla approach to telling stories on the screen—normal in documentary but antithetical to the assembly line traditions of the features business—allows the low-budget independent to prosper and can lead directly to cutting-edge creativity in film art. This is strikingly apparent in the digitally enabled work of Mike Figgis, Steven Soderbergh, the Danish Dogme Group (principally Lars Von Trier and Thomas Vinterberg), Wim Wenders, Spike Lee, Michael Winterbottom, Gary Winock, Rick Linklater, and many others. For speed and convenience in compositing, George Lucas shot his *Star Wars: Episode II Attack of the Clones* using high-definition (HD) digital camcorders, and he came out a convert to HD, having shot the equivalent of 2 million feet of film in a third less shooting time and with $2.5 million saved in film costs.

LOCATING THE HELP YOU NEED

When any aspect of production reveals specific difficulties, try solving your problem by going to:

- The checklist for the part that concentrates on that stage of production
- The chapters handling that area of activity, via the Table of Contents for the part
- The Index
- The Glossary
- The Bibliography
- The Internet. Though a Web site guide is included, Web sites die and resurrect with bewildering speed, so be prepared to use a good search engine, such as Google, to flush out sources of information. As always, cross check any important information with other sources.

THANKS

Anybody who writes a book like this does so on behalf of the communities to which they belong. These, in my case, number at least four—my college, international colleagues in the film teaching profession, my publishers, and my friends and family.

Many ideas in this book grew from teaching relationships at Columbia College Chicago and New York University with past and present students who are now so numerous their names would halfway fill this book. I also benefited inestimably from interaction, advice, and criticism from many dear colleagues, most recently at Columbia's Film/Video Department. Particular help for this and previous editions came from Doreen Bartoni, Robert Buchar, Judd Chesler, Gina Chorak, Dan Dinello, Chap Freeman, T.W. Li, Emily Reible, Joe Steiff, and Diego Trejo, Jr.

That I mostly kept my sanity during four years of upheaval and changes as chair of the Film/Video Department at Columbia College Chicago was particularly owing to Ric and Eileen Coken, Charles Celander, Joan McGrath, Margie Barrett, Sandy Cuprisin, and Micheal Bright. Thanks also to Wenhwa Ts'ao, Chris Peppey, T.W. Li, Joan McGrath, and Sandy Cuprisin for help finding pictorial matter. Successive administrations have given our department an extraordinary level of faith and material support, in particular Executive VP Bert Gall, Dean Caroline Latta, Dean Doreen Bartoni, Provost Steve Kapelke, and three successive presidents—the late Mike Alexandroff, who founded the college in its modern form, and his successors Dr. John B. Duff and Dr. Warrick L. Carter.

I also want to thank my successor Bruce Sheridan, whose experience, energy, wit, and wisdom in the chairmanship are taking the 2,100-strong Film/Video Department community to new levels of achievement.

I learned greatly from the many impassioned teaching colleagues I encountered in the 14 countries where I have taught and from all the good work done by those who organize and attend the conferences at CILECT (the International Film Schools Association) and UFVA (University Film & Video Association of North America). All of us, I think, feel we are slowly coming to grips with the octopus of issues involved in teaching young people how to act on audiences via the screen. Particularly must I thank Nenad Puhovsky, Henry Breitrose, Joost Hunningher, and Aleksandar Todorovic for the invaluable help I got from their 200-page report on behalf of CILECT's Standing Committee on New Technologies. Their report, and much else of value, can be found on CILECT's Web site (www.cilect.org).

Enduring thanks to my publishers, Focal Press. Thanks to Ken Jacobson for advice on the book's original substance, and Karen Speerstra, Marie Lee, and most recently Elinor Actipis for unfailing support, encouragement, and great publishing work.

Among friends and family in Chicago, thanks go to Tod Lending for teaching me more about dramatic form and Milos Stehlik of Facets Multimedia for pictorial assistance. Thanks also go out abroad to my son Paul Rabiger of Cologne, Germany for our regular phone discussions and advice on composing for film, and to my daughters Joanna Rabiger of Austin, Texas and Penelope Rabiger of Jerusalem for far-ranging conversations on film, education, and much else. Over four decades their mother, Sigrid Rabiger, has also influenced my beliefs through her writings and practice in art therapy and education.

Lastly, undying appreciation to Nancy Mattei, my wife and closest friend, who puts up with the solitary and obsessive behavior by which books of any sort take shape and whose support and valuations keep me going and keep me right.

To anyone unjustly overlooked, my apologies. After all this help, any mistakes are mine alone.

Michael Rabiger, Chicago, 2003

PART 1

ARTISTIC IDENTITY

CHAPTER 1

THE JOB OF THE DIRECTOR

You are in love with the movies and want to try your hand at directing. This book, written by someone who has spent many years helping people try their wings, will help you. Affordable technology for learning by experiment is available and conditions for learning have never been better. Now the only way to find out if and where you belong in filmmaking is to roll up your sleeves and do it. This book is written with the firm belief that you learn best by doing, either in a film school with fellow students or out of it working with a few friends.

Becoming a good screen director demands a strong, clear identity in relation to the world around you and a clear grasp of what drama is. Developing these will figure very largely in this book. You will need other skills, too, but let's first examine the job and what the working environment is currently like for filmmakers. Whenever I speak of filmmakers and making film, I include film and video production together because each is just a delivery medium drawing on a common screen language.

THE CINEMA NOW

Cinema, at the start of the 21st century, is indisputably the great art form of our time, the preferred forum for mass entertainment, and a major conduit for ideas and expression. Occupying a status formerly monopolized by the novel, the screen is now where dreams of every shape, hue, and meaning leap into the public mind—crossing language and cultural barriers to excite hearts and minds as art must, and as no medium has ever done before.

The cinema has earned this place because it is a collective, not an individualist's, medium. Cinema production is a place of encounter, collaboration, and compromise among writers, dramatists, actors, image and illusion makers, choreographers, art directors, scene builders, sound designers, make-up artists and costumers, musicians, editors, artists, and technicians of every kind. They willingly yield the greater part of their lives to serve the screen story in its many incarnations. To complete this Noah's Ark, there are distributors, exhibitors, business people, financiers, and speculators. They make filmmaking possible because they make sure it finds its audience, nationally and internationally.

The medium gets its strength from the interplay at the center of its process. Ingmar Bergman likens film production to the great undertaking in the Middle Ages when large teams of craftsmen gathered to build the European cathedrals. These were specialists who didn't even leave us their names. The cinema, says Bergman, is a collective endeavor with shared creativity out of which something emerges that is greater than the sum of its parts. A similar process generated most of the early theater and dramatic poetry whose inheritance, if you think of the Arthurian legends and the tradition of romantic love, we are still using. So the artist as an embattled individualist is a very recent invention and is not the only or best source for enduring artwork.

LEARNING ENVIRONMENT

There has never been a better time to study filmmaking. The film industry thoroughly accepts that filmmakers of new talent will emerge from film schools and that these students are more broadly educated, versatile, and capable of radically developing the cinema than any preceding generation. Film school alumni have created such a stellar track record that the question is no longer *whether* the aspiring filmmaker should go to film school but only which one would be suitable.

Film schools, so recently founded in comparison with those for other arts, are usually good at teaching history and techniques. The better institutions try to liberate their students to recognize their own experience and to express their sharpest perceptions of the world around them. These schools are likely to be those that include practicing professionals among their teachers, and place their best students as interns in professional production.

That said, you can also teach yourself and develop a style and a film unit without any film school backing. It's difficult, but so is anything worthwhile. Novices now have access to low-cost video equipment and stand in relation to filmmaking as would-be musicians stood in relation to sound in the 1960s. From such unprecedented access flowed a revolution in popular music that, in its turn, accelerated profound social changes.

FILMMAKING TOOLS

The changing tools of filmmaking make this book's approach ever more practical. Digital camcorders, digital audiotape (DAT) sound recorders and computerized editing have slashed the cost of hands-on experience and massively accelerated the student's learning curve. Films shot and postproduced in the digital domain are presently transferred at great expense to 35 mm film for projection in cinemas, but electronic projectors are appearing that improve on many aspects of 35 mm. There is no weave in the image, colors do not deteriorate, the print does not become scratched, and it cannot break. There are no changeovers between reels, and focus does not rely on the judgment of a projectionist. Sound is phenomenal, and the entire show can be delivered to the home or cinema via satellite, saving a fortune in shipping. Multiple languages are easier to support, and cheating by exhibitors and piracy of bootleg copies will be more difficult. The present barrier is the high cost of equipping new theaters, but this is a repeat of the cost of re-equipping cinemas for sound in the 1920s. Digital systems will some day soon rival the 65 mm Imax experience, which draws crowds with the sheer exhilaration of the cinematic experience, just as they first came at the start of the twentieth century.

As film production has moved beyond the control of the studio system, so film financing and distribution show strong signs of becoming decentralized and more like book publishing. With more diverse distribution available via videotape, DVD, and movies on demand through the Internet or satellite, more productions will be "narrowcast" to more specialized audiences, just as book production has been for centuries.

INDEPENDENT FILMMAKING

THE GOOD NEWS

The decade of the 1990s saw a steep rise in the number of "indie" or independently financed and produced productions, and their Mecca was the Sundance Film Festival. These movies now outpace studio productions in number and sometimes quality, originality, and prizes, too. Digital production is sometimes replacing film because of its lower costs and greater flexibility. Notable cinema productions shot digitally include: Thomas Vinterberg's *The Celebration* (1998), Lars von Trier's *The Idiots* (1998), Mike Figgis' *Time Code* (2000) and *Hotel* (2001), Spike Lee's *The Original Kings of Comedy* (2000), Rick Linklater's *Waking Life* (2001), Steven Soderbergh's *Full Frontal* (2002), and George Lucas' *Star Wars II* (2002). Lucas used Sony CineAlta high-definition video cameras and pronounced them not only trouble-free but so liberating that he could not imagine returning to shooting on film (Figure 1–1). You can find more news about digital filmmaking at *www.nextwavefilms.com.*

THE BAD NEWS

These encouraging signs are offset by the mournful fact that most independent features are unwatchable and never find a distributor. Better access to the screen has produced a *karaoke* situation in which anyone can stand up and sing—though the audience may not stay to listen. In Tommy Nguyen's *American Cinematographer* article "The Future of Filmmaking" (September 19, 2000), cinematographer after cinematographer affirms a similar belief: Cinema tools will change, but the art of the moving image is already well established and controlling it can only improve. One after another they stress how necessary good stories are and that they are in terribly short supply.

And so you and I squarely face the problem that follows any liberation: How to use the new freedom effectively. How to prepare, how to exercise your

FIGURE 1–1

The Sony CineAlta HD CAM ® HDW-F900 high-definition video camera.

capacities, how to train for the marathon. How not to run over the cliff with the herd. That's what this book is about. Let's look at some sobering facts:

- Most film school recruits are unduly influenced by the occasional *wunderkind* who leaps, fully armed, from school to public prominence, and film schools capitalize on this.
- Nothing is more hazardous to your future than a meteoric start.
- Everyone entering film school wants to direct. Baptismal ordeals show most that they belong in one of the other craft skills.
- The insights and skills required to be a minimally competent director are staggering.
- Becoming good enough to direct films for a living is a long, uncertain, and uphill process.
- Most film school alumni who eventually direct take a decade or two working their way up from editing, camerawork, or writing.
- It takes this long because directing requires a knowledge of life that most 20-somethings do not have until they are 40-something or more.
- Virtually nobody gets financial backing to direct without first having proved themselves in one of the allied crafts.
- Reaching professional competency as a director takes about the same amount of work and dedication as becoming a concert musician. Many are called, few are chosen.

Like any long journey, you've got to really like the trek. Before you commit time and funds to getting an education in filmmaking, read this book very carefully, beginning immediately with Part 8: Career Track. Absorbing what it says will prepare you to use your whole period of education in preparation for work. Following what everyone else says or does by not planning ahead is not a wise move because it guarantees you won't be distinguishable. Most people follow along, delay making important preparations and choices, and wake up to the realities in the last year of their studies, or later still.

WHO CAN DIRECT

Directors come in all human types—tall, short, fair, dark, introvert, extrovert, loquacious, taciturn, male, female, gay, straight. Today anyone with something to say and access to modest production equipment can direct a movie of some kind—that is no longer the barrier. To be successful means having inventiveness and tenacity, an ability to get the best out of a team, a strong sense of vision, and an abiding love for the process of making films. In a multi-disciplinary medium requiring strong social skills, as well as intellect and character, it is seldom possible to predict who will emerge as truly capable. More men than women presume to have these qualities, but happily this is changing. Film school entry tests are far from definitive, as many a working director will attest. If you are turned down and deeply want to direct, find another way. Do not give up.

The best way to prove your capacity is to just do it. Making cinema, like swimming or dancing, is not something you can learn from theory but something you have to do over and over again—until you get it right.

This book assumes you are without prior knowledge of the component crafts, so you will need to acquire some screencraft basics. It contains many projects to develop your directing skills, but no instructions for operating equipment. For this, many good manuals exist (see the Bibliography). Don't listen to those who say you must learn the tools before you can have anything to say. People, not tools, make films. In the beginning, don't agonize over form, techniques, or polish; if you can find something to say, you will figure out better and better ways to say it.

You will have to reverse the abstract, literary thinking of a lifetime, and instead practice getting strongly visualized stories together. This material—usually, though not invariably, a screenplay—will need to be thoroughly felt, comprehended, and believed in. Then you will need a competent crew, a well-chosen cast, and the skills and strength of character to get the best out of everybody. You will need to understand actors' frames of reference and the various states of consciousness they pass through. For directing means bringing together people of very different skills and mentality. It will be a struggle to keep everyone going while you hold onto your initial vision.

A good director knows how to keep demanding more from the cast and crew while making each person feel special and valuable to the whole. After shooting, you need the skill, persistence, and rigor in the cutting room to work and rework the piece with your editor until the notes have become the concerto. Never *ever* let anyone tell you that you do or don't have talent. Patience and hard work are infinitely more important than talent, which is always ephemeral.

For all this you need the self-knowledge, humility, and toughness that commands respect in any leader. You will have to know your troops, lead by example, and understand how to fulfill the emotional, psychological, and intellectual needs of the common person—that is, your audience. Happily, the members of that audience are a lot like you.

Expecting to find all these qualities in one human being is a tall order. The beginner confronting all those skills often feels like an inept juggler. Your first efforts (of which you were so proud) soon embarrass you with their flat writing, amateurish acting, and turgid dramatic construction. If you are doing this outside a film community, reliable guidance may be hard or even impossible to find.

This book, thoroughly and exhaustively used, can be your best friend because it has advice, examples, and explanations to cover most predicaments. It cannot, however, provide the perseverance and faith in yourself that characterize those who prosper in the arts and crafts. This you must supply.

PARTICULARLY FOR THE EXCLUDED

Like many desirable professions, filmmaking has long been a white male preserve, but women and minorities are infiltrating and bringing their blessedly different ways of seeing. Is this you? My hope is that your sensibility and real-life experience will dislodge the sick preoccupation with power and violence that presently dominates mass culture. Apologists claim that entertainment does not lead society but reflects it. Were this true, advertising would fail. Of course appetites can be created by endlessly repeating the same ideas and iconic images. But just as pornography temporarily fascinates societies newly emerged from repression, so the present obsession with violence could have something to do with widespread feelings of powerlessness. After the real violence of September 11, 2001, in New York, guns disappeared from American cinema advertising and reappeared in Afghanistan. Coincidence?

In every era it will take new voices and new visions to show us who we really are. Are you ready?

WITH LOW BUDGETS IN MIND

Most who use this book will be working with modest equipment and slender budgets. Take this as a badge of honor, for you can still make excellent films without elaborate settings or expensive props, costumes, equipment, or special effects. The ability to make much out of little is a vital one and shows up throughout cinema history. For this reason, most film examples in this book come from classic or modern low-budget cinema.

SHORT FILMS OR LONGER?

Anyone serving on a festival jury discovers that most films bare their shortcomings in two or three shots. Within as many minutes the whole panoply of strengths and weaknesses is complete. The jury wonders (sometimes aloud) why people don't stop at 5 minutes instead of taking a mind-numbing 50. The message is clear: Short films require their makers to conquer the full range of production, authorship, and stylistic problems poetically and in a small compass. The economy lies in shooting costs and editing time, not in brainwork, for you must still establish characters, time, place, and dramatic situation and set tight limits on the subject. These are tough skills to learn. They take much thought and practice but pay off handsomely as you approach longer forms. Poets always do well in longer forms, whether they are plays, novels, or films.

Getting your work seen is the precursor to getting your abilities valued, and two good short films have far more chance of a festival showing than one long one. Film schools are not the best place to learn brevity because students and faculty alike are drawn to the medium by features, and film schools mostly use features as examples. Students not attuned to the merits of brevity invariably make what I think of as zeppelins—enormously long films without weight, beauty, or agility. There is a special section, called Short Forms, in Chapter 16 with a list of suggested films. Short films, whether you like it or not, will be your calling card, so you may want to look for recent examples on the Internet.

FILM OR VIDEO?

Passions still run high over what medium to use, so it is worth running over the pros and cons—especially as they affect the way you learn. Shooting a feature film on high-definition (HD) video saves 20–35% of the time and some of the money needed to use camera stock. For features, 35 mm film is still the preferred camera medium, even though postproduction now takes place almost wholly in the digital domain. Film currently records a more detailed image and has a nicer look, but this superiority only shows up in a well-equipped, well-run film theater, and most are neither. Because so much viewing is in the home and on video, the superiority of film is a moot point unless all the other attributes such as writing, acting, and staging are of an equally high order. Directing methods are identical for film and video, so only the scale of operations and path to completion are likely to differ.

Historically, anything shot on film has been widely regarded as of higher *class* than video, so film has been the medium of choice for the festival circuit (where most short films begin and end their careers). But as videomakers learn to shoot and edit to cinema standards of economy, this prejudice is waning. Audience consumption patterns will inevitably influence future production methods. Pornography, for instance, is a huge market that is cheaply produced using small digital cameras. Customers don't expect spectacle because their interests are, um, strictly local. For the large, bright, detailed image that characterizes the cinema, film has been a necessity, but the latest video projection is comparable to, or even exceeds, 35 mm quality. Should movies on demand really arrive—downloadable from satellite, cable, or the Internet—the cinema experience will become ever more widely and cheaply available, and primarily in the home. Home theaters will draw audiences away from the cinema unless the theaters can indeed offer the kind of spectacular experience that Imax now does. Though cinemas may have to specialize in spectacle, more and more films will be needed to feed the rest of the entertainment monster, and they will have to be made on ever lower budgets. Those who do well in the low-budget area will graduate to larger budget productions.

Let's look at the ground level, where you come in. Digital video allows the filmmaker-in-training to shoot ample coverage and edit to broadcast standards without much regard for expense. The major costs are acquiring the story and paying the cast and crew. This is revolutionary because it democratizes film production. Though 35 mm film is still special and wonderful, the digitizing, editing, and *matchback* process (in which digital numbers become the sole guide to cutting the negative) can be complex and prone to irreversible mistakes. Until recently, most video editing was offline, that is, editing was done initially at a low resolution to cram a lot of screen time on a restricted computer hard disk. You worked to produce an artistically viable fine cut but of degraded technical quality. Once this was achieved, an *Edit Decision List* (EDL) was used to re-digitize selected sections of the camera's original tape at high resolution to produce a fine-quality final print.

With computer storage capacities going up and prices coming down, it's now quite possible to store a whole production digitally in the highest quality form and edit a broadcast-quality version in one process. This means that with some experience and a lot of drive, you can use small-format digital video to produce sophisticated work. This you can use to argue persuasively for support in a more expensive format like HD video or film. What matters most is getting as much filmmaking experience as possible.

WHY USING HOLLYWOOD AS A MODEL CAN'T WORK FOR BEGINNERS

To appreciate how you learn best, let's compare the professional feature team's process with that of a lean, independent production. The differences show up in schedules and budgets. Priorities in feature films are mostly set by economic factors, not artistic ones: Scriptwriting is relatively inexpensive and can take time, while actors, equipment, and crew are very costly. Actors are cast for their ability to produce something usable, immediate, and repeatable. Often the director must shoot a safe, all-purpose camera coverage that can be "sorted out in the cutting room" afterward.

Locked into such a production system, the director has little option but to fight narrowly for what he (only rarely she) thinks is achievable. It is hardly surprising that Hollywood-style films, too profitable to change from within, are often as packaged and formulaic as supermarket novels, and reflect this onscreen. A box office success can return millions to its backers in a few weeks, so a producer will sooner back the standard process than the new or the personal.

Consider how professionals acquire and maintain their craft skills. During a feature shoot, about 100 specialists carry forward their particular part of the communal task, each having begun as an apprentice in a lowly position and having worked half a lifetime to earn senior levels of responsibility. Many come from film families and absorb the mindset that goes with the job with their orange juice. Apprenticeship is a vital factor in the continuity of skills, but it's also a conditioning force that deeply discourages self-evaluation and change. None of this is evident to the newcomer, or to the old-timer who grew up in the industry. Both think a film school should naturally emulate the professional system. But it cannot and should not.

Production aspect	90-minute, low-budget professional feature	Typical 30-minute student film
Script development period	6 months–several years, innumerable drafts	2–6 months, probably two drafts only
Preproduction period	4–12 weeks	3–5 weeks
Rehearsal period	Little or none	0–7 days
Shooting period	6–12 weeks	7–15 days
Postproduction period	4–6 months	3–14 months
Format	35 mm	16 mm or DVCAM
Budget	$8 million	$35,000

FIGURE 1–2

Typical professional and student productions compared.

Take a look at the beginner's production schedule in Figure 1–2. The big giveaway is the postproduction period. Enormous time and effort is spent in the cutting room trying to recover from problems embedded in the script (beyond the writer's or director's experience), inadequate acting (poor casting and/or insufficient rehearsal), and inconsistent shooting (hasty, too much coverage early, or too little later). With this example I mean only to warn, not to discourage or disparage. The poor director had to control a slew of unfamiliar variables and could not have helped but underestimate the process.

VITAL DIFFERENCES FOR THE LOW-BUDGET FILMMAKER

Because the low-budget (or no-budget) production seldom has a wide choice of crew or actors, the director must use methods that shape non-professionals into a well-knit, accomplished team. Non-professional actors need extended rehearsals in which to develop empathy with their characters and the confidence and trust in the director that alone give their performances conviction and authority.

Perhaps you have seen these masterpieces in international cinema that use non-professional actors:

Italy

- Luchino Visconti: *La Terra Trema* (1948)
- Vittioria De Sica: *The Bicycle Thief* (1948), *Umberto D* (1952)
- Francesco Rosi: *Salvatore Giuliano* (1961)

France

- Robert Bresson: *Pickpocket* (1959); *Balthazar* (1966), *Mouchette* (1967)

Iran

- Abbas Kiarostami: *Where is the Friend's House?* (1987); *Taste of Cherry* (1997)
- Bahram Beizai: *Bashu, the Little Stranger* (1991)
- Mohsen Makhmalbaf: *Gabbeh* (1996)
- Jafar Panahi: *The White Balloon* (1995)
- Bahman Ghobadi: *A Time for Drunken Horses* (2000)

Extraordinary performances in these films are from non-professional actors, some of whom are Iranian or Kurdish villagers, nomadic tribespeople, or Italian peasants. Under such circumstances the director cannot afford to be immovable about the script: Cast limitations require that it be responsive to the actor rather than vice versa. Strictly speaking, a script is only a blueprint and by its literary nature impossible to fulfill except through intelligent (which means flexible) translation. You can minimize these shortcomings by choosing a subject and treatment that require no elaborate events or environments. You can schedule more time for rehearsal (if you know how to use it), and so on. But setting the whole low-budget situation alongside big-industry norms, it is overwhelmingly apparent that low-budget filmmakers absolutely must work differently, set different priorities, and use special strategies if they are to convert initial handicaps into advantages.

ALTERNATIVE ROUTES IN THIS BOOK

To aim at professional-level results, you must use trial and error as a developmental process and find strength from experiment. As we shall see, a convincing human presence on the screen is only achieved (by amateur and professional actor alike) when *the director can see the actors' problems and remove the blocks causing them.* Left undisturbed, these obstacles always sabotage the entire film, no matter how glossy the rest of the production process might be.

The development processes outlined in this book create bonds among members of the ensemble and give the director and writer (if they are indeed two people rather than one) a positive immersion in the singularities of each cast member. The director must, in turn, be ready to adapt and transform the script to capitalize on cast members' individual potentials. What the Hollywood filmmaking army does with its marines and machines can be matched if the low-budget filmmaker enters the fray as a guerrilla combatant using cautious, oblique, and experimental tactics. Once this principle of organic, mutual accommodation is accepted, the rest of the process follows logically and naturally.

Actually, there is nothing in this book that is radical or untried. A little reading will show how similar strategies have served major names like Allen, Altman, Bergman, Bresson, Cassavetes, Fassbinder, Fellini, Herzog, Leigh, Loach, Resnais, Soderbergh, and Tanner, as well as the other directors mentioned previously who chose to use non-professional casts.

ABOUT DRAMATIC PRESENTATION AND DIRECTING

The director's main task in relation to actors is often misunderstood. It is not to spur actors into doing the extraordinary but rather to give feedback and remove myriad psychological and other obstacles. These block both the ordinary and the extraordinary from happening. Effective screen acting lies not in a range of arcane techniques but in their absence. When an actor is relaxed, honest to his or her emotions, and free of misconceptions, he or she is no longer acting but *being*, a far more powerful condition. A misguided self-image, for instance, can put actors' attentions in the wrong place and make them behave unnaturally.

The normal psychological defenses that everyone develops are therefore a major barrier to relaxed acting, and even more so are popular ideas about acting itself.

Novice actors in particular—and even trained actors who should know better—often feel they must produce something heightened to merit attention. Instead of just *being,* players discharge their responsibility onscreen by "signifying," which means projecting thought and emotion. This is thought-laden and artificial and precludes any of the true experiencing that makes a stage or screen performance "live." Self-critical and divided even as he or she acts, another part of the actor anxiously watches, criticizes, and plans the next phase of the performance. The camera pitilessly reveals the truth about this divided and unnatural state of affairs. Michael Caine presents some compellingly illustrated arguments on this and other aspects of his craft in *Acting in Film: an Actor's Take on Movie-Making* (BBC TV tape, New York: Applause Theatre Publishers, 1990).

When actors "signify," it is not necessarily because of inexperience or misguided effort. The impulse to stylize dramatic material has a long and respectable history in live theater where performance is often non-naturalistic. Until modern staging and lighting arrived in the 19th century, stage performance made little attempt to be naturalistic. Greek drama was played in masks that concealed the actors' psychological identity and projected archetypal human qualities like nobility, wisdom, or greed. Japanese *Kabuki* theater used elaborate, ritualized costumes and an operatic verbal delivery that, as in Western opera, invites the audience to attach to the groundswell of human passions beneath the surface. Likewise, medieval Christian mystery plays, mime, mummers, and the Italian *commedia del arte* all employed traditional characters, gestures, episodes, and situations. All of this was deliberately non-realistic and not concerned with the actors' psychological identities.

Why should the person of the actor be concealed, yet the interpretation of a stock character be so prized by audiences? Prior to the Renaissance the very idea of individual worth was a vanity amounting to blasphemy against God's purpose. The transience of life and the religious tenets that explained this bleak state of affairs made people see themselves as ephemera in a God-determined whole. A life was just a brief thread in God's great tapestry, with each individual destined to carry out a role allotted by accident of birth but conditioned by such human constants as ambition, compassion, love, and jealousy. Realistic presentation, at least to a small audience, was never impossible, but it's clear that verisimilitude and psychological accuracy were irrelevant to the predicament audiences knew as their own.

With the focus shifting toward the potential of the individual that began during the Renaissance, and particularly after the impact of Darwin in the 19th century, audiences were increasingly interested in investigating the significance of the individual life and willing to see it as a struggle for survival, rather than as a temporary stay during which to earn merit for an afterlife. Writers increasingly reflected ideas about the individual's inner life and about his (rarely her) individually wrought destiny. Acting styles were, however, slower to change and remained declamatory and stylized as late as the early phase of the movies.

In early 20th-century Russia, just after the revolution, came a time of bold rethinking in the arts, allied with advances in psychology. Stanislavsky developed the modern theory of the actor's consciousness that underlies any distinctive performance. The advent of the sound cinema brought audiences eyeball to eyeball with the grisly remains of feigned naturalism, and both actors and dramatists were forced to give new attention to what could pass as a credible human interchange.

Modern audiences now expect screen characters to be as believable as people captured unaware in a documentary. So unless a film strives for a subjectively perceived environment (as in German Expressionist cinema of the 1920s and 1930s or any of the non-realist modern genres such as horror or slapstick comedy), audiences expect to encounter real people behaving realistically in real settings. This, so easy to understand, is exceptionally hard to produce.

Rightly or wrongly, the preponderance of cinema aims at the appearance of verisimilitude, so the student director's priority should be to handle realism. Done well, it looks effortless, and students make the fatal mistake of thinking this must come from using a professional camera. But a camera only magnifies: A good performance is made larger, and a bad one looks larger, too.

Filmmaking compels a circuitous artifice to arrive at the effortless and natural. With shooting fragmented by lighting changes, talent availability, and budget, cinema is not even a good training ground for actors. The best usually come from strong theater backgrounds, where the continuity of performance and the closed loop of communication with an audience have made them trust their own instincts. The film actor, on the other hand, must perform in fits and starts. No audience feedback is possible during filming because only the director, crew, and other actors are present. The actor must, in any case, dismiss the director and crew from consciousness while the camera is rolling.

Acting for the camera should be like living life without knowing you are watched. The camera sees everything, spying at close range upon characters in their most private and intense moments. Actors can afford no lapse in experiencing their characters' inmost thoughts and feelings. Such a lapse, called *losing focus*, is immediately visible. Focused actors can shut out the technical process. During his apprentice days, Aidan Quinn did an improvised scene of considerable power with a woman actor in a directing class of mine. It was taped documentary style (more about this later). During a long and very intense scene, the camera snaked around the actors and came within two or three feet of them. After the student director called "cut," the actors took deep breaths as they returned to the present, and then said, "We should have taped that one." They had been utterly unaware of the camera's presence.

As in documentary, the camera-as-witness and a determined director will compel actors to make a choice between focusing on tasks at hand or becoming disengaged and self-conscious. The actor either stands outside the situation and observes from a position of safety what is being presented (which is disastrous) or he or she jumps in and undergoes a series of actual and sometimes scary emotions that blot out everything extraneous to the character. Movie actors can seldom wear a mask, either actual or psychological. Instead they must go naked and merge with the part—whether that character is good or bad, attractive or ugly, intelligent or stupid. This does not mean that actors' intelligences are switched off. Far from it: Actors in focus are both inside their characters and still somewhat aware as a craftsperson from the outside.

Here we face a problem that is particularly acute in love scenes: how to behave spontaneously and have real emotions before camera and crew in take after take. This throws formidable demands upon the actor's concentration, ego, and self-assurance, for it is unacceptable to merely signify villainy, impersonate weakness, or mime erotic attraction. The actor has to dig deeply into his or her own emotional range in order to uncover whatever is demanded. Many are afraid, and all have areas of fear. Searching within for an "unpopular" or revealing emotion, the actor may have to confront embarrassing or even hateful aspects of the self. Ralph Fiennes, who so powerfully played the Nazi camp commander Amon Goeth in Spielberg's *Schindler's List* (1993), found his part emotionally excruciating because he despised his character so much. Some of the Polish extras hired to play townspeople are said to have wept after having to yell anti-Semitic abuse at actors playing Jewish prisoners.

A further threat to the actor's ego may be that of accepting and building upon critical feedback from an undemocratic audience of one: the director. A far-ranging, seemingly effortless performance onscreen will thus be the result of an extraordinarily disciplined mind drawing widely upon its owner's emotional experience. For actor and director to achieve such a performance, they must trust and respect each other as they navigate a minefield of fascinating problems together.

ON MASKS AND THE FUNCTION OF DRAMA

There is an important purpose behind stylized theater's masks and stock characterizations. By screening out the banal, psychological identity of the actors, these devices encourage us to fill in the details from our imaginations. This type of theater gives us characters held at a distance so we look not for specific human attractiveness or malevolence but for the immeasurably richer beauty and terror seen by our own imagining minds. Ancient dramatists discovered something the infant cinema has to learn—that dramatic art can only fulfill its potential if it evokes universals. It is insufficient to simulate reportage; it must evoke the audience's co-creation.

In various ways throughout this book I shall seek to demonstrate a curious and little-appreciated fact: *A cinema audience does not really go to see the film but goes to see into itself, to imagine, think, and feel as others may do. Its members go to become* other, *just for a while.* This is like the reader of a novel who reads not to see language or print, but to participate in that structured, waking, and intensely speculative dreaming that we call reading. Film, with its hypnotic appeal to the senses, has often been likened to dreaming.

Here we collide head-on with the cinema's limitation. The prosaic realism of the camera, showing literally and to the last open pore whatever is placed before it, constantly threatens to pull us away from myth and back into the material and banal. Used unintelligently, the camera conveys a glut of the real and lets nothing become metaphorical or metaphysical. This is a severe handicap for an art medium. Think of the phrase, "She was incomparably beautiful." How can

FIGURE 1–3

Carné's *Children of Paradise,* a story of unattainable love based on the Pierrot and Columbine archetypes (courtesy Museum of Modern Art/Film Stills Archive).

you possibly *show* incomparable beauty? Films that successfully break out of the stockade of realism always connect us to myth and archetype. These are the stock of tragi-comic human equations constructed somewhere in the distant past that unfailingly trigger our deeper emotions. The character of Garance in Marcel Carné's *The Children of Paradise* (1945) will be undyingly lovely as long as one print survives and one audience member lives to see her (Figure 1–3). This is not just because the actress, Arletty, is beautiful or because the black-and-white cinematography and the lighting are unearthly, but because her enigmatic character hides so much. She is the legendary character of Columbine reborn, the fickle, unattainable, free spirit whom poor Pierrot can never hold because he's too foolishly sincere and earthbound. In short, she evokes the poignancy of our own unattained loves.

DEVELOPING CINEMA ART

A progressive cinema activates the audience's imagination, opening up interior spaces and questions that can only be filled from the hearts and minds of the viewers. Here we are talking not just about withholding full perception but about a cinematic language that shows less so it can imply more about the crucial ambiguity of human character and theme. Only thus can a narrative direct the audience toward something of greater worth than the superficial, sensational, or polemical. We are talking about looks, glances, averted profiles, turned backs, enigmatic silences, the suggestive voices of nature, and of primeval landscapes inhabited or abandoned by humans. We are talking of a narrative art that can alert us to what exists at the very edges of our perception, and beyond.

The more the cinema invites the audience to dream, exercise their judgment, and draw on their own instincts, the more it approaches the emotional release of music or matches the intellectual power of literature.

The cinema is several arts rolled into one, and to develop your potential as an artist you need to look for component parts that lie outside cinema. You will have to step back in time to consider how other arts function and how they act upon us, and you will need strong, clear, and critical ideas about your contemporaries and their time. This, the core of artistic identity and the story material it chooses, will be the subject of the next two chapters.

THE *AUTEUR* AND AUTHORIAL CONTROL

This book, intended to take you from beginner to advanced levels of filmmaking, may seem to offer many encouragements to *auteur* filmmaking. This term was coined in the 1950s during the French New Wave and refers to the writer/director wanting to exercise an integrated control across the spectrum of the writing and realization processes. Such control can only be exercised when you have thoroughly internalized how work of depth and resonance is created, how screen works become individual, and how the narrative form itself might be expanded and developed.

In filmmaking of any technical complexity, the *auteur* concept is just that—a concept and not a reality. However, generations reared in the Romantic tradition of the artist as the isolated and controlling individualist have confused directing films with exercising total control. But how can a director control the characters as a novelist does while leading a team of near-equals?

Curiously, the nearest thing to *auteur* exists at the beginner level, when you can do it all yourself, and again—but differently—at the pinnacles of accomplishment in the world film industry. It doesn't hold in the middle ground. A typical evolution begins in film school where the filmmaker starts as a Renaissance figure: writing, shooting, and editing a tiny film. Then, wanting to produce more sophisticated work, he or she has to divide up the tasks among people specializing in one of several crafts. The director comes to specialize in, say, editing. Competently handled, this becomes his or her bridge into the film industry where our filmmaker initially makes a slender living as a freelancer. Eventually becoming a respected specialist, the director becomes known and established and his or her living less precarious. Through years of working and continuous learning, the drive to direct results in an opportunity, but early directing work is necessarily cautious and commercial, for death at the box office means plunging down the ladder again. With two or three modest successes, our director, like someone standing up in a boat, expands cautiously into more personally meaningful work. Even when limited by survival instincts and money interests to doing popular work, the astute director can flex artistic muscle and learn to control the medium. This is even true to a more limited degree in commercials.

As our greying director gains a mature command of the medium, and as the path of his or her life reveals what he or she has to say through the work, audiences begin to thrill to an exciting authorial identity at work. The filmmaker who in film school had total control over a very small film now has perceived control in an immensely expensive and popularly significant medium. The *auteur* seems to have re-emerged, driving a better car. In fact this same person is humbled from years of teamwork, and would be embarrassed to proclaim him or herself an *auteur*—even though the director will never have more authority. Those heartfelt thanks during Academy Awards given to the team are no meaningless ritual. They acknowledge the true source of creativity in a collaborative art form.

DRAMATURGY ESSENTIALS

BEATS, THE KEY TO UNDERSTANDING DRAMA

What drama is and how you make it are for some reason almost universally misunderstood. It's the single most disabling ignorance. The problem seems to arise from unexamined assumptions lodged, virus fashion, somewhere in popular culture. Faced with making drama, most people use it to make escapist entertainment or to supply moral improvement that illustrates right and wrong. Both approaches produce typical characters in typical situations who have typical problems. The result is depiction, explanation, and boring stereotypes but not drama. Ideologically driven work, unless artfully packaged to make it stylish, witty, futuristic, or frightening, is something audiences simply reject from long experience of clumsy salesmanship. They know it from preaching, political, polemic, and advertising propaganda.

In a more innocent time, medieval morality plays used this approach to elevate consciousness by showing the life of a saint dealing with temptation and the struggle between good and evil. Epic morality plays in the cinema, like George Lucas' *Star Wars* (1977) or Peter Jackson's 2001 adaptation of Tolkien's *Lord of the Rings,* rely on spectacle, a strong plot, and special worlds involving journeys in space, androids, puppets, creature costumes, or computer animation to deflect our attention from the simplistic nature of the underlying messages. By making their stories as epic fables, and by using distancing devices, the plots can be clothed, and we are ready to contemplate notions of courage, loyalty, power, evil, and the other grand abstractions that seem to perennially inhabit human imagination.

But the low-budget filmmaker faces more immediate and universal problems. Not having intergalactic space available, unable to afford even a spade-full of Middle Earth, he or she must instead find drama in the familiar. For this we turn to methods of finding drama all around us, which often means the problems of family and work relationships. This alerts us to the usefulness of the dramatic arc worked out by Greek playwrights 2500 years ago.

First, however, we should talk about the *dramatic unit* and its key component, the *beat*, which, by the way, has nothing to do with rhythm, nor does it, as some screenplay usages suggest, mean a moment of rest. A beat is a moment of dramatic fulcrum, a changed awareness following mounting pressures that have culminated in a changed balance of forces. That awareness can reside in one of the characters or in the audience when they understand more than the characters.

INTRODUCING THE GOBLIN TEASMADE™

This heartbeat of drama is something few people outside acting understand. When film students grasp what a beat is and how to use it, they have a sense of revelation. I will illustrate the notion of a beat by describing the action of that iconic gadget, still to be found in British bed and breakfast establishments, the Goblin Teasmade™. This automatic tea maker, first brought forth in 1902 by an enterprising gunsmith, is perfect to illustrate a dramatic unit culminating in a beat. Here's how it works:

> Before bed, the brave user fills a metal canister with water, puts dry tea in a china teapot, places them side by side and sets an electric clock for wake-up time. At the appointed hour, the clock silently turns on a heater. Initial rumbles soon turn to hissing as the water comes to a thunderous boil and decants itself by steam pressure into the adjacent teapot. The water, shifting weight from one vessel to the other, tilts a platform that turns off the current. The shaken guest then ventures out from under the covers to enjoy a fresh pot of tea.

Can you see the beat in this machine's performance? It's not when the current switches on, or when the water heats up, for those are the preliminaries. The beat comes at the moment of maximum threat when the shifting weight of water audibly switches the contraption off. At that moment the guests perceive the change that renders the machine harmless and themselves safe to enjoy another day. The full Goblin Teasmade story can be found at *www.teasmade.com/models.html/*, and yes, people collect these things.

Dramatic scenes center on someone with an *agenda*—something this person wants to get or do. Our guests, being British to the core, want to wake up to a nice hot cup of tea. The scene becomes dramatic because there is some degree of *conflict*. Getting tea means running the gauntlet of steam power, and the guests are intimidated by the explosive nature of the tea's arrival. Dramatic scenes require there to be a *problem*. The problem here is that a modest desire to have tea appears to be life-threatening, and the users suffer feelings of fight or flight that reach their zenith at the machine's moment of maximum activity. Now any *major change of consciousness* in one (or more) of the characters in a scene is a beat. The beat may be subtle, comic, or melodramatically extreme, but it represents a definite forward step up drama's developmental ladder. In the Teasmade scenario, the beat can be placed at the moment of realization that the threat has passed, tea is served, and the war is won.

Now see if you can spot the two beats in this little narrative:

> Two bleary and unshaven men, George and Phil, sprawl in a rusty Dodge full of empty beer cans as they drive across a hot, empty landscape. They notice that

> the car is running on Empty and hope to make it to a gas station they can see in the distance. But the old clunker coughs to a halt before they get there.
>
> Excitable George curses fate and pounds the steering wheel, but phlegmatic Phil steps into the blinding sunlight and walks to the gas station, where he asks for a can of gas.
>
> Don, the sleepy youth on duty, says they don't keep cans. So Phil and George, sweating and cursing, have to push the creaking behemoth to the pumps, where they fill up and then drive away exhausted.

What is the agenda, what is the problem, and where do the major changes of consciousness occur? George and Phil's *agenda* is simply to get wherever they are going. Their *problem* is that they are running out of gas and must find more. One *beat* happens when the car dies short of the gas station. This intensifies their *problem* and changes its nature. No longer can they get the car to the gas, now they must get gas to the car. George howls at the gods but Phil *adapts* to this, and puts a new plan in action—to get a little gas in a can so they can drive the last few hundred yards. The second *beat* comes when Phil realizes from Don's answer that his plan has failed, and he cannot take gas to the car. This raises the question, "Now what will they do?" It is answered when the narrative jumps forward to them implementing their solution, which is to push the car to the gas (the dramatic terminology is italicized so you see how it's used).

What is the *conflict* in this scene? Surely it's two shiftless guys up against the heavy, inert car. We see it played out as a Herculean struggle, and the *resolution* comes when they arrive panting at the pump and are able to fill the car and drive onward to further pursue their *agenda*.

We therefore have several *dramatic units*, each posing questions in the spectator's mind, which is always the key to effective drama:

> **Unit 1** establishes that they are running out of gas. Q: Will they make it? A: No, they won't, and the problem escalates when the car dies. This dramatic unit ends at the first beat when they realize this. Q: How will they solve the problem?
>
> **Unit 2** deals with the answer, how they *adapt* to the *new circumstances*. After some heated discussion involving mutual blaming, Phil steps out into the roasting heat and walks to the gas station. The next beat comes after a brief discussion during which Phil realizes that this plan won't work either. Q: What he will do?
>
> **Unit 3** jumps forward in time to show the answer: pushing the heavy car in stages into the forecourt where they can fill up. Q: Do they even have money to fill the tank?
>
> **Unit 4** is the answer, or *resolution* to the scene as they drive away with the problem solved. Q: What will happen to them next?

Notice the question-and-answer dialogue activated in the audience's minds. This is inherent in good storytelling and can be traced in any skillful telling of a joke. Laying bare the dramatic components of any scene means answering the following questions, which I have applied to our travelers George and Phil:

Main character is	[Phil, because he takes the main action and develops most]
Agenda is . . .	[To complete their journey]
Problem or issue is . . .	[George's lack of foresight means they run out of fuel]
Conflict is between . . .	[Between men and machine, between fallible, imperfect human beings and the unforgiving demands of their journey]
Complicating factors are . . .	[Car dies far from gas station, nobody can bring gas, and no help is available]
Beats are . . .	[See previous discussion in text]
Resolution is . . .	[Expending superhuman energy to refill tank, driving onward]
Dramatic units are . . .	[See previous discussion in text]

You can remember this with a mnemonic device in the letters bold-printed above: MAP CC BiRD.

A dramatic unit can be likened to the tree-felling process. It includes:

- Defining the problem (needing to cut down the tree)
- Overcoming the obstacles that prevent solving the problem (notching the trunk to make it fall the right way; axing or sawing through the trunk)
- Reaching the fulcrum point when the all-important change happens (the tree groans and begins to crash to the ground)
- Finding the resolution (the tree must now be dismantled and carted away—new conditions that inaugurate the next dramatic unit's set of problems)

Further dramatic units might be: struggling to turn the tree into planks; turning the planks into a home for a family; the family now having its particular problems, each of which will be dealt with in a new set of dramatic units.

Each dramatic unit has a *developmental arc* to completion. An example might be the moment in Mike Newell's *Four Weddings and a Funeral* (1994) when Charles realizes that Carrie has given him up and is going to marry her wealthy fiancé after all. The buildup of forces—establishing the situation, pressure building, then an irrevocable change of consciousness that produces new pressures—can only be accomplished if the characters have mismatched volitions and therefore harbor the potential for conflict. *Conflict is the very heart of drama*, and may be:

- External conflict between persons
- External conflict between persons and an environment
- Internal conflict between one part of a person and another

We will later use the material in this chapter to analyze drama and make analytical graphics. If you wish, look ahead to a page of screenplay analyzed and broken down in Chapter 24, Figure 24–1.

If you can apply these principles, no matter what genre, your work will be head and shoulders above most. One way to practice is to find examples of dramatic units in the everyday life around you.

BEATS HAVE NARRATIVE FUNCTIONS

Douglas Heil, in his article "Dramatic and Melodramatic Beat Structures"[1] (*Creative Screenwriting*, Volume 3, Number 4, January, 1997), has quoted Smiley's *Playwriting: The Structure of Action* (Prentice-Hall Inc., New Jersey, 1971) to show that beats can be characterized in three different ways: as plot beats, character attitude beats, and character thought beats. For our purposes, this means that each beat has a different implication for the narrative, and can be summarized thus:

1. *Plot Beats*	
a. Story beat	Advances the story, often connected to the disturbance or complication
b. Preparation beat	Establishes the beginning of a sequence or provides foreshadowing
c. Expository beat	Provides information about past circumstances
d. Crisis beat	Presents conflict
e. Mood beat	Establishes emotional circumstances
f. Reversal beat	Reverses action (This may well be associated with a plot point)
2. *Character Attitude Beats*	
a. Dispositional beat	Reveals a personality bent
b. Motivational beat	Expresses desires and provides reasons for actions
c. Deliberative beat	Expresses a reflective or emotional thought
d. Decisive beat	Indicates a significant decision
3. *Character Thought Beats*	
a. Emotive beat	Expresses what a character feels
b. Reflective beat	Expresses what a character concludes, considers, discovers
c. Informative beat	Presents information relevant to the (film)
d. Exaggerational beat	Expresses maximizing or minimizing of a topic
e. Argumentative beat	Contains conflict

Some of these are fine points and difficult to separate. What, for instance, is the difference between a deliberative beat involving thought and a character thought beat involving reflection? When these distinctions help you clarify the line of action through a scene, use them. When they simply pose boundary problems, don't. As always, we seek clarity of purpose, not taxonomy for its own reason.

In the same article, Heil draws a useful difference between drama and melodrama. He argues that drama is the modern day substitute for tragedy because

[1] My thanks to Doreen Bartoni for drawing my attention to this article.

today's social and psychological forces have replaced antagonists who are supernatural or divine. While drama has complex characters and may concern right fighting right, melodrama "assumes that right and wrong can easily be discerned in any situation." In melodrama, characters are often one-dimensional and pursuing their objectives without reflection or emotion. Drama is more likely to concern everyday conflicts arising from contradictory human desires and situations and to be at a lower pitch than melodrama.

THE THREE-ACT STRUCTURE

The classic *three-act structure* was developed in theater but can be applied to a whole film or the contents of a single sequence. Here are the divisions:

Act I establishes the *setup* (characters, relationships, and situation and dominant problem faced by the central character or characters).

Act II escalates the *complications* in relationships as the central character struggles with the obstacles that prevent him or her solving the main *problem*.

Act III intensifies the situation to a point of *confrontation*, and *resolves* it, often in a climactic way that is emotionally satisfying.

When you begin applying these divisions to films you see and to events you witness or experience, you will see how fundamental they are to all aspects of life.

CHAPTER 2

IDENTIFYING YOUR THEMES AS A DIRECTOR

DOING SOMETHING YOU CARE ABOUT

While you are learning how to use the screen you will want to shoot projects with some special meaning. Filmmaking is too long and arduous to commit your energies to doing just anything. In any case, people are attracted to the arts for good reasons. Human beings are by nature seekers, and though the nature and direction of everyone's quest is different, everyone seeks meaning in our brief sojourn. The more urgent and fatal the attraction to this journey, the more intense the work is likely to be. When we find an answer, it glitters—but only for a while. Soon we face the more profound question underlying it. The truths we find for ourselves are relative, never absolute. Perhaps it is the search more than the discoveries that lend us grace.

Make your earliest filmmaking not just an exercise in skills but *about* something. Whether you write your own stories, have someone else write a script, or choose something to adapt, you will always face these central questions: How am I going to use my developing skills in the world? What kind of subjects should I tackle? What can I be good at? What is my artistic identity?

Those with dramatic life experience (say, of warfare, survival in labor camps, or of being orphaned) seldom doubt what subject to tackle next. But for those of us whose lives seem ordinary, finding an identity for your undoubted sense of mission can be baffling. You face a conundrum; you can't make art without a sense of identity, yet it is identity itself you seek by making art.

Many people gravitate to the arts because they feel a need for self-expression or self-affirmation. This is treacherous ground, for it suggests that art and therapy are synonymous. They overlap, but they are different. Art has work to do out in the world, while therapy is self-referential and concerned with personal wellbeing. There's nothing wrong with this when that's what you need, but self-affirmation in the guise of art leads down the slippery slope of self-display.

Trying to establish your individuality and worth by making films about yourself is risky because it invites you to compare yourself with the ideals, role models, and ideologies that make up the received wisdom of your time. Making an inventory of your beliefs and achievements inevitably produces homily. This comes from the anxiety, comparison, and competitiveness that fuel the misguided quest for individuality in a society (in the West, anyway) that marches in ideological lockstep. For we live in an age that idealizes the notion of individuality. It tells us that our Self is that which is different from everyone else's. Historically this idea gathered force when humankind began questioning older notions of God and placed man at the center of the universe. The Hindus believe differently; to them, Self is that which you *share* with all creation. Significantly, their ideology is inclusive while the Western one is isolating. Most people trying to create something actually subscribe to both ends of the spectrum. They want to be individual and recognized, but also to create something universal and useful to others.

You may be asking, "Does all this philosophy and psychology stuff really matter this early in my career?" Yes, I truly think it does. Your beliefs about creative expression, whether you are aware of them or not, will determine whether you will be happy and productive working in a collaborative medium like film.

After observing generations of film students at work, I have come to believe that few fail because they cannot handle the work or the technology. Mostly they fail because they are ill-equipped to work closely with other people. The root problems are usually control issues related to a fragile ego and an unwillingness to make or keep commitments.[1]

No doubt the reasons for this inability lie deep in family, social, and even colonial history. Wherever survival depends on jockeying for a favorable position in the eyes of an overlord or something else entirely, it is only human to be competitive, especially if there is no countervailing religion or other system of humane belief to help keep larger aims in view. Nobody living in the long shadows cast by the hierarchies of a farm, plantation, factory, corporation, military unit, class system, political party, social institution, or dysfunctional family has evaded the experience of having power abused, nor have they failed to learn how to curry favor and make headway by stabbing the unwary back.

Antisocial habits, as they emerge in work or marriage, are things anyone can reject or modify, *if they matter enough*. Indeed, much of the group work in a film school program exists to sort through these problems and help students locate their best partners. The importance of this cannot be overstated. George Tillman, Jr. and Bob Teitel, the writer/producer/director team responsible for *Men of Honor* (2000), were a black student and a white student who met in my college's second-level production course. After leaving Columbia College Chicago, they began their professional output with *Soul Food* (1997) and have worked successfully together ever since meeting. People find whom they look for, and countless relationships that have persisted over decades have come from similar beginnings.

[1] I am indebted to my Buddhist colleague Prof. Doreen Bartoni for enlightening conversations on this subject, as well as to her example of egoless leadership as a dean at Columbia College Chicago.

Most film students, when asked *what* they want to create, are not only confident that they know, but insulted by the question. They see directing as learning to use the tools of cinema and the rest following naturally, but their work is content to imitate a genre they enjoy. Unless you have strong persuasions about cause and effect in life, you will remain invisible to film audiences, no matter how competent you become with the tools. How, then, can you define your outlook to make yourself ready to direct fictional films?

Really, your options at any given time are mercifully few and simply need uncovering. Each person's life has marked them in unique ways, and these marks—whether you are aware of them or not—determine how you live your life, what quest you are pursuing, and what you have to say authoritatively through an art form. You can ignore this or deny that you carry any special marks, but this does not affect their power over you. Or, you can acknowledge that there is an emerging pattern in your life. When this happens—alone, with a friend, or with a therapist—we suddenly feel the rush of relief and excitement that comes from seeing what has been driving us. A man's character, said Heraclitus, is his fate. In a close community, everyone can see over time how others act according to the marks they carry, but only with difficulty do we see it in ourselves. Thus, we play a major part in making our own path anyway.

This was not something I appreciated myself until I was into my 30s. As part of a study program, I was required to watch all my documentary films and write a self-assessment. Though they were all about different topics, I was astonished to find they had a common theme that had hitherto completely escaped me. It was that "most people feel imprisoned, but the inventive are able to adapt, rebel, and escape."

How could I have made more than 20 films and never noticed this one constant? The explanations came sailing in like homing pigeons. I had grown up in a family relocated by World War II into an English agricultural village. We were middle class and isolated among the rural poor. For the first several years my father, a foreigner, was away serving on merchant ships, and my mother found nothing in common with her neighbors. Going to a local school, I had to contend with kids who jeered at the way I spoke. I was derided, my possessions envied, and sometimes I was ambushed. Thinking we were "better" than the local people, at some point I drew several conclusions: that I was different and unacceptable to the majority, that fear was a constant, and that I must handle it alone because adults were preoccupied. I found I could get out of tight spots by making people laugh, and that outside home it was best to become a different person. Later, when I read the history of English rural misery and exploitation, I understood the hostility to what I represented. Losing my fear, and with it an inculcated sense of class superiority, my relationships with my fellow conscripts in the Royal Air Force—where the whole thing might easily have been repeated—was quite different and very gratifying.

The common thread in my films came from having lived on both sides of a social barrier and empathizing with those in similar predicaments: the black person in a white neighborhood, the Jew among Gentiles, the child among adults. Any story with these trace elements quickens my pulse. But for many years (and more than 20 films) I was quite unaware that I carried a vision of life as a succession of imprisonments, and that from each there is always the possibility of escape for the determined few. Perhaps this mark is in my family, for each generation seems to move off to another country.

A biography by Paul Michaud about the late François Truffaut links such films as *The 400 Blows* (1959), *Jules and Jim* (1961), *The Wild Child* (1969), and *The Story of Adèle H.* (1975) with pain Truffaut suffered as a child upon being estranged from his mother. His characters' rootless lives, their naïve impracticality, and Adèle Hugo's neurotic, self-destructive hunger for love all reflect aspects of the Truffaut his friends knew. This does not reduce or "explain" Truffaut so much as point to an energizing self-recognition at the source of his prolific output and to show that self-recognition can always be turned outward to develop stories that are universally accessible.

You may wonder whether it's helpful or destructive to "understand" your own experience too well, and whether it's productive to seek professional help in doing so. There is a different answer for each individual here, but psychotherapy is hard work, and those who pursue it usually only do so to get relief from unhappiness. Making art is different, for it concerns curiosity and the fundamental human drive to create order and suggest meanings. You should do whatever prepares you best for this. Below are some techniques for clarifying your sense of direction and the imprint that life has made on you. If you find them interesting, you can explore them in greater depth in my book *Developing Story Ideas* (Focal Press, 2000).

FIND YOUR LIFE ISSUES

You carry the marks of a few central issues from your formative experiences. Reminders unfailingly arouse you to strongly partisan feelings. They are your bank account of deepest experience, and finding how to explore and use them in your work, even though they seem few and personal, can keep you busy for life. We are *not* talking about autobiography, but about having a core of deeply felt experiences whose themes have endless applications.

There are, of course, right and wrong ways to gain possession of your own particular life issues. A wrong way is to entrust someone else with deciding what you should be or do. To find what your own life issues really are means confronting yourself honestly and paring away whatever is alien to your abiding concerns. This is not easy because of the shimmering, ambiguous nature of what we call reality. What is real? What is cause and what is effect? Perhaps because film appears to look outward at the world rather than inward at the person or people making the film, many filmmakers seem content with a superficial understanding of their own drives. But if drama is to have a spark of individuality, it must come from a dialogue—with yourself and with an audience.

PROJECTS

The following are some exercises that you may find helpful.

PROJECT 2-1: THE SELF-INVENTORY

To uncover your real issues and themes, and to therefore discover what you can give others, make a non-judgmental inventory of your most moving experiences. This is not as difficult as it sounds, for the human memory jettisons the mundane and retains only what it finds significant.

1. Go somewhere private and write rapid, short notations of each major experience just as it comes to mind. Keep going until you have at least 10 or 12 experiences by which you were deeply moved (to joy, to rage, to panic, to fear, to disgust, to anguish, to love, etc.).
2. Stand back and organize them into groups. Give names to each grouping and to the relationships among them. Some moving experiences will be positive (with feelings of joy, relief, discovery, laughter), but most will be painful. Make no distinction, for there is no such thing as a negative or positive truth. To discriminate like this is to censor, which is just another way to prolong the endless and wasteful search for acceptability. Truth is *Truth*—period!
3. Examine what you've written as though looking objectively at someone else's record. What kind of expressive work should come from someone marked by such experiences? You should be able to place yourself in a different light and find trends, even a certain vision of the world, clustering around these experiences. Don't be afraid to be imaginative, as though developing a fictional character. Your object is not therapy, but to find a storytelling role that you can play with all your heart.

Even though you may have a good handle on your underlying issues, try making the inventory anyway. You may get some surprises. Honestly undertaken, this examination will confirm which life-events formed you, and this in turn will focus your work on exploring the underlying issues they represent. You will probably see how you have resonated to these issues all along in your choice of music, literature, and films, not to mention in your friendships, love affairs, and family relationships.

PROJECT 2-2: ALTER EGOS

Try taking an oblique approach to your deeper aspirations and identifications. Because particular characters or particular situations in films, plays, or books often trigger a special response in us, these offer useful clues to our own makeup, though the larger part will always remain a mystery. The purpose of this project is to discover some of your resonances.

1. List six or eight characters from literature or fiction with whom you have a special affinity. Arrange them by their importance to you. An affinity can be hero-worship, but it becomes more interesting when you are responding to darker or more complex qualities.
2. Do the same thing for public figures like actors, politicians, sports figures, etc.

3. Make a third list of people you know or have known, but leave out immediate family if they complicate the exercise.
4. Take the top two or three in each list and write a brief description of what, in human or even mythical qualities, each person represents, and what dilemma seems to typify them. If, for instance, O.J. Simpson were on your list, he might represent someone whose jealous passion destroyed what he most loves.
5. Now write a self-profile based on what the resonances suggest. Don't hesitate to imaginatively round out the portrait as though it were a fictional character. The aim is not to define who you are (you'll never succeed) but to build a provocative and active picture of *what you are looking for and how you see the world.*

PROJECT 2-3: USING DREAMS TO FIND YOUR PREOCCUPATION

Keep a log of your dreams, for in dreams the mind expresses itself unguardedly and in surreal and symbolic imagery. Unless you have a period of intense dream activity, you will have to keep a record over many months before common denominators and motifs begin showing up. Keep a notebook next to your bed, and awake gently so you hold onto the dream long enough to write it down. If you get really interested in this work, you can instruct yourself to wake in the night after a good dream and write it down. Needless to say, this will not be popular with a bedroom partner.

Dreams frequently project with great force a series of tantalizing images that are symbolically charged with meaning. The British novelist John Fowles started both *The French Lieutenant's Woman* and *A Maggot* from single images, one of a woman gazing out to sea toward France and the other of a mysterious group of horsemen crossing a hillside accompanying a lone woman. Whole complex novels came from investigating the characters "seen" in these alluring glimpses. You too have hidden patterns and propitious images waiting in the wings to be recognized and developed.

THE ARTISTIC PROCESS

Practitioners in every area of the arts agree that there is an artistic process, and that to find it is to plug into the heartbeat of being alive. Craftspeople report the same exhilaration, and who is to say they are not artists, too. Being on the path of the artistic process is like finding you are on the most significant journey of your life, one that opens up doors to meaning, one that reveals connections to a larger whole.

This search for your own path, for the truths underlying your formation and patterns, starts feeding itself once you make a commitment to expressing something about it. This willingness to begin the journey sustains the artistic process; at the beginning you get clues, clues lead to discoveries, discoveries lead to movement in your work, and movement leads to new clues. A piece of work—whether a painting, a short story, or a film script—is therefore both the evidence of movement and the engine of progress during the search for meanings. Your work becomes the trail of your own evolution.

As you get ready to produce, search for that special element that fascinates you. It might be expressed through mountaineering, the rescue of animals, something involving water and boats, or love between school friends. You explore that fascination by producing something external to your own thoughts: the piece of work. What begins as a circumscribed personal quest soon leads outward. You might take two opposing parts of your own character during a trying period of your life and make them into two separate characters, perhaps making imaginative use of two well-known political or historical characters to do so. Making profiles of historical personalities, social assumptions, political events, or the temperaments of the people most influential in your life will all contribute to sharpening and shaping your consciousness. Doing such things well entertains and excites your audience, who are also—whether they know it or not—pursuing a private quest and starving to go on similar journeys of exploration.

CHAPTER 3

DEVELOPING YOUR STORY IDEAS

THE DEVELOPMENTAL PROCESS

Because a director is a leader responsible for the overall dramatic statement of a film, he or she must know how to choose a piece of writing for the screen and how to shape and develop it. This involves knowing how to critique, deconstruct, and reconstruct a chosen piece, and how to develop its full cinematic potential in collaboration with the writer. This is difficult until you know, as an insider, how writers think and work. In your early training as a director you should write your own scripts. This is excellent exposure to the basics of the screenwriter's craft, about which myths abound. There's no better way to understand something than by doing it.

You will discover that writing is an organic rather than linear process. Accomplished writers switch rapidly between different types of thinking and change hats as a matter of course. The three major modes of writing are as follows:

- **Ideation** or idea development, which means finding a promising idea and theme as the kernel for a screen story. This is something a writer periodically revisits to check whether the core idea has changed as a result of the writing process.
- **Story development**, which is the expansion of the idea into characters, dialogue, situations, and events.
- **Story editing**, which involves revision, structuring, pruning, shaping, and compressing the overall piece. A screenplay will routinely go through many drafts before it is considered ready for filming.

These operations call on different human attributes. Ideation and story development call on taste and instincts and require that you freely follow inspiration, intuition, and emotional memory rather than objectivity and logic. Story editing, on the other hand, takes analytic and dramaturgical skills. You must objectify yourself to judge how best to structure and cadence the work for maximum impact on a first-time audience. This is not possible unless you develop a strong interest in how others assimilate and react. These results, in turn, may or may not tally with what the work first intended to deliver. Changes in any one stage can affect what seemed stable in the others, so writing is a circular—not linear—activity.

IDEATION

In this chapter we will concentrate on ideation. Screenwriting manuals often suggest that an outline is the starting point, but this omits the all-important area of ideation. Ideas often take shape from nothing more substantial than a persistent image, mood, strong feeling, interest, or persuasion. Born from an inner source like this, the beginning is a fragile flame and is easily snuffed out. The best ideational work usually emerges from habits of rigorous self-questioning and examination. As the actor and directing teacher Marketa Kimbrell likes to say: "You can't put up a tall building without first digging a deep hole." She means you must burrow down into your very foundations before moving upward to shape the superstructure of a film.

Striking authorship never emerges from market surveys, wizard screenwriting methods, or industry insider knowledge. Nor will any amount of desire to excel get you there; writing is no more susceptible to willpower alone than is athletics. If you don't believe me, try it. Sit down to write something "new" and purely from imagination. You will soon be paralyzed by thoughts of how someone else has already had every idea you can come up with. The problem is you are not trying to create, you are trying to excel. Stop it! Truly, no story is original, so put aside all thoughts of being "good" or "original" or any of those other competitive and self-judgmental words.

Ideation begins when you set aside some quiet, self-reflective time from the hubbub of normal life. Many of us live in a welter of noise and activity to *avoid* reflection, so a part of you will want to reject this stage. Busywork activity is a narcotic that tells you to take refuge in being useful—doing anything rather than being quiet and introspective.

Once you achieve a quiet, reflective mood,

- examine without judgment the marks your life has made on you.
- write how your experiences have specially formed you.
- from these, list:
  the kinds of stories you are qualified to tell.
  the kinds of characters that particularly attract you.
  the situations you find especially intriguing.
  the genres you want to work in (comedy, tragedy, history, biography, film noir, etc.).
- now, go over your answers and substitute something better for anything at all superficial or clichéd and give proper particularization to everything you specify.

Quick, reflex answers usually jump out of the pool of clichés we all carry. Consider them a starting point from which you can refine and sharpen what you are reaching for. Little by little, something that is itself, something you don't have to reject, will emerge. The process of giving birth to a core idea is like becoming a parent. You don't want to crush your children by demanding they become winners. It is wiser to nurture them, get to know their preferences and subtleties, and encourage them to reach for their own best potential. To do this you must work quietly and persistently. Be patient, loyal, and persistent, and stay open to surprises and changes of direction. Good ideas are not ordered into existence, they are beckoned, and the better ones hide out among the stereotypes, where it's your job to recognize them.

It may be reassuring to know you are not alone. You swim in a historical stream, and knowingly or unknowingly, you draw on the well of humanity's story—that is, from life and from other creators. In Chapter 10 of this book, there is a list of the available themes, plots, and situations—just to show how few there really are. But that doesn't limit you, for there are an unlimited number of fascinating characters walking the face of the earth, and an unending number of variations and combinations you can extract from the basics.

At first, when you search for stories it may seem you have nothing dramatic in your life to draw upon. Perhaps the tensions you have witnessed or experienced never matured into any action. But the writer's gratification—and it may even be the chief reward of authorship—is to make happen what should have happened but didn't. Because an event or situation is etched into your consciousness, it can be shaped into something expressive of some theme or vision of life. This, depending on your tastes and temperament, may be tragic, comic, satiric, realistic, surreal, or melodramatic. By projecting the original characters and events into the confrontation and change that could have happened (even if it did not), you can follow the road not taken and investigate the originals' unused potential.

Any real-life situation containing characters, events, situations, and conflicts has the elements of drama and the potential to become a full-blown story. Change one or two of the main elements in this borrowed framework, develop your own characters, and the meaning and impact of the entire work will begin to evolve in their own special direction.

For example, you know two married people who are totally incompatible. You imagine a film that takes their differences to some point of resolution. Because they have never expressed anything more than irritation with each other, you do not know how to do it. In the newspaper you happen to see a true story about a peaceable civil servant, married for 38 years, who flipped and did the unthinkable. This catches your eye because you're fascinated by what makes people conform all their lives and then at some triggering moment shear off into uncharted waters. One Thanksgiving, this man suddenly rose from the dinner table because his wife put the salt shaker back in the wrong place on the table. Irrevocably crossing some inner threshold, he left home without explanation. Later, friends found he had gone to look for a childhood sweetheart. Because this piques your interest, and the article doesn't tell you why it happened, you decide to write a story that makes all this comprehensible.

Now you face a dilemma. You can digress imaginatively from a biographical structure or you can stick closely to it. Here are examples of feature films that followed the biographical path.

- John Boorman's *Hope and Glory* (1987) is modeled on the lives and emotional evolution of his family during World War II when he was a boy. The film explores with imagination and sympathy his mother's unfulfilled love for his father's best friend.
- Michael Radford's *Il Postino* (1994) is about the enlightening relationship that developed between a postman and the Chilean poet Pablo Neruda while he was exiled to a Mediterranean island.
- Michael Haneke's *The Piano Teacher* (2001) is a film in which Isabelle Huppert plays a repressed and sexually perverted piano teacher who falls for a charming student. The script is based on a novel by Elfriede Jelinek, herself formerly a pianist and teacher.

What makes these films outstanding is what distinguishes any story. They embrace biography as something dramatic and express distinct ideas about the underlying causes of their characters' dilemmas. Without sensitivity to the nuance of the actual, and to how unexpectedly actual people behave under pressure, the writer will fall into stereotype. Those who study real life know that nothing is more mysterious and full than the actual, and that nothing is so untrue as a stereotype.

COLLECTING RAW MATERIALS

If you are by nature a storyteller, you are probably doing what I am about to describe. Here are ways to collect and sift through material that can be made into a story, *the* story you need to tell, given the limitations you must work within. If you are not yet a storyteller, you can adopt the habits of one. Everyone has a story, always. All you need do is summon the concentration and energy to begin. People work in fiction rather than autobiography because you are not tied to the literal truth and can take artistic license wherever more important truths need telling.

The seeker searches for a larger picture among the many baffling clues, hints, and details that life provides. Some pursue personal respite and may enlist a therapist or support group, others do it out of a need or sense of obligation to entertain—that is, to share with others what it means to be alive. The stories you need probably won't be on hand when you want them. It will take a resolute and indirect search process. Your best materials will emerge piecemeal and from unexpected sources.

Because of the singularity of your identity, you may find you have only one story in you. But—and this is an article of faith—telling it successfully will open the way for the next. The most prolific artists often mine a single, deep-seated theme, and their work becomes a sustained pursuit of ever-deeper understanding.

You will have to collect materials and examine your collection diligently as it grows. You are actually searching for the outlines of the collector, the shadowy self that is implacably assembling what it needs to represent its own preoccupations.

JOURNAL

If you don't train yourself to record things, you will come up empty-handed when you most need story materials. Keep a journal and note anything that strikes you, no matter what its nature. Carry your journal at all times, and be willing to use it publicly and often. Typing material later makes you explore it and will help you remember it better. By transferring your notes to a computer, you can also file incidents in a database under a variety of headings. Then you can call up material by particular priorities or in a particular order.

Because inspiration is a most unreliable handmaiden, most working writers develop their own routines to keep their minds active. Reading your journal is a renewable journey through your most intense ideas and associations. This primes the creative pump and suggests alternatives when you run dry. The more you consciously note what catches your eye, the nearer you move to your underlying themes and interests. This is an example of changing hats—when you move from collecting to analyzing. Good analysis also helps you know what you need to collect!

NEWSPAPERS

There is nothing like real life for a profundity of the outlandish and true. Keep clippings or transcribe anything that catches your interest and classify the information by groups or families. Listing and classifying is a vital activity because it helps reveal underlying structures. Going through 50-year-old newspapers, for instance, will supply you with a profusion of rich sources that nobody else is using. Maybe you'll find a story about two business partners, one of whom absconds with the company bank balance to blow it all in Las Vegas. It reminds you of your best friend's father and the ruin a similar incident caused her family. That sets you thinking about your role in trying to help her through the period of disaster and what you both learned. Here, you realize, is a plot from one source, characters, and even a point of view from another.

The agony columns, the personals, the local crimes page, even the ads for lost animals can suggest subjects and characters. Newspapers are a cornucopia of the human condition at every level, from the trivial to the global. Local newspapers are particularly fertile because the landscape and characters are accessible and reflect local economy, conditions, and idiosyncrasies.

With every new source you have the same possibility: to cross-pollinate ideas by bringing together your overall interests with plots, characters, and situations available elsewhere.

HISTORY

History isn't really something that happens, it's a retrospective view selectively told for ulterior motives. Consider *why* history is written and you see not objective truth but someone's interpretation. History is all about point of view. The past is a rich repository of figures who have already participated in the dramas that interest you. The playwright John Osborne explored the predicament of the anti-establishment rebel through Martin Luther; Alan Bennett resurrected George III to investigate paternal authority as it veers over the brink of insanity; and Steven Spielberg brought alive Oskar Schindler so he could explore the awful predicament of being Jewish in Nazi-dominated Europe. Jane Campion recreated the dark and isolated beginnings of fellow New Zealander Janet Frame in *An Angel at My Table* (1991), and in *The Piano* (1993) she uses a 19th-century setting to develop themes of isolation and eroticism. In both films she explores a woman's point of view in breathtakingly imaginative ways (Figure 3–1).

No matter what happens to fascinate you—be it charismatic leaders who go wrong, practical jokers who get taken seriously, crooked doctors who find real cures, polygamous family groups who end up at war, neglected inventors, or old ladies who fill their houses with stray animals—there is a wealth of fully realized characters already tied to great themes. A little diligent research and you can find just what you want in the great casting agency of the past.

MYTHS AND LEGENDS

Legends are inauthentic history. By taking a historical figure and developing your own version of this person's life and actions, you are fabricating legend. Every culture has its icons (George Washington, Al Capone, Robin Hood, Queen Victoria, William Tell, Adolf Hitler) who reflect the national sense of demons and geniuses. Why not make your own?

Myths frame conflicts that each generation finds insoluble and whose immovable dialectic must therefore be absorbed into regular life. The human truths in Greek mythology (for instance) do not lead to easy or happy resolutions, but leave a bittersweet aftertaste that is perversely uplifting. Each culture has its favorite myths, and they often translate effectively into a modern setting. Each generation regenerates myths and uses them to frame contemporary characters and action, particularly when the issue in question is irresolvable. This quality of paradox and the unanswerable is peculiarly modern. Happily, we have left an age of anodyne resolutions and entered one that recognizes that we face more questions than answers.

FAMILY STORIES

All families have favorite stories that define people and moments. One of my grandmothers was said to find things before people lost them. Conventional in all respects, she loved foraging for flowers and fruit, and during breaks in long journeys she would hop over garden walls to liberate a few strawberries or a fistful of chrysanthemums. How a family explains and adjusts to such foibles might be the subject of a short film.

Another grandmother began life as a rebel in an English village, became an Edwardian hippy, and then married an alcoholic German printer who beat her and abandoned her in France, where she stayed the rest of her life. She and her children lived lives too richly fantastic to be believable in fiction, but there are many single aspects I could borrow and develop.

Family tales can be heroic or very dark, but as oral history, they are usually vivid. Sometimes the surviving information is so trenchant that it begs for a

FIGURE 3–1

In *The Piano's* bold premise, a mute woman and her child arrive in 19th-century New Zealand with little more than a piano (The Kobal Collection/Jan Chapman Prods/CIBY 2000).

fictional development. One of my 19th-century forebears was a Scots milliner who migrated south to sell ribbons and fabric from a pony and trap. Nobody said that he liked drink. Instead they said that his horse would embarrass him when he took his family out for a Sunday drive by stopping automatically outside every pub. He had eight children, all of them earthy and jolly. The daughters grew up to be huge and shake when they laughed, while the sons collected pubs and could navigate southern England from a list of pub names. Yet none was an alcoholic. What kind of man was their father?

CHILDHOOD STORIES

Everyone emerges from a childhood war zone. If you write down two or three of the most intense things that happened, you will have several ready-made short film subjects that are meaningful, have a strong and inbuilt visualization, and contain great thematic significance for your subsequent life.

One that springs to mind is how, at the age of five or so, I found a pair of scissors and cut my own hair. My mother was so dismayed that I clapped a hat on my head and kept it on when my father came home. Thereafter when my hair was unruly my mother would sigh and say it was because I had once cut it myself. This incident lay, emblematically, at the root of a discomfort with my body and appearance for decades after. *I had cut my own hair and ruined it.* What a childish absurdity. But wait, let's look deeper. Behind it is the idea that you can make a single fatal, self-mutilating mistake for which you must suffer ever afterward. And it turns out my mother—I am realizing this as I write it for you—had in fact made such a mistake. As an 11-year-old, she let her foot be run over by a streetcar, hoping that an accident would bring her feuding parents together. Repairing and setting the broken foot caused her agony, and did bring her parents together, but only for a couple of years, and the streetcar driver who had been her friend was devastated. So many invisible influences direct our destiny. How far have you explored yours?

DREAMS

Your dreams are a sure indicator of your underlying concerns, obliquely expressed in imagery and action. Keep a notebook by your bed and write each dream down while you still remember it. You can even train yourself to wake during the night after a good one. Don't edit or try to shape them, just scribble down the essentials. Look back over an accumulation of entries and you will see a pattern of recurring motifs and archetypal characters. Here are your deepest concerns expressed in surreal visual language. What more could a filmmaker ask?

SOCIAL SCIENCE AND SOCIAL HISTORY

If, for example, you are interested in how factory workers have been exploited, you can find excellent books and case studies on the subject, many with bibliographies that will lead you to other accounts, perhaps in both fiction and nonfiction. The more modern your source, the bigger the bibliography. Many books now contain filmographies, too.

Case histories can be a good source of trenchant detail. If you are writing a part for a shoplifter, reading about actual shoplifters will supply you with what is typical (you need to know that) and also with detail that is quirky and interesting, so your shoplifter character doesn't get stuck as a stereotype.

Case histories generally come with an interpretation, so the dramatist finds good material *and* guidance as to its significance. Social scientists are chroniclers and interpreters; their work can confirm your instincts and provide the kind of background information that allows you to root your fiction in what we know about the real world.

SUBJECTS TO AVOID

Many subjects come to mind easily because they are in your immediate surroundings, are being pumped up by the media, or lend themselves to moral propaganda. Despite this, avoid:

- Worlds you haven't experienced and cannot closely observe
- Any ongoing, inhibiting problem in your own life (find a therapist—you are unlikely to solve anything while directing a film unit)
- Anything or anyone "typical" (nothing real is typical, so nothing typical will ever be interesting or credible)
- Preaching or moral instruction of any kind
- Films about problems to which you have the answer (so does your audience)

Your films will be your portfolio, your precious reel that alone tells others who you are and what you can do. If you aim to reach audiences beyond your peer group, you will be making short films that are accessible to a wider audience. Try taking something small that you learned the hard way and apply it to a character quite unlike yourself. Through this, try to make a comment on the human condition. In doing so you should be able to avoid the narcissistic tunnel vision that afflicts many student films.

DISPLACE AND TRANSFORM

After a period of careful inquiry and reflection, take the best issues you discover as if they were your own. Even though they may prove temporary and subject to change, treat them as if they are substantial. When working directly from events and personalities in your own life, *displace the screen version from the originals*. Deliberately fictionalizing frees you from self-consciousness and allows you to tell underlying truths that might offend the originals. Most importantly, it allows you to concentrate on developing dramatic and thematic truths instead of getting tangled in questions of biographical accuracy.

You can further liberate your imagination and obscure your sources by giving characters alternative attributes and work, by making them composites by amalgamating the attributes of two life models, by placing the story in a different place or epoch, or even by switching the sex of the protagonists. One student director whose script told his own story—about choosing to abandon a suburban marriage and a well-paying job to become a film student—inverted the sex of the main characters and made the rebel into a woman. In rethinking the situation to give her credible motivations, he made himself inhabit both the husband's and wife's positions and came to more deeply investigate what people trapped in such roles expect out of life. The displacement principle forced him into a more empathic relationship with all his characters. This raised the level of his film's thematic discourse.

CHECKLIST FOR PART 1: ARTISTIC IDENTITY

The recommendations and points summarized here are only those most salient or most commonly overlooked. To find more about them or anything else, go to the Table of Contents at the beginning of Part I, or the index at the back of the book.

To Get on Target to Become a Director:

- Get hands-on knowledge of all the production processes you are most likely to oversee.
- Accept that you'll need to know writing, acting, camerawork, sound, and editing.
- Confront your temperament and creative track record to decide which specialty to adopt as your craft stepping-stone toward eventual directing.
- Resolve to make lots and lots of short films.
- Investigate how new technology can liberate expression in those who embrace it intelligently.
- Remember that hard work can get you places, talent almost never.
- Don't wish for too much success; work for it, and hope it comes slowly.
- See what the herd is doing and make something different.
- Settle in for the long haul, and pace yourself accordingly.

As a Director You'll Need To:

- Become a tough-minded leader.
- Be ready to function even when feeling isolated.
- Be ready to make much out of little.
- Stop thinking in literary abstracts and start thinking in filmable, concrete steps.
- Become interested in and knowledgeable of other art forms.
- Become a good leader—one who liberates the best from people around you.
- Develop original and critical ideas about your times. Lots of them.

To Make Educational Progress:

- Use video and finish lots of film projects. The delivery medium isn't as important as producing lots of work.
- Use short works to argue for your competency at directing longer ones.
- Be ready to adapt and improvise when working with a low budget (people and imagination make films rather than equipment).
- Be ready to rewrite the script around the actors.
- Shoot rehearsals documentary-style and learn from the screen how to make right judgments when you see a living performance unfold.

- To arrive at professional-level results, invest in a long, experimental development period prior to production.

When You Deal with Actors:

- Learn to see actors' obstacles and discover how to remove them.
- Learn to be an acting coach; unless you can afford top talent, you'll need it.
- Learn to work with non-actors; you'll learn from them most of what you need to direct actors.
- Lower actors' fears and create an ensemble with an intense period of development prior to shooting.
- Remember, the camera sees and hears everything; actors must *be*, not perform.
- Actors' egos are threatened when they play contemptible characters or reveal their characters' bad parts.
- "Nothing human is alien to me" (Terence c. 190-159 B.C.). For complexity, find the good in the bad character, and the faults in the good one.

To Entertain Your Audience Means:

- Giving the audience mental, emotional, and imaginative work to do, as well as information and externals.
- Inviting the audience to co-create the movie, which means planting many questions and delaying the answers.
- Making films that activate the mind and heart.
- Using myth and archetype to underpin anything you want to be powerful.
- Using screen language that suggests, not just shows, so your audience can imagine.

Authorship Essentials Require:

- Being willing to reject idea after idea until you get something fresh.
- Learning to operate in different modes: one associative and free as the generating mode and the other disciplined and calculating for the shaping, editorial mode.
- Making use of all available resources and constantly trying out new ideas.
- Using your work to search for what you passionately care about, not illustrating what you know.
- Developing something you sincerely want to say. Simple and heartfelt is always better than big and bombastic.
- Picking a special form after you've found a story—form follows function. Every form you use should be special, not picked off the rack.
- Understanding beats and dramatic units. Practice recognizing them in the life unfolding around you.

- Understanding the creative process and letting it direct you when you, and it, need it to.

Questions to Help You Travel Inward and Develop Your Ideas:

- What marks has your life left on you?
- What ongoing dialogue are you privately having with yourself?
- What is the unfinished business in your life? (Your next story can use and further this quest but it's best to do it in a displaced rather than autobiographical form.)
- From your self-inventory, what authorial role do you see for anyone marked by your kind of emotional experience?
- What major conflicts do you face or which ones seem to perennially interest you?
- What kind of heroes or heroines do you respond to, and what does this say about the issues and needs you understand?
- What constants keep turning up in your dreams?
- What visual images remain with you, charged with force and mystery, waiting for you to investigate and develop them?
- What areas of life do you find abidingly fascinating?

Avoid:

- Self-consciousness and libel by displacing the actual into the fictional, so you can be truthful.
- Worlds you don't know—unless you're willing to do a great deal of research.
- Any personal topic for which you really need a therapist.
- Anything or anyone typical. Nobody and nothing is.
- Anything or anyone generalized instead of specific.
- Preaching. Remember what Louis B. Mayer said, "If you want to send a message, call Western Union."
- Illustrating what you know. That's just another disguise for preaching.
- Any idea, situation, or character already familiar or clichéd.
- Clichés. All thinking begins with clichés, but only hard work brings something better.

Resources to Probe:

- What genres fascinate you?
- What themes and preoccupations emerge as constants in your journal?
- What kind of characters and themes turn up regularly in the clippings you make from newspapers?
- Whom do you identify with in history?
- Whom do you detest in history? (A nemesis can be important.)

- What mythic or legendary figures are peculiarly your own, and which would you like to develop?
- What major characters or situations can you use from your family history?
- What are the childhood stories that seem to epitomize your growing up?
- What constant themes emerge?

PART 2

SCREENCRAFT

This part (Chapters 4 through 6) contains a detailed moviemaking workout, beginning with the origins of screen language as an approximation of human perceptual processes. Once you grasp the idea, you can practice applying it to your own consciousness at any time and in any place. Next, we look critically at film language and see how well the makers of a film have used film techniques to approximate human perceptual habits. This is when you analyze a film minutely, a radically different activity from free-associating with what you remember from a viewing. A study project in this part compares the original screenplay of a film with how the director interpreted and transformed it. This allows you to peer speculatively into the complicated act of making a film and to hazard what decisions were made. There is practice at naming and identifying types of lighting, which have so much to do with mood and rendering of time and place. Finally there are shooting projects, all of which can be developed into more than one version. This is to get you used to executing different points of view and purposes in the cutting room, where a film finds its final voice.

There is a lot of work here, but you'll come out with skills that would take you years to acquire by a more haphazard route. Before doing any project, be sure to check its Assessment Form in the appendix. This will help focus your work. Do make use of the checklist at the end of this part for salient reminders from the chapters. Anything else you need is likely to be in the index or glossary at the end of the text.

CHAPTER 4

A DIRECTOR'S SCREEN GRAMMAR

SCREEN LANGUAGE

As children we learn to communicate because language is a tool to get or accomplish things. My elder daughter's first sentence was, "Meat, I like it." Effective, if a little shaky in syntax. All languages operate under conventions, and those determining screen language began developing in the 1890s as camera operators and actors competed to rush elementary stories before paying audiences. Soon they were joined by directors and editors as movies became big business and a production line evolved requiring greater division of labor. Though the first movies were very simple, most of today's screen language emerged in the first two decades of silent cinema.

Separately, in the world's various centers of production, filmmakers felt their way toward the same movie grammar through trial and error. During the 1920s, needing an efficient common language to communicate with a vast, multilingual, and mostly illiterate population, filmmakers in the post-revolutionary Russian government made a concerted effort to formulate screen language. Their theoretical writings do not make easy reading and are of limited use. Even today, theory among working filmmakers is mostly conspicuous by its absence—hardly surprising as languages flowered for millennia before anyone needed philology.

FILM AS A REPRODUCTION OF CONSCIOUSNESS

Like any language, film's is evolving to enable the stories we want and the form we want them in. It uses the juxtaposition of images, actions, and sounds, as well as spoken and written language. The visual and behavioral aspects of film are universally accessible because human beings everywhere have common processes of perception and emotion. Proof of this is that those in the industry discuss a film in progress in terms of "what works." Be it an action, rhythm, shot, line, or character's motivation, the dialogue hinges on what *works*. Each person calls on his or her bank of life experience to recognize what is authentic and organic to the story and its characters, and what is off kilter. Without this innate ability to recognize authenticity in a stream of events on the screen, neither the cinema nor drama itself could exist.

Isn't film language easy to use if it relies on something common to everyone? To use it superficially is easy, but to use it more profoundly is not easy at all. That's because we lack a detailed knowledge of our own perceptual and emotional processes. Our perceptions work automatically and feed our feelings, but we have no need to know how they work together—not, that is, until we want to make effective film.

THE NEED FOR A HUMANE VOICE

Because film is realized technologically, the beginner sees its obstacles as technological, too. Therefore, this is what most schools and most beginning film students attend to, unless enlightened teaching places their attention on larger issues. But there are endless reasons to keep your eyes lowered: logistical and financial details and the need for persistence, empathy, humility, and self-knowledge to lead other people—all this is needed to construct even the shell of a fiction story.

Most people start directing by modeling themselves on admired filmmakers. This is natural and necessary, but it holds the same dangers as when actors study other actors. Stanislavsky warned that actors must learn from life, not from the tricks used by other actors. If acting and film language are rooted in human perceptions, actions, and reactions, then *life itself* is the primary resource, and the works of those who simulate it are secondary.

This is liberating because it means whenever you become aware of how your perceptions and emotions interact, you are working at developing film language and film subjects. An active involvement in unraveling consciousness and a willingness to make many short films are the path toward an individual—as opposed to mechanical—writing or screen "voice," one with the force of simplicity and truth. Then other people's work becomes not a model to emulate but an example of a solution to particular problems you are trying to solve.

Cinema language is really the most evolved model we have developed of human consciousness at work. Human experience and human communicating always involve a *point of view*, and what is put on the screen should, too. By point of view I mean more than a political outlook or philosophically influenced way of seeing, which can be learned or copied. Your point of view on your family, for instance, cannot be copied because it is too individual and too informed by complex experience. What you have to say about your family is almost certainly interesting, even arresting, and will tell the listener much about your outlook, beliefs, and vulnerabilities. A point of view is simply a full human perception, with all its inbuilt convictions, loyalties, and contradictions. It is not a manifesto or teaching strategy and is not meant to educate or improve others. It is a human soul, something invariably present in work that audiences and critics have always instinctively valued.

Any endeavor that sets out to involve the human heart requires that the members of its authorial team be treading the demanding path of self-realization. How you use narrative to address your audience will only be as engaging as the concerns in the hearts and minds of your team. Many professionals are unaware of this because the film industry uses assembly-line methods that provide their own momentum and meaning. Thus, most filmed fiction is soulless because it lacks an honest heart and an overarching human point of view.

Yet an authorial voice of sorts is often present in students' first works. Sadly, it disappears when their attention moves toward glossier skills. To help you avoid this dehumanization in your work and to focus you always on what is human in the process, here is an unconventional screen grammar that relates every aspect of film language to human behavior and perception. By picking subjects with special meaning to you, and by assimilating and using the analogies for human consciousness in the next section, you will always be evoking the psychological and physical viewpoint of an involved observer, which is how a point of view is constructed.

THE ELEMENTS OF FILM LANGUAGE

Let's look over the elemental units of film language. They correspond to glancing, reacting, studying, walking, looking around, whirling about, stepping back, rising, sinking, scanning, running, gliding, and a host of other expressive bodily and psychological interactions. Film is a reproduction of consciousness, and whatever is within a human being also has its outward, bodily expression. Conversely, a person's outward movement, when it's authentic, always expresses his or her inner state. Film happens in the here and now and expresses human feeling though a texture of seeing, hearing, and moving.

FIXED CAMERA POSITION

A fixed camera position gives the feeling you get when you stand in one spot and look around. Depending on the context, a static shot can variously convey being secure, fixed, trapped, contemplative, wise, or just plain stuck. Yasujiro Ozu's famous *Tokyo Story* (1953), about an elderly couple discovering that none of their married children can make time for their visit, is shot from a single camera height and contains just one movement, a gentle pan, throughout the movie. See the film to realize how natural such stasis can be. It makes you aware of how routinely camera movement is debased through overuse.

A shot is a framed image, which might be taken by accident, or more often is an image recorded by someone for whom it had meaning. Think of a shot as equivalent to a glance, which can be short or long and lingering. Of course, looking at anything or anybody starts any number of thoughts, questions, and feelings (such as curiosity, fear, boredom, wonder, weary acceptance). Shots evoke more than their subject, for they make us wonder who is doing the seeing, and why.

Brief Shots are like the cursory glance that ends immediately once we know what we were seeking. We do this all the time. Often we do this to orient ourselves in a new situation or to look in many places in search of something. Think about where your eye goes and how long it stays as you search, coupon in hand, for the new, low-sodium Nutty Wheatlets in the supermarket.

Held Shots are like the long looks we indulge in. Maybe we are too weary to look around anymore or something significant or interesting requires sustained attention, such as some mystifying street graffiti. Maybe we watch a store customer we suspect of shoplifting with the hope of catching him. Maybe it's a friend leaving for a long journey whose last smile we want to commit to memory. Long looks therefore break into two classifications: resting looks and studying looks.

Close Shots reproduce the feeling of taking a close and intensive look. Maybe it's something small requiring close attention like a watch face, or something large such as the surface of a great weathered rock. There are also other, more psychologically determined reasons to dwell on something. Imagine a person who waits by a phone in a large room. When it rings, the person waiting will learn the results of a medical test. All that exists for that person is the phone and its terrifying aura of power. In this case the close shot reproduces a kind of emotional focus that makes us blind even to grandiose surroundings.

Wide Shots approximate the way we take in something large, busy, or distant. We look at it until we have located what we need to examine in more detail. Coming out of a dark church into a busy street, for instance, takes adapting to the new circumstances while we work out the direction home. Often we must establish the nature of our new surroundings, hence the common term *establishing shot.* Think of this shot as the long moment upon arriving at a party when you establish the room, establish who is there, and establish who is talking to whom.

MOVING CAMERA

Camera movements, like their human-movement equivalents, never happen without a motivation. Camera movements divide into three kinds of motivation, which resemble active and passive ways of being present at an event:

- *Subject-motivated*, in which camera movement responds to stimuli provided by the action. The camera might follow a moving subject or adapt to a changing composition. It is a relatively passive mode of interaction that adapts and is subject-driven.
- *Search-motivated*, in which the camera's "mind" actively pursues a logic of inquiry or expectation. This is a more active mode that probes, anticipates, hypothesizes, or interrogates the action.
- *Boredom-motivated*, in which the camera simulates the human tendency to look around when we run out of stimuli.

Camera movements generally have three phases, each with its own set of considerations:

- Starting composition (held for a particular duration before the movement)
- Movement (with its particular direction, speed, and even its subject to follow, such as a moving vehicle)
- Finishing composition (held for a particular duration after the movement)

Camera Movements from a Static Position

These movements convey the feeling of looking from a fixed position and include turning, looking up and down, and looking more closely.

Pan (short for panoramic) shots happen when the camera pivots horizontally, mimicking the way we turn our heads when scanning a horizontal subject such as a landscape or bridge. Direction of travel is indicated as "pan left" or "pan right."

Tilt shots are like a pan shot except the camera pivots vertically, reproducing the action of looking up or down the length of a vertical subject like a tree or high building. Direction of travel is indicated as "tilt up" or "tilt down."

Zoom ins or zoom outs are made with a lens of adjustable focal length. Although zooming gives the impression of movement toward or away from the subject, picture perspective actually remains identical because the proportion of foreground compared with background objects stays the same. For perspective to change as it does when we walk, the camera itself must move.

TRAVELING CAMERA MOVEMENTS

These occur when the whole camera moves—up, down, forward, sideways, or backward through space, or in a combination. Traveling camera movements impart a range of kinesthetic feelings associated with walking, running, approaching, climbing, ascending, descending, retreating, and so on.

Craning (up or down) is a movement in which the camera body is raised or lowered in relation to the subject. The movement corresponds with the feeling of sitting down or standing up—sometimes as an act of conclusion, sometimes to "rise above," sometimes to acquire a better sightline.

Dollying, tracking, or trucking are interchangeable names for any movement by which the camera moves horizontally through space. In life, our thoughts or feelings often motivate us to move closer to or farther away from that which commands our attention. We move sideways to see better or to avoid an obstacle in our sightline. Associations with this sort of camera movement include walking, running, riding a bike, riding in a car, gliding, skating, sliding, sailing, flying, floating, or drifting.

Crab dollying is when the camera travels sideways like a crab. The equivalent is stalking someone or accompanying them and looking at them sideways as you walk.

SHOTS IN JUXTAPOSITION

When any two shots are juxtaposed, we look for a relationship and meaning between them. In this way A + B does not equal AB, but C—a third meaning. In the documentary film about the September 11, 2001 sabotage of the World Trade Center by Jules and Gedeon Naudet, *9/11* (2002), a single shot reveals how a crumpled aircraft engine cowling has landed next to an equally crumpled waste bin whose sign says, "Do Not Litter." These images juxtaposed within a single shot are a comment not only about the irony of fate, but about the larger irony in which airliners smash into New York life.

Juxtaposing is used extensively in advertising to implant associations: the richly attired couple next to the Mercedes; the bag of fertilizer standing amid a rich green lawn; the bride in her wedding dress running barefoot on the beach outside a hotel. A comic strip juxtaposes a series of key frames to compress a lengthy process and suggest its essence. Each new frame makes us imagine the progression from the previous one.

Film's favorite form of juxtaposing is the cut from one image to another, and the juxtaposing of scene against scene, making the cinema master of time and space. At this juncture we are trained to expect a narrative intention. Figure 4–1 and the remainder of this section show some examples with explanations and illustrate an engaging disagreement between two early Russian editing theorists.

Continuity and expository editing: Examples 1 through 5 (see Figure 4–1) illustrate Pudovkin's categories of juxtaposition in which exposition (building the information of a story line) and continuity are paramount. With the coming of sound and theatrical moviemaking, the illusion of continuity during dialogue scenes with many changes of angle became paramount, and most editing focused on creating continuity.

Dialectical editing: Examples 6 through 12 (see Figure 4–1) show the preferred methods of Eisenstein, for whom the essence of narrative art lay in dialectical conflict. His juxtapositions therefore highlight contrast and contradiction, and as they inform, they argue by creating contrasts and irony.

Action match editing: Editing that is too obvious can easily draw unwelcome attention to authorial manipulation. Early filmmakers discovered that the best way to edit from a tight shot to a wide shot, or vice versa, was to place the cut not in the static part of the action, but right in the most dynamic. Like a pickpocket whose craft is most safely practiced during a flurry of activity, or a conjuror using sleight of hand, the action match cut allows an image change to pass unnoticed under a cover of compelling action. When you want the eye not to notice something, seduce it with movement.

Ear and eye together: The mind has only so much processing power, so you can take our attention away from sound by showing the eye some compelling action (during an unpleasant atmosphere change, for instance), or you can mask a bad picture cut by introducing a new sound element. You will in each case direct our critical faculties away from the fiasco.

Sound juxtaposing: Sound in film realism simply backs up the picture—what you see determines what you hear, so nothing you would expect is missing. But sound effects, music, and language are also frequently juxtaposed against picture to create not an imitation of reality, but a composite set of impressions for the audience to interpret. Director Robert Altman is famous for developing dense picture and sound counterpoint in his films.

POINT OF VIEW

Meaning and signification are a cultural work in progress and thus are always in slow but inexorable evolution. Effective film communication depends on maintaining collusion between audience and communicator by providing a set of

	Shot A	Shot B	Shot B in relation to shot A	Type of cut
1	Woman descends interior stairway	Same woman walking in street	Narrates her progress	Structural (builds scene)
2	Man runs across busy street	Close shot of his shoelace coming undone	Makes us anticipate his falling in front of a vehicle	Structural (directs our attention to significant detail)
3	Hungry street person begging from doorway	Wealthy man eating oysters in expensive restaurant	Places one person's fate next to another's	Relational (creates contrast)
4	Bath filling up	Teenager in bathrobe on phone in bedroom	Shows two events happening at the same time	Relational (parallelism)
5	Exhausted boxer takes knockout punch	Bullock killed with stun-gun in an abattoir	Suggests boxer is a sacrificial victim	Relational (symbolism)
6	Police waiting at road block	Shabby van driving erratically at high speed	Driver doesn't know what he's going to soon meet	Conflictual (still vs. the dynamic)
7	Giant earthmoving machine at work	Ant moving between blades of grass	Microcosm and macrocosm coexist	Conflictual (conflict of scale)
8	Geese flying across frame	Water plummeting at Niagara Falls	Forces flowing in different directions	Conflictual (conflict of graphic direction)
9	Screen-filling close-up of face, teeth clenched	Huge Olympic stadium, line of runners poised for pistol start	The one among the many	Conflictual (conflict of scale)
10	Dark moth resting on white curtains	Flashlight emerging out of dark forest	Opposite elements	Conflictual (dark vs. light)
11	Girl walks into funfair	Distorted face appears in funfair mirror	The original and its reflection	Conflictual (original vs. distorted version)
12	Driver sees cyclist in his path	In slow motion driver screams and swings steering wheel	Event and its perception	Conflictual (real time vs. perceived time)
13	Driver gets out of disabled car	Same image, car in foreground, driver walking as a tiny figure in distance	Transition—some time has gone by	Jump cut

FIGURE 4–1

Examples of juxtaposed shots or cuts.

conventions the audience can "read." Ethnographers noticed, after projecting edited footage to isolated tribespeople, that their subjects understood the "story" until the film cut to a close-up. The tribespeople lost concentration because they failed to understand why the camera eye suddenly "jumped close." They were unaware that a close-up does not necessarily collapse space; it can act like a telescope that diminishes and intensifies the field of attention and clears away what surrounds and obscures the center of interest.

But *whose* center of interest? You might reply, "The audience's," but the answer is more complex and much more useful to film directing because it places the persona of a storyteller ahead of the audience's reception of the story.

Perception by a camera is a mechanical process in which sensitized film at the focal plane is affected by incoming light. Perception by humans is radically different because, unlike a machine, we are able to evolve an intellectual and emotional framework within which to organize what our senses bring us. The conventional narrative or inner internal monologue (also called *voice-over*) illustrates this because it verbalizes the process.

THE CONCERNED OBSERVER AND THE STORYTELLER

Witnessing: Let's say that human perception *is the inner dialogue of ideas, feelings, and intentions we maintain as we navigate the tests posed by an environment.* This interior activity is not simply a reaction or a discrete parallel activity, for it forms our resolve and initiates our actions. We are seldom dispassionate observers, but are usually concerned and involved.

The literary or oral storyteller is a little different, for he (or she, of course) seeks to affect the listener by a selective presentation of bygone events. Think of how a comedian might describe a wedding. Through the telling, he aims to sustain and modulate a funny event in the reader's imagination.

Storytelling by a camera is by comparison an anomaly. Film is always *now* and appears to show us an uninflected, ongoing present. Unless you force the past tense on what the audience sees with a past tense narration, film always lapses into the present tense. How can you *retell* the present? The most you can do is observe, react, and navigate, which is what the camera does unless it serves to reproduce what a character is experiencing. A camera and editing can do all this without so much as a word, causing any apparent mediation to vaporize, even though a selective intelligence is silently guiding our eyes and ears as much as any literary mediator could.

The Concerned Observer: Let's place this involved, perceptual process in a notional figure we'll call the Concerned Observer. Seeing and hearing, this onlooker forms ideas and anticipations. But a witness only experiences and doesn't necessarily relay anything. How and why the Concerned Observer witnesses will be important, but it won't be any form of communication until witness turns into communicator.

The Storyteller: In this situation our Observer changes from informed witness to an active, opinionated Storyteller, like a comedian who describes a wedding and makes the audience laugh. A Storyteller is someone through whose active, creative intelligence we perceive the film's events.

WHY DIRECTING MUST BE STORYTELLING

Creating the narrative wit, intelligence, and emotional involvement of a Storyteller is central to conscious, integrated film directing. This is where the events cease to be mechanically reflected through technique and appear through the prism of a human heart and intelligence. I want to make perception as personal and non abstract as possible in a film because in everyday life, perception is so routine that we seldom notice *how* or why we observe. Even the word "observe" has misleadingly passive, scientific association, when in reality it is a highly active process and freighted with an intricate interplay of feelings, associations, and ideas—all leading constantly to actions.

Something you have to deal with in filmmaking is the existence of not just one axis in cinema, but many. This is where we'll employ the Concerned Observer.

SCENE AXIS ESSENTIALS

LINES OF TENSION AND THE SCENE AXIS

Notice, when two people have an animated conversation near you, how your attention shifts back and forth between them. Figure 4–2 represents Person A and Person B being watched by observer O, who might be yourself but whom it may be helpful to think of as a child because children are highly observant, have strong emotions, and are often invisible to their seniors. As O your sight line plays back and forth from A to B and back again as they talk. Your eye is following an invisible line of tension between them, the active pathway of their words, looks, awareness, and volition. In film parlance this is called the *scene* or *subject-to-subject axis*.

Every observed two-person scene has additionally an observer-to-subject axis, which in my example (see Figure 4–2) is at right angles to the scene axis between A and B. This is called the *camera* or *camera-to-subject axis*. The term *axis* depersonalizes the situation and makes it sound technical when all along it is intensely human. The observer (you involved in watching two people in conversation, for instance) has a strong sense of relationship to each person, to the invisible connection between them, and to what passes between them. When you are watching this way, you become the Concerned Observer, to whom all these connections are significant.

In turning to look from person to person, the Observer can be replaced by a camera *panning* (that is, moving horizontally) between the two speakers. Now let's see in Figure 4–3 what happens when O moves closer to A and B's axis.

Not to miss any of the action, the Observer must switch quickly between A and B. When they do this, human beings blink their eyes to avoid the unpleasant blur as the eye is swished between widely separated subjects. To the brain, momentarily shutting your eyes produces two static images with virtually no period of transition between them. And so you have—the cut! Cutting between two camera angles taken from the same camera position reproduces this familiar experience. The cinematic equivalent probably emerged when someone tried

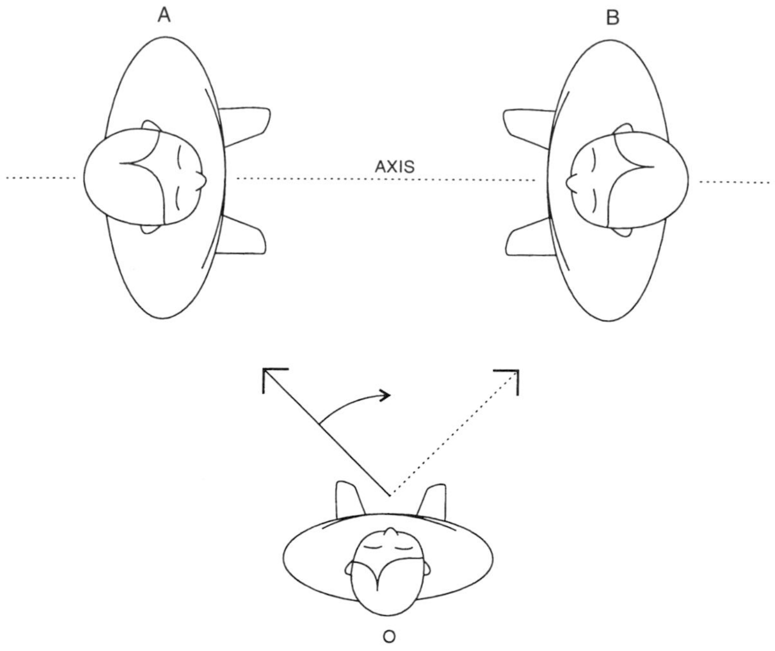

FIGURE 4–2

The Observer watching a conversation.

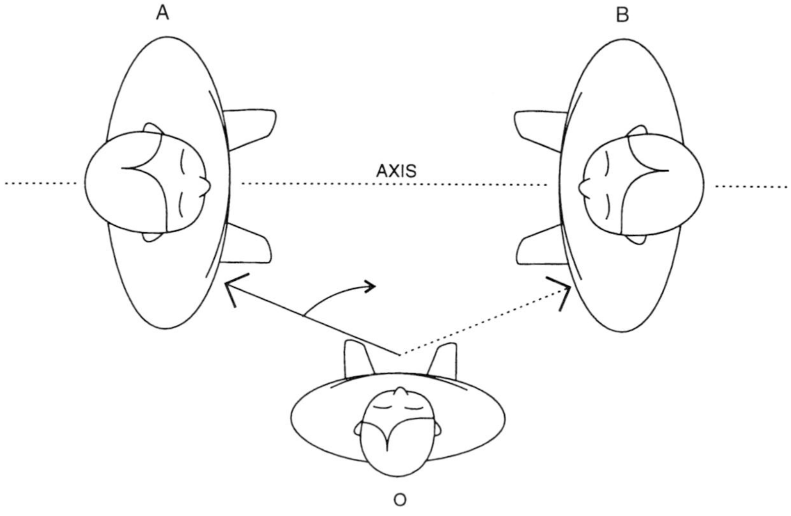

FIGURE 4–3

The Observer moves close to the characters' axis.

cutting out a nauseatingly fast pan between two characters. It "worked" because its counterpart was already embedded in human experience.

CROSSING THE LINE OR SCENE AXIS

In life, we are used to occupying an observing position in relation to events, as O does to A and B. The camera generally mimics this treatment of space by staying on one side only of a scene axis. So long as O stays on one side, A will always be looking left to right (L-R) in the frame and B always right to left (R-L). In Chapter 30, Figures 30–3A and 30–3B, you will find a ground plan and storyboard that show what happens if you *cross the line*, shoot a shot from the other side of the scene axis, and then intercut it. If there is an observational logic, it need not be a disaster, and in any case there is an established device that allows you to cross the axis, or line, if you need to. See the following sections on Screen Direction and Changing Screen Direction. In the meantime, let's continue with the figures at either end of the scene axis, or line.

THE ACTOR AND THE ACTED-UPON

Consider the different ways you follow a conversation. Sometimes you merely look toward whomever speaks next. Other times, when the talk becomes heated, you find yourself looking at the listener, not the speaker. What's going on here?

A human interaction can be likened to a tennis game. At any given moment, one player *acts* (serves the ball), and the other is *acted upon* (receives it). When we see a player prepare to make an aggressive serve, our eye runs ahead of the ball to see how the recipient will deal with the onslaught. We see her run, jump, swing her racquet, and intercept the ball. When it becomes certain she's going to succeed, our eye flicks back to see how the first player is placed and how she will handle the return. The cycle of actor and acted-upon has been reversed because our eye jumps back to the original player before the ball returns.

Unconsciously, we monitor every human interaction the same way because we know everybody is *constantly trying to get or do something*, no matter where, what, or who is involved. A game ritualizes this interchange as a competition, but to the film specialist (which you are now becoming) every conversation has potential to be equally complex and structured.

Of course, we nice, middle-class people hate to think of ourselves making *demands*. We picture ourselves as patient, tolerant victims being worked on by a greedy and selfish world. Seldom do we see how we act on others, except during our occasional triumphs. But the fact is—and you must take this to heart if you intend to work in drama—that *everyone acts upon those around him, even when he uses the strategy of passivity.*

To the analytic, any time one person acts on another, there is always an actor and an acted-upon. Usually, but not always, the situation alternates rapidly, but it is through actions and reactions that we measure another person's character, mood, and motives.

Now see how you watch two people conversing. Your sightline switches according to your notion of who is acting upon whom. As in watching tennis, you'll find that as soon as you've decided how A has begun acting on B, your eye switches in mid-sentence to see how B is taking it. Depending on how B adapts and acts back, you soon find yourself returning to A. Once you can identify this in action, most shooting and editing decisions become obvious.

TEXT AND AUTHORSHIP ESSENTIALS

SUBTEXT

While observing a conversation, you are really searching for behavioral clues to unlock the hidden motives and inner lives of the characters. Beneath the visible and audible surface lies the situation's *subtext*, or hidden meaning—something we are always seeking. Most of the work a director does is not with the text but in response to the subtext.

The text is what the characters do or what action they take verbally. But why do they say what they say and do what they do? This is the purview of subtext. This hidden life—the character's hidden agenda, whatever it is they are trying to get or do—is something developed by the director and the actors, and something that continues developing during rehearsal, shooting, and even in editing. It is the editor's job, in addition to putting the pieces together, to liberate the subtextual possibilities that eluded everyone else. Lengthening a reaction before a character speaks and allowing for a more complex subtext may implant a quite different idea of her interior action and motivation.

Shot Point of View is the how and why of the way we look at something. It is the intention behind the combination of a shot's content and form. At a photo exhibition you are guessing what the photographers were thinking and feeling as they decided to take each shot. You assess this from what each shot includes and *from what it excludes or implies*. For instance, a shot of a man staring offscreen focuses our attention on *how* rather than *what* he sees. Shot point of view is also used more prosaically to imply where the shot was taken from, such as from a high building down into a plaza.

Shot Denotation and Shot Connotation describe different ways to register an image. If we see a bus, a pair of worn-out shoes, and a man in a wheelchair, we may only see what those images denote. If their context encourages us to ascribe special meanings to them, such as vacation, poverty, and power brought low, then we are reacting to associations those images connote. Denotation is *what* a thing is, connotation is *what it seems to mean*, a cultural set of associations the image-maker uses to channel the spectator into a particular path of speculation.

When we see carefully framed shots of a flower or of a hand lighting a candle, they denote a flower and a hand lighting a candle. But a flower on a battlefield might connote a single, fragile life, natural beauty, devotion, or a host of other ideas. The hand lighting a candle in the trenches of that battlefield might connote, depending on context, hope being kept alive, remembering the dead or more prosaically the risk of getting shot. Responding to connotation means going beyond what is literally there and calling on the larger framework of implied meanings.

AUTHORIAL POINT OF VIEW

Connotations of an image that imply a symbol or metaphor prompt us to wonder about the heart and mind that chose to take note of the flower or the hand lighting the candle, each in its particular context. This is the authorial point of view, the Storyteller's sense of what is finally significant.

ORGANIC AND INORGANIC METAPHORS

The flower and lighting candle images mentioned previously are acceptable because they are organic to the battlefield situation. If instead you interpolated a naked baby into the battlefield to *symbolize*, say, how vulnerable humanity is, it would look like a heavy-handed editorial comment because babies, naked or dressed for dinner, do not belong with and are not *organic* to, trench warfare. In any case, because these images I have chosen are clichés, they use worn-out language and are not acceptable. From a sophisticated modern audience they might even draw a groan.

UNACCEPTABLE POINT OF VIEW

The more remote material is in terms of time and place, the more easily you can see how a film imposes meanings, and how pervasive were the received truths of the day. Any footage taken in colonial days is likely to disclose the unreflecting racial supremacy of the day, in which natives were treated at best like children. Nobody at the time questioned the favoritism of the filmmaking, for it was "true" in the eyes of the white beholders.

The parallel should give us due warning: What we view of present-day footage of familiar scenes may seem objective and value-free. But representations, whether of actuality or of life enacted or re-enacted, are always *constructs*. This means they are always subjective and imply a triangular relationship among content, Storyteller, and viewer. You must be able to identify what an implied point of view is, decide what biases it incorporates, and assess its overall credibility. In Scorsese's *Taxi Driver* (1976), Travis Bickle, the narrator, is so crazed that he is plainly what literature calls an "unreliable narrator." Usually a point of view, especially one established through camerawork alone, is much more subtle and difficult to pin down.

Imagine you are hunting through archival World War II shots in a film library, as I once did at the Imperial War Museum in London. After you recover from the atmosphere of a place so packed with sad ghosts, you notice that by today's standards, the cameras and film stock from this era were less developed. Even so, each shot testifies, in addition to its subject, to different kinds of involvement from its makers, that is, different emotions, emphases, and agendas.

You run a shot that some librarian has neatly labeled "Russian soldiers, vicinity of Warsaw, running into sniper fire." From the first frame you notice how emotionally loaded everything seems: It's shot in high-contrast black-and-white that accentuates the mood, and the air is smoky because lighting comes from behind the subjects. Here as elsewhere, filming is undeniably a mechanical process of reproduction, but everything has been polarized by the interrelationship among human choice, technology, subject, and environment. All these things contribute to the powerful feelings you are getting. The camera enters the soldiers' world because it runs jerkily with them instead of shooting from a sheltered tripod. You catch your breath when a soldier falls because the cameraman almost trips over his fallen comrade. The camera recovers and continues onward, leaving the wounded soldier to his fate. Then suddenly it plunges to the ground. Framing some out-of-focus mud, the camera motor runs out. With slow horror you realize you have just accompanied a cameraman in his last seconds of work. Desolated, you replay his shot several times. As you stop on particular frames, it seems as though time and destiny can be replayed, re-entered, and relived. Even when you replay something and know full well what's going to happen, *film is always and forever in the present tense.* Film permits destiny to be played and replayed.

Now someone brings you a photo of a dead cameraman lying face down on the battlefield, his camera fallen from his hands. You recognize the knob of mud from his last seconds of film. It's him, your poor cameraman. Left alone with him, you ponder what made him willing to gamble his life to do his work. You wonder whom he left behind and whether they ever learned how he died. Now you are his witness because you died with him. Somewhere inside you his work, his good intentions, his gamble that ended in death will always be with you. You are aching with sadness, but he has given you something and you have grown. Now you carry him in the recesses of yourself. You have *become* him. There can be a world of meaning in a single shot. Here authorship and the author's fate converge.

SCREEN DIRECTION AND ANGLES

Screen direction is a term describing a subject's direction or movement, especially when a subject's movement links several shots, as in a chase (Figure 4–4). An important screen convention is that *characters and their movements are generally observed from only one side of the scene axis.* Let's imagine you ignored this and intercut one part of a parade moving across the screen L-R (left to right) with another going R-L. The audience would expect the two factions to collide, as when police move into a position where they can block a demonstration.

Now suppose you run ahead of the parade to watch it file past a landmark. In the new position you would see marchers entering an empty street from the same screen direction. But in life, you might cross the parade's path to watch it from the other side. This would be unremarkable because you initiated the relocation. But in film, cutting to a camera position across the axis must be specially set up or it reverses some screen directions and causes disorientation for the spectator.

CHANGING SCREEN DIRECTION

You can make a parade change screen direction by filming at an angle to a corner (Figure 4–5). The marchers enter in the background going screen right to screen left (R-L), turn the corner in the foreground, and exit L-R. In essence they have changed screen direction. If subsequent shots are to match, their action will also have to be L-R.

Another solution to changing screen direction is to dolly during a gap in the parade so the camera *visibly* crosses the subject's axis of movement (Figure 4–6). Remember that any change of observing camera orientation to the action must

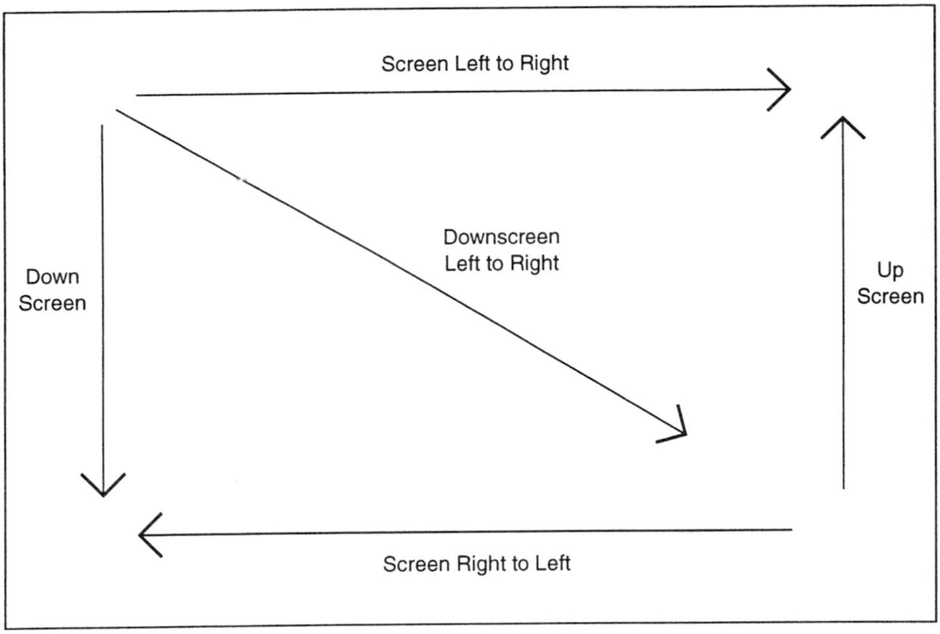

FIGURE 4–4

A range of screen directions and their descriptions.

be shown onscreen. Screen direction can be changed without trouble if we see the change onscreen.

DIFFERENT ANGLES ON THE SAME ACTION

So far we have found everyday human correlations for every aspect of film language. But can there be one to justify using very different angles to cover the same action? We said earlier that cutting together long and closer shots taken from a single axis or direction suggests, by excluding the irrelevant, an observer's changed degree of concentration. But now imagine the scene of a tense family meal that is covered from several very different angles. Though it's a familiar screen convention, surely it has no corollary in life? Ah, but wait. This narrative device—switching viewpoints during a single scene—was a prose convention long before film was invented; so probably it has rather deep roots.

In literature it is clear that multiple points of view imply not physical changes of vantage point but shifts in psychological and emotional points of view. The same is true when this strategy is used onscreen. But film is misleading because, unlike literature, it seems to give us "real" events and a "real" vantage point, so we must constantly remind ourselves that film gives us a *perception* of events, a "seeming" that is not, despite appearances, the events themselves.

Here's an example from your own life. When you are a bystander during a major disagreement between friends, you get so absorbed that you forget all

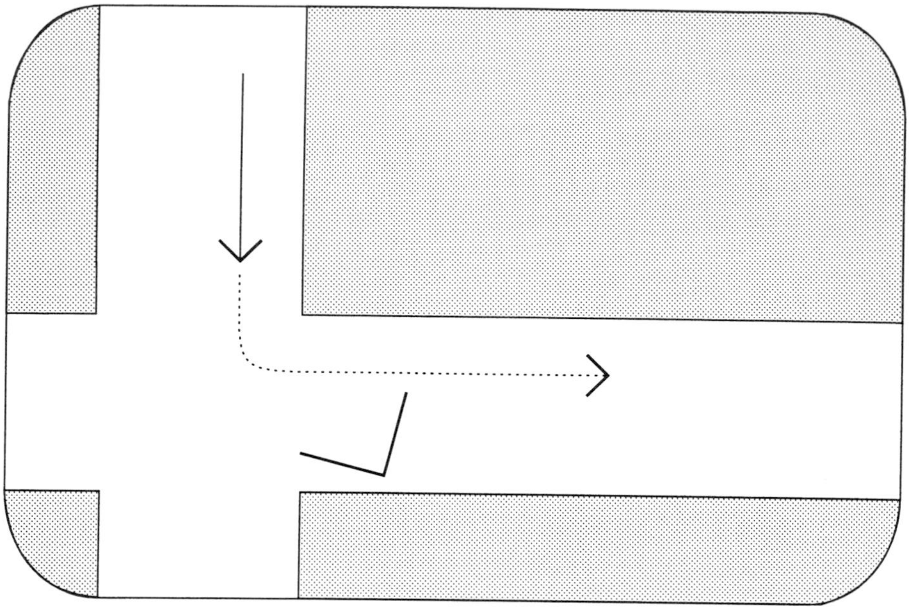

FIGURE 4–5

By shooting at a corner, a parade or moving object can be made to change screen direction.

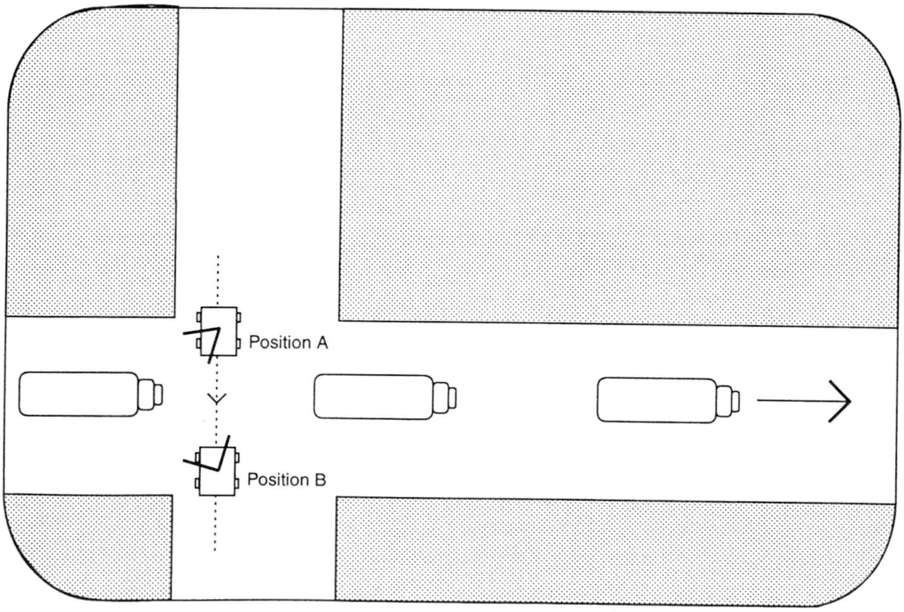

FIGURE 4–6

Dollying sideways between floats in a parade changes the parade's effective screen direction, but the dollying movement must be shown.

about yourself. Instead, you go through a series of internal agreements and disagreements, seeing first one person's point, then another's. You get so involved that you virtually experience each of the protagonists' realities. Screen language evokes this heightened subjectivity by employing a series of physically privileged views. These correspond, we have learned, with the way an observer can identify with different people as time progresses. Under such close examination, our sympathy and fascination migrates from person to person. What's important is that an empathic shift must be rooted in an identifiable point of view—usually one of the characters—if it is to pass as natural and integrated. This state of heightened and all-encompassing concentration is not one that anyone normally maintains for long.

ABSTRACTION

The alternative pole to this state of probing emotional inquiry is that of withdrawal into mental stocktaking or abstraction. We alter our examination from the whole to a part, or a part to the whole—whatever suffices to occupy our reverie. Watch your own shifts of attention; you will find that you often do this to escape into a private realm where you can speculate, contemplate, remember, or imagine. Often a detail catching your eye at this time turns out to have symbolic meaning, or is a part made to stand for a whole. Thus a car door immersed up to the door handle in swirling water can stand for a whole flood. This oft-used principle in film is called *synecdoche* (pronounced sin-ECK-doh-kee). It arises when our eye alights on something symbolic, that is, something conventionally representative, much as a scale represents justice or a flower growing on an empty lot might represent renewal.

Abstraction can arise for different reasons. Going into reverie may represent withdrawal or refuge by the Observer, but also taking refuge inward as one makes an intense search for the significance of a recent event. Selective focus is a device used to suggest this state. When an object is isolated on the screen, with its foreground and background thrown out of focus, it strongly suggests abstracted vision. Abnormal motion—either slow or fast—has rather the same effect. These are ways to represent how we routinely dismantle reality and distance ourselves from the moment. We may be searching for meaning, hiding from pain, or simply regenerating ourselves through imaginative play.

SUBJECTIVITY AND OBJECTIVITY

Our world is full of dualities, oppositions, and ironic contrasts. You drive your car very fast at night, and then, stopping to look at the stars you become aware of your own insignificance under their light, which has taken millions of years to reach your eye. Human attention shifts from subjectivity to objectivity, from past to present and back again, from looking at a crowd as a phenomenon to looking at the profile of a woman as she turns away. There is screen language to replicate every phase of the Observer's attention. If as a filmmaker you make the shifts in the image-stream consistent with human consciousness, your audience will experience an integrated being's presence—that of our invisible, thinking, all-seeing Concerned Observer.

DURATION, RHYTHM, AND CONCENTRATION

Human beings are directed by rhythms that begin in the brain and control heartbeat and breathing. We tap our feet to music or jump up to dance when the music takes us. Everything we do is measured by the beat, duration, and capacity of our minds and bodies.

Screen language is governed by other human capacities. The duration of a shot, for instance, is determined by how much attention it demands, just as the decision of when to cross the road is governed by how long we take to scope out the traffic. The speed of a movement on the screen is judged by its context, where it is going, and why.

Speech has inherently powerful rhythms. The Czech composer Leoš Janáček was so fascinated by language rhythms that his late compositions draw on the pacing and tonal patterns of people talking. Films—particularly those with long dialogue scenes—are composed similarly around the speech and movement rhythms of the characters. Screen language mimics the way an observer's senses shift direction and follows the way we maintain concentration by refreshing our minds through search. Complex dialogue scenes are always the most difficult to get right in editing because subtextual consistency depends on delicate nuances.

Rhythm plays an important role in helping us assimilate film, but this comes from an old, established principle. Archaic narratives like Homer's *Odyssey*, the Arthurian legends, and the Norse sagas were composed in strict rhythmic patterns. This not only made memorization easier for the troubadours who recited them from court to court, but language with a strong rhythmic structure helped audiences concentrate longer.

Film language makes use of every possible rhythm, not only speech. Many sounds from everyday life—bird song, traffic, the sounds from a building site, or the wheels of a train—contain strong rhythms to help in composing a sequence. Even static pictorial compositions contain visual rhythms derived from the sensations of symmetry, balance, repetition, opposition, and patterns that intrigue the eye.

SEQUENCE AND MEMORY

In life there is an everlasting flow of events, and only some of them are memorable. A biography takes only the significant parts of a life and jumps them together. The building blocks are segments of time (the hero's visit to the hospital emergency room after a road accident), the events at a location (the high points of his residency in Rome), or of a developing idea (as he builds their home, his wife loses patience with the slowness of the process). Because time and space are now indicated, there are junctures between the narrative building blocks that must either be indicated or hidden as the story demands. These junctures are transitions, to be emphasized or elided (glided over).

Actually this process of *elision* is also faithful to human experience because our memory casts off whatever is insignificant. If you think back on the sensations you had during an accident, you'll find your *recall* keeps only the significant parts, almost like a shot list for a film sequence. The memory is a fine editor.

Once, advising two students who were feeling defeated in front of their 70 hours of documentary dailies, I surprised them by telling them not to use their logs at all, but to write down what they remembered. What they wrote down was, of course, that minority of the footage that "had something," and this became the core of a successful film.

When we have a dream or tell an experience, we relay only the tips of what we recall, never the troughs.

TRANSITIONS AND TRANSITIONAL DEVICES

The transitions we make in life—from place to place, or from time to time—are either imperceptible because we are preoccupied or come as a surprise or shock. Stories replicate this by hiding the seams between sequences or by indicating and even emphasizing them. An action match between a woman drinking her morning fruit juice and a beer drinker raising his glass in a smoky dive minimizes the scene shift by drawing attention to the act of drinking. A dissolve from one scene to another would signal, in rather creaky language, "and time passed." A simple cut from one place to the next leaves the audience to fill in the blank. However, imagine the scene of a teenager singing along to the car radio on a long, boring drive, followed by flash images of a truck, screeching tires, and the youngster yanking desperately at the steering wheel. The transition from comfort to panic is intentionally a shock transition and reproduces the violent change we undergo when taken nastily by surprise.

Sound can be used as a transitional device. Hearing a conversation over an empty landscape can draw us forward into the next scene (of two campers in their tent). Cutting to a shot of a cityscape while we still hear the campsite bird song gives the feeling of being confronted with a change of location while the mind and heart lag behind in the woodland. Both these transitional devices imply an emotional point of view.

Each transition, like the literary phrase, *and then*, is a narrative device with its own way of handling the progression between two discontinuous story segments. Each transition's style also implies an attitude or point of view emanating from the characters or Storyteller.

SCREEN LANGUAGE IN SUMMARY

Screen language is routinely confused with professional packaging and can easily lack soul when used offhandedly to present events to an audience. But whenever we sense the sympathy and integrity of a questing human intelligence at work, life onscreen becomes human and compelling instead of mechanical and banal.

Imagine that you go to your high school reunion and afterward see what another participant filmed with his little video camera. It was his eyes and ears, recording whatever he cared to notice. Afterward you find that his version of the events gives a strong idea of his personality. You see not only whom he looked at and talked to, but based on how he spent time with each person and event, you see his mind and heart at work and even into the inner workings of his character.

Likewise, the handling of events and personalities in intelligent fiction always implies an overarching heart and mind behind the perceiving. Under the *auteur* theory of filmmaking, this is the director's vision. But controlling how a whole film crew and actors create the perceptual stream is simply beyond any one person's control, so I prefer to personify the intelligence behind the film's point of view as that of the Storyteller. This is not the simple "I" of the director, but a fictional entity as complex and dependent on the director's invention as any of the film's characters.

Less obviously this is also true for documentary and other nonfiction forms. All are constructs, even though they may take their materials directly from life. At its most compelling, *screen language implies the course of a particular intelligence at work as it grapples with the events in which it participates.* People who work successfully in the medium seem to understand this instinctively, but I have never heard or read what I have just written. If you happen to lack such instinct, simply pattern your work around the natural, observable processes of human perception, human action, and human reaction. You can't go far wrong if you are true to life. As you do this, your film will somehow take on a narrative persona all its own, and as this emerges you should augment it.

RESEARCHING TO BE A STORYTELLER

You could prepare yourself for the responsibility of storytelling by reading all of Proust and Henry James. If you don't have the time, simply form the habit of monitoring your own processes of physical and emotional observation, especially under duress. You'll constantly forget to do this homework because we are prisoners of our own subjectivity. In ordinary living we see, think, and react automatically, storing our conclusions but remaining oblivious to how we arrived there. Now compare this with what you usually see on the screen. The camera's verisimilitude makes events unfold with seeming objectivity. Well used, it gives events the force of *inevitability*, like music that is perfectly judged.

Students often assume that the cinema process and its instruments are an alchemy that will aggrandize and ennoble whatever they put before the camera. But cameras and projectors simply frame and magnify. Truth looks more true and artifice more artificial. Small is big, and big is enormous. Every step by a film's makers relentlessly exposes their fallibilities along with their true insights. To use the medium successfully you will need to understand a lot about the human psyche. You must develop an instinct for what your audience will make of anything you give them. This is rooted not in audience studies or theory, but in your instinct for human truth and human judgments.

Let's say it again: A film delivers not only a filtered version of events but also, by mimicking human consciousness, it implies a human heart and mind doing the observing. Screen some of the world's first films and you'll comprehend this. Louis and Auguste Lumière are palpably present behind their wooden box camera, winding away at the handle until their handmade filmstock runs out. It is through their minds as much as their cameras that we see workers leaving the Lumière factory in Lyon or the train disgorging passengers so casually unaware of the history they are making.

Film conventions are modeled on the dialectical flow of our consciousness whenever we are following something of importance to us. Our emotional responses play a huge part in this by literally directing our sight and hearing. You can test this. Try noting what you remember from a striking event you experienced. What most people write down about an accident, for instance, is highly visual, abbreviated, selective, and emotionally loaded. Just like a film!

WHY DOCUMENTARY TRAINING IS USEFUL

Unfortunately there is a perception on the part of would-be fiction filmmakers that documentary is a lesser form. Actually, some *direct cinema* experience, if you can get it, is very useful. Direct cinema is also called *observational filming*, and it demands that the camera is subservient to the action and does not intrude into or alter any of the processes it films. John Cassavetes' earliest films, such as *Shadows* (1959), *Faces* (1968), and *Husbands* (1970), were made in this way and remain powerful and disturbing to this day. He believed that the stock Freudian, psychological keys to character are bogus, and instead character is formed or even found in the interstices of human interaction. Ray Carney in *The Films of John Cassavetes* (Cambridge University Press, 1994) has written with rare insight about how Cassavetes' characters plunge into experiences in order to learn about them:

> But the openness of Cassavetes' characters is much more radical than their merely being open to change or defying prediction, and that leads to the second difference between Cassavetes' characters and those in virtually all other American feature films. The Cassavetean self is open in the sense of pulling down the walls that normally separate one character from another. Like onstage performers, characters like Lelia, Mabel, and Gloria make themselves up and revise themselves in a continuous process of dramatic improvisation in response to the different audiences before which they appear. Their identities are relational; they are, at least in part, negotiated with others. Cassavetes' leading characters figure an extreme degree of awareness of, sensitivity to, and responsiveness to others; yet that is not to put it strongly enough. Cassavetes' characters are so open to external influences and so willing to make adjustments in their positions that it would be better to say that it is as if their identities are not theirs alone, but shared with others. They are not in complete control of their selves, but turn over part of the control to others. Their selves are not solid and bounded, but soft and permeable; others reach into them, affect them, change them, and at times even inhabit them . . . Their identities are supremely vulnerable—continuously susceptible to violation or deformation.
>
> (Introduction, pp 21–22)

Perhaps only an extremely experienced and passionately committed actor could possibly create characters with such a truthful degree of human volatility and at the same time understand the futility of stock forms of illustrative characterization.

Your ability to see actors at work and challenge them to create between themselves will be enhanced if you use improvisation techniques and a documentary technique that captures what actually happens. For you, documentary can:

- Offer a rapid and voluminous training in finding stories and telling them on the screen.
- Develop confidence in your abilities and show the rewards of spontaneity and adapting to the actual.
- Demand that its makers use intuitive judgments.
- Develop your eye for a focused and truthful human presence.
- Offer a workout in the language of film and demand that you find a means of narrative compression.
- Offer the opportunity for fast shooting but slow editing and time to contemplate the results. Fiction, conversely, is slow to shoot but fast to edit.
- Require much inventiveness and adaptability in the area of sound shooting. Sound design can be quite intensive in documentary, and location sound inequities teach the preeminent importance of good microphone choice and positioning.
- Show you real characters in real action. Character is allied with will or volition, and each is best revealed when the subject has to struggle with some obstacle. You'll also see Carney's observation in action: that individual identity is somehow developed between people and is not a fixed and formed commodity that functions the same way in all circumstances.
- Face you with the need to capture evidence of character-making decisions. Gripping observational documentary usually deals with the behavior of people trying to accomplish things. Documentaries expose the elements of good dramatic writing by revealing these principles at work in life.
- Allow you to see how, in active characters, issues flow from decisions, and decisions create new issues.
- Demonstrate how character-driven documentaries are no different from character-driven fiction. Well-conceived documentary is thus a laboratory of character-driven drama.
- Show how editing must impose brevity, compression, and rhythm. In fiction, this has to be injected at the writing stage. Thus documentary teaches why the elements of good writing involve brevity, compression, and action.
- License a director and camera crew to improvise and spontaneously create.
- Give directors advance experience of participants simply being, a crucial benchmark for knowing when actors have reached that state during the search for spontaneity.
- Teach the director to catalyze truth from participants, so a fiction director can learn to do the same with actors.
- Pose the same narrative problems as fiction, thus giving what is really writing experience.
- Help the whole crew to see all human action as dramatic evidence.
- Be shot in real time, when drama must be plucked from life. This accustoms directors to thinking on their feet.
- Establish that the risk/confrontation/chemistry of the moment are the stock in trade of both documentary and improvisational fiction.

Documentary coverage of fiction film rehearsals is useful for:

- Discovering the best camera positions.
- Practicing camera framing and movements as something subservient to actors.
- Revealing performance inequities on the screen.
- Demystifying the relationship between live performance and its results on the screen.
- Seeing need for rewrites based on the screen results.
- Giving experience in working with non-actors or actors who are marginally experienced.
- Helping to spot clichés, bad acting habits, and areas that are forced or false.
- Helping prepare actors for the presence of camera—thus lowering the regression that follows the introduction of a camera when shooting begins.
- Posing problems of adaptation to a here-and-now actuality.

In later chapters I strongly advocate shooting continuous-take documentary coverage of rehearsals, from which (if you follow my advice) you will see the value of your work in the points above. Should documentary catch your interest, the companion volume to this book will expand the points above (Michael Rabiger, *Directing the Documentary* 3rd edition, Burlington, MA Focal Press, 1998). Incorporating a documentary attitude to human truth could change how you think about fiction and put you with the modern masters of the cinema who are moving cinema away from its theatrical beginnings.

CHAPTER 5

SEEING WITH A MOVIEMAKER'S EYE

The four study projects in this chapter will make you familiar with the essentials of composition, editing, script analysis, and lighting. Collectively they yield the basics of seeing with a moviemaker's eye and will be immensely useful to your confidence when you begin directing.

PROJECT 5-1: PICTURE COMPOSITION ANALYSIS

A stimulating and highly productive way to investigate composition is to do so with several other people or as a class. Though what follows is written for a study group, you can do it solo if circumstances so dictate.

Equipment Required: For static composition, a slide projector and/or an overhead projector to enlarge graphics are best but not indispensable. For dynamic composition you will need a video or DVD player.

Object: To learn the composition of visual elements by studying how the eye reacts to a static composition and then how it handles dynamic composition, that is, composition during movement.

Study Materials: For static composition, a book of figurative painting reproductions (best used under an overhead projector so you have a big image to scan), or better, a dozen or more 35 mm art slides, also projected as large images. Slides of Impressionist paintings are good, but the more eclectic your collection, the better. For dynamic composition, use any visually interesting sequences from a favorite movie, though any Eisenstein movie will be ideal.

ANALYSIS FORMAT

In a class setting it's important to keep a discussion going, but if you are working alone, notes or sketches are a good way to log what you discover. Help from books on composition is not easily gained because many texts make composition seem intimidating or formulaic and may be difficult to apply to the moving image. Sometimes rules *prevent* seeing rather than promoting it, so trust your eye to see what is really there and use your own non-specialist vocabulary to describe it.

STRATEGY FOR STUDY

If you are leading a group, you will need to explain what is wanted something like this:

> We're doing this to discover how each person's visual perception actually works. I'll put a picture up on the screen. Notice where your eye goes in the composition first, and then what course it takes as you examine the rest of the picture. After about 15 seconds I'll ask someone to describe what path his eye followed. You don't need any special jargon, just let your responses come from the specifics of each picture. Please avoid the temptation to look for a story in the picture or to guess what the picture is "about," even when it suggests a story.

With each new image, pick a new person to comment. Because not everyone's eye responds the same way, there will be interesting discussions about the variations. There will usually be a great deal of agreement, so everyone is led to formulate ideas about visual reflexes and about what compositional components the eye finds attractive and engrossing. It is good to start simply and graduate to more abstract images, and then even to completely abstract ones. Many people, relieved of the burden of deciding a picture's "subject," can begin to enjoy a Kandinsky, a Mondrian, or a Pollock for itself, without fuming over whether or not it is really art. After about an hour of pictures and discussion, encourage your group to frame their own guidelines for composing images.

After the group has formed some ideas and gained confidence from analyzing paintings, I usually show both good and bad photos. Photography, less obviously contrived than painting, tends to be accepted less critically. This is a good moment to uncover in striking photography just how many classical elements arise from what first appeared to be a straight record of life.

Here are questions to help you discover ways to see more critically. They can be applied after seeing a number of paintings or photos, or you could direct the group's attention to each question's area as it becomes relevant.

STATIC COMPOSITION

1. After your eye has taken in the whole, review its starting point. Why did it go to that point in the picture? (Common reasons: brightest point in composition, darkest place in an otherwise light composition, single area of an arresting color, significant junction of lines creating a focal point.)
2. When your eye moved away from its point of first attraction, what did it follow? (Commonly: lines, perhaps actual ones like the line of a fence or an outstretched arm, or inferred lines such as the sightline from one character looking at another. Sometimes the eye simply moves to another significant area in the composition, going from one organized area to another and jumping skittishly across the intervening disorganization.)

3. How much movement did your eye make before returning to its starting point?
4. What specifically drew your eye to each new place?
5. If you trace an imaginary line over the painting to show the route your eye took, what shape do you have? (Sometimes this is a circular pattern and sometimes a triangle or ellipse, but it can be many shapes. Any shape at all can reveal an alternative organization that helps you see beyond the wretched and dominating idea that every picture tells a story.)
6. Are there any places along your imaginary line that seem specially charged with energy? (These are often sightlines: between the Virgin's eyes and her baby's, between a guitarist's and his hand on the strings, between two field workers, one of whom is facing away.)
7. How would you characterize the compositional movement? (For example, geometrical, repetitive textures, swirling, falling inward, symmetrically divided down the middle, flowing diagonally, etc. Making a translation from one medium to another—in this case from the visual to the verbal—always helps you discover what is truly there.)
8. What parts, if any, do the following play in a particular picture?
   - repetition
   - parallels
   - convergence
   - divergence
   - curves
   - straight lines
   - strong verticals
   - strong horizontals
   - strong diagonals
   - textures
   - non-naturalistic coloring
   - light and shade
   - human figures
9. How is depth suggested? (This is an ever-present problem for the director of photography (DP) who, if inexperienced, is liable to take what I think of as the firing squad approach: that is, placing the human subjects against a flat background and shooting them. Unless there is something to create different planes, like a wall angling away from the foreground to suggest a receding space, the screen is like a painter's canvas and looks what it really is—two-dimensional.)
10. How are the individuality and mood of the human subjects expressed? (This is commonly through facial expression and body language, of course. But more interesting are the juxtapositions the painter makes of person to person, person to surroundings, or people inside a total design.)
11. How is space arranged on either side of a human subject, particularly in portraits? (Usually in profiles there is lead space, that is, more space in front of the person than behind them, as if in response to our need to see what the person sees.)

12. How much headroom is given above a person, particularly in a close-up? (Sometimes the edge of a frame cuts off the top of a head or may not show one head at all in a group shot.)
13. How often and how deliberately are people and objects placed at the margins of the picture so you have to imagine what is cut off? (By demonstrating the frame's restriction you can make the viewer's imagination supply what is beyond the edges of the "window.")

VISUAL RHYTHM: HOW DURATION AFFECTS PERCEPTION

So far I have stressed the idea of an immediate, instinctual response to the organization of an image. When you show a series of slides without comment, you move to a new image after sufficient time for the eye to absorb each picture. Some pictures require longer than others. For a movie audience, unless shots are held for an unusual length of time, as pioneered in Antonioni's *L'Avventura* (1960), this is how an audience must deal with each new shot in a film.

Unlike responding to a photograph or painting, which can be studied thoughtfully and at leisure, the filmgoer must interpret the image within an unremitting and preordained forward movement in time. It is like reading a poster on the side of a moving bus: if the words and images cannot be assimilated in the given time, the inscription goes past without being understood. If, however, the bus is crawling in a traffic jam, you may have time to absorb and become critical or even rejecting of the poster.

This tells us that there is an optimum duration for each shot to stay on the screen. It depends on the complexity of a shot's content and form and how hard the viewer must work to extract its significance and intended meaning. An invisible third factor also affects ideal shot duration—that of expectation. The audience may work fast at interpreting each new image, or slowly, depending on how much time the film has allowed for interpreting preceding shots.

The principle by which a shot's duration is determined according to content, form, significance, and expectation is called *visual rhythm*. A filmmaker, like a musician, can either relax or intensify a visual rhythm, and this has consequences for the cutting rate and the ideal tempo of camera movements.

Ideal films for studying compositional relationships in film and visual rhythm are classics by the Russian director Sergei Eisenstein, such as *The Battleship Potemkin* (1925), *Que Viva Mexico* (1931–1932), *Alexander Nevsky* (1938), and *Ivan the Terrible* (1944–1946). Eisenstein's origins as a theater designer made him very aware of the impact upon an audience of musical and visual design. His sketchbooks show how carefully he designed everything in each shot, down to the costumes. More recent films with a strong sense of design are Ingmar Bergman's *The Seventh Seal* (1956), Stanley Kubrick's *A Clockwork Orange* (1971), and David Lynch's *Blue Velvet* (1986).

Designer's sketches and the comic strip are the precursor of the storyboard (see example in Figure 6–2 in the next chapter), which is much used by ad agencies and conservative elements in the film industry to lock down what each new frame will convey. Storyboarding is particularly helpful for the inexperienced, even when your artistry is as lousy as mine and doesn't run much beyond stick figures.

DYNAMIC COMPOSITION

With moving images, more compositional principles come into play. A balanced composition can become disturbingly unbalanced should someone cross the frame, or leave it altogether. Even the turn of a figure's head in the foreground may posit a new eyeline (subject-to-subject axis), which in turn demands a compositional rebalancing. Then again, zooming in from a wide shot demands reframing because compositionally there is a drastic change, even though the subject is the same.

To study dynamic composition, find a visually interesting sequence, such as the chase in John Ford's *Stagecoach* (1939) or William Friedkin's *The French Connection* (1971) or almost any part of Andrew Davis' *The Fugitive* (1993). Here your VCR's slow-scan function will be very useful. See how many of these aspects you can find:

1. Reframing because the subject moved (look for a variety of camera adjustments)
2. Reframing as a consequence of something or someone entering the frame
3. Reframing in anticipation of something or someone entering the frame
4. A change in the point of focus to move attention from background to foreground or vice versa. (This changes the texture of significant areas of the composition from hard focus to soft.)
5. Strong movement within an otherwise static composition (How many can you find? Across frame, diagonally, from background to foreground, from foreground to background, up frame, down frame, etc. Eisenstein films are full of these compositions.)

In addition, ask yourself the following questions:

1. How much do you feel identified with each kind of subject movement? (This is a tricky issue, but in general the nearer you are to the axis of a movement, the more subjective is your sense of involvement).
2. How quickly does the camera adjust to a figure who gets up and moves to another place in frame? (Often camera movements are *motivated* by changes from within the composition, and subject and camera moves are made synchronous, with no clumsy lag or anticipation. When documentary covers spontaneous events, such inaccuracies are normal and signal that nothing is contrived.)
3. How often are the camera or the characters blocked (that is, choreographed) to isolate one character? What is the dramatic justification?
4. How often is the camera moved or the characters blocked so as to bring two characters back into frame? (Good camerawork, composition, and blocking is always trying to show *relatedness*. This helps to intensify meanings and ironies and reduces the need to manufacture relationship through editing.)
5. How often is composition angled down sightlines and seeing in depth, and how often do sightlines cross the screen and render space as flat? (Point of view often shifts at these junctures from subjective to objective.)

6. What do changes of angle and composition make you feel about (or toward) the characters? (Probably you will feel more involved, then more objective.)
7. Find several compositions that successfully create depth and define what visual element is responsible. (An obvious one is where the camera is next to a railroad line as a train rushes up and past. Both the perspective revealed by the rails and the movement of the train create depth. In deep shots, different zones of lighting at varying distances from the camera, or zones of hard and soft focus, can also achieve this.)
8. How many shots can you find where the camera changes position to include more or different background detail to comment on the foreground subject?

INTERNAL AND EXTERNAL COMPOSITION

So far we have been looking at composition that is internal to each shot. Another form of compositional relationship is the momentary relationship between an outgoing shot and the next, incoming shot. This relationship called *external composition*, is a hidden part of film language. It is hidden because we are unaware of how much it influences our judgments and expectations.

A common usage for external composition is when a character leaving the frame in the outgoing shot (A) leads the spectator's eye to the very place in shot B where an assassin will emerge in a large and restless crowd. The eye is conducted to the right place in a busy composition.

Another example might be the framing of two complementary close shots in which two characters have an intense conversation. The compositions are similar but symmetrically opposed. In Figure 5–1 the two-shot (A) gives a good overall feel of the scene, but man and child are too far away. The close shots, (B) and (C), retain the feel of the scene but effectively cut out the dead space between them. Note that the heads are not centered: each person has lead (rhyming with "feed") space in front of his face, and this reflects his positioning in the two-shot. The man is high in the frame and looking downward, and the child lower in the frame and looking up—just as in the matching two-shot.

Other aspects will emerge if you apply the questions below to the film sequences you review. Use the slow-scan function to examine compositional relationships at the cutting point. Go backward and forward several times over each cut to be sure you miss nothing. Try these for yourself:

1. Where was your point of concentration at the end of the shot? (You can trace where your eye goes by moving your finger around the screen of the monitor. Your last point in the outgoing shot is where your eye enters the composition of the incoming shot. Notice how shot duration determines the distance the eye travels in exploring the shot. This means that on top of what we have already established about shot length, it is also a factor in external composition.)
2. What kinds of symmetry exist between complementary shots (that is, between shots designed to be intercut)?
3. What is the relationship between two different-sized shots of the same subject that are designed to cut together? (This is a revealing one; the inexperienced

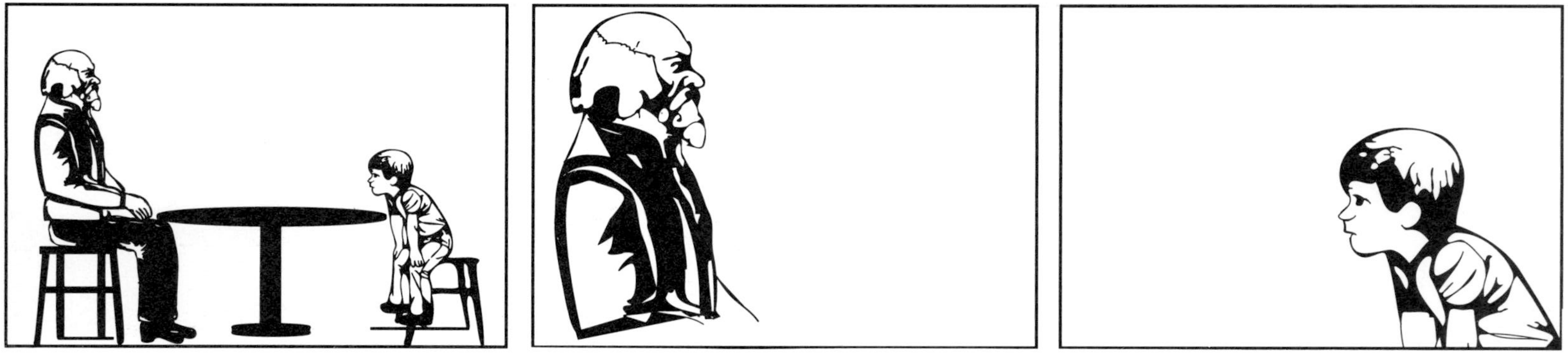

A B C

FIGURE 5–1

Wide shot and two complementary close-ups (CUs). Notice the lead space in front of each CU character and how the height and placing in the frame of each replicates the composition of the master shot.

camera operator will produce medium shots and close shots that cut poorly because the placements of the subject are incompatible.)

4. Examine a match cut very slowly and see if there is any overlap. (Especially where there is relatively fast action, a match cut, to look smooth, needs about four frames of the action repeated on the incoming shot. This is because the eye does not register the first three or four frames of any new image. This built-in perceptual lag means that when you cut to the beat of music, the only way to make the cuts look in sync with the beat is to make each cut around three or four frames *before* the actual beat point.)
5. Find visual comparisons in external composition that make a Storyteller's comment (for instance, cut from a pair of eyes to car headlights approaching at night, from a dockside crane to a man feeding birds with arm outstretched, etc.)

COMPOSITION, FORM, AND FUNCTION

Form is the manner in which content is presented, and visual composition as part of form is not mere embellishment but a vital element in communication. While it interests and even delights the eye, good composition is an important organizing force when used to dramatize relativity and relationship, and to project ideas. Superior composition not only makes the subject (content) accessible, it heightens the viewer's perceptions and stimulates his or her imaginative involvement, like language from the pen of a good poet.

I believe that form follows function, and that you should involve yourself with content before looking for the appropriate form to best communicate it. Another way of working, which comes from being more interested in language than content, is to decide on a form and then look for an appropriate subject. The difference is one of purpose and temperament. Content, form, structure, and style are analyzed in greater detail in Chapters 12 to 16.

So far we have looked at pictorial composition, but a film's sound track is also a composition and is critically important to a film's overall impact. The study of sound is included in the next editing study project.

PROJECT 5-2: EDITING ANALYSIS

Equipment Required: VCR or DVD player as in Project 1

Objective: To produce a detailed analysis of a portion of film using standard abbreviations and terminology; to analyze the way a film is constructed; and to distinguish the conventions of film language so they can be used confidently

Study Materials: Any well-made feature film containing dialogue scenes and processes that have clear beginnings, middles, and ends will do, but I recommend these films for their excellent development of characters and settings:

- Terence Malick's *Days of Heaven* (1978) for its awe-inspiring cinematography of the Texas landscape, its exploration of space and loneliness, and its unusual and effective pacing. The film uses the younger sister Linda as a narrator.

- Peter Weir's *Witness* (1985) for its classically shot dialogue scenes, its exploration of love between mismatched cultures, and the superb Amish work sequences.
- Stephen Daldry's *Billy Elliot* (2000) has interesting character studies and dynamic dance sequences.

FIRST VIEWING

First, see the whole film without stopping, and then see it a second time before you attempt any analysis. Write down all the strong feelings the film evoked, paying no attention to order. Note from memory which sequences sparked those feelings. You may have an additional sequence or two that intrigued you as a piece of virtuoso storytelling. Note these down, too, but whatever you study should be something that hits you at an emotional, rather than a merely intellectual, level.

ANALYSIS FORMAT

What you write down will be displayed on paper in *split page format*, also known as *TV script format*. All visuals are placed on the left half of the page and all sound occupies the right half (Figure 5–2).

First, transcribe the picture and dialogue—shot by shot and word by word—as they relate to each other. Your draft transcript should be written with wide line spacing on numerous sheets of paper so you can insert additional information on subsequent passes. Once this basic information is on paper, you can turn to such things as shot transitions, internal and external composition of shots, screen direction, camera movements, opticals (such as fades, dissolves, superimpositions), sound effects, and the use of music. You will need to make a number of shot-by-shot passes through your chosen sequence, dealing with one or two aspects of the content and form at a time.

Because your objective is to extract the maximum amount of information about an interesting passage of film language, it is better to do a short sequence (two to four minutes) very thoroughly than a long one superficially. Script formats, whether split page or screenplay, show only what can be seen and heard. Some of your notes (for example, on the mood a shot evokes) will clutter the functional simplicity of your transcript, so keep them separately.

MAKING AND USING A FLOOR PLAN

For a sequence containing a dialogue exchange, make a *floor plan* (also called a *ground plan*) sketch (Figure 5–3). In the example, the character Eric enters, stands in front of William, goes to the phone, picks up a book from the table, looks out the window, and then sits on the couch. The whole action has been covered by three camera positions. Making a floor plan for a sequence allows you to: recreate what a whole room or location layout looks like, record how the characters move around, and decide how the camera is placed. This will help you decide where to place your own camera in the future, and it reveals how little of an environment needs to be shown for the audience to create the rest in their imaginations. This is the co-creation discussed earlier in Chapter 1.

TB Sanatorium Sequence

ACTION	SOUND
Fade in LS ruins of sanatorium. Camera pans left around buildings, stops with two small figures walking slowly.	Birdsong, distant jet, sounds of distant softball players.
Cut to two pairs of feet walking on brick path, weeds growing up.	Fade in sound of elderly man coughing.
2S Sylvia and Aaron in profile.	Young Man's Voice: "Dad? Dad?"
POV shot residential building, windows broken.	Aaron: "This is where I came to see him...
Telephoto shot of gutter with ferns growing against skyline.	....last. You know what he missed the most?"
	Sylvia: "Your mother?"
LS through ruined greenhouse, Sylvia and Aaron in BG.	Aaron: "No, his garden. His damned garden."
POV shot sapling growing up through broken glass roof.	Aaron: "Why did they let this place go? It used to be so beautiful."
CS Aaron's hand opening creaky gate.	Sylvia: "How long did you come here?"
WS enclosure with vegetable plots, one old man working in BG. Sylvia and Aaron enter shot from camera right.	Aaron: "Just over a year. He had a vegetable plot here. Towards the end I had to do everything for him."
	Sylvia: "That's how you became such a gardener?"
2S, Aaron looks off camera left, Sylvia follows his gaze.	Aaron: "I used to see that thing all the time while I was digging...
POV shot, high chimney next to large building.	...It seemed to be waiting for him to die."
Neglected rock garden, pond dry with weeds growing out of cracks.	Aaron: "When I was a kid and Dad had left us, I used to try and hate him, but I never could. (Pause) Sylvie, it was a mistake to come back here."
Frontal 2S, Sylvia puts her arm around Aaron, who has become very sad.	

FIGURE 5–2

Split page format, also known as TV script format. Picture is always on the left, sound on the right. (LS = long shot, MS = medium shot, CS = close shot, 2S = two shot, that is, shot containing two people, POV = point-of-view shot.)

STRATEGY FOR STUDY

Your split page script should contain:

1. Action-side descriptions of
   a. each shot (who, what, when, where)
   b. its action content
   c. camera movements
   d. optical effects (fades, dissolves, etc.)

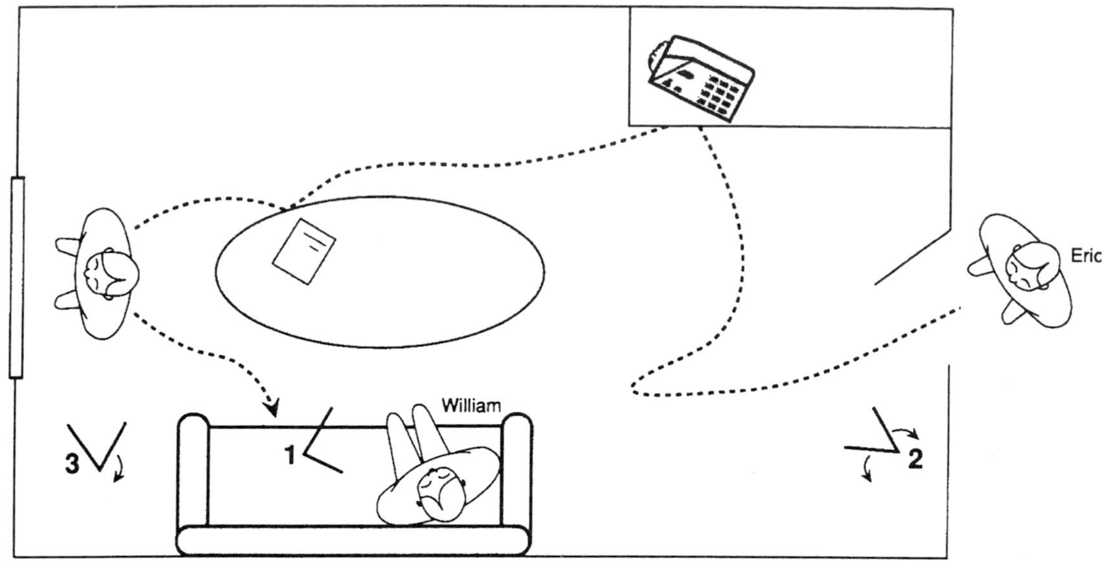

FIGURE 5–3

Floor or ground plan showing entry and movement of character Eric and the camera positions to cover the action.

2. Sound-side descriptions of:
   a. dialogue, word for word
   b. positioning of dialogue relative to the action
   c. music starting and stopping points
   d. featured sound effects (that is, other than synchronous, or "sync" sound)

Sound that is native to the location is called *diegetic sound.* Non-diegetic sound is that which has been applied as counterpoint, for example, the sound of a loud heartbeat placed over a man trapped in an elevator.

Very important: *Read from the film rather than reading into it.* Film is a complex and deceptive medium; like a glib and clever acquaintance, it can make you uneasy about your perceptions and too ready to accept what should be seen or should be felt. Recognize what the film made you feel, then trace your impressions to what can actually be seen and heard in the film. To avoid overload, scrutinize the sequence during each pass on just a few of the aspects listed below. Try to find at least one example of everything so you understand the concepts at work. Though I have listed them in a logical order for inquiry, reorder my list if you prefer.

First Impressions

What was the progression of feelings you had watching the sequence?

Definition and Statistics

- How long is the sequence (minutes and seconds)?
- What determines the sequence's beginning and ending points?
- How many picture cuts does it contain?
- Is its span determined by:

  Being at one location?

  Being a continuous segment of time?

  A particular mood?

  The stages of a process?

  Something else?

The duration of each shot and how often the camera angle is changed may be aspects of the genre (what type of film it is) or a director's particular style, or suggested by the sequence's content. Try to decide whether the content or its treatment is determining the frequency of cutting.

Use of Camera

- How many different motivations can you find for the camera to make a movement?
- Does the camera follow the movement of a character?
- Does a car or other moving object permit the camera to pan the length of the street so that camera movement seems to arise from action in the frame?
- How does the camera lay out a landscape or a scene's geography for the audience?
- When does the camera move in closer to intensify our relationship with someone or something?
- When does the camera move away from someone or something so we see more objectively?
- Does the camera reveal other significant information by moving?
- Is the move really a reframing to accommodate a rearrangement of characters?
- Is the move a reaction—panning to a new speaker, for instance?
- What else might be responsible for motivating this particular camera move?
- When is the camera used subjectively?
- When do we directly experience a character's point of view?
- Are there special signs that the camera is seeing subjectively? (For example, an unsteady handheld camera used in a combat film to create a running soldier's point of view.)
- What is the dramatic justification for this?
- Are there changes in camera height?
- Are they made to accommodate subject matter?

- Do they make you see in a certain way?
- Are they done for other reasons?

Use of Sound

- What sound perspectives are used?
  Do they complement camera position? (Use a near microphone for close shots and far from microphone for longer shots, thus replicating camera perspective.)
  Do they counterpoint camera perspective? (Robert Altman's films often give us the intimate conversation of two characters seen distantly traversing a large landscape.)
  Are sound perspectives uniformly intimate (as with a narration, or with voice-over and *thoughts voices* that function as a character's interior monologue) or are they varied?
- How are particular sound effects used?
  To build atmosphere and mood?
  As punctuation?
  To motivate a cut (next sequence's sound rises until we cut to it)?
  As a narrative device (horn honks so woman gets up and goes to window where she discovers her sister is making a surprise visit)?
  To build, sustain, or diffuse tension?
  To provide rhythm (meal prepared in a montage of brief shots to the rhythmic sound of a man splitting logs; last shot, man and woman sit down to meal)?
  To create uncertainty?
  Other situations?

Editing

What motivates each cut?

- Is there an action match to carry the cut?
- Is there a compositional relationship between the two shots that makes the cut interesting and worthwhile?
- Is there a movement relationship that carries the cut (for example, cut from car moving left-to-right to boat moving left-to-right)?
- Does someone or something leave the frame (making us expect a new frame)?
- Does someone or something fill the frame, blanking it out and permitting a cut to another frame that starts blanked and then clears?
- Does someone or something enter the frame and demand closer attention?
- Are we cutting to follow someone's eyeline to see what they see?
- Is there a sound, or a line, that demands that we see the source?
- Are we cutting to show the effect on a listener? What defines the right moment to cut?

- Are we cutting to a speaker at a particular moment that is visually revealing? What defines that moment?
- If the cut intensifies our attention, what justifies that?
- If the cut relaxes and objectifies our attention, what justifies that?
- Is the cut to a parallel activity (that is, something going on simultaneously)?
- Is there some sort of comparison or irony being set up through juxtaposition?
- Are we cutting to a rhythm (perhaps to an effect, music, or the cadences of speech)?
- Other reasons?

What is the relationship of words to images?

- Does what is shown illustrate what is said?
- Is there a difference, and therefore a counterpoint, between what is shown and what is heard?
- Is there a meaningful contradiction between what is said and what is shown?
- Does what is said come from another time frame (for example, a character's memory or a comment on something in the past)?
- Is there a point at which words are used to move us forward or backward in time? (That is, can you pinpoint a change of tense in the film's grammar? This might be done visually, as in the old cliché of autumn leaves falling after we have seen summer scenes.)
- Any others?

When a line overlaps a picture cut, what is the impact of the first strong word on the new image?

- Does it help identify the new image?
- Does it give the image a particular emphasis or interpretation?
- Is the effect expected (satisfying, perhaps) or unexpected (maybe a shock)?
- Is there a deliberate contradiction?
- Other effects?

Examine at least three music sections. Where and how is music used?

- How is it initiated (often when characters or story begin some kind of motion)?
- What does the music suggest by its texture, instrumentation, etc.?
- How is it finished (often when characters or story arrive at a new location)?
- What comment is it making? (Ironic? Sympathetic? Lyrical? Revealing the inner state of a character or situation? Other?)
- From what other sound (if any) does it emerge (or *segue*)?
- What other sound does it merge (or segue) into as its close?

Point of View and Blocking

Blocking is a term for the way actors and camera move in relation to each other and to the set. As discussed earlier, *point of view* seldom means whose literal eyelines the audience shares. More often it refers to whose reality the viewer most identifies with at any given time. The director's underlying statement is largely achieved through the handling of point of view, yet how this is done can be deceptive unless you look very carefully. A film, like a novel, can have a main point of view associated with a main, point-of-view character and also expose us to multiple, conflicting points of view anchored in other characters.

Sometimes there is one central character, and one point of view, like the mentally handicapped Karl in Billy Bob Thornton's *Slingblade* (1997). Or there may be a couple whose relationship is at issue, as in Woody Allen's *Annie Hall* (1977). Successive scenes may be devoted to establishing alternate characters' dilemmas and conflicts. Altman's *Nashville* (1975) has nearly two dozen central characters, and the film's focus is the music town of Nashville being their point of convergence and their confrontation with change. Here, evidently, we find the characters are part of a pattern, and the pattern itself is surely an authorial point of view that questions the way people subscribe to their own destiny. Both Quentin Tarantino's *Pulp Fiction* (1994) and Robert Altman's *Short Cuts* (1993) use serpentine storylines with characters who come and go and appear in different permutations. Each sequence is liable to have a different point-of-view character. Both films deal with the style and texture of groups, and their time and place.

Following are some ways to dig into a sequence to establish how it covertly structures the way we see and react to its characters. But first, a word of caution. Point of view is a complex notion that can only be specified confidently after considering the aims and tone of the whole work. Taking a magnifying glass to one sequence may be misleading unless you use it as an example to verify and justify your overall hypothesis. How the camera is used, the frequency with which one character's feelings are revealed, the amount of development he or she goes through, the vibrancy of the acting—all these factors could play a part in enlisting our sympathy and interest.

In your sequence for study, to whom, at different times, is the dialogue or narration addressed?

- By one character to another?
- By one character to himself (thinking aloud, reading diary or letter)?
- Directly to the audience (narration, interview, prepared statement)?
- Other situations?

How many camera positions were used? (Use your floor plan.)

- Show basic camera positions and label them A, B, C, etc.
- Show camera dollying movements with dotted line leading to new position.
- Mark shots in your log with the appropriate A, B, C camera angles.
- Notice how the camera stays to one side of the *subject-to-subject axis* (an imaginary line between characters that the camera usually avoids crossing)

to keep characters facing in the same screen direction from shot to shot. When this principle is broken, it is called *crossing the line, crossing the axis,* or *breaking the 180-degree rule,* and it has the effect of temporarily disrupting the audience's sense of spatial relationships.

- How often is the camera close to the crucial axis between characters?
- How often does the camera subjectively share a character's eyeline?
- When and why does it take an objective stance to the situation (that is, either a distanced viewpoint, or one independent of eyelines)?

Character and Camera Blocking
How did the characters and camera move in the scene? To the location and camera movement sketch you have made, add dotted lines to show the characters' movements (called blocking). Use different colors for clarity.

- What points of view did the author engage us in?
- Whose story is this sequence, if you go by gut reaction?
- Considering the camera angles on each character, with whose point of view were you led to sympathize?
- How many psychological viewpoints did you share? (Some may have been momentary or fragmentary, and perhaps in contradiction to what you were seeing.)
- Are the audience's sympathies structured by camera and editing, or more by acting or the situation itself?

FICTION AND THE DOCUMENTARY

Most of these analytical questions apply equally to the documentary film because the two forms have much in common. This is more than a similarity in film language, for some of the important questions cannot be applied to most nature, travelogue, industrial, or educational films. These other genres generally lack what distinguishes the fictional and documentary forms—an authorial perspective. That is, they often lack a point of view, a changing dramatic pressure, and a critical perspective expressed about what it means to be human.

This critical relationship to the characters and their world is crucial to providing the feeling of a distinctly human sensibility unifying the events it shows, even though (and we must never forget this) the making of a film is collaborative. We sense the presence of a Storyteller's sympathy and intelligence, so what in lesser hands might be technical or formulaic becomes vibrantly human. This kind of vision is the best sort of leadership, for without egoism and by example it invites us to see a familiar world with new eyes.

PROJECT 5-3: A SCRIPTED SCENE COMPARED WITH THE FILMED OUTCOME

Objective: To study the relationship between the blueprint script and the filmed product.

Study Materials: A film script and the finished film made from it on videotape. Don't look at the film until you have planned your own version from the text. The script must be the original screenplay and not a *release script* (that is, not a transcript made from a finished film). A suitable script can be found in Pauline Kael's *The Citizen Kane Book: Raising Kane* (New York, Limelight Editions, 1984). Another is Harold Pinter's *The French Lieutenant's Woman: A Screenplay* (Boston, Little, Brown, and Co., 1981). The latter has an absorbing foreword by John Fowles, the author of the original novel. It tells the story of the adaptation and describes, from a novelist's point of view, what is involved when your novel makes the transition to the screen.

If obtaining an original script is a problem, an interesting variation is to use a film adapted from a stage play and study an obligatory scene, that is, one so dramatically necessary that it cannot be missing from the film version. Good titles are:

Arthur Miller's *Death of a Salesman*

- Laslo Benedek's 1951 film version with Fredric March.
- Wim Wenders' 1987 TV version with Dustin Hoffman. It is interesting for its expressionist sets and because a theatrical flavor is retained.

Edward Albee's *Who's Afraid of Virginia Woolf?*

- Mike Nichols' 1966 film version.

Peter Schaffer's *Equus*

- Sidney Lumet's 1977 film version.

Tennessee Williams' *A Streetcar Named Desire*

- Elia Kazan's 1951 film version.

STRATEGY FOR STUDY

Study the Original

Try to select an unfamiliar work and read the whole script (or stage play). Choose a scene of four or five pages.

1. Imagine the location and draw a floor plan (see Figure 5–3 for an example).
2. Make your own shooting script adaptation, substituting action for dialogue wherever feasible and making use of your location environment. (See Figure 7–1 in Chapter 7 for standard screenplay layout.)
3. Mark characters' movements on floor plan.
4. Mark camera positions (A, B, C, etc., and indicate camera movements), and refer to these in your shooting script.
5. Write a brief statement about (a) what major themes you think the entire script or play is dealing with, and (b) how your chosen scene functions in the whole.

Study the Film Version

First see the entire film without stopping. Then run your chosen scene two or three times, stopping and rerunning sections as you wish. Carry out the following:

1. Make notes on film's choice of location (Imaginative? Metaphoric?).
2. Make a floor plan and mark camera positions and movements of characters.
3. Using a photocopy of the scene, pencil in annotations to show what dialogue has been cut, added, or altered.
4. Note actions, both large and small, that add significantly to the impact of the scene. Ignore those specified in the original, as the object is to find what the film version has added to or substituted for the writer's version.
5. Note camera usage as follows:
    a. Any abnormal perspective (that is, when a nonstandard lens is used. A standard lens is one that reproduces the perspective of the human eye. Telescopic and wide-angle lenses compress or magnify perspective respectively)?
    b. Any camera position above or below eye level?
    c. Any camera movement (track, pan, tilt, zoom, crane)? Note what you think motivated the camera movement (character's movement, eyeline, Storyteller's revelation, etc.).
    d. Note what the thematic focus of the film seems to be, and how your chosen scene functions in the film.

Comparison

Compare your scripting with the film's handling and describe the following:

1. How did the film establish time and place?
2. How effectively did the film compress the original and substitute behavior for dialogue?
3. How, using camerawork and editing, is the audience drawn into identifying with one or more characters?
4. Whose scene was it, and why?
5. How were any rhythms (speech, movements, sound effects, music, etc.) used to pace out the scene, particularly to speed it up or slow it down?
6. What were the major changes of interpretation in the film and in the chosen scene?
7. Provide any further valuations of the film you think worth making (acting, characterization, use of music or sound effects, etc.).

Assess Your Performance

How well did you do? What aspects of filmmaking are you least aware of and need to develop? What did you accomplish?

PROJECT 5-4: LIGHTING ANALYSIS

Though directors do not have to understand techniques of lighting, they must be able to ask for particular lighting effects and discuss lighting using the terminology a DP understands.

Equipment Required: VCR as in previous projects. Turn down the color saturation of your monitor so that initially you see a black-and-white picture. Adjust the monitor's brightness and contrast controls so the greatest possible range of gray tones is visible between video white and video black. Unless you do this you simply won't see all that is present.

Objective: To analyze common lighting situations and understand what goes into creating a lighting mood

Study Materials: Same as in previous project (a film script and the finished film made from it on videotape), only this time it will be an advantage to search out particular lighting situations rather than sequences of special dramatic appeal. The same sequences may fulfill both purposes.

LIGHTING TERMINOLOGY

Here the task is to recognize different types and combinations of lighting situations and to apply standard terminology. Every aspect of lighting carries strong emotional associations that can be employed in drama to great effect. The technique and the terminology describing it are therefore powerful tools in the right hands. Here are some basic terms:

Types of Lighting Style

High-key picture: The shot looks bright overall with small areas of shadow. In Figure 5–4 the shot is exterior day, and the shadow of the lamppost in the foreground shows that there is indeed deep shadow in the picture. Where shadow is sharp, as it is here, the light source is called *specular.* A high-key picture can be virtually shadowless, so long as the frame is bright overall.

Low-key picture: The shot looks dark overall with few highlight areas. These are often interiors or night shots, but in Figure 5–5 we have a backlit day interior that ends up being low-key, that is, having a large area of the frame in deep shadow.

Graduated tonality: The shot has neither bright highlights nor deep shadows, but consists of an even, restricted range of midtones. This might be a flat-lit interior, like a supermarket, or a misty morning landscape as in Figure 5–6. In that example, an overcast sky diffuses the lighting source, and the disorganized light rays scatter into every possible shadow area so there are neither highlights nor shadow.

Contrast

High-contrast picture: The shot may be lit either high- or low-key, but there must be a big difference in illumination levels between highlight and shadow area, as in Figure 5–7, which has a soot-and-whitewash starkness. Both Figures 5–4 and 5–5 are also high-contrast images, although the area of shadow in each is drastically different.

FIGURE 5–4

High-key scene: hard or specular lighting, high-contrast. Notice compositional depth in this shot compared with the flatness of Figure 5–5.

FIGURE 5–5

Backlit, low-key scene: Subject is silhouetted against the flare of backlit smoke.

FIGURE 5–6

Graduated tonality scene: It is low-contrast because key light is diffused through morning mist.

Low-contrast picture: The shot can either be high- or low-key, but with a shadow area illumination level near that of the highlight levels. Figure 5–6 is high-key, low-contrast.

Light Quality

Hard lighting: This is any specular light source creating hard-edged shadows, such as sun, studio spotlight, or candle flame. These are all called *effectively small* light sources because a small source gives hard-edged shadows. Figure 5–4 is lit by hard light (the sun), while the shadow under the chair in Figure 5–5 is so soft as to be hardly discernible.

Soft lighting: Any light source is soft when it creates soft-edged shadows or a shadowless image, as in Figure 5–6. Soft light sources are, for example, fluorescent tubes, sunlight reflecting off a matte-finish wall, light from overcast sky, or a studio soft light. Do not confuse soft lighting with lighting that is of low power. A candle is a low-power, hard-lighting source.

Names of Lighting Sources

Key light: This is not necessarily an artificial source, for it can be the sun. The key is the light that creates intended shadows in the shot, and these in turn reveal the angle and position of the supposed light source, often relatively hard or specular (shadow-producing) light. In Figure 5–4 the key light is sunlight coming from the rear left and above the camera. In Figure 5–5 it is streaming in toward the camera.

FIGURE 5–7

High-contrast image with very few midtones because of backlighting and no fill.

Fill light: This is the light used to raise illumination in shadow areas. For interiors it will probably be soft light thrown from the direction of the camera, because this avoids creating additional visible shadows. There are shadows, of course, but the subject hides them from the camera's view. Especially in interiors, fill light is often provided from matte white reflectors or through diffusion material such as heat-resistant fiberglass. Fill light can also be derived from bounce light, which is hard light bounced from walls or ceilings to soften it.

Backlight: This is light thrown upon a subject from behind—and often from above as well as behind, as in Figure 5–5. A favorite technique in portraiture is to put a rim of backlight around a subject's head and shoulders to separate them from the background. Rain, fog, dust, and smoke (as in this case of garage barbecuing) all show up best when backlit.

Practical: This is any light appearing in the frame as part of the scene; for example, table lamp, overhead fluorescent, or, as in Figure 5–8, the candles on a birthday cake. Practicals generally provide little or no real source of illumination, but here the candles light up the faces but not the background.

Figure 5–8 illustrates several lighting points. The girl in the middle is lit from below, a style called *monster lighting*, which is decidedly eerie for a birthday shot. The subject on the left, having no backlight or background lighting, disappears into the shadows, while the one on the right is outlined by *set light* or light falling on the set. The same light source shines on her hair as a backlight source and gives it highlights and texture.

FIGURE 5–8

Practicals are any lights seen in the frame, like these birthday candles. Strong set light prevents the background from going dark.

Types of Lighting Setup

In this section the illustrations are of the same model lit in various ways. As a result, the effect and the mood in each portrait vary greatly. The diagrams show the positioning of the key and fill lights. A floor plan can show the angle of throw relative to the camera-to-subject axis, but not the height of light sources. These can be judged from the screen image by assessing the positioning of highlight and shadow patterns.

Frontally lit: The key light in Figure 5–9 is so close to the camera-to-subject axis that shadows are thrown behind the subject and out of the camera's view. Very slight shadows are visible in the folds of the subject's shirt, showing how the key was just to the right of camera. Notice how flat and lacking in dimensionality or tension this shot is compared with Figures 5–10 and 5–11.

Broad lit: In Figure 5–10 the key light is some way to the side, so a broad area of the subject's face and body is highlighted. Key light skimming the subject lengthens his face, revealing angles and undulations. There are areas of deep shadow, especially in the eye sockets, but their effect could be reduced by increasing the amount of soft fill light.

Narrow lit: The key light in Figure 5–11 is to the side of the subject and beyond him so that only a narrow portion of his face receives highlight. The majority of his face is in shadow. The shadowed portion of the face is lit by fill light, or we would see nothing. Measuring light reflected in the highlight area and comparing it with that reflected from the fill area gives the *lighting ratio*. Remember

FIGURE 5–9

Frontal lighting flattens the subject and removes much of the face's interest. Most flash photography is frontal and correspondingly dull.

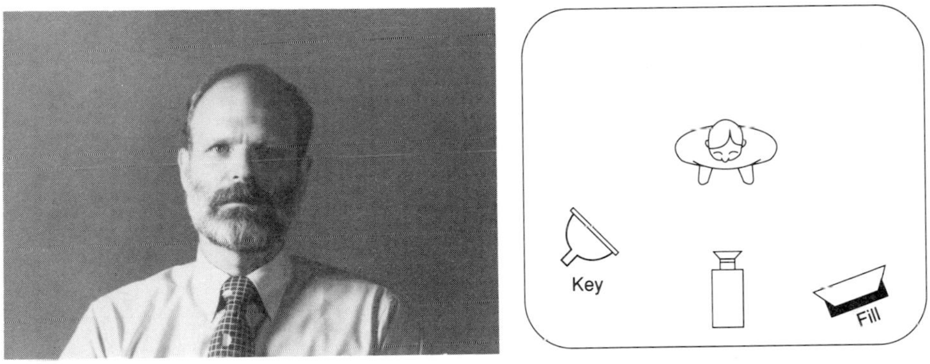

FIGURE 5–10

Broad lighting illuminates a broad area of the face and shows the head as round and having angularities.

FIGURE 5–11

Narrow lighting illuminates only a narrow area of the face. More fill used here than in Figure 5–10. The effect is decidedly dramatic.

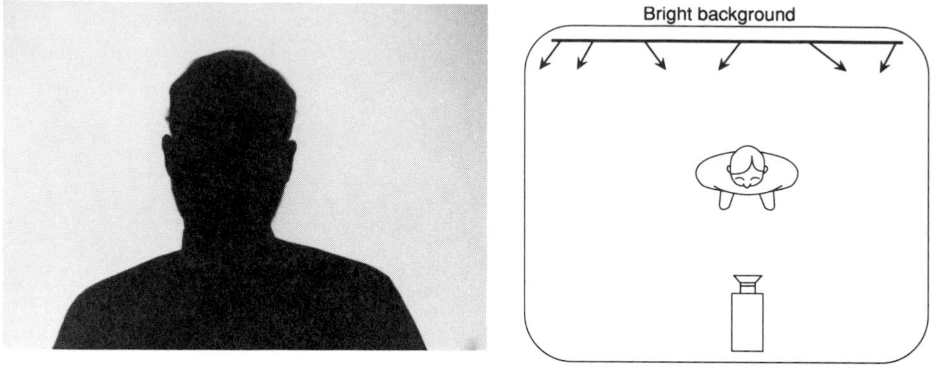

FIGURE 5–12

Silhouette: All light is from the background and none reaches the subject's face.

when taking measurements that fill light spills into highlight areas but not vice versa, so reliable readings can only be taken when all lights are on.

Silhouette: In Figure 5–12 the subject reflects no light at all and shows up only as an outline against raw light. This lighting is sometimes used in documentaries when the subject's identity is being withheld. Here it produces the ominous effect of someone unknown confronting us through a bright doorway.

Day for night: Shooting exteriors using daylight (day-for-day) presents few problems, but direct shooting at night or in moonlight is virtually impossible because neither film stocks nor video cameras approach the human eye's sensitivity. One solution is to shoot *night-for-night* by carefully modeling bluish artificial light to cast long, hard-edged shadows that simulate those cast by the light of the moon. *Day-for-night* shooting is easiest in black-and-white, because you can use early morning or late afternoon sunlight when shadows are long, underexpose by several stops, and use a red or yellow filter to turn blue skies black and increase all-round contrast. Day for night in color uses a similar lighting and exposure strategy, and a graduated filter to darken the sky, but seldom looks very convincing. A more effective color day-for-night effect results from using the so-called *"magic hour,"* a period of little more than 10–20 minutes just before there is too little light to shoot. In urban scenes, streetlights and car headlights are on, and the whole landscape is still visible under what is often a gorgeous reddish sky. Any dialogue scenes of more than a line or two in a single shot must be taken later in close-up with artificial lighting and backgrounds that match the long shots.

STRATEGY FOR STUDY

Locate two or three sequences with quite different lighting moods, and using the previously discussed definitions, classify them as follows:

Style:	High-key/low-key/graduated tonality?
Contrast:	High- or low-contrast?
Scene:	Intended to look like natural light or artificial lighting?
Setup:	Frontal/broad/narrow/backlighting setup?
Angles:	High/low angle of key light?
Key quality:	Hard/soft edges to shadows?
Key source:	Source in scene is intended to be ______
Fill light:	Fill source is where?
Practicals:	Practicals in the scene are ______
Time:	Day for day/night for night/dusk for night/day for night? ______
Mood:	Mood conveyed by lighting is ______
Continuity:	Any discernible differences of lighting between complementary angles that show lighting has been handled differently?

After analyzing several sequences in black-and-white, see if you can spot further patterns by turning up the color. This often reveals how the DP and art director have employed the emotional associations of the location, costuming, and decor in the service of the script. Predominant hues and *color saturation level* (meaning whether a color is pure or *desaturated* with an admixture of white) have a great deal to do with a scene's effect on the viewer. For instance, David Lynch's *Blue Velvet* (1986) portrays its Lumberton in stark, bright toy-town colors as a surreal setting for sadistic sex and loneliness. Robert Altman's *Gosford Park* (2001) uses the low-key interiors and crowded sets of a Victorian country mansion as the setting for this convoluted family tale. The predominant tones are dark red and brown.

Two classically lit black-and-white films are Orson Welles' *Citizen Kane* (1941) with deep-focus cinematography by the revolutionary Gregg Toland, and Jean Cocteau's *Beauty and the Beast* (1946) whose lighted interiors Henri Alekan modeled after Dutch paintings. A much more recent black-and-white film with lighting by Alekan is Wim Wenders' poetic *Wings of Desire* (1987).

CHAPTER 6

SHOOTING PROJECTS

If you've dipped into this book and want to jump right into the "doing" part, its design is meant to encourage you to do just that. Although one kind of learner likes to read, understand, and be thoroughly prepared before entering practical work, there are others (like myself) who must learn things by doing them. So start production here if you wish, and usc the rest of the book to solve problems as you encounter them. That, after all, is how the film industry evolved.

Each project in this book explores different techniques of expression, but you should make each one a vehicle for your own ideas and tastes. I have included discussion of the topics, a list of skills you can expect to learn, and questions after each to help you probe your work's aspects, strengths, and weaknesses.

These projects and their variations represent a fairly complete workout in basic filmmaking. You can use them to explore building a character, a situation, and the audience's involvement through non-verbal, behavioral means. They allow you to build an authorial point of view and the disparate perspectives of the characters themselves. The latter are not basic at all.

HOW BEST TO EXPLORE THE BASICS

Production, the seat of learning in the school of hard knocks, teaches you teamwork and how important it is to be organized. As a director you should make creating *a gripping human presence on the screen* your No. 1 priority. For this you will need knowledge of actors, the ability to see what is credible and what isn't, and the ability to find solutions to problems actors encounter.

Good screen fiction requires multidimensional characters striving visibly after their own goals in truthful and interesting ways. It looks so easy and natural in the cinema, but it's really difficult to produce.

ASSESSMENT

In the Appendix are assessment sheets, listed by chapter and project. Each project below lists an assessment sheet that you should study carefully because it lists the outcomes your work should aim to demonstrate. Outcomes assessment shows you how well you are succeeding in all the major areas and where your directorial or other skills might need more work.

ON DEVELOPING YOUR ABILITIES

Techniques: The projects that follow will help you develop a broad and representative range of directing and editing skills. Technique should never become an end in and of itself. "Art," said Thomas Hardy, "is the secret of how to produce by a false thing the effect of a true." This applies perfectly to the artifice that goes into screen narrative. Good technique is transparent and goes unnoticed by the audience because the film grips the viewer's imagination. Poor technique or virtuosity misapplied is technique that draws attention to itself and confounds the film's purpose.

The first projects explore basic technique and embody modest subject matter, but do not be deceived into thinking they are beneath you.

I have supplied requirements, procedures, and hints, but I leave much of the problem solving—always the most rewarding area of learning—to your ingenuity and resourcefulness. Where a project requires lighting, keep it basic and simple so you avoid getting sidetracked by the delights of cinematography.

Critique sessions: Finished projects are best assessed in a group or class so you get used to working with collaborators and giving and taking critique. If any project has a great number of critical assessments and there are too many to monitor while watching a cut, solve this by having each person in a group watch for a few particular facets. This ensures a discussion of depth from which everyone learns—particularly the maker, whose job it is to listen, take notes about the audience reaction, and say nothing. Never, never explain what the audience *should* have understood. You are responsible for anything your audience missed.

Further help: For additional information, use the table of contents at the front of the part dealing with the appropriate production phase or the glossary and index at the book's end.

PROJECT 6-1: BASIC TECHNIQUES: GOING AND RETURNING

This project is without dialogue and asks that you establish the character and situation of a woman who looks forward to arriving at a building, but discovers she has lost her keys. During the discovery and returning to her car to look for them, she can go through a range of subtle emotions—irritation, anxiety, relief, perhaps even amusement. While creating this character you give yourself a workout in film grammar basics such as preserving the screen direction of characters and action and of matching movement at action-match cuts. (See "Cutting on Action" and "Match Cut Rules" subheadings in Project 6-1A.)

Skills to develop:

- Maintaining relevant screen direction.
- Panning and tilting to follow action.
- Picture framing and composition to suggest depth.
- Editing:
  action match cutting.
  cutting together different sizes of similar images using action as a bridge.
  cutting together complementary angles on the same action.
- Telling a story through action and behavior, not words.
- Ellipsis (compressing real time into a more cinematic shorthand).
- Editing to music.
- Making a long version (first assembly) and a short version (fine cut).

6-1A: PLAN, SHOOT, AND EDIT THE LONG VERSION

Assessment: Use **Assessment 6-1A/B (Editing)** in Appendix

A car draws up. Mary, its occupant, gets out and approaches a house, looking up at a window in anticipation. She mounts a flight of steps to the front door. There she discovers she does not have her keys. Perplexed, she returns to her car, which she expects to be open. Finding the door locked, she reacts in frustration, thinking her keys are locked in. But looking inside, she sees the ignition is empty. Patting her pockets and looking around in consternation, she spots her keys lying in the gutter. She picks them up, relieved, and returns to the house.

Figure 6–1 is a specimen floor or ground plan. Adapt yours to your location (mine is a one-way street to allow the driver to drop her keys in the nearside gutter). The floor plan shows Mary's walk and the basic camera positions to cover the various parts of the action. No sound is necessary.

Figure 6–2 is a *storyboard* of representative frames for each camera position. For your coverage, make your own ground plan and show camera positions and storyboard key frames. Here is a sample shot list related to the ground plan and key frames A through G.

- Establishing shot of locale from camera position A with car arriving as in Frame A.
- Medium shot (MS) panning with Mary left to right (L-R). When she turns the corner in the path she changes her effective screen direction, ending up as in Frame B.
- Medium close shot (MCS) of Mary's feet walking R-L and L-R on sidewalk and up steps as an all purpose *cut-in* (also called insert) shot, as in Frame D1.
- Big close-up (BCU) panning, telephoto shot of Mary's head as she walks, looking up at window as in D2.
- Feet enter shot descending steps, camera tilts down to follow action, Frame G.

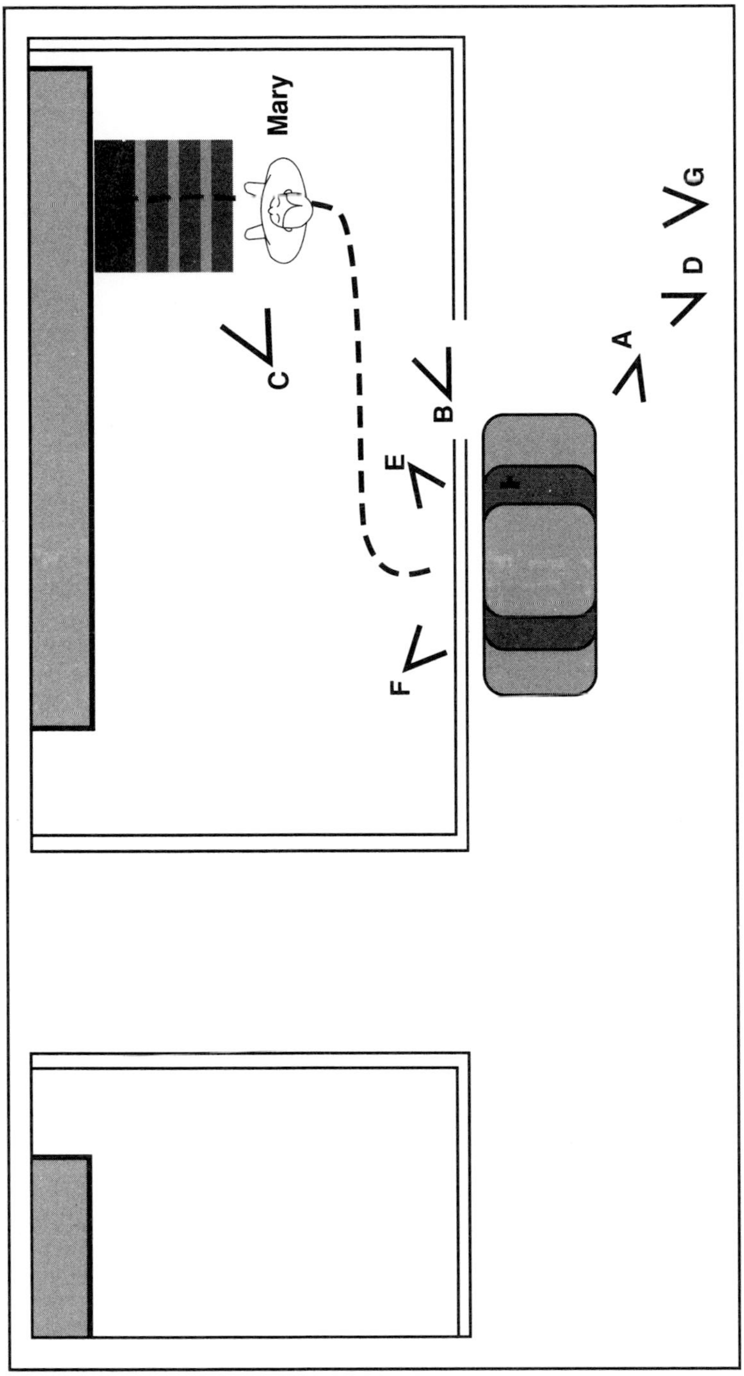

FIGURE 6–1 Specimen floor plan for the "Mary sequence." Camera positions are marked as A through G.

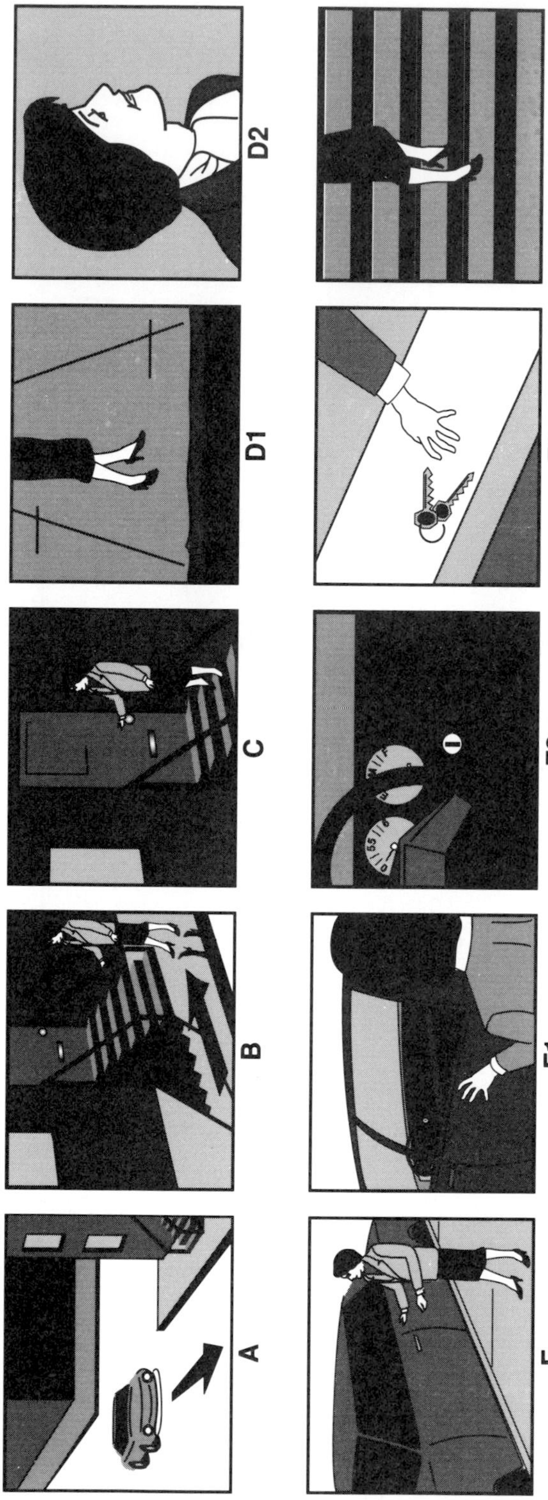

FIGURE 6–2

Storyboard frames showing setups for the various camera angles in Figure 6–1.

- Overshoulder (OS) shot of empty ignition, F1.
- Point-of-view (POV) shot, F2.
- BCU keys in gutter, hand reaches into frame and takes them, F3.

In its simplest edited form, the abbreviated sequence might look something like this:

Camera Position	Shot Number	Action
A	1	Car arrives, Mary gets out, slams door, exits bottom right of frame.
B	2a	Mary enters L-R, begins crossing frame.
D2	3	CU Mary looks up at window.
B	2b	This is the rest of shot 2a. Mary continues L-R, turns corner of path, walks R-L toward steps and up them.
C	3	Mary rises into frame from R-L, fumbles for keys, can't find them, looks back at car, turns back out of frame.
B	4	Mary descending steps across frame L-R, turns corner, crosses frame R-L.
E	5a	Mary arrives from screen R, walking R-L toward car, fails to open door, curses.
F1	6	She crosses frame, repositions herself looking R-L to see if key is in ignition, peers inside.
F2	7	Her POV of empty ignition.
E	5b	Mary straightens up, pats pockets, sees something out of frame on the ground.
F3	8a	CU keys lying in gutter from Mary's POV.
E	5c	Mary reacts, stoops down.
F3	8b	CU of keys, hand enters frame, takes them back up.
E	5d	Mary straightens up looking relieved and exits into camera, making frame go black. End of sequence.

Notice that shot 2 is intercut with a CU, while the action in shot 5 has been intercut three times. When directing for intercutting like this, don't shoot individual reactions to slot into the script. Instead shoot a large section or even the whole action in the two different sizes of shot, afterward selecting the fragments you require from the continuous take during editing. The more sustained the acting, the more you will get actors *in focus*, that is, unselfconsciously lost in their characters' realities.

Notice how at the end of shot 5, when Mary returns with the keys, her movement is used to black out the screen by walking right up to the camera lens. To continue the transition in the following shot, have the actor back up against the lens and then on "Action" walk away from the camera. In the transition the screen goes from action to black, then from black to a new scene. This is one of many transitional devices of which the simplest is the humble cut. Overuse the fancy ones and you run the risk of being tricksy.

- Cut this first, long version together, taking into account cutting from shot 2a to 3.
- Maintain Mary's walking rhythm across cuts and be careful you don't make the poor woman take two steps on the same foot. Rhythm consciousness is needed for editing all walking shots, or anything where rhythms are involved.
- When cutting from 5a to 6, there will probably be an action match. Below are some of the few rules in filmmaking.

Cutting on Action: This is always preferable to cutting at points of stasis. When an attention-commanding action flows across a cut, the eye hardly notices the changes of composition or subject. Action matches work best when the outgoing shot initiates the movement, and the incoming shot takes over and completes most of the action.

Match Cut Rules: For the best action match, follow these steps.

> **Step 1:** Let the outgoing shot run until the start of the action is established. Use no more of the action than is necessary for us to recognize *what the action is going to be.* This is important because *the eye stops being critical whenever we know what is happening next.*
>
> **Step 2:** Complete the majority of the action with the incoming (closer or longer) shot, but be aware that if the action flowing across the cut is at all fast, you must *repeat three or four frames of the action at the head of the incoming shot.* This overlap is necessary because the eye does not register the first three or four frames of any new image. Though a frame-by-frame analysis shows a slight action repeat, shown at normal speed the action will appear smooth and continuous.

Cutting from 5c to 8b, use the same principle. Let Mary just begin to stoop and then cut to keys with hand entering at top of frame shortly afterwards. If you leave too much footage before the incoming hand appears, you will imply that Mary is 8 feet tall.

Criteria: Run your cut version. Make an exact minutes and seconds count of its length. Now try rating your agreement for each of these criteria on the 1–5 scale outlined in Assessment 6-1A, and B (Editing) in the Appendix. Circling the scores will give you clues to which aspects of your work are strong and which need more work.

6-1B: EDITING A MORE COMPRESSED VERSION

Assessment: Use **Assessment 6-1A/B (Editing)** in Appendix.

Run your cut and consider which moments in the action are vital and which are link material. Surely a lot of the walking is of secondary importance. If, for instance, Mary turns to look back in the direction of the car, we don't need to see her cover every inch of ground to arrive there. Amend the first cut by making a compressed version. Here's where the unused bridging close-ups come in, signified in this new, abbreviated list with an asterisk:

Camera Position	Shot Number	Action
A	1	Car arrives, but cut before it comes to a complete halt.
B	2a	Mary enters L-R, begins crossing frame.
D2	3	CU of Mary smiling up at window.
D1	*	Her feet L-R.
B	2b	Mary arrives at corner of path, turns R-L; cut immediately to . . .
C	3	Mary almost at door, fumbles for keys, can't find, looks back at car and turns.
G	*	Feet descending a couple of steps.
D1	*	CS feet walking on sidewalk R-L.
E	5a	Mary almost at car, fails to open door, curses.
F2	7	CU to her POV of empty ignition.
E	5b	Mary straightens up, pats pockets, sees something on ground.
F3	8a	CU keys lying in gutter, her hand enters frame to pick them up.
E	5d	Mary leaving car walks into camera, turning screen black.

Discussion: How long is the sequence this time? It should be 30–50% shorter, yet lose nothing of narrative importance. See if you can cut it down further, to perhaps as little as 30–60 seconds overall. Keep running it and you will find shots or parts of shots that can be eliminated. Set the audience up to infer what is not visible, and they will. This way, instead of passively witnessing something that requires no interpretation, the audience actively participates and uses its imagination to fill in points of elision. This is treating your audience as active and intelligent collaborators rather than passive vessels to be filled up with information.

6-1C: SETTING IT TO MUSIC

Assessment: Use **Assessment 6-1C Music** in the Appendix.

Having discovered how much leeway there is to the length of many of the shots, you can now turn Mary into a musical star. Find a piece of music with a strong beat that enhances the mood of the sequence. Re-edit the materials, placing your cuts and major pieces of action on the beat or on the music's instrumental changes. Be aware that *for any cut to appear on the beat, it must occur three or four frames before the actual beat point.* This is owing to the *perceptual lag* inherent when you cut to a new image. The only non-negotiable aspects of your earlier cut are the action match cuts. There will be one way only to make them look right.

Discussion:

- How tightly does the action fit the music?
- Does cutting on the beat become predictable? If so, try cutting on a musical subdivision.

- How much compromise did you have to make with the tight version to adjust the action to fit the music?
- What does the music add to the earlier version's impact?

PROJECT 6-2: CHARACTER STUDY

Skills to develop:

- Revealing a character through action
- Using mobile *cinéma vérité* handheld coverage
- Blocking camera and actor for mutual accommodation
- Developing counterpoint between words and action
- Imposing a second point of view

6-2A: PLAN, REHEARSE, AND SHOOT LONG TAKE OF CHARACTER-REVEALING ACTION

Assessment: Use **Assessment 6-2A (Blocking, Acting, & Camerawork)** in the Appendix.

Alan, alone, makes breakfast in his own way. Depending on your actor, this is an opportunity to show someone amusingly smart, dreamy, pressured, ultra-methodical, or slovenly making his breakfast in a particular state of mind and emotion. Develop your ideas in rehearsal:

- First decide what Alan's character is going to be.
- Then decide on his situation.
- Then figure out how to externalize these as action without telegraphing what the audience is meant to notice. Put the accent on credibility as though this was reality being shot by a hidden camera.

Camera coverage should adapt to what the actor improvises, and blocking should evolve from mutual accommodation between camera and actor. You may also find that some actions won't look normal on the screen unless they are slowed down.

You may need to re-block the action, that is, have the actor turn some actions into the camera or have him move away from a close position to a marked point so the whole of the action is visible without the camera having to move or make choices. You may need some lighting. For this semi-documentary approach, try placing light stands in a tight group against the least interesting wall so your camera has maximum freedom to move around without picking up telltale stands and supply wires. Bounce the light off a white ceiling or reflector so you work relatively shadowlessly under soft light.

Have fun with this shoot, and in your coverage incorporate:

- Action of about 4 minutes that is emotionally revealing of Alan's basic character, particular mood, and immediate past and future

- Idiosyncratic interaction with objects (no other people, no phone conversations)
- A single, nonstop, handheld take using wide-angle lens only
- Camera movement (pan, tilt, handheld tracking shot, etc.) to follow or reveal as necessary
- Close and long shots produced by altering subject-to-camera distance as necessary. This may be done by moving the camera in and out, or by blocking Alan to move closer or farther from a static camera.
- Thorough exploitation of the domestic setting
- Lots of rehearsal with camera to make all of the above look smooth and natural
- Safety cutaways, point-of-view shots, and inserts

The difference between an insert, cutaway, and point-of-view shot is that:

- An *insert* takes detail already inside the main shot and magnifies it usefully.
- A *cutaway* shows something outside the main shot's framing.
- A *point of view* shot replicates what a character sees from his or her eyeline.

If they are not to look arbitrary and contrived, cutaways, insert shots, and point-of-view shots need to be motivated by a character's actions or through a consistent logic of storytelling. If, for instance, Alan glances up and out of the frame in wide shot, you can use this glance to motivate cutting to his point of view (and a cutaway shot) of a clock.

Discussion: Try to extract findings from the specifics of your work.

- What in general can make fluid camerawork intrusive or objectionable?
- What is the drawback of long-take coverage?
- What are its advantages?
- What is the difference in feeling when the action takes place across the frame instead of down its depth?
- What are the consequences of framing and camera movement?
- When can the camera look away from Alan and take its own initiative, make its own revelations? (It might, for instance, show that while Alan is searching for eggs, the frying pan is smoking ominously.)
- When is it legitimate for the camera to be caught by surprise or to show it knows what is going to happen next?
- Does the audience feel it is spying on Alan unawares, or is there guidance, a feeling that the camera has its own ideas about him and is deliberately showing particular aspects of him?
- What might determine which storytelling mode to use?
- How much of the take is dramatically interesting and where are the flat spots of dead or link material?

6-2B: ADDING AN INTERIOR MONOLOGUE

Assessment: Use **Assessment 6-2BC (Interior Monologue)** in the Appendix.

Going further: Now add an interior monologue track as a voice-over (VO) in which we hear Alan's thought process. In planning this, you will need to consider the following:

- Which actions does he do automatically from long habit?
- Which actions require thought?
- On what grounds is each decision made?
- At what points are a character's thoughts in the present?
- At what points do they fly away elsewhere, and why?
- When do we consciously note what we are doing, and why?

Do not forget to shoot monologue "presence track" or atmosphere (also known as *buzz track* or *room tone*) to serve as a necessary "sound spacer" should you want to extend pauses in the VO.

When you have completed the assignment, assess or discuss the following:

- Where the interior monologue voice is over-informing the audience
- Where it is under-informing
- Is there redundancy in what you hear because it can be inferred from the action?
- Is VO used skillfully to set up the audience to notice or interpret something that would otherwise be missed? Could it have been?
- Did you show then tell, or tell then show? Which is best?
- Are any losses offset by gains in information, humor, or other aspects?
- Did you use too much or too little VO overall?

6-2C: VOCAL COUNTERPOINT AND POINT OF VIEW

Assessment: Use **Assessment 6-2BC (Interior Monologue)** in the Appendix.

Going further: Working again with the original piece, now write and record an alternative VO track that this time doesn't complement what you see, but instead contrasts revealingly with it. When action suggests one meaning, and Alan's VO another, the conjunction of the two yields a more complex set of possibilities. The aim here is to develop tensions between picture and sound, a series of deliberate ambiguities or even contradictions that invite the audience to develop its own ideas about the discrepancies. Now you impel the audience to actively develop ideas about Alan's character. Suggested voices are:

- Alan telling his psychiatrist how his compulsions are going away when clearly they aren't.

- Alan rehearsing how to convey his efficiency and foresight in an upcoming and important job interview.
- Alan's mother telling him how to eat well now that he is on his own.
- Alan's wife loyally telling a friend how easy it is to live with him.
- A private eye interpreting Alan's culpability from his innocuous actions.

Unless you are using a character reading from a diary or letter, you will want to avoid the mechanical sound of an actor reading. Even the most professional actors have trouble making a text sound like spontaneous thought. Happily, there is an easy way around this difficulty. Show the actor the ideas and discuss them, then have him or her improvise thoughts, perhaps from headings alone. Do several versions and redirect your actor between takes. Edit them to the action. This reliably produces spontaneity. Do not forget to shoot *room tone* as a necessary sound spacer should you want to extend pauses in the VO. Also known as *buzz track* or *presence track*, room tone is a simple recording of the set at prior recording level, when no action or dialogue is happening. Every sound location has its own relative silence; you can't extend a track with a silence from another place or even microphone position because they will sound different.

Of course there is ample scope for comedy here, but did you create sympathy for your central character or does he come off as a buffoon? The VO has to be carefully developed and rehearsed. Be aware that though the first two options are apparently Alan's view of himself, they should allow the audience to develop an independent sense of Alan that might confirm what a psychiatrist or job interviewer suspected. The remaining three suggestions are perspectives that might better serve to profile the speaker than Alan.

Discussion:

- Using VO were you able to inject interest into periods of bridging action so they were as entertaining as the best action? (It's wise to use VO to raise the dull parts and let eloquent actions speak for themselves.)
- Did you leave interesting sound effects (Alan dropping his shoes) in the clear? (To do this, lay in the VO as a second sound track, which leaves salient portions of the sync or original dialogue track "in the clear." Raise levels of the sync track in the spaces between blocks of VO so the *foregrounded* track may either be VO, featured dialogue, or action from the sync track.

PROJECT 6-3: EXPLOITING A LOCATION

Skills to develop:

- Developing a mood
- Shifting the mood from objective to subjective
- Making use of cause and effect
- Capitalizing upon inherent rhythms
- Implying both a point of view and a state of mind
- Suggesting a development

- Using sync sound as effects
- Using music to heighten or interpret the environment

6-3A: DRAMATIZING AN ENVIRONMENT

Assessment: Use **Assessment 6-3A (Dramatizing an Environment)** from the Appendix.

Select an interesting location, which can be any authentic interior or exterior setting. It might be a harbor, motorcyclists' café, farmyard, teenager's bedroom, stock exchange, fairground, book shop, airport lounge, or anything else that is mainly a physical entity rather than a human event. This assignment has considerable documentary aspects and you will need to spend some hours just observing with a notebook in hand. Afterward, work your observations into a script that incorporates whatever interesting is likely to happen. You can use a POV Observer character of your own deciding so long as he or she looks unquestionably credible. Without using any speaking characters, develop a mood sequence of about 2 minutes that has a structure organic to the location's daily life and that changes and intensifies. In planning your sequence, consider the following:

- What is inherently present that might structure the sequence? (Passengers arriving in an airport, then leaving at the departure gate? Time progression? Increasing complexity in the action? Forward exploratory movement of camera?)
- What cause-and-effect shots can you group together into sub-sequences? (Within a winter forest scene, you establish icicles melting, drops of water falling past a shack's window, drops falling in a pool, rivulet of water flowing through ice, etc.)
- Are there inherent rhythms to be exploited (water dripping, cars passing, a street vendor's repeated cry, dog barking, etc.)?
- Do the sequences move from micro to macro view, or the reverse? (Start with BCU water droplets and develop to view of entire forest; or conversely, start with an aerial view of the city and end on a single, overfilled trash can.)
- Can you create a turning point that marks the onset of a heightened or altered sensibility? (For instance, in a deserted sandy cove, the camera discovers a single, smoking cigarette butt. Thereafter, coverage suggests the uneasiness of wondering if there is a lurking human presence.)

Here fiction merges with documentary; the environment has become a character studied by the Storyteller. We make the same dramaturgical demands, asking that the view of the location grow and change so it draws us into reacting and becoming involved.

The classic *three-act structure* was developed in theater but can be applied to the contents of a single sequence, a short film, or even a full-length fiction film.

Act I Establishes the *setup* (establishes characters, relationships, situation, and dominant problem faced by the central character or characters)

Act II Develops the *complications* in relationships as the central character struggles with the obstacles that prevent him or her from solving the main problem

Act III Intensifies the situation and *resolves* it, often in a climactic way that is emotionally satisfying

It's important to say that the main character need not be human. In Pare Lorentz's classic ecology documentary *The River* (1937), the Mississippi River in all its awesome power and changing moods is the central character. Lorentz traces it from a trickle at its start to a roaring torrent that in full flood sweeps away homes and lives.

As always, contrasts and contradictions are the richest stimulant to awareness. In a seaside scene it might be the juxtaposition of frenetic game players with corpulent sun-worshipers that provides the astringent comparisons, or the waves compared with the stillness of the rocks. Every setting, like every character, contains dialectical tensions whose irreconciled and coexisting opposites define the subject's scope and subjective meaning to the observer.

Depending on your storytelling Observer (a child, an old man, a foreigner, a cat, an explorer, someone revisiting his past, etc.), the environment can be interpreted very differently. Through what you show, you can suggest the observing consciousness of a particular person in a particular mood, even though that person is seldom or never seen.

Discussion:

- Was the sequence dependent on the impressions each image and activity suggested or upon the movements and words of a central human subject?
- Did you find inherent rhythms in the material?
- Did you let shot durations be decided by their context?
- Was there a beginning, a middle, and an end to the sequence? (as if you were writing a dramatic scene, but ideally the developments are not imposed but come from the rhythms and activities inherent in the setting)
- The sequence should come from a response to the location and not be an attempt to impose some spurious story or usefulness on it.

6-3B: ADDING MUSIC

Assessment: Re-use **Assessment 6-1C (Music).**

Going further: Now try adding music to your sequence, choosing it carefully. Don't use any songs; the aim is to work with emotional associations and behavioral narration, not a verbal one. Try different pieces roughly against your scene to determine which works best before downloading onto your hard drive. When you lay the music against the sequence, do the following:

- Be ready to let particular sound effects bleed through the music in appropriate places.

- Decide where and why you want pure music, with no diegetic sound at all. Making these decisions raises important points about when music needs to be "pure" and when its impact and meaning is enhanced by sounds from the "real" world.
- Be ready to adjust shot lengths and cutting points to accommodate the structure of the music you've chosen. Music is never just applied; there should always be mutual responsiveness between visuals, diegetic sound (where used), and music.

Music can do the following:

- Augment what has been created pictorially and act illustratively
- Suggest something hidden that the audience must hunt for. Example: A peaceful harvest scene accompanied by an ominous marching tune, or abandoned houses in a blighted urban area seen against an impassioned Bach chorale
- Suggest what is subjective either to a character in the film or to the Storyteller. Example: that young farm workers go off to die on foreign battlefields, or that poverty and failure are somehow part of God's plan for mankind

Music is easy to begin and a lot less easy to conclude. The start and stop of a camera movement or subject movement can motivate music in- and out-points, as can the ending or beginning of a strong diegetic sound effect. Study feature films for further guidance.

Discussion:

- What rules do you feel govern the legitimacy of using music?
- When is using music illegitimate?
- When is music being used creatively rather than programmatically (that is, as mere illustration)?
- What should music's relationship be to dialogue?
- How should music relate to diegetic sound effects (that is, effects natural to the scene)?
- When should music belong to the world of the characters and when can it come from beyond their world?
- Can music be motivated by the storytelling "voice" of the film?
- Can you mix periods (use modern music on a historic subject, for instance)?
- What determines the texture and instrumentation of a music piece?

PROJECT 6-4: EDITED TWO-CHARACTER DIALOGUE SCENE

Skills to develop:

- Planning and shooting dialogue exchanges

- Camera placement
- Using verbal rhythms and operative words in editing
- Controlling the scene's point of view

6-4A: MULTIPLE COVERAGE

Assessment: Use **Assessment 6-4AB** in the Appendix.

Overview: This project, though short, covers a lot of ground and will take effort, invention, and organization. It will help if you have read ahead in this book, all the way into the Production phase, in fact (Chapters 26–31). Do not shortchange yourself in the planning stage, for you can learn much from making plans, carrying them out, and then realizing what you'd do differently next time.

1. Write a short dialogue scene (approximately 3 minutes) that makes use of an active indoor game. Make one character realize that the other is bluffing and does not know how to play. You must imply why this situation has arisen and what it means to each person.
2. Mark the shooting script with your intended pattern of cutting. This frees you during shooting to overlook weak sections that fall in the part of an angle you don't intend to use. Having this information at hand will help you decide immediately whether to call for another take.
3. Shoot the whole scene from at least three angles. This style of coverage was once the Hollywood norm. The editor was expected to find a point of view later within the all-purpose coverage. Today shooting a scene this way is considered decision-less coverage that wastes actors' energies, crew time, and filmstock. Such broad coverage here is useful because it allows you leeway to experiment in editing.
4. About pacing a scene: Comedy should be paced about a third faster than things would happen in life if it is to look right on the screen. Conversely, serious scenes often must be slowed, particularly at beat points, so that pauses, silences, eyeline shifts, or an exchange of glances can be fully exploited. Experienced directors know where the truly high points are in a scene and how to alter the pacing to their advantage. Beginners often reverse these priorities and strive to ensure that no silence, or silent action, ever threatens to "bore" the audience. Nothing could be further from the truth.
5. A word about stretching or compressing time in editing: Having double coverage in the cutting room lets you double a pregnant moment when it isn't pregnant enough. To do this, use all of the moment in the outgoing shot, then cut to the matching, incoming one at the beginning of the moment. That way you can double its screen duration, a key technique for stretching time at strategic points. Conversely, if the moment was held overlong in a shot, you can abbreviate it by cutting tight to the matching angles and using editing as an elision device.
6. Actions, reactions, and subtexts: Although editors cannot speed up or slow down the way words in a sentence emerge, they can control the rhythm and balance of action and reaction, which is a huge part of implying a subtext. Surefooted editing can make a vast difference to the degree of thought and

feeling the audience attributes to each character, and greatly improve the sense of integration and consistency in the acting.

Steps:

- Cast the actors.
- Decide the location.
- Write a script that implies where the characters come from (their *backstory*) and where they might be going next.
- Make several copies of the script and mark up one with the *beats* (more about this useful theatrical term later, but for now, treat a beat as that point at which one of the characters undergoes a major and irreversible realization).
- Rehearse the scene.
- Develop the accompanying action, going beyond what the script calls for.
- Make a floor plan of the location showing characters' moves and intended camera positions (see Figure 5–3 as an example).
- Define what you want the scene to accomplish and whose point of view at any given point the audience is to (a) mainly and (b) partially share and understand.
- Using another copy of the script and colored pens for each camera position, mark up the script with your intended editing plan. Figure 6–3 provides an example.
- Plan to cut between angles at times of major subject movement so cuts will disappear behind compelling action.
- Be sure to shoot a generous action overlap at the intended cutting points or you will have insufficient choice in places to cut. This can spell disaster if the cut is to be an action match.
- Shoot, playing the whole scene through in each major angle, thus allowing yourself to experiment widely during the editing.
- Edit strictly according to your plan.
- Solicit audience critique.
- Re-edit according to what you now feel should be done.
- Solicit new audience critique.
- Write directorial guidelines for your next directing project based on what you learned.

Discussion: Directing and editing a convincing dialogue scene is one of the most challenging tasks a director faces. How did you do?

- How difficult was it to achieve consistent success throughout a take?
- How right was the pacing of the scene?
- Were the significant moments effectively exploited, and if not, why not?
- How did your writing sound in the mouths of your actors?

- Would the acting in this scene pass as documentary shot with a hidden camera?
- What did you learn about directing actors from this experience?
- What did you learn about directing from a text?

6-4B: EDITING FOR AN ALTERNATIVE POINT OF VIEW

Assessment: Use **Assessment 6-4AB** in the Appendix. See if you did better the second time around.

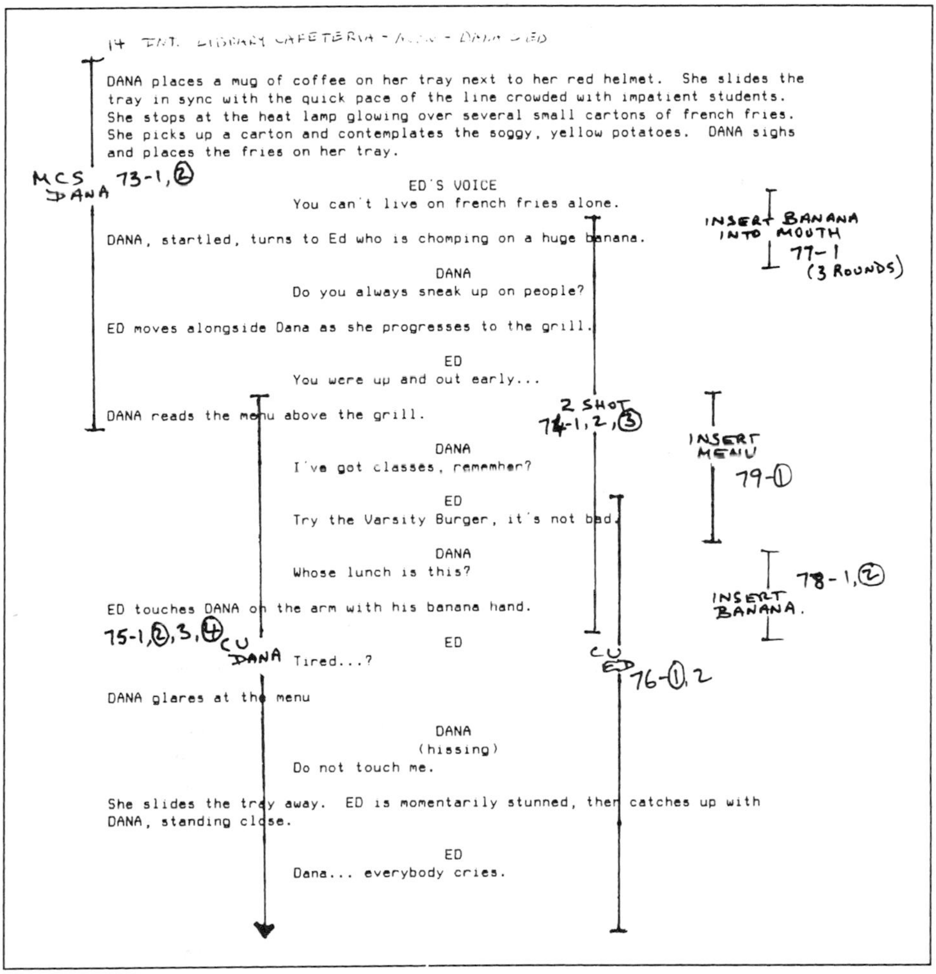

DANA places a mug of coffee on her tray next to her red helmet. She slides the tray in sync with the quick pace of the line crowded with impatient students. She stops at the heat lamp glowing over several small cartons of french fries. She picks up a carton and contemplates the soggy, yellow potatoes. DANA sighs and places the fries on her tray.

ED'S VOICE
You can't live on french fries alone.

DANA, startled, turns to Ed who is chomping on a huge banana.

DANA
Do you always sneak up on people?

ED moves alongside Dana as she progresses to the grill.

ED
You were up and out early...

DANA reads the menu above the grill.

DANA
I've got classes, remember?

ED
Try the Varsity Burger, it's not bad.

DANA
Whose lunch is this?

ED touches DANA on the arm with his banana hand.

ED
Tired...?

DANA glares at the menu

DANA
(hissing)
Do not touch me.

She slides the tray away. ED is momentarily stunned, then catches up with DANA, standing close.

ED
Dana... everybody cries.

FIGURE 6–3

Marked-up script showing intended cut and generous overlaps to allow action matches and other kinds of alternatives in editing.

Re-edit your scene to make the audience identify with a significantly different point of view, such as the secondary character's or an omniscient Storyteller's point of view.

Discussion: Apply the same criteria as in Project 6-8A, but also propose additional coverage or differences in acting that might make the audience engage better with the new point of view.

PROJECT 6-5: AUTHORSHIP THROUGH IMPROVISATION

Skills to develop:

- Involving actors in script idea development
- Spontaneous and creative interaction between actors and director
- Directing an event for direct cinema coverage, useful where actors must merge, for example, with an uncontrollable public event
- Editing documentary-style coverage
- Script development from taped improvisations
- Stylistic decision making
- Working intuitively and thinking on your feet

6-5A: DEVELOPING A SHORT SCENE

Assessment: Use **Assessment 6-5ABC (Improvised Scene)** in the Appendix.

Authorial goals: Set up guidelines for a 3 to 4 minute improvised scene between two people that incorporates an emotional transition in one of the characters from cheerful to angry. The goal is not to produce great drama, but to experiment with camera coverage and editing. Should you need guidance in directing an "*improv*," read the introductory part of Chapter 21, then follow the instructions for Exercise 21–15: Bridging Emotions. When you have run through your scene several times so it has become reasonably stable and secure, use a handheld camera to cover the complete scene, doing this at least three times to favor three different angles: on character A, on character B, and on both as a two-shot.

The goal is obtaining sufficient coverage to allow freedom in cutting the scene together and to cope with the unavoidable variations inherent in multiple takes of an improvised piece. You will have to rely on your camera operator for the quality of the coverage, so it is best to bring him or her in early to shoot rehearsals.

Camera use: With the advance of Steadicam use, and with high definition (HD) video being used increasingly in feature films, handheld coverage is increasingly common. Stylistically it usually projects a strong feeling of spontaneous human observation, as opposed to the godlike omniscience implied by the tripod's perfect composition and rock steadiness. It also injects an interesting sense of fallibility and subjectivity into the coverage. Sometimes, of course, this is intrusively wrong—for instance, during a sequence of misty mountain landscape shots at daybreak when nobody is supposed to be about. In that case, tripod shots are a must.

In *direct cinema* documentary, also known as *observational* camera coverage, the director cannot line up each shot, so creative initiative passes to the camera operator, who must have the mind of a dramatist, not just that of a technician or still photographer. A director quickly finds out whether the operator sees only composition through the viewfinder or whether he or she is finding dramatic meaning and focus within a scene. Some do and some can learn, but many camera operators will remain detached visual designers.

Sound coverage: Here it's catch-as-catch-can (something your sound recordist will find a real challenge). While the camera adapts to the action, the microphone operator must stay out of frame and pick up good sound in a swiftly changing, unpredictable situation. Pay attention to sound balance before you show your work to an audience or discrepancies will make them misread the piece's inherent qualities. One solution is to use a DAT multi-track recorder and put a wireless microphone on everyone who speaks, recording each on a separate channel.

Editing: Edit together a complete version, keeping to the form and length of the original, and apply **Assessment 6-5ABC (Improvised Scene).**

Discussion: Exposition

- Was all the expository detail included by the actors so the audience understands the situation? (It is fatally easy in improv to overlook something vital.)
- Was each new piece of expository information concealed artfully enough?
- Did the information come too early or too late in the edited piece?

Camera coverage

- When was mobile, handheld footage stylistically appropriate and when not?
- What conclusions can you draw to help you make guidelines for the future?
- Was the spontaneous coverage adequate or is the operator sometimes caught by surprise?
- What effect do these moments have on the audience?
- How much does the unpredictability of the characters' movements prevent you from more deliberately showing their environment?
- To what degree can you construct an integrated point of view?
- Did you manage to grab enough close detail? By grabbing close-ups, *insert shots*, and *cutaways* as you shoot, you will give your editor a variety of material by which to control the substance and rhythms of the scene. An insert shot enlarges significant detail within an existing shot. For example, the watch face a character is consulting. The editor inserts it into the main action. A cutaway shot might convey similar information, but does so by

showing something outside the existing shot. For example, if a character looks up out of frame, you would shoot her eyeline view of the clock. This shot is a cutaway because the clock is outside the main action and to show it requires cutting away from the immediate action.

- Does the composition succeed in showing a revealing relationship between people (crestfallen son, for instance, in foreground, angry mother in background)?
- Or between objects (miner grandfather's tombstone in foreground, the coal mine that killed him in background)?

Sound

- How acceptable is the dialogue track?
- How hard was it to cover speakers whose movements are spontaneous?

Point of view

- Whose scene is it?
- Does point of view arise more from the performance than from the camera treatment? (This is extremely hard to pinpoint, but nevertheless, too important to neglect).
- Or between people and some aspect of their environment? (for instance, a forlorn, withdrawn child standing in a playground that looks like a concentration camp)

Improvising

- What did you gain, what did you lose from improvising a scene?
- What did you gain, what did you lose from handheld coverage?
- How credible were the characters?
- How consistently did the dramatic problem between the characters develop and did it resolve?
- How consistent was the density of the piece and how much did you find yourself wanting to edit around plateaus in the pacing or development?

Time your first cut for comparison with the next assignment.

6-5B: EDITING A SHORTER VERSION

Assessment: Use **Assessment 6-5ABC (Improvised Scene)** in the Appendix again.

Going further: Now edit your initial cut down, trying to make it tighter and more functional by eliminating verbal and behavioral padding. To do this you will have to decide with your editor the dramatic function of much that is said and done on the screen and devise methods of eliminating whatever does not deserve to be there. You are also free to restructure the piece if repositioning exposition or other elements improves the dramatic curve.

Discussion:

- What percentage of the original length did you eliminate?
- In what ways is the new cut more effective?
- How consistent is the pace of dramatic development now?
- What did you feel about the acting?
- What would you do differently?

The strength of improvisation is the spontaneity and realism of the acting and the conviction of the characters. Discuss which of the following weaknesses turned up in your work and whether they could be eliminated:

- The difficulty of achieving a satisfying development. Improv often suffers from irregularly paced dramatic growth, with long plateaus during which both actors and audience feel the pressure for something to happen.
- The temptation for actors, when desperate, to resort to manipulating moments to get the piece moving again.
- The difficulty of reliably hiding exposition inside ongoing events.

You do not want your audience to feel the presence of an editorializing hand during verbal exchanges, feeding such giveaway lines as, "Isn't it rough being out of work for three months, Ted?" and, "The last time we met—you remember—it was at the supermarket. You got mad because I couldn't give you back the money you lent me in September."

Even if no clumsy authorial hand comes occasionally crashing through the backdrop of your piece, the probability is high that you will be dissatisfied with the dialogue. At times it is skimpy and over-compressed, at other times prolix and flaccid. Though editing can usually remove padding, it may also reveal inadequate joints and structural problems. However, if things go reasonably well, you end up with interestingly developed characters and a story line. Whatever you have by now is the basis for the next stage.

6-5C: FROM IMPROV TO SCRIPT

Assessment: Use **Assessment 6-5ABC (Improvised Scene)** in the Appendix.

Transcribe the scene from the previous exercise onto paper and rewrite it, aiming to keep the words the actors used, but compress verbiage into pithy lines. Distribute and camouflage any expository information, and wherever possible, transform dialogue into actions that do not require accompanying words. This way characters can show their feelings instead of telling them to each other. Now, using the same cast and location, rehearse and shoot the scene as in Project 6-6.

Discussion: Compare the two versions of the same scene.

- What was lost by turning an improvised performance, shot documentary style, into a scripted and more formally controlled scene?
- What was gained?
- How did your cast handle their lines and action this time?
- What did you learn about authorship and directing through doing this project?

PROJECT 6-6: PARALLEL STORYTELLING

Skills to develop:

- Intercutting two narrative lines
- Counterpointing two moods or activities to imply a storytelling commentary
- Advancing two story lines concurrently so each acts as a cutaway for the other and both are kept to brief essentials
- Showing separate, concurrent events developing toward a moment of convergence

6-6A: SEEING THE SCENES AS SEPARATE ENTITIES

Assessment: Use **Assessment 6-6ABCD (Parallel Storytelling)**, but omit the last section, Parallel Stories.

Either write or improvise two whole scenes with content that will intercut meaningfully and provoke the audience to see a connection. Suggested pairs of subjects:

- man getting ready for a date
- woman in very different mood getting ready for the same date
- burglars getting ready to rob a house
- detectives making preparations to trap them
- man rehearsing how he will ask for a raise
- two managers discussing how they will fire him

Write each as a complete, 3-minute, stand-alone scene. Now cast, shoot, and edit each scene separately and assemble them so that one whole scene follows the other. Do a reasonably tight edit on each sequence and then consider them as follows:

Discussion:

- What difference is there in implication when you run the sequences as AB or BA? (The detectives, for example, may have arrived too late, and the firing may follow the request for a raise, instead of precede it.)
- How long is each sequence?
- What do you gain in dramatic buildup by staying with each unbroken sequence?

6-6B: LONG INTERCUT VERSION

Assessment: Use **Assessment 6-6ABCD (Parallel Storytelling)** this time *with* the last section, Parallel Stories.

Going further: Now loosely intercut the two sequences losing nothing of the original material.

Discussion:

- What ironies were you able to create? (Perhaps you counterpoint the fact that the woman preparing for the date has bought a new dress while the man forgets to clean his shoes.)
- What meaningful comparisons do you create? (Both the man asking for a raise and his managers think he is underpaid.)
- What causes and effects does the audience link together? (Both detectives and burglars have radios.)
- Do both sequences appear to be happening at the same time, or is one retrospective in comparison with the other? (For instance, a son from abroad searching for his parents finds that his father is already dead. His father's death is intercut with his mother's account of it, which is softened to spare the son's feelings.)
- Does one sequence foretell the outcome of the other? (In Nicholas Roeg's *Don't Look Now* (1973) the famous lovemaking scene is intercut with the couple getting dressed afterward.)

6-6C: SHORT VERSION

Assessment: Use **Assessment 6-6ABCD (Parallel Storytelling)** with the last section, Parallel Stories.

Going further: Now reassess the cut. Because it is no longer necessary to maintain the illusion of continuous time, you can pare away anything the audience can infer and which is thus nonessential. You will probably see new and improved points at which to cut between the parallel stories.

Discussion:

- How much shorter is the new version compared with the old?
- How many of the ideas for your new cut arose from the shooting, blocking, and playing of the scene?
- How many of your intercutting ideas were germinated while writing, and how many came afterward?
- What kind of dramatic capital has been gained and what lost through intercutting?
- Knowing what you know now, how should a writer plan the raw materials for such sequences?

6-6D: DISCONTINUITY AND USING JUMP CUTS

Assessment: Use **Assessment 6-6ABCD (Parallel Storytelling)**, but not the last section, Parallel Stories.

Going further: Now experimentally reassemble each sequence in chronological order, retaining only the pieces you chose for the intercut version as a *discontinuity* version using *jump cuts*. A jump cut is any discontinuous edit that signals a significant piece of time has been discarded between the scenes and that we have jumped forward in time. By doing this you are moving from continuity narrative to an episodic narrative using discontinuous time.

Discussion: What are the effects of eliminating the slack material between the high points? Surely this accelerates the story, and by discarding objective time it probably accentuates an authorial attitude toward what moments matter. Flat-footed realism and its linear, continuous time have given way to something more impressionistic and subjective.

If you hate this version of your sequences, it may be because the jump cuts make ugly visual leaps. How true would this be had you written the film with this in mind and designed each jump cut's composition? Here are some options to consider:

> **Similarity of Frame:** You might, for instance, have cut from a bed with two people reading, to the same bed with them asleep, to a morning shot with one still there and the other dressing in the background. Older convention would dictate a long, slow dissolve between the three setups (which should be taken with the camera locked down in the exact same position so each composition is exactly the same), but the same narrative content can be conveyed in a fraction of the time by jump cutting. This makes the jump cut a formal storytelling device of great agility.
>
> **Difference of Frame:** With a bold difference of composition you can simply jump cut elsewhere in space and possibly in time as well. During a wide shot of people preparing to fire a piece of pottery, you can cut to a close shot of the oven. Somebody opens it, and the pot is already fired. We understand that a block of insignificant time has been eliminated, even though dialogue continues with an unbroken sentence across the cut into the new time plane. The TV commercial has familiarized audiences with cinematic shorthand like this.

Freed from the literalness and "objectivity" of present-tense realism, discontinuity allows a wealth of possibilities for a fleeter and more staccato storytelling style. These developments are very significant if as a writer, director, or editor you want to co-opt the audience's imagination by using a cinematic language of greater flexibility. Jean-Luc Godard was the first director to use this style intensively in *Breathless* (1959).

CHECKLIST FOR PART 2: SCREENCRAFT

The points and recommendations summarized here are only those most salient. Some are commonly overlooked. To find them or anything else in the text, go to the Table of Contents at the beginning of this part or try the index at the back of the book.

Screen grammar

- Every so often when you have time, make yourself aware of the different aspects of your consciousness and decide what film language would best serve your stream of consciousness.
- What did your consciousness make you do? (Move in, move away, avert your eyes, listen, think, remember . . . ?)
- Pretend you are handling a camera in everyday life and line up shots. Determine their aspects and motivations according to the emotional context of an Observer.
- Practice seeing every shot for its connotations, not just denotation.
- Look for metaphors or symbols in movies and analyze whether they are organic to the situation or imposed.
- Make yourself classify shot juxtaposition by their type, such as illustrative, counterpoint, contradiction, associative, tense-shifting, etc. (See Chapter 4, Figure 4–1 and supporting text for types of cut).
- See how established directors handle the axis, particularly crossing the scene axis. Multiple character scenes with a number of character or camera moves can get very complicated.
- Practice dividing up scenes in everyday life into their possible axes (subject-to-subject, and observer-to-subject). You may want to unobtrusively scan from different vantage points.
- Make yourself aware of what makes a scene discrete. (Is it defined by time, location, mood, other?)
- Screen language implies a particular intelligence, grappling with events in which it also participates.

Seeing with a moviemaker's eye

- Notice when composition on the screen is being adjusted because of changing internal elements.
- See a feature film and count how many types of scene or time transitions it uses.
- Notice when visual rhythm is inherent to the subject matter or when it is being varied for authorial reasons.
- Notice external compositional relationships (the juxtapositional commentary created by two compositions cut, dissolved, or otherwise associated together).

- For practice, make a floor plan of two rooms you live in, showing electrical outlets, windows, and direction of ambient light, furniture placement, and door swing.
- Practice being conscious of the layering in movies' sound tracks.
- Practice being aware of different kinds of light and lighting, in movies and in life, and make a mental note of the emotional associations.
- Notice in different situations how you experience time—what extends it and what truncates it.
- See a movie by a famous director and decide (a) what the Storyteller's identity was and (b) what in the movie communicated it to you.

Shooting fundamentals

- Plan everything and make lists of everything you need to remember.
- Do floor plans showing lighting placements for all your shooting. Name the lights.
- Mark intended camera positions on a floor plan.
- Always check an exterior location for light direction at the time of day when you plan to shoot.
- Check location for unwanted sound intrusions (like being in the flight path of an airport!).
- Be sure to shoot sound presence tracks for every location.
- Don't forget to get written permission for locations if you need them.
- Dialogue scenes are the hardest to shoot and cut well.
- Remember to inhabit your Storyteller's character while you direct. Shoot and see from his or her point of view. This won't be easy to remember.
- Become aware of who is acting and who is being acted upon at any moment and in any situation.
- Remember that characters are alive when they are seeking to do or get.
- Direct to imply the subtext.
- Make storyboards if you are doubtful about how a sequence will cut together. Draw stick figures if this is the best you can do.
- Remember to shoot generous action overlaps between matching shots when you mean to cut them together.
- Decide when long, comprehensive takes are called for and when a more fragmented style suits the situation being filmed.
- Give your major attention to the actors and after initial consultation for each shot, leave directing the camera to the DP.
- Look carefully for what you may have forgotten before striking any camera position or set.
- Keep all the versions you edit.
- View all your rushes again before you lock down a final cut—there is always an unused gem.

- If you want to place a cut on the beat of music, you must make it three frames ahead of the beat if it's to look right.
- In match cutting on movement, overlap (that is, repeat) the first two or three frames of movement to allow the eye to catch up.
- See how far you can go with discontinuity and still keep your audience. Have showings to find out what you can get away with. What permits the audience to fill in the gaps?

PART 3

WRITING AND STORY DEVELOPMENT

Part 3 (Chapters 7 through 11) deals with the director's responsibility to the script, that all-important document that initiates virtually all fiction films. The first step in creating anything at all—whether bridge, chair, song, or film—is to develop a full vision of the finished article. Subsequent work bridges the gap between the plan and its realization and makes the vision a reality. The fiction script is the vision and represents, in a standard and shareable form, the film developed in your head. Unlike documentary, which reflects a world already in existence, a fictional world must first be envisaged before it can be filmed, and the script is vital to this.

Problematic films almost invariably have problematic scripts, and knowing how to fully develop all the script elements before filming is a vital skill for any aspiring director. There is a great deal to learn, and as always, the best learning is by immersion in direct experience. If you are writing your first screen works, this chapter will get you started. If you are directing from someone else's screenplay, you'll find criteria throughout this part to help you assess how practical and well-written it is, and how to set about developing it from a director's perspective. Although I often address the reader as a screenwriter, my hope is that the director will become an expert at judging and developing scripts, rather than the writer of his or her own screen projects. This, as will be explained, gives you the best chance to win recognition as a director.

When you need reminders of the advice in this part, be sure to use the checklist at the end.

CHAPTER 7

SCREENWRITING CONCEPTS

WHEN YOU DIRECT FROM YOUR OWN WRITING

As a beginner, you will need to write and direct your own short films. Though your first films will be simple, read the chapters on writing, form, and structure. Sometimes people are impatient and look down on exercises and projects as "not real films," but every piece for the screen, no matter how short, faces you with options in point of view, genre, plot, and style, all of which are treated in the coming chapters. There is a huge amount to learn from making short films, but be prepared to profit as much from negative experiences as from positive ones. Later I will argue for collaboration with a screenwriter, but for now, let's assume you are a writer-director.

For any story to work well on the screen, no matter how short, allow much time and a number of drafts in which to complete the writing process, and *seek out honest criticism* at key stages. Doing so is like exposing your film to audience reactions in advance. Film is an audience medium, yet beginning directors tend to hide from exposure as long as possible. One way to get criticism is to *pitch* your work, which means you describe its essentials orally in brief and exciting form to another person. Today this has become a vital skill for a director, producer, or screenwriter to possess. See the beginning of Chapter 8 for more details.

DECIDING ON SUBJECTS

As you make exercise films to learn the basics of film technique and grammar, take care to choose subjects you care about. You will have to live with your choice and its ramifications for some time. Once you start shooting, you should complete the film, no matter what. If this commitment sounds scary, it can be explored with the option of retreat all through the writing and rewriting stages. Writing and rewriting as you move among the three dimensions of screenplay, step outline, and concept (explained in detail later) will allow you to *inhabit* a text, something virtually impossible from one or two detached readings. As always, when you translate from one mode of representation to another, you will discover a range of aspects hidden from the more casual reader, no matter how expert he or she may be.

Whether your film is to be comedy, tragedy, horror, fantasy, or a piece for children, it must embody some issue with which you identify. Everyone bears scars from living, and everyone with any self-knowledge has issues within, awaiting exploration. Your work will best sustain you when connected to something that moves you to strong feelings. This might be racial or class alienation, a reputation for clumsiness, fear of the dark (horror films!), rejection, an obsession, a period of intense happiness, or a brief affair you had with someone very beautiful. It might be a stigma such as illegitimacy, being foreign, or being unjustly favored—I repeat, *anything that has moved you to strong feelings*. Start a list. You will probably be surprised at two things: how many subjects you have to draw on and the themes that emerge when you look for common denominators.

Directing films demands both creation and contemplation—an outward doing and a parallel inner process of search and growth. This is the foundation of the *artistic process*. Your validity as a storyteller begins with the scars of experience rather than from ideas or ambitions that lack the bedrock of experience. We have all passed through war zones, so work in any corner of existence about which you know something and want to learn more. Avoid debating problems or demonstrating solutions. The object is not to produce a film that preaches or confesses but one that deals—in some suitably displaced way—with something you care deeply about. To feel satisfying to an audience, your story should show evidence in its main character of some change or growth, however minimal or even negative this may be.

START MAKING WORKING PARTNERSHIPS

After a year or two of production, most film students have a better idea of their interests and limitations and also realize they will need to work professionally in one of the allied crafts before anyone considers them mature enough to direct. You are helped in this by the virtual impossibility of finding directing work unless you emerge with a sensational piece of student work, as Robert Rodriguez did at the Sundance Film Festival with *El Mariachi* (1993). If you are committed to directing professionally, start looking now for your natural collaborators in writing, cinematography, and editing.

WHY READING A SCRIPT IS DIFFICULT

Whether you want to raise funds or just put your intentions before a crew and cast, communicating the nature of your film depends on the script. It seems simple—you just hand someone a script, don't you? But this may accomplish nothing useful; scripts are very demanding to read and a well-written one is purposely minimal. Because actors, director, camera crew, and even the weather all make unforeseeable contributions, the astute scriptwriter leaves a great deal unspecified. A script should consist of dialogue, sparse or nonexistent stage directions, and equally brief remarks on character, locations, and behavior. Until the shooting stage there will be no directions for camerawork or editing. The reader must supply from imagination what is missing, something that key crew members such as the director, technicians, and actors, do as part of their creative contribution to the project.

A screenplay is a verbal blueprint designed to seed a nonliterary, organic, and experiential process. Rarely if ever does it give more than a sketchy impression of what the film will really be like. Nor does it give many overt clues to the thematic intentions behind the writing. These must be inferred by the reader, again at considerable effort. The lay reader, expecting the detailed evocations of a short story or novel, feels that inordinate mental effort and experience is demanded to decompress the writing. More arduous than reading poetry and much less rewarding, reading scripts is not pleasurable. Inside the film industry and out, most people resist reading any more scripts than necessary. Most production companies, receiving several hundred a week, throw the unsolicited ones away or give them no more than a cursory glance, perhaps scanning every 10th page. Because the likelihood of finding anything usable is so small among the 50,000 or so scripts copyrighted annually, professionals will usually only look at work forwarded by a reputable agent.

To earn money by screenwriting, you must first write well enough to win the respect of a good agent. If you are a director looking for a script, expect a lot of hard and discouraging reading. In the film industry, first-rate scripts are extremely rare and their qualities immediately apparent. There is a terrible shortage of distinguished work. If you are in film school, start talent scouting.

STANDARD SCRIPT FORMS

The industry standard for layouts is simple and effective and has evolved as the ultimate in convenience. Do not invent your own.

SCREENPLAY FORMAT

The sample page in Figure 7–1 illustrates the following rules for screenplay form:

Typeface: **Screenplays** always use the old-fashioned typewriter font called 12-point Courier. The industry has never moved away from this because one page in this format runs approximately a minute onscreen.

Scene heading: Each scene begins with a flush-left, capitalized scene heading that lists:

- Number of the scene
- Interior or exterior
- Location
- Time of day or night
- Main characters involved

Body copy: This material, which includes action description, mood setting, and stage directions, is double-spaced away from scene headings and dialogue and runs the width of the page.

Character names: Outside the dialogue these should appear in all capitals.

11. INT. LIBRARY CAFETERIA NOON DANA & ED

DANA places a mug of coffee on her tray next to her crash helmet. She slides the tray in sync with the quick pace of the line crowded with impatient students. She stops at the heat lamp glowing over several small cartons of french fries. She picks up a carton and contemplates the soggy yellow potatoes. DANA sighs and places the fries on her tray.

ED'S VOICE
You can't live on French fries alone.

DANA turns startled to find ED next to her chomping on a huge banana.

DANA
Do you always sneak up on people?

ED moves alongside DANA as she progresses to the grill.

ED
You were up and out so early...

DANA reads the menu above the grill.

DANA
I've got classes, remember?

ED
Try the Varsity Burger, it's not bad.

DANA
Whose lunch is this?

ED touches DANA on the arm with his banana hand.

ED
Tired?

DANA glares at the menu.

DANA (hissing)
Do not touch me.

She slides the tray away. ED is momentarily stunned, then catches up with her again, standing close.

ED
Dana...everybody cries.

FIGURE 7–1

Sample page of screenplay (from an unproduced screenplay, *A Night So Long* by Lynise Pion).

Dialogue sections:

- Should be headed by the speaker's name, centered and in all capitals
- Should be centered within extra margins
- Should be preceded and followed by a double space
- Are accompanied, when strictly necessary, by a stage direction inside brackets

Shot transitions: Terms like *Cut to* or *Dissolve to* are placed either flush left or flush right and are only included when unavoidable if the script is to make sense.

Figure 7–1 is a page in pure screenplay form. There are no camera or editing directions. Industry practices vary; some commercial scripts are hybrid creatures trying to dramatize their contents by moving closer to a shooting script. This may help to sell a particular script in a particular quarter, but in most places it has no practical value. Do what is normal from the beginning.

A TRAP FOR THE UNWARY

The screenwriter's most treacherous friend is the screenplay format itself, for its appearance and proportions suggest that films are built theatrically around dialogue. While this may be wretchedly true for soap opera, it is quite wrong for good screen drama, which is primarily behavioral. Actors and directors can also be lulled into assuming the primacy of the spoken over the behavioral. I do not mean to devalue the screenplay as the genesis of successful screen drama. Nobody has yet demonstrated that you can effectively coordinate actors and crew without a central structure, but this structure must be cinematic, not literary or theatrical. In fact, there are ways to reach it apart from the traditional one of writing, but that we'll explore later.

SPLIT-PAGE OR TV SCREENPLAY FORMAT

The *split-page format* (see Figure 5–2) is frequently used in multi-camera television studio shooting when a complex drama must be enacted in real time. For this reason the format is sometimes called a *television* or *TV format* script. In multi-camera television, all production elements have to be pre-envisioned and present because there is no postproduction. In cinema-style shooting, in which each shot is created discretely and the final version composed meticulously afterward in the cutting room, this density of detail is usually irrelevant.

Split-page format, however, is the best layout for logging and analyzing a finished movie. Unlike the screenplay, it allows clear representation of the counterpoint among images and among images and various sound elements. Notice that the left-hand picture column contains *only what you would see* and the right-hand sound column contains *only what you would hear.* Do not transpose them or the point of having a standard is lost.

Chapter 5, "Seeing With a Moviemaker's Eye," strongly recommended that you make a split-page transcript of a few sequences from your favorite contemporary movies. If you did it, you discovered how dense film language is. The exercise also demonstrates how effectively the split-page format can toggle the reader's attention between dialogue and action. If you like alternative cinema, which often uses dialogue, music, and effects while intercutting different levels of footage (past, present, archive, graphics), you may find writing in screenplay format difficult or even paralyzing. Try using the split-page format in the planning stage, and convert it to screenplay format later if you need to.

SCRIPT FORM CONFUSIONS

Publishers have caused confusion by making no distinction between the original screenplay and *continuity scripts* or *reader's scripts.* Both the latter are transcriptions of the finished product and not the all-important blueprint that initiated it. The glossary in this text explains the differences. If you study scripts, make sure you know what you are reading; otherwise, you may form the appalling idea that films are written and made by omniscient beings. To compare a film with its original screenplay is to contemplate the multiplicity of changes and modifications that took place after the blueprint. Whereas cars are first designed, then manufactured, films are redesigned and evolved throughout the process, from the first idea all the way to final mixing and color balancing the print.

PREPARING TO INTERPRET A TEXT

After your first reading of a screenplay, examine the imprint it left on you:

- What did it make you feel?
- Whom did you care about?
- Whom did you find interesting?
- What does the piece seem to be dealing with under the surface events?

Note these impressions and read the screenplay once or twice again, looking for hard evidence to go with your first impressions. Next ask yourself the following:

- What is the screenplay trying to accomplish?
- What special means is it using to accomplish its intentions?

Again, note your answers. Now leaf through the screenplay and make a flow chart of scenes, giving each a brief, functional description (Example: Scene 15: Ricky again sees Angelo's car; realizes he's being watched). From this list of scenes and their dramatic intentions, you are more likely to pinpoint the screenplay's dramatic logic, something difficult to abstract any other way. If you can't find it, this is a bad sign. If you can see some logic that the screenwriter seems unaware of, this is quite usual and is the reason directors and writers work together on rewrites of the script.

Having established some initial ideas about a screenplay's structure and development, we can now look at significant details.

GOOD SCREENPLAYS ARE NOT OVERWRITTEN

Because a screenplay is a blueprint and not a literary narrative, it is important to ruthlessly exclude embellishment. A good screenplay:

- Includes no author's thoughts, instructions, or comments
- Is reticent with qualifying comments and adjectives (over-describing kills what the reader imagines)
- Leaves most behavior to the reader's imagination and instead describes its effect (for example, "he looks nervous" instead of "he nervously runs a forefinger round the inside of his collar and then flicks dust off his dark serge pants")

- Under-instructs actors unless a line or action would be unintelligible without guidance
- Contains no camera or editing instructions
- Isn't written *on the nose* (over-explicitly, telling everything instead of leaving the viewer with interpretive work to do)
- Uses brief, evocative language whenever the body copy wants the reader to visualize

The experienced screenwriter is an architect who designs the shell of a building and knows that others will choose the walls, interiors, colors, and furnishings. A good reason to avoid over-instructing your readers is that you prevent them from filling deliberate ambiguities with positive assumptions. Inexperienced screenwriters tend to be control freaks who, in architectural simile, design the doorknobs, lay carpet, hang pictures, and end up making the building uninhabitable by anyone but themselves.

The writer-director might seem to be a special case. Because he or she should know exactly what is to be shot, where it is to be shot, and how, why not write very specifically? This overlooks the realities of filming. Without unlimited time and money, nothing much works out as you envision, so it's foolish to specify anything you may not be able to deliver.

Overwriting is not just impractical, it's hazardous. Any highly detailed description conditions your readers (money sources, actors, crew) to anticipate particular, hard-edged results. The director of such a script is locked into trying to fulfill a vision that disallows variables, even those that would contribute positively.

LEAVE THINGS OPEN

How a script is written sends messages to actors. An open script invites the cast to offer their own input while the over-specific, closed one expects actors to conform to the actions and mannerisms minutely specified in the text, however alien they may be. Challenging actors does not mean trying to minutely control them; on the contrary, it means getting from each a different and distinct personal identity. The good screenplay assists this by leaving the director and players to work out how things will be said and done. This encourages the creativity of the cast and catalyzes an active process between cast member and their director.

WRITE BEHAVIOR INSTEAD OF DIALOGUE

The first cowboy films made a strong impact because the American cinema recognized the power of behavioral melodrama. The good screenplay is still predominantly concerned with behavior, action, and reaction. It avoids static scenes in which people verbalize what they think and feel, as in soap opera.

PERSONAL EXPERIENCE NEEDS TO BE ENACTED, NOT SPOKEN

Everyone is moved by aspects of their own life, and every writer includes autobiography in their writing. But a writer must distinguish between the intensity of life experienced subjectively and that which remains powerful or exciting when seen only externally in the cinema. In a moving personal experience, you are actively involved and acted upon, feeling powerful pressures subjectively and within. In screen drama, the characters' inner thoughts and emotions can only communicate to outsiders as they do in life itself—through outwardly visible behavior. Drama is about *doing*, so what matters most on the screen is what actions people take. Every screen character who is at all compelling is *trying to get or do something*. All the time. Just as you are in your life, year to year, day to day, minute to minute. The trouble is, we are very aware when we feel something but are blindly unaware of nearly everything we do or did in pursuit of our objectives.

RECOGNIZING CINEMATIC QUALITIES

A simple but deadly test of a script's potential is to imagine shutting off the sound and assessing how much the audience would understand (and therefore care) about what remains. Submitting each sequence to this test reveals how much of it is conceived as behavior and how much as dialogue. This is not to deny that we talk to each other or even that many transactions of lifelong importance take place through conversation. But *being* one of the protagonists is one thing, and *looking* at someone on the screen is another. An onlooker is convinced by characters' actions more than their words, and it is through actions that we gain reliable insight into another person's inner life. Making effective drama means making the inner struggles of characters visible through their outward actions. Dialogue should therefore be used only when necessary, not as a substitute for action. *Dialogue should itself be action*, that is, it should be people acting upon each other, never people narrating their thoughts and feelings to each other.

CHARACTERS TRYING TO DO OR GET

We judge a screen character as we do someone in life, by first assessing all the visible clues—appearance, body language, clothes, and how they wear them. We look into the person's face, belongings, and surroundings to form initial impressions.

Watching how someone handles obstruction, we are primed to interpret available details of their background, such as their formative pressures, assumptions, and associations. We try to decide which among these the person chose and which were thrust upon them. How the person reacts—in particular to the unexpected or threatening—tells us much, as do the attitudes of their friends and intimates. These interactions also help to establish the goals, temperaments, and histories of the other characters.

A character's path is not determined by personal history alone; there is nature as well as nurture. Temperament, an active component in anyone's make-up, exerts its own influences in the face of conditioning at the hands of family and society. "Character," said Novalis, "is destiny." The astute writer never forgets this. Most of all, we make character judgments from the moral quality of a person's deeds. Each unexpected predicament a person faces is really a test of his or her moral strength, and what he or she does modifies or even subverts what hitherto appeared true. It may change what that person "is"—even to himself or herself.

To produce this evidence, dramatists strew the paths of their characters with obstacles. Your job as a dramatist is to dream up credible acts, situations, and environments that will propel your protagonist forward as he or she tries to get or do what lies on the agenda. Building lifelike contradictions into a character helps the audience to see human complexity—quite different from the illustrative portrayal that reeks of "message." Contradictions in a character's actions and beliefs are necessary if the person is to have inner conflicts. In heroic drama, conflicts are drawn as good characters against evil ones. But characters in contemporary realism need to be complex and have inner conflicts if they are to seem whole and have any magnitude.

STATIC CHARACTER DEFINITION—ONLY A BEGINNING

When deciding a screenplay's potential, assess the characters by more than their *givens* (such as age, sex, appearance, situation, and eccentricities). These are only a static summation, something like a photograph that typifies them but makes their development seem already closed and complete. Watching this kind of character in a film is like seeing a photomontage in which each person is fixed in a typical role and attitude. This constriction is unavoidable in the TV commercial, which must be brief and propagandistic. There each character is set by one or two dominant characteristics so that everyone is typical: a typical mother, a typical washing machine repairman, a typical holiday couple on a typical romantic beach. Homes, streets, meals, and happy families are all typified—which is to say, stereotyped.

When drama is conceived in a closed and illustrative form, players struggle in vain to breathe life into their characters, for everything their characters do and everything that befalls them falls back into that dominant and static conception. This prescriptive tendency denies and paralyzes the willpower, tensions, and adjustments present in even the most quiescent human being, and it prohibits the growth and change essential to being alive and inherent in real drama.

DYNAMIC CHARACTER DEFINITION—CHARACTER IN ACTION

What we need is a dynamic conception of character, one focusing on flux and mobilizing the potential for development instead of paralyzing it. The secret, so vital to writers and actors alike, is to go beyond what a character *is* and formulate what that character is trying to *get* or *do*. This is dynamic and interactive and deals with what the person is trying to accomplish and perhaps become.

In good drama you can see and feel each main character's will pitted against the surrounding obstacles. It's like studying an ant moving through gravel. We can see where the character is going and what he faces every step of the way, and we can become deeply involved in how he solves all the obstructions. This won't be true of writing in which the writer does not grasp how central volition is to characters and to drama itself. To uncover this kind of inner structure (or its absence) in drama, pick an active moment in a scene and apply the following questions:

- What is this character moving away from?
- What is this character moving toward?
- What is this character trying to get or do, long term?
- What is this character trying to get or do, this moment?
- What is this character facing as a new situation?
- What is this character obstructed by?
- What does the character want next?
- How is this character trying to overcome the obstacle?
- How is this character adapting to the obstacle? (Successfully? Unsuccessfully?)
- How is this character faced with a new situation after trying to adapt?
- How is this character changed in terms of goals by this experience?

Applying these *what* and *how* questions probes a character's development, moment by moment, and uncovers the character's immediate goals, as well as those that are longer term. Soon you can see how thoroughly a piece of dramatic writing has been thought through, and what weak areas need analyzing in the next step, which is identifying solutions and toughening a script's internal structure.

CONFLICT, GROWTH, AND CHANGE

Every rule has its exceptions, but dramatists generally agree that all stories need at least one character who shows some degree of growth and change or the story will seem hopeless. This learning is called a character's *development*. In accomplished writing, even minor characters pursue an *agenda*; that is, they struggle for something, face inner conflict or outer opposition, and they may even learn something, too. A short film, like a short story, needs only one character who shows a degree, however small, of development. A feature film, being longer, has a more complex architecture.

The screenwriter's job is to supply clues to evolving tensions in the characters. The 10 *how* and *what* questions listed previously are designed to detect evidence of this vital conflict and movement. When the answers for what each character says and does are consistent, you sense that you are completing a join-the-dots puzzle. As the evidence mounts, the character becomes someone struggling for consistent ends and who communicates the touching qualities of a living human being.

No story of any genre will have the power to move us unless its main or *point-of-view* character has to struggle, grow in awareness, and change. Particularly in a short film, this development may be minimal and symbolic, but its existence is the cardinal sign of a strong story. That a character learns something and grows a little seems to answer our perennial craving for hope and counters the many otherwise discouraging elements of contemporary life.

To breathe life into each character in a drama, the company and its director must create the whole from the clues embedded in the characters' words and actions. Most importantly, this must be conceived in the actors' own coin and cannot be dictated by the writer or director, who are midwives to truth, not its final creators.

PLANNING ACTION

At its most eloquent, the screen is a behavioral medium—one that shows rather than tells. Look at the list of sequences in a script and rate how readily each could be understood without sound. In some sequences the film's narrative is evident through action. In others the issues are handled verbally and could use translating into action. For example, in a breakfast scene, while a father gives his young son a sermon about homework, you could work out *business* in which the boy tries to rearrange and balance the cutlery and cereal boxes, while the father, trying to get his full attention, attempts to stop him. Though we don't see the precise subject in dispute, the conflict between them has been externalized as action.

Now whether this is best kept as work with the actors or whether it calls for script revision depends on your judgment. Will solving a particular problem encourage or inhibit your actors' creativity? Too little margin for imagination is stultifying; but too open, static, and empty a text may pose overwhelming problems of interpretation.

Usually a dialogue scene is always improved when reconceived as action. Say the boy comes home to find his father waiting with the schoolbooks set out. Reluctantly he sees what is at issue and silently takes the books into his room. Later his father looks in and finds his son sprawling in headphones listening to music. At breakfast the boy avoids his father's eye, but, unasked, goes to the doorstep to get his father the paper with guilt and remorse in his action. Now the need for confrontation and interaction has been turned entirely into a series of situations and actions, and it avoids the theatrical set-piece conversation.

However you solve the problem, try to substitute action for every issue handled verbally. It may be minimal facial action, it may be movement and activities of a revealing metaphorical nature, or it may be movement that the actor thinks will heighten his character's interior tension by concealing rather than revealing his true feelings.

Action and conflict are inherently interesting because action is the manifestation of will. Actions become even more interesting when they conflict with what a character says. Such contradiction can reveal both inner and outer dimensions, the conscious and the unconscious, the public and the private.

The antithesis of this principle is the script in which a tide of descriptive verbiage drowns whatever might be alive and at issue.

```
                         ROSE
Uncle, I thought I'd just look in and see how you are. It's
so miserable to be bedridden. You're Dad's only brother and
I want to look after you, if only for his sake.

                         UNCLE
You're such a good girl. I always feel better when you look in.
I thought I heard your footsteps, but I wasn't sure it was
you. It must be cold outside—you're wearing your heavy coat.
```

```
                         ROSE
You are looking better, but I see you still aren't fin-
ishing your meals. It makes me sad to see you leave an
apple as good as this when you normally like them so much.

                         UNCLE
I know dear, and it makes me feel almost guilty. But I'm
just not myself.
```

I wrote this to show the worst abominations. Notice the redundancies, how the writing keeps the characters static, how there is no behavior to signify feelings, and no private thought separate or different from the public utterances. Neither character signifies any of the feelings or hidden agenda that gives family interaction its rich undercurrents. Even between people like these, who like each other, there are always tensions and conflicts. But this writing grips the audience in a vice of literalness, lacking even unspoken understandings for the observer to infer. Most damning, nothing would be missed by listening with eyes closed. It is the essence of bad soap opera.

By reconceiving this scene to include behavior, action, and interaction, you could prune the dialogue by 80% and end up with something animated by a lot more tensions. If the scene is meant to reveal that the old man is brother to Rose's father, there must be a more natural way for this to emerge. At the moment, editorial information issues from her mouth like ticker tape. Perhaps we could make her stop in her tracks to stare at him. When he looks questioningly back, she answers, "It must be the light. Sometimes you look so much like Dad." His reaction—whether of amusement, irritation, or nostalgia—then gives clues about the relationship between the brothers.

DIALOGUE

In most movies, people speak to each other a lot, and this raises the question of how to write good dialogue and how to write *different* characters because most writers create characters who all speak with the same voice.

Cinema dialogue sets out to be vernacular speech. Whether the character is a young hood, an immigrant waitress, or an academic philosopher, each will speak in their own street slang, broken English, or strings of qualified, jargon-laden abstractions. What type of thought, what type of speech, will each character use?

Dialogue in movies is different from dialogue in life. In the cinema it must sound true to life yet cannot include life's prolixity and repetitiousness. Cinema dialogue is highly succinct though just as informal and authentically "incorrect." Dialogue must always steer clear of what the camera reveals and avoid imposing redundant information ("You're wearing your heavy coat," as in the previous example).

Because each character needs his or her own dialogue characteristics, writing good dialogue is an art in itself. Vocabulary, syntax, and verbal rhythms for each character have to be special and unlike another's. Getting this right takes dedicated observation or an extraordinary ear. Eavesdropping with a cassette recorder will give you superb models, and if you transcribe everything, complete with *ums*, *ers*, laughs, grunts, and pauses, you will see that normal conversation is not normal at all. People converse elliptically, often at cross-purposes, and not in the tidy ping-pong exchanges of stereotypical drama. In real life, little is denoted and much connoted. Silences are often the real "action" during which extraordinary currents are flowing between the speakers. To study how people really communicate is a writer's research.

You will learn much by taking some eavesdropped interchanges and editing them. You are doing on paper what an editor does when editing a radio documentary, that is, editing out what is redundant yet retaining the individual's sense and idiosyncrasies. Any documentary editor will tell you how much stronger characters become when reduced in this way to their essence. This is the secret of a master of dialogue like Harold Pinter, or any good mimic or comedian. They truly listen, and in listening, search out the keys to the person's behavior and thinking. Comedians make us laugh by revealing the characteristics of a type of person such as the office bore, the mother convinced that her child is a genius, the organic food nut, and so on.

The best dialogue is really *verbal action* because in each line the speaker is aiming to get something. It is pressure applied even as it seeks to deflect pressure being experienced. It is active and structurally indispensable to the scene, never a verbal arabesque or editorial explanation of what is visible. Least of all is it verbal padding.

The best way to assess dialogue is to speak lines aloud and listen to their sound. Afterwards apply these questions:

- Is every word in the character's own language?
- What is this character trying to do or get with these words?
- Does the dialogue carry a compelling subtext (that is, a deeper underlying connotation)?
- Is what it hides interesting?
- Does it make the listener speculate or respond emotionally?
- Is there a better balance of words or sounds?
- Can it be briefer by even a syllable?

PLOT

Plot is a complex issue and is closely allied to a film's structure. It is handled at length in Chapter 14, "Structure, Plot, and Time," but here is a quick introduction. The *plot* of a drama is the logic and energy driving the story forward, and its job is to keep the audience's interest high. A screenplay's plot only becomes fully visible when you make an outline. Every step the characters take must be logical and inevitable, for anything that is unsupported, arbitrary, or coincidental will weaken the chain of logic that keeps them in seemingly inevitable movement.

In a plot-driven story, sheer movement of events usually compensates for lack of depth or complexity in the characters. By giving attention to the plot in a character-driven movie, the audience has something other than characters and their issues to find interesting, and you can often appreciably strengthen the whole.

PLOT POINTS

A plot point is a moment in which a story, moving in one direction, suddenly goes off on an unpredictable tangent. If, for example, in a story about a happy young couple going on their first holiday together, the man suddenly freezes on the steps of the airplane and will go no farther, we have an unpredictable turn of events. It turns out that he has concealed his claustrophobia, and they must somehow go abroad by sea instead. On the steps of the boat, the young woman clings to the rail on the quay: She has concealed her agoraphobia. Another plot point. What will they do next?

Plot points are not only recommended in Syd Field's work on screenwriting—their placing is recommended, too. The point is that tangents and the unexpected are useful as a means of shaking things up, of periodically demolishing the predictability that a story adopts. They help to keep dramatic tension high. Keep 'em guessing.

METAPHORS AND SYMBOLS

What makes the cinema so powerful is that the inner experiences of the main characters can often be expressed through artfully chosen settings, objects, and moods. These function metaphorically or symbolically as keys to deeper issues. I suspect this is the magic that draws people to camerawork and is where cinematography must serve more profound purposes than the training people are able to get usually includes. The parched, bleached settings in Wim Wenders' *Paris, Texas* (1984) are emblematic of the emotional aridity of a man compulsively searching for his lost wife and child. In John Boorman's *Hope and Glory* (1987), the beleaguered suburb and the lush riverside haven dramatize the two inimical halves of the boy's wartime England. They also betoken his split loyalties to the different worlds and social classes of his parents. The film has many symbolic events and moments, one being as the boy disinters a toy box from the ruins of the family's bombed house. Inside are lead soldiers charred and melted in eerie mimicry of the Holocaust. Though the image is only on the screen a few seconds, everyone remembers it. For it perfectly represents war and loss not only for the boy, the son of a soldier, but also for all those immolated in warfare—particularly the victims of the Nazi Holocaust. It also suggests the poignant irreversibility of change itself and the loss of childhood.

Symbols and symbolic action have to be artfully chosen because advertising has equipped audiences to decisively reject the manipulative symbol or over-earnest metaphor even before it has fully taken shape. Most importantly, *metaphoric settings, acts, and objects need to be organic*, that is, drawn from the world in which the characters live. They cannot be imposed from outside or they become contrived and editorial.

One of the most breathtaking integrations of metaphor into screen drama is in Jane Campion's *The Piano* (1993), which sweeps the viewer up in its earliest scenes. That power is visible in the briefest summary: Ada, a young immigrant Scot who won't or can't speak, arrives with her illegitimate daughter and her piano on the wild New Zealand seashore of the 19th century. She is there to marry a man she neither knows nor loves and who refuses to bring home her piano. Instead it goes to another man's home. Inevitably, it is he and not her husband who listens to her music, and it is to him that she gives her body and soul.

We are in a realm where nature is truly savage, love is denied by decorum, subtlety is beyond the reach of language, and the soul reaches out by way of music and suppressed eroticism. Who could ask for a more potent canvas?

FOUNDATIONS: STEP OUTLINE, TREATMENT, AND PREMISE

Though a screenplay shows situations and the quality of the dialogue writing, it offers little about point of view, that is, about the subjective attitudes that must be conveyed through acting, camerawork, and editing. Still less does it explain the subtexts, ideas, and authorial vantage point we are supposed to infer and that presumably motivated the writing in the first place.

If you are starting production work from a completed script, you will need to generate some short-form writing yourself to help you develop dramatic oversight of the piece in hand.

STEP OUTLINE

Writing methods vary considerably, but at some point many directors or writers make a *step outline*, which is a summary that:

- Is told in short-story, third-person, present-tense form
- Includes only what the audience will see and hear from the screen
- Allots one numbered paragraph to each sequence
- Summarizes conversations, never gives them verbatim

Making a step outline invariably leads to all kinds of fresh ideas and evolutionary changes. A step outline should be periodically rewritten to reflect the changes between drafts of the screenplay.

The step outline should read as a stream-of-consciousness summation that never digresses into production details or the author's comments. Remember to put down only what the audience will see and hear. Write no dialogue, just stick to essentials by summarizing in a few words each scene's setting, action, and an overview of any conversation's subject and development.

Step Outline for THE OARSMAN

1. At night, between the high walls of an Amsterdam canal, a murky figure in black tails and top hat rows an ornate coffin in a strange, high boat. In a shaft of light we see that MORRIE is a man in his late 30s whose expression is set, serene, distant.
2. Looking down on the city at night, we see a panoramic view over black canals glittering with lights and reflections, bridges busy with pedestrian and bike traffic, and streetcars snaking among crooked, leaning, 17th-century buildings. As the view comes to rest on a street, we hear a noisy bar atmosphere

where, in the foreground, a Canadian woman and a Dutch man are arguing fiercely.

3. Inside the fairly rough bar with its wooden tables, wooden floor strewn with peanut shells, and wooden bar with a line of old china beer spouts, is JASMINE, a tough but attractive young Canadian in her late 20s. She is trying to leave the bar during a bitter argument with her tattooed and drugged-looking Dutch boyfriend MARCO. She says she's had enough.

Each numbered sequence represents a step in the story's progression, and the whole step outline becomes a bird's eye view of the balance and progression of the material, whether the screenplay is a work in progress or a final draft. Actually, the only final draft is the finished film. Everything else is in evolution.

TREATMENT

A *treatment* is a narrative version written in present-tense, short-story form. It, too, concentrates on rendering what the audience will see and hear and summarizes dialogue exchanges. It is briefer than a screenplay to read and easier to assimilate. Confusingly, the term *treatment* is also used for the puff piece a writer may generate to get a script considered by a particular production company. Geared toward establishing the commercial potential of the film, some treatments function like a trailer that advertises a coming attraction, and they often present the screenplay idiosyncratically for whomever is being targeted.

PREMISE

Neither screenplay, treatment, nor step outline articulates the ideas underpinning the film's dramatic structure and development. This, directly defined as the *premise*, is sometimes called the *concept*. It is a sentence or two expressing the dramatic idea behind the scene or behind the whole movie. The premise behind Robert Altman's *Gosford Park* (2001) might be "When a leader or magnate uses power corruptly he will eventually be toppled, no matter how far-reaching his power, and no matter how cynically he buys off his supporters."

Like everything else in this organic process, the premise often mutates as you journey ever deeper into the material. After you and your writer have been working together, make a point of revisiting the premise. Seeking it will always yield the paradigm of your latest labors and let you know if and how your work is thematically focused. This is one of the most magical aspects of working on narratives.

CHAPTER 8

THE WRITING PROCESS

Authorship starts with the writer at a keyboard, develops through the director's process of *mise en scène* (design for directing), and reaches its apotheosis under the hand of the editor during postproduction. Already there are three people involved with a professional production, and we could add the DP, art director, actors, and many others to the authorial process.

Screenwriting, once a discrete craft, is now commonly included in a larger authorial process that the director often shares and influences. Some cinema directors write their own material, but the majority work closely with writers. Whether a script is generated by a director, alone or in partnership with a writer, its attributes will largely determine the movie. A good script is the visionary blueprint that unites everyone involved in realizing the film.

PITCHING

Whether you are a writer beginning a script or a director or producer with a finished property (script they have paid for) looking for finance, you will constantly have to "sell" a current project. Called *pitching* a project, the word comes from baseball and means projecting the essentials of a screen story rapidly and attractively. You may get 10 minutes to convey a feature screenplay in professional situations, and 20 minutes maximum for a pitch to studio executives. You should be able to pitch a short film in 3–5 minutes.

Pitching is neither easy nor comfortable, but under any circumstances it is an excellent exercise. There is no set formula, and part of the challenge is to handle the idea in the way that best suits it. The most important quality to convey is your passion and belief in the special qualities of the story. Here's what you might cover for a short film:

- Title and brief overview (Example: "This story is called *Deliverance* and is about four urban businessmen celebrating freedom by canoeing through unspoiled Appalachia. When they find they are the prey of degenerate, vengeful mountain men, each must put notions of manhood to the test as they struggle against the odds to survive.")

- Genre
- Main character and the problems that he or she faces in life generally
- Main character's problem or predicament
- Obstacles main character must overcome
- Why these obstacles matter, what is at stake, and why an audience should give a damn
- Changes the main character undergoes
- Resolution: how he or she is at the end
- Cinematic qualities that make the film very special

Pitch over and over again to anyone who will listen to you until you are fluent. From each new listener's face, attitude, and body language, you will be able to tell whether your idea grips them and where it fails. If it's not working, change whatever is wrong until you get it right. These are your first audiences, and you know you have a good idea once listeners are excited and spontaneously enthusiastic.

There are innumerable screenwriting Web sites, but here are two that deal with pitching to studio executives: *breakingin.net/tswpitching.htm* and *www.sydfield.com/artofpitching.htm.*

The more you read, the more you understand how vital pitching is and how irregular it is in practice.

Go to screenwriting workshops and especially festivals that feature pitching sessions, and trawl the Internet for screenwriting competitions. If you fancy yourself a writer, win recognition for it. *Filmmakers Magazine* has an annual contest (see *www.filmmakers.com/contests/short/2002/*) and the rules are fairly typical. Read every contest's rules very carefully, and if you sign a legal release, be absolutely sure you understand all the implications because you may be giving away your baby. The entry fee for screenwriting contests is usually \$18–\$50, and you usually win a cash prize or have the script submitted for professional consideration. Rules usually specify that you are over 18, have not adapted the idea, write in English or another given language, and that your opus is of a specified length. It is absolutely vital that you write in standard screenplay form, following the specs for format, binding, and cover minutely and to the last brass staple. Always check to be sure you can make the deadline: Old Internet postings never die, and you could be entering something that's already history.

The Screenwriter's Forum (*www.screenwritersforum.com/*) is one Web site with a contest, but you can find many of them by using Google or other search engines and the keywords "screenwriting contest" or "screenwriting." Another supportive organization for screenwriters is Cinestory (*www.cinestory.com/*), and it, too, has contests, as well as events and online information to aid and encourage the new writer. More is written about writing for the screen than any other aspect of filmmaking, so screenwriters have many resources.

WHY NOT WRITE ALL YOUR OWN SCREENPLAYS?

You may be thinking, "For a student, can there really be an argument for using someone else's screenplay?" The short answer is no, not for your first films. While you scramble to learn the basics you won't have time to wait for someone else to write them. Besides, at entry level it's important to have hands-on experience with all the creative crafts, writing included. Quite soon, though, the pace slows and the stakes become higher. Nobody will tell you that writing isn't your strong point, and it's easy to hide from that fact. Ambitious directors shoot themselves in the foot by using only their own writing. Particularly when your directorial learning curve is steepest, you need all your concentration and more for that most difficult and complex craft in filmmaking—directing. Find a strong script that you really like and direct it.

Why is there such an aversion to this? Seemingly the *auteur* mythology about filmmaking elevates the integrity and control of one person's vision, and leads many to assume that directing is not legitimate unless you both write and direct. Major film schools around the world have realized that this fails to produce the best films from their student population, and worse, sends students out into the world ill-equipped to function. Many schools are instituting a different nexus for project inception. At the very least they are making conditions more favorable to group productions with separate people in writing, producing, directing, and editing roles.

However, many students resist this out of cultural assumptions about being an artist and insist on writing and directing all their own work. They gamble everything, and if they don't win recognition, throw in the sponge. Afterwards nobody can say whether or not a perfectly viable screenwriter, director, or editor might have developed, had the person not tried to wear all three hats. Who in their right mind would try to learn juggling with knives while also learning to ride a unicycle across a high wire? Some skills must be mastered separately before trying to combine them.

The *auteur* notion of filmmaking was a useful antidote to industrial filmmaking in the 1950s and '60s but was never a working reality. Fiction films have always been made by creative teams that get behind a script or improvisational scripting process. I am only exaggerating a little if I liken directors to sailing ship figureheads: out front and highly visible, of great symbolism, but wholly dependent on who and what propels them. As a director you have so much to control that you depend on the creative input of others. Directing means giving control of their parts to actors, of the camera to a camera operator, lighting to a DP, sound recording to a recordist, the editing to an editor . . . and writing to a writer. As a director you coordinate the work of all these people, and you work through them. You need their skills and you need their values. Their separate judgments help you attain some distance on the material so you can retain a sense of how it must strike a first-time audience.

THE RISE OF THE ENTREPRENEURIAL PRODUCER

Another contemporary movement in world film schools, as in my own, is to make entrepreneurial producing a major element in film school education. My college has a thriving undergraduate producing program that includes residential study and internship in Hollywood (see the Semester in LA program via *www.filmatcolumbia.com*). Producers are needed in low-budget filmmaking not only to manage money or do the public relations legwork, but to shop for promising scripts, develop creative teams around them, and work at the business model that will make them viable. This means working at the fundraising, co-funding, and pre-sales that today make professional filmmaking possible.

To the *auteur* student, the producer has figured no higher than a production manager. Now the producer is becoming a leading entrepreneurial figure who specializes in the business (yes, it's a business) of getting projects afloat and who is not a frustrated director or a frustrated anything else. There is wide support for this cultural shift. The Brussels-based international association of film schools CILECT (Centre International de Liaison des Écoles de Cinéma et de Télévision—see *www.cilect.org*) initiated the Triangle Project expressly to investigate the entrepreneurial partnerships that lie behind many successful European films. Like so many independent films, they cannot draw upon Hollywood financing. CILECT'S favored model is a three-person team of producer, screenwriter, and director. The Triangle idea (as it's called) is to cultivate collaborative project teams that have several projects afloat at any time, rather than the traditional approach, which is to bet the bank on a single horse.

DAMMIT, I WANT TO BE A HYPHENATION

Are you still determined to become a writer-director (or *hyphenation*)? Why not make it a goal for 10 or 20 years into your career? For now, as you try to improve on the basics in film school or as an independent, you really should shop for a writer just as you seek all your other collaborators. If you want to develop as a writer, why not write material for your best friend to direct?

Still not convinced? Consider this: Most people's early writing uses autobiographical sources, naturally enough. Without some distance from your work, you will find yourself trying to reanimate remembered situations and expecting your actors to reproduce something only you can know about. The mere presence of a writer as a collaborator will help displace the original where it belongs: as drama running under its own fictional imperatives. You need confidence when you direct. If the script is a vital part of your life, anyone who queries it will seem to challenge your plausibility as a person. Do you want to risk annihilating your self-esteem and negating your authority as a director?

The screen's overwhelming strength, success, and relevance, since its inception, has come from the process's division of labor. This is an additive process of creation, where the whole is greater than the sum of its parts. The process tempers each contribution with checks and balances that are vital to an audience medium.

THE DOGME GROUP AND CREATIVE LIMITATION

In 1995, the founding members of the Danish Dogme 95 Cinema Group (Figure 8–1) were Thomas Vinterberg, Lars von Trier, Christian Levring, and Søren

FIGURE 8–1

Lars von Trier, a founding member of the innovative Danish Dogme 95 Cinema Group (The Kobal Collection).

Kragh-Jacobsen. In the next few years, the group members produced such extraordinary films as *Breaking the Waves* (Lars von Trier, 1999), *The Celebration* (Thomas Vinterberg, 1998), and *The Idiots* (Lars von Trier, 1999). They began by playfully setting up rules of limitation, rather as the photographers Edward Weston, Imogen Cunningham, Ansel Adams, and Willard Van Dyke had done in 1932 for their group, f/64. The photographers—tired of pictorial work in which photography tried to make itself look more like painting, charcoal sketches, or etching—proclaimed that photography would only be liberated to become itself by rejecting everything borrowed from other pictorial forms, so they concentrated on developing photography's own attributes.

Compare this with the Dogme Group's "Vow of Chastity," which appears in various versions and translations. I have taken minor editorial liberties to render it into vernacular English:

- Shooting must be done on location. Props and sets must not be brought in, but shooting must go where that set or prop can be found.
- Sound must never be produced separately from the images or vice versa. Music must not be used unless it occurs where the scene is shot.

- The camera must be handheld. Any movement or immobility attainable by handholding is permitted. The action cannot be organized for the camera; instead the camera must go to the action.
- The film must be in color. Special lighting is not acceptable, and if there is too little light for exposure, the scene must be cut or a single lamp may be attached to the camera.
- Camera filters and other optical work are forbidden.
- The film must not contain any superficial action such as murders, weapons, explosions, and so on.
- No displacement is permitted in time or space: The film takes place here and now.
- Genre movies are not acceptable.
- Film format is Academy 35 mm.
- The director must not be credited. Furthermore, I swear as a director to refrain from personal taste. I am no longer an artist. I swear to refrain from creating a "work," as I regard the instant as more important than the whole. My supreme goal is to force the truth out of my characters and settings. I swear to do so by all the means available and at the cost of any good taste and any aesthetic considerations.

Signed ____________________

The last clause is interesting because it forswears a leadership hierarchy, personal taste, and strikes a mortal blow at ego. Instead, it passes preeminence to the cast. Of course, in practice any number of contradictions will appear, but the group's work, and the high praise it called forth from actors, demands that we take the spirit of the manifesto seriously. Thomas Vinterberg, interviewed by Elif Cercel for *Director's World*, said:

> We did the "Vow of Chastity" in half an hour, and we had great fun. Yet, at the same time, we felt that in order to avoid the mediocrity of filmmaking not only in the whole community, but in our own filmmaking as well, we had to do something different. We wanted to undress film, turn it back to where it came from and remove the layers of makeup between the audience and the actors. We felt it was a good idea to concentrate on the moment, on the actors and, of course, on the story that they were acting, which are the only aspects left when everything else is stripped away. Also, artistically it has created a very good place for us to be as artists or filmmakers because having obstacles like these means you have something to play against. It encourages you to actually focus on other approaches instead. *(stage.directorsworld.com)*

Following this vow put Danish film at the forefront of international cinema and induced the Danish government to increase State funding by 70% over the next 4 years. The moral? All undertakings profit from creatively inspired limitations. Some are inbuilt, some encountered, and the best are chosen to squeeze your inventiveness. The Dogme Group's rules de-escalated the importance of filming in favor of working with actors and handed their excellent actors a rich slice of creative control. The actors responded handsomely.

So, what creative limitations will you set yourself?

WHAT SCREENWRITING IS

When writing a screenplay, you try to put on paper the movie you see in your mind. You can only set down what can be put in words, and words can describe only a portion of cinema's capabilities. Even then, something effective in writing may not translate into effective cinema. How, for instance, could you ever film "By the light of a melancholy sunset she broods upon the children she will never have"?

Screenwriting needs to be guided by knowledge of film, both as a medium and as a production process. A screenplay is a blueprint, not a complete form of expression. It will be turned into a polished, professional movie by many specialized and idiosyncratic minds working together—actors as well as camera, sound, art direction, props, and so on. Dialogue that a writer may imagine has a set meaning can, in the mouth of an accomplished actor, acquire an unforeseen range of shading and subtlety. These nuances, even if you happen to think of them, are impossible to specify in a screenplay.

Open the screenplay to criticism early and often. You and your partner cannot please everybody, but you can listen, and you can recognize real problems early, particularly when several critics are saying the same thing. This is learning from an early audience, much as a playwright will evolve a new play in the light of audience reactions. For once a movie is completed, it becomes a fly set in amber. To survive and prosper, you must submit drafts of your work to representative readers or audiences, seek out its weaknesses, and attend to them while you can. Regrettably, this is the least practiced of necessary arts among film students, who walk in mortal terror of an idea being stolen. This is not completely unrealistic, but the dangers are very much exaggerated and should never inhibit you from profiting from intensive discussions. Reinvigorated cinema, like any art form, always seems to come from a group's profound exploration of fundamentals, a discourse that no individual would have the time, energy, or inventiveness to sustain alone.

WRITING A SCREENPLAY

Writing is a major part of the creative process in fiction filmmaking, and results are deeply affected by how you set about it. Anyone at all serious about directing should be writing all the time, for the act of writing is really the mind contemplating its own workings—and thus willfully transcending its own preliminary ideas and decisions. People who don't write and rewrite are people who don't care to think in depth.

To write you must learn touch typing. It takes 10 or 15 hours of lessons, and if I learned it, believe me, anyone can. With computers making writing (and particularly rewriting) so much faster, touch typing is absolutely the most useful skill you will ever acquire. A word processor gives you easy changes, a thesaurus, and spelling checks to catch typing errors. It also gives you the capacity to make an outline and collapse it down to essentials or expand it with different levels of detail.

Set aside regular periods of time and make yourself write, no matter whether the results are good or bad. The first draft is the hardest, so do not wait to feel inspired, just keep hacking away. Write scenes that interest you, and write fast rather than writing well or in scene order. Get it down any old way. Once a few things are down, you can edit, develop, and connect what you have written.

It is very important to always write as if for the silent screen. Writing for the camera, rather than thinking in conversational exchanges, means dealing with human and other exteriors. To make your characters' inner lives accessible, keep in mind that a person has no inner experience without outward signs in his or her behavior. Keep writing until you find them. If this or any other advice stops you from writing, then write early drafts any way you can. Write any way, anywhere, anyhow—just write, rewrite, and rewrite again.

IDEA CLUSTERING, NOT LINEAR DEVELOPMENT

Most people who want to write but cannot are suffering the damage of doctrinaire teaching. The most common block results from trying to write from an outline in a linear fashion—beginning, middle, and end. At some point the writer ends up in a desert with nowhere to go. Perfectionism, which is the fear of your own judgment and that of others, is another virulent paralyzer. Remember, most unhappiness comes from comparison. Perfectionism is fine in its place—polishing your crafted product to its ultimate form—but when applied to early work it's a killer. Most writing manuals are very prescriptive and will actually stop you from writing.

At any stage, when you hit the brick wall, you can always resort to your associative ability. Where the pedestrian intellect fails, the exuberant subconscious will obligingly run rings around it. Here is a way to turn it loose:

- Take a large sheet of paper and write whatever central idea you are dealing with in the middle. It might be "happiness" or "rebuilding the relationship."
- Now, as fast as you can write, surround it with associated words, no matter how far removed or wacky. The circle of words should look like satellites around a planet.
- Around each associated word, put another ring of words you associate with it. Soon your paper will be crammed with a little solar system.
- Now examine what you have written and turn it into a list that structures the ideas into a progression of families, groups, and systems—anything that speaks of relationship.
- While engaged in this busywork all kinds of solutions to your original problem will take shape.

WRITING IS CIRCULAR, NOT LINEAR

Finished writing is linear, but the process of getting there is anything but. Scripts are not written in the order of concept, step outline, and screenplay, nor as beginning, middle, and end. Although the odd screenwriter may work this way, he or she is just as likely to write the most clearly visualized scenes first, making an outline to gain an overview, and finally filling in the gaps and distilling the concept from the results.

Like any art process, scriptwriting—indeed filmmaking itself—looks untidy and wastefully circular to the uninitiated, and quite alien to the tidy manufacturing processes dear to the commercial mind (your producer, perhaps). This produces much friction and misery in the film industry, where artists handling people and concepts must work within financial structures imposed by managers from law or business backgrounds who can only see inefficiency.

CREATING CHARACTERS

Fiction, when not plot-driven, is driven by characters. Write down everything you can see or imagine about your characters as a way of getting to know them. Include in your list:

- What they look like
- What they wear
- What they like
- How they live
- Where they come from
- What experiences have marked them
- What they crave
- What they are trying to get or accomplish
- In what part of their spirit they ache

Strong characters will assist or even create the plot, but a plot will not create characters. Indeed, it may cramp and desiccate them.

WORK TO CREATE A MOOD

Settings that are bland or unbelievable compel the audience to struggle with disbelief at every scene change, something unavoidable in the theatre but eminently unnecessary when watching the screen. Using locations and sound composition intelligently can provide a powerfully emotional setting and hurl the audience into the emotional heart of a situation.

Whenever you are out and about, make a point of noting any place or situation that makes an impact. Later these can be incorporated into what you write. Like actors, good dramatists pay extremely close attention to what is around them and are constantly observing and researching in pursuit of their work. Making art is all about paying attention to life, something our escapist culture works so diligently to negate.

WRITE FOR THE CINEMA'S STRENGTHS

To avoid creating filmed theater, try turning conversations into behavioral exchanges that a deaf person could follow. This means writing as though for a modern, but silent cinema. Not only should dialogue be minimal, the storytelling itself should use images to drive the story forward. David Mamet protests that "most Hollywood films are made . . . as a supposed record of what real people really did" (*On Directing Film*, New York: Viking Penguin, 1992, p. 2). Mainstream features tend to be expository realism, a stream of passively informational coverage that occupies our attention without challenging our judgment or imagination. Mamet advocates telling a story in the way that "Eisenstein suggested a movie should be made. This method has nothing to do with following the protagonist around but rather is *a succession of images juxtaposed so that the contrast between these images moves the story forward in the mind of the audience*" (Mamet's emphasis). He goes on to say:

> You want to tell the story in cuts, which is to say, through a juxtaposition of images that are basically uninflected. Mr. Eisenstein tells us that the best image is an uninflected image. A shot of a teacup. A shot of a spoon. A shot of a fork. A shot of a door. Let the cut tell the story. Because otherwise you have not got dramatic action, you have narration. . . . Documentaries take basically unrelated footage and juxtapose it in order to give the viewer the idea the filmmaker wants to convey. They take footage of birds snapping a twig. They take footage of a fawn raising his head. The two shots have nothing to do with each other. They were shot days or years, and miles, apart. And the filmmaker juxtaposes the images to give the viewer the idea of great alertness. . . . They are not a record of how the deer reacted to the bird. They're basically uninflected images. But they give the viewer the idea of alertness to danger when they are juxtaposed. That's good filmmaking. (*On Directing Film p. 2*)

This approach produces a dialectic of images and action that challenges you to discern the underlying authorial intent. It also happens to reflect daily experience in which our attention, combined with the assessments we make, causes us to jump from object to object to person to face to hand to doorway—and so on. We can only interpret people by telltale details of their external appearances and deeds. Perhaps this is why Herzog did not telephone or write to his beloved mentor, Lotte Eisner, when she lay sick, but trudged on foot from Munich all the way to her bedside in Paris.

Characters in a movie should be seen in action; their actions should give clues to their inner tensions. When they speak it should be to act on each other. They should not speak for the sake of realism or atmosphere, and never because their author needs to speak through them. (If you want to send a message, use Western Union.) Dialogue is best when it is a form of action, and sparse dialogue raises words to high significance.

These are widely held views for you to consider. Decide what qualities you really enjoy on the screen and regulate your filmmaking with creative limitations to take advantage of them.

TAKING STOCK

After some exploratory writing, distill a dramatic premise. This is a sentence or two encapsulating the situation, characters, and main idea on which the whole movie is founded, such as, "An unfulfilled man adopted as a child is now having a troubled marriage. He sets out to find his biological mother. So different is she from what he imagined that he returns to his wife with new appreciation."

Next make a step outline, which is a third-person, present-tense description of each sequence's action with dialogue summarized and a new paragraph for each sequence. Quite often a full draft of the screenplay precedes the step outline, which becomes a defining process rather than a planning one. Reducing your ideas to their essence allows you to gain control over what the script is truly about. It sounds paradoxical that writers should need to discover their own work's themes and meanings, but the creative imagination functions on different levels, and some of its most important activity takes place beyond reach of the conscious mind.

The summarizing, winnowing process of making outlines and concept statements is a discipline that will raise the submerged levels into view and make them more useful. The amended step outline and premise you make after a new draft will energetically point the way to your next bout of revision and rewriting. Winnowing and summarizing makes analysis and development inevitable. Only when the characters have been created and the action and plot roughed out is it wise to begin a screenplay.

SCREENPLAY: FORM FOLLOWS FUNCTION?

Unfortunately, because of the priorities and theatrical layout of the conventional screenplay, dialogue appears to be the major component. Here form doesn't follow function, form *swallows* function. Anyone trying to write in the Eisenstein mode is impeded, not helped by the prevalence of dialogue. A better way to draft initial ideas is to use the split-page format, adding a third column in the early stages of writing where you draft the Observer's developing perceptions, as in Figure 8–2.

Using this layout, you can work out what you want your audience to think, feel, question, decide (both rightly or wrongly), or remember from earlier in the film. The word processor's drag-and-drop function is excellent for experimentally moving materials around, but an agreeably low-tech alternative is to put your shots or sequences on index cards and move them around on a large table. Being equipped to experiment with ideas and intentions is vital to developing your own creative process and style. If you have special qualities as a storyteller, here rather than during shooting is where they will emerge.

WITH THE AUDIENCE IN MIND

If the drama you write is to get beyond the egocentricity of therapy, you will have to consider your audience intensively. This does not lead automatically to exploiting them or to some kind of fatal artistic compromise. It simply means trying to conceive works that participate in modern thought and modern dilemmas, prompt pertinent questions and ideas, cut across conventional thought, and resonate vividly in the hearts and minds of those watching your movie.

The only real way to picture this audience is to write for an audience of people very much like yourself in terms of their values and intelligence, but who

Picture	Sound	Observer notices . . .
Wide shot car graveyard	Birdsong, turns into the regular breathing of someone sleeping.	A mood of decayed hulks, family cars worn out and cast aside
Shots of cars, their headlights making them look like faces	Mumbling, as of a dreamer	Do cars have ghosts?
Grass and ferns growing up through floors. Glass splintered in black sedan.	Male group making businessman conversation. Sound diminishes to silence	Important people once used this car.
Executive at head of boardroom table waits for respectful silence.	Child's voice begins nursery song, then . . .	What does all this have to do with abandoned automobiles?
Bangs his hand down on table. Everyone jumps	Bang!!	Why is he angry?
Car graveyard again. A pair of gloves on a dusty seat. A plane passes through top of frame.	Pigeon wings flapping, a voice in a large room says, "Are we all ready?"	Someone has left a pair of gloves . . . another voice from another time . . . what's going to happen?
A muffled figure rises from back seat, stretches, yawns.	Sync sound	Ah, someone lives here. A new character. Is this street person going to connect with those boardroom types?

FIGURE 8–2

A draft of a screenplay in split-page format gives precedence to shots and their association to sound. In a third column the writer sketches the Observer's interior process while following the story.

do not have your specific experiences and knowledge. Some would-be filmmakers by nature share much with the greater world, and some share little. There is nothing you can do about this except to embrace living and struggle mightily to leave the cocoon we all grow up in. Popularity in the cinema (or out of it) is nothing you can plan. All you can do is to use all your potential, take all the risks you need to take, and be true to yourself. If you make "Nothing human is alien to me" your creed, you will have a lifetime's work ahead, opening your mind to the human condition. Walking that road with all your heart will put you in touch with many good companions and reveal what is awful and wonderful in being human. This willingness to see comprehensively is at the very center of the artistic process.

STORY LOGIC AND TESTING YOUR ASSUMPTIONS

During the composition process you write from experience, imagination, and intuition, as well as assumptions stored in the unconscious. What is least certain is not the original experience or what you want to say about it, but whether your intentions will get across to the audience. Most miscommunication arises from being unaware of assumptions the audience can't or won't share and failing to provide a timely exposition as framing. For instance, though a screenwriter knows her character Harry would never perjure himself in court, her audience knows nothing of the sort. His honesty must first be established (the word *establish* appears a lot in screenwriting). To do this she might make Harry go back into a store after unthinkingly carrying a newspaper out with his groceries. Now his honesty is attested by his action of paying for it. She can even make him a white-collar criminal who has siphoned thousands from his corporation but who still goes out of his way to pay for his newspaper at the corner store. Complex moral codes are always interesting.

A story is a progression of logic that raises questions and offers clues, the full significance of which is often skillfully delayed. This logic you design and test through your planning process's third column. You will need to fulfill the audience's basic expectations for every human situation you set up. For instance, a film about a man adopted in childhood who searches for his biological mother would hardly remain credible if he failed to look for his birth certificate and never questioned his foster parents. These are basic steps that you either show or establish that they have been accomplished without satisfactory result.

Later, when our adoptee finds his mother, it would be equally illogical for him to become happy and fulfilled. Everyone of any maturity knows that people finding their biological parents have very mixed emotions, not the least of which are pain and anger. Lasting euphoria is untrue to human nature and makes the character simple-minded. Either the character or the moviemakers are naïve. If it's the latter, the audience will quickly realize they are smarter than the movie—and move on.

CREATING SPACE FOR THE AUDIENCE

Whether a story is told through literature, song, stage, or screen, the successful storyteller always creates significant spaces that the audience must fill from its own imagination, values, and life experience. Unlike the reader of a novel, film spectators do not have to visualize the physical world of the story, so it's all the more important that they speculate about the characters' motives, feelings, and morals. As a painting implies life beyond the edges of its frame, so dramatic characters and the ideas they engender should go beyond what we can see and hear.

CREDIBILITY, MINIMIZING, AND RAISING STORY TENSION

A fictional world, though self-contained, still runs according to rules drawn from life at large. The writer cannot capriciously violate the audience's knowledge of living. The story and its characters must be interesting, representative, and consistent if they are to remain credible. Other genres, such as documentary or folk tale, are hardly less free; each is true in some important way to the spirit of reality, and all are governed by rules the audience recognizes as "true." Paradoxically this means the coincidences that occur in life become suspect in fiction.

While you write, anything you want to imply must first be named and fully explored before you move to minimize it. The writer always knows far more than he or she shares with the audience, but initially it is best to over-specify. Arthur Miller's plays start out at 800 pages before he cuts and compresses them down to a manageable stage time. Good storytellers withhold whatever they can and as long as possible because successful storytelling depends on creating tension and anticipation. Wilkie Collins, the father of the mystery novel, put it succinctly: "Make them laugh, make them cry, but make them wait."

DIRECTING FROM YOUR OWN SCREENPLAY

If you are directing from your own script, work hard to distance yourself by exposing it to tough criticism. By carrying out all available analytical steps you can, with difficulty, gain an objective understanding of your own work. Be as ruthless with its faults as you would with anyone else's work. Unless you have learned to be professionally rigorous with your own writing, there will be many unexamined assumptions waiting to explode later into full-blown problems, and these, under public exposure, can badly sabotage the writer-director's confidence and authority.

YOUR WORK IS NOT YOU

Your writing is not you; it is only the work you did at a particular moment in your life. Your work is an interim representation. The next piece will show changes; it will be a little stronger and sharper. Truffaut admitted late in life that it is just as difficult to make a bad film as a good one, and he became a kinder critic after he had experienced the failures that prepare us to succeed. The integrity and perseverance of the explorer is what matters.

Keep going, no matter what. All writers say one thing: You must write to a schedule. Some days it produces bad writing. Some days, trying to write produces little or nothing. Other days it pours out. But you must learn to love the process and make yourself keep writing. Good writing only comes from rewriting bad writing.

INVITING A CRITICAL RESPONSE

Exposing your work in its different stages to criticism from trial readers or audiences is an important part of confirming that you are in touch with a first-time audience. Developing a story in isolation from feedback is risky and can be catastrophic. Getting confirmation that your instincts are right isn't difficult and is usually energizing.

TEST EXHAUSTIVELY ON OTHERS

It is a good practice to pitch one's ideas to anyone who will listen and be critical. If "the unexamined life is not worth living," the unexamined story idea is not worth filming. Hearing yourself is the very best way to see your ideas from another's point of view. Repeatedly exposing your ideas to skeptical listeners also flushes out the clichés in your thinking (the power of positive embarrassment!). After all, your first thoughts are the same junk as everyone else's. Original ideas come to those who work hard at rejecting the unoriginal.

As with initial ideas, so with the screenplay. In seeking responses:

- Find mature readers whose values you share and respect.
- Keep your critics on track; you cannot be too interested in the film the respondent would have made.
- Ask what he or she understands from the script.
- Ask what the characters are like.
- Ask what seems to be driving them.
- Ask which scenes are effective.
- Ask which are not.

From this process you should acquire a complete and accurate sense of what the audience knows and feels at each stage of the proposed film. Critical readers will have to be replaced over time as they become familiar with the material. Remember, shooting an imperfectly developed screenplay is opening a Pandora's box of problems. It's heartbreaking to try curing them in the cutting room when it's too late.

ACT ON CRITICISM ONLY AFTER REFLECTION

In an audience medium, the director hopes for understanding by a wide audience whose experiences do not debar them from entering the most arcane world if it is carefully presented. Seeking responses to a script can be very misleading and also a test of self-knowledge. If you resist all suggestions and question the validity of the responses, you are probably insecure. If you agree with almost everything and set about a complete rewrite in a mood of self-flagellation, or worse, scrap the project, it means you are very insecure. If, however, you continue to believe in what you are doing but recognize some truth in what your critics say, you are progressing nicely. There will still be plenty of anguish and self-doubt. No gain without pain, they say.

Never make changes hastily or impulsively. Let the criticism lie for a few days, then see what your mind filters out as valid. When in doubt, delay changes and don't abandon your intentions. Work on something else until your mind quietly insists on what must, or must not, be done.

Do not show unfinished work to family or intimates. They will want to save you by getting you to hide your faults and naiveté from public view. Almost as damaging as reckless criticism is total, loving, across-the-board praise. The best way to show friends and family your work is with a general audience whose responses will help shape your friends and family in theirs. How many artists have had nothing but resistance and dissuasion from their family only to see it all magically evaporate when they hear an audience clapping ("Well, now, I never thought you'd do anything with that damned guitar . . .").

TESTING WITH A SCRATCH CAST

Before proceeding to production you should assemble a *scratch cast* to read the script through, preferably with a small, invited audience of friends who will tell you candidly what they think. Each actor, however inexperienced, will identify with one character and show your script in an unfamiliar light. You should be able to wholeheartedly justify every word of dialogue and every stage direction in the script.

Large cities with a theater community often have screenplay readings and writers' groups that exist to critique each other's work. Actors and theater organizations usually know about such facilities, as do film schools and film cooperatives.

REWRITE, REWRITE, REWRITE

Be ready to keep changing the screenplay all the way up to the day of shooting. A script is not an artwork with a final form; it is more like plans for an invasion that must be altered daily in light of fresh intelligence. Finished films cannot be product-tested with audiences the way plays can, so testing and reshaping must be accomplished during the script development and cast rehearsal periods. Editing, compressing, or expanding your material where needed, simplifying, and even wholesale rewriting will shape the material to take advantage of the way players enact the piece. Feature films I have worked on were regularly undergoing rewrites the day before shooting. Writers loathe this compulsive rewriting, but their standards for completion arise from habits of solo creation, while filmmaking is an organic, physical process that must adapt to the unfolding reality of cast and shooting—in both their negative and positive implications.

Rewriting is frequently omitted or resisted by student production groups because of inexperience or because it threatens the writer's ego. If this happens, the director should take over the script and alter it as necessary. In the professional world, the writer delivers a script and then loses control of it. There is a good reason for this, but few writers will agree.

FIGHT THE CENSOR AND FINISH

Finishing projects is very important. Work left incomplete is a step taken sideways, not forward. It is tempting halfway through a project to say, "Well, I've learned all I can learn here so I think I'll start something new." This is the internal censor at work, your hidden enemy who whispers, "You can't show this to other people, it isn't good enough; the real you is better." Your work seldom feels good for long, but do not let that make you halt or change horses. Only intermittently will you feel elation, but finishing will always yield satisfaction and knowledge.

CHAPTER 9

ADAPTATION FROM ART OR LIFE

ADAPTING FROM LITERATURE

There is a constantly growing supply of plays, novels, and short stories that might adapt well to the screen. Libraries and the Internet have an amazing range of offerings, and someone somewhere has already analyzed, indexed, or published (by characters, subject, or theme) the very thing you are interested in. All you need to do is find it. Short stories, for example, are indexed by theme.

The short story is a favorite source of material for both short and full-length films. Like all good literature, it can be a quicksand to the unwary, for the magic of language can seduce the filmmaker into assuming the story will make an equally fine film. Effective adaptation may actually be impossible if the author's writing style and literary form have no cinematic equivalency. A story relying on a subtly ironic storytelling voice, for instance, might be a bad choice because there is no such thing as ironic photography or recording.

Effective literature never automatically contains the basis for a good film. Most of the criteria for judging material for an adaptation remain the same as those used to assess any script:

- Does it tell its tale through externally visible, behavioral means?
- Does it have interesting, well-developed characters?
- Is it contained and specific in settings?
- Are the situations interesting and realizable?
- Is there an interesting major conflict, and is it dramatized rather than internal?
- Does the conflict imply interesting metaphors?
- Does the piece have a strong thematic purpose?
- Is the thematic purpose one you can relate to strongly?

- Can you invent a cinematic equivalency for the story's literary values?
- Can you afford to do it?
- Is the copyright available?

FAITHFUL ADAPTATION

Any well-known work comes with strings attached. Should J.D. Salinger personally hand you the rights to *The Catcher in the Rye*, you would not have a free hand at adaptation. Because the book has touched so many people, meeting their expectations would be well nigh impossible. For this reason alone, literature adapted to the screen almost always disappoints its fans. Other works, long or short, may pose narrative or stylistic problems that can only be solved through radically altering the form suggested by the original. For instance, John Korty's version of John Updike's five-and-a-half-page story "The Music School" takes a story that happens contemplatively inside a man's mind, develops it into interwoven events, and propels them upon a musical theme of increasing texture and confidence. The result is a short film gem no less profound than Updike's extremely compressed original, a good deal more accessible, and yet true to the original's spirit.

Karel Reisz's 1981 screen version of John Fowles' *The French Lieutenant's Woman*, however, suffers badly. Fowles' novels tend to overflow with ideas, and this one more than any. The movie version, although scripted by the supremely intelligent Harold Pinter, is forced by time limitations to strip away most of the sociological and philosophical speculation by which the novel assesses the 19th century against its 20th-century offspring. Like most adaptations, the movie concentrates on plot and action at the expense of discourse and emerges with a bad case of malnutrition.

FREE ADAPTATION

A more fertile union of literature and screen can happen when, instead of processing literary or theatrical icons, the filmmaker uses aspects of a written work to seed a fully autonomous film. Inventive, original cinema takes what it needs from anything and everything, while great novels or plays processed for the screen are always diminished—like paintings made into tablecloths. Godard's groundbreaking movies of the 1960s included free adaptations of theater or sociology, works by Alberto Moravia and Guy de Maupassant, and most interestingly, transformations of pulp fiction. The Quentin Tarantino movie *Pulp Fiction* (1995), however, adopts the style and values of pulp fiction without apparently having anything in its back pocket beyond style. Its undoubted professionalism and panache lead to an emptiness and an exaltation of what it wants us to laugh at.

USING LITERATURE OR ACTUALITY AS A SPRINGBOARD

When you take over a story framework (from a literary work or from a life situation) and substitute your own choice of main elements, an entirely new work can emerge because everything else, including the main issues, will be affected. In the search to integrate all the parts, the work will inevitably evolve and begin to impose its own demands that the writer must satisfy. Elements you might alter could be:

Characters: Placing a new character in any situation creates pressure for new outcomes (and therefore a changed destiny). Strong characters can steer a story to new conclusions that, in turn, express a different resolution and meaning.

Situations and conflicts: Changed characters almost certainly generate changes in the events and changes in some or all of the main conflicts.

Period: One can tell an old story in a modern setting, as Leonard Bernstein did by adapting Shakespeare's *Romeo and Juliet* to a New York setting in the musical show *West Side Story.*

Settings: New characters demand their own settings to express what is particular to them. Changes of class, changes of region, or changes of occupation all have far-reaching consequences. A change of setting will produce changed pressures on the characters.

Point of view: In *The Wide Sargasso Sea*, novelist Jean Rhys reinterprets the situation in Charlotte Bronte's *Jane Eyre* by taking the viewpoint of the mad, imprisoned Mrs. Rochester. A radically different story arises from Rhys' outrage at the injustices suffered by neglected wives, something she personally experienced during her early years in Paris. Any story that draws you emotionally into its web is capable of being reinterpreted, especially if you want to contest the meanings drawn by the original author.

Thematic purpose: You might keep similar characters but adjust the situations to produce a different thematic outcome. Here you may be attracted to interpreting the same events differently.

You are surrounded by rich resources for storytelling. You can legitimately borrow and adapt from any source, providing the new entity gains its own entire identity and purpose. If it remains visibly, identifiably indebted to a copyrighted source, you must, of course, obtain permission as described in a later section.

Your feeling should no longer be "Help, I don't have any stories to tell" but instead, "What is the basis for my choices and adaptations?" and "Why do I like this particular story so much?" Whatever causes a deep response in you throws light on your underlying storyteller's identity. Growing self-knowledge will draw into your work whatever else fascinates you. The aim is to design a vehicle freighted with personal significance so that you become possessed by it, answering to characters, events, and situations that propel themselves forward to their own conclusion. Indeed, the sign of an effectively rigorous writing process is that your characters detach themselves from their originals and become autonomous within their own world.

COPYRIGHT CLEARANCE

If you make an adaptation bearing a likeness to its original, you must procure the legal right to use it. Copyright law is changed periodically. In the United States you can obtain current information from the Copyright Office, Library of

Congress, Washington, D.C. 20559. Many works first published 56 years ago or more are old enough to be in the public domain, but do not assume this without careful inquiry, preferably through a copyright lawyer. The laws are extremely complicated, especially concerning a literary property's clearance in other countries.

ACTOR-CENTERED FILMS AND THEIR SCRIPTS

Another potential influence on the script is the cast. This source of help will be explored in depth later, but this chapter would be incomplete without establishing the importance of actors' personalities and traits to an existing idea or script. Look at it this way: Your vision reaches the audience through what you put on the screen, and most of this will be the human presence. The credibility and quality of that human presence makes or breaks any film, yet seldom is the individuality of the very actors who bring it alive allowed to modify the text. Invariably, unless a powerful star is involved, the actors must adapt to the text. This is because most films are manufactured in a unidirectional process, and actors are fitted to a finished and funded script. This is neither desirable nor true for the low-budget filmmaker.

Actors whose effortless-looking performances we take for granted arrive on the screen through a rigorous apprenticeship and ruthless winnowing process. But beginning or low-budget filmmakers must try to match this professionalism using actors with little or no experience. Most try doing this by following the industry's assembly line operation, though there's really something already wrong with professional norms. Jessica Lange, a film actress as professional as they come, has deplored the lack of rehearsal time in which to reach into the emotional life of her characters (see her interview in *American Film*, June 1987). So anyone using inexperienced actors, or non-actors, can hardly bring together people unknown to each other *and* unfamiliar with the process of filming *and* expect them to be relaxed and focused in their roles. You need an induction process that will bring anxiety levels down and build an ensemble able to be playful in its seriousness.

For the inexperienced cast, there's an urgent need to explore and interact, so the prudent director plans time and activities through which cast and script can evolve. *Careful and intensive rehearsal is a must.* Use intelligent discussion and improv work to explore the ideas and emotional transitions in the script and to liberate that magic quality of spontaneity.

Here is a scripting method that uses human beings as well as the computer. Though nontraditional, it is increasingly used and with significant results.

INTEGRATING THE CAST INTO THE SCRIPT

Some distinguished directors already write in an unconventional, actor-centered way, foremost among them Bergman, who does not favor the screenplay:

> If . . . I were to reproduce in words what happens in the film I have conceived, I would be forced to write a bulky book of little readable value and great nuisance. I have neither the talent nor the patience for a heroic exercise of that kind.

> Besides, such a procedure would kill all creative joy for both me and the artists.
> (Introduction, *Four Stories by Ingmar Bergman*, New York: Doubleday, 1977)

Bergman develops his films from an annotated short story. For *Cries and Whispers* (1972) he supplied notes about the artistic approach, intended characters and their situations, settings, and time period. There are also fragments from Agnes' diary, details of a dream, and the dialogue and narrative of the events. Bergman hands these materials to all participating, and the developmental work begins from a thorough discussion and assimilation of their possibilities. Much of the creation of characters and action then lies with actors whose careers and talents (and children!) Bergman has been instrumental in developing.

In the United States, actor-director John Cassavetes also gave primacy to his actors, either having them improvise completely, as in *Shadows* (1959), or basing a written script on structured improvisations as he did in *A Woman Under the Influence* (1974). "The emotion was improvised," he said. "But the lines were written."

Alain Tanner, a Swiss director who came to feature films through television documentaries, has gradually evolved his fiction works toward the spontaneity of his documentary beginnings. For *Jonah Who Will Be 25 in the Year 2000* (1976) he showed photos of his chosen cast to writing collaborator John Berger. The associations Berger made with each face became the basis for a script (Figure 9–1). In his later film *In the White City* (1985) Tanner used no script at all, relying instead upon the ability of his fine actors to improvise on a framework of specified ideas. This takes expertise all around.

In Britain, Mike Leigh's films started out with bittersweet comedy but have developed into a darker criticism of English life. *High Hopes* (1988) and *Life is Sweet* (1991) are comedies of character that make a poignant critique of English working class powers of adaptation and survival when the mainstays of dignity—work and a place in the order of things—begin to disappear. *Naked* (1993) projects an apocalyptic vision of characters lost and in torment in a London where the have-nots roam the streets like hungry, wounded wolves. Leigh comes from the theater and bases his work on particular actors. His results show none of the hesitancy of pacing, bouts of self-consciously bravura acting, or the uncertainty of structure visible in the work of Cassavetes and other improv-based filmmakers.

Before you line up behind any particular creed, it may be useful to glance at some fundamentals of modern realistic cinema. If the object is to create believable life on the screen and to expose credible contemporary issues, there must not only be viable ideas and situations, but above all, credible characters. Today's audience has spent upwards of 18,000 hours watching the screen and is expert at judging acting. People are quite unmoved by the representational styles that audiences loved years ago. So unless an actor finds an adequate emotional identification with his character, we will reject his performance, and with it, much or all of the film.

Unsophisticated or untrained actors tend to model their performances not on life but on ideas gleaned from other admired actors. They will signify a character's feelings and "perform" at the mass audience they imagine existing just beyond the camera lens. The director must develop strategies for each actor to

FIGURE 9–1

Tanner's *Jonah Who Will Be 25 in the Year 2000*, a film developed from its actors' improvisation (courtesy New Yorker Films).

break through to something true. Their particular qualities and limitations should guide how you realize your authorial intentions. Even your intentions may need rethinking if they are to align with the intrinsic and highly visible qualities of your cast.

As a developing director you must, as a matter of survival, give first priority to developing your actors' potentials. Good film acting looks like being, not like acting at all. Your film can survive indifferent film technique, but nothing can rescue it from lousy acting—not good color, not good music, not good photography, not good editing. None of these—separately or combined—can change the true state of consciousness and the inherent human qualities you cannot avoid capturing, documentary fashion, with your camera.

A SCRIPT DEVELOPED FROM ACTORS IMPROVISING

Let us imagine you are going to make a film about the conflicts and paradoxes in a young man leaving home, and you want to show it as an ordeal by fire. It is possible and even desirable to begin without a full-fledged script. Leaving home is so universal that most cast members will have strong feelings on the subject. You decide to find an interesting cast, knowing that each actor's ideas are going to be engaged in developing your thematic concerns. John Cassavetes' *A Woman*

Under the Influence (1974) began this way. Cassavetes and his wife, actress Gena Rowlands, who plays the wife in the film, were interested in what happens in an Italian-American blue collar family when the ideas of women's liberation penetrate the home. The wife becomes aware that her role as wife and mother is preventing her from growing into an autonomous adult. The resulting script was founded on the experiences and personalities of the players. Uneven as the movie is, Gena Rowlands' performance is disturbingly memorable.

By finding an interested cast and by posing the right questions, it is possible to draw out their interests and residual experience of life. When you turn up interesting and credible situations, you can have your cast experimentally play them out. As this happens, consistent characters begin to emerge from each player, and in emerging, they demand greater clarity and background. You and your cast will find your attention turning from ideas to character development, from character development inevitably to situations, and from situations and characters to the specific past events—personal, cultural, political—that seeded each character's present. Gradually you form a world out of the tensions and conflicts, and the world belongs to everyone taking part because each has had a hand in its creation.

A ship with several oarsmen needs a firm hand on the tiller. Directing a project of this nature takes subtlety, patience, and the authority to make binding decisions. Dramatically the results may be a mixed bag, but at the very least this process is a tremendous way of building rapport among cast and director. The cast tends to retain what is successful by consensus, so that what began as improvisation gradually metamorphoses into a mutually agreed text. This is truly fascinating, for this surely rediscovers how folk drama was produced for hundreds of years.

Another more open-ended method is to start, not from a social theme or idea, but from a mood or from the personality and potential of individual cast members. If "character is fate," let your characters develop their fates. By getting each to generate an absorbing character and by letting situations grow out of the clashes and alliances of these characters, themes and issues inevitably suggest themselves. A project like this is good for a theater company used to working together, or as a follow-up film project when the cast and director have come to trust each other and want to go on working together (not always the case!).

Though there are only 36 basic dramatic situations in the world, there is no limit to possible interactions among characters. Alternatively, both characters and issues might be developed from the nature and resonance of a particular location, say a deserted gravel pit, the waiting room in an underground car park, or a street market. Very potent is the site of an historical event, such as a field where strikers were gunned down or the house where a woman who had apocalyptic visions grew up.

Experiments of this kind are excellent for building the cast's confidence to play scripted or unscripted parts with unselfconscious abandonment and giving them the daring to act upon intuition—all priceless commodities. Playful work of this nature generates energy and ideas, and when the dramatic output is rounded up and analyzed, a longer work can be structured. Firm guidance is imperative or the results will lack integration and fail to make any recognizable statement. This is true for all improv-generated ideas. Techniques useful for this kind of work appear throughout Part 5: Preproduction and particularly in Chapter 21, "Learning about Acting."

THE VIDEO NOVEL: AN IMPROV APPROACH

Just as the theater in England was once revitalized when local companies turned their backs on cocktail plays in favor of more explosive local issues, it now seems possible that local fiction might emerge to begin producing the modern equivalent of the regional novel. Amber Films has done this in the industrial north of England (*www.amber-online.com/html/index.html*) with their films *Eden Valley* (1994) and *Like Father* (2001).

In America as elsewhere, there are a host of obstacles standing in the way of this, but the main one is the sheer lack of proficiency in filmmaking outside the few metropolitan areas where films are produced. Most regional film production remains imitative and third-rate. A few first-rate contemporary voices would send distributors rushing to invest in a new source of product, and make no mistake, they need it. With ever more channels, not to mention the inevitability of movies on demand through the Internet, the people of the world want to see themselves, not just Hollywood forever.

The most likely point of origin is city theatres producing works of contemporary social and political criticism and having a fairly stable ensemble. It has been done before. Both the German director Rainer Werner Fassbinder and the fine actress Hanna Schygulla, who played in his *Marriage of Maria Braun* (1978), emerged from such an institution, the Munich *action-theater*, which later became the *anti-theater*. The company made no fewer than six of Fassbinder's early films together, and his astonishingly prolific and creative film career was plainly rooted in the experience of creating instant theater from contemporary personal or political issues.

If it can be done in Munich, why not elsewhere? Of course, there will always be many arguments against a grassroots screen drama movement. Funding, distribution, the continuity of the ensemble, and homogeneity of vision are all difficult to sustain. Rather than debate these points, I will just point out a possible niche for an enterprising group, given that the means of production are now within reach.

Let us take an example. During the last 20 years in Chicago, where I live, the steel industry has gone silent, and the hardworking ethnic communities that clustered around it have gone through a period of unemployment. They participated in the American Dream for two or three generations, and now heavy industry and the notion of real work being mills and factories has all but died. What happens to such people? What happens to their sons and daughters? What happens when people whose sense of virtue was founded in hard, dirty labor now have no more "man's work" in the offing? How do they explain their losses? This is a story being repeated all over the industrialized Western world as it changes from a manufacturing to an information society. Such people and their fate are of wide significance and also of wide interest. It is not hard to find out about them, for their survivors have ample time for the researcher.

At first sight it seems more of a Barbara Kopple documentary subject, but when you begin to read articles and interviews, to visit with union leaders, local historians, doctors, and clergymen, as well as with the unemployed steelworkers and their families, you find that the story is diffuse and complicated. Some of the men still live on false hope. Some drink too much. Some, to keep up their work ethic, have taken meaningless jobs that pay a fraction of what they once earned. The wives now go to work, and the family dynamic has changed. The young people either stay because for one reason or another they cannot leave, or they go off to college, leaving their parents' decaying neighborhood ever farther away, yet feeling guilty for betraying their embittered, once-proud parents.

Here is a situation with many possibilities, indeed so many things happening that the only way to select is to decide which are especially interesting and make a dramatic construct out of those. What we begin to see is perhaps a representative family whose members are composites inspired by people we met and who left an indelible impression. We make up a list of key events in the life of a composite fictional family, which span many years. Covering half a lifetime is something that fiction can do rather well. Here are some key events:

- Father loses job
- Believes his skills will soon be needed elsewhere
- No job comes, no job can be found
- Scenes of mounting economic and emotional pressure in the family
- Mother finds a job as a checkout clerk at a supermarket
- Daughter begins going to a college downtown
- Daughter becomes increasingly critical of her family and its assumptions
- Son drops out of high school and hangs out on street corners, identifying more and more with racist gang messages of revenge and hatred

We have built up a series of pressures. Now we urgently need ideas about how these pressures will resolve, what kind of contortions this family and this bereaved community are going to suffer, and what "coming out the other side" may mean. A fictionalized treatment of these very real circumstances must, therefore, have an element of prediction to propose to its audience, a prediction about the way human beings handle slow-motion catastrophe.

Becoming a social analyst or prophet is an exciting job to give yourself. Do it well and you will arouse much interest, but you'll need the abilities (or the help) of journalist, sociologist, documentarian, or novelist to make it work. But look what is already available: a host of characters to play minor roles; a landscape of windswept, rusting factories and rows of peeling houses; and a circuit of bars, dance halls, and ethnic churches with their weddings, christenings, and funerals. Sound too depressing? Then go to the amateur comedian contests and make Dad into an aspiring stand-up comic. The community where you are going to film has all sorts of regular activities to use as a backdrop, and within the wide bounds of the possible, you can make the characters do and be anything you want.

Actually, people who lose their jobs, provided they are resilient, sometimes say afterward when they have found a new life, "That was awful and it hurt, but looking back it was the best thing that ever happened to me." It's important when telling stories to offer hope, and this resolution is indeed hopeful. One way to sugar the pill is to use the genre of comedy. Many recent British comedies have been set in similar surroundings and use humor to deal with serious situations. Mike Leigh's *Life is Sweet* (1990), Mark Herman's *Brassed Off* (1996), Peter Cattaneo's *The Full Monty* (1997), and Stephen Daldry's *Billy Elliot* (2000) have all been about local characters in failing rust belt settings. Indeed, *The Full Monty* was so successful and so universal in its appeal that its central idea has been recycled as a musical about steelworkers in upstate New York.

What is happening in your area that needs to be understood? A rash of teenage suicides? A cult? A new and dangerous form of racing? A cosmetician who has found a way to get rich quick? A UFO society? An archeological hoax by a hitherto reputable academic? A sexual purity movement among teenagers? Industrial espionage? An aging beauty queen who has run away with her priest? A computer nerd reorganizing the town's bank accounts for no personal profit?

Among novelists there have always been committed regionalists. You could become one. You could reach out to inhabit interesting, broadly significant local situations that can be filled out from imagination and experience. Newspapers, magazines, and bookshops are full of models, and you need only to choose well from the local storehouse. Intelligently realized, the deeply local subject becomes the truly universal one.

CHAPTER 10

STORY DEVELOPMENT STRATEGIES

While creating a story, the writer alternates between generating story materials and editing them in pursuit of character development and plot unity. In the generating mode, give free rein to inspiration and write organically and disconnectedly as ideas, scenes, characters, and situations appear in your imagination. This is letting the work help to create itself.

Then, once the blitz of a generating phase is over, you begin editing; that is, you review and analyze what you have produced to develop it. Like a manic potter who produces flawed and surplus goods among the useful, there comes a time when production must be halted to allow someone to organize, classify, tidy up, and throw out the junk. Here you need methods by which to re-impose order. Whether potter or writer, nobody creates in a vacuum. Virtually all characters and situations, no matter how up-to-date, are variations of archetypal patterns. To deny this or hide from it is not preserving your originality so much as refusing the help of parentage that even great artists welcome. Later in the chapter we will look at how to find and use archetypes.

If you are assessing a completed script or working on your own writing, you will need to get a dramatic oversight of the piece. This is equally true whether you have five pages or 150. You will need to apply the analytical tools of the step outline, premise, concept, and treatment.

The step outline is like the framework of headings I used to begin writing this book. Any extended writing is a slow, circular activity like fumbling your way through a dense forest. Even after starting from a clear plan I regularly lost sight of the overview of what I was doing, and I had to create content lists to see exactly where I had been and where I still needed to go. When you first picked up this book, you probably looked in the list of chapters, tables of contents, and index to see whether it contained what you wanted. These summations functioned for you and me both. Writing a story is a lot more complex than writing a manual, and it needs periodic reorganizing and overview all the more.

EXPANDING AND COLLAPSING THE SCREENPLAY

The step outline is an excellent starting point for writing a screenplay, but it is an equally useful tool for traveling in the opposite direction, that is, for simplifying the essentials of a completed screenplay draft. Working in screenplay format means the basic structure often becomes obscured, particularly from its own progenitor. When a screenplay presents problems (and which one doesn't?) it will help to make a step outline that reveals the plot and inherent structure.

Reducing the screenplay to step outline and then further reducing the step outline to a ruling premise are vital steps in testing a story's foundations. (See Chapter 7, "Script Development Essentials.")

STORY ARCHETYPES

Major work has been done in the last few decades surveying story archetypes. While archetypes are especially helpful to fiction writers in the editing and structuring phase of their work, you will almost certainly find them inhibiting as a starting point. Their completeness can be paralyzing. That's why I've waited to present this material until a section dealing with story-editing tools. When you write initial drafts, put formulae out of your mind and follow your inclinations. Create first, no matter how poorly; then shape and edit later when the world you have set in motion is firmly established. Myths and archetypes become most helpful for a story with difficulties or when you become stuck.

In the Notes and Queries section of the international newspaper *Guardian Weekly*, a reader asked if it was true that there are only seven basic stories in fiction. An obliging reader responded with eight:

1. Cinderella—virtue eventually recognized
2. Achilles—the fatal flaw
3. Faust—the debt that catches up with the debtor
4. Tristan—the sexual triangle
5. Circe—the spider and the fly
6. Romeo and Juliet—star-crossed lovers who either find or lose each other
7. Orpheus—the gift that is lost and searched for
8. The Hero who cannot be kept down

To these other readers added:

9. David and Goliath—the individual against the state, community, system, etc.
10. The Wandering Jew—the persecuted traveler who can never go home

Another reader pointed out that it is fictional themes, not stories, that are said to be limited to seven. They are:

1. Revenge
2. Survival
3. Money

4. Power
5. Glory
6. Self-Awareness
7. Love

Yet another reader referred to Georges Polti's *The Thirty-Six Dramatic Situations* as the definitive listing of dramatic possibilities (Figure 10–1). Written in French and copyrighted in an English translation in 1921, this hard-to-find book is a seminal analysis of dramaturgy. Polti lists each situation of human conflict with its elements, plus wonderfully categorized examples and variations. Here, to whet your appetite, are the situations and elements.

Lists like this may seem limiting, but myths, conflicts, and themes are the DNA of human experience. Human beings will never stop enacting them and will never stop needing stories that explore their implications. You could make a long list of films for every one of the 36 situations noted in Figure 10–1. Most films contain multiples of the basic situations.

Once you know which situations and theme (or themes) your script is handling, you can look up its collaterals. This will certainly give you ideas about modifications or additions. These are unlikely to change the nature or individuality of your piece; instead, you are more likely to find and overcome your piece's weaknesses. Merely examining and testing the fabric of your story will toughen it and increase your authority as its director.

THE HERO'S JOURNEY

The lifetime work of Joseph Campbell, author of *The Mythic Image*, *The Masks of God*, and *The Hero with a Thousand Faces*, was to collect myths and folk tales from every imaginable culture and reveal their common, symbolic denominators. "The hero," he says, "is the [person] of self-achieved submission." The terms of this submission may vary, but they reflect that "within the soul, within the body social, there must be—if we are to experience long survival—a continuous recurrence of birth (*palingenesia*) to nullify the unremitting recurrences of death" (*The Hero with a Thousand Faces*, Princeton, New Jersey: Princeton University Press, 1972, p. 16).

Campbell recognizes that the hero's journey (he also means heroine's) always deals with a central character's struggle for regeneration against the forces of darkness. My purpose here is not to summarize his work, but to draw your attention to its profound implications for the makers of screen works. Just as Stanislavski found the psychological and practical elements of acting from studying successful actors, Campbell discovered the recurring spiritual and narrative elements held in common by so many of the world's tales. If something you have created shares some of the archetype, you may find it useful to see what elements are missing and whether their inclusion would strengthen your story. Campbell alleges that the hero generally makes a circular journey during his or her transformation. It includes departure, initiation, and return. You could apply this principle to a child going to her first day of school or to a cosmonaut making the first journey to a distant planet. Both go through severe trials and return changed.

	Situation	Elements
1	Supplication	A persecutor, a suppliant, a power in authority whose decision is doubtful
2	Deliverance	An unfortunate, a threatener, a rescuer
3	Crime pursued by vengeance	An avenger and a criminal
4	Vengeance taken for kindred	Avenging kinsman, guilty kinsman, remembrance of the victim, a relative of both
5	Pursuit	Punishment and fugitive
6	Disaster	A vanquished power, a victorious enemy or a messenger
7	Falling prey to cruelty or misfortune	An unfortunate, a master or a misfortune
8	Revolt	Tyrant and conspirator
9	Daring enterprise	A bold leader, an object, an adversary
10	Abduction	The abductor, the abducted, the guardian
11	The enigma	Interrogator, seeker, and problem
12	Obtaining	A solicitor and an adversary who is refusing, or an arbitrator and opposing parties
13	Enmity of kinsmen	A malevolent kinsman, a hated or reciprocally hating kinsman
14	Rivalry of kinsmen	The preferred kinsman, the rejected kinsman, the object
15	Murderous adultery	Two adulterers, a betrayed husband or wife
16	Madness	Madman and victim
17	Fatal imprudence	The imprudent, the victim or the object lost
18	Involuntary crimes of love	The lover, the beloved, the revealer
19	Slaying of a kinsman unrecognized	The slayer, the unrecognized victim
20	Self-sacrificing for an ideal	The hero, the ideal, the "creditor" or the person or thing sacrificed
21	Self-sacrificing for kindred	The hero, the kinsman, the "creditor" or the person or thing sacrificed
22	All sacrificed for a passion	The lover, the object of the fatal passion, the person or thing sacrificed
23	Necessity of sacrificing loved ones	The hero, the beloved victim, the necessity for the sacrifice

FIGURE 10–1

Georges Polti's *The Thirty-Six Dramatic Situations*. Reproduced by kind permission of The Writer, Inc., Boston. Copyright © 1977, 1993 by The Writer, Inc.

24	Rivalry of superior and inferior	The superior rival, the inferior rival, the object
25	Adultery	A deceived husband or wife, two adulterers
26	Crimes of love	The lover, the beloved
27	Discovery of the dishonor of a loved one	The discoverer, the guilty one
28	Obstacles to love	Two lovers, an obstacle
29	An enemy loved	The beloved enemy, the lover, the hater
30	Ambition	An ambitious person, a thing coveted, an adversary
31	Conflict with a god	A mortal, an immortal
32	Mistaken jealousy	The jealous one, the object of whose possession he is jealous, the supposed accomplice, the cause or the author of the mistake
33	Erroneous judgment	The mistaken one, the victim of the mistake, the cause or author of the mistake, the guilty person
34	Remorse	The culprit, the victim or the sin, the interrogator
35	Recovery of a lost one	The seeker, the one found
36	Loss of loved ones	A kinsman slain, a kinsman spectator, an executioner

FIGURE 10–1 (Continued)

A few of Campbell's chapter headings in *Hero with a Thousand Faces* show just how flexibly his analysis fits many film ideas:

Departure

The Call to Adventure
The Refusal of the Call
Supernatural Aid
The Crossing of the First Threshold
The Belly of the Whale

Initiation

The Road of Trials
The Meeting with the Goddess
Woman as the Temptress
Atonement with the Father
Apotheosis
The Ultimate Boon

Return

Refusal of the Return

The Magic Flight

Rescue from Without

The Crossing of the Return Threshold

Master of the Two Worlds

Freedom to Live

If this calls to you, read it for yourself. If you would like to apply the ideas directly to a screen work without getting lost in the fascinations of world literature, look into Christopher Vogler's *The Writer's Journey: Mythic Structure for Storytellers and Screenwriters* (California: Michael Wiese Productions, 1998). This is an intelligent and well-written book by an experienced story analyst. Vogler's enthusiasm, his many examples from classic and contemporary films, his willingness to share everything he knows with the reader, and his ability to keep the reader focused on the larger picture of human endeavor make this an unusually useful book. Vogler concludes by saying, "The beauty of the Hero's Journey model is that it not only describes a pattern in myths and fairytales, but it's also an accurate map of the territory one must travel to become a writer or for that matter, a human being."

CHARACTER DEVELOPMENT PROBLEMS

A common problem is the character who refuses to develop and becomes a bore even to his creator. This usually happens because characters are being conceived to illustrate ideas rather than to dramatize situations, that is, to struggle with issues and conflicts. Contrast this with what Stuart Dybek says in introduction to his story "We Didn't," published in *Best American Short Stories 1994* (New York: Houghton Mifflin, 1994). "As image begot anecdote, and as anecdote begot characters, I decided to let the characters take over and tell their story. They would have anyway, whether I'd let them or not." Commonly authors feel like servants to their characters, but this can only happen when the characters are charged up with needs and desires that render them highly active. By the way, the annual *Best American Short Stories* book always contains superb and inspiring examples of short (and not-so-short) tales.

What to do when the characters are grounded?

Volition: Find out what the characters want, and what they are trying to get or do. Note for each scene what they should be trying to get from each other or from their situation.

Contradictions: All interesting characters contain conflict and contradictory elements. It's always what you can't reconcile in someone that makes them interesting.

Flaws: Each major character should have some interesting character flaws. The definition of a tragic figure is, after all, a character of magnitude with a fatal flaw. Flaws don't have to be fatal and characters don't have to be tragic, but they should be fresh, interesting, and above all, active.

Vital mismatches: One way to guarantee conflict is to make each character a different personality type.

- Astrology offers a whole system of personality types and destinies that can jolt your thinking and help you break out of monolithic characterization.
- Another system is that of the Enneagram, an ancient Sufi psychological system. Don Richard Riso and Russ Hudson's *Personality Types* (Boston: Houghton Mifflin, 1990) outlines the system and considers character in terms of nine basic types: the reformer, the helper, the status seeker, the artist, the thinker, the loyalist, the generalist, the leader, and the peacemaker. Each type is broken down by healthy and unhealthy characteristics, all offering a wealth of insight and developmental possibility for the screenwriter.
- Go to *www.amazon.com* and look up "personality types" among book titles, and you will find a wide range of choices.

THE MOST COMMON FLAW

The research I've cited previously—focusing as it does on the paradigms of drama—further confirms what all the screenwriting manuals proclaim: that above everything, the central characters must be active, doing, seeking, and therefore in conflict, rather than illustrative, passive, or acted upon.

In my experience this screenplay failure can be traced to a writer's limited concept of self. These writers see themselves (and therefore their point-of-view character) as someone *acted upon*, someone unable to significantly influence his or her destiny. When this is how you see yourself, you are going to create characters in that mold. In these scripts, if something good happens it is because of good luck rather than something earned by a character's actions. If something bad happens, it is because bad things always happen to good people.

Why is the culture of passivity so pervasive? Maybe it's because our collective unconscious was formed by ancestors living under intense subjection, who believed they must never antagonize "them," the powerful. Even the lack of facial affect in some cultures can, I suspect, be traced to forms of slavery. Any expression of feeling implied independence and led to punishment.

Growing up myself in a nation still tied to feudal attitudes toward authority and knowing that a part of myself is conditioned to passive victimhood, I have pondered this question often, both personally and professionally. As a European, I was accultured to a fatalism that is anathema to Americans. At a Munich film conference, a delegate complained about the Americans taking over the European film market. Another speaker said it was because European films were too boring, and "because we don't know how to tell a story." It set me thinking about storytelling and about the polarity between free will and fatalism.

Why *do* world audiences prefer Hollywood fables? This cannot be explained any longer as an international capitalist conspiracy. Surely the implications are more complex and interesting. Humankind has always had to resist being overcome by fatalism, and maybe as populations grew and the stress of competition increased, our sense of insignificance and powerlessness grew, too. Religion helped us deal with this until Darwin convinced us we were just another species fighting to survive, red in tooth and claw. The growth of the anti-globalization movement shows how outraged people feel at being exploited as consumers by global sales systems controlled somewhere else by "them" in business suits. Joseph Campbell's work argues that secular narrative evolved to help the individual fight back against feelings of powerlessness. Tales about heroes remind both teller and listener that an individual has potential. But notice that until the 20th century, regeneration was never accorded anyone who ignored the moral laws of the universe.

An immigrant civilization like the United States, trying nobly to function under its extraordinarily visionary constitution, is by historic accident a laboratory of these values—and of their antitheses. Free will is an article of faith with Americans. An old-worlder like myself, married to an American, will frequently play out the profound philosophical differences; under pressure I hide behind irony and what I imagine to be elegant fatalism. My American wife's instinct is to move to combat and overcome the circumstances. A small example: When I am ill, I generally accept what the hospital says it can do for me. But my wife goes into battle armed with pointed questions. Guess who uses more energy, and guess who gets better results from institutions?

The central question here is of great moment to writers: Do your characters accept circumstances or do they struggle against them? Neither course taken heedlessly will yield better consequences. Revolution can be tragic and so can tractability. So perhaps the energy of self-willed heroes comes as refreshment to civilizations weary from bowing to successive tyrannies. Somehow the better part of the American entertainment industry, so often led by immigrants with the energy and courage to reject the circumstances of their birth, has always offered visions—spurious or otherwise—of escape and moral triumph. How strange that this energy and optimism, widely equated with American immaturity, is the very nourishment found in the world's folk tales.

Dramaturgy is the art of orchestrating the contest of moral and emotional forces. For the competition to be serious, the contest must be balanced, as in Agnieszka Holland's *Europa, Europa* (1991), in which the young Solomon Perel repeatedly escapes the dark force of his Nazi tormentors by a combination of luck and inspired ingenuity. Less experienced writers creating from unexamined assumptions about passivity and victimhood deprive their audience of any true conflict. When you next examine a piece of screen writing, do the following:

- Assess each scene for what the main characters are trying to do or get, and summarize it each time as a tag description in the margin.
- Survey the whole constituted by these tags alone and the movement they create.
- Use the tools describing archetypes to help see deeper into the underlying dramatic structure.
- Mend and re-energize what is deficient.

THE ETHICS OF REPRESENTATION

Acquiring the education to make films is expensive, so most of those who make it into the film industry are from the comfortable middle classes. The result is that a nation's feature film output, with few exceptions, tends to represent as "normal" only what the privileged see as such. Anybody lucky enough to make movies for a living has a certain kind of power, and power used responsibly is power used for the greater good. Fiction filmmakers should sometimes speak for those without a voice and should certainly be careful not to perpetuate stereotypes. In documentaries this obligation is obvious, in fiction less so.

All storytelling begins from assumptions about what will be familiar and acceptable to the audience. Look back a few decades and see how many people, roles, and relationships in movies are represented in archaic or even insulting ways, though they excited little remark at the time. Women appear as secretaries, nurses, teachers, mothers, or seductresses. People of color are servants, vagrants, or objects of pity with little to say for themselves. Criminals or gangsters are ethnically branded, and so on—all this is very familiar. These stereotypes come from what some film faculty members at the University of Southern California call *embedded values*, or values so natural to the makers of a film that they pass below the radar of awareness. Jed Dannenbaum, Carroll Hodge, and Doe Mayer of USC's School of Cinema and Television have an excellent book, *Creative Filmmaking-From the Inside Out: Five Keys to the Art of Making Inspired Movies and Television* (New York: Simon & Schuster, 2003). One section of the book poses some fascinating questions that I have adapted below.

Embedded values, easy to see in another field, creep into our own work with surprising ease. The point is not learning to be politically correct, which is just another kind of suffocation, but to avoid feeding into whatever is still "normal" and just shouldn't be. Take a few steps back and consider how your script represents what is listed below and whether the world in your script would look stereotypical or credibly complex on the screen to an astute person from another culture. This is particularly addressed to filmmakers of the First World whose preoccupations circle the globe, causing bitterness and even hatred.

Characters:

Class: What class or classes do they come from? How are differences handled? How are other classes represented?

Wealth: Do they have money? How is it regarded? How do they handle it? What is taken for granted? Are things as they should be, and if not, how well does the film express this?

Appearances: Are appearances reliable or misleading? How important are appearances? Do the characters have difficulty reading each other's appearances?

Background: Is there any diversity of race or other background and how is this handled? Do other races or ethnicities have minor or major parts?

Belongings: Do we see the characters work or know how they sustain their lifestyle? Do their clothes, appliances, and cars belong with their characters' breadwinning ability? What do their belongings say about their tastes and values? Is anyone in the film critical of this?

Talismans: Are there important objects, and what is their significance?

Work: Do the characters seem skilled and expert enough? Are they capable of sustaining the work they purportedly do?

Valuation: For what are characters valued by other characters? Does the film question this or cast doubt on the inter-character values?

Speech: What do you learn from the vocabulary of each? What makes the way each thinks and talks different from the others? What does it betray?

Roles: What roles do characters fall into, and do they emerge as complex enough to challenge any stereotypes?

Sexuality: If sexuality is present, is there a range of expression and how is it portrayed? Is it allied with affection, tenderness, and love? Or is it shown as disembodied lust? Is it true to your experience?

Volition: Who is able to change his or her situation and who seems unable to take action? What are the patterns behind this?

Competence: Who is competent and who not? What determines this?

Environment:

Place: Do we know where characters come from and what values are associated with their origins?

Settings: Will they look credible and add to what we know about the characters?

Time: What values are associated with the period chosen for the setting?

Home: Do the characters seem at home? What do they have around them to signify any journeys or accomplishments they have made?

Work: Do they seem to belong there, and how is the workplace portrayed? What does it say about the characters?

Family Dynamics:

Structure: What structure emerges? Do characters treat it as normal or abnormal? Is anyone critical of the family structure?

Relationships: How are relationships between members and between generations portrayed?

Roles: Are roles in the family fixed or do they develop? Are they healthy or unhealthy? Who in the family is critical? Who is branded as "good" or "successful" by the family, and who "bad" or "failed"?

Power: Could there be another structure? Is power handled in a healthy or unhealthy way? What is the relationship of earning money to power in the family?

Authority:

Gender: Which gender is shown to have the most authority? Does one gender dominate, and if so, why?

Initiation: Who initiates the events in the film, and why? Who resolves them?

Respect: How are figures with power depicted? How are institutions and institutional power depicted? Are they simple or complex, and does the script reflect your experience of the real thing?

Conflict: How are conflicts negotiated? What does the film say about conflict and its resolution? Who wins, and why?

Violence: Who is violent and why? What does it say about your values that you let them settle something this way?

In Total:

Criticism: How critical is the film toward what its characters do or don't do? How much does it tell us about what's wrong? Can we hope to see one of the characters coming to grips with this?

Approval/Disapproval: What does the film approve of, and is there anything risky and unusual in what it defends? Is the film challenging its audience's assumptions and expectations, or just feeding into them?

World View: If this is a microcosm, what does it say about the balance of forces in the larger world of which it is a fragment?

Moral Stance: What shape does the film's belief system take in relation to privilege, willpower, tradition, inheritance, power, initiative, God, luck, coincidence, etc.? Is this what you want?

Making fiction is proposing reality, and this is as true for fantasy as it is for realism. Films about chainsaw massacres or teenage shooting rampages gradually alter the threshold of reality for those attracted to such subjects, as a rash of high school shootings has demonstrated internationally. What do you want to contribute to the world? Are the elements you are using working as you desire?

These considerations are at the core of screen authorship, and *Creative Filmmaking–From the Inside Out* has some very pertinent ideas. It asks not that you change what you wish to say, but that you know and take responsibility for the ethical and moral implications of your work.

FUNDRAISING AND WRITING THE PROSPECTUS

Raising funds for a production is a special area of writing that varies greatly according to the scale of the production and the intended market for the film. To attempt covering it adequately would greatly increase the size of this book, which instead concentrates on the conceptual side of fiction filmmaking. There is, however, a written presentation that very much affects your success at arousing interest and raising funds, no matter how you go about it. This is the prospectus, a presentation package or portfolio you put together that communicates your project, its purposes, and personnel to prospective funders. It should create enthusiasm not by waxing lyrical, but through the eloquence of the arguments and detail it presents. It should be as personable, word perfect, graphic, and tasteful as something that would make you linger in a bookstore. It should contain the following:

Cover Letter: This succinctly communicates the nature of the film, its budget, the capital you want to raise, and what you want from the addressee. If you are targeting many small investors, this may have to be a general letter, but wherever possible, fashion a specific letter to a specific individual.

Title Page: Finding a good title usually takes inordinate effort but does more than anything to arouse respect and interest. An evocative photo or other professional-looking artwork here and elsewhere in the prospectus can also do much to make your presentation exciting and professional.

One-liner: A simple, compact declaration of the project. Some examples:

- A woman in a small New England town who discovers that her husband is gay must start a new life and conquer what it means to be alone.
- Four 12-year-old friends cut school for a day to find a home for a pony they mistakenly think is unwanted.
- A 40-year-old man conspires to leave his possessive mother and marry the woman of his dreams—who is in prison for something she didn't do.

Synopsis: Brief recounting of the story that captures its flavor and style.

History and Background: How and why the project evolved and why you feel compelled to make this particular film. Here is the place to establish your commitment.

Research: Outline what research you've done and what it contributes. Include stills of locations or actors that will help establish the look of your film. This is the opportunity to establish the factual foundation to the film if there is one, as well as its characters and their context. If special cooperation, rights, or permissions are involved, you should assure the reader that you've secured them.

Budget: Summary of main expected expenditures. Don't understate or underestimate—it makes you look amateur and leaves you asking for too little.

Schedule: Day-by-day plan for shooting period and preferred starting dates.

Cast: Pictures and resumes of intended cast members, paying special attention to their prior credits.

Resumes of Creative Personnel: In brief paragraphs, name the main creative personnel and summarize their qualifications. Append a one-page resume from each. Your aim is to present the team as professional, committed, exciting, and specially suited.

Copy of Screenplay: This is optional because most potential investors don't have the expertise to make sense of a barebones screenplay. The fact that it exists and looks fully professional may be a deciding factor for some. If it's an adaptation, be explicit that you have secured the rights to film it.

Audience and Market: Say what particular audience the film is intended for, and outline a distribution plan to show the film has a waiting audience. Copies of letters of interest from distributors or other interested parties are helpful here.

Financial Statement: Outline your financial identity as a company or group, make an estimate of income based on the distribution plan, and say if you are a not-for-profit company, or working through one, because this may permit investors to claim tax breaks.

Means of Transferring Funds: To save potential investors from having to compose a letter, enclose a sample letter from an investor to your company that commits funds to your production account.

If you approach foundations or other funding agencies, bear in mind that:

- Each is likely to have its preferred form of presentation.
- You should research the fund's identity and track record to know how best to present your work.
- Every grant application is potentially the beginning of a lengthy relationship, so your prospectus and whatever else you send should be consistent and professional in tone.
- Always write to a named individual and include a reprise of your project and your history with them to date.
- Though each prospectus is tailored for different addressees, be careful not to promise different things to different people.
- Your prospectus should have professional-looking graphics and typesetting.
- Have everything triple-checked for spelling or other errors. At this stage *you are what you write*, so secure desktop publishing facilities, and use the best available stationery.

CHAPTER 11

SCENE-WRITING EXERCISES

One challenge the professional writer faces is climbing into situations and characters to which he or she may not immediately relate. This takes effort and research, but the truly imaginative writer should be able to discover something gripping and vital in almost any character and circumstance.

The game in this chapter was inspired by the random access methods of the I Ching. To generate a short scene-writing exercise you can either simply pick the ingredients you want or, more interestingly, create them haphazardly by a lottery method. This will challenge you to develop ideas flexibly and spontaneously and to venture beyond autobiography.

A class or workshop facing writing problems together will quickly move into interesting discussions about the demands that arise. Much useful learning can come from these, as well as a greater trust and closeness among writers. Successful writers often work in partnerships or teams, and who knows, this exercise might just be the beginning of that experience.

SKILLS

- Writing to preset form and ingredients, as a series screenwriter would
- Working beyond concepts of self and autobiography
- Creating credible people in interesting predicaments
- Working consciously in a genre
- Creating within a time constraint
- Controlling where the scene crisis, or high point, is placed
- Creating a beat or beats
- Making a setting organic to character(s) and situation
- Orchestrating a conflict
- Handling time

- Expressing a theme
- Writing dialogue in the characters' own voices
- Delivering some sort of impact
- Experiencing the reactions of an audience of fellow writers
- Contributing as a critic to someone else's work
- Working with other writers on common problems and perceptions
- Rewriting
- Extending the original idea to a subsequent scene

ASSESSMENT

Use **Assessment 11–1 Scene Writing** in Appendix 1.

TO PLAY

H and *T* in the second column of the following table signify heads and tails, so *HHT* means the coins you threw came up as two heads and one tail. If you throw an unlisted coin combination, make a free choice for that section.

For a random scene-writing assignment:

1. Write down any number between 1 and 30.
2. Starting at item 1 in the left column, toss the appropriate number of coins to get a selection. Write down what you get.
3. Continue onward doing the same thing for items 2 through 10, gathering parameters for a piece of writing.
4. For item 11, use the title for your scene that corresponds with the random number you wrote down in step 1.

Assignment arising from coins I threw:	Write a 2-minute tragedy scene set late at night with two characters and the point-of-view (POV) character a male of age 15–20. The conflict is between the POV character and his environment, and the crisis is placed one third of the way through the scene. There is one beat, and the scene title is "Live Now, Pay Later."

You can see that my assignment leaves open whom the second character is (maybe his father or mother or a girlfriend) and where they happen to be late at night (a car sinking into a bog, a police station, halfway up Mount Everest). As a writer I can choose blatant melodrama and lower the challenge, or I can do something more unexpected that takes more invention.

Write the final in standard screenplay form, but work out the action in treatment form first if that's easier.

SCENE-WRITING GAME

To decide . . .	Toss these coins . . .	And follow these instructions
1. Ratio of dialogue to behavioral language	H	Use up to 60% of screen time in dialogue.
	T	Use sound, music, and effects but no more than two lines of dialogue
2. Gender of POV character	H	Gender same as yours
	T	Different from yours
3. Age of POV character	HHH	Age same as yours
	HHT	2–10
	HTH	10–15
	HTT	15–20
	TTT	20–35
	TTH	35–50
	THT	50–65
	THH	Over 65
4. Genre	HHH	Comedy
	HHT	Tragedy
	HTH	Mystery
	HTT	Horror
	TTT	Film noir
	TTH	Sci-fi
	THT	Detective
	THH	Realism
5. Screen time	HH	Duration 2 minutes
	HT	3 minutes
	TT	4 minutes
	TH	5 minutes
6. Scene crisis placement	HH	Crisis near beginning
	HT	One third in
	TT	Two thirds in
	TH	At end
7. Number of beats	H	One
	T	Two or more
8. Number of characters	HH	Two characters
	HT	Three
	TT	Four
	TH	Your choice

9. Time	HHH	Morning
	HTH	Afternoon
	HHT	Late night
	HTT	Small hours
	TTT	Discontinuous (short overall time period)
	TTH	Discontinuous (long overall time period)
10. Conflict	HH	Conflict between characters
	HT	Between POV character and environment
	TT	Internal to POV character
	TH	Internal to other character
11. Title (Use the number 1–30 you were asked to pick at random.)	1	First Time
	2	The Truth at Last
	3	Interlude with a Stranger
	4	Moment of Danger
	5	Last Bus
	6	No Turning Back
	7	Never Forget
	8	Saved
	9	Finally
	10	Darkest Hour
	11	Embarrassing Moment
	12	Let It Be
	13	Paradise Lost
	14	Revisitation
	15	What Goes Around, Comes Around
	16	Live Now, Pay Later
	17	Bad Omens
	18	Go-Between
	19	Meant to Be
	20	Visitor
	21	Outsider
	22	Temptation
	23	First Love
	24	Persistence Pays
	25	Learning the Hard Way
	26	Jealousy
	27	Memory
	28	Bliss
	29	Alienated
	30	Speechless

When your first draft is finished:

- Put it away for a day or two.
- Re-read it.
- Read it out loud, acting the movements and speaking the dialogue (if there is any), and time the whole scene. If it's under-length, develop it. If it's too long, prune.
- Write more drafts.
- Wherever possible, replace dialogue with action.
- Contract dialogue wherever you can, even by a syllable.
- Contract body copy wherever you can, even by a syllable.

Now go to Appendix 1 and use Assessment Form 11-1 to rate your own work; have an honest critic in the class rate it, too. Compare the two sets of ratings.

DISCUSSION

How did your assessment match that of a critic's? Try to be a tough but fair judge when you assess someone else's work and be ready to explain your values. If you don't know each other well enough to be candid, score scenes as a group, and then have a diplomatic group spokesperson deliver the group's verdicts. No one person will feel responsible, and the writer will get a true audience reaction.

Numerical totals matter less than discussion about aspects that scored exceptionally high or low. Discuss the points raised by the assessment form, then ask the following:

- Could readers see the scene every step of the way in their mind's eye?
- Did it falter anywhere?
- Did they find the characters interesting, and if so, why?
- Did the scene have dramatic tension, and what generated it?
- What is the likely backstory for the scene?
- Does the scene suggest where the story might go next?

WRITER'S NOTES

Take notes of everything your critics say and work at being completely receptive. This is your audience, and your role now is not to argue or explain because you've had your say in the scene you wrote. Listen with an open mind and absorb what your audience wants to tell you.

This qualitative feedback, and seeing how readers' reactions matched your intentions while writing, are the springboard from which to develop better drafts.

GOING FURTHER

Wait a day or two to let the critical reaction to your writing settle. Now write the following:

- A second draft that addresses only the criticism that you found constructive and convincing.
- The scene that follows (involving one or more of the original characters).

REVIEW

- What was gained and what was lost in the second draft of the original scene?
- How much did audience reaction play a part in helping the second draft develop?
- How successful was the new scene?
- How organically did the second scene grow out of the first?
- What is most helpful in a critic for the writer, and what is least helpful?

CHECKLIST FOR PART 3: WRITING AND STORY DEVELOPMENT

The points and recommendations summarized here are only those most salient. Some are commonly overlooked. To find them or anything else, go to the Table of Contents at the beginning of this part or try the index at the back of the book.

Writing as a process

- What creative limitations does this project require?
- Investigate what differing techniques and permutations of characters can offer by doing the game-of-chance writing assignments (Chapter 11).
- Write sparely and leave actions open for the actors to interpret.
- Know what the characters are trying to do or get every step of the way.
- What is each character's major conflict?
- Use dialogue as the vehicle for action with one character acting on another.
- Try writing a step outline first, rather than a screenplay.
- First drafts are dreadful.
- Write no matter what.
- Circle among screenplay, step outline, and premise, and revise each as necessary.
- Don't be afraid to write by association: Let things happen and see where they lead.
- Really make us see the characters.
- Work to create a mood.
- Write visually and behaviorally, which is where the cinema excels.
- Write for the silent screen and let yourself resort to dialogue later.
- Distill a dramatic premise for the piece and one for each scene.
- Don't produce characters just as you need them; write them so they function earlier.
- Pitch your idea to anyone who'll listen. You'll learn a lot from their reactions.
- Make your audience laugh, make them cry, but make them wait (for explanations).
- Keep the audience in suspense and anticipation about as much as possible (but not past the point of patience).
- Never use a line where an action could function just as well.
- Don't cave in to critics. Wait to see what you feel is true.

The screenplay

- To begin with, write and direct your own short works, 3–10 minutes maximum.

- Choose subjects you really care about, but avoid autobiography unless you have at least 5 years' distance on the events.
- Look for a reliable, compatible writing collaborator.
- Write about what calls to you, and write about what you need to explore.
- First work on a step outline; do *not* write a script straight away.
- Start developing the premise once you have the events mapped out.
- Rewrite the piece as successive drafts.
- Just keep writing and rewriting regularly; don't wait for inspiration.
- Work on your characters first and foremost. Interesting characters are bound, sooner or later, to develop into a good story if you let them.
- Aim to tell a good story—don't set out to preach or advocate ideas.
- Look for actions or objects that can function as a ruling image or a symbol of something larger embedded in the scene or story.
- Practice pitching your idea (describing it briefly and well).
- Use standard screenplay or split screen formats only for your final drafts.
- Write behaviorally, as if for the silent screen, and allow yourself to add dialogue later.
- What do you want your audience to feel, and what do you want them to think?
- How well does the screenplay pose questions for the audience to solve?
- How open is the screenplay for the audience to think, listen (sound design), and hypothesize solutions to questions that arise?
- Create a version of the script with a third column that details what the Observer (and therefore the audience) must notice.
- Write a premise.
- Write a treatment. You may solve problems in writing the treatment that lead you back to a rewrite of the screenplay.
- Test out your screenplay with a dramatic reading and a critique session. You may learn something important.
- Take part in script readings and critique sessions of other people's work so you know how you want to handle such a session for your work.

Adapting a book, play, or short story

- Adapting anything well known presents many problems, and you will probably have to stay faithful to the original.
- Cutting and compressing are always acceptable.
- A free adaptation is more courageous, if the piece warrants it in translating to the screen.
- Short stories often make great adaptations, but get copyright clearance and make sure you are choosing for cinematic, not literary, reasons.
- You can base a film on adaptations or improvisations from your actors' lives.

- A documentary approach involving research can be a potent way of laying the foundations for a good script.

Story development

- Early versions of stories always need development.
- Make sure you begin with an up-to-date step outline.
- Classify your tale according to the nearest basic dramatic theme and situation, as well as any myths, legends, or folk tales that parallel yours.
- Put the outline of your screenplay next to its archetypal collaterals and see what you can learn from an outline of the other work.
- Most stories are forms of journey, so check your piece against the archetypal Hero's Journey steps.
- Make sure major characters have interesting character flaws and contradictions.
- Be ready to alter scenes to make better use of the actors.
- Apply the scene assessment criteria (Appendix 1: Assessment 11-1).
- Submit your work to as many objective readers as you can, making sure they don't lose their objectivity by reading more than one or two drafts.
- Make sure you can live with the representations in your script and you don't violate your own ethics and standards.

Fundraising

- Put together a prospectus complete with photographs; you will be surprised what you discover when you set out to sell something.
- See if you can raise some funds; begin with family members if need be.

PART 4

AESTHETICS AND AUTHORSHIP

Part 4 (Chapters 12 through 16) examines the aspects of form that must be brought under control because a film is not just content, but form, too. This often-neglected area embraces how the film will look, how its story will be told, and why. The chapters consider point of view, authorial purpose, genre options, the place of conflict in drama, and the ethics of representation.

A book on narrative I have found inspiring and challenging is Michael Roemer's *Telling Stories: Postmodernism and the Invalidation of Traditional Narrative* (Lanham, Maryland: Rowman & Littlefield, 1995). Chapter 1 begins:

> Every story is over before it is begun. The novel lies bound in my hands, the actors know all their lines before the curtain rises, and the finished film has been threaded onto the projector when the houselights dim.
>
> Stories appear to move into an open, uncertain future that the figures try to influence, but in fact report a completed past they cannot alter. Their journey into the future—to which we gladly lend ourselves—is an illusion.

Behind these illusory figures in their enchanted hinterland stands the invisible and little-understood role of the cinematic storyteller. Part 4 examines the aesthetic choices that flow from taking on this role and facing fundamental dramatic considerations: the relationships among plot, structure, and time in a film; the significance of space and environment; and their relationship to the characters, whether presented naturalistically or non-naturalistically. Part 4 concludes with an overview of visual and sound design and the varying relationships with the audience a film strikes when it uses either a short- or long-take style of filming.

Be sure to make use of the checklist at the end of Part 4 during the preproduction and production cycles of your films. In a brief, prescriptive form it summarizes much useful advice for any developing work you have in hand. Appendix 2 includes a Form and Aesthetics Questionnaire. It will help you set out the basic properties of any film you have in mind.

CHAPTER 12

POINT OF VIEW

A point of view (POV) shot in film is a view from a character's physical location in the scene. But film has its own version of literary point of view: a set of more diffuse and empathic impressions experienced by an audience sharing a character's feelings. The effect is easy to describe, but it is harder to say how it came about. Harder still is to write, direct, and control it. This is because, unlike literature, the screen communicates in multiple ways. The printed page at least stands still as you analyze it, while film language is a complex interplay of moving images accompanied by the infinite modifiers of words, symbols, sounds, color, movement, and music. How all this interacts in our minds is simply beyond verbal analysis and formulation, as semiotic analysts found out.

But however indirect POV may be on the screen, it remains within your influence, and you will need to have some ideas and intentions about controlling it. For some helpful parallels, let's first look at how point of view works in the older and better-understood medium of writing.

POINT OF VIEW IN LITERATURE

In literature there are two basic sources for a story's narrating POV. One is *omniscient* and comes from the storyteller who is outside the story, while the other is by way of a *character within the story.*

OMNISCIENT

The omniscient storyteller, like God, has unrestricted movement in time and place, and can look into every aspect of the characters' past, present, and future. The Omniscient Storyteller can even address the reader directly. There are some variations:

- The *self-effacing storyteller* who shows the tale without comment, remains essentially characterless, and by so doing encourages us to make our own interpretation.

- The *character within the story* who has omniscient powers. This is easier to accept when the tale is in the past tense because the "tall tale" convention permits the narrator to affect greater knowledge and ability than would be credible in the events' present.

CHARACTER WITHIN THE STORY

A character within the story offers a more partisan and limited perspective routed through what characters in the tale experience, see, hear, and understand.

- The *naïve narrator* is someone (like Forrest Gump) who doesn't understand all the implications of his or her situation.
- The *knowing narrator* may pretend naïveté but be more acute than he or she lets on.
- The *epic hero* is at the sharp end of competency—someone such as Homer's Odysseus or Superman—who is cunning, heroic, or superhuman in some other way. In *film noir* the epic hero is typically the cool detective whose only vulnerability is a pretty woman in trouble.

TYPES OF NARRATIVE AND NARRATIVE TENSION

There are two classes of narrative in literature:

- *Simple narrative*, which is primarily functional and supplies an exposition of events, usually in chronological order. Simple narrative exists to inform.
- *Plot-driven narrative*, which may depart from chronology to reveal the events according to the story's type and plot strategy. Plot-driven narrative sets out to entertain by generating tension.

In literature, a rich source of tension lies between the story's elements and the attitudes the storyteller implies or manifests toward them. In all storytelling, withholding information is an important way to generate tension.

POINT OF VIEW IN FILM

Screen language has some advantages over literature but also some major handicaps. Although the screen image's comprehensiveness allows it to set up a situation and a mood in seconds, thereby dispensing with literature's lengthy tracts of exposition, photography's indiscriminate inclusiveness presents the eye with a bewildering catalogue of detail. Part of the function of framing, camera movement, and editing is to keep the eye where it should be and to discourage it from wandering off into byways. When wandering is encouraged, as in Antonioni's *L'Avventura* (1959), the environment begins to overwhelm the characters.

To successfully disentangle the subject from a surfeit of detail, a film must therefore direct the audience's attention. A caricaturist would face the same problem if requested to work through life photography instead of line drawing.

The "insistently descriptive nature of the film image," as James Monaco puts it, "inundates both subject and subtext with irrelevant detail. Ideas and authorial clarity are therefore harder to achieve in film than in literature." When I first saw Terence Malick's *Days of Heaven* (1978) in the cinema I saw a beautiful and moving film, but only by viewing it later on a television monitor did I fully grasp its underlying themes and allusions. The reduced image and greater prominence of sound allowed me to look *into* rather than *at* it.

Because cinema relies on montage to channel our attention, the natural strategy for its narrative style is an omniscient POV with occasional forays into individual characters' viewpoints. Indeed there is said to be only one pure character-within-the-film POV movie, the actor-director Robert Montgomery's 1947 mystery *The Lady in the Lake*, in which the camera is the detective Philip Marlowe and characters address the camera when talking to him. We see him only when he looks at himself in the mirror.

Fiction films need the advantages of omniscience, but since German Expressionist times, films have freely used the power of a psychologically subjective vantage point. It remains easier to imply what a character notices and feels than for the audience to explore what the character feels. Let's look at the variations in POV available to the filmmaker and examine their authorial implications.

CONTROLLING

The controlling point of view in a film is usually that of a central character. In *Anna Karenina* it would probably be Anna's but it could be Karenin's or anyone else's. In the novel *Wuthering Heights*, the story is ostensibly told by a sympathetic servant who acts as a surrogate mother in a motherless household.

Like literature, film often temporarily switches POV whenever the shift usefully augments the viewer's perceptions. This can be achieved through parallel action (cutting to another story happening concurrently) or by an angle or subjective coverage that places us with the alternate character. Still more subtly, the switch can be made by an interaction that invokes our sympathy and needs no attention-shifting technique such as a special angle or shot. POV is, after all, intended to create an empathic insight into a character's feelings and thoughts—it isn't only concerned with what he or she sees.

Some films, like Truffaut's *Jules and Jim* (1962) or Alan Pakula's *Sophie's Choice* (1982), use a character's first-person voice-over narration to drive the film and locate its focus. Where there is no verbal narration, the controlling POV is seldom made so obvious. More often such films follow the lead of omniscient literature and locate POV in the consciousness of the person or persons at the center of the work. An example is Lewis Carroll's Alice passing through the looking glass and entering a world of inverted logic that we experience from her perspective. To the child in us, *Alice Through the Looking Glass*'s looming, swollen personages are alarming magnifications of those encountered in our own childhood. Alice's bizarre world takes most of our attention, but the way she copes with it helps us see empathically into her psyche. What she confronts, and how she deals with it, are the two sides of a single coin, which is why content and form are so inseparable.

This is more easily seen in Victor Fleming's *The Wizard of Oz* (1939). When Dorothy makes a journey, like Alice's, through a bewitched landscape, she is joined by the Lion, the Tin Man, and the Scarecrow—alter egos whom she inspires to continue but who represent the threatened aspects of Dorothy's Self. When she awakens at the end of the movie we understand that her dream has been the means of reordering aspects of herself. Oz is therefore the setting for an allegorical quest for selfhood in which she seeks answers she needs in her "real" life on the farm.

Alice and Dorothy, the locus of attention in their particular worlds, become surrogates for ourselves, each heroine acting as a lens of temperament. As so often in narrative, each character's journey begins after irreversibly crossing a threshold (as in Joseph Campbell's analysis of folk stories), each becomes a lens into their world, and each initiates, then passes, trials that prove essential to their maturity.

Many films establish powerful worlds through the eyes of vulnerable young people, notably de Sica's *Bicycle Thief* (1949), Ray's *Pather Panchali* (1954), Truffaut's *400 Blows* (1959), Saura's *Cria* (1977), Schlöndorff's *The Tin Drum* (1979), Babenco's *Pixote* (1981) (Figure 12–1), Bergman's *Fanny and Alexander* (1983), John Boorman's *Hope and Glory* (1987), and many recent Iranian films, most notably those of Abbas Kiarastami. In the American cinema, M. Night Shyamalan's *Sixth Sense* (1999) is outstanding for the haunted state of mind of its 9-year-old central character, Cole.

A few films that create powerful worlds through an adult's point of view are Truffaut's *The Story of Adèle H.* (1975), Resnais' *Providence* (1977) (Figure 12–2), Wenders' *Paris, Texas* (1984), Forman's *Amadeus* (1984), Paul Leduc's *Frida* (1987) (Figure 12–3), and Jane Campion's unnervingly visceral *The Piano* (1993).

VARIATIONS

POV variations show the physical viewpoint of a secondary character and elicit an alternative emotional understanding, that is, they make us feel what another character may be feeling at a particular moment. Good fiction brings minor characters alive, reminding us that they, too, have lives, feelings, and agendas to fulfill.

BIOGRAPHICAL

A biographical point of view implies the critical study of a central character who stands for larger qualities and ideas. Werner Herzog's *Kasper Hauser* (1974) focuses on the progress of a famous person who emerged after being kept isolated in a pig sty throughout his youth. The film's philosophical contentions emerge from Kasper's collisions with different small-town factions and by amassing a catalogue of their reactions. Boldly and poetically, the film imparts the violence of Kasper's sensations and the chaos of his inner life, beginning with a lyrical shot of a field of blowing corn. Over pastoral music a quotation is superimposed: "But can you not hear the dreadful screaming all around that people usually call silence?" At a stroke, Herzog establishes the juxtaposition of summer beauty and inner despair that will tear Kasper apart.

FIGURE 12–1

Survival through the eyes of a street urchin in Babenco's *Pixote* (1981, courtesy New Yorker Films).

In the simple narrative sections we see Kasper objectively in his interactions with others, but Herzog's issue-driven plot and his use of music imply what Kasper feels and cause us to infer Kasper's subjective experience. Herzog the storyteller frames and juxtaposes these viewpoints and intersperses sections of textual quotation to imply that Kasper is an undefended and innocent Everyman. This makes an impassioned and poetical comparison between the nobility of a human's potential and the muddle and corruption we call civilization. What could be more movingly appropriate from someone who grew up in Nazi Germany?

CHARACTER WITHIN THE FILM

A film's apparent vantage point may come from a character within the film who directs us through the events, sometimes by narrating them. Some of the most moving guides are children. In Malick's *Days of Heaven* (1978) the fugitive's young sister provides voice-over narration. The country lawyer's daughter is the narrator of Mulligan's *To Kill a Mockingbird* (1963), and the boy houseguest writing in his diary narrates Losey's *The Go-Between* (1971). In Truffaut's *Jules and Jim* (1961) the narrator is a novelist and participant in the love triangle. His

FIGURE 12–2

A novelist transforms his family into the characters of dark fiction in Resnais' *Providence* (1977, courtesy Almi Distributors).

limitations and distorted perceptions make us aware of his subjectivity and vulnerability, creating a rising sense of dramatic pressure. A character in extremity may perceive magic and monsters, and to portray these is really to dramatize that character's state of mind.

MAIN CHARACTER'S IMPLIED POINT OF VIEW

Omniscient cinema characters and their issues are often established through a meaningful juxtaposition of realistic events. Their world is "normal" and undistorted by how they perceive it. The coolness and distance of this mode allow the audience to think as much as feel. Audience members long remain nonidentifying observers but eventually merge with the main characters through empathy. Jiri Menzel's *Closely Watched Trains* (1966) is about a youth adapting to his first job in a railroad station. Obsessed by the shameful fact of his virginity, he finds himself surrounded by the sex lives of others. This seems more the humor of the gods than a situation he has influenced. Tony Richardson's *A Taste of Honey* (1961), on the other hand, focuses on a provincial teenager who gets pregnant at a time of great loneliness, is abandoned by the baby's father, and then is befriended for a while by a homosexual boy. As it shows how she is led by raw emotion from one situation to another, the film credits her destiny to the random interaction of environment, chance, and character. Her world, like that

FIGURE 12–3

Leduc's highly visual *Frida*: love and art through the transcendent vision of the Mexican painter Frida Kahlo (1987, courtesy New Yorker Films).

of the young Czech railwayman, is still an alien environment with which she must struggle, but she bears more responsibility for her destiny. Strangely, this film (on which I worked as cutting room assistant) lost some of its documentary power in transition from the first raw material of the dailies to edited final version. Editing increases what we can see but fragments the inherent power of a moment.

Each of Hitchcock's two most famous films hinges on the fallibility of a POV character's judgment. In *Rear Window* (1954) an injured photographer confined to his room is compelled to look at the building opposite and becomes so convinced that a murder has taken place that he takes on some of the guilt of the murderer. In *Psycho* (1960) Marion Crane battles to deny her instincts that something malign is afoot in the Bates Motel. In each case, the audience must constantly decide the nature of reality in relation to appearances, until at the end Hitchcock provides the famous keys that unlock the suspense.

DUAL

In Malick's *Badlands* (1974), Penn's *Bonnie and Clyde* (1967), and Godard's *Pierrot le Fou* (1965), the subjects are partnerships and so there are two POV characters. All three films involve road journeys that end in self-destruction. In the two American films, the partnerships seem to exist to define male and female roles within a dissident or criminal subculture, while Godard's work uses the same self-immolating subculture as a vehicle to explore the incompatibilities between male and female psyches. Each film studies the tensions generated among characters and uses the way each step is (or is not) resolved to energize the next move. *Pierrot le Fou* in particular makes a rewarding study of dramatic form because character and dramatic tension are developed from action between the characters rather than from pressures applied externally by the chase.

Wim Wenders' *Alice in the Cities* (1974) (Figure 12–4) is another journey, but the dialogue is between characters initially quite unequal: a 9-year-old girl and a reluctant journalist helping her search for her grandmother. Managing to avoid the pitfalls of kitsch sentiment, the film explores the initial gulf between adults and children. By creating two lost and uncertain characters of wonderful dignity, it shows how adults and children can achieve trust and emotional parity.

MULTIPLE

In Alain Tanner's *Jonah Who Will be 25 in the Year 2000* (1976), Altman's *Nashville* (1975), and later in his *Gosford Park* (2001), a dominant POV is

FIGURE 12–4

A child's and an adult's world compared in Wenders' *Alice in the Cities* (1974, courtesy Museum of Modern Art/Film Stills Archive).

deliberately excluded because each character exists as a fragment within a mosaic. All three films have a cast of characters reaching into double figures, and all focus on the patterns that emerge during a collective endeavor rather than on the consciousness and destiny of any individual. This concern with the flow and interaction of collective destiny can also be seen in Quentin Tarantino's *Pulp Fiction* (1994) and Paul Thomas Anderson's *Magnolia* (1999). Both are concerned with coincidence and irony.

AUTHORIAL

A film's authorial POV is difficult to separate from its characters' individual points of view, but here, for the sake of argument, are three very different films—each dealing with ideas about humanity rather than the individuality of any protagonist. Orson Welles' *Citizen Kane* (1941) teases us with the enigma of a dead person's character by focusing on reporters trying to assemble a portrait of a deceased newspaper magnate. Charles Foster Kane is a mystery to be unraveled, a great man whose driving motives remain tantalizingly obscure to the little people in his shadow. Welles has a key to Kane's mood of unassuageable deprivation and shows it only to the audience. Through the symbol of a sled, epitomizing the loss of Kane's home as a boy, Welles clinches his argument that pain fuels human creativity.

Pedro Almodóvar's films have the common qualities of speeded-up farce, melodramatic plots, and a penchant for characters who seem to be parodying themselves. Yet among his druggie girls, harried housewives, battling lesbians, and streetwise prostitutes, there is a real humanity. In *All About My Mother* (1999) he focuses on a mother and teenage son whose father has become a transvestite prostitute. All of Almodóvar's customary circus takes place, but a clear and touching vision emerges of love between unlikely partners, with a message that kindness and loyalty are paramount even in a world of freaks.

Ethan and Joel Coen's *O Brother Where Art Thou?* (2000) takes the journey motif of Homer's *Odyssey* and makes it the story of escaped convicts in Depression-era Mississippi. The focus is on the epic hero who is able to wriggle out of every confrontation, including a memorable encounter with the Ku Klux Klan. Featuring a fabulous bluegrass music track, the film calls on every stereotype of the period to demonstrate how legends are spun.

These storyteller POV films, concerned with the mapping of cause and effect, employ characters to exemplify patterns of behavior rather than to be objects of sympathy, although of course we must sympathize with the characters to care about the ideas they exemplify. The same might be said of Hitchcock's films, which dwell on the subtle, misleading interplay of human constants rather than seeking to confer recognition on human individuality. Hitchcock is a polemicist whose passions are more of the head than the heart.

Where a director's intelligence and character are repeatedly stamped in a body of work, you can trace the recurring signs of vision and philosophy. This we think of as the directorial POV. Like that of a character, this POV may be interestingly polarized and in conflict. A storyteller like the novelist F. Scott Fitzgerald, who also wrote for Hollywood, may create a world of which he disapproves. Though Fitzgerald participated enthusiastically in the hedonism of the

1920s flapper generation, part of him loathed its privileges and egocentricity, and this ambivalence fuelled his writing. Such ambivalent critique by an artist is not unusual.

AUDIENCE

There is still another POV to be considered—that of the audience, which assesses the storyteller, his or her cinematic tale, and the assumptions the film expresses. To look at a patriotic World War II film is to experience an eerie gap between our values and those guiding the film. Individually and collectively, we as an audience have our own cultural and historical perspective into which we fit the entirety of an artwork. Enclosed with the work is the authorial frame of reference by which it was originally fashioned.

SUMMING UP

POV can be likened to the enclosing nature of Russian dolls.

- The audience's POV encloses the storyteller's (or film's) POV.
- The storyteller's POV encloses the characters' POV.
- The POV character's viewpoint embraces that of the subsidiary characters.
- Each character, however, holds up a mirror to the others.

POV emerges by default in run-of-the-mill films and results from the subject at hand and the idiosyncrasies of the actors and team that made the film. POV is difficult but important to bring under control, and probably the most practical approach is to think in terms of thematic statement and applied subjectivity. To expose this we might ask the following questions at any point while planning how to tell the tale:

- What belief or outlook does the story seek to express?
- From whom or what does this thematic concern emerge?
- Who is the main character and what makes him or her important?
- Whose mind is doing most of the seeing?
- What are the idiosyncrasies in the way they see?
- What disparity is revealed between their world and that of others?
- What is the function of a particular moment of subjective revelation?

This chapter discussed four different POV dimensions. Starting within the film frame and backing away toward the audience, we find them in the following order.

MAIN CHARACTER(S') OR CONTROLLING POINT OF VIEW

When shown from his or her POV, the main character's subjectivity affects the mood of both what is shown and how it is shown. This controlling POV influences both content and form of the film and shows up in a number of ways:

- It may be explicit, in the form of a character who speaks as a narrator to the audience.
- More often it is implicit, as the audience empathizes with a particular character or characters.
- Usually artful *mise en scène* (directing, scene design, and blocking) contributes heavily (see Chapter 29: Mise en Scène Basics).
- The film may feature a retrospective POV (the body of the film is perhaps a diary or memoir).
- A character may directly address the audience.

SUBSIDIARY CHARACTERS' POINTS OF VIEW

The subjectivity of subsidiary characters is called upon when useful to heighten or counterpoint that of the main character. Sometimes a movie lacks a central character or characters and concentrates on a texture of equal points of view.

AUTHORIAL OR STORYTELLER'S POINT OF VIEW

Authorship of a film is a collective effort, like that of an orchestra under a conductor, so the origin of authorial viewpoints remains uncertain. Authorial POV has two main polarities that often overlap:

- A personal or *auteur* POV may be the means by which the film expresses a central personality and attitude toward the characters and their story.
- Authorial POV may be vested more diffusely in the handling of archetypes and archetypal forms in genres such as the film noir or the western.

AUDIENCE POINT OF VIEW

This is the critical distance the audience senses between itself and the film. Films that seek to engulf the audience in sensation often manipulate the viewers to *identify* with (lose their identity in) a heroic figure and thus try to annihilate the audience's critical faculties. Other kinds of film follow the lead of Eisenstein (or Brecht in the theater) by stressing that the cinema is a construct, not a substitute reality. The polemicist blocks the spectators' tendency toward identifying and invites them instead to take on a heightened and critical awareness.

CHAPTER 13

GENRE, CONFLICT, AND DIALECTICS

MAKING THE VISIBLE SIGNIFICANT

Memorable cinema communicates an integrated point of view not just as the occasional garnish by subjective camera angle or interior monologue, but as a feeling of access to a fellow spirit's inward eye and outward vision. We're not talking about heroic and idealized characters enshrined by the star system, but rather the kind of cinema that makes you see unfinished business in your life or society.

How else can you go about reflecting such things on the screen? Robert Richardson defines the heart of the problem: "Literature often has the problem of making the significant somehow visible, while film often finds itself trying to make the visible significant" (*Literature and Film*, Bloomington, Indiana: Indiana University Press, 1973, Chapter 5, p. 68). Film's surfeit of realistic detail is inclined to deter the audience from looking any deeper than the surfaces rendered so minutely and attractively by the camera. This can lead to simplistic valuations. There are many subtle ways, of course, that film authorship can draw our attention to a film's subtext, but without using film language astutely, an underlying discourse can go completely unnoticed.

The fiction film, the documentary, and the short story have something in common. All are consumed at a sitting and so perhaps carry on the oral tradition, which at one time constituted (along with religion) the entirety of the ordinary person's education. Like the oral tale, these forms seem best suited to representing history that is personally felt and experienced rather than issues and ideas in abstraction. Any short, immediate form must entertain if it is to connect with the emotional and imaginative life of a mass audience. Like all entertainers, the filmmaker either understands the audience or goes hungry. Richardson argues convincingly that the vitality and optimism of the cinema, in contrast to other

20th-century art forms, is a result of its collaborative authorship and dependence on public response.

The cinema's strength and popularity lie with its power to make an audience see and feel from someone else's point of view. In the cinema we see through different eyes and experience visions other than our own. For significant sections of the world, recently divested of thousands of years of spiritual beliefs, this is a reminder of community and of something beyond self whose value cannot be underestimated. Just as importantly, the best cinema is relativistic, that is, it allows us to experience other related but opposing points of view. Used responsibly, this is an immensely civilizing force to offset the conformity imposed by merchandisers striving to convert us into a compliant admass.

OPTIONS

Anyone planning even the shortest film must make fundamental aesthetic choices at the outset. These are by no means completely free because all films depend on screen conventions. There are choices in screen language, but other choices are driven by the type of story. Storytelling has deep roots that precede film, printing, and even written history. Let's examine the notion of story as it reaches us from the screen.

At its best, the screen exercises our consciousness so successfully that a recently seen movie can afterward feel more like personal experience. Through the screen we enter an unfamiliar world or see the familiar in a new way. We share the intimate being of people who are braver, funnier, stronger, angrier, more beautiful, more vulnerable, or more beset with danger and tragedy than we are. Two hours of concentrating on a good movie is 2 hours during which we set aside the apparent unchangeability of our own lives, assume other identities, and live through a different reality. This world can be wonderfully dark and depressing, light and idealizing, or one that plumbs the unanswered questions of the present with wit and intelligence. We emerge from a good movie energized and refreshed in spirit.

This cathartic contact with the trials of the human spirit is a human need no less fundamental than eating, breathing, or making love. It is what helps us to live fully. In our daily lives an excess of emotional movement or a lack of it will send us to the arts looking for reflected light. Quite simply, art, of which the cinema is the newest form, nourishes us in spirit by engaging us in surrogate emotional experience and implying what patterns lie behind it. It helps us make sense of our past, deal with our present, and prepare us for what might await us in our future. It shows us that what seemed isolatingly personal is really inside the mainstream of human experience. Art allows us to pass into new realities, become *other*, and return to ourselves knowing more about the human family.

All art grows out of what went before it, even when the artist is deemed highly original. This means that you must choose an area in which to work, a language through which to speak to an audience, and perhaps some changes or variations you want to make to the genre. Pushing the envelope of form cannot be done unless you are intimate with conventions and why they exist.

GENRE AND POINT OF VIEW

Realism presents a story in documentary fashion as a set of interesting events in a world we accept as real or typical. Other genres project us into special worlds running under particular conditions. A slapstick or screwball comedy, a gothic romance, or a *film noir* each has emphases and limitations that are well understood by the audience. These arise from the area of life the genre deals with, but also from the heightened and selective perceptions of its protagonists. There is nothing inherently unreal, untruthful, or distorted about a genre once you accept that in life, people not only contend with reality but also create it through the force of their own perceptions. If "character is fate," then a collection of characters can collusively create their own reality. History and the newspapers are full of examples.

We enjoy genres like historical romance, sci-fi, or buddy movies because we need to experience worlds beyond the suffocatingly rational one of everyday life. Sometimes we need to enter a "what if" world running under selectively altered circumstances. We buy into it by emotional choice, just as we learn the most vivid lessons from emotional immersion rather than from intellectual instruction. Watching Tolstoy's *Anna Karenina*, we expect to enter the adulterous heroine's sufferings, not simply be told she is immoral. We want to know how it feels to be a young woman married to a stuffy older man, to feel isolated and loveless, and then to be approached by a romantic admirer. What does it feel like to be tempted—and then viewed by society as the temptress?

When a movie is good, we imaginatively experience these conditions and come away expanded in mind and heart. To make this happen, the cinema must project us into a main character's *emotional* predicament, for our main and perhaps only desire is to inhabit the worlds of others. In a love triangle like *Anna Karenina* there is more than one emotional situation because separate and different perceptions are possible by each character—that is, Anna's, her husband's, and her lover, Vronsky's. With the husband, Karenin, we might view Anna's liaison as a betrayal; with Vronsky, as a romantic adventure that turns sour; and with Anna, feel night turn into brightest day, then change into a long, bloody sunset.

A story has dimensions beyond those understood by its protagonists. In *Anna Karenina* there is the overarching watchfulness of the storyteller, Tolstoy, and still others superimposed by anyone subsequently reinterpreting the novel. Altered perspectives often require no change in the interactions specified by the original novel. They simply impose a slant or filter drawn from a contemporary mood or conviction.

Finally, as discussed previously, the audience brings a POV to the piece. This is affected by national culture, as well as social, economic, or other contexts. A Chinese village audience does not interpret the film the same way as a San Francisco or Turin audience does. Stories, domestic or foreign, are consumed by a culture to find reflected aspects and meanings for itself, which is why a Shakespeare play can be set in recent times and still resonate loudly in modern India.

To control a genre, a director must know what the special conditions of that genre are, and how to create and handle points of view within the film

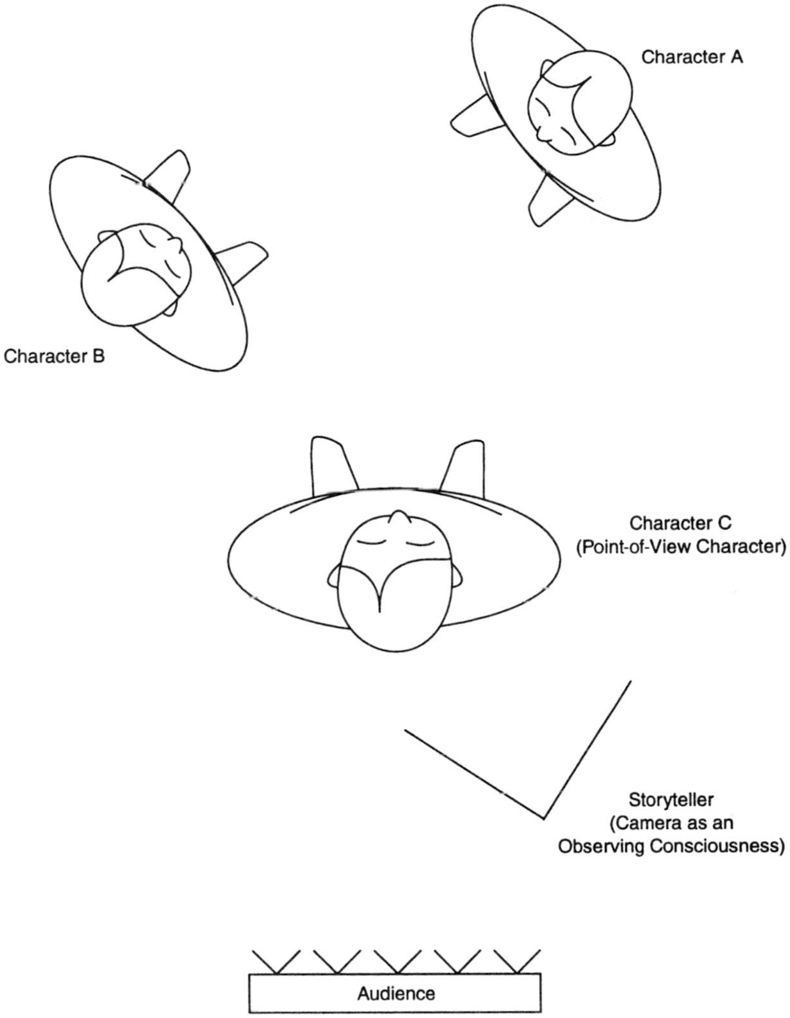

FIGURE 13–1

Diagram of characters, POV character, and storyteller.

to build the subjectivity of a special world. The director must analyze a story or screenplay and know whose subjectivity is important at any given point (Figure 13–1).

GENRE AND DRAMATIC ARCHETYPES

In French, *genre* simply means kind, type, or sort, and in English the word is used to describe films that can be grouped together. James Monaco's *How to Read a Film* (New York: Oxford University Press, 2000) lists under *genre*:

black film	gangster film	thriller
buddy film	horror film	war film
chase	melodrama	westerns
comedy (screwball)	musicals	youth
detective story	samurai	
film noir	science fiction	

For television it lists:

action shows	docudrama	soap opera
cop shows	families	
comedy (sitcom)	professions shows	

Each category is archetypal because it contains characters, roles, or situations somewhat familiar to the audience. Each therefore promises to explore *a known world running under familiar rules and limitations.* The buddy film is usually about same-sex friendships, though it may contain works as diverse as Kramer's *The Defiant Ones* (1958), Hill's *Butch Cassidy and the Sundance Kid* (1969), and Hughes' *Planes, Trains and Automobiles* (1988). Ridley Scott's *Thelma and Louise* (1991) is a female version.

The gangster film, the sci-fi film, and the screwball comedy all embody subjects and approaches that function dependably within preordained limits. Screen archetypes have their roots in a cultural history infinitely longer than that of the cinema. Audiences have always craved alternatives to realism, so it is hardly surprising that horror and fantasy have been staples throughout cinema's short history. They are cinema's variation on folk tales and folk drama, forms through which humankind still indulges its appetite for demons, ogres, wizards, and phantom carriages. Under the guise of futurism, Schaffner's *Planet of the Apes* (1968) and Lucas' *Star Wars* (1977) are really old-fashioned morality plays whose settings obscure, but do not efface, their ancient origins. Even the revolutionary Godard in *A Woman Is a Woman* (1961) explores well-worn ground in his young couple setting up house together, but it's done with characteristic humor and playfulness (Figure 13–2).

Though fiction cinema allows you to vicariously experience most imaginable fates, there has been a conspicuous silence on nuclear attack and on the Holocaust, at least until Spielberg's *Schindler's List* (1994). Even so, the film focuses on one of the few uplifting stories to emerge from that period of brutality and shame. True horror, it would seem, is nothing we really care to contemplate.

Comedy in its different forms offers worlds with constants to which we can turn with anticipation. Chaplin, Keaton, Mae West, W.C. Fields, Red Skelton, Laurel and Hardy, as well as Tati, Lucille Ball, Woody Allen, John Cleese, and Steve Martin all play types of characters that are recognizable from film to film. Each new situation and dilemma pressures a familiar and unchanging personality with a new set of comic stresses.

Comedy's underlying purpose is said to be making audiences laugh at their own deepest anxieties and trauma. Harold Lloyd hanging from Manhattan skyscrapers and Chaplin working frantically to keep up with a production line or playing the dictator are obvious examples. But recent sex comedies in which women take over male preserves, homosexual couples take on parenthood, or sitcoms involving men taking over women's roles and identity all confirm how comedy functions as a safety valve for anxieties about social change.

FIGURE 13–2

The human condition according to Jean-Luc Godard in *A Woman Is a Woman* (1961, courtesy Museum of Modern Art/Film Stills Archive).

That audiences should want to vicariously investigate anxiety, fear, or deprivation is easier to understand than other kinds of experimenting. The sexploitation film with its portrayal of women as willing objects of misogynistic violence and the "slasher" film portraying sadistic brutality prompt disturbing questions about manipulation and responsibility for the darker side of the (mostly male) human imagination. Perhaps secular, middle-class living has so effectively banished fear and uncertainty that we recreate the primitive and supernatural to allay that worst of all bourgeois ills: terminal boredom.

Brecht's question remains. Is art a mirror to society or a hammer working on it? Does art reflect what is, or does it create it? The answers are likely to vary with the makers of the artwork, and with history and even the age of those involved. What we can say with confidence is that in every period and in every part of the world, art has supplied a surrogate experience to exercise hearts and minds. Sometimes actuality is dramatic and mysterious enough on its own (as during war or an unimaginable event like the World Trade Center destruction); at other times we gravitate toward works presenting elaborate metaphors for our condition, particularly as we approach taboos.

But how does the poor filmmaker, surrounded by the paraphernalia of scripts, budgets, and technical support, know when to abandon the kitchen sink realism so generic to photography? What we need are guidelines to put individual perception into a manageable frame. I wish there were a magic formula, but instead we must talk about dialectic worlds animated by the creative tensions of opposition.

DUALITY AND CONFLICT

Have you ever received one of those photocopied family newsletters around Christmas time?

> The Russell News for the Year
>
> David received his promotion to area manager but now has a longer drive to work. Betty has completely redecorated the dining room (with an avocado theme!) after successfully completing her interior decorator course at Mallory School of the Arts. Terry spent the summer camping and canoeing and thoroughly enjoyed being a camp counselor. In the fall he learned he had a place at Hillshire University to study molecular biology. In spite of what the doctor said, Joanne has successfully adapted to contact lenses. . . .

What makes this insufferable is that the writer insists on presenting life as a series of happy, logical steps. In the Russell photo album, everyone faces the camera wearing a smile. There will be nothing candid, spontaneous, or disturbing. The newsletter events are not untrue, but the selection method renders them lifeless, especially if you happen to know that David's drinking problem is getting worse.

By avoiding all hint of conflict, the account is rendered insipid. It totally suppresses the dissent, doubt, and eccentricity that makes every family turbulent. Family life is like a pond; calm on the surface but containing all the forces of warring nature below the surface. So, too, is an individual. A person's life does not move forward in linear steps like an adding machine. Instead it moves like a flying insect in a zigzag pattern formed by conflicting needs and random conditions. Joanne Russell needs her mother's emotional support, but cannot bear the way she criticizes her. Terry Russell wants to go to college, but dreads leaving friends and home behind him. Each has conflicting feelings over these issues, and each feels contradictory impulses in dealing with them.

The individual psyche is like a raft on the ocean moving irregularly under the conflicting wills of those (the passions) rowing on all four sides. Most row peaceably together in one direction, but a few dissidents struggle to send the raft in their own direction. Imagine now several such rafts in conflict with each other, and you have a family.

MICROCOSM AND MACROCOSM

Because drama reproduces on a large scale the warring elements found in an individual, the screenwriter could make drama from something like an exploded diagram of a single human being. By selecting aspects of the complex subject's personality (usually modeled to his or her own) and expanding them into separate characters, one can be set in conflict with the others. This takes what would normally be an internal and mental struggle and transforms it into outwardly visible action—so necessary for the screen.

Conversely, when a diffuse, complex situation needs to be presented coherently, it can be miniaturized by reversing the process to make the macrocosm a microcosm. Oliver Stone's *Wall Street* (1988) concentrates and simplifies trends in the stockbrokering industry into a parable. A young stockbroker is seduced into illegal practices by the charisma of a powerful and amoral mentor. His counterbalancing influence is his pragmatic, working-class father. Interestingly, a similar configuration of influences vie for the hero's soul in Stone's *Platoon* (1987). In each case, a complex and otherwise confusing situation is simplified and made accessible because characters are created to represent moral archetypes. As the Everyman central character makes choices, we see him tempered in the flame of experience.

If you make a character into a torchbearer for a human quality, take care that he or she doesn't become monolithic and flat. It is not enough for one quality to predominate; each character must be complex and facing some vital conflicts of his or her own.

HOW OUTLOOK AFFECTS VISION: DETERMINISM OR FREE WILL?

When a piece is character-driven, the storyteller's vision of the particular world will depend on the POV character. When the piece is plot-driven, the storyteller's vision will hinge more on settings, situations, and the idiosyncrasies of the plot. Temperamental and cultural factors also influence the filmmaker's choices. The political historian or social scientist, for instance, may see a naval battle as the interplay of inevitable forces, with victory or defeat being the result of the technology used and the different leaders' strengths and weaknesses. This is a deterministic view of human behavior that might produce a genre film. It is relatively detached and objective and will express itself similarly whether it works through comedy, mystery, or psychological thriller.

Other dramatists, concerned with the individuality of human experience, treat a battle differently—going below decks, looking into faces and hearts, and seeking out the conflicts within each ship and within each sailor, the great and the humble. Such a film might place us in the heat of battle to show not the constants in human history or the eternal repetition of human error, but the human potential inherent in moral choice. This kind of film is likely to show a more individual vision and a less predictable world because it wants to raise questions about character and potential rather than demonstrate the repetition of historical patterns.

Whether you show a deterministic world or one where individuals influence their destinies will be a matter of your temperament and the story you want to tell. It is also, as I say often, a matter of what *marks* life has made on you and therefore what stories you need to tell. Luckily there are many limitations on choice.

DRAMA, PROPAGANDA, AND DIALECTICS

Drama and propaganda handle duality differently: Drama sees the live organism of the sea battle while the propagandist, knowing before he starts where the truth lies, drives his audience single-mindedly through a token opposition to arrive at a prescribed victory. His drama is not a process of exploration but of jostling the spectator into accepting a predetermined outcome, much as salesmen's stories are directed at selling their merchandise. Television or cinema with a message arouses our defenses because we are being sold cheap goods under the guise of entertainment, and instinctively we resent it.

The dramatist, valuing the complexity, integrity, and organic quality of struggle and decision, treats audiences more respectfully. Truly dramatic writing evolves from exploring the author's fascination with particular ambiguities. To some degree it is always a journey toward an unknown destination. The absence of this quality makes most well-intentioned educational and corporate products stultifyingly boring. The makers have either forgotten or are incapable of recreating the sense of discovery. The viewer is treated like a jug, a passive receptacle to be filled with information, and not an active partner in discovery. The educator with a closed mind wants to condition us, not invoke our free-ranging intelligence. This is why art under totalitarianism comes from the dissidents, never the establishment.

We face a range of artificial oppositions between which any film will ambiguously be suspended. Here are those mentioned so far, as well as a few extra.

Either	**Or**
Auteur (personal, authorial stamp)	Genre (film archetype)
Subjective (character's) POV	Objective (storyteller's) POV
Non-realistic, stylized	Realistic
Duality requires audience judgment	Conflicts are generic and not analyzed
Conflicts are interpersonal	Conflicts are large-scale and societal
Conflicts are divergent and unresolved	Conflicts are convergent and resolved
Outcome uncertain	Outcome satisfyingly predictable but not reached without struggle

Notice that these columns are neither prescriptions for good and bad films, nor do many films fall into predominantly one column or the other. They are simply alternates. How do you decide which oppositions to invoke in your particular piece of storytelling?

At the point of deciding what story and what kind of world the protagonists of the story inhabit, it is unimportant. This will emerge later. What matters is to keep in mind that everything or everybody interesting always has contradictions at the center, and that every story must be routed through the intelligence experiencing the story as it unfolds. We have personified this intelligence as the Concerned Observer.

BUILDING A WORLD AROUND THE CONCERNED OBSERVER

You will recall that, relieved of corporeal substance, the Observer is invisible and weightless like a spirit and sees all the significant aspects of the characters. Feeling for them, the Observer sometimes leaves the periphery to fly into the center of things, but remains mobile and involved and always in search of greater significance and larger patterns of meaning.

Developing empathy with the characters and knowledge of them, the Observer passes through a series of experiences that invoke identification with the characters, strain his or her powers of understanding, and stress his or her emotions. Following are some invented examples for discussion.

SURVIVAL FILM

You have set your film in the rubble after World War III. You have chosen to use realism to allow the audience no escape and to make the audience identify with a family that has survived through a freak occurrence. There are some interpersonal conflicts (over what is the best direction to follow in search of water), but most of the struggle is between the family and the hostile environment. The trials faced are for survival and involve bravery and ingenuity rather than self-knowledge and human judgment. You want your audience to be affected by the bleakness of the environment, the tragedy of humankind having wiped itself out, and the futility of your lone family's efforts. Their hope is to meet others. Their fear is not finding enough food or shelter to survive an endless winter. You want to show the resourcefulness and compassion of a family unit under extreme duress.

LOTTERY WINNER FILM

An elderly widower goes from genteel poverty to stupendous wealth by winning the lottery. He decides to indulge his two best friends with everything they have ever wanted. Each, according to his minor flaws, becomes distorted by the bounty in a major way, and each finds that getting what you want brings more trouble than it is worth. In the end the three are forced to separate and begin new lives apart.

Here you can show three different characters in three different phases of reality, all very subjective, and you can occasionally drop back to a more objective storyteller's mode. The conflicts each character suffers are mostly internal—over suddenly having to opt for what makes them happy. There is much doubt and self-examination and perhaps conflict among the three friends as they find themselves in deep waters. The lottery winner feels responsible, and often we will see things through his eyes. The world, which is first a desert, becomes a cornucopia of delights; then it becomes complicated and troublesome. The lottery winner finds he likes his friends less and less until they all agree to give up the life they have taken on. The price of affluence is isolation.

Your intention is to show how security and a sense of self-worth comes from facing problems, and that people fall on their faces when there is nothing left to push against. This is a subtle subject, for it shows how fragile people become when accommodating an excess of good fortune.

Neither of the above are unusual subjects, yet the world you show and the roles in which you place the audience enable you to create a progression of experiences that explore the human condition. The same would be true for any form of film you choose, provided you decide not only upon the characters' careers, but also the role of the subjective, watching audience—a role that normally emerges by default rather than by conscious design.

OBSERVER INTO STORYTELLER

While the literary storyteller always tells a story that has already happened, the film storyteller summons us into a story that is happening here and now. In this respect, screen language is alien to human experience, for we never experience an account except through someone else's persona and in retrospect. Film violates this in two ways: One, we see through other eyes yet seem to see directly; two, we see in the present, not the past tense. This is clear from the example in a previous chapter of seeing someone's documentary coverage of his class reunion party. We experience the party happening not *then*, but here and now, and we have to remind ourselves that what we see is not objective truth but something filtered through a particular temperament.

Audiences and filmmakers resolve this psychic non sequitur by disregarding the storyteller—the subjective filter through which the world is seen in a certain way. Though you may not like every distinguished cinematic author such as Hitchcock, Godard, Resnais, Bergman, Fellini, Antonioni, Altman, Almodóvar, and Kiarastama, you never doubt whose hands you are in when watching one of their films. But much work for the cinema, and virtually all fiction made for television, lacks any individuality of vision whatsoever. As Mamet says, such movies are made "as a supposed record of what real people really did." A film of this kind is a faceless newsreel documenting the story and characters and at best does a good job of being a Concerned Observer. Mamet's knowledge does not save him from falling into the same trap when he directs, so understanding the problem is far from being the solution. I think the answer lies in three areas:

1. **Create a definite Storyteller:** A director must make the film's Storyteller have the subjectivity of a strong and interestingly biased personality, as is common to all effective storytelling voices. To obtain it for the film, the director must "play" the part while planning the film and directing it. That means imaginatively getting inside the storytelling sensibility like an actor. Any David Lynch film has a powerful sense of Lynch's storytelling presence. When such a subjective vision is there from the beginning all the way through shooting, a good editor will recognize it with delight and work to enhance it. Editors are usually trying to *create* the storytelling voice because it is absent.
2. **Take control:** The director must psychically control the filmmaking process, not be controlled by it. This is a matter of having a strongly realized design for everything and having the confidence, clarity, and obstinacy to get this vision realized during the production process. The more professional the crew and actors feel they are, the more likely is the tail to wag the dog when the director fails to impose the necessary POV.
3. **Aim to go somewhere:** With a destination in mind, you'll go where you aim. If you only want your film to look professional, you will eventually do so—but facelessly. Make your priority a good story seen in a specially discovered way, and you will be readily forgiven any lack of professionalism.

CHAPTER 14

STRUCTURE, PLOT, AND TIME

STRUCTURE

The definitive structure of a film results from the interplay of many considerations, starting with the script and its handling of time. However, during editing, a film may change drastically. Even the eventual shape of a single unit such as a sequence is determined late in the process by its dramatic content, composition, visual and aural rhythms, amount and complexity of movement within the frame, and length and placement of shots. Little of this can be more than hazily present in the filmmaker's mind at the outset. Therefore, the intention of this chapter is to deal only with the largest determinants of a movie's structure—plot, time, and thematic purpose.

Many filmmakers (though not general audiences) tend to resist the idea of a tightly plotted narrative because it can feel manipulative and contrived. When they find that screenwriting manuals prescribe three acts, each of a certain length, with page numbers specified for the *plot points* (points at which the story goes off at a tangent), many would-be screenwriters head for the hills. If such obsession with control over form seems reductive and formulaic, some context is missing from this picture. Nobody starts with the three-act form and the page numbers in mind. Writers begin with ideas, images, feelings, and perhaps some incidents in their own or a friend's life. The first draft may be in short story or outline form, or may be written as a treatment; every writer generates material however they can. Next, the writer figures out what *problems* the characters face and are trying to solve. This is usually very difficult, but once it is identified, the trajectory of a plot becomes clearer. Then the writer starts to story-edit using a dramatist's toolbox to spot the narrative elements and archetypes, and to assess how to increase their effectiveness.

These archetypes are as embedded in new stories as they are in old ones. Freud and Jung were highly conscious of them, and Joseph Campbell made it his life's work to trace them in world mythology and folk tales. Hollywood has come to similar conclusions by studying what audiences like. So much about film form is hotly debated, but, "if anything is natural," says Dudley Andrew "it is the psychic lure of narrative, the drive to hold events in sequence, to traverse them, to come to an end" (*Concepts in Film Theory*, New York: Oxford University Press, 1984). There are narrative and so-called non-narrative approaches to storytelling, but non-narrative cinema is not without structure. Consider this from a review of Richard Linklater's *Slacker* (1991):

> An original, narratively innovative, low budget movie from the fringe, *Slacker* is a perfectly plotless work that tracks incidental moments in the lives of some one hundred characters who have made the bohemian side of Austin, Texas, their hangout of choice. . . . The two forces that hold the film together are its clear sense of place (specifically Austin, more generally college towns) and its intimate knowledge of a certain character type; the "slacker". . . . But the film's improvisatory, meandering style is actually carefully constructed. (James Pallot and the editors of *The Movie Guide*, New York: Perigee, 1995)

Slackers is artfully constructed to complement Linklater's ideas about his characters and their values, but there are innumerable ways to pattern drama. Traditional Indian drama, dance, and music is often structured by a sequence of moods. Peter Greenaway's *A Zed and Two Noughts* (1985), which is structured around an operatic concatenation of events taking place between characters who work in a zoo, interweaves Greenaway's favorite fascinations: numbers, coincidence, philology, painting, wildlife, decay, and taxonomies—just to mention a few of the topics that help structure this bizarre film.

As long as audiences consume films in a linear fashion, an organizing structure and a premise will be inescapable. The over-formal Hollywood structure is really a paradigm abstracted from experience in cinemas, and that happens—not surprisingly perhaps—to reflect developments in the public consumption of the other time arts (dance, theater, music, radio, and television). Some central organizing factor is essential, especially for the short film, which, like poetry, must accomplish much in a brief time.

PLOT

The plot of a drama is the design that arranges or patterns the incidents befalling the characters. Michael Roemer in *Telling Stories* (Lanham, Maryland: Rowman & Littlefield, 1995, p. 39) says plot is "devised or constructed to manipulate, entertain, move, and surprise the audience." He equates the notion of plot with the sacred, the ineluctable rules of the universe against which the characters are fated to struggle. As proof of this, discussions about plot always seem to center on what is likely, what usually happens in such circumstances, and what, morally or ethically speaking, *should* happen.

Because a film cannot show everything that happens to its characters, it must select certain incidents and actions while implying a whole world outside its purview. By concentrating our attention, a film's plot therefore acts as a lens through which to focus authorial intentions.

The emphasis on plot may be light or heavy. Heavy plotting tends to stress the logical and deterministic side of life. In more character-driven drama, plot may be de-emphasized in favor of a looser and more episodic structure in which chance, randomness, and the imperatives of character play a larger part. When you develop an idea for a film, your sense of cause and effect in life is bound to be reflected in the type and degree of plotting you choose.

Though a film may ardently promote a theory of randomness in life, cause and effect cannot be random in regard to the language it must use. The relationships among shots, angles, characters, and environments in film language are fashioned according to film language precedents. And though you have some latitude to modify the language, there's no more randomness in the basics than with any other language. You have to use the rules of English if you are to be understood by English-speakers. Film language results from a historically developed collusion between filmmakers and audiences, but like all live languages, it is in evolution. Plot plays its part in the pact not just by reconciling the characters' motivations—why character A manipulates a confrontation with character B, for example—but by steering our attention to the issues at hand. It should also maintain the tension that keeps the movie moving forward by making us want to see more.

Because characters' temperaments largely determine their actions, plot must be consonant with character. Conversely, characters cannot be arbitrarily plugged into any plot because plot and character must work hand in hand. Certain characters do certain things, and unless this appears natural, the plot will be forced. As the story advances, each event must stand in logical and meaningful relationship to what went before and lead with seeming inevitability to what follows. Plot failures will be those weaknesses in the chain of logic that disrupt credibility and leave the audience confused or feeling cheated.

There is a distinction between how things happen in reality and what is permissible in drama. If in real life an oppressed, docile factory worker suddenly leaps to the center of a dangerous strike situation and averts a tragedy by delivering an inspired oratory, you will ponder what signs of latent genius his co-workers overlooked, but you cannot doubt it could happen. If, however, we base a fiction film on such material, our audience will reject this event as untrue to life. Because the film is fiction, we shall have to carefully rearrange or even add selected incidents to show that our hero's potential was visible (although nobody noticed it), and it took the pressure of particular events to free him up to realize it.

Common weaknesses found in plotting are an excessive reliance on coincidence, or on the *deus ex machina*, the improbable action or incident inserted to make things turn out right. Audiences sense when a dramatist forces a development in this way, so you must ask a great many searching questions of your screenplay to ensure that its plot is as tight and functional as good cabinetry and that each character is true to his or her nature.

The well-crafted plot has a sense of inevitable flow because it includes nothing gratuitous or facile. It generates a sense of energizing excitement, and each step—by obeying the logic of the characters and their situation—stimulates the spectator to actively speculate what will happen next. This desirable commodity, called *forward momentum* in dramaturgy, is something that everyone works hard to generate.

THEMATIC PURPOSE

The theme of a work is the topic of its discourse or representation. When directing, you need to be well aware of your film's intended final meaning or thematic purpose. Some features, meant for a materialist and secular audience, employ a realism that leaves little room for metaphysical suggestion, yet audiences—whether they know it or not—crave the resonance of deeper meanings and crave drama that contains the seeds of hope.

Former generations, reared on the allusions and poetry of religious texts, were more attuned to thinking on multiple levels, as also happens in repressive societies in which people get used to indirect communication and accustomed to sniffing out the veiled allusion smuggled past the nose of authority. The artist who wants to be noticed today must recapture this skill, which really means using poetic thinking to relay visions of what the world is or can be. Allegory and parable (from *parabola*, meaning curved plane or comparison) can hit a nerve in audiences very powerfully, as shown by Robert Zemeckis' otherwise predictable *Forrest Gump* (1994). Its theme is that the gods protect a man without guile, and all things eventually come right.

When considering the thematic purpose of a screenplay, it's helpful to fashion a graphic image or diagram to represent the movement of elements and characters in the story. The developmental curve for tragedy (Figure 14–1) is familiar to anyone who has studied dramaturgy, but you can create your own coordinates according to the story at hand. Figure 14–2 takes time as the horizontal axis and pressure on two characters as the vertical one, and it shows the development of an initially weak character in relation to a stronger one.

By making yourself translate from drama to a graph or other representation, you tackle the director's fundamental responsibility of making visible the film's underlying thesis, which can never be done except by deep and sustained

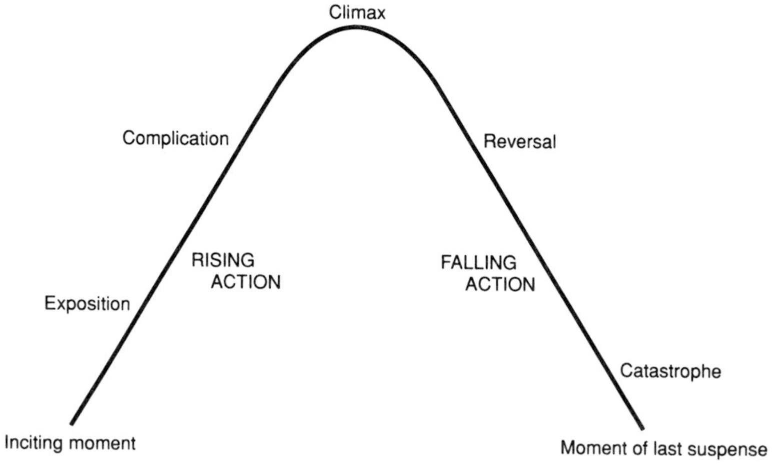

FIGURE 14–1

Development curve for the traditional tragedy.

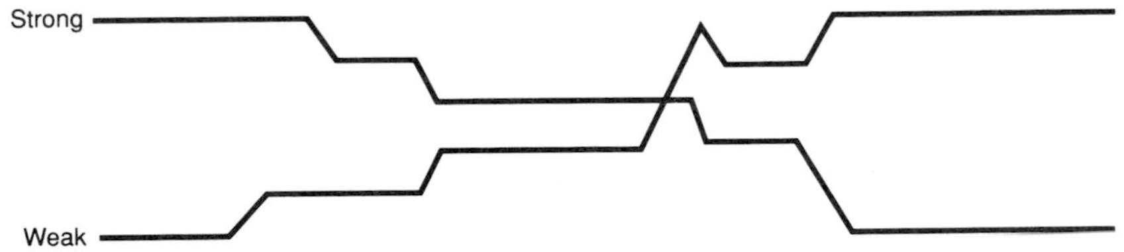

FIGURE 14–2

Graph representing the development of an initially weak character in relation to one stronger.

thinking—something we all avoid. An image for *The Wizard of Oz* (1939) could come from the way each of the characters exerts—for good or ill—different pressures on Dorothy, who metaphorically speaking is like the hub at the center of a spoked wheel. Movement in the film is like a journey during which the wheel revolves a number of times, with each spoke bearing on her more than once. The image usefully organizes ideas about how *The Wizard*'s thematic design applies a rotation of pressured experiences, each testing Dorothy's stamina and resourcefulness.

Drama put under pressure of inquiry will always yield additional thematic elements that cross-modulate within the larger pattern. Each work's full design emerges at the end of postproduction: A problem in editing turns out to be a misjudged scene that subtly disrupts and negates the overall pattern, and it must either be changed, moved, or eliminated. Often by discovering a disruptor, you establish harmony elsewhere, like one false note in an experimental chord progression that confirms by its wrongness the rightness of everything else.

Before you ever direct, make more than one detailed, written analysis of sequences or short films that move you (see Chapter 5: Seeing with a Moviemaker's Eye). True critical interaction will help enormously when you need to externalize the thematic development of a script you intend to film. During developmental work, follow the initial script, make a graphic representation of the whole film's changing pressures and development, and then write about it. As always, the act of writing will further develop what had initially seemed complete and devoid of further development potential. Defining a film's thematic progression in a script and representing it though action, symbol, and metaphor are major steps toward identifying a good structure for your film because theme and structure are symbiotic.

TIME

Every intended film has an optimal structure, one that will best represent the dramatic problem, its working out, and outcome. Arriving at it always involves deciding how to handle time. As with all design problems, less is more, and the simplest solution is usually the strongest.

LINEAR TIME

A linear time structure is one in which a film's sequences proceed through time in chronological order, though usually with unimportant passages removed. This produces a relatively cool, objective film because the narrative flow is not interrupted or redirected by plot intentions. Effect follows cause in a predictable and unchallenging arrangement.

Sometimes the conservative, linear approach does not do a story justice, though departing from it courts disorientation in your audience. Volker Schlöndorff's film of Heinrich Boll's novel *The Lost Honor of Katharina Blum* (1975) abandoned the novel's flash-forward technique as too complex, substituting a conventionally linear structure that unfortunately muted the novel's contemplative, inquiring voice. What emerged was a polemical film in the Costa-Gavras tradition.

NONLINEAR TIME AND THE PAST

Frequently a story's chronology is disrupted and blocks of time are rearranged to answer the subjective priorities of a character's recall or because the storyteller has a narrative purpose for reordering time. Resnais, perennially fascinated by the way the human memory edits and distorts time, intercut *Muriel* (1963) with 8 mm movie material from the Algerian war to create a series of flashback memory evocations. In his earlier *Hiroshima Mon Amour* (1959), the French woman and her Japanese lover increasingly recall (or are invaded by) memories of their respective traumas—his, the dropping of the bomb on Hiroshima; hers, a love affair with a German soldier in occupied France. These intrusions from the past are central to the present-day anguish suffered by each, and Resnais' premise implies that extreme lives are propelled by extreme trauma. The placing and frequency of these recollections indicate the movement of the characters' inner lives and provoke us into searching their developing love affair for what must be bringing these withheld memories to the surface. Both films pose questions about the effect of repressed personal history on present behavior.

NONLINEAR TIME AND THE FUTURE

A scene from the future can be a useful foreshadowing device. A familiar comedy routine illustrates this. After we see a man start walking, the film cuts ahead to a banana skin lying on the sidewalk. Cutting back and forth between the man and the banana skin creates expectation so that when he falls on it, we are in a state of receptive tension and laugh when chance takes its toll. We can subvert the expectation of the genre by making him step unaware over the banana skin at the point where the pratfall should occur.

Because the victim is unaware of the banana skin, the revelation of what threatens him necessarily arises from a storyteller's point of view, not that of the character. This is a game between storyteller and audience seemingly at the victim's expense, but turns out to be a joke on the audience. This, by the way, is a plot point. If instead the banana skin has been laid as a trap by a hidden boy, the flashing back and forth between victim and banana skin can only be the waiting boy's point of view and has become a piece of continuous present. Point of view here determines the *tense* of the footage.

In an example of dramatic foreshadowing, Jan Troell's *Journey of the Eagle* (1985) starts with unexplained shots of human bones in a deserted arctic encampment. The film is about an actual balloon voyage to the arctic at the turn of the century, a hastily prepared expedition that concluded with the death of the aviators. We see the actual aviators' fate first, then the fictional film reconstructing their tragic destiny.

Alain Tanner uses different foreshadowing in *The Middle of the World* (1974). The authorial narration at different stages counts down how many days remain in the affair we witness between the engineer and the waitress. Because the ending in both films is foreknown, our attention focuses on human aspiration and fallibility rather than, as it normally would, on whether the couple will stay together or the aviators will survive.

An interesting flash-forward technique is used in Nicholas Roeg's *Don't Look Now* (1974). The lovemaking scene is repeatedly intercut with shots of the couple getting dressed later in a state of abstraction. The effect is complex and poignant and suggests not only the idea of comfortable routine but also that each is preoccupied with what must be done after they have made love. The sequence implies that each act of love has not only a beginning, middle, and end, but a banal aftermath waiting to engulf it.

NONLINEAR TIME AND THE CONDITIONAL TENSE

A favorite device in comedy is to cut to an imagined or projected outcome, as in John Schlesinger's *Billy Liar* (1963), whose hero takes refuge from his dreary undertaker's job in fantasy. This technique is used altogether more somberly in Resnais' *Last Year in Marienbad* (1961), in which a man staying in a vast hotel tries to renew an affair with a woman who seems not to know him. Sometimes maddeningly experimental as it moves between past, present, and future, the film extends multiple versions of scenes to suggest repeated attempts by the central character to remember or imagine. Here Resnais uses film as a research medium and provides us with an expanded, slowed-down model of human consciousness at work on a problem.

TIME COMPRESSED

All time arts select and compress their materials in pursuit of intensified meaning, ironies exposed through juxtapositions, and brevity. Film does this supremely well. Presumably this came about because newsreels at the beginning of film history proved that audiences could infer the whole of something, such as a boat sinking, from key fragments of the action. The audience imagined not only what was between scenes and beyond the edges of the frame, but they inferred ideas from the dialectical tension among images, compositions, and subjects. Over the decades this film shorthand has become more concise as audiences and filmmakers evolve an ever more succinct understanding. Ironically, this process has been helped and accelerated by that thorn in our flesh, the TV commercial. In the cinema, Godard probably did more than anyone to demonstrate that cumbersome transitional devices were superfluous. Because the jump cut (already familiar from home movies) showed a time leap for a single cut or for a transition from one scene to the next, a more compressed overall editing style became inevitable. But narrative agility is useless if a film is otherwise based on a ponderous scripting style that over-explains and relies on hefty dialogue exchanges.

For a sustained narrative style that is elegant, compressed, and highly allusive, Jean-Pierre Jeunet's delightful *Amalie* (2002) uses every trick in the book. When the heroine must cut up paper, for instance, the camera shows her in comic fast motion. The script jump-cuts from scene to scene in tribute to the French New Wave cinema of earlier times that is clearly its inspiration.

American experimental cinema of the 1960s and 1970s rebelled against the conservatism of Hollywood and tried drastically altering assumptions about audience attention and the length of films and their parts. Eight hours of the Empire State Building made a statement at the long end of the spectrum, while Stan VanDerBeek's two-frame cuts and manic compression of scenes stand (or should I say streak) at the other. As the cinema has disentangled itself from television, the most conservative dramatic techniques have been left behind for the little screen and its older audience, though MTV and the advertising used to attract the consumer's attention has become demented. Cinema films have matured and are longer, more reliant on mood and emotional nuance, and less tied to the laborious plotting associated with screen narrative formulae.

The danger with too much narrative compression is the risk of distancing the audience from a developing involvement with personalities, situations, and ideas, and of generating a general, even ritualized drama, like the western serials that at one time dominated television. Compressing or even eliminating prosaic details should not simply allow makers to shoehorn ever more plot into a given time slot; it should make way for the expansion of what is significant. Here the Godard films of the early 1960s reign supreme.

TIME EXPANDED

The expansion of time onscreen allows a precious commodity often missing in real life—the opportunity to reflect in depth while something of significance is happening. Slow-motion cinematography is an easy way to do this, but we are a little tired of lovers endlessly floating toward each other's arms. The same hackneyed device bloated the race sequences of Hugh Hudson's *Chariots of Fire* (1981).

Yasujiro Ozu's *Tokyo Story* (1953) (Figure 14–3) and Michelangelo Antonioni's *L'Avventura* (1959) subverted the popular action form by slowing both the story and its presentation to expose the more subtle action within the characters. Both films center on the tenuousness of human relationships, something impossible to achieve with a torrent of action. Needless to say, an unattuned audience will find such films boring. *L'Avventura* was ridiculed at the Cannes Film Festival, but later found success in Paris and became a cornerstone in Antonioni's career.

OTHER WAYS TO HANDLE TIME

There is *literal time*, something seldom tackled in film form. Agnes Varda's *Cleo from 5 to 7* (1961) shows exactly 2 hours in the life of a woman who has just learned she may be dying of cancer. Jafar Panahi's *The White Balloon* (1996)

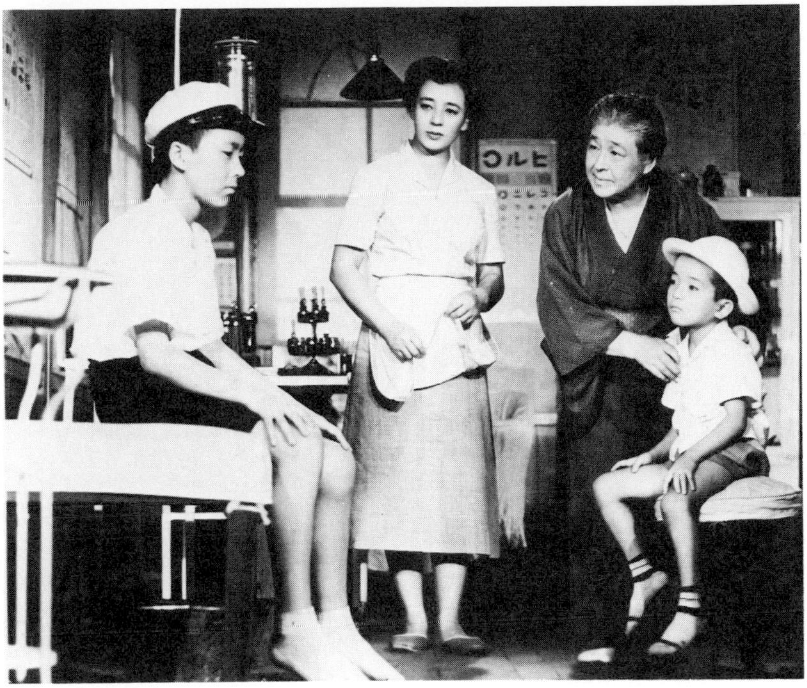

FIGURE 14–3

Technical minimalism and a slow pace concentrate attention on the tragedy of two old people in Ozu's *Tokyo Story* (1953, courtesy New Yorker Films).

shows a feisty 7-year-old going through one maneuver after another to get the goldfish she absolutely must have to celebrate the Iranian New Year. This film, too, is in real time, and Jonathan Rosenbaum thinks Panahi wanted to explore the difference between real time and subjective time—how long some experiences feel.

Christopher Nolan's *Memento* (2001), about a man with memory loss trying to piece his way backward to the moment of his wife's rape, is in *retrograde time*, or time played backward to a source point. Harold Ramis' very funny *Groundhog Day* (1993) contains a *time loop*. A jaded TV weatherman sent to witness the groundhog finds he is condemned to keep returning to the same key moment, each time learning a little more about himself, until finally he escapes a purged and happier man.

There is *continuous time*, or rather the illusion of it, in transparent cinema. This aims to rid its techniques of any evident cinematic contrivance. The appearance of real time masks the *time expanded* and *time contracted* behind the look of continuity. And there is *parallel time*, or parallel storytelling, as pioneered by D.W. Griffith, who acknowledged his debt in this regard to Dickens. Because the screen treatment of subjective experience is inseparable from perceived time and memory, there must be other designs for screen time yet to be explored.

CHAPTER 15

SPACE, STYLIZED ENVIRONMENTS, AND PERFORMANCES

SPACE

Film abridges time in the interest of narrative compression and can be equally selective with space. A protagonist eating dinner who suddenly remembers he hasn't put a coin in the parking meter will not be shown covering every step on his way to rectify the situation. Instead we will see him leap to his feet, his dropped spoon splashing soup, follow his feet running downstairs, then cut to join him in the middle of an argument with the meter maid. Even when locations are used to set our expectations about characters, the movie may only show us key aspects. Three scenes in a baronial hall will be set against the fireplace, the great stairway, and a doorway flanked with suits of armor; our imagination will create the rest of the space. Afterward we may distinctly remember seeing a wide shot of the whole hall, though it is a point of view supplied by our ever-ready imagination.

In Scorsese's black comedy *After Hours* (1985), the hapless office worker Paul escapes one dark, tangled New York situation only to fall into a worse one, and no location is shown more than minimally. It feels afterward as if you have seen every inch of Kiki's studio, but Scorsese actually gives us very little. The spectator is always completing what has been suggested, and with only a few well-chosen clues our minds will construct a whole town, as in David Lynch's *Blue Velvet* (1986). Every setup in his small town America is obviously and garishly contrived to be surreal, and this speaks of Lynch's origins as a painter. The film's early and brilliant predecessor is Lang's *Metropolis* (1926), in which the stylized environment is so pervasively visionary that it becomes a leading component in the film's formal argument.

Expressionism, especially in a film set in the present, creates a *reality refracted through an extreme subjectivity*. Lynch's first film *Eraserhead* (1978), about an alienated man reacting to the news that his girlfriend is going to have a baby, takes subjectivity to the limits of imaginable psychosis. Stylization is often present in the sound treatment, and *Eraserhead* also makes full and frightening use of the potential of sound. As Bresson said, "The eye sees but the ear imagines," and our imagination is the ultimate dramatist. (*Notes on Cinematography*, New York: Urizen Books, 1977). It is what we imagine that is most memorable and moving.

Film is such a relativistic medium that specific aural or visual devices can only be judged in their specific contexts, something beyond the scope of this book. This chapter will touch some issues that arise constantly for the film author and suggest some guidelines that show, I think, that point of view and environment are inextricably intertwined. Making rules and drawing demarcation lines between the realistic and the stylized, subjectively observed environment is too ambiguous unless tied to a specific example. Even then, a detectable stylization may be traced to nothing more remarkable than a choice of lens, a mildly unrealistic lighting setup, or an interestingly unbalanced composition.

STYLIZED WORLDS

A genre is a specialized world, and stylization serves to create that world by reflecting the special way in which characters perceive and interact with their environment. This illuminates their temperaments and moods and makes their world a projection of their collective reality. In Polanski's chilling *Repulsion* (1965), the apartment occupied by its paranoid heroine becomes the embodiment of threatening evil. Logically you see how events are being created by her deluded mind, but you are nonetheless engulfed by what she perceives. The outcome is a sickeningly unpleasant sense of the psychotic's vulnerability. All this is *demonstrated* by the film's Storyteller—presumably for a larger purpose than merely to prove his power over our emotions. That Polanski's wife was later murdered raises unanswerable speculation about the roots of art in its maker's subconscious.

The screen does not and cannot render anything objectively because time, space, and the objective world are all refracted through particularities that may be human, technical, or just plain random. The outcome is a partly deliberate, partly arbitrary construct. Every aspect of a complex film is likely to resonate with every other one, like the stresses in a tent when one guy rope is tightened. For this reason alone, film has eluded attempts at objective analysis.

These chicken-or-egg questions are irrelevant to an audience, but bothersome to anyone trying to gain an overview of authorial method. The best advice is to accept that, no matter what film histories and books of criticism say, your only *control* over a live-action film is to abort it. To control a film is like trying to control your life. You can't control either, but you can guide them. Your films will be a true record of how successfully you envision something and then capitalize on chance, which is why this book stresses planning a vision, advancing your self-knowledge, collaborating with others, and being willing to improvise.

The ordinary viewer, however, sees a clear spectrum of possibility—with films of objective affect at one end and films of invasively subjective impact at the other. As if sampling Mexican food, let's start with mild and move toward hot.

OCCASIONALLY STYLIZED

In mainstream, omniscient cinema the stylized environment usually makes only a passing appearance—perhaps as a storytelling inflection to point out a character's temporary unbalance (euphoria, fear, insecurity, etc.) or to share confidential information with the audience, as a novelist might do in a literary aside. Withheld from characters, this privileged information (symbolic objects, foreshadowing devices, special in-frame juxtapositions) heightens tension by making us anticipate what the characters do not yet know is in store. By using a character's subjective vision minimally, realism lets us enter the main character's reality without giving up our observer's superior sense of distance and well-founded judgment. In the famous shower scene in *Psycho* (1960) we temporarily merge with the killer's eyeline after he begins stabbing. Then the point of view switches to show the last agonized images seen by Janet Leigh's character. Finally, the killer runs out, and as Janet Leigh's character is now dead, we are left with the Storyteller's point of view: alone with the body in the motel room.

This brief foray into immediate, limited perceptions—first of the killer, then of his victim—is reserved for the starkest moment in the film, when Hitchcock boldly disposes of the heroine. Elsewhere we are allowed more distance from the characters. Were we to remain confined to the characters' points of view, we would be denied Hitchcock's signs and portents of the terror to come. Often a storyteller raises the audience's awareness above that of the characters themselves and makes of the audience a privileged witness.

The deranged or psychotic subjectivity of *Psycho* and *Repulsion* is of course a favorite mechanism for suspense movies. Many of the films listed in previous chapters under single-character point of view (POV) expose us only sparingly to the POV character's circumscribed vision, leaving most of the drama to be shown from a more detached standpoint. In Carpenter's *Halloween* (1978) we mostly identify with the babysitter, but occasionally circle and stalk her along with the vengeful but unseen murderer, occupying his reality even to the point of sharing the sensation of his breathing. While the switch to a subjective POV catapults us into vulnerable perspectives at times of peak emotion, an audience's overall empathy builds in response to the character's whole situation, not just at peaks or during close-ups. The island scene in Carroll Ballard's *The Black Stallion* (1979) creates the boy's love for the stallion through a lyrically edited vision of the horse galloping free in the waves of the island shore, yet the camera is usually distant from both boy and horse.

So far we have dealt with movement from a safe base of normalcy into a character's subjectivity and back again, just as the close-up takes us temporarily closer than would be permitted in life to explore some development of high significance in a character or (in the case of an object like a clock or a time bomb) some high significance to the mood or advancement of the story.

You must rely on the full range of storytelling to do this, not just editing. Indeed, to avoid stereotyped thinking about camera coverage and editing, it's important that you closely research what lies behind an audience's identification with a particular character. While getting an audience to identify with a main character is usually desirable, it is emphatically *not* the only purpose of drama. Brecht insisted that drama also exists to spur thought, memory, and judgment, and these, he contended, were in abeyance whenever the audience ceded their identity to that of a hero. But Mother Courage, for all her universality, is still a woman in a series of predicaments, and we must still empathize with her if we are to relate to the very human decisions she makes and are to make political judgments about emotion and expediency.

Sympathy and involvement in a film character's situation don't automatically arise because you happen to see from a character's location in space; they come about because we have learned from her actions what she is made of and from her situation what she must still face. Stylized camera coverage and editing do not alone create this, but they do serve it.

FULLY STYLIZED

Some films—to the purist, maybe all—set aside realism for a stylized environment throughout. Usually such a film is deliberately distanced in time or place. Period films fall readily into this category, from Griffith's *Birth of a Nation* (1915) and Victor Fleming's *Gone with the Wind* (1939) to more recent examples such as Anthony Minghella's *The English Patient* (1996) or Ang Lee's fable set in ancient China, *Crouching Tiger, Hidden Dragon* (2000).

Because we more readily grant artistic license to what is filtered through imagination or memory, any story profits from being distanced in time and place from what is familiar. Indeed the word *legend* is defined as unauthentic history. The cinema is thus furthering the notion of oral tradition in which actual events are freely shaped and embellished to serve the narrator's artistic, social, or political purpose.

ENVIRONMENTS

EXOTIC

Another way to achieve tension between figures and their environment is, instead of transporting the story in time, to place them in a specialized or alien setting, such as Bogart and Hepburn in Africa for Huston's *African Queen* (1951) or Antonioni's *L'Avventura* (1960), which imprisons its urbanites on an uninhabited island. Whenever the topic is a confrontation between antagonistic values, an alien setting allows the film to be impressionistic and create powerfully subjective moods. Vincente Minelli's *An American in Paris* (1951) allowed Gene Kelly to make Paris into a dream city of romance, while John Boorman's *Deliverance* (1972) thrust his four Atlanta businessmen into Appalachia's wilderness to put their "civilized" values to the test of survival. A quite different setting distinguishes Spike Jonze's *Being John Malkovich* (1999) in which an unemployed puppeteer finds a way into the actor John Malkovich's head and rents out the view from his eyes.

FUTURISTIC

The flight from the here and now includes not only myth but also the future. Fritz Lang's *Metropolis* (1926) is the classic, but there is no shortage of other good examples. Chaplin's *Modern Times* (1936), Godard's *Alphaville* (1965), Kubrick's *2001* (1968), Truffaut's *Fahrenheit 451* (1966), Lucas' *Star Wars* (1977), Scott's *Blade Runner* (1982), and Gilliam's *Brazil* (1986) all hypothesize worlds of the future. Each shows Kafkaesque distortions in the social, sexual, or political realms that put characters under duress. Plucked from the familiar and invited to respond as immigrants to a world operating under different assumptions, we are often shown the totalitarianism of dehumanized governments made powerful through technology. However, in the drive to illustrate a thesis, secondary characters often emerge as unindividualized, flat archetypes. If tales are traditionally vehicles for exploring our deepest collective anxieties, the realm of the future seems reserved for nightmares about the individual alone during a breakdown in collective control.

EXPRESSIONIST

Some films construct a completely stylized world. Kubrick's strange, violent *A Clockwork Orange* (1971) is a picaresque tale played out by painted grotesques in a series of surreal settings. Even if you quickly forget what the film is about, the visual effect is unforgettable and owes its origins to the Expressionism of the German cinema earlier in the century. Robert Wiene's *The Cabinet of Dr. Caligari* (1919) borrowed its style from contemporary developments in the graphic arts, which explored a wholly altered reality—an endeavor utterly justified by subsequent events in Nazi Germany. In these films characters may have unnatural skin texture or move without shadows in a world of oversized, distorted architecture and machinery. Fritz Lang's *Dr. Mabuse* (1922) and Murnau's *Nosferatu* (1921) sought to create the same unhinged psychology with a more subtle use of the camera. The proportions of the familiar have utterly changed in these films, and we find ourselves enclosed in a fully integrated, nightmarish world expressing an alien state of mind. They made their political and satirical comment, much as Kokoschka, Grosz, and Munch did through the graphic arts of the 1920s and 1930s.

Whereas Travis Bickle in Scorsese's *Taxi Driver* (1976) insanely misreads a familiar world, the hero in an expressionistic film such as David Lynch's *Blue Velvet* (1986) tries to feel at home in an arbitrary and distorted cosmos. The audience joins him in setting aside normalcy for a heightened and subjective world vibrant with ominous metaphor. Central characters in expressionist films are often under attack by a world running according to inverted or alien rules and peopled by characters who neither reflect nor doubt. Expressionism is clearly akin to the fairy tale world of Hans Christian Andersen or the brothers Grimm. In the cinema, Victor Fleming's *The Wizard of Oz* (1939) stands out as the classic of the genre, and more recently Steven Spielberg has made a whole industry out of providing modern fairy tales, most notably *E.T.* (1982).

ENVIRONMENTS AND MUSIC

Past, future, or distant settings are easiest to selectively distort in the service of a biased caricature. But there are ways to remain in the present, yet display everyday transactions as heightened and non-realistic. Musicals are one way. Jacques Demy's *The Umbrellas of Cherbourg* (1964), though visually formal and lyrical in composition and camera movement, tells a conventional small-town love story using natural dialogue. The difference is that it is sung, giving the effect of a realistic operetta (if that is not a contradiction in terms). The Gene Kelly films do something similar, but with dance, and they use unashamedly abstract, theatrical sets. Busby Berkeley's dance films, on the other hand, veer toward fantasy by merging human beings into kaleidoscopic patterns.

Music itself, when its use surpasses conventional mood intensification, can impose a formal patterning of emotion on the life onscreen. In Losey's *The Go-Between* (1971), Michel Legrand's exceptionally fine score starts with a simple theme from Mozart and develops and modulates it hauntingly, carrying us through a boyhood trauma and onward to the ultimate tragedy—the emotionally withered, unused life of the old man who survives. Peter Greenaway's use of Michael Nyman's minimalist scores in *The Draughtsman's Contract* (1983), *A Zed and Two Noughts* (1985), and *Drowning by Numbers* (1991) powerfully unites the mood of characters moving like sleepwalkers through worlds dominated by mathematical symmetry and organic decay.

THE STYLIZED PERFORMANCE: FLAT AND ROUND CHARACTERS

Perhaps the least stylized performances are those caught, documentary fashion, by a hidden camera, as Joseph Strick did in *The Savage Eye* (1959). Here we face a paradox: If the subject is unaware he is being filmed, he is not acting but being. Performers know they are performing and make choices about what they present, consciously and unconsciously adapting to the situation. All performance is therefore stylized to some extent.

Here I'll draw a working distinction between the performance that strives for realism—the art that hides art—and that deliberately heightens for dramatic effect. The adaptations of Dickens' novels, such as George Cukor's *David Copperfield* (1934) or David Lean's *Oliver Twist* (1948), have a young person as their POV character and use him as a lens on the adult world. Fagan, Bill Sykes, and the other thieves verge on the grotesque, while Oliver remains a touchingly vulnerable innocent caught in their web. These are good examples of what E.M. Forster called *flat* and *round* characters, the round character being complex and psychologically complete and the flat characters being more dimensionless because they are filtered through Oliver's partial and vulnerable perception.

How much a secondary character should be played as subjective and distorted can be decided fairly easily by examining the controlling POV. In Welles' version of Kafka's *Trial* (1962), it is the character of Joseph K. with whom we identify and through whose psyche all the characters are seen. Likewise, in *The Wizard of Oz* (1939), Glenda the Good Witch and the Wicked Witch of the West are designed to act in oppositional ways upon Dorothy and dramatize her conception of benevolence and evil.

In films in which a polarization is implied between the POV character and those in the surrounding world, oppositional characters or *antagonists* can be analogues for the warring parts of a divided self. Often in dialectical opposition

FIGURE 15–1

Lovers amid encroaching darkness in Cox's 1985 film *Cactus* (courtesy Spectrafilm).

to each other, they will bear on the (usually vulnerable) main character like the spokes of a wheel in relation to its hub. The morality play form, with its melodramatic emphasis on setting the innocent adrift among hostile or confusing forces, is a particularly useful way to externalize the flux within an evolving personality because the cinema, with its emphasis on externals, does not otherwise handle interior reality particularly well.

It is the writer's and director's task to set the levels of heightened characterization and to determine the nature and pressure of what each spoke must transmit to the hub or POV character. It will be crucial, too, that the level of writing and playing be consistent and that there be change and development throughout the film so that no part, whether spokes or hub, becomes static and therefore predictable.

Flat characters usually have simple characteristics and represent particular human qualities as they apply to a main character. They remind us of the early theater's masks and stock characters discussed in the section of Chapter 1 titled On Masks and the Function of Drama. Non-realistic or flat characters are likely to function as metaphors for the conflicting aspects of the round character's predicament and thus to forewarn us of a metaphysical subtext we might otherwise miss.

NAMING THE METAPHORICAL

If characters play metaphorical roles in an allegory—and it is invariably revealing to analyze *every* script as though this were true—it is important for the director to find metaphors to epitomize each character and assign each character an archetypal identity. These are potent tools for clarification and action, and the process is equally useful for the worlds the characters inhabit. Paul Cox's *Cactus* (1985) portrays the developing relationship between an angry and desperate woman losing her sight and a withdrawn young man who is already blind (Figure 15–1). The man makes his refuge a cactus house, and she visits him there to see what he can tell her about her fate. The cacti are dry, hostile, and spiky, but also phallic, and the setting becomes emblematic of his predicament. In a sexually charged world, he has turned his back on intimacy and intends to survive self-punitively in a place devoid of tenderness or nourishment.

Having settings and predicaments dramatized, and explanatory metaphors in hand will greatly help you explain to actors how you want each to play their role and why. We shall explore this principle much more fully in upcoming chapters on analyzing the script and working with actors.

CHAPTER 16

FORM AND STYLE

FORM

Form is the manner in which content is presented. For a short film to maintain a memorable and intriguing outlook on the human life it portrays, the makers must choose a form unique to the story's purpose and nature. Norman McClaren's *Neighbors* (1952) or *Pas de Deux* (1969) make stunning use of pixilation and optical printing respectively to enhance what they have to say about men and territory and about dance. Chris Marker's unforgettable *La Jetée* (1962) is a futuristic fable told entirely in still photographs with just a few seconds of movement in one shot. Robert Enrico's moving *Occurrence at Owl Creek Bridge* (1962) will be mentioned later in this chapter.

Though formal variations seem unlimited, they are, in fact, usefully confined by allied concerns, some of which we have already considered. Designing a film's form involves more than figuring out where to put the camera and what lens to use before shooting. It means articulating a clear and provocative purpose for telling the tale, which in turn means considering the subject, point of view, and the genre that will best serve your authorial purpose.

If, for instance, we want to show a holdup in a grocery store, we would first need to decide whose was the controlling point of view. It could be that of the store owner, the frightened clerk, a short-sighted old man out to buy a lottery ticket, the off-duty policeman there getting a loaf of bread, or the robber himself. For each the events have a different significance, so each would tend to notice different things. This way of noticing lets the audience infer the nature and dilemma of each character. Point of view thus usefully limits and shapes your decisions, and the choice of lenses, camera positions, angles, and lighting all contribute to the cumulative impression you are building for the audience. Together they add up to a progression of distinct moods and to a particular way of seeing. Lighting would flow from the kind of place and the kind of interaction. How the camera was handled would also flow from point of view and the kind of comment the director wants to make.

In deciding on form we must always consider how to structure time. A crime, for instance, need not be shown in chronological order—you might also show it in discontinuous portions, as remembered by a survivor, perhaps, or from the stage-by-stage retrospect of the court case following the arrest of the robber. Different witnesses might have conflicting memories of key actions, and so on. Screen order, as these examples show, is affected by point of view.

Of overarching concern is the Storyteller's nature and premise, for this constitutes an agenda and purpose distinct from those of the characters or even the director. The Storyteller's POV might shift narrative focus among three of the characters, treating the point of view of each as equally important. The controlling point of view and the limitations inherent in the story's structure largely determine the form of any film, but good formal choices are seldom obvious nor can they be made without analysis and decisions.

FORM, CONFLICT, AND VISION

Events do not achieve significance just because someone frames them. An average audience is primed to know that good fiction is not a reproduction of life *but an enactment of ideas about it.* If your topic is robbery, your audience expects you to reveal something fresh about what robbery means—socially, culturally, or emotionally. Who carries it out, where, in what way, and why—these are questions of basic story philosophy, all of which run back to the audience's hope that the film will offer some interesting ideas about life.

To determine such issues you should review the major characters' basic makeup. Every human being is a mix of innate temperament, environmental influence, and what his or her peculiar history has instilled. Most of what is visible about people's characters—what moves them to act the way they do and what causes them to forge their own destinies—arises from their personal baggage of unresolved conflicts, both the internal ones they carry and the external ones they confront or cause.

Such conflicts already exist in you as you read these words. They are your unfinished business in life. However old or young you may be, however much you feel yourself to be lacking in "interesting" experience, you are stigmatized in certain ways and carry within you buried memories of events that still smolder. Their cause and effect you still feel deeply, and you will best find their significance by telling analogous tales. By this token, *the Storyteller tells a tale not just to entertain, but to grow in spirit.*

A film's form is therefore highly functional. It serves the tale you are really trying to tell, what you want to show through telling it, and reveals the best framework and visual or aural language to impart these things. The following examples highlight the elements of form you should take into consideration.

VISUAL DESIGN

This is something people readily notice, and it is determined by lighting, choice of lenses, camera height and movements, art directing, costuming, set dressing, and by the locations and terrain themselves. A film gains power when it finds visual equivalencies to its thematic concerns. Wim Wender's *Paris, Texas* (1984) finds in the arid and depopulated desert of Texas the perfect counterpart to the dehydrated emotions of the numbed, inarticulate man stumbling in search of his lost wife and child. Bergman's *The Seventh Seal* (1956) is set in the Middle Ages, when superstition and fear of the plague ruled men's hearts, so the story takes place amid gloomy forests and high contrast scenery. The dark figures, and low-key black-and-white photography prime us to anticipate the mixture of magic and superstitious terror at a time when life was "nasty, brutish, and short" (Thomas Hobbes, 1588–1679).

Jacques Rivette's *Celine and Julie Go Boating* (1974) has an ingenious and effective development in its visual style (Figure 16–1). Two young women break into a shuttered house where a stagey domestic drama is slowly unfolding. Becoming absorbed by the characters and wanting to know the "play's" outcome, they are compelled to keep returning. Then they discover they can enter the play's action quite unnoticed by the other characters. As the piece develops, and as missing links drop into place, the characters and their setting gradually become more and more unnatural in color. What starts as realism gradually becomes more surreal, distanced, and artificial until the main characters have merged into a dynamic genre painting. The film's theme seems to be that living with passionate and active curiosity turns life into art.

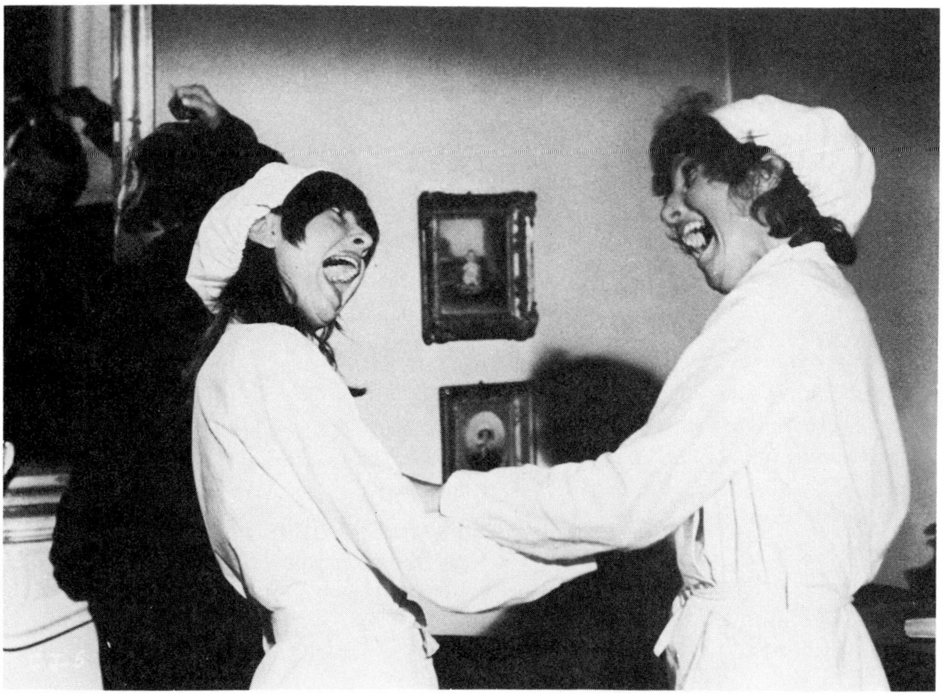

FIGURE 16–1

Two friends discover each is playing the same part in the drama they have infiltrated. Rivette's *Celine and Julie Go Boating* (1974, courtesy New Yorker Films).

Richard Linklater's *Waking Life* (2001) has an unusual visual design that takes a college-age man on a walk through a series of philosophical conversations. The movie was rotoscoped (filmed, then traced as animation) so it has an animated feel that is initially beautiful, but as you get deeper into its 99 minutes a sort of fatigue sets in from the constantly shimmering imagery.

Films by painters such as Robert Bresson and David Lynch are often noticeably visual in a way entirely lacking in filmmakers who start from ideas rather than imagery.

SOUND DESIGN

Too much film sound is diegetic, slavishly providing everything that logically could accompany what we see on the screen. In this scenario, you must hear a *miaow* whenever a cat appears and hear every type of passing vehicle in a traffic scene. Every footfall in an interior is rendered, and it changes for every kind of surface the character traverses. The effect, far from the realism it aspires to, is cluttered and suffocating.

TEXTURAL DESIGN

Bresson said, "The eye sees, but the ear imagines." Think what the imagination supplies for these sounds: the cooing of doves floating in through a sunny bedroom window, footfalls in a church, children distantly playing hide-and-seek, or muffled weeping in a darkened room. They work miracles on our imagination and receptivity. Against these perceptions by an acute mind, dialogue stands in poetic counterpoint. Sometimes the sound track can go quiet, presenting us with the shock and tension of silence. This is *musique concrète*, the texture and impact of which are poles away from the literal world of diegetic (realistic) film sound.

Sound designer Randy Thom complains with full justification that he is too often brought on to a production when it has been edited into wall-to-wall dialogue—and he can do nothing. Quite apart from the audience fatigue this produces, he recommends deliberately writing for sound. That is, characters should listen, and quiet spaces should exist when the picture is deliberately withholding information so narrative momentum can come through the sound track. Again, David Lynch's films are very sound-sensitive and make good examples of movies that included sound in their original design. Sound should sometimes be a foreground player, not a late cosmetic applied to a stage play. See Thom's "Designing a Movie for Sound" at *www.filmsound.org/*.

RHYTHMIC DESIGN

The term *rhythmic design* probably suggests music or sound such as footsteps and clocks ticking, all used to supply a rhythmic identity to a scene. But other elements in a film can create a rhythmic design.

Rhythms of:

- sound effects
- speech patterns
- breathing patterns
- music, if used
- scene alternation (long scenes interspersed with short ones, for instance)

Frequency of:

- sound changes
- picture cuts

Inherent rhythm of:

- shot (affected by content and its movement and its composition)
- camera movements
- action
- particular characters (varies according to their temperament, mood, time of day, predicament, etc.)

Cinematic rhythms emanate from multiple sources at any given time. A good editor and an experienced director are acutely sensitive to their combined effect, and they know as instinctively as any musician when the combined effect is, or is not, working.

An audience's involvement, as any performer will tell you, is best sustained by variety. Shakespeare—who supported a large company of actors by satisfying the tastes of the common people—switches scenes from action to monologue to comedy, interspersing long scenes and short scenes, group scenes and duologues, duologues and soliloquies. Even while making a continuous thematic development, he juxtaposes very different textures and rhythms. Without the sustaining music of consummate form and poetically dense language, Shakespeare could never have delivered such profound themes and ideas to unlettered audiences.

Good film technique also refreshes the ear and eye with variations and comparisons. These cause us to pass through a succession of perspectives and moods. Similar to variations in rhythm is the idea of changes in dramatic pressure. You can increase or relax the audience's sense of pressure by bringing the appropriate rhythmic changes. Surely this is why Bergman insists that film is a musical rather than a literary medium: "Film is mainly rhythm; it is inhalation and exhalation in continuous sequence" (*Four Screenplays of Ingmar Bergman*, New York: Simon & Schuster, 1960, Introduction).

MOTIFS

Motifs are devices placed by the Storyteller to signify thematic aspects. For example, shots of flowing water might signify the theme that "life goes on no matter what." Any formal element, aural or visual, can signify a motif, and one that recurs is called a *leitmotif*. They help to project ideas and interpretation into the insistently material world that film gives us.

AURAL MOTIFS

In Carpenter's *Halloween* (1978), a strange synthesizer sound accompanies the presence of the vengeful escapee. It is a *non-diegetic* sound (meaning it is heard by the audience and not by the characters) and serves to heighten our sense of their danger. Most film music uses the leitmotif principle, that is, a special instrumentation and/or special musical theme running through the film is assigned to a particular character, situation, or sentiment. Prokofiev's delightful orchestral *Peter and the Wolf* uses motifs for the main characters and was composed for children to demonstrate the different instruments of the orchestra and their tonal range using the medium of a fable.

VISUAL MOTIFS

Certain camera movements can be a motif, like the crabbing shots through the trees in Enrico's *Occurrence at Owl Creek Bridge* (1962) that signify a guilty, uneasy voyeurism. In Abraham Polonsky's *Tell Them Willy Boy Is Here* (1969), the motif is the action of running. The fugitive Indian is on the run throughout the film, so running itself becomes emblematic of his existence (as it once was for Polonsky, badly victimized during the McCarthy witch-hunt years). Shots of trickling sand in Teshigahara's *Woman in the Dunes* (1964) repeatedly characterize the woman's threatened situation. In Roman Polansky's *Tess* (1979) the use of color becomes a motif, as Thomas Hardy, in fact, specifies in the original novel. The young peasant heroine, moving unconsciously between what society sees as innocence and sin, is repeatedly associated with either white or red (the white dresses in the opening May walk, the red of the strawberry Alec puts between her unwilling lips, for example). The color red is also a motif connoting danger throughout Roeg's *Don't Look Now* (1973). Compositional balance or vantage (looking through foreground objects, for instance) or the use of sound and silence might all be pressed into service as motifs.

BRECHTIAN DISTANCING AND AUDIENCE IDENTIFICATION

Cinema, unlike literature, generally views characters from the outside and subsequently favors action over contemplation. The suspense film and the action thriller go further, for they aim to make you *identify* with a particular character, and to "lose yourself," as the alarming success of the James Bond films testifies. You might assume that all films promote audience identification, as theater tended to do until Berthold Brecht (1898–1956) set out to subvert this in a Germany succumbing to the Nazis. Realizing he could not make audiences critical if they were trained to abdicate their autonomy to a show, Brecht set out to redefine theater itself. Alert to the murderous simplifications of fascism, he needed to make people consider the collective currents of political and social life, not to let them dream their way through the fate and fortunes of a unique individual. So he devised a theater of mixed and constantly changing forms to keep the audience aware they were watching not an imitation of life but a show with an urgent dialectical purpose.

In a Europe seared by the after-effects of two world wars, a Brechtian discourse is still present in the work of Kluge, Godard, Gilliam, and Greenaway, to name just a few. Their styles may employ authorial narration, titles, songs, musical interludes, or surreal events peopled with bizarre, allegorical, or historical characters. Often elliptical, these films deliberately disrupt the audience's ever-present desire to lapse into that waking dream of identification that Brecht, surrounded as he was by incipient fascism, saw as suicidal escapism. Mass audiences are not yet drawn to Brecht's demanding alternative to traditional narrative form, but his work and that of those under his influence can be immensely moving and invigorating.

Keeping an audience thinking and not just feeling is a rare skill that awaits development on a wider scale in the cinema. Wim Wenders' two films about the angels over Berlin, *Wings of Desire* (1988) and *Faraway, So Close* (1993), point most excitingly in this direction.

LONG TAKES VERSUS SHORT TAKES

Without abandoning his wish to keep the audience at a distance, Alain Tanner in *Jonah Who Will Be 25 in the Year 2000* (1976) adopted a quiet and non-confrontational technique by playing whole scenes as single takes. Using only the simplest of camera movements he lets us stand back and consider the meaning of the characters' lives rather than urging us to participate in their emotions. The result is a cool and welcome distancing that invites you to ponder with the characters how they should live out their ideals when their 1968 social revolution has failed.

To eliminate the need for editing, the long take needs astute blocking and rehearsal. In conventional technique, editing and mobile camerawork inject nervous excitement and enable the point of view to zigzag around a central character—two classic ways of luring the spectator into identifying. Tanner uses some minor camera movement so locations won't appear flat like a backcloth. Otherwise he uses one take per scene; yet you feel no loss of the conventional apparatus of cinema. Because you can't intercut takes in this method, the director must closely maintain the level and consistency of playing. Actors and technicians may, at any time, abort not just a take but a whole scene, so this apparently simple approach may save nothing in time or filmstock. Hitchcock, in 1948, made his thriller *Rope* in the same way, but more as a technical challenge than because the story, based on the Leopold and Loeb murder case, called for it.

In the long take, the audience sees everything in its context so far as practicable. Close-ups are produced by blocking characters to move close to the camera. However, the conventionally shot and edited scene reveals only enough important fragments (of a room or of an action, for instance) to let us infer the whole. By completing their context in your mind you unconsciously enter the reality of the person whose experience the scene represents. In so doing, Brecht would say we yield intellect to sensation.

Somewhere between these extremes—Eisensteinian fragmentation with its control and exploitation of the spectator's sensibilities at one end of the spectrum, and the unbroken, uninflected presentation of Brechtian cinema at the other—lie choices reflecting not just convenience, but your storyteller's stance in relaying the story to the audience. There is a place for the emotions *and* the intellect in any intelligent film, though maybe not in every single scene it contains. Depending on the point of view and content of each scene, there may be room in your film for quite different language at different points.

SHORT FILM FORMS: A NEGLECTED ART

The short film is closest to poetic form because it requires deft characterization, a compressed narrative style, and something fresh and focused to say. Sadly, the short film subject is often overlooked by new directors with serious intentions. This is like would-be novelists rejecting poetry or the short story as forms unworthy of attention. Here are some classic short films, compiled with the help of Peter Rea and David K. Irving's excellent book, *Producing and Directing the Short Film and Video*, 2nd edition (Boston: Focal Press, 2001). Because distributors change so rapidly, look for these films via the Internet or in specialized film listings, such as Facets Multimedia (*www.facets.org*), where you can often buy famous films in collections, or at Amazon (*www.amazon.com*), which also lists short film collections on DVD. Because the films come from several countries, I have included alternative titles.

Block, Mitchell: *No Lies* (USA, 1972, B&W, 16 minutes). It looks like a documentary as the director crudely presses a raped woman for an account of her misfortune, but it's all acted and for a purpose.

Bunuel, Luis: *Un Chien Andalou/The Andalusian Dog* (France, 1928, B&W, 20 minutes). A surrealist experiment in shocking imagery, undertaken with Salvador Dali, that consciously avoids any linear story logic.

Davidson, Alan: *The Lunch Date* (USA, 1990, B&W, 12 minutes) A deceptive encounter over a salad between a woman and a homeless man at Grand Central Station.

Deren, Maya and Alexander Hammid: *Meshes of the Afternoon* (USA, 1943, B&W, 13 minutes). Seminal work in which the mother of American experimental cinema plays a woman who dreams of being driven to suicide by loneliness and adversity.

Enrico, Robert: *An Occurrence at Owl Creek Bridge/La Rivière du Hibou* (France, 1962, B&W, 27 minutes). A soldier in the American Civil War makes a miraculous escape from hanging—or does he? A fine film and a veritable catalogue of judiciously used sound and picture film techniques. From a tale by Ambrose Bierce.

Godard, Jean-Luc: *Tous les Garçons s'Appellent Patrick/All the Boys Are Called Patrick* (France, 1957, B&W, 21 minutes). Two girls find they are dating the same man.

Lamorisse, Albert: *Le Balon Rouge/The Red Balloon* (France, 1956, color, 34 minutes). A lonely boy in Paris makes friends with a balloon, which begins to reciprocate his attentions. No words.

Marker, Chris: *La Jetée/The Jetty/The Pier* (France, 1962, B&W, 29 minutes). A film almost entirely in stills about a survivor of World War III whose childhood memories allow him to move around at will in time. One shot has motion, and Georges Sadoul rightly says "the screen disarmingly bursts into sensuous life."

Metzner, Ernö: *Überfall/Accident/Police Report/Assault* (Germany, 1928, B&W, 21 minutes). A man wins some cash in a beer hall, but it brings him nothing but bad luck. Almost a catalogue of camera techniques.

Polanski, Roman and Jean-Pierre Rousseau: *The Fat and the Lean/Gruby i Chudy* (France, 1961, B&W, 15 minutes). This allegory about a fat and a thin man explores the relationship of dependency between master and servant, and what stops the servant from escaping.

Polanski, Roman: *Two Men and a Wardrobe/Dwaj Ludzie z Szafa* (Poland, 1957, B&W, 15 minutes). Another allegory in which two men appear out of the sea, struggling with a bulky wardrobe, avoiding humanity and unable to solve their problems.

Renoir, Jean: *Une Partie de Campagne/A Day in the Country* (France, 1936, B&W, 37 minutes). A Paris shopkeeper takes his family for a day in the country, and his daughter—who already has a fiancé—falls in love with another man. Sadly, the relationship has no future. Renoir's debt to his famous father emerges, as well as to other Impressionists. From a tale by Guy de Maupassant.

Beginners work in short forms because they are inexpensive and place high demand on the control of craft and storytelling essentials. They also send you rapidly through the entire production cycle and are good learning vehicles. The dates in the films listed above tell you how few good short films there are. Any decent short film will readily earn a place in film festivals over an equally good but longer film because it is easier to schedule and very popular with audiences. To earn recognition, you must win prizes; so please be kind to yourself—save time and money, get invaluable experience, and compete in the less restricted arena.

Think of it this way: if you could make five 8-minute films for the price of one 60-minuter, you have increased your chances of recognition at least fivefold. After these you will handle a long film five times as well because you have tackled five sets of characterization, blocking, dramatic shape and flow, and editing challenges. You will also have directed a host of actors and given life to a gallery of characters.

What makes a good short subject? Much like a good short story, a short film needs:

- A limited but evocative setting
- Characters engaged in a significant form of struggle
- A character who develops—however minimally

- A resolution that leaves the audience pondering some aspect of the human condition

Such a film can be a farce, a dark comedy, a lyrical love letter, a Chaplinesque allegory (like Polanski's early shorts), a sitcom—anything. However, it must declare its issues and its personalities quickly and deftly. It should be well acted, interestingly shot, and tautly edited. A superb short film is the ultimate advertisement for what you could do with a bigger canvas. Two wedding videomakers in my area were invited to make a feature after circulating free copies around Hollywood of their deft comedy about a script doctor.

Finding your best short film subjects means defining what situations you know that best reveal a given character. This will almost certainly include some turning point, where pressures have built up and the main character is forced to take action. When he or she acts, there follow the inevitable consequences to which he or she must adapt. Because the turning point marks the onset of change, it may be the true starting point of the story (the buildup is only a prelude). In Polanski's dialogue-free *The Fat and the Lean* (1961) the thin man serves the fat man in all manner of humiliating ways, all the while visibly yearning to escape toward the Paris skyline. Eventually, to our joy, he runs away—only to be recaptured by the fat man who is roused to action by the loss of his slave. On one level a vaudeville comedy, on another a grisly political allegory, the film shows how neither slave nor master are free. Who can wonder that Polanski was soon entrusted with bigger things?

STYLE

The word *style* is often and confusingly interchanged with *form*. Godard when apparently speaking of form said, "To me, style is just the outside of content, and content the inside of style, like the outside and inside of the human body—both go together, they can't be separated" (Richard Roud, *Jean-Luc Godard*, London: Secker & Warburg, 1967, p. 13).

The style of a film is really the visible influence of its maker's identity. The distinction is made messy by the fact that film authorship is collective. But a Godard or a Lynch film, even if you hate it, is immediately recognizable. Partly this is content, partly it's the kind of tale and the characteristic forms each chooses, and partly it's because the films have the mark of individual personalities and tastes written all over them. It is this last, virtually uncontrollable, element that is properly known as *style*.

Just as you can't choose your own identity at any meaningful level, so you should let your film style take care of itself. You can and should locate your film within a genre and design its content and form to be an organic whole. If over the period of its creation you serve each controllable aspect of your film well, people will come to recognize in a succession of your films a continuity that is hard to pin down, but that will be called your style. From your audience and your critics you may even learn what it is—rather as (at considerable risk to your equilibrium) you extract a sense of your character from the reactions of friends, enemies, family, flatterers, and detractors.

Setting out to strike a style or artistic identity, as students often feel they must do in fine art schools, leads to superficialities and attention-demanding gimmicks. Far more important is to develop your deepest interests and make the best cinema you can out of the imprint left by your formative experience. Working sincerely and intelligently is what can truly connect your work to an audience. Even with these qualities you must expect a long evolution while you internalize all the technical and conceptual skills.

CHECKLIST FOR PART 4: AESTHETICS AND AUTHORSHIP

Note: There is an important set of prompts in the Form and Aesthetics Questionnaire in Appendix 2. It will greatly help you during the development and preproduction stages of your film. The recommendations and points summarized here are only those most salient or the most commonly overlooked from the chapters in this part. To find more about them or anything else, go to the Table of Contents at the beginning of this part, or try the index at the back of the book.

Point of View:

- Making the audience experience a character's point of view (POV) means making it experience a character's emotional situation as if it were their own.
- Complex drama often shows multiple POVs, which become poignant when the drama also shows characters' limitations, misperceptions, and miscommunications.
- The eyes and mind through which we view the film's events (personified as the Storyteller) also add up to a very important POV, which may be philosophical, critical, amused, ironic, detached, excited, terrified, etc.
- Everyone's POV, including that of the Storyteller, is stimulated and qualified by their own particular context (which is why juries are so carefully chosen).
- In daily life, make a point of backtracking whenever you get a sharp sense of someone else's reality to find out what opened the door for you.
- Make yourself aware of how POV is implied in literature, painting, photography, and theater, as well as film. There are common denominators arising out of audience response that will strengthen your command in film.
- It's important that the audience come to care deeply about at least one person in a story.
- Often films center on a main character's predicament and this person becomes the film's controlling POV. This does not exclude contrasting POVs, which can easily sharpen that of the main character or characters.
- That we care about your characters and care whether they overcome their difficulties is a major part of generating suspense and dramatic tension.
- To control POV takes a God-like ability of the story's creator(s) to see both from the character's viewpoints and also from the audience's.
- An omniscient POV gives the Storyteller the ability to be anywhere, see all, and know all (like God).
- A subjective POV means that the character through whom we are seeing is subject to special and very human limitations and passions.
- An audience has its own subjectivity that the filmmaker may or may not be able to anticipate, depending on how distant the audience is from the filmmaker's own culture.

Subtext and Making the Significant Visible:

- The audience must know what it is looking for in a story, so the story must declare its intentions.
- Merely *showing* events will probably leave the events' meaning buried under an avalanche of banal reality (a great hazard in filmmaking).
- Much of what is meaningful in human life goes on below the surface and requires interpretation and judgment—skills that an audience loves to exercise.
- What is cause and what is effect are plot considerations, but above these are moral implications, which interest us above everything else.
- The events chosen, their artful juxtaposition, irony, and humor are all ways to signify an underlying meaning or set of values.
- Allegory, analogy, metaphor, and symbol are more ways for the Storyteller to signify meanings.
- The struggle between right and wrong is not as morally testing as that between right and right.

Genre:

- A genre is a type of film the audience recognizes as a world running according to particular rules or norms.
- Film genres are often extensions of traditions begun in other media like painting, literature, music, or theater.
- Genre permits framing an area of life and seeing it through a particular prism of concerns or values.
- Subjectivity is inherently interesting and fertile in determining genre. "The public" as seen by an overworked postal clerk is a vastly different species from that seen by a newly ordained priest.

Duality and Conflict:

- The clash of values or temperaments is the stuff of drama.
- If drama is to be about people trying to get or do things, there must always be obstacles, difficulties, and unforeseen consequences, just as in life. This is conflict.
- Conflict does not have to be something negative; we learn through solving problems and every problem involves solving conflicts "Fire is the test of gold; Adversity of strong men" (Seneca 4 B.C.–A.D. 65).
- The core of every interesting personality is in his or her conflicts and "unfinished business."
- Every credible person and situation contains contradictions and opposites—an actor playing a "bad" character must find the good in him, and if playing a good character, must find his weaknesses.

Microcosm and Macrocosm:

- The same truths are reproduced in large and small scales. An individual might represent a whole people, and dancers might be used to represent atoms. This can be useful.
- Nations behave with the passions of a myopic individual.
- An individual's complex psyche can be split up and represented as a group of characters, each representing different dominant traits.

Drama, Propaganda, and Dialectics:

- Representation and typifying can lead to flat characters unless you create interestingly ambiguous characters. In melodrama, however, characters tend to have one assigned characteristic and stand either for good or bad.
- Like yourself, cinema audiences are drawn to the ambiguities in their own lives and not to other people's certainties (for which one joins a church).
- If you must promote ideologies, make their opposition strong and intelligent.
- Your audience is as intelligent as yourself. It's wiser to reflect human predicaments than be caught trying to tell people how to live.
- Duality and ambiguity in a movie invite the audience to make judgments. Using your judgment is an important part of being gainfully entertained.

The Difference Between Observer Filmmaking and Storytelling:

- There is no right or wrong way to make any film, only effective and ineffective stories, and effective and ineffective forms for those stories.
- Some events are so powerful they need only to be relayed. They need little or no framing or implied commentary.
- Most fiction, however, needs a moral purpose in the telling and a moral attitude on the part of the teller. This should never be simplistic—even for young audiences.
- A story gains much from the added dimension brought by the critical intelligence of its Storyteller (good social criticism is less concerned with right and wrong than with enabling us to ponder ironies).
- When the Storyteller draws us emotionally into the film's world, we experience what it is like to be someone else. The audience longs to experience being *other*.
- The story, characters, and human predicaments in your movie are always going to be more important to get right than technique, which is at best a transparent vehicle for these.

Structure, Plot, and the Handling of Time:

- Plot is the arrangement of incidents and the logic of causality, which needs to seem credible and inevitable at every step.
- You can't be sure you have control of your movie's plot unless you maintain an up-to-date outline. This allows you to see it unobstructed.

- A film's structure should create forward momentum by posing questions and appropriately delaying their resolution.
- Plot structure should never be needlessly complicated unless the film's form is deliberately a maze.
- Clarity of Who/What/When/Where helps the audience concentrate on the thematic issues and the Why, which usually centers on the characters and their situations.
- How time is handled is a major organizing principle for any story.
- Departing from chronological time usually signals that the film is routed through someone's subjectivity, either that of a character or of the Storyteller.
- Flashbacks generally slow and weaken the forward momentum of a story.
- Heavy use of flashbacks (past tense) usually goes with a heavily determinist or even Freudian outlook (she does this *now* because of what happened to her *then*).
- Have you graphed the intended rise and fall of pressures in your film?
- Have you faced the faults this reveals?

Thematic Purpose:

- The thematic purpose is your Storyteller's motive for telling the tale.
- The Storyteller is not necessarily you; more likely he or she is a dramatized intelligence who has particular needs to fulfill through telling the tale. Make sure you elucidate what they are because this is the persona you are going to serve (play) when you direct, and it is the aura of this intelligence that gives the film an identity all its own.
- You won't be in control of your movie's thematic purpose unless you maintain an up-to-date premise or concept.
- Examine your outline and screenplay for how well the movie serves the thematic purpose.
- Thematic purpose is often best discovered by searching for appropriate metaphors.
- These metaphors will almost certainly suggest sound and visual motifs and even leitmotifs.
- A well-developed theme unifies and justifies your movie.
- It's important to your energy and focus that your movie serves a thematic purpose in which you deeply believe.
- Strong things are usually simple; don't feel your theme must be complex and all embracing.

Space, Stylized Environments, and Performances:

- Decide what kind of spaces your characters inhabit and what impression these should give.

- Depending on the film's system of POVs, you may want to show most, or very little, of the detail in each location.
- Characters can notice very little of their surroundings through familiarity, confusion, or preoccupation.
- Characters can notice very much about their surroundings because they have time on their hands, are in new surroundings, or have special reasons to take stock.
- Space may go noticed or unnoticed simply because that's the habit or temperament of the POV character.
- Stylization generally means departing from the unremarkable.
- In a movie a whole world or only aspects of it may be stylized.
- Stylization signals subjectivity on the part of the characters, the genre, or their Storyteller.

Music:

- Music can be misused as a dramatic crutch.
- It can legitimately suggest the interior state of the POV character.
- It can also signal the Storyteller's feelings about the story, impelling the audience to investigate what they're watching in particular ways.
- For the audience, music is like a drug habit; pleasant in the beginning and painful when perceived to be withdrawn.
- Music can illustrate or it can counterpoint.
- Music can accompany and enhance whatever is inherently strong in emotion.
- Avoid music that duplicates what we can see or hear (for instance, lush pastoral music over shots of cows in a wide meadow).
- Music can provide historical, social, or emotional context.
- Most music sold in music libraries is so bad, it isn't worthy of the name.
- Better to have no music than bad music.
- Too often bad music survives because it came free from a friend.

Form and Style:

- Form follows function.
- Less is more.
- Simple is strong.
- Kill your darlings. That is, remove anything you love that is not functional.
- Listen to your characters for what they need.
- Know where the movie belongs and where it departs from its genre.
- Don't neglect visual style; your cinematographer should be your ally here.
- Don't confuse visual style with directing; it's only part of the job and can lead you to neglect content and character.

- Design the sound track like a sound play, don't just leave it to trail after a picture.
- Remember that rhythms underlie everything in screen language, *everything*.
- Decide whom or what you want your audience to identify with.
- If you want to counter identification, you will first have to create it and subvert it.
- Only use long takes if your movie needs them; there are many other rewarding ways to challenge yourself.
- Short films are harder to make than long films; poetry is more demanding than prose.
- Short films get shown much more easily than longer ones.
- Let your film tell you its style, not vice versa.
- As far as your own style is concerned, you can only strive to become authentic to yourself. Personal style will take care of itself. In filmmaking you dress to impress at your peril.

PART 5

PREPRODUCTION

Part 5 (Chapters 17 through 27) covers the vast amount of work that goes into a movie after a script has been accepted and up to the moment when shooting must begin. It covers digging deeply into the script to find all the life below the surface—all the structures and meanings without which the movie would be just a hollow facade. There is the process of casting, which alone can cause a film to succeed or fail definitively, and how to work with actors, whose performances are the key to your audience's accepting the world the film depicts.

The relationship between actors and their director will likewise make or break your film. Actors, being all too human, have human problems, and the director must deal with these constructively. If that fails, the director must risk unpopularity and deal with them with the best interests of the project in mind.

To help the novice director learn from doing, there are many improvisation exercises. Any director afraid to improvise will be badly handicapped at directing actors who are using improvisation. The improvisation exercises for student directors will free you and empower you to use your cast's powers of improvisation, so often a lifesaver when you face an impasse. There are also exercises with a text. Whether you happen, at any given moment, to be directing or acting, these exercises will reveal the world the actor lives in and make acting both familiar and fascinating.

Then comes the vital process of rehearsal and development so often omitted by professionals and novices alike. It is strongly recommended that you videotape all rehearsals that are "off book" (the actors have learned their lines). A methodology is given to make this an exciting prospect. There are guidelines for actor and director preparing a scene and then guidance on planning coverage. The last roundup comes in the all-important preproduction meeting.

If you are in preproduction, do remember to use the checklist at the end of Part 5: Preproduction. It will remind you of many things, not least that a little time taken to survey your work can sometimes reveal embarrassing oversights.

CHAPTER 17

INTERPRETING THE SCRIPT

THE SCRIPT

If you have already made the step outline and concept as described in Chapter 7, you are coming to grips with the script's inner workings and practical implications. If you have not, do so now. Because the screenplay is skeletal and open to a wide spectrum of interpretation, you will need all the help you can get to assess its potential and build on it methodically and thoroughly.

FIRST IMPRESSIONS

If the screenplay is new to you, read it quickly and without interruption, noting your random first impressions. First impressions are intuitive and, like those about a new acquaintance, become significant as familiarity blunts your clarity. Define the film's premise and make sure you have an up-to-date step outline showing each sequence's function.

DETERMINE THE GIVENS

Reread the script and carefully determine the *givens*. This is your hard information directly specified in the screenplay. Givens include:

- Epoch
- Time of day
- Locations
- Character details revealed by their words and actions
- Clues to backstory (events prior to the period covered by the film)
- Words and actions used by characters

For each actor, for instance, the script provides everything known about the character's past and future. A character, after all, is like the proverbial iceberg—four-fifths out of sight. What is visible (that is, *in* the script) allows the actor to infer and develop what is below the "water line" (the character's biography, motives, volition, fears, ambitions, vulnerabilities, and so on). The givens are fixed and serve as the foundations determining everything else. Much is deliberately and wisely left unspecified, such as the movements and physical appearance of the characters and the treatment to be given the story in terms of camerawork, sound, and editing. The givens must be interpreted by director, cast, and crew, and the inferences each draws must eventually harmonize if the film is to be consistent.

BREAK INTO MANAGEABLE UNITS

Next, divide the script or treatment into workable units by acts, locations, and scenes. This helps you plan how each unit of the story must function and initiates the process of assembling a shooting script. If, for example, you have three scenes in the same day-care center, you will shoot them consecutively to conserve time and energy, even though they are widely spaced in the film. This will be laid out in the *breakdown* or *crossplot* (see Figure 17–4) described later in this chapter. When production begins, everyone must be well aware of the discontinuity among the three scenes or the actors may inadvertently adopt the same tone, and the camera crew may shoot and light them in the same way. In storytelling, you are always looking for ways to create a sense of contrast, change, and development.

PLAN TO TELL THE STORY THROUGH ACTION

Truly cinematic films remain largely comprehensible and dynamic even when the sound is turned off, so you should *devise your screen presentation as if for a silent film*. This will force you into telling your story cinematically rather than theatrically—that is, through action, setting, and behavior rather than through dialogue exchanges. This may require rewriting, which is a director's prerogative but most writers' idea of sabotage. Be sure to warn your writer of this likelihood well in advance. You don't want to find yourself battling your writer before you've even begun shooting.

DEFINING SUBTEXTS

You should keep in mind that every good text is a lifelike surface that hides deeper layers of meaning or *subtext* below. It reminds us that we are dramatists whose first purpose is to make evident the submerged significances flowing beneath life's surface. Much of the subtext arises out of what each character is really trying to do or get.

THE DISPLACEMENT PRINCIPLE

In life, people very rarely deal directly with the true source of their tensions. Characters often don't know themselves, or they keep what they do know hidden from other characters (remember life with your family?). What takes place is thus a displacement or an alternative to the characters' underlying desires. Two elderly men may be talking gloomily about the weather, but from what has gone before, or from telltale hints, we realize that one is adjusting to the death of a family member and the other is trying to bring up the subject of some money owed to him. Although what they say is that the heat and humidity might lead to a storm, what we infer is that Ted is enclosed by feelings of guilt and loss, while Harry is realizing that once again he cannot ask for the money he badly needs. This is the scene's subtext, which we can define as "Harry realizes he cannot bring himself to intrude his needs upon Ted at this moment and his situation is now desperate." We cannot interpret the subtext here without knowledge gained from earlier scenes, and this emphasizes the degree to which well-conceived drama builds and interconnects its subtexts.

ESTABLISHING CHARACTERS AND MOTIVES

An important aspect of considering a script is to trace each event and character backward to see that the requisite groundwork has been laid. If a cousin arrives to show off a new car, and in so doing, reveals his uncle's plan to sell the family business, that cousin needs to be established earlier, and so does the family's dependence on the business. Drama that uses coincidence or wheels in a character purely for plot requirements looks shoddy and contrived. Like threads in cloth, you want to make your tapestry appear seamless and untailored.

AMBIVALENCE OR BEHAVIORAL CONTRADICTIONS

Intelligent drama exploits the way each character consciously or otherwise tries to control the situation, either to hide underlying intentions and concerns or, should the occasion demand it, to draw attention to them. Once, as director and actor, you know the subtexts, you can develop behaviors to manifest the tensions between inner and outer worlds, between what the character wants and what impedes him.

Ambivalences like these are clues to the audience about a character's hidden life and underlying conflicts. When actors begin to act on (not merely think about) their characters' conflicts and locked energies, scenes move beyond an illustrative notion of human interaction and begin to truly manifest the characters' tensions. The work now begins to imply the pressurized water table of human emotion below the aridly logical top surface. This underlying tension may demand preserving a logical exterior in which the character is rational, mannerly, and inscrutable. This is all part of how a person keeps their agendas hidden. We all do it, and most of the time.

BREAK THE SCREENPLAY INTO ACTS

To refresh your memory:

Act I	Establishes the *setup* (characters, relationships, situation, and dominant problem faced by the central character or characters)
Act II	Develops the *complications* in relationships as the central character struggles with the obstacles that prevent him or her from solving the main problem
Act III	Intensifies the situation and *resolves* it, often in a climactic way that is emotionally satisfying

DEFINE A PREMISE OR THEMATIC PURPOSE

Another concept vitally important to the director is that of the thematic purpose, or *superobjective*, to use Stanislavski's concept. This is the authorial objective powering the work as a whole. You might say the superobjective of Orson Welles' *Citizen Kane* (1941) is to show that the child is father to the man, that the power-obsessed man's course through life is the consequence of childhood deprivation that no one around him ever understands.

However short your film, it is vital to define its thematic purpose while it remains in script form or you won't capitalize on the script's potential. Usually you have a strong intuition about what the thematic purpose is, but you should have it stated and to hand when you survey all the scene subtexts together. Side-stepping this brainwork will cost you dearly later.

To some degree, a script's thematic purpose is a subjective entity derived from the author's outlook and vision. In a work of some depth, neither the subtexts nor the thematic purpose are so limited that interpretive choices for the director and cast are fixed and immutable. Indeed, these choices are built into the way the reader reads and the audience reacts to a finished film because everyone interprets selectively what they see from a background of particular experiences. These are individual but also cultural and specific to the mood of the times.

Franz Kafka's disturbing story *Metamorphosis*—about a sick man who discovers he is turning into a cockroach—might be read as a parable about the changes people go through when dealing with the incurably sick or as a science fiction "what if" experiment that imprisons a human sensibility in the body of an insect. In the first example, the thematic purpose might be to show how utter dependency robs the subject of love and respect, while the second shows how compassion goes out to a suffering heart only when it beats inside a palatable body.

Whatever you choose as your thematic purpose, you absolutely *must* be able to articulate something interesting with utter conviction. It must be consistent with the text and stimulating to your creative collaborators. Superficial readings of the screenplay will produce divergent, contradictory interpretations, so you must shepherd your ensemble toward a shared understanding of the story's purpose or you won't have an integrated story. No matter how much work you put in, probing and intelligent actors will take you further into unexamined areas. That's part of the excitement of discovery.

GRAPHICS TO HELP REVEAL DRAMATIC DYNAMICS

Following are a couple of ways to expose the heart and soul of each scene. These methods for exposing what would otherwise remain undisturbed and unexamined are consciousness-raising techniques that allow the director to confront the implications of the material. They take time and energy to implement, but will repay your effort.

BLOCK DIAGRAM

Make a flow chart of the movie's content, with each sequence as a block. To do this conveniently, photocopy the Story Line/Editing Analysis Form (Figure 17–1). In the box, name the scene, and under "Contributes" write two or three lines to describe what the audience will perceive as its dramatic contribution to the story line, as in Figure 17–2. This goes further than the step outline because it is predominantly concerned with dramatic effect rather than content. Expect to write descriptive tags concerning:

- Plot points
- Exposition (factual and setup information)
- Character definition
- Building mood or atmosphere
- Parallel storytelling
- Ironic juxtaposition
- Foreshadowing

Having to write so briefly makes you find the paradigm for each tag a brain-straining exercise of the utmost value. Soon you will have the whole screenplay diagrammed as a flow chart. You will be surprised by how much you learn about its structure and its strengths. The following are common weaknesses and their likely cures:

Fault	**Likely cure**
Expository scenes that release information statically and without tension	Make the scene contribute action and movement to the story, not just factual information. You may need to drop the scene and bury the exposition in a more functional sequence.
Unnecessary repetition of information	Cut it out. However, some information may be so vital to the plot that you may want to cover yourself and only edit it out later if the audience proves not to need it.
Information released early or unnecessarily	Wilkie Collins said, "Make them laugh, make them cry, but make them wait." Making the audience wait is axiomatic

STORY LINE OR EDITING ANALYSIS FORM Page ________

Production title________________________________ Length ________mins

Writer/Editor________________________________ Date _____/______/2_____

Sequence definition (brief line title)	Sequence's contribution to the film's developing "argument."
Seq. #_______	Contributes: ____________ Length____mins_____secs
Seq. #_______	Contributes: ____________ Length____mins_____secs
Seq. #_______	Contributes: ____________ Length____mins_____secs

FIGURE 17–1

Form for script or editing analysis.

	for all drama, so it comes down to deciding how long.
Factual information that comes too late	When an audience is unduly frustrated they may give up. Another judgment call.
Confusions in time progression	This can be disastrous. Better to be conservative in shooting, knowing you

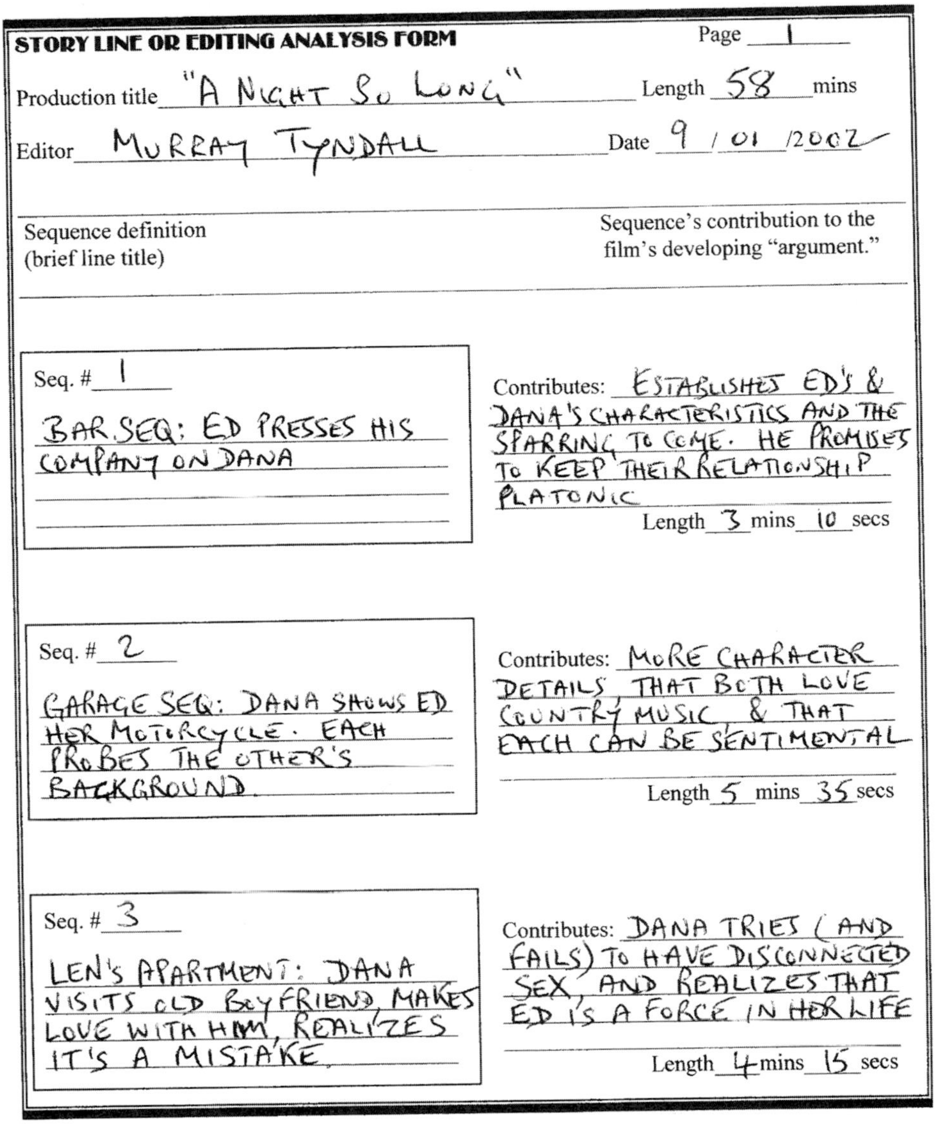

STORY LINE OR EDITING ANALYSIS FORM Page 1

Production title "A NIGHT SO LONG" Length 58 mins

Editor MURRAY TYNDALL Date 9 / 01 /2002

Sequence definition (brief line title) | Sequence's contribution to the film's developing "argument."

Seq. # 1
BAR SEQ: ED PRESSES HIS COMPANY ON DANA

Contributes: ESTABLISHES ED'S & DANA'S CHARACTERISTICS AND THE SPARRING TO COME. HE PROMISES TO KEEP THEIR RELATIONSHIP PLATONIC
Length 3 mins 10 secs

Seq. # 2
GARAGE SEQ: DANA SHOWS ED HER MOTORCYCLE. EACH PROBES THE OTHER'S BACKGROUND.

Contributes: MORE CHARACTER DETAILS, THAT BOTH LOVE COUNTRY MUSIC, & THAT EACH CAN BE SENTIMENTAL
Length 5 mins 35 secs

Seq. # 3
LEN'S APARTMENT: DANA VISITS OLD BOYFRIEND, MAKES LOVE WITH HIM, REALIZES IT'S A MISTAKE

Contributes: DANA TRIES (AND FAILS) TO HAVE DISCONNECTED SEX, AND REALIZES THAT ED IS A FORCE IN HER LIFE
Length 4 mins 15 secs

FIGURE 17–2

Sample of block-diagram analysis of a script.

	can reorder time during editing if experience shows your story profits by it.
Bunching of similar scenes, events, or actions	You'll only spot this if you force yourself to tag each scene with a premise. The cure is to drop the weaker scenes or give them different purposes.

Characters disappearing for long periods until needed	This can be a sign of having too many characters (amalgamate some?) or of characters who are conveniences rather than active in their own right.
Characters invented to serve a limited dramatic purpose	Amalgamate, thin out cast, or reconsider who does what.
Use of coincidence to solve a dramatic problem ("Guess what, I've won the lottery!")	Something is drastically wrong with the plotting unless the piece is about the degree to which life is determined by chance. Coincidence must never be allowed to carry a major plot point.
A lack of alternation in mood or environment	See if you can reconfigure the order or chronology of scenes to produce a more varied progression.
Excitement too early leading to anticlimax	Climaxes in scenes or in whole screenplays are quite often wrongly placed. You will have to reposition any that undercut the whole.
Similarity (and therefore redundancy) in what some scenes contribute	Remove the weaker of any redundant material.
Multiple endings because of indecision over what (and therefore how) the story must resolve	This is a problem emanating from having an ill-defined premise or multiple and incompatible premises. Sometimes endings depend on the nuance of the playing, and it may be legitimate to shoot more than one ending—even to include them all, depending on the genre of the piece.

GRAPHING TENSION AND BEATS

A good way to dig below a script's surface is to graph the changing emotional pressures or temperatures of each scene. Do it after several readings of the script and before you start work with the actors. If a scene remains problematic, it's good to graph it collaboratively with the actors after some initial rehearsal. Time is the graph's baseline and tension is the vertical axis. Do the overall scene in black, then use a different color for each main character. If, for instance, you have a comedy scene between a dentist and a frightened patient, you could graph the rise and fall of the patient's anxiety, then rehearse the action to progressively escalate the patient's fear and link to it the rising irritation of the dentist. Each dramatic unit within the scene culminates in a *beat* or moment of decisive realization for one or another of the characters. One such beat might take place in the reception area when the already nervous patient hears a yell from the surgery and decides to make a run for freedom once the receptionist's back is turned. Another might come when, finding she has already locked the door, he must face her contempt.

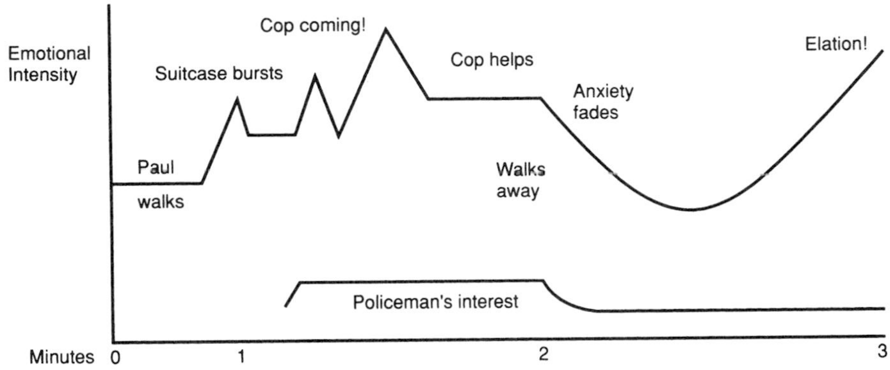

FIGURE 17–3

Graph expressing changes of emotional intensity in two characters.

Before you begin shooting, make a barometric chart for your whole film's emotional dynamics. It won't be easy because you will have to designate graph coordinates to reflect the issues in your particular scene. You will be surprised at how much this reveals. I discovered why you need this exercise the hard way: in the cutting room when I found I had directed a film where scene after scene had surreptitiously adopted a uniform shape. They were simply restating the same emotional information.

As an example, here is a scene based on a wartime experience of my father's in World War II in London. Food was scarce and often acquired on the black market. Note that for a film treatment we put it into the present tense.

> Paul is a sailor from the docks setting out for home across London. Onboard ship he has acquired a sack of brown sugar and is taking it home to his family. Food of all kinds is rationed, and what he is doing is very risky. He has the sugar inside a battered old suitcase. The sugar is as heavy as a corpse, but he contrives to walk lightly as though carrying only his service clothing. In a busy street one lock of the suitcase bursts, and the green canvas sack comes sagging into view. Dropping the suitcase hastily on the sidewalk he grips it between his knees in a panic while thinking what to do. To his horror, a grim-faced policeman approaches. Paul realizes that the policeman will check what's inside the suitcase, and Paul will go to prison. He's all ready to run away, but the policeman pulls some string out of his pocket and gets down on his knees, his nose within inches of the contraband, to help Paul tie it together. Paul keeps talking until the job's done, then thanking him profusely, picks up the suitcase as if it contained feathers and hurries away, feeling the cop is going to sadistically call him back. Two streets later he realizes he is free.

The graph in Figure 17–3 plots the intensity of each character's dominant emotion against the advance of time. Paul's emotions change, while the unaware policeman's are simple and placid by contrast. Paul's stages of development, roughly, are:

- Trying to walk normally to conceal weighty contraband
- Sense of catastrophe as suitcase bursts
- Assuming policeman is coming to arrest him
- Realizing his guilt is not yet apparent—all is not yet lost
- Tension while trying to keep policeman's attention off contents
- Making escape under policeman's ambiguous gaze
- Sense of joyous release as he realizes he's gotten away with it

Notice that the treatment contains some realizations that cannot be explicitly filmed without breaking the sequence into "what if" sequences where Paul imagines himself arrested, being tried, and being put in prison. Better would be to plant the consequences of thieving earlier in the action.

A visual like Figure 17–3 brings clarity to where and how changes in the dominant emotions must happen and shows:

- The need to create distinct rising and falling emotional pressures within the characters
- Where characters undergo major transitions or beats
- Where the cast must externalize beats through action

Clarifying the unfolding action in this way helps overcome a major problem with untrained actors: They often try to play *all* their character's characteristics *all* the time, no matter what is happening at any given moment. This muddies and confuses the playing and renders it an intellectual approach. Good playing deals with one situation and its attendant emotions at a time and finds credible ways to transition from one to the next. The director must often rein in actors and help them concentrate on the specifics of their character's consciousness, moment by moment.

In the scene above, the policeman feels only a mild, benign interest, which falls away as the sailor with the successfully mended suitcase goes on his way. It is a very different situation for Paul. He must pretend he's an innocent man with a luggage problem. Knowing something the policeman does not know, the audience empathizes with the sailor's anxiety and appreciates his efforts to project petty concerns. What is missing from the scene is the knowledge of (1) the nature of the contraband, (2) where he is going with it, and (3) what he risks if he is caught. For the scene to yield its full potential, all these plotting points would need to be established as exposition earlier.

POINT OF VIEW

We could add a dimension to our scene by underscoring Paul's subjectivity and raising the stakes of the scene. By having the policeman appear threatening as he approaches, we could make him seem to be testing Paul's guilt by offering to help. Only late in the scene would we reveal his benign motives. Camerawork juxtaposing the bulging, insecure suitcase against the approaching policeman would suggest visually the thoughts uppermost in Paul's mind.

Here we are trying to reveal Paul's point of view (POV), which means *relaying evidence that makes us identify with him.* By switching to the policeman's point of view, we can also investigate his reality and show the POV of an apparently unsympathetic character as well as that of our hero. This is an important departure from the good/evil dichotomy of the simple morality play where only the main character is a rounded portrait and subsidiary characters remain flat.

In my example the audience has been led to participate in Paul's inner experience while seeing all the time how he conceals what he is feeling. Actors and directors of long experience intuitively carry out this duality. The clarity and force of subjectivity revealed in this way will contribute much to a satisfying performance. For the novice actor lacking an instinct for this, nothing less than a detailed, moment-to-moment analysis with his director will enable him to effectively mold his character's consciousness at the core of the scene.

FATAL FLAW: THE GENERALIZED INTERPRETATION

Inexperienced players will, as I have said, approach a scene with a correct but generalized attitude gained from a reading or discussion. Applied like a color wash and without regard to localized detail, the unspecific, monolithic interpretation produces a scene that is fuzzy and muted where it should be sharp and forceful. When you see this as you direct, you will have to demand that each actor develop clear specific goals from moment to moment within each scene. You can get this by asking actors to speak their character's subtextual thoughts out loud, as in Project 22-3: "Improvising an Interior Monologue." This may have to be done one-on-one so the actor does not feel humiliated in front of more experienced players. Be careful, by the way, that your role as coach is not appropriated by actors who consider themselves more experienced or you will soon have multiple directors.

CROSSPLOT OR SCRIPT BREAKDOWN IN PREPARATION FOR REHEARSAL

Take the script and make a breakdown of characters appearing in each scene, like the one in Figure 17–4 made for a treatment of *Northanger Abbey.* A scene breakdown like this, allowing you to see at a glance which scenes require which location and what combination of actors, will be essential for planning the rehearsal schedule and the eventual shoot. It also indicates the film's inherent pattern of interactions and is yet another aid to discovering the work's underlying structures.

FIRST TIMING

A film's length absolutely determines what festival or market it can enter. Television has strict length requirements, so learning to keep control over length is vital. Already you need to know how long the script will run. You can get a ballpark figure by allowing a minute of screen time per screenplay page. This should

Scene	Location	Script Pages	Catherine	Isabella	John Thorpe	Henry Tilney	James Morland	Eleanor	Mrs. Allen	General Tilney	Mrs. Thorpe	CHARACTERS PER SCENE
1	The Dance	1-2	✓						✓			2
2	Lower Rooms	2-6	✓			✓						2
3	Pump Room	6-7		✓							✓	2
4	Mrs. Allen's	7-13	✓	✓	✓		✓					4
5	Pump Room	13-20	✓	✓		✓	✓	✓				5
6	Mrs. Allen's	20-24	✓	✓	✓		✓		✓			5
7	On the Journey	24-25	✓		✓		✓					3
8	At the Theater	25-27	✓			✓			✓			3
9	Mrs. Allen's	27-30	✓	✓	✓		✓	✓		✓		6
10	Out Walking	30-35	✓			✓		✓				3
11	Mrs. Allen's	35-37	✓	✓								2
12	In the Street	37-40	✓		✓							2
13	At the Tilneys'	40-41	✓					✓		✓		3
14	Mrs. Allen's	41-43	✓	✓								2
	NUMBER OF SCENES PER CHARACTER		13	7	5	4	5	4	3	2	1	

FIGURE 17–4

Typical scene and character breakdown table shows which characters, locations, and script pages are necessary for each scene.

average out across many pages but will not necessarily work for specific passages such as a rapid dialogue exchange or a succession of highly detailed images with long, slow camera movements. You can get a more reliable figure by reading over each scene aloud, acting all the lines, and going through the actions in imagination, or better, for real. Using a stopwatch, make a notation for each sequence, then add up the total.

Be aware that *rehearsal and development invariably slows material* by adding business not specified in the script. This kind of action must be present if the characters are to be credible and the film cinematic rather than theatrical. Make new timings periodically to avoid unpleasant surprises.

If rewriting makes a scene too long, re-examine every line of dialogue to see if newly developed action makes any of it redundant. Likewise, in rehearsal, never hesitate to cut a line if its content can be delivered by an action.

CHAPTER 18

CASTING

WHY CASTING MATTERS

Good casting contributes massively to the success of any film. Beginning directors often do it poorly by settling for the first person who seems right or who is reliable.

The object of auditioning is to find out as much as you can about the physical, psychological, and emotional make-up of each potential cast member so you can commit yourself confidently to the best choice. Doing this means initially putting many actors through a brief procedure to reveal their character and to indicate how each handles representative situations. Later there will be semifinal and final rounds of auditioning. The first aim is to identify broad characteristics:

- Physical self (features, body language, movements, voice)
- Innate character (confidence, outlook, reflexes, rhythm, energy, sociability, imprint made by life)
- Type of intelligence (sensitivity to others, perceptiveness of environment, degree of self-exploration, and cultivation of tastes)
- Grasp of acting (experience, concepts of the actor's role in drama, craft knowledge)
- Directability (interaction with others, flexibility, defenses, self-image)
- Commitment (work habits, motivation to act, reliability)

THE DANGERS IN IDEALS

There are two ways to approach casting.

1. **Can this actor play the father in my script?** Naturally you wonder whether this particular man is right for the character of the father in your script. There is, however, a hidden bias in this attitude. The actor is being held up to an ideal of the character, as though the character were already formed and the

actor either right or wrong. This puts emphasis on a premeditated image of the character and makes you view the actor through a cookie cutter. By this measurement the actor will always fail. Casting a film from a mental master plan is like marriage for the man who knows what Ms. Right must be before he has met her.

2. **What kind of father would this actor give my film?** By this approach you acknowledge that the role is capable of many possible character shadings. Casting becomes development rather than fulfillment. Very importantly, you are already treating the actor's physical and mental being as an active collaborator in the process of making drama.

THE CASTING PROCESS

Casting is a predictable process. It involves circulating character descriptions and finding actors to fill each part and to bring both tangible and intangible assets to what is in the blueprint. This is always an anxious time, but it's important to see what kind of character a person will produce because of who and what they inherently are. You want to ensure that you can work with cast members and that they are enthusiastic about the character they will play.

DEVELOPING CHARACTER DESCRIPTIONS

Before you can search for possible actors, make basic character descriptions to post in appropriate places (newspapers, theater, or acting school billboards) or to give over the phone. A typical list might look like this:

Ken, 15, tall and thin, nervous, curious, intelligent, overcritical, obsessed with science fiction

George, late 20s, medium height, medical equipment salesman, lives carefully and calls his parents each Friday; husband of Kathy

Kathy, early 30s, but has successfully lied about her age; small-town beauty queen gone to seed after a steamy divorce; met George through a dating service

Ted, 60s, bus inspector, patriot, grower of prize chrysanthemums, disapproving father of George

Eddie, 40s, washing machine repairman, part-time conjuror and clown at children's parties; too self-involved to be married, likes to spread home-spun philosophy

Angela, 70s, cheerful, resourceful, has a veneer of respectability that breaks down raucously after a couple of drinks; in early life made a fortune in something illicit and determined to live forever

Thumbnail sketches compress a lot into a few words and allow the reader to infer possible physical appearances. They also present an attractive challenge to people who would like to fill these roles.

ATTRACTING APPLICANTS

In every aspect of filmmaking, supply yourself with an abundance of choice. Apply this principle particularly to casting because the human presence on the screen is mostly how you command your audience's attention. Though the audience might be inexpert in screen technique, they are an absolute authority on the validity of the human presence. Here you can easily be more naive than your audience, especially if you cast a friend or loved one in a main part. I once edited a film where the director simply couldn't see how inadequate his wife was in the main part and fiercely resisted being told.

Casting among beginners is usually the least rigorous part of the whole process. Feeling uncomfortable with the power to choose among fellow aspirants, the embarrassed newcomer settles too early and too easily for actors who look right. Age and appearance matter, but this is only the beginning. All 40-year-old men are not alike, and to presume you can take the right face and make its owner into the script's sentimental, spendthrift father is asking for trouble.

Inadequate casting usually arises from a lack of:

- Confidence in your right to search far and wide
- Knowledge about how to discover actors' underlying potential
- Self-knowledge about who you can work with and who you cannot

Learning how to audition helps to remove the crippling sense of inadequacy and embarrassment about making human choices. Using a video camera delays decision making until you can, if you wish, enlist the opinions of key production members.

PASSIVE SEARCH FOR ACTORS

If you live in a city, you can spread a large net simply by putting an advertisement in the appropriate papers. Be warned that large nets bring in some very odd fish and sometimes bring in nothing at all.

ACTIVE SEARCH FOR ACTORS

If there is a fair amount of theater in your area, there is probably a monthly auditions broadsheet, Web site, or other professional contact method. In it, describe the project and give the number, sex, and age of the characters in a few words and a phone number to contact.

Apart from the oldest and youngest in the sample cast described earlier, the rest are drawn from an age bracket normally immersed in daily responsibilities. Three of the adults are blue-collar parts, a social class least likely to have done any acting and most liable to feel inadequate and self-conscious. These are generalizations whose only function is to help focus the search and indicate what kind of inventiveness is needed to locate the exceptions with the necessary qualities and spare time.

Anyone who lacks a liberal budget must be resourceful in finding likely people to try out. Wherever possible, save time and frustration by actively seeking out likely participants. First contact key people in theater groups. Locate the casting director and ask if you can pay a brief visit. Whoever handles casting will have a wealth of information about local talent, but be careful to clarify that you will take care not to poach in their preserves. The next most knowledgeable people are the producers (who direct in the theater) and other committed theater workers. Knowledgeable members will often respond enthusiastically with names you can invite to try out. When a theater group is successful enough to use only professional (union) actors, the response is likely to be cautious or even downright unfriendly. Theaters don't like their best cast members seduced away by screen parts and may want to avoid prejudicing their relationship with the actors' union. Don't be surprised if you get a tight-lipped referral to the actors' union.

If your budget is rock bottom, you will have to work hard. Actors well suited to specific parts can always be found, but it takes ingenuity and diligence. Never forget that if you have a good script, *your film's credibility comes not from your film technique, but from how believable you can make the human presence on the screen.* Good film technique simply provides a seamless storytelling medium. The better it is, the more the audience dwells on that all-important human presence.

For the character of 15-year-old Ken, I would track down teachers producing drama in local schools and ask them to suggest boys able to play that character well. The teacher can ask the child, or the child's parents, to get in touch. This allays the nightmare that their child is being stalked by a coven of hollow-eyed pornographers.

Elderly people are more of a problem. Because most cultures sideline the old, many become physically and mentally inactive. Your first task in casting Ted and Angela will be to locate older people who keep mentally and physically active. You may be lucky and find a senior citizen's theater group to draw upon or you may have to track down unusual individuals.

For Ted, I would look among older blue-collar men who have taken an active and extroverted role in life, perhaps in local politics, union organizing, entertainment, or salesmanship. All these occupations require some flair for interaction with other people and a relish for the fray.

Angela is a hard person to cast, but try looking among retired actresses or vocal women's group members such as citizen's and neighborhood pressure groups—anywhere you could expect to find an elderly woman secure in her life's accomplishments and adventurous enough to play a boozy, earthy woman with a past.

While you cast, remind yourself periodically that hidden among the gray armies of the unremarkable there always exist a few individuals in any age group whose lives are being lived with wit, intelligence, and individuality. Such people rise to prominence in the often-unlikely worlds to which exigency or eccentricity has taken them. Angela, for instance, might be the president of the Standard Poodle Fanciers Club, and Ted might be discovered through attending an amateur comedian contest or a poetry slam.

Werner Herzog's actors, for instance, include non-professionals drawn from around him. The central figure in *The Mystery of Kasper Hauser* (1974) and *Stroszek* (1977) is played by the endearing Bruno S—, a street singer and Berlin transport manager whose surname has remained undisclosed to protect his job.

Robert Bresson, who refused to cast anyone trained to act, used lawyers in *The Trial of Joan of Arc* (1962) to play Joan's inquisitors. A lifetime spent defining details gave them just the right punctiliousness in their cross-examining. In his *Notes on the Cinematographer* (Los Angeles: Green Integer, 1997), Bresson gives a compelling rationale, akin to a documentary-making attitude, for using "models" (his word for players) who have never performed before.

SETTING UP THE FIRST AUDITION

FIELDING PHONE APPLICANTS

Many people who present themselves as actors are minimally experienced. The world is full of dreamers looking for that path to stardom; these should be avoided except for very brief, undemanding parts. A rigorous audition helps weed out the half-hearted. Add the obviously unskilled to a waiting list so you can audition those claiming experience first. As each person calls, you must be ready to politely abort the procedure at any stage. Try informing potential cast in this order:

- **The project and your experience.** Be direct and realistic. If you are a student group, say so. Use this as leverage to find out the person's experience in acting. If they claim film experience, ask their impressions of the process.
- **Time commitment and any remuneration offered.** Be truthful about the time rehearsal and shooting will take, and emphasize that filming is slow at the best of times. Any cool responses or undue negotiating are a danger bell indicating the applicant's high ego or low level of interest.
- **The role in which the actor is interested.** Question the actor to find out whether his or her characteristics are appropriate, and be ready to suggest an alternate part if the person sounds interesting.
- **An audition slot if the person sounds appropriate.**
- **What the audition will demand.** A first call might ask actors to perform two contrasting 3-minute monologues of their own choosing and take part in a cold reading.

CONDUCTING THE FIRST AUDITION

This session aims to net as many people as practical so you can later have call-backs for those deemed suitable. Many respondents, in spite of what they said on the phone, will be devoid of everything you require or quite unrealistic about their abilities and commitment. In this winnowing operation, expect much chaff for very little wheat.

GATHERING INFORMATION

Schedule people into slots so that they arrive at, say, 10-minute intervals and can be individually received by someone who can answer questions. Have actors wait in a separate area from the audition space, and give each a form to complete, so later you have on file the following information:

1. Name and address
2. Home and work phone numbers
3. Acting experience and any references
4. Role for which actor is trying out
5. Special interests and skills

The last is purely to get a sense of what attributes the actor may have that indicate special energy and initiative. You might also have a section asking actors to write a few lines on what attracts them to acting. This can reveal values and how serious and realistic the person is.

A good plan is to have trusted assistants in the holding area who can chat informally with incoming actors. This helps calm actors' fears and lets your assistants form impressions of how punctual and organized the actors seem and what their personalities are like. These can be most valuable later.

STARTING THE AUDITION

The actor can now be shown into the audition space where he or she will perform. Videotape the performances so you can review your choices later and make comparisons, especially when you see a lot of actors for one part.

Most people are trying to cover up how nervous and apprehensive they are at auditions, but this is not necessarily negative because it shows they attach importance to being accepted. The presence of a camera increases the pressure.

MONOLOGUES

It is good to see two brief monologues of the actor's choice and that show very different characters. These can tell you:

- Whether an actor habitually acts with the face alone or with the whole body
- What kind of physical presence, rhythm, and energy level he or she has
- What his or her voice is like (a good voice is a tremendous asset)
- What kind of emotional range he or she spontaneously produces
- What the actor thinks is appropriate for him- or herself and for your piece

Whether their choice of material is well or badly performed and whether you can "see" the character the actor is playing are very important. The actor's choice and handling of material also indicate what they think they do best. The choice may reflect intelligent research based on what the actor has found out about your production, or it may indicate an enduring self-image. A man trying out for a brash salesman who chooses the monologue of an endearing wimp has probably already cast himself in life as a loser whose best hope is to be funny. This will hardly do for, say, the part of someone vengeful. Here you may sense a quality of acquiescence that makes the actor psychologically and emotionally unsuitable for this part, though perhaps interesting for another.

COLD READING

For this you will need several copies of several different scenes. Depending upon whom is in your waiting room, you might want to try combining two men, two women, a man and a woman, an old person with someone young, and so on. It is a good idea *not* to use scenes from your film, but instead to find something from theatrical repertory that is analogous in mood and characters. You don't want whomever you choose to become fixed by early impressions of your script.

Your assistant can decide, based on whom is waiting, which piece to read next and give each actor a copy of the scene in advance.

In the cold reading you will:

- See actors trying to give life to a character just encountered and having to think on their feet
- See the same scene with more than one set of actors, and thus what each brings to the part
- Have the opportunity to compare what quickness, intelligence, and creativity are evoked by the bare words on the page
- Hear how each actor uses his or her voice
- See how some will use their bodies and inject movement
- Find out who asks questions about their character or about the piece from which the scene is drawn

Performances and behavior will affect you differently and often in ways that pose interesting questions. In a reading with two characters of the same sex, you can switch the actors and ask them to read again to see if the actors can produce appropriate and different qualities at short notice.

After actors have auditioned, always:

- Thank them
- Give a date by which to expect news of the outcome
- Make a note of something positive about their performance to help you be supportive of those you have to reject

DECISIONS AFTER FIRST ROUND OF AUDITIONS

If you have promising applicants, run the tapes of their contributions and brainstorm with your project coworkers. Discussing each actor's strengths and weaknesses usually reveals further dimensions of the candidates, not to mention insights into your crew members and their values.

Now comes the agonizing part. Call everyone who auditioned and tell them whether they were selected for callback auditions. Telling the bad news to those not selected is hard on both parties; mitigate the disappointment by saying something appreciative and positive about the person's performance. With the people you want to see again, set a callback date for further auditioning.

DANGERS OF TYPECASTING

Be careful when casting characters who have prominently negative traits. It can be disastrous during shooting if an actor slowly becomes aware that he was cast for his own negative qualities.

To varying degrees, all actors go through difficulties playing negative characteristics because of the lurking fear that these characteristics are really within their own make-up. The less secure the individual is, the more likely such self-doubts will become acute. A sure sign of this insecurity is when an actor makes a personal issue of his or her character's qualities and argues to upgrade them.

To protect yourself, ask any actors you are considering to outline their ideas about their character's negative traits. Their underlying attitudes may influence your choice. Villains are easy to play, but playing a stupid or nasty character may either be viewed as an interesting challenge or as a personal sacrifice by the actor. There are no small parts, said Stanislavski, only small actors.

LONG- OR SHORT-TERM CHOICES

It can be tempting to cast the person who is ahead of the pack because he or she gave something specially attractive at the audition. This actor may be brilliant or may later emerge as glib and inflexible, developing less than a partner whose audition was less accomplished. Caution dictates that you investigate not only what an actor wants to do, but also how well they handle the unfamiliar and how willing and interested they are to push beyond present boundaries. All actors of any experience are fervently committed in principle, but in practice may reveal something different. Acting involves the whole person, not just ideas, and you may find that a genially accomplished personality coming under the threat of the unexpected suddenly manifests bizarre forms of self-defense and resistance (see Chapter 20: Actors' Problems).

THE DEMANDING PART OF THE CHARACTER WHO DEVELOPS

Many parts require little in adaptability to direction. To cast a surly gas station attendant for one short scene requires little growth potential, whereas the part of a young wife who discovers her husband is dominated by his mother will call for extended and subtle powers of development. This character must go through a spectrum of emotions during which she changes and experiences deep feelings, so the director must find an actor with the openness and emotional reach to undertake a grueling rehearsal and performance process.

FIRST CALLBACK

When you are ready to call back the most promising actors who auditioned, you will need to prepare some additional testing procedures.

A READING FROM YOUR SCRIPT

Give some background to the scene, which should be demanding but only a few minutes in duration.

- Ask each actor to play the character in a specified way. After the readings, give critical feedback and directions to further develop the scene.
- Have them play the scene again and look for how the actors build on their initial performances, holding on to what you praised but altering the specified areas.
- For a further run-through, give each actor a different mood or characteristic to see what he or she produces when given a radically different premise.

IMPROVISATION

Give two actors brief outlines of characters in the script and outline one of the script's situations that involve them. Then:

- Ask your players to improvise their own scene upon the situation in the (unseen) script. The goal is not to see how close they get to the scripted original, but how they handle themselves when much of the creation is spontaneous.
- After they have done a version, give them feedback about aspects you see developing in their version, and ask for a further version, specifying some change in behavior and mood. Now you will be able to see not only what they can produce from themselves but how well they incorporate direction.

SECOND CALLBACK

INTERVIEW

By now you have formed ideas about each individual, which you want to confirm and amplify. Give your best candidates the script to read, but tell them *not* to learn any lines, because this will fix their performance at an embryonic stage.

After they have read the script, spend time informally and alone with each, encouraging him or her to ask questions and to talk about both the script and himself or herself. Look for realism, sincerity, and a genuine interest in drama. It is a good sign if an actor is sincerely excited because the script explores some issue that is genuinely central to his or her own life. It is also very important that the actors feel they have something to learn from working with you and your project.

Be wary of those who flatter or name-drop, who seem content with superficial readings, are inflexibly opinionated, or leave you feeling that they are stooping to do you a good turn. Avoid like the plague anyone who seems to be looking over your shoulder for something better.

MIX AND MATCH ACTORS

When you have multiple contenders for a lead part, try them out in different permutations so you can assess the personal chemistry each has with the others. In part, this is to see what they will communicate to an audience. I once had to cast a short film about a man in his 30s who becomes involved with a rebellious teenage girl. We rejected a more accomplished actor because there was something indefinable in his manner that made the relationship seem sinister. Another actor paired with the same actress changed the balance to give the girl the upper hand, as the story demanded.

You also mix and match in search of the most interesting chemistry between the actors themselves. Sometimes two actors simply don't communicate well. Actors cast to play lovers must be tried out extensively with each other. There may be temperamental or other differences that render them unattractive to each other, but whatever the cause, the result will be a wariness and stiffness in their playing that could utterly disable your film. You always want to cast players who are responsive and interested in each other. Even when this is accomplished, you may still encounter problems. In Alain Tanner's *The Middle of the World* (1974), the male lead usually produced his best work in an early take while the woman playing opposite him slowly worked to her peak over a number of takes, sometimes leading to frustration all round (Figure 18–1).

FIGURE 18–1

Actors have different development rates. Philippe Leotard in Tanner's *The Middle of the World* (1974, courtesy New Yorker Films).

FINAL CHOICES

REVIEW YOUR IMPRESSIONS

Before making a final choice, review your impression of each actor's:

- Physical and temperamental suitability
- Impact
- Imprint on the part in relation to the other actors
- Rhythms of speech and movement
- Quickness of mind and directability
- Ability at mimicry, especially if he or she is to maintain a regional or foreign accent
- Voice quality (extremely important!)
- Capacity to hold on to both new and old instructions
- Ability to carry out his or her character's development, whether it is quick and intuitive or slower and more graduated
- Commitment to the project
- Long-term commitment to acting as a discipline
- Patience with filming's slow and disjunctive progress
- Ability to enter and re-enter an emotional condition over several takes and camera angles
- Compatibility with the other actors
- Compatibility with you, the director

CAMERA TEST

To confirm that you are making the right choices, shoot a short scene on videotape with the principal actors. Even then you will probably remain somewhat uncertain and feel you have to make difficult decisions.

If you have an overwhelming urge to cast someone that your intuition says is risky, you should tactfully but directly communicate your reservations. You might, for instance, feel uncertain of the actor's commitment or feel that the actor has a resistance to authority figures and will have problems being directed. Confrontation at this early point shows you how the actor handles uncomfortable criticism and paves the way should that perception later become an issue or, God forbid, should replacement become a necessity. An actor who seems arrogant and egocentric will sometimes gratefully admit, when faced with a frank reaction to his characteristics, that he has an unfortunate way of masking uncertainty.

More than anything, people in all walks of life crave recognition. If the director is able to comment on the potential and on any deficiencies that mask it, the serious actor will respond with warmth and loyalty. Sharing and honesty is a goal in director-actor and actor-actor relationships because it is the basis for trust and a truly creative working relationship. Every committed actor is looking for a director who can lead the way across new thresholds. This is development not just in acting, but in living. If you can perform this function, that actor will place great loyalty with you and be your best advocate to other actors.

ANNOUNCING CASTING DECISIONS

When you make your final decisions, personally notify and thank all who have taken part. This signals your professionalism and maintains your good standing in the community. Needless to say, rejection is painful, and all the more so for those who made it to the final round. Actors are used to rejection, and someone who does it thoughtfully and sensitively is someone worth trying again in the future. Filmmaking is a village, and your reputation is important when you return to the well.

CHAPTER 19

DIRECTING ACTORS

Apart from a knowledge of filmmaking, the most useful understanding any director can acquire is of acting. You can and should read about it, but more important is to take classes and actually do it. Acting is a well-documented craft, so what follows is a brief digest of useful ideas and practices.

IN SEARCH OF NATURALNESS

While an animator creates a complete world according to an esoteric vision, live action cinema must fashion its tales from people and objects captured by photography. The theater uses the same means but boldly forces the spectator to accept something patently untrue. Go to *Hamlet* and you must suspend disbelief and accept that you can see through invisible walls what's happening in a medieval Danish court. However, a cinema Shakespeare such as Kenneth Branagh's *Much Ado About Nothing* (1993) has little choice but to use authentic locations and costumes or to risk doing a modern production. Film's intimacy and fidelity to the actual forces the need for realistic settings. Authentic settings make audiences expect psychological realism in the acting. The unwillingness of audiences trained to high standards to suspend disbelief faces film productions unable to afford experienced screen talent with problems. You will need to understand acting and become a drama coach if your characters are to meet your audience's basic expectations.

THEATER AND FILM ACTING COMPARED

When you see a fine theater production on TV or film, some quality in the acting intrudes to make the performances false to the screen. Actors are doing something that they had to abandon early in the 20th century as film and its audiences matured. The difference between acting for theater and film is now very significant and is a psychological matter rather than one of technique. The difference is in where actors find support for what they do. One has an audience, one does not, and this makes a world of difference.

- In the theater *actors invoke the audience's support in sustaining belief in their roles.*
- In fiction film *actors draw belief in their roles as in life, from within themselves and from other characters.* There is no audience.

Fiction film is not different from documentary in that it demands conviction from within, not externally. When a theater actor first enters the film situation, he feels robbed of support and may suffer doubt over his ability and worth. The director is now the only audience and must wean the actor to a new, more personal and internalized way of sustaining focus and belief. A non-actor will feel no different because we are used to getting other people's reactions in unfamiliar situations. Film crewmembers, each busy with their jobs, are at first strangely impersonal and remote. The director will need some methods to support non-actors as well as trained actors.

DIRECTING IS REMOVING OBSTACLES

In general, film actors don't need special techniques or arcane information from their director. What they require is authoritative help in casting off any layers of human insecurity so they can *be* rather than perform. Quite simply, freedom from tension is what permits this. The film actor should have no sense of performing for anyone other than you, the director. The biggest surprise to anyone watching a scene being filmed is the smallness and apparent inconsequentiality of the action. I remember as a young cutting room assistant sneaking on to the set to watch a close-up being shot. It was all very static and after some mumbling from the actors the assistant director called "Cut" and I thought, "Nothing happened—they can't have been filming." Yet when I saw the scene huge on the screen the next day, *everything* happened. The fiction camera captures life as intimately and completely as if you are seeing a documentary—and then some. What the director evokes is human truth, which in everyday life takes place within a small compass. It's hard to believe that a huge Panavision camera can be such a perfect and intimate voyeur.

MAINTAINING FOCUS BY DOING

The film actor cannot lose focus even for a moment because the camera registers everything and there is nowhere to hide. An under-occupied actor being stared at by a camera becomes fatally aware of how she may look. This is a vicious circle, for the actor becomes self-consciously aware of how destructive it is to be thinking such things. Now fatally divided, one half of the actor's attention is fixed on trying to act while the other half is trying *not* to be a judging audience. The battle against self-consciousness is lost until the actor can escape back into her character's state of natural preoccupation. The character's inner and outer actions offer a useful escape because they tend to engage her in the character's state of mind, deflecting the mind from consciousness of self. *Doing is therefore the path to being*. To stay in character, all actors need a continuous flow of internal or external actions, of things to *do*.

FOCUS AND RELAXATION

Paradoxically, mental focus leads to an overall relaxation of mind and body, which further assists the actor in finding and maintaining the character's mental focus. To know where actors are, study their body language until you know instantly their particular signs of tension—particularly in their shoulders, face, hands, and walk.

Usually you can undo this tension by redirecting their attention or by using indirect ways to reassure actors that their work is effective. When they care too much, they get tense. Have some improv games ready as a refresher to solve extreme cases. Be on your guard, for a relaxed actor can also be one who is not trying and doesn't care about the production.

The experienced actor avoids the onset of paralyzing self-judgment by maintaining a flow of the character's physical tasks. He or she works hard to invent just the right action or task to resonate the character's present state of mind.

EMOTIONAL MEMORY

Not only is the actor freed from self-contemplation by maintaining a flow of actions, but the truest actions release powerful, authentic emotion during performance. Stanislavski named this curious psychic reflex *emotional memory*. Of his many discoveries about acting psychology, this is the most frequently misunderstood. To do it justice we must look at how the human mind works when an actor is *being* rather than *signifying*.

THE MIND-BODY CONNECTION

A person's body invariably expresses his or her state of mind. A brother knows what kind of day his sister has had from the way she dismounts her bicycle or eats a sandwich. A class knows what mood the teacher is in when he puts down his books. This knowledge of body language is developed in our earliest years. Indeed young children react intuitively to what adults express non-verbally and only become confused when the adult uses contradictory words. When people reach their teens they have learned to value cerebral control above what is intuitive and emotional.

Remember that *no inner state exists without outward evidence*. To the alert, we always show what we feel. This means that when an actor's mind and emotions are correctly engaged and his actions are appropriate, his body will unconsciously express all that his character feels. Directing should therefore be concerned with arriving at a character's true state of mind by helping the actor develop the actions that truly accompany it. Emotions are enlisted by actions, not the other way around, as most people think. Exactly how you cover your mouth with your hand when you have spoken out of turn will bring on the feeling of embarrassment. Try it. Now try feeling embarrassed and letting your feeling direct your hand. It's a non-starter because *one cannot choose to feel an emotion.*

BUSINESS

Actor and director must generate plenty of *business* (or appropriate action) while preparing each role. Don't move on when an actor correctly describes what the character feels unless you have also explored what the character might *do* in the circumstance. Doing will usually involve a small but significant action, like dropping the eyes, turning to glance out a window, feeling for change in a pocket, or recalling the image of an indulgent aunt. Many actions will be interior as well as exterior, and interior ones are just as important. Deciding why you want to go for a walk can be an interesting and informative thing to watch if done authentically and well. Good actors love this kind of challenge.

STAY BUSY IN CHARACTER

As an actor, the key to maintaining your character's flow of consciousness is not just to keep busy, but to *keep busy in character*. To exist realistically as a new character, you must have your attention fully occupied by your character's thoughts, memories, inner visions, and outward actions. Given any opportunity, your ever-anxious mind will detach and begin to imagine how you must appear to those watching (foolish, undignified, heroic, handsome, deeply moving, etc.). This is disabling and leads immediately to the black hole called *loss of focus*.

LOSING AND REGAINING FOCUS

Signs of Lost Focus: When an action comes across as false, the actor has either chosen poorly or has lost focus. Losing focus (ceasing to experience a character's thoughts and emotions) shows in the whole physical being, in everything the actor says and does. An audience, no matter how uninformed, will register this. Being focused is not peculiar to acting because it underpins everyone's sense of normalcy. In everyday life we maintain actions and pursue relationships from assumptions about who we are and how we appear to others. These are only challenged under exceptional circumstances.

Reasons for Lost Focus: When someone we respect watches us, or when we must speak to a group, we may become so self-aware that we stop functioning automatically and harmoniously. We cease, in fact, to behave normally. The implications are major for the film director, whose work so often centers on getting actors to reproduce the processes and feel of real life under conditions of intense scrutiny. Actors lose focus for a reason. Something in the text doesn't sit right or someone has done something to shake them out of their character. Your job is to find out the reason. Insecurity of all kinds, even the fear of losing focus, leads to loss of focus: “The only thing we have to fear is fear itself . . . ” (Franklin D. Roosevelt, 1882–1945). In a moment, the audience sees a believable character crumble into a beleaguered actor. Unless the actor has learned how to recover, she can feel completely exposed.

Regaining Focus: An effective way for an actor to regain focus is to look closely at something nearby, such as a carpet pattern or the texture of her sleeve. Because it is real, something in her character’s here and now, the actor’s attention is stabilized. Now she can broaden her attention by stages to include her character’s larger sphere of awareness.

USING THE ACTOR’S EMOTIONS AS THE CHARACTER’S

What should the actor do when an irrelevant emotion intrudes itself, such as pain from a headache, surprise over an unexpected move by a partner, or confusion from a misplaced prop? Part of any good actor’s training is learning to employ every genuine emotion as part of the character’s present. This means, in effect, embracing and co-opting the invader instead of struggling to screen it out. Because every real emotion is visible, struggling to put a lid on the inappropriate will also be visible. The tactic of incorporating external emotion is thus inevitable.

By using every facet of an actor’s self to maintain the character’s physical and mental action, and by reacting to every nuance of any other characters’ behavior, the actor stays so busy every time the scene is played, and so aware on multiple levels, that he or she no longer worries about remembering lines or whether anyone is watching. Everything in the intense, subjective sphere of the character’s reality recedes from consciousness. This intense state of focus is readily available for beginners to experience in improvisation work (which is what makes improv so valuable). It takes more discipline within the regimen of a text, especially when multiple takes and angles stretch beyond a day of movie work.

NEVER DEMONSTRATE

The director should always encourage actors to find their own solutions to a problem. Unless desperate, the director should never step forward and demonstrate what she wants. This implies you are an actor and want a mimicry of yourself, when actually you need something unique to the actor.

NEVER SAY, “BE YOURSELF”

This innocent request can set actors worrying: What did he really mean? How does he see me? Which me does he really want? Always focus your actor on aspects of the character’s experience.

SET SPECIFIC, POSITIVE GOALS

Avoid negative instruction of all kinds ("Could you not be so noisy opening the closet?"). You can get what you want by saying, "See if you can open the door softly this time."

Convey your wishes through redirecting attention to a particular kind of action ("I'd like to see you more irresolute as you turn away."). Less effective would be to say, "Be irresolute" without locating the character's doubt in particular moments of the scene. The actor may not agree but you can negotiate another specific place. Another way to get a change is through suggesting a different subtext, such as "Try making your refusal more ironic" or "Try closing the door on him with finality instead of regret."

ACT AS IF NOBODY'S PRESENT

Instruct actors never to look at the camera, to ignore the crew's presence, and to act as if they were alone in real life. This prevents them from falling into the trap of playing to an audience.

OBSTACLES: HABITS OF BEING

MANNERISMS

Certain kinds of people do particular kinds of jobs, and some jobs generate mannerisms that are a liability in filmmaking. Lecturers and politicians tend to address invisible multitudes, instead of talking one-to-one as they did in rehearsal. Firemen talk in clipped, official voices; salespeople may be ingratiating; and so on. Unfamiliar circumstances like filming cause people to fall back on their conditioning, and many ingrained behaviors are hard or even impossible to change. The positive aspect is that many of the qualities for which you cast a particular person will survive the unnatural procedure of filming and appear just as you wanted them on the screen.

Many actors also have particular mannerisms that you may have to live with. To eliminate them would mean changing something so basic that you would disrupt their talents. Here the director must exert careful judgment before speaking up. As always, try to relocate actors' attention in the positive, rather than asking them to suppress the negative.

LIMITING AN ACTOR'S SPHERE OF ATTENTION

When an actor's misconception of his relationship to the camera must be altered, try to guess what is ingrained habit and what is only a misperception about filming and correctable. For instance, the theater-trained actor who addresses an audience can usually be redirected by saying, "Imagine there is a small bubble of space only big enough to enclose you and your partner. There is only one person, him, listening to you. Talk only to him, there is no one else, no camera present, just you two." Usually this reminder does the trick and keeps theatrically trained actors using authentic, unmagnified voices and actions. Interestingly, the scene intensity rises noticeably, which shows that poor theatrical technique can also function as a retreat from the danger of real feelings.

TACKLING SERIOUS ARTIFICIALITY

With an incurable voice projecter or anyone habitually artificial, the best solution is to bang yourself over the head and recast. If that is impossible, some selected video playback to the actor may forcibly communicate the problem. Be aware, however, that many are shocked and depressed when they first see themselves on the screen, so showing an unsatisfactory performance should be a last resort, done privately and supportively.

Sometimes you will cast someone to play a small part, and this person's concept of acting comes from TV commercials. Valiantly your housewife in the short scene projects a wacky personality. If she is playing a stage mom this could be just what you wanted, but in most other circumstances it would be a disaster. Take her aside and get her to talk through the character, perhaps getting the actor to recall someone similar whom she knows and upon whose image she can model herself. Trying to become an idea of the part is what is phony. Get your actor to develop her character's interior process through improvising an interior monologue or *thoughts voice* (see Chapter 22, Exercise 22–3: Improvising an Interior Monologue). Once she is busy maintaining her character's interior processes, the actor can no longer stand outside herself and make a presentation, which is at the root of the problem. Fully inhabiting her character, she begins to speak and act out of a genuine consciousness. This at the very least takes care of realism.

CHAPTER 20

ACTORS' PROBLEMS

Sartre said "Hell is other people," and working under high pressure with a range of temperaments shows how true this is. This chapter is about the mines in the minefield of human relations—concentrating on actors who are the director's main concern. Their job is far from easy, and they will present you with difficulties, most of them interesting and rewarding to solve. You will be unlucky indeed if you hit much that can't be solved with goodwill, but you should be alert to one or two ticking time bombs.

PERCEPTIONS OF ACTING

The public, seeing accomplished performances as a matter of course, assumes acting is easy and pleasant. But actors' work places them under a physical and psychic scrutiny that is rare in ordinary life. The attention that is the profession's initial allure also leaves actors vulnerable. Faced with a demanding part and an unwelcome self-image, actors may dread their ability to even function. Under such conditions it is regrettably human to deny, evade, or blame others.

THE IDEAL

The ideal actors are ready for these trials and are not on the defensive. Their training taught them humility, self-knowledge, and self-discipline with almost religious fervor. They maintain emotional and intellectual flexibility during criticism and do not try to hide the nature or degree of problems. They stand still to confront the worst rather than finding ways to resist the director's demands. Few actors, especially those available to the low-budget filmmaker, have this degree of training or spiritual evolution. And there is no one walking the face of the earth who does not have lapses.

MERE MORTALS

Resistance to the work at hand is a remarkable human constant and takes many forms. You will need to treat it (in crewmembers or actors) with understanding and respect because it almost always arises from self-doubt and not ill will. Make no mistake, acting is a demanding and self-exposing craft. It aims to expose human nature, and the vulnerability of the actor is never far from that of the character being played. That said, one person's needs and insecurities cannot dominate those of the group or threaten the viability of the project. Your tough-love ability to take actors beyond what they consider their limits will earn you their love and respect. They know when your work has helped them to grow and become more employable.

TENSION

Tension is the most common and insidious problem and saps the actor's confidence. It should dissipate after the initial period of uncertainty when everyone is becoming acquainted. As actors come to know each other, the crew, and their director, they are increasingly able to move between play and work without freezing up. For your part, being willing to attend to the actor's problems and always giving a series of playable objectives will help a lot.

NOT LISTENING

Actors who don't listen to other players during a scene are a serious problem because they are in isolation and giving nothing back to co-actors. The actor is often quite unaware of this and responds to help, especially when you make use of an improvisation game. Not listening often comes from anxiety over knowing lines. Once actors get used to playing the scene rather than the lines, the insecurity (and insecurity's deafness) departs. Another way to press actors into listening is to get them to speak their characters' thoughts by identifying the subtext in the other players' lines before speaking their own. Thus their motivation comes, as in life, through the nuances of how others are acting upon them.

LINES AND INSECURITY

Sometimes actors claim to need the book long after they should have learned the lines. This is a common insecurity symptom and completely arrests a scene's development. If at a subsequent rehearsal and after due warning the same individual still claims to need the book, simply take it away and ask him or her to improvise the scene. The difficulty and embarrassment of floundering through a scene in this way normally motivates the actor to come thoroughly prepared the next time. Insecure actors usually find it liberating to deal with the spirit of a scene rather than feel they are being tested to the letter.

When an actor again claims to need the book I say, "Well, you know what the scene's about so you'll just have to make something up so we can rehearse the scene." The actor first looks appalled, but the results are often surprisingly good. Either the actor knows the scene better than he or she thought or, compelled to improvise from a general idea, takes a heightened interest in the text. This strategy should not be undertaken punitively, however irritating the behavior, but used as necessary to get on with the rehearsal.

CLINGING TO THE LETTER OF THE SCRIPT

Clinging to the letter of the text or to "what we already decided" is another form of resistance. The actor who is afraid to think, feel, and explore in character will often take refuge behind a structure of perceived "rules." These may be what the actor thinks he or she learned from mentors elsewhere, and the implication is that they are greater than you. Rightly, you will take this as a challenge to your authority and must deal with it as such. Stick to what you want, and be clear and unyielding about it. Let the actor get there in his or her own way, or if that fails, get another actor.

FEAR OF CHANGES

Sometimes your request to alter the performance in some way or to change something previously set will trigger an irrational unwillingness to adapt. Some people have a pattern of discomfort with authority figures (of which you are now one) and always have to rebel. Bear with this person—he may be scared and doing the best he can. However, he may also be testing you in the only way he knows how.

One way to disarm people with patterns of rebellion (or patterns of any kind) is to name the pattern, as affectionately as you can, when it next appears. "Uh oh, Anne's having another attack of existential doubt!" The company will laugh delightedly, and if you are lucky Anne will admit her problem instead of blaming the screenwriter. To carry this off, you need to be sure the actor is insecure rather than angry.

ACTING IN ISOLATION

An actor who doggedly carries out what he or she has prepared regardless of the nuances of other performances is wound too tight to listen, watch, and work from life going on around. This actor will not feel the cup in his or her hand, smell the morning air, or feel the touch of his or her lover's lips. Holed up inside a set of mental constructs, he or she will reconnect with the here-and-now only through listening fully to acting partners and physical experience of right detail. It is particularly dangerous to let this person learn lines too early because internalizing the text is part of the armor. This person is afraid of improvisation and badly needs the relaxed security that having "played around" can bring.

OVER-INTELLECTUALIZING

The tendency to intellectualize is another way an actor puts off the fearsome task of experiencing the character's (and his or her own) emotions. The actor who wants to debate every point feels safer discussing than doing, and may try to involve the whole cast in arguments about niceties of interpretation. These are delaying tactics, a bid to wrest control from the director, or both. Keep returning the cast to work if this is happening.

THE ANTI-INTELLECT ACTOR

This actor scorns discussion and the search for underlying structures and may be someone intellectually insecure (lacking formal education, for instance) or someone unusually intuitive. It will be important to prevent this person, whose aura of conviction can be very influential, from intimidating other cast members who work differently. As the director, avoid debates on method and stress the individual's freedom to use whatever method delivers the goods. Avoid the authority struggle that some actors seek and remain accepting of each actor's different needs.

CONTROL BATTLES

The actor who tries to control scenes, manipulate other actors, or resist directorial criticism is probably afraid to place trust in working partnerships of any kind. If you do not set limits, this person may absorb a disproportionate share of everyone's energies. This individual will try to direct other actors or to challenge the director's authority in public. Such a challenge in private can make a truly creative contribution, but it depends on the underlying spirit. Genuinely creative personalities sometimes overflow their territory and may need and want a firm hand to contain them. Combative energy of all kinds is not necessarily bad because it usually gets the company's adrenaline flowing. Control battles sometimes happen when the director mistakes informality for friendship and lets professional boundaries drop.

PLAYWRITING

The actor who *playwrites* is one who acts against the flow of either a scripted or improvised scene, manipulates other actors, introduces inappropriate material, or in other ways undermines the validity of what others are doing. How you assert your authority will be important. Again, there may be a responsible spirit here who is working in inappropriate ways. Be careful not to be crushing.

INAPPROPRIATE HUMOR

Humor is usually the precious elixir that gets people through difficult circumstances (hang out with nurses and you'll know what I mean). But jokes or other diversions that disrupt the working atmosphere are often a means of delaying and diffusing a situation the actor finds threatening (like working without the book). When you are certain that sabotage is what is happening, cut into the saboteur's rigmarole and sharply rally the cast to work.

WITHDRAWAL

The actor who repeatedly deals with problems by going into withdrawal may be asking for special consideration or may habitually evade the responsibility for solving problems. Try holding a one-on-one meeting and naming the pattern. Confrontation, when sympathetic, sometimes releases the actor to talk about a more serious underlying problem. You can only resolve what you know, so this can be a most positive development leading to greater mutual trust. As in any important relationship, if the actor will only withdraw under any kind of criticism and refuses discussion, you should recognize that he or she is using antisocial control tactics and should be replaced.

UNPUNCTUALITY AND COMMITMENT PROBLEMS

This is a very, very serious pattern and something only a Marilyn Monroe can get away with. Take such offenders to a private place, look them in the eye, and name stringent conditions for retaining them. If an actor puts up a stream of explanations, tell him or her that "people only accomplish what matters to them." Do this early and without compromise, and make everyone else aware of the conditions you have set.

Retaining an unreliable person devalues the commitment of others and daily hands increasing leverage to the offender. If the actor mends his or her ways after the warning, be warmly supportive of the accomplishment and cross your fingers.

Never go along with an actor or crewmember who shows a poor respect for the film but intimates that he or she wants to do you a good turn. Invariably this pale motivation runs out at the least convenient moment.

ROMANTIC ENTANGLEMENTS

As Truffaut's *Day for Night* (1973) shows so well, romances or other excluding alliances in the cast, or between cast and crew, can be very damaging. They tilt what should be a level playing field of professionalism and tend to incubate jealousies and intrigues that can threaten the production. Suicidally destructive is an open romance between director and cast member. Now instead of being the cast's director, you have conferred the ultimate mantle of favor on one actor at the expense of the others. Work will become a jealous hell for everyone, especially your inamorata.

PROFESSIONALS

Committed actors are the best company—the warmest, most intelligent, and most vibrant people in the world. They love their profession and give up many good things in life to pursue it. Appreciate them, be good to them, and they will treat you royally.

CHAPTER 21

LEARNING ABOUT ACTING

ACTING AND DOING

Drama is the artful presentation of fictional characters, their conflicts, and their struggles, and its themes are derived from human truths made visible because of pressures in real life. Conventional education, stressing the intellectual, is a woeful preparation because it suggests that you become competent by learning something theoretically, and then demonstrate what you know.

Life is not lived in this way. You don't learn about breaking your leg before going to the hospital to have it set. You don't learn the theory of falling in or out of love before doing it, nor do you have the luxury of preparing for many of life's surprises before having them thrust upon you. The fact is that we are almost never mentally, intellectually, or emotionally prepared for the left-handers that life throws us. We learn how to handle them by handling them, and somehow we get by.

Interesting, truthful acting cannot be studied up like a chemistry exam, and then carried out to the satisfaction of an audience. It's something you must do because it requires imagination, intuition, and the quick reflexes we use in any tight spot. Nothing in formal education prepares us to rely on these more intuitive resources, which are going to be vital not just in acting, but in filmmaking in general. Making films even at the highest levels of sophistication is itself an improvisational activity, so there are many parallels with acting.

Actors must practice handling unforeseen situations where they find out about their abilities and learn to trust their instincts. Directors must have some firsthand knowledge of these things, and playing improv games is a delightful way of discovering basic principles. It later allows you to approach trained actors from a respectful and informed perspective.

Solving any dramatic problem requires generating a range of possible solutions. Usually we can recognize what is truthful, but we seldom know how to get there more directly. Filmmaking involves making repeated attempts to produce some effect until our inbuilt capacity recognizes what is authentic and says, "Ah, yes, that's it!"

Even if you don't expect to do these actor's exercises, read this chapter carefully because there is a wealth of information embedded in the exercises and the discussion topics that go with them.

WHY IMPROVISATION IS VALUABLE

The improv exercises in this chapter are skill-building games. Treat them as educational fun, but be serious-minded enough to take risks and pump the collective adrenaline. They are valuable because:

- There are only a few major principles, but they take repetition and courage to absorb.
- Players are fully *in* the moment. The nature of improvisation precludes thinking ahead, and for some this will be a scary experience. However, when actors are *not* present in the moment, their acting invariably suffers.
- Players develop *communion* (a useful Stanislavski term for actors listening and watching other characters so they react to what the others actually do or imply).
- The players develop *adaptation* (the ability to adjust in a lifelike way to unforeseen obstacles as they arise).
- All actors in a scene must remain active and never become passive so that someone else must take the initiative.
- The group generates its own dramatic vocabulary so that learning is memorably embedded in shared experience.
- Solving problems takes failures. Everything can go wonderfully wrong in a game, but people learn without humiliation.
- Like jazz, everyone knows when a piece is "cooking."
- Safe successes are not really successes at all.
- Courageous failures are successes.
- Successful improvs have a natural ending.
- Improv is not limited and can be made to span most of the territory of drama.
- Improv games used during production can refresh the cast or help them to problem-solve.

WHAT AN ACTOR LEARNS FROM IMPROV WORK

Once it has been written, drama becomes the director's and actors' responsibility. A really good actor can take a poorly written part in a poorly directed movie and still produce a character full of life and depth. As an aspiring actor, however inexperienced you are, you can expect to learn the following from improv games:

- What it's like to be watched
- How to enjoy being silly and that finding the courage to do this is the key to tackling larger things

- How improv lowers the stress of self-consciousness
- The need to let go of hiding and self-preservation, which prevent actors from exploring their characters' emotions in public—which is what acting is all about
- That each character must act on the other or the passive actor cedes control to the more active
- Taking control is as much the product of insecurity as relinquishing it
- Common hang-ups and situations that actors get into
- That each character must adapt to the obstacles and problems the other presents (adaptation)
- If a player takes refuge in preconceptions he will manipulate the other by "play-writing" (See Chapter 20: Playwriting)
- Anybody can be equal to the unexpected when relaxed enough for his or her imagination to work freely
- Improvs, like scripted scenes, often get stuck on the same few crucial elements, but actors can learn what's needed to unstick the piece and make it develop
- Actors can experience being inside their characters *and* simultaneously conscious of the dramatic problems that only they can solve
- That a group can rapidly and enjoyably discover each other's abilities and temperaments
- That playing together helps dissipate the competitiveness that comes from insecurity
- That actors can see when and why drama gets blocked
- How very difficult acting is, especially if you must also hit chalk marks at particular points in a scene
- What an actor feels like under different kinds of directors
- What an actor hopes for and what he or she fears
- What trust or distrust from other actors feels like
- How incidences of failure are a valid part of your development
- What qualities and approaches might best solve particular acting problems
- What the director can do to unlock situations that are blocked or going in wrong directions
- That even without any preparation you can find the resources to handle almost any situation
- What rejection feels like
- How good it feels after hard work and taking risks to get a round of applause

WHAT A DIRECTOR LEARNS WHEN ACTORS IMPROVISE

For a directing instructor or a student director using improv to tackle cast or interpretational problems, improv is something of a Pandora's Box when you first use it. But it is such a powerful and useful tool that you should definitely get experience.

A director must know how to ask for different versions of something while in search of what works, what fits. That goes for every creative stage—writing, art direction, rehearsal, camerawork, lighting, acting during the production, *blocking* (the placement of camera and actors in relation to each other), and editing afterward. Every aspect of making film drama involves experimenting and generating a range of options and solutions.

Good directors know a lot about acting and about each actor in their cast. They learn to sense when an individual isn't living up to potential and move to actively eliminate the blockages. As a director of improvisations, you can expect to find out:

- How good you are at giving feedback to the cast, and what you need to improve
- How to earn the trust of actors and crew
- What it feels like when an actor doesn't trust your judgment or challenges you
- How each actor responds to different kinds of communication
- How much actors depend on your feedback in their work
- How actors either accept or avoid responsibility in a scene
- How to change a passive actor into an active one
- How to get an interior monologue going inside an actor who isn't generating any interior life for his or her character
- How divisive personalities function and what you can do to avoid being controlled by one
- How each actor has habits and patterns that limit him or her
- What a director can do when actors think they cannot surpass a limit
- How it feels to take someone over a threshold of fear and how good you both feel
- The overload you feel when trying to monitor multiple characters and lines of development
- How guilty you feel when actors give their all and you don't like what you see

Directors can learn to spot any problem from experience gained using improv. They also learn that anyone can act—anyone at all—once the fears subside and the armor is laid down. When you have done some acting yourself, directing other people becomes a matter of diligently and empathically spotting the right keys to unlock each individual's potential.

In a class or shooting situation, there is always an audience of sorts. Each person in the ensemble will need to support and appreciate the others, particularly when it involves pushing limits. Onlookers must be absolutely still and silent, yet contribute every iota of their attention in support of the players. This is really the essence of *crew etiquette*.

Because discovering and maintaining spontaneity are so important, the first 20 exercises are improvisational. Many involve experimenting with vulnerability and will be familiar to anyone with an actor's training.

ANALYZING BEATS AND DRAMATIC UNITS

Throughout the upcoming exercises, the director will search for beats—those special moments of flux or dramatic change. The director's and actors' major responsibility is to completely understand an improvisation or a text in terms of the main character, where he or she is changing, and why. If you need to refresh you knowledge, refer to the section in Chapter 1, Beats, the Key to Understanding Drama.

THE JOURNAL

If you are part of a directing class, keep a journal. In it describe honestly your thoughts, observations, and feelings about assignments and peers. Periodically the instructor can collect these and report any trends or significant observations to the class. No confidences or names are ever disclosed without the writer's prior permission.

The journal functions as a safety valve, a channel for feedback that allows the instructor to be fully aware of common insecurities and personal triumphs. Through it the instructor gets to know everyone on his or her own terms and can write confidential replies.

NOT ALL ACTING IS A DUET

The following acting exercises suggest that acting only takes place between two people. Many times an actor will either be alone or in a large group and sustaining many interactions, but to allow for all this would produce unreadable English, so I have treated the duet as if it were the standard.

IMPROVISATION EXERCISES

WHAT THEY ARE

Sometimes these exercises incorporate a degree of premeditated structure, and sometimes the actor has virtually no guidelines beforehand. Some exercises will be referred to later in the book because they make useful tools when actors get hung up during rehearsal or shooting.

ACTORS, MAKE YOUR AUDIENCE SEE

Using no props, see your surroundings and the things you handle with such conviction that the audience is able to see them, too. When the actor sees, the audience sees, believes, and is captivated.

MIX IT UP

Be sure to change partners from exercise to exercise so you work with people you do not know. Wear loose, comfortable clothing that you don't mind getting dirty. Try occasionally to play people whose characters, ages, and circumstances are well removed from your own.

STAY FOCUSED

The biggest challenge is to achieve and *maintain focus*, that is, to:

- Think your character's thoughts
- See your character's mental images
- Experience your character's feelings
- See and hear the other characters and react to what they are giving you, here and now

Improvisation constantly faces the actor with surprises, so you are repeatedly flushed out of your hiding places. Through improv you can learn to trust your instincts, discover the supportiveness of other cast members, and gain confidence that dealing with the unexpected need not cause you to lose focus and fall out of character.

THE DIRECTOR'S ROLE

To direct an improv seems like a contradiction in terms. Most of these exercises need nothing beyond an assurance that the actors understand and keep to the ground rules for the exercise and feedback afterward. The more advanced exercises, however, will benefit from having a director select and coordinate cast ideas and take spot decisions so the piece can start without delay.

Remember, the director is really the surrogate for an audience. All exercises will benefit, after each performance, from directorial feedback so the cast can tackle specific problems in subsequent versions.

DURATION OF SKETCHES

Either the instructor can call, "Cut!" or, as confidence develops, audience members give a show of hands when a piece runs its course. This way actors get used to satisfying audience demands and directors learn to make independent judgments rather than relying on their instructor.

ASSESSMENT AND DISCUSSION

During an exercise, look for the combination of spontaneity and intensity that comes when actors are fully accepting the demands of a role. Reward courage with a round of applause at the end of the piece. After each exercise, brief and concentrated discussion is valuable, but the audience should speak about what was communicated and *avoid making valuations like good and bad.* During feedback:

- Avoid all theorizing. When discussion becomes academic it drains away the momentum.
- Stick to the specifics of what happened.
- Say what particularly struck you (impact).
- Describe what stages the piece went through (its structure).
- Say not only what happened, but *what it made you feel* at each stage (what it delivered).
- Listen attentively to feedback and as either actor or director, aim never to argue or justify what you did. In all your work, you aim to learn what you are doing from your audience.

EXERCISE 21-1: SEE OR BE SEEN

Purpose: Exploring the idea of focus.

Activity: Half the class is in the audience and remains seated. The other half, the performers, stand in a row facing the audience and looking above them into space. Audience members should carefully study the faces and body language of the performers.

- The instructor tells the performers to empty their minds and concentrate on simply being themselves.
- After a minute or two, the instructor tells the performers to mentally visualize a room they know well and everything in it.
- After another minute or two, the instructor tells the audience and performers to switch roles and repeats steps 1 and 2 with the other half of the class.

Discussion: Address these questions to the following groups.

Performers:	How did it feel to focus on being yourself?
Audience:	How did the performers' feelings show in their behavior and appearance?
Both:	What did you see when the performers switched to visualizing?
Performers:	What kinds of work can an actor legitimately undertake to avoid feeling self-conscious?

This exercise shows everyone how disturbing it is to have someone watch you when your mind is unoccupied. You fantasize how stupid and ungainly the watcher thinks you must be. This is the curse of being self-conscious. It results in mental and even physical discomfort and is utterly disabling to actors. Having or making mental work helps occupy the judge we all carry within, and lets you become relaxed and normal again. *Actors always need mental and physical work!*

EXERCISE 21-2: DOMESTIC APPLIANCE

Purpose: To become in spirit something you are not.

Activity: First, study a domestic appliance in its full range of action. Announce in class what you have been assigned to do, then give a full impersonation using your whole body and vocalized sound effects. Try to convey the appliance's spirit as well as its shape, actions, and sounds. The class should choose someone to be the instructor, who breaks the ice by going first (more than once I have been asked to be a flushing toilet). It is quite normal to feel foolish and painfully self-conscious. Use what you learned from Exercise 21-1 to maintain focus.

Examples that can be assigned:

Coffee percolator
Toilet flushing
Electric can opener
Rubber plunger opening drain
Washing machine changing cycles
Toothbrush at work
Nutcracker
Honey pouring
Coffee grinder
Corkscrew
Garbage disposal unit
Overfilled garbage bag removed
Cold car engine that will not start
Tomato sauce pouring
Dripping faucet
Upright vacuum cleaner
Electric toaster
Rusty door lock
Steam iron
Photocopier
Blender with lumps
Clock radio coming on

Discussion:

1. When and why was the actor self-conscious?
2. Where in his or her body could you locate tension from self-consciousness?
3. Did he or she get into focus, and if so, how?
4. Which part of the impersonation made you see the real thing?

EXERCISE 21-3: FLYING BLIND

Purpose: Exploring trust and dependency.

Activity: The rehearsal space is made into a disordered jumble of obstacles. Divide into pairs. One person is blindfolded and turned several times to disorient him or her. He now walks as fast as he dares with his partner not touching him but whispering instructions on which way to move. A variation is for the seeing partner to guide through touch. After a few minutes, switch roles on the instructor's command.

Discussion:

1. Actor: What were your feelings and sensations, being so utterly dependent on another person?

2. Instructor/Audience: What did the body language differences tell you about different people's reactions to dependency?

EXERCISE 21-4: "TIMBER!"

Purpose: Exploring trust, equal partnership, and tactile defensiveness.

Activity: Using pairs (same sex or different), one person is a piece of timber, and the other must try to balance the timber upright. You can use any part of your body except your hands to catch and steady the falling timber. After a few minutes, swap roles on command.

Discussion:

1. What are your thoughts and feelings, being in bodily contact with someone you do not know well?
2. How free and true to gravity was the timber? (How much did he or she protect the two of you by making it easier?)
3. How willing was the timber to trust you to catch him or her? To fall backward and stay rigid?
4. Was one partner tending to control the situation?

Actors must be able to make physical contact and even play love scenes with people they may neither know nor find attractive. In any acting situation, each must share control equally, being ready to "catch" a partner or be caught, yet neither taking more than momentary initiative. Neither should fall into a habitually dominant or a submissive acting relationship. When things are working right, both actors are sensitive to each other, actively creating, conscious of the unique nuance of the moment, and able to work from it. This confidence comes from the relaxation that goes with having trust in your partners and in the audience's approving reaction.

EXERCISE 21-5: MIRROR IMAGES

Purpose: Close observation and moment-to-moment adaptation without anticipating.

Activity: You arrive in front of the bathroom mirror, coming close to its surface, and go through your morning routine. Your partner is your image in the mirror, doing everything you do as you do it, inverted as a mirror image inverts. Swap roles after a few minutes.

Discussion:

1. How successful was the mirror at replicating the actions?
2. How difficult did the mirror find it to neither anticipate nor lag?
3. Did the person stay in character?

4. How frank and complete was the person's routine? Who took risks and was therefore self-revealing?
5. What analogous situations is an actor likely to face?

EXERCISE 21-6: WHO, WHAT, WHEN, AND WHERE?

Purpose: Immediate character and situation development without props.

Activity: Instructor designates an actor, then asks successive people to supply a who, what, when, and where. The actor then carries out some appropriate action, in character, for a minute or two. The instructor calls "Cut!" when the action is long enough or if development levels off. The class reports what it saw happening and what was communicated. The actor then says briefly what he or she intended. Example:

Who [is present]?	Mary Jo Sorensen, 35
Where [is she]?	In an airport lounge
When [is this]?	Christmas Eve, late at night
What [is happening]?	Waiting for her parents. She must tell them she has lost her job.

Our designated actress thinks a moment, then slips into character. She sits moodily, tearing up a Styrofoam coffee cup, looking sidelong with fatigue and distaste at some people nearby. From another direction she notices evidence of some change and stands apprehensively, straightening her skirt.

Discussion:

1. What seemed to be going on inside the character?
2. What was convincing, and what were false notes?
3. What intentions did not come across as natural?
4. Did the actor carry out all of the assignment?
5. Did he or she remember to interact with the environment?
6. Was there a significant change or development?

Typical discussion: On balance the class believed that Mary Jo had not told her parents about the change in her employment, and they liked her action with the Styrofoam cup, which most "saw" in her hands. They also liked her irritability, but were unclear as to what was its source. One person thought it was because of cigar smoke, another thought it was carousers the worse for drink. However, most felt that the change of awareness was imposed and that the actor lost focus at that moment.

The actress said she had believed in her character while she had the cup in her hands, but then had imagined a man with a loud voice but had been unable to see his image. In confusion she had decided to make her parents appear at the arrival gate, but this image, too, refused to materialize because she had forced it.

EXERCISE 21-7: SOLO, NO WORDS

Note: From this exercise onward, a piece can be ended when, by raising their hands, the majority of the audience signifies that dramatic development has well passed its peak.

Purpose: Use unremarkable, everyday action to communicate something of the inner thoughts and feelings of a character whose life is quite unlike that of the actor.

Activity: From an action (the what) and using no props, invent a who, where, and when to sustain your character sketch for 3 minutes. Avoid storytelling or high drama of any kind. An actor must be able to carry out everyday actions and make them interesting to watch. Try any or all of these:

- Alone in someone's house (whose?) where you explore: (a) the refrigerator, (b) the bathroom, (c) someone else's bedroom that you have been given
- Finding a box of your childhood toys you haven't seen for many years
- Unwrapping a long-awaited parcel
- Waiting in the dentist's office
- Making a grocery list
- Trying on a new coat
- Taking medicine
- Caring for a pet
- Taking a bike out after the winter
- Cleaning out the attic
- Wrapping a gift
- Cleaning shoes
- Looking out the window
- Waiting for a phone call
- Dividing up the laundry
- Watching a sport
- Overhearing an interesting conversation in a store

Discussion:

1. In a particular performance, what was interesting, and what did it make you see?
2. When did the player break focus?
3. Why?

EXERCISE 21-8: DUO, NO WORDS

Purpose: To communicate through interaction something of the inner thoughts and feelings of two characters using an everyday action that involves some element of conflict.

Activity: From an action (the what) and using no props, invent a who, where, and when to sustain your character sketch. Avoid storytelling or high drama of any kind and use action and minimal dialogue. Try these:

- Mending a car
- Making a double bed
- Buying a magazine
- Pulling a sliver out of a finger
- Carrying a heavy garbage can
- Washing the best dishes after a special meal
- Washing a child's hair
- Photographing a model
- Putting up a tent
- Playing pinball
- Maneuvering heavy furniture through a doorway
- Waiting in a doorway for a heavy rainstorm to ease
- Writing out a speeding ticket after the talking is done
- Watching a TV program: one likes it, the other does not
- A stranger in a plane who is falling asleep against you

Discussion: Did the actors create:

1. Two distinct character identities (who)?
2. A believable and recognizable environment—country, area, city, place, or room—and use it (where)?
3. A distinctive period and time of day (when)?
4. A believable tension?
5. A situation in which speech was not called for?
6. An interaction in which neither was controlling the movement of the sketch?
7. Was there communion and adaptation?

EXERCISE 21-9: GIBBERISH

Purpose: To use the voice as an expressive instrument and to compel the actors to use their bodies and voice quality as tools of communication. Too often, once actors have lines to speak they cease to act with the whole body. This exercise stimulates speech but de-emphasizes verbal meaning in favor of underlying intention.

Activity: Using the examples in Exercise 21-8, carry out an activity with a conflict, using gibberish as the characters' language.

Discussion: As in Exercise 21-8.

1. How did the actors handle the gibberish conversations?
2. Did they become natural?

EXERCISE 21-10: SOLO, WITH WORDS

Purpose: To create a character, employing the usual who, where, when, and what, and using both actions and speech.

Activity: In creating your character, remember to develop him or her through actions. Do not sit still and rely on a monologue. Here are some suggestions:

- A difficult phone conversation (phone has a long cord)
- Reconstructing a painful conversation
- Writing the opening remarks of an important speech
- Rehearsing in front of the bathroom mirror for a traffic court appearance
- Planning a dinner party
- Getting ready to tell someone about a betrayal or infidelity
- Working up to approaching your boss for a raise
- Rehearsing the way you will evict a rich, peppery relative who came to visit and has long overstayed
- Explaining to your new employer why you must start a new job in a gorilla costume
- Imagining different approaches to someone who attracts you deeply but whom you hold in awe
- Your head is stuck between the railings enclosing a war memorial. Someone has gone to call the fire department, and you are trying to figure out an explanation.
- It is Judgment Day, and you are rehearsing an explanation of your sins to a recording angel.
- You are preparing to audition for the role of "Talk Show Host with a Difference."
- A practical joke has misfired, and you must explain to the irate victim.

Discussion: Did the actor:

1. Create a believable character?

2. Keep up a developing action?
3. Make the situation develop?
4. Make you see all the physical objects and surroundings?

EXERCISE 21-11: DUO, WITH WORDS

Purpose: To maintain conversation and a developing action at the same time.

Activity: Each of these sketches requires both a conversation and accompanying physical action, which should be purposeful. Do not take it too fast, and do not feel you have to be talking all the time. Examples to try:

- Eating a meal and discussing a prearranged topic
- Demonstrating a kitchen appliance to a family member
- Cleaning the car, discussing something
- Getting a large piece of furniture through an awkward doorway
- Discussing your son's or daughter's rotten grades
- Asking for some money that you are owed
- Buying something embarrassing from a pharmacist
- Rearranging a room
- Showing someone they have not done a good job of work
- Teaching a friend to drive
- Discussing a change in hairdo
- Teaching someone a dance step
- Meeting someone you had hoped to avoid
- A confession you would rather not hear

Discussion: Did they:

1. Keep both the topic and the actions going?
2. Keep the physical world they created consistent?
3. Listen to and work off each other?
4. Share the initiative equally?
5. Allow the piece to develop spontaneously?
6. Develop interesting characters?

EXERCISE 21-12: MAKE YOUR OWN CHARACTER

Purpose: To place the actor, as a character, in the hands of the audience.

Activity: Go before the class, in costume, as a character based on someone you know or have met who made a powerful impression on you. The class asks you probing questions about yourself. You answer in character.

Each character should be onstage for about 10 minutes, and two or three performances per session is the maximum, as the interaction can be very intense.

Discussion: This, honestly undertaken, can be really magical, a powerful exercise in portrayal that tells much about the actor's values and influences. There may be little need for discussion if the exercise goes well. Play it by ear.

EXERCISE 21-13: ENSEMBLE SITUATIONS

Purpose: To engage the whole group in a collective creation.

Activity: These are situations in which individual characters contribute to a whole. The where and when will need to be agreed on beforehand. The aim is to keep up your character while contributing to the development of the piece. You might want to reuse a character developed earlier, perhaps the one from Exercise 21-12. Sample situations follow:

- A tug of war
- Dealing with an obstreperous drunk
- Someone is hurt in the street
- Surprise party
- A person faints in a crowded train
- Bus driver stops bus because passenger will not pay
- Unpopular coach berates a team
- Party interrupted by protesting neighbor
- Busy hotel kitchen with waiters and waitresses coming and going
- Airline with badly delayed flight dealing with irate passengers
- Exercise class in an institution for severely disturbed people
- Policeman tries to arrest person at demonstration; crowd argues
- Subway train stops in tunnel due to power cut
- Someone arrives with news that may have serious consequences

Discussion:

1. How many subordinate actions were going on during the main action?
2. Did everyone stay in character? (The temptation is to lose focus unless you are important.)
3. How did the piece develop?
4. What compromises did people make to sustain the whole?

EXERCISE 21-14: DEVELOPING AN EMOTION

Purpose: Actors are asked to improvise a scene that culminates in a given emotion in one or more of the characters.

Activity: This exercise should not be attempted until the class has developed considerable rapport and experience. The players must invent characters and a situation, then develop it to the point where the specified emotion is reached. The class can stop the sketch when the emotion is reached or if the piece is not going anywhere. Emotions one character might feel include:

Anger	Suspicion	Sympathy
Relief	Jealousy	Condescension
Rejection	Love	Regret
Disbelief	Friendliness	Release
Superiority	Empathy	Inferiority

Discussion: This is a tricky demand because it asks that actors build to a known conclusion, and this tempts them mightily to escape by manipulating the situation. All the prior criteria apply, but important considerations here are:

1. Was the interaction credible?
2. Did it arrive at the specified emotion?
3. If not, why not?
4. Was the development even or uneven?
5. Was the initiative shared equally?

This exercise will highlight the cardinal weakness of improvisation: an unevenness of inspiration that produces an inconsistent pace of development. The symptoms are lengthy periods when the actors are circling a problem, unable to break through or, alternatively, forcing their way through by decision instead of using the characters' process. This happens from frustration or panic at making the audience wait. A sign of confidence in both players and company (audience) is that the players do not short-circuit the process in pursuing the goal, and the audience remains supportive.

EXERCISE 21-15: BRIDGING EMOTIONS

Purpose: To make a credible change from one emotion to another.

Activity: Same as Exercise 21-14 except the players start in the middle of one emotion and find their way to the next. Start with two emotions, and then, if you want to make it truly challenging, specify three.

Discussion: Same as Exercise 21-14.

EXERCISE 21-16: SURFING THE CHANNELS

Purpose: To involve a group in immediate and unpremeditated invention.

Activity: Divide the class into players and audience. The audience is watching a TV program that leads to one of the following generic situations. The players are TV actors who must instantly become a program showing the chosen situation. When the situation is running out of steam, an audience member may seize the remote control and change the channel, announcing what the new program is. The players must now develop the same situation in the new program format, until someone changes the channel again. After a while, students swap roles. Here the accent is on experiencing the same situation and probably the same emotions through very different characters, and feeding into different but set expectations in the audience. Suggested situations:

Persuasion	Being authoritative
Trapped	Avoiding something
Returning	Complaining
Interview	Disaster
Making a difficult request	Surprise
Successfully stopping an argument	Laughing out of relief
Jeering	Cheating

Discussion:

1. How inventive were the players?
2. How authentic were the situations to actual TV programs?
3. How quickly were they able to make the change?
4. How equally were roles distributed?
5. Did some actors fall into controlling or passive roles?

EXERCISE 21-17: VIDEO CONVENTION

Purpose: Same as Exercise 21-16.

Activity: Same ideas as Exercise 21-16, except the situation is a huge video dealer's convention offering unsold video programs at big discounts. The audience is composed of potential buyers at a stand where everything imaginable on video is on sale:

- Do-it-yourself kitchen rehab
- Car tune-up
- Nature films
- Social documentaries
- Comedies
- Tragedies
- Slasher films
- Soft-core porn films for all sexual orientations
- Biology lessons
- Sales motivation
- Music videos

- Teen romances
- Farces
- Beauty procedures for those over 50

When the audience decides to see a new sample, an audience member calls out the title of the new video.

Discussion: Similar to Exercise 21-16. Accent is on spontaneity and speed of adaptation. Because these are videos that have not sold, they probably are obscure or third rate and full of genre clichés. Did the cast contribute equally?

EXERCISE 21-18: BLIND DATE

Purpose: To work with interior monologue.

Activity: A man and a woman have been set up by friends on a blind date. They meet in a bar and discuss how to spend the evening together. Character A has several conflicting personality traits, each spoken by a class member who sits behind him. As the conversation between the two slowly proceeds, each of the voices chimes in, speaking its biased reaction or tendentious thought. Character A must take time and listen to these interior voices, react realistically to these "thoughts," and act upon the most appropriate in his next words or action. Character B disregards everything except what Character A says or does. Character A may initially get a chorus of "inner voices," or there may initially be none. The voices may overlap and argue with each other. Character A should take all the time needed to assess and react to them, while remaining in character. The personality traits (with a voice for each) could include any four of:

The need to be liked	Fear of being manipulated
Fear of rejection	Worry about expense
The need to be unique	Guilt (feeling bad about something you've done)
The need to be normal	Shame (feeling bad about who you are)
The need to make a conquest	Pride

Discussion: This exercise is a lot of fun and demands tremendous concentration from all concerned. It is a key to understanding that *an actor who keeps his character's interior voices going will never lose focus* and will consistently bring a richness of ambiguity to each moment of the part. Remember, *the real action of any part is interior action, which goes on behind the character's outward words and physical actions.*

1. How did Character A handle all the input?
2. What were his or her most noticeable influences?
3. Where did Character A break character?
4. Did Character B provide a good foil?
5. What were the most interesting and convincing interior actions?

Once more: Now Characters A and B go through their scene again, but this time Character A internalizes the interior voices by imagining them. Often the scene will be strikingly rich in implications and shows what real inner conflict brings to an actor's work.

EXERCISE 21-19: INNER CONFLICT

Purpose: To portray a character's contradictory tensions but never directly reveal them.

Activity: An actor is designated to play an intelligent person who wishes to be correctly understood. The character can be modeled upon someone prominent in the news. In this exercise, inspired by Richard Nixon and his "I am not a crook" speech, the character has gone through life denying certain aspects of his or her character, so sometimes "puts a good face on things" and rationalizes what he or she cannot change. The character begins with the sentence, "Because I think you may have the wrong idea about me, I'm going to tell you what most people don't know." After he or she has spoken for a while, the audience can help by asking questions. The actor must portray his or her character's conflicts by denial, which must flow from the character's rationale about what can or cannot be admitted in public.

Discussion:

1. When was the character sincere?
2. When suppressing the truth?
3. How did you know?
4. When was the actor's performance believable?
5. When did it look contrived?
6. What was interesting, what was less so?

EXERCISE 21-20: THROWN TOGETHER

Purpose: To bring together two characters in a common activity that each is using to gain emotional satisfaction from the other. The exercise seeks to explore the idea that in real life we almost never express what weighs on our minds; instead we recreate our own unsolved issues through the situation at hand and use them to seek satisfaction, occasionally with success.

Activity: Take two of the least compatible characters developed in Exercise 21-12 or 21-19 and put them together in a credible work situation. Within the bounds of ordinary, decent, civilized behavior, each follows his or her usual agenda in relating to other people. The actors should take the time to keep up an interior (and silent) monologue. No issues are ever named; their needs and reactions must be expressed through the work they are doing together. Whether they get along or whether they find mutual accommodation should not be predetermined.

Discussion:

1. Did each character develop?
2. Did each find a way to play out his or her issues through their work?
3. Did each choose a credible path?
4. Did they stay in focus and in character?
5. Did they find a believable way of cooperating?
6. Did you believe the outcome?
7. Did one "win"?
8. Did either or both find satisfaction? Neither?
9. What was the obligatory moment in the scene?
10. What made it the obligatory moment?

Again: Have the two actors play the scene again, this time adding their thoughts out loud in an undertone. Then play the scene as before, with silent, interior monologues.

Discussion: Did having to improvise thoughts change or improve the scene? Can you see using this method to solve a problem in a scripted scene?

CHAPTER 22

EXERCISES WITH A TEXT

These exercises develop particular skills and will be useful later when you have to deal with common problems that emerge during rehearsals or shooting. They are done in the moment in front of the class or group.

TEXTS

Because you should learn the rehearsal process without ever having to doubt the quality of the writing, it's smart at this stage to use a good one-act theater piece rather than your own writing. It won't be cinematic, but in this phase of your work you aim to discover the potential of text and cast, so this doesn't matter. Use something short so discussion can be narrowly (and therefore deeply) focused. Avoid comedy because playing it begs for a live audience, and you don't want your actors playing to the gallery. Harold Pinter's short works are ideal, and I like *The Dumb-Waiter* for this work. Pinter is fascinated by the disparity between what characters say and what is being hatched in their minds.

READ-THROUGH

Each cast member should carefully read the whole play and make brief definitions of the characters. Then hold an ensemble read-through. Actors must *not* learn lines until instructed or they will internalize an unexamined understanding of the piece. Give plenty of time for discussions because they will reveal much about both text and actors.

DEVELOPMENTAL PROCESS

Allow the exploration process to take its own course. Particularly if you are directing actors of some training and experience, it is unwise to arbitrarily impose any developmental technique, as they may feel it is unnecessary or beneath them. Watch and listen very carefully, letting your actors get as far as they can with minimal directing. When problems arise, choose an appropriate technique to break the logjam. After one or two successes, your credibility will rise.

"USEFUL WHEN"

Each exercise can serve as a resource to help solve common problems during rehearsal or production. Its "medicine chest" utility is provided under the heading Useful When.

EXERCISE 22-1: WHAT THE ACTORS BRING

Useful When: You (as the director) want to adjust your thematic intentions for the piece around the cast and make use of what each individual brings.

Purpose: To make decisions about the special qualities and characteristics of the actors for use in your thematic interpretation.

Activity: After the read-through:

1. Make notes for yourself that capture the intrinsic quality of each actor. This, for example, concerns an actor called Dale:

   ***Dale** has a slow, quiet, repressed quality that masks a certain pain and bitterness. He is watchful, highly intelligent, intense, and his first reaction is often a protective cynicism, but really it matters very much to him that he be liked. He reminds me of a stray cat, cornered and defiant, but hungry and cold, too.*

2. Make a projection of how the actors' qualities can legitimately be used to polarize the performances, and how this will affect your thematic interpretation of the piece. For example:

   ***Dale** has the quality of honorable victimhood, and this stacks the cards interestingly against the father, whom we assume has practiced subtle violence against his son in the distant past, without the mother being aware of it.*

EXERCISE 22-2: MARKING BEATS IN A TEXT

Useful When: Actors cannot be relied on to make a complete dramatic analysis of a text.

Purpose: To find the beats, those fulcrum points of emotional change. You may want to review the definition and examples of *beat* and *dramatic unit* in Chapter 1. Beats are extremely important to the actors and will need special consideration in the *mise en scène* (the combination of acting, blocking, camera placement, and editing that produces the dramatic image on film).

Activity: Director and actors should separately study the scene looking for the beats. These moments of irrevocable change may be triggered by dialogue, an action, or outside information coming in, such as a phone call. Emotional change does not happen continuously and smoothly like the hands of a clock. It is more like the movement of a heavy object being pushed across a rough surface. Pressure against its immovability mounts and mounts until suddenly it slides a few feet. Those pushing regroup themselves and start exerting pressure again, until—boom!—again it moves.

In dramatic terms, the beat is the moment of yielding when emotional pressures overcome resistance and compel a moment of changed awareness. This requires each character to have a conception of what conflict they face, like two wrestlers who must make contact to compete. Finding beats, therefore, means finding the important moves in the match and defining the strategy, from each protagonist's point of view, leading to each meaningful strike and counterstrike.

There may be one beat or there may be several in a scene. All the beats may belong to one character, or there may be beats for both, some even simultaneous and mutual. Either character may remain unconscious of the other's change of consciousness, though the audience should be aware of changes in both.

Discussion: In rehearsal, agree where the beats are and what causes them.

EXERCISE 22-3: IMPROVISING AN INTERIOR MONOLOGUE

If you were to study only one of these exercises, this is the most significant. When an actor claims to have created an interior monologue, and the results are still not making sense, asking for it out loud will reveal what part of their understanding needs changing. Generally this actor has failed to make sense of what her partner means or to build on her character's history. Here the director can be of great help. Demanding that an inner monologue be kept up is a sure way to immediately upgrade a so-so performance. It also helps stabilize players of unreliable timing because it supplies a repeatable interior process that will pace each forward step of a character's external behavior. This is work that actors habitually evade or forget, but the mere possibility that you will again ask them to do it aloud and in front of other actors usually keeps them working at it.

Useful When: A text refuses to come alive and you need a powerful method of getting actors to externalize their understanding. Also useful for unlocking intransigent trouble spots in rehearsal. Asking a cast member to speak his inner monologue usually reveals a crucial lack of understanding at that point in the text and helps you figure out how to help. Sometimes the problem lies with the actor's understanding and sometimes with the writing itself.

Purpose: What a character says and does is only the surface of his or her existence. In reality, we have a rich inner life going on all the time, and no fictional character can be interesting or complete without also having one. This exercise compels actors to fill the gaps between their lines and actions with the character's inner thoughts and feelings. Having to invent an inner monologue forces an actor to articulate the character's inner life. Because everything other characters do helps *cause* that inner life, it also ties the actor into the surrounding action.

Activity: At a troublesome part of the text, have your actors improvise their characters' interior monologues. Ask them to use a full voice for the "out loud" line and a soft voice for the "thoughts voice" or interior monologue. The cast will at first find this hard or baffling, and the scene will go at a snail's pace. But having to create publicly and on the spot always yields deeper understandings, and a high degree of commitment is unavoidable.

Discussion:

1. Do the inner monologues show that your actors are on the same wavelength?
2. Are you and your cast making the same interpretations?
3. What did you (the director) learn from the actors?
4. What did you learn about your actors?
5. What did your actors learn about you and your approach?

EXERCISE 22-4: CHARACTERIZING THE BEATS

Useful When: You need to clarify and energize a scene or a passage that is muddy and lifeless.

Purpose: To give each dramatic unit and its beats a clear intention and identity, which in turn sharpens each beat and turning point. To focus attention on subtext and on the actor's body language, movement, and voice range.

Activity:

- Ask the actors to devise a brief tag line for each step in the rise of pressure leading toward each beat. Try to phrase these tags so they always express volition. (Examples: "Leave me alone!"; "I need you to notice me"; "You're not going to hoodwink me again.") Be sure each tag is in the active, not passive voice ("Let me go to sleep." not "I am being kept awake.") so it expresses active will even when the character is being victimized. Each tag line should contain an element of "I want."
- The actors now approximate the actions and movements of the scene from memory, but use only the tags as dialogue. Actors may have to say, "I need you to notice me" half a dozen times, changing the sense of the tag through bodily action and language, until they bargain up to the beat point. Where the text used verbal logic, now pressure is applied or parried by action supporting the tag that uses the voice and body as instruments. This device causes interesting developments in the actors' range of expression, shifting it from verbal and logical to physical and emotional, with a corresponding increase in power.
- Now have the actors play the scene as scripted, keeping the body and vocal expression developed previously—and marvel at the difference.

Discussion: What did you learn:

1. About the actors from the movements they used this time?
2. About how they extended their emotional range?
3. About their communion when the exercise forced it into continuous existence?

EXERCISE 22-5: ACTIONS AT BEAT POINTS

Useful When: A scene seems monotonous, wordy, and cerebral, and actors are playing the scene "in general." This is because the actors are approaching the scene with correct but generally applied ideas. A scene must be built out of behaviorally authentic blocks, each containing a clearly defined sequence of human strivings. A scene in which one character shows several emotions will only be effective when he or she builds each separately.

Purpose: To focus and physicalize the beats and demarcate the phases of the scene behaviorally. This technique returns the spotlight to the turning points.

Activity: When the beat points are located and tagged, ask the actors to devise several possible actions for their character during each beat, or change of awareness. These can start out multiple and exaggerated so the director can choose which feels best. The chosen action can then be brought down to an agreed level of subtlety. When actors invent from their own emotional range, the action becomes authentic to both actor and character.

Discussion:

1. What is really at stake for each character at each beat?
2. How much interpretational leeway is there at important beats?
3. What is the range of options in terms of behavior that could be appropriate?
4. Of the range presented, did the director choose the most telling? If not, why not?

EXERCISE 22-6: GIVE ME TOO MUCH!

Useful When: One or more of your actors is under an emotional constraint and the scene is stuck in low gear.

Purpose: To release actors temporarily from restrictive judgments they are imposing and give them permission to overact.

Activity: Tell the actors that you feel the scene is bottled up and you want them to reach for the same emotions but exaggerate them. Exaggeration brings clarity and licenses actors to go to emotional limits they fear would look absurd if produced under normal conditions.

Discussion: You can now tell your cast what to change and at what new levels to pitch their energy and emotions. Often exaggeration alone clears a blockade. Ask actors how it felt to go so far beyond their previous levels. When actors switch from dabbling fearfully in the shallows to leaping with abandon off the top diving board, they often find they can now do the elegant dive and let go of a specific fear.

EXERCISE 22-7: LET'S BE BRITISH

Useful When: A scene has become over-projected, artificial, and out of hand. Actors may have begun to feel the scene will never work, that it is jinxed. It's time to pull back.

Purpose: To return the actors to playing from character instead of striving for an elusive effect.

Activity: Ask your actors to play the scene in a monotone, with emotion barely evident, but fully experiencing their character's emotion underneath the reticence.

Discussion:

1. Does repressing emotions sometimes heighten them?
2. Did the scene that had turned into sound and fury go back to basics?
3. What did the actors feel?

EXERCISE 22-8: SPOT CHECK

Useful When: A line or an action repeatedly does not ring true. This exercise is like a breathalyzer test, jolting the actors into keeping up the inner lives of their characters for fear you will pull them over. Use sparingly.

Purpose: To stick a probe into an actor's process at a particular moment.

Activity: Simply stop a reading or an off-book rehearsal at the problem point, and ask each actor what his or her characters' thoughts, fears, mental images, etc. were at that moment.

Discussion:

1. Did this flush out a misconception?
2. A forced emotional connection?
3. Did the actors' concentration change afterward?
4. What other effects did this exercise produce?

EXERCISE 22-9: SWITCHING CHARACTERS

Useful When: Two actors seem stalemated and not properly aware of the character each other is playing. This can arise when a defensive actor's over-preparation precludes him or her from adapting to nuances in a partner's playing. This situation arises when actors distrust each other or feel incompatible.

Purpose: To place each actor temporarily in the opposite role so later he or she empathizes with another character's predicament and achieves an interesting duality.

Activity: Simply ask actors to exchange parts, without regard for sex, age, or anything else. Then have them return to their own parts to see if the reading changes.

Discussion:

1. Actors: Each should say briefly what you discovered about the scene from the other person's role.
2. Actors: Did you have any new revelations about your own part?
3. Director: What did you notice after the actors resumed their own parts?

EXERCISE 22–10: TRANSLATING A SCENE INTO AN IMPROVISATION

Useful When: The cast seems tired and unable to generate emotions the scene calls for. Keep improv scenes up your sleeve for any scene that may give trouble. Actors may initially resist your request, but they usually come to enjoy the refreshment after a scene has become oppressive and immobile. Most will be impressed when you whisk out an alternative approach like this. At the very least, this exercise will release the malaise that builds up from repeated failures with the formal text.

Purpose: To free the actors from the letter of the scene to recreate its spirit. Refreshes a rehearsal session when energies are flagging. The less experienced your cast, the less they can concentrate and develop during long rehearsal sessions.

Activity: Take the main issue in the scene, or the one that is causing a problem, and translate it into two or three analogous scene subjects for improvisation. If, for example, you are having trouble in a scene of conflict between a daughter and her suspicious and restrictive father, you might assign analogous improvs on:

- A scene between an officious nurse and a patient who wants to leave the hospital
- A bus driver and a rider who wants to get off the bus before the next stop
- Two customers in a supermarket checkout line, the younger of whom wants to jump in line because she only has three items

Each of these situations has a built-in conflict hinging on rights and authority, and tackling them rapidly one after another will generate a wider emotional vocabulary that can be imported back into the original scene. A useful variation is to let the actors invent analogous scenes. You can get further mileage if you do the improvs a second round with the roles reversed.

Discussion:

1. Which improv worked best?
2. What came of switching roles?
3. What were the differences when the cast returned to the text?

CHAPTER 23

REHEARSAL AND CAST DEVELOPMENT

Rehearsal for fiction film production is a misunderstood activity, perhaps because the word suggests the aridity of repetition and drilling. A better expression would be *cast development.* A low-budget production that forgoes this stage prior to shooting is courting a death wish. When all theater production, even improvisatory theater, grows from rigorous rehearsal, you might wonder why big-budget filmmaking does not do so. The professional cinema argues that because film actors can learn the next day's lines just before shooting, rehearsing the cast as an ensemble is a waste of money.

But even famous screen actors study and rehearse intensively. Dustin Hoffman, Meryl Streep, and Gary Sinise—to mention only a few exceptional talents—make extensive preparation and believe, with the late Rod Steiger, that acting is a highly demanding craft. Ingmar Bergman, Robert Altman, and Mike Leigh command unusual loyalty from their actors because they take time to develop the ensemble prior to filming.

If top professional directors and actors need preparation, novices need it even more. Few seem aware of this, and the acting in student or novice directors' films is generally appalling. Expensive cameras and computerized editing are no alchemy, and they won't transform lead into gold. Filming simply magnifies, so good looks bigger and better, and bad looks bigger and worse.

For rehearsals to work, the director must understand the importance of tapping into actors' creativity. If you shape your ensemble to have a history together and a dynamic of relationships before you start filming, the company can absorb dramatic situations into its own reality. Characters' and actors' relationships become indistinguishably authentic, and that is our goal in this developmental work. The stages that follow aim to produce a disciplined, creative team. The results of the quest are channeled through the sensibility of the director, who becomes coordinator, midwife, and first audience.

PLANNING AND SCHEDULING REHEARSALS

As soon as parts are cast, your assistant director (AD) should log everyone's availability and work out rehearsal times. Actors are generally busy people and prefer working on a predetermined schedule. Making a schedule signals your professionalism. Schedule enough time for the film's performances to evolve; a rule of thumb is to invest one hour of rehearsal for every minute of screen time. A demanding 3-minute scene thus needs at least 3 hours of rehearsal. Make sessions brief and frequent rather than long and comprehensive because doing unfamiliar work tires some people and makes them unable to concentrate. The 3 hours' work for the one scene might be most productive as three sessions interspersed with work on other scenes. Use your instincts.

After every rehearsal, remind the actors of the next session and make sure each has a printed schedule. Also be sure everyone has a full list of cast and unit email addresses and phone numbers (especially cell phones).

Lastly, warn actors that all aspects of filming are very slow, and they should bring good books, crossword puzzles, and so on to tide them through down time when shooting begins.

FIRST MEETING

CAST RESEARCH

For the first meeting, ask the cast to develop intensive notes on all aspects of their character and a detailed biography to substantiate their conceptions. Review these collectively and then later with each cast member separately. You don't want to risk publicly bruising someone's confidence so early in the process.

DEALING WITH "NEGATIVE" ASPECTS OF A CHARACTER

Be ready to deal with actors wanting to parlay a negative trait in their character into something more, well, admirable. The Roman poet Terence said, "Nothing human is alien to me." Use this to help your actors see truth as neither positive nor negative, but as simply human and part of the job.

FIRST READ-THROUGH

After everyone has had time to study the script, the first read-through will show how each actor interprets the piece and how well the nascent characters fit together. Expect to get glimpses of where your biggest problems will lie—in particular scenes, in particular actors, or both.

Depending on the length and complexity of the screenplay, try for a complete reading in one sitting. Give little or no direction; you want to see what ideas and individuality each cast member brings to the role and to the piece. This shows that you respect their ideas and don't want actors to passively depend on minute instructions. Have a list of fundamental questions handy to pose. Most actors are thrilled when their director sees them as partners in problem-solving, which is at the heart and soul of creativity.

Although you have strong ideas of your own, keep quiet and listen to your actors' input. You want them to dig into the piece and thoroughly explore what kind of person each character is. They, not you, have to develop what motivates their characters, and you want each to have a stake in defining what purposes lie behind the script as a whole. Serious actors will love this approach. Keep an eye open for anyone who feels insecure and inadequate at the outset and might need special support.

Urge your cast to develop as much physical movement as they can, even though the primary focus may be on the meaning of words. Holding a script will inhibit this, but the emphasis on movement reminds the cast to act using the whole body, not just the voice and face.

KEEP NOTES

It's tough holding on to the impressions that arise during a rehearsal. Because so much is happening simultaneously, early impressions get erased by later ones, and when you get tired it's easy to face your actors with a mind void of everything except the last impression. Save yourself this embarrassment by carrying a large scratch pad. Without ever taking your eyes off the performance, scribble a key word or two. Glance down momentarily and place your pen at a starting point ready for the next note. Afterward you will have pages of large wobbly prompts. These should trigger the necessary recall.

DIRECT REHEARSALS BY ASKING QUESTIONS

Through probing questions, you can guide the cast into discovery of what you already know. Posing questions also gives you time to think ahead as the actor searches for an answer. Because of the diversity a group brings, your question will flush out a range of aspects and ideas that would not occur to you, and learning becomes a two-way street. Your cast probably reads more like an audience and may catch the omissions or contradictions you were unable to see.

Throughout production, even when everyone feels there can be nothing left to discover, the piece will continue to deepen, growing stronger as you and your cast stumble upon yet more meanings and interconnections. With only a little luck, you will have an exhilarating sense of shared discovery and closeness, something that people will recall nostalgically years later.

Asking challenging questions is always more effective than reeling off instructions. Because of their authoritarian nature, orders can be resisted or misunderstood, especially if modified or superseded. But people never forget what they discovered for themselves. That is the philosophy of learning behind everything in this book.

NO LEARNING OF LINES YET!

At this stage, be absolutely clear that you still want nobody to learn lines. Committing lines to memory transfixes whatever action and interpretation the actor has reached. Making changes subsequently is much harder after initial memorization. At this early stage much is still in flux, so nobody has sufficient knowledge to risk this.

FOCUSING THE THEMATIC PURPOSE

A film's theme is the overall thrust of meaning the piece delivers to an audience, and you arrive at its optimal form by exploring what the text can support. To communicate a theme you will have to get everyone behind it. Stating the thematic purpose will require defining the steps and focus of the whole piece and paraphrasing what these are. It's wise to hold back on doing this while you learn more from the rehearsal process.

A story represents a limited but intense vision that is made coherent by an underlying value system of cause and effect. Most stories are experimental in that telling them is a way to construct a working model of your beliefs. If others are moved to conviction, the principles behind the model are vindicated and may be accepted as having vision. That is the best anyone can do.

Your thematic purpose need not encompass universal truth ("in our Western way of life the rich get richer while the poor get poorer") or be morally uplifting ("if people would just vent their real feelings, everyone could be free"). Audiences will resent being preached at, especially if the film should fall short of the global nature of its message. Don't forget that something as timeless and elemental as "Frankie and Johnny were lovers, but he done her wrong" still raises goosebumps if it's followed up well.

Limited, specific, and deeply felt aims will have the most impact. Your thematic statement will be all the stronger for focusing on a simple principle with profound consequences ("sometimes marriage between two good people is not practical and everyone suffers" or "because his ideas are held so inflexibly, he is dangerous to those who love him"). By investigating a small truth and deeply investigating it, you can indicate larger truths of wider resonance. Put another way, *an absorbing and convincing microcosm will call up the macrocosm.*

Now that the cast has had time to study the script:

1. Ask the players to informally discuss the meanings and purposes of the whole story and its characters. This will reveal what spectrum of opinion exists. Encourage all points of view and impose none of your own. You will acquire additional insights because each actor is an advocate for a single character. Your notion of the piece's thematic purpose comes from knowing the text, but there's no guarantee that it's universal. Though you may have to tell players with tiny parts what the piece is about, you can't do this to anyone with a major role, for it suggests that the actor must suppress any original or contrary impressions. A well-founded disagreement may point to problem areas in the script, so you need this dialogue as much as your cast does.
2. A wise approach to leadership is to form your own ideas and then either parlay your cast into accepting them or into forming alternatives that are just as acceptable. Don't tell anyone until later, but their ideas may be superior! Again, reiterate that nobody learns any lines until interpretations, meanings, and characters have been thoroughly explored and agreed on.
3. Ask cast members to formulate their characters' *backstories* (what seems to have happened before they appear).

4. Ask each actor to profile his or her character and deliver a brief character biography for another meeting. Let the cast debate each other's characters and motivations—it will deepen the texture and integration.
5. Turn the cast's attention to successive key scenes and ask the players to develop the subtextual matter for each.
6. Ask the cast to again review the main themes of the piece and explore their hierarchy. During this process you can be more authoritative as you unify the body of opinion into a coherent thematic purpose for the piece.

If you cannot achieve agreement about everything at this stage, agree to differ and let it go. Goodwill disagreements provide a creative tension that spurs closer examination during the next phases of work. Actors will probably be too busy with more immediate concerns to make it a running fight, and everyone will eventually arrive at a tacit agreement through shared problem-solving or, failing all else, simple fatigue.

You are now ready to begin developing the piece and testing your ideas through rehearsals. You have designed your plane, and now you want to see how it flies.

ENCOURAGE ACTORS TO DEVELOP THEIR CHARACTERS' BACKGROUNDS

An essential resource for any conscientious actor is the character's biography, which he or she prepares. Without an explicit request, some may not make the effort, especially if they have yet to understand its benefit. Others do the job inadequately or go off on a tangent through misreading the piece. This is a good time to meet alone with each actor to check his or her ideas and to encourage, develop, or redirect. It is also a good time to discuss how the actor's character sees the other characters.

VALUES AND HAZARDS OF WORKING ONE-ON-ONE WITH ACTORS

Much of a part's future direction will develop from one-on-one exploratory sessions. Inevitably, the larger the cast, the less the director's undivided attention is available to all cast members. Because feedback is so vital to actors, most feel inadequately recognized most of the time. If one actor sees another actor alone with the director, he or she may resent the special attention unless there is an awareness that the session is remedial. Because of these pressures, the beginning director should work with a small cast and capitalize on relationships with good actors by using them again in subsequent productions.

A good solution to the demand for individual attention is to see everyone alone, even minor parts, at the outset. You will want to check the actor's ideas and approach and establish a personal and supportive relationship. From then on, try to rehearse collectively, reserving private discussion for special support and the exchange of ideas or suggestions about problem areas. You should develop something personal and supportive to tell each actor just before shooting begins.

During shooting you can inject new tensions into a scene by briefing an individual and leaving the others in ignorance of what is to come.

REHEARSING ONE SCENE AT A TIME

Initially, try to rehearse scenes in script order. Later, when the piece is thoroughly familiar, adopt a plan of convenience and work around people's schedules. You will need to give priority to key scenes and those presenting special problems.

At this stage the cast is still working with "the book." Actors are searching for their characters' full range of motivations and developing a knowledge of how each scene functions in the piece as a whole. Film scenes often seem very fragmentary, especially to actors used to theater. It may allay fears to show them clips from analogous productions.

DEAL ONLY WITH TOP-LEVEL PROBLEMS

At each run-through, deal only with a scene's most major problems, or you risk burdening actors with too much information and blurring the priorities. A rehearsal spirals backward and forward, oscillating between particular details and the more abstract areas of meaning and philosophy. As major problems get solved, others of secondary significance, such as lines or actions that lack credibility, will move to the top of the heap and claim everyone's attention. The rehearsal process is thus one of continuous discovery and refinement.

FROM BEAT TO BEAT, THE DRAMATIC UNIT

Once a scene's major difficulties are brought under control, you should go over everything within each beat, one unit at a time. You can only do this effectively if the major players understand the text in terms of beats. Make tactful inquiries to find out if anyone needs a little coaching. Inevitably there will be debate about beats and units. Much of the value of working on each separate unit lies in preventing the actors' growing and embracing knowledge from pervading everything they do. This is happening when the scene becomes muddy and lacking in dynamics. Characters should live keenly and restrictedly within their immediate present, experiencing one discovery after another and reacting to what they do discover. They should develop one emotion after another and one action after another, never a blend or soup.

THE ADVANTAGES OF VIDEOTAPING REHEARSALS

Once your cast is off book and becoming reasonably confident, cover rehearsals with a video camera using the documentary style called direct cinema. This is a continuous take with a handheld camera, moving close for close ups, and backing away, panning, or tracking as the action requires. This treats the rehearsal as a happening to be recorded without intervention on behalf of the camera. Because the camera tries to be in the right place at the right time, this coverage needs no editing. Taping produces quite a range of advantages:

From the director's point of view:

- A dramatically complete version is viewable within moments of calling "Cut!"
- You can judge what works on the screen from *seeing* what works on the screen.
- You can privately run and rerun rehearsals.
- You get early sight of mannerisms, clichés, trends, as well as subtleties that would otherwise only make themselves known in rushes or (God help us) postproduction.
- You can expect the cast not to regress when you start shooting and to give natural and unstrained performances from the first day.

From the actors' point of view:

- A mobile and unobtrusive camera encourages them to move as they wish.
- The camera is choreographed into the process, rather than appearing later as a dominant and inhibiting newcomer.
- They work alongside key crewmembers and get to know and trust them.

From the crew's point of view:

- Camera and sound principals can be integrated early, seeking each scene's optimal form in terms of camera angles, movement, lenses, lighting, and sound coverage.
- The crew learns the imperceptible indications each actor gives when about to move or speak and what sightlines and movements can be expected.
- The crew learns during rehearsals (along with the director) how to cover more action with fewer angles and longer takes.
- The crew gets advance warning of what compromises an actor must make in speed or destination to overcome a camera or microphone problem.

By the time formal shooting begins,

- Everyone is an old hand at shooting and being shot.
- Camera placements and movements that show the scene to advantage are known, not theoretical.
- First shooting is from a living reality, instead of something based on the static, heroic concepts of the storyboard approach.
- Dealing with the unexpected is easy when everybody thoroughly knows the foundations.

Especially when a group intends to function as a repertory company (as in Fassbinder's early films), the cycle of performance and critical viewing can be a superb way of helping people get beyond shock and fascination of seeing with their own image and to begin working instead on the places where their resistances lie.

WHEN NOT TO SHOW ACTORS THEIR PERFORMANCES

Taping rehearsals is not without risks, and if there is any insecurity in the cast, it may *not* be a good idea to let them see themselves acting until you have finished shooting:

- Cast members clamor for a showing, but are usually appalled on first seeing themselves onscreen.
- Actors who depended on your judgment may lean the other way and attempt to apply their own corrective action, giving you new problems.
- Inexperienced or untrusting actors can begin to direct not only themselves but, worse, other actors.
- Knowing they will be seen on the screen by other cast members may make staying inside their characters' thoughts and experiences more difficult.

If you show rehearsal tapes, you must persuade everybody well before the shoot to relinquish monitoring and judging their own performance and pass that responsibility to you. You are the director, and you represent the first audience. The actor who fails to do this, locked in defensiveness and mistrust, is a liability. Often this person has, or imagines she has, star status and is terrified of losing her reputation. But this you won't face for a while!

Taping, showing rehearsals to actors, and debating the outcome is an evolutionary process that works well with a dedicated ensemble, but it takes time. If you are taping rehearsals, but your schedule won't allow this degree of development, use the following procedure:

- Warn that it is normal to hate the way you look on the screen.
- Make a little footage available early in rehearsals for the curious.
- Be clear that you will show no tape footage later and no rushes during the shoot.
- If there is protest, remind the cast that actors in feature films are normally barred from seeing rushes because it is too unsettling.

PLEASE DON'T COPY THE FILM INDUSTRY

As we have said, the professional film industry usually does without rehearsals to save costs and preserve spontaneity. Don't be influenced by this practice unless you have a top-level cast and crew whose professionalism makes up for a lack of fundamental development. In all other situations you should undertake development with your cast and videotape what you do or risk having amateurish, inconsistent theatrical performances that look terrible on the screen.

Here's why: A director formerly a cameraperson or assistant director has spent years observing actors and setups. That person, having also seen how each take looked afterward on the screen, has the experience to make good judgments about performances as he or she first directs. But the new director who never apprenticed in the industry and who didn't tape rehearsals or even rehearse, will inevitably judge performances in front of the camera by live-performance criteria. The resulting artificiality cannot be changed in the cutting room.

Another pitfall you can avoid: New directors often delay evolving a *mise en scène* (camera treatment) until the last moment. This makes for a late and highly theoretical fragmentation of the material and coverage that may err on the side of caution or be thin and unbalanced. Any production filmed under these conditions will probably overshoot, have a choppy look, and lack an integrated point of view. Extended coverage is also expensive, takes longer, uses more film stock, and exhausts crew and cast. The editor tries to compensate for uneven performances and the film emerges over-cut.

Now tell me honestly, can you afford *not* to tape rehearsals?

If you doubt that this is professional, remember that many directors use a video assist at film shoots. This is a picture feed from the camera's viewfinder that lets the director see the action on a video monitor instead of watching the take live from alongside the camera. If *they* need to see what is actually going on film, can *you* afford to do otherwise?

CHAPTER 24

DIRECTOR AND ACTOR PREPARE A SCENE

For collaborative work to be truly effective, actors and the director should each work alone on the text before trying out a scene together. Their preparatory work will overlap, creating checks and balances in which action, motivations, and meanings come under multiple examinations. This helps avoid omissions and draws usefully partisan perceptions from the actors. Their viewpoints may not all be compatible with yours or each other's because each sees the world of the text more from their own character's perspective. The director leads the process of coordinating and reconciling these viewpoints, making it a creative dialogue rather than a battle of wills. For this the director should be evenhanded, holistic, and speaking for the needs of a general audience.

Following are the responsibilities that director and actor bear at the outset of rehearsal. If this seems unduly weighted toward the intellectual, much will become instinctive once you gain experience.

THE DIRECTOR PREPARES

GIVEN CIRCUMSTANCES

Know the script so you're quite certain what locations, time frame, character details, acts, and so on are specified and what other detail is implied or must be invented by director and cast.

BACKSTORY

Using your intimate knowledge of the script, infer the *backstory*, that is, the events preceding the script's action. Biographical details that substantiate the backstory fall into the domain of the individual character's biography, which is best generated by the actor playing the part. Directors need to be ahead of the game if the cast is to consider them authoritative.

NATURE OF CHARACTERS: WHAT EACH WANTS

It isn't enough to know what a character *is*; you must know what each character *wants* and is *trying to get* or *do*. This gives the character not just a fixed, static identity worn like a monogrammed t-shirt, but an active, evolving quest that mobilizes willpower to gain each new end, moment to moment. There is a great difference between "Paul is afraid" and "Paul's fear makes him try to deflect the policeman's attention away from his suitcase." In the static example, the actor playing Paul has only generalized fear to work with, while the active description provides a series of definite ends to gain, each specific to the moment. A person's acting is transformed by a succession of limited, precise goals because it transforms the character into someone dynamic who shows new evidence of inner life at every step.

COMMUNICATING THE NATURE OF ACTS

Screen actors must develop behavior authentic to their characters and situations, for each right action, no matter how small, helps to create a rich and unique identity for its doer. *An evocative simile or analogy gives a precise and imaginative coloration to an action or line.* Verbal labels become a potent way to direct as you help each actor decide what works. To say that a man "leaves the table during a family feud" is not enough, for it provides no special information. But naming it his "tactical retreat" or "the first step in leaving home" makes it memorable and specific. A possessive mother's behavior when receiving her son's fiancée for the first time might be called "the snake dance," and a son entering a funeral parlor where his father lies dead might be "crossing into the underworld."

THE NATURE OF CONFLICT

The engine of drama is conflict, so the director must know precisely how and where each situation of conflict develops. The classic descriptions and their modern equivalencies are:

- Man against Nature (conflict between a character and the situation)
- Man against Man (conflict between characters)
- Man against Himself (conflict between the opposing parts of a character)

For conflict to exist in a dramatic unit (or in a larger unit such as a whole scene, of course) you must define its pattern of oppositions so you can orchestrate them. We'll use my father and his contraband sugar in "Graphing Tension and Beats" from Chapter 17 as an example:

Define the unit's . . .	By asking . . .	Example
Situation	What, when, and where?	During WWII a young sailor called Paul is leaving London docks with contraband sugar hidden in a suitcase.

Primary point of view	Whose experience are we sharing?	The sailor's
Secondary point(s) of view as resource	Who else's viewpoint might we share?	(1) Bystanders (2) Policeman (3) Hungry seagulls
Main problem	What is main character trying to accomplish?	He wants to get it safely home to his family.
Conflict	Where is the main conflict?	Though afraid of breaking the law, he wants to bring home a special treat to his family.
Obstacle	Obstacle that he or she faces?	Just when his suitcase bursts he encounters a policeman.
Stakes	The price of failure?	If he's caught he may go to jail.
Complications	How do the stakes rise as the situation moves toward the apex or crisis point?	The policeman seems helpful, but may be playing cat and mouse. He ties up the suitcase while Paul sweats. Paul starts walking away. Has he gotten away with it? He walks jauntily, in dread of hearing "Stop!"
Beat	How does a main character's consciousness change?	Turning into the next street, he realizes that he is free.
Resolution	How does the situation end?	At last he can breathe freely and look around him again.

The three-act concept works well here, even in the smallest dramatic unit. It provides a wonderful set of tools for developing dramatic focus and tension. Try applying it to these situations:

- Striking a match in the dark
- Getting a locked door open in an emergency
- Getting a picky cat to sample a cheaper brand of food
- Getting an injured person across a rickety jungle bridge
- Finding a banknote in a crowded street
- Finding gravel in your shoe on the way to the altar
- Losing your partner in a supermarket
- Waking up in no man's land during a battle
- Practicing a seduction that almost works

Approached with dramatic insight, almost any situation can be developed into a fine short film and can be any genre—farce, tragedy, domestic realism—anything you like.

The dramatic unit's course has been usefully likened to the cycles of an internal combustion engine (John Howard Lawson, *Theory and Technique of Playwriting,* New York: Hill & Wang, 1960).

1. The piston draws in explosive gases (exposition, setting the scene)
2. Compression stage and building of pressure inside the cylinder (rising action)
3. Ignition at maximum pressure followed by explosion (beat, or climax if it's a scene)
4. Motor is forced forward into a new cycle of intake, compression, and explosion (resolution leading to next dramatic unit or scene)

This diagram works equally well for a single beat inside a dramatic unit, or to represent a complete scene with its build, climax, and resolution.

DRAMATIC TENSION AND FINDING BEATS

For this section you may first want to refresh your memory by reading the end of Chapter 1 beginning with the section, Beats, the Key to Understanding Drama.

A situation of tension between two individuals is like a fencing match—much strategic footwork and mutual adaptation punctuated by strikes. Each strike threatens to alter the balance of power and puts the match's likely outcome in a different light. Likewise in drama, a scene's nature and possible outcome alter with each impact or beat. Whenever a character feels a strike, it alters the balance of power. And this moment of altered consciousness has a heightened significance for at least one character. Each beat is a moment of "crisis adaptation," and there may be one or many per scene.

CHARACTERIZING THE BEATS

In Chapter 1, we spoke of assigning a function to each beat, and that they can be expected to belong in one of these categories.

1. *Plot Beats*

a. Story beat:	Advances the story, often connected to the disturbance or complication
b. Preparation beat:	Establishes the beginning of a sequence or provides foreshadowing
c. Expository beat:	Provides information about past circumstances
d. Crisis beat:	Presents conflict
e. Mood beat:	Establishes emotional circumstances
f. Reversal beat:	Reverses action (this may well be associated with a plot point)

2. *Character Attitude Beats*

a. Dispositional beat:	Reveals a personality bent

b. Motivational beat:	Expresses desires and provides reasons for actions
c. Deliberative beat:	Expresses a reflective or emotional thought
d. Decisive beat:	Indicates a significant decision

3. *Character Thought Beats*

a. Emotive beat:	Expresses what a character feels
b. Reflective beat:	Expresses what a character concludes, considers, or discovers
c. Informative beat:	Presents information relevant to the (film)
d. Exaggerational beat:	Expresses maximizing or minimizing of a topic
e. Argumentative beat:	Contains conflict

Characterizing each beat and classifying it according to plot needs, character attitudes, or character thoughts will focus what needs to happen in each beat. It should also consolidate your sense of the scene's trajectory, explain the development of a character's will, and clarify what effect you intend for the audience. Tagging each beat with a characterization may just as easily show unwanted reiteration and thus explain why a portion of the scene suffers from aimlessness. It's worth trying, but don't worry if you can't make sense of your screenplay using these particular tools.

FINDING THE DRAMATIC UNITS

Between one beat and the next is a transition that includes winding down from the old beat and winding up to the new. This, in the barometric language of drama, is the falling action of the old unit and the rising action of the new. All communication involves both intellectual and emotional modes of operation. Beware seeking to control your audience intellectually. To direct, you *must* be able to enter the emotional realities of each character, see through their eyes, feel their feelings and changes. The *audience's ideas change deeply only when they are emotionally engaged.*

Each dramatic unit can be minutes or seconds long.

- **Find the beats.** First identify the beat points in your script and see how the scene's forward movement becomes a series of dramatic thrusts at the audience's emotions. This waveform is often most palpable in domestic comedy. It can be predictable and manipulative or done so well that it becomes movingly true to human life. The difference is a matter of honesty, purpose, and taste both in the writing and the playing.
- **Know what kind of beat it is.**
- **Determine the dramatic units.** If a scene has three beats, it probably has three dramatic units. Each beat is a high point, and one of them is probably the scene turning point, or *obligatory moment.*
- **Find the subtexts and nominate functions for each dramatic unit.** Good drama is like machinery: Everything has a purpose and a function. Everything in a machine has a name; give names and functions to each part of your dramatic machinery. It will make you a good director.

IDENTIFYING SUBTEXTS

Figure 24–1 is the first page of a scene in which two characters get lost while driving in a city's outskirts. It shows a dramatic unit with its beat typically marked up. Husband and wife have a fight because Tod, as the typical male, won't stop and look at the map. The beat comes at the pivotal moment in which Tod realizes that Angela is seriously upset and that he must do something differently. There are several steps on the part of each character toward this moment, and they are decided by making an analysis of *subtexts*. A subtext is the underlying truth behind what the characters actually say or do. The beat has been defined in handwriting, and the steps in the subtext as it ramps up to the beat are all characterized with an interpretative *tag*.

See if you agree that:

- Angela's first three lines are all fueled by the same underlying idea, "I'm afraid we're really lost."
- Once she realizes their directions mention a supermarket, and that neither this nor the gas station are anywhere to be seen, her subtext changes to "We've got to get help."
- Tod makes adjustments to Angela's increasing frustration, and his will is pitted against hers.
- The beat comes when he realizes he's let things go too far. Typically, there's always a significant action at the obligatory moment. Here it's when he changes his mind and stops the car.
- At this point, a new dramatic unit begins.

Trained actors know how to do this work, either instinctively or deliberately with a pencil, as I did. Untrained actors won't have the first idea about this stuff, and you will have to work with them tactfully until they understand both the method and its importance. Putting a screenplay on the block reveals how tight or loose its cabinetry is and what you and your actors must do to fix it. Learn this by heart:

- Dramatic analysis is vital because it can define *a clear set of actable steps.*
- Each new step is a new action *fueled by a new volition and emotion.*
- A character's complex of emotions is like a melody: It only exists if the notes are sounded in sequence, not all at once.
- Acting is sequencing one clear intention after another, one clear and appropriate action after another, one clear emotion after another.

Though this is true to life, only trained actors understand it. The layman gets it wrong because he *remembers* a situation in abstract, summary form in which all the fine, distinct experiences have been mulched together into a static description. This is what you, as a director, must so often work to tease apart and make dynamic.

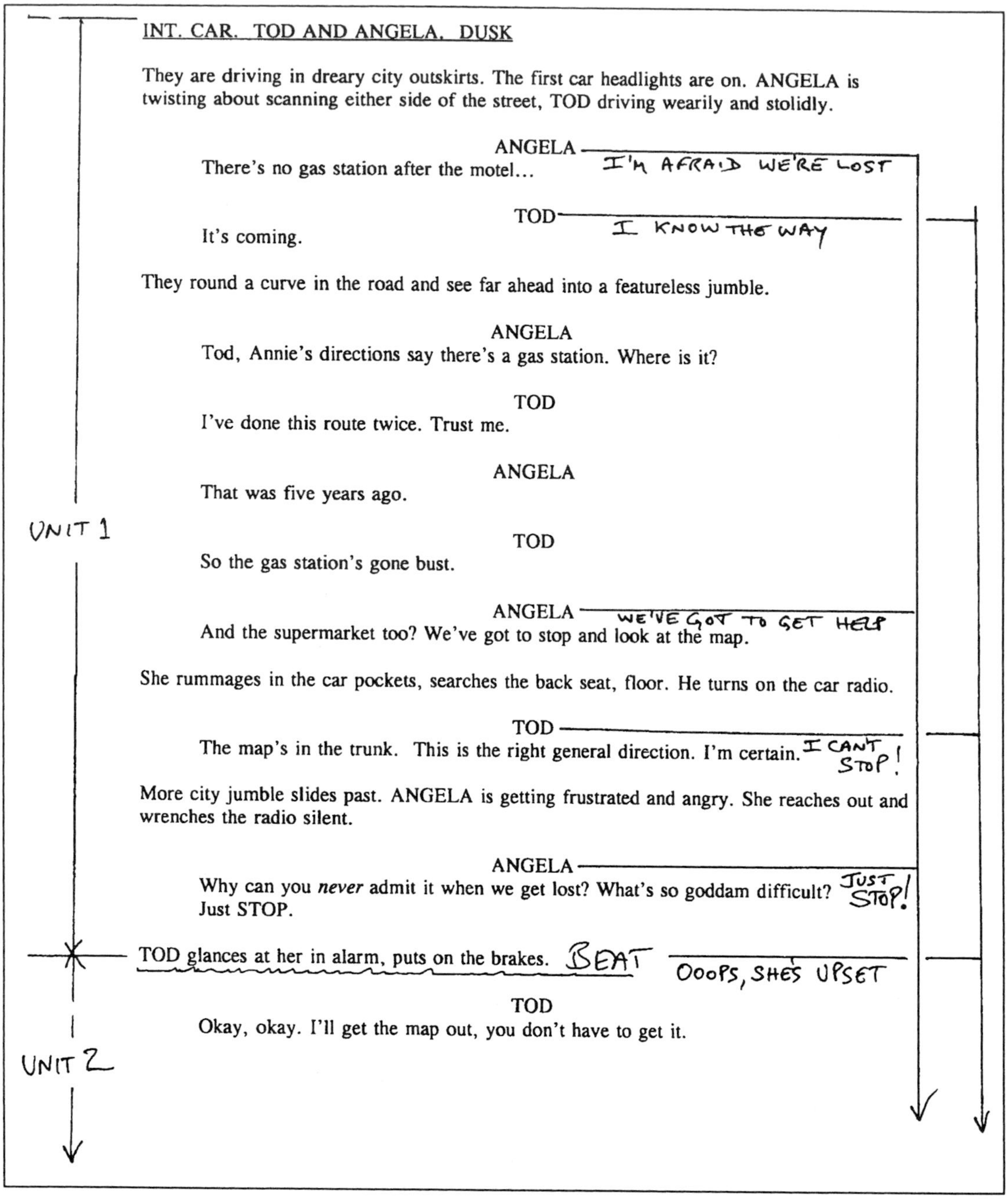

INT. CAR. TOD AND ANGELA. DUSK

They are driving in dreary city outskirts. The first car headlights are on. ANGELA is twisting about scanning either side of the street, TOD driving wearily and stolidly.

ANGELA
There's no gas station after the motel...

TOD
It's coming.

They round a curve in the road and see far ahead into a featureless jumble.

ANGELA
Tod, Annie's directions say there's a gas station. Where is it?

TOD
I've done this route twice. Trust me.

ANGELA
That was five years ago.

TOD
So the gas station's gone bust.

ANGELA
And the supermarket too? We've got to stop and look at the map.

She rummages in the car pockets, searches the back seat, floor. He turns on the car radio.

TOD
The map's in the trunk. This is the right general direction. I'm certain.

More city jumble slides past. ANGELA is getting frustrated and angry. She reaches out and wrenches the radio silent.

ANGELA
Why can you *never* admit it when we get lost? What's so goddam difficult? Just STOP.

TOD glances at her in alarm, puts on the brakes.

TOD
Okay, okay. I'll get the map out, you don't have to get it.

I'M AFRAID WE'RE LOST
I KNOW THE WAY
UNIT 1
WE'VE GOT TO GET HELP
I CAN'T STOP!
JUST STOP!
BEAT
OOOPS, SHE'S UPSET
UNIT 2

FIGURE 24–1

Script page with marked beat, dramatic units, and steps within the first unit delineated as tag lines.

To strengthen your skills, make a point of observing—in yourself as well as in others—how realizations, emotions, and actions are sequenced in real life. After observing actuality you won't accept the mishmash rendering anymore.

To feel secure, you must always be ahead of your cast, breaking down each scene and knowing precisely what drives each step forward for each character within each unit. You may learn something when you review the work the actors have done on their own, but they will be deeply impressed that you understand their parts so well. From preparation you derive conviction about what you want, and from this comes your authority to direct.

Actors seek clarity and decisiveness from their director, as well as clear, detailed feedback about their work, but they feel they never get enough. The director who comprehends what each actor is giving, who can describe it accurately to the cast, is like the orchestral conductor who hears every instrument and can tell the fourth cello afterward what wrong note she played. This is not a skill anyone is born with, but something you must work mightily to acquire. Doing your homework diligently on the script is the absolute foundation.

CHANGES IN A CHARACTER'S RHYTHM

Every character has rhythms for speech and action. These vary according to mood (whether, for instance, the character is excited or tired) and the pressures exerted by the situation. It is an actor's responsibility to keep the character's rhythms distinctive and varying according to the character's inner state, which will always change if he or she has a beat point. Put another way, monotony of rhythm usually means that the actors are performing by rote, so you must know where to expect rhythmic changes. The problem has become acute when all the actors in a scene fall into the same mesmerizing rhythm.

OBLIGATORY MOMENT

One of Lawson's intake explosion cycles described previously will be the scene's *obligatory moment*, that is, the major turning point for the scene. This is the moment for which the whole scene exists. Determine what is the obligatory moment by seeing whether the scene still makes sense without it. If you axe the obligatory moment, the scene becomes disabled or redundant. Make sure your directing has the right focus by being sure what each scene's obligatory moment is.

NAMING THE FUNCTION OF EACH SCENE

Like a single cog in the gear train of a clock, each scene in a well-constructed drama has its correct place and function. Defining how power courses through the piece, scene by scene, enables you to interpret each scene confidently and to know how it feeds impetus into its successor in the larger pattern. Giving a tag name to each scene defines it for you and lets you communicate its nature to cast and crew. Dickens' chapter titles from *Bleak House* make good examples: "Covering a Multitude of Sins," "Signs and Tokens," "A Turn of the Screw," "Closing In," "Dutiful Friendship," and "Beginning the World." Ideas about *mise en scène* and scenic design flow effortlessly from charged descriptors like these.

THEMATIC PURPOSE OF THE WHOLE WORK

The director decides and shapes the authorial thrust of the whole work. This interpretation must remain consonant with the screenplay's content and be accepted by the cast. Unlike a published play, a screenplay is not a hallowed document and directors often take considerable liberties with one after a property (a revealing name for a screenplay) has been acquired, which causes much bitterness among screenwriters. Once the piece is in rehearsal and on its way to shooting, the director alters the thematic purpose of the whole at his or her peril.

THE ACTOR PREPARES

A NOTE TO DIRECTORS

Many concepts important to actors are similar to those mentioned for directors, and so they appear in the following section in abbreviated form. Though I have written in the third person as if myself addressing an actor, these notes are for your instruction. Any trained actor should know all this anyway.

By the nature of their work actors are vulnerable, so avoid openly top-down instruction. When you must instruct, couch it respectfully as something to try. This is particularly important when you enter areas of technique or emotion that you haven't experienced yourself. Your function as a director lies primarily in recognizing the authenticity of the result, not dictating how the actor gets there. So from here on, my language addresses actors.

BACKSTORY

Know the events that brought your character to the script's present.

YOUR CHARACTER'S GIVEN CIRCUMSTANCES

Know at every point what circumstances and pressures determine your character's physical and mental state.

BIOGRAPHY

Make up a full life story for your character that supports the backstory details implied by the script. This ensures that you know a great deal more about the character you are creating than is required, and that everything your character says or does has proper roots in the past. Without this integrity of experience and motivation, your character will lack depth and credibility. Your director will often question you during rehearsal about your character's background, always probing what is not yet coming across well.

BE ABLE TO JUSTIFY EVERYTHING YOUR CHARACTER SAYS AND DOES

You should know the specific pressures motivating your character's every action and line. This process of justification has already been used to build your character's biography, and this biography in turn helps govern your character's choices and decisions. The script usually contains the relevant clues, but occasionally your character's action must be completely defined by you and your director.

DEFINE EACH ACTION WITH AN ACTIVE VERB

Onscreen actions are the most eloquent expressions your character ever makes, so the linguistic tags by which you plan them matter very much. Take this poor example: "A woman is seen stepping away from her tipsy husband in embarrassment at a party when an indiscretion passes his lips." This flat description uses the passive voice and is minimally informative. An enterprising actor might describe the action as, "sidestepping the landmine," "she absorbs a punch in the gut," "she springs toward the bar," or "she reels aside after stepping in filth." These descriptions employ active verbs to illuminate the behavior and its motivation.

What about common actions like opening a closet door? To perform the action in general, that is, without a specific motivation, is false to life. Giving even small actions an active description helps invest each with a specific identity and meaning. For instance, "He eases the door open" shows caution and perhaps apprehension. Substitute such verbs as *jerks, rips, shoves, barges, slides, elbows, flings, dashes, heaves*, or *hurls* and you have a spectrum of relationships between person and door, each particularizing the action to great effect.

Filmmakers expect actors to remain consistent over many takes and many angles, and a single 3-minute scene may take a whole day to shoot. Consistency becomes a major problem for the actor, especially if inexperienced. Verbal tags help stabilize this situation, especially as fatigue sets in. Make them part of your preparation and each action will remain clear in quality and motivation so you remain emotionally consistent. Having tags to hand also makes you a joy to work with because communication with your director is quick and clear.

WHAT IS MY CHARACTER TRYING TO GET OR DO?

Answering this commonplace little question is the key to persuasive acting. In everyday life most of us are unaware of how unceasingly inventive we are in pursuing what we want. Instead, we see ourselves as civilized, long-suffering victims who sacrifice happiness and fulfillment to the voracious demands of others. But you are not called an *actor* for nothing. Your character is always trying *actively* to get what he or she wants (a smile, a cup of coffee, a sympathetic reaction, a rejection, a sign of guilt, a glimpse of doubt) using a strategy peculiar to your character alone, as he or she tries to realize the desire of the moment. As circumstances alter, the character's needs change and adapt. Incidentally, being active like this is the only viable method to portray a passive person, who differs only in strategy.

WHAT ARE OTHER CHARACTERS TRYING TO DO TO ME OR GET FROM ME?

Your character must remain alive to the real and unpredictable chemistry of the acted moment. If you scan the other characters for signs of their will and intention, your character will be fresh and alive. In real life this process is constantly within us, happening automatically and unconsciously. But in a role, these reflexes must be deliberately patterned until your character's actions and reactions are internalized. Then a scene shot in untold takes and angles can still be alive at the end of a long working day because you and your partners are still working from the actual, not just from the rehearsed.

KNOW WHERE THE BEATS ARE

See the section on "Finding the Beats" in the previous director's portion of this chapter, but be aware that as an actor sustaining a single consciousness, you sometimes see peaks of consciousness in your character that have been overlooked by your director. Don't be afraid to play these or be an advocate for your character.

HOW AND WHERE DOES MY CHARACTER ADAPT?

Every character has goals to pursue or defend and will read either victory or defeat into the course of things. To accommodate changes in other characters, you must make strategic adaptation within the frame of the writing. Spotting where and how to make these adaptations helps build a dense and changing texture for your character's consciousness. Maintaining this is so much work that you can stay effortlessly in focus throughout many takes.

KEEP YOUR CHARACTER'S INTERIOR VOICE AND MIND'S EYE GOING

In real life, people are enclosed in their own ongoing thoughts, hopes, fears, memories, and visions, some of which are occasionally verbalized as an interior monologue. The good actor builds and maintains his or her character's stream of consciousness or *interior action.* Hear or even speak your character's conflicting thoughts internally. Summon up mental images from your character's past, remember and imagine in character, and you will be continuously convincing and interesting to an audience. Another consequence is that your actions and reactions will become consistent and true in pacing. A properly structured consciousness in turn liberates genuine feeling. The actor's art is nothing less than maintaining a disciplined consciousness, and this is why acting is so difficult and psychically demanding.

KNOW YOUR CHARACTER'S FUNCTION

Know all your character's objectives. Know what the scene and the whole film are meant to accomplish and what your character contributes. Don't work to inflate or change it.

KNOW THE THEMATIC PURPOSE OF THE WHOLE WORK

The responsible actor knows that characterization must merge effectively with the thrust of the whole work. You must cooperate, not compete, with the other actors to realize this. Your director is the arbiter of these matters, and also your only audience. Seek feedback from the director alone. Ignore anything told you by crew, onlookers, or other actors.

REHEARSING WITH THE BOOK

EARLY WORK WITH THE BOOK

By now the actors should have done their homework. You (the director) have not yet given them the go-ahead to learn their lines because, as we have said, this leads to actors internalizing an undeveloped and unproven interpretation. Learning lines also fixes an actor's attention prematurely on words when, for screen acting, behavior (of which language is only a part) is preeminent.

The cast may be bursting with questions and ideas. Run through scenes "with the book" (that is, actors reading from the script) and see what each actor's conception of his or her character and of the scene is. You should never have to struggle to understand something. If the words or actions don't communicate, something is invariably wrong with the actor's understanding. Early rehearsal should be geared toward finding the focus and interpretation you want. At this stage, *learning the scene is more important than learning lines*. Character consistency is an issue because it requires reconciling a character's actions in one scene with those in other scenes. Expect discussion and disagreement over the nuances of motivation behind the action and dialogue. This is not people subverting your authority, but the heady and untidy excitements of discovery.

REHEARSAL SPACE

It is an advantage to rehearse in the locations to be used, but this is often impractical. Make still photos to show actors what the location is like. This helps them imagine the proportions in which the scene is to take place and feeds the overall image of their characters' lives. Rehearsal itself often takes place in a large, bare space that is borrowed or rented. Indicate placement of walls, key pieces of furniture, doors, and windows with tape on the rehearsal room floor.

The advantage of a minimalist rehearsal like this is that there is nothing to distract from attention to the text and its characters. The disadvantage is that its abstract quality can lead some to compensate by projecting theatrically toward an imagined audience.

WHICH SCENES FIRST?

At the first rehearsal you will probably cover one or two scenes chosen for their centrality to the piece as a whole. These should emerge naturally while you made your dramatic breakdown and definition of thematic purpose. Work on these, and the turning points within them will provide a sure framework for other linked scenes. Like laying the foundations for a building, rehearsal deals with important issues first.

MOVEMENT AND ACTION

Although reading from a text hinders actors from moving with freedom, get each cast member to develop actions that reflect his or her character's internal, psychological movement. These are vital at the beats. For example, a man being questioned one evening in the kitchen by his possessive mother decides he must confess he is engaged to marry. The text reveals what he says, but it's from what he does that we know how he feels during these stressful minutes. The screenplay does not specify. Does he start drying the dishes, repeatedly handing items to his mother so her hands are never empty? Let's try that to see how it works. When she becomes especially probing, he goes silent, so maybe he should let the water out of the sink, watching it drain away. As the last of it gurgles away, he turns and blurts out his secret. The domestic scene, the way he purges himself of the family china, the water running away, all combine both as credible action and as metaphors for the pressure he feels to act on a "now or never" decision.

Spontaneous invention first produces clichés, so the director must demand fresher and less predictable action from the cast than the example I have invented here.

While hampered by the book and unable to truly interact with each other, actors' readings will remain inadequate, so content yourself with rough sketch work at this stage. As soon as you are satisfied that character, and motivation and the right kind of ideas for action are agreed, instruct the cast to learn their lines for a scene.

REHEARSING WITHOUT THE BOOK

When work begins without the book, watch out that the increased meaningfulness of the lines don't usurp the development of physical action. Encourage the actors to approach the scene from a behavioral rather than textual standpoint. This confirms the importance of having a clear idea of the setting—what it is, what it contains, and what it represents to the characters themselves. Insist on exploring the meaning and spirit of lines, not on their strict accuracy. You can always tighten the readings later. You'll find Chapter 21, Exercise 21-9: "Gibberish" a useful resource here.

TURNING THOUGHT AND WILL INTO ACTION

Only a few significant actions are specified in the average script, and unless director and actors approach the script as an extremely spare blueprint requiring extensive development, characters will move into position, deliver their speeches in an overwrought manner, and be done. This reliably produces a hollow, unconvincing movie.

The true power behind both speech and action is will. Imagine you have a domestic scene between a mother and son under development. It might well develop as follows: When Lyn tells her son Jon that the car bumper is twisted, she is trying to make him feel shocked and guilty. You and your cast know this from the rest of the script, but you want to translate this into action. At the beginning of the scene, Jon hears his mother walk to the garage, but instead of hearing her drive away, he hears her footsteps return. Now she must force her angry state of mind upon her son. You get your actress to slow her entry and make it wordless, accusatory. She stands in the door looking at him. Now he must repel or subvert the pressure she is applying. The actor tells you he feels that his character wants to be busy. You decide he is building a model car and painting the kit parts, keeping this up so he can avoid his mother's accusing gaze.

How does she command his attention? From intuition you suggest to her, "Try throwing the car keys next to the box of parts." This rudely interrupts his evasive activity and creates a charged moment culminating in a beat as their eyes meet. You and your actors are elated because you feel instinctively that you have created a strong moment. Now when the mother says, "The front bumper's all twisted," she is no longer supplying information but pushing home an accusation that began with her silent re-entry. We no longer have words as neutral information or words initiating action. We now have action culminating in words that themselves seek an effect. Driven by conscious needs, *words become a form of action* seeking the gratification of a reaction. This is why a well conceived dialogue contains much that is *verbal action.*

Good actors and good directors try to develop those pressures in the characters that produce dialogue. And in good writing, all dialogue is specific and acts on the person addressed. Thus lines of dialogue become *verbal actions*. Dialogue supplies momentum by energizing action in the person addressed.

Developing a scene is therefore more than knowing the dialogue and where to move on such and such a line; it is working out a detailed flow of action to evidence the internal ebb and flow of each character's being. Primarily this is each actor's responsibility, but final choice and coordination is the director's job. Proof of success is when an audience senses what is going on without hearing a word. I do a lot of international travel, and I seldom bother listening to the sound tracks of in-flight movies. Instead I watch them silently to learn as much as possible from their non-verbal side.

SIGNIFICANCE OF SPACE

How characters use space in this flow of action becomes highly significant. Continuing the previous scene, the mother and son are half the room apart when she enters, but she walks up to him in silence. The pressure from her proximity can cause him to make a painting error, and he lays down the work, looking up at her accusingly. "It's not my fault; you parked it too close to the wall," he says, continuing to look up. She turns away in frustration and turns on the TV. Both stare at the silent picture for a moment or two, hypnotized and taking refuge in habit before they return to the divisive issue of how the car got damaged.

It is now the action rather than the dialogue that is eloquent of their distress, yet no more than a few bald lines of dialogue appear on the page. Action has been created to turn implication into behavior—*behavior being the ebb and flow of will.* If some dialogue is now redundant you can cut it. So much the better.

A CHARACTER'S INNER MOVEMENT

If you break down a single moment of inner movement in a character, you find four definite steps:

1. **Feels Impact:** An expectation (someone's words or actions) impacts character's consciousness.
2. **Sees Demand:** This, filtered through his temperament, mood, and current assumptions, is translated (correctly or otherwise) into a demand ("She wants . . .").
3. **Feels New Need:** Forms a new need ("Now I must . . .").
4. **Makes Counter-Demand:** The new need is expressed through an action (physical or verbal) that the character expects will get fulfilling results.

Commonly when an actor looks unconvincing, steps 2 and 3 are absent because the inner process isn't happening. Let's look at an example, a discussion between a couple about an outing they have planned.

> It is early Friday evening. Brian and Ann disagree about which movie they should see. She wants them to drive out to the farther cinema and see a new comedy. Not really wanting to go out, he says the comedy was not well reviewed, so they might as well go to one of the nearer films. She finds the newspapers and says that, on the contrary, the movie got three stars in both papers. Looking at him, seeing he is not changing his mind, she turns abruptly and moodily kicks her shoes into the closet, saying that he never wants to go out with her. He looks concerned and protests that it is not true. They end up going to the movie she wanted to see, and he enjoys it more than she does.

Let's analyze the moment when Ann suggests the film at the faraway cinema. Brian, whose job we know requires him to make a long commute, now wants to watch TV and relax. His interior changes call for something like the following interior monologue:

> **Feels Impact:** "Drive 10 miles to see a movie when I could settle down and watch the news? Oh boy, this is really something to come home to."
>
> **Sees Demand:** "It's her day off, and she wants us to do something together. It's the old complaint that I never consider her situation, but that's not true. . . ."
>
> **Feels New Need:** "I really can't get back into that traffic again for 40 minutes. I've really got to put this off somehow. . . . It's not even a decent movie."
>
> **Makes Counter-Demand:** (Speaking to Ann while looking ineffectually through the accumulation of newspapers) "You know, I seem to remember that David What's-his-name in the *Times* only gave it one star."

Brian does not signal his feelings, but instead makes a direct, action-oriented leap between what he perceives to be happening and what he must do to cope with it. In general our feelings are followed by action and only require conscious examination when we are in internal conflict. Brian is not conflicted until he realizes that Ann is nearly crying with disappointment and frustration. To make him realize this and to move him to action will require that we first see Ann's changes and his adaptations to what she feels and does.

Of course, not all human interaction centers on disagreement, but it often happens in drama because all drama centers on conflict, no matter what the genre. Even when characters appear to be in harmony, one may be buying time, that is, going along verbally while turning the whole matter over in his or her mind. Because inner states always find outward expression, it is important to find a fresh, subtle action to evidence (not telegraph or illustrate!) what the character is experiencing inside. Only troublesome moments need to be worked over in fine detail like this one.

ADAPTATION

In the adaptation between characters, we have to picture something like two people trying to stand up in a small boat. Each must compensate for the changes of balance caused by the movements of the other. This causes many feints, experiments, surprises, and mistakes. A script says nothing about these because it is the actors' work to create whatever adaptations lead to the next line or specified action. This is not as difficult as it may sound because we are all experts in recognizing what is or isn't authentic to characters in a situation. The actors suggest and the director accepts, rejects, or modifies.

WHEN A CHARACTER LACKS AN INNER LIFE

Trained actors know how to maintain their characters' inner lives, but for others you have to ask for an inner monologue, that is, the conscious internal enunciation of the characters' thoughts and perceptions. The symptoms of an actor without an interior life are that the character:

- Seems to have no credible thought process
- Comes to life only when he or she has something to say
- Switches off while waiting for the next cue
- May be actually visualizing the script page—certain death for movie acting

A sure way to shift an actor out of this mode is to request an out-loud *thoughts voice* between lines, as in Chapter 22, Exercise 22-3: "Improvising an Interior Monologue." This is also a superb way to examine a point at which an actor repeatedly loses focus or when you suspect there is a skewed understanding of a certain passage.

REACTIONS

Working in a big studio, I noticed that the better actors could make reaction shots interesting, while others could not. An actor's character remains alive during reaction times only if they remain internally active and in character. If an actor's reaction shots are disappointing, attend to what they are doing within.

USEFUL MISPERCEPTIONS

As in life, dramatic characters often make errors of judgment for a wide range of reasons—out of nervousness, fear, misplaced confidence, wrong expectation—and read a fellow character's intentions wrongly. A character laboring under a misapprehension can produce very good dramatic mileage. Other equally productive misapprehensions come from a characters' unfamiliarity with the culture or with the personality of the antagonist, and to this we could add inattention, preoccupation, partial or distorted information, habit, or inebriation, to name just a few other reasons for myopia. Misperception is a fertile source for comedy (think of Basil Fawlty in the *Fawlty Towers* series), and just as easily it produces tension by provoking others into action that, far from neutralizing a situation, drives matters forward to new heights of revelation about the characters' differences and inner lives.

The work of Harold Pinter, like that of many modern dramatists, exploits the tensions between the characters' surface conformity and the dark, groping, private worlds existing beneath. In *The Dumbwaiter*, two hired assassins are left waiting interminably in a disused kitchen for further instructions. The lengthening wait, punctuated with bizarre, unfulfillable requests sent down in the dumbwaiter, acts upon the two men's private fears and distrust. While trying to maintain the faltering normality of their working partnership, each is gnawed by increasing fears, and we see them regress out of sheer insecurity.

The subtext deals with masters and servants, order and chaos, security and insecurity. It presents the characters as an analogy for mankind waiting nervously to learn God's will. But the piece can misfire as a light comedy of manners if director and actors fail to play the subtexts.

EXPRESSING THE SUBTEXT

An actor must develop not just an idea of a subtext but the physical expression of it, so he or she enters an intensive, created world where thoughts and feelings of the character can be lived out. The actor creates the character, yet also *is* that character and so can speak for them and be guided by a growing intuition about what is authentic. This means finding what action (both given and received) truly sustains the flux of the character's emotions. Conversely, it means sensing what is going against the character's grain and which he needs to examine and change. Like ambitious parents to their child, each actor is shepherd and champion for his or her own character. The director encourages this, but also deals evenhandedly with the rest of the cast so that a spirit of destructive competition doesn't set in.

CHAPTER 25

FINAL REHEARSALS AND PLANNING COVERAGE

THE DIRECTOR AS ACTIVE OBSERVER

So far our rehearsal priorities have given primacy to the actors' sense of what their characters must do, moment to moment, with the director observing and steering the results by way of critical feedback. Soon you must turn from interpreting characters and text to planning their presentation on the screen.

Habit will make you want to sit while observing and taking notes, but this is dangerous because it leads to experiencing the action like a theater-goer and to choreographing the action for a static camera placement. Clearly this is not cinematic and arises largely out of the director's immobility.

So, *as the action unfolds, move around* and adjust your viewing position. Take the most involved and privileged view, whether of the whole or significant parts. This leads naturally to finding a point of view for the scene itself and the camera angles that reveal it. Your mobility also prevents actors from habitually relating to you as their audience in one flat plane, which they will do if you are known to occupy a fixed position. No longer knowing where you are, their action becomes enclosed as they play to and for each other—just as it happens in real life.

When you get to the point of fine-tuning the blocking of actors and camera in relation to each other and to breaking the action into separate shots, it should all proceed with few conceptual problems.

FORM: SEEING IN AN UNFAMILIAR WAY

What makes films fresh and memorable is often not *what* is told, but *how* it is told. This is form as opposed to content and should be your concern all through the conceptualization of the movie. Innovative Storytellers seek language that uniquely serves the tale at hand. Cinema storytelling form is influenced by many determinants such as photography, lighting, set and costume design, choice of location, story construction, and editing style.

The question of form—what options exist for best presenting a story's particular world—is at the very heart of original cinema, indeed of art itself. If you haven't already read it, Chapter 16: Form and Style, contains a detailed account. Here I want to draw your attention again to form's importance, because not even dialogue scenes should get the all-purpose industrial treatment. The whole film should aim for a kind of revelation that is somehow special to its content and nature and to your purpose for telling the tale.

Remember that first you occupy the position of the Observer; then, as your Observer gains an active storytelling purpose, you become a surrogate for the tale's Storyteller. Create a personality sketch for this person and make him or her someone other than yourself.

BLOCKING

This ugly word, suggestive of building Stonehenge, refers to positioning actors and camera in relationship to each other. In my outline of a scene's development, the director encourages the actors to freely develop movement and action without initial regard to filming restrictions. Where each character moves, and why, comes from what each actor feels his or her character needs and what the director sees as necessary. With repeated rehearsal—and especially if the rehearsal is taped—this organic and experimental development will eventually settle into a tacitly agreed pattern of actions that express the flow of the characters' internal movements (perceptions, thoughts, feelings, will).

However, what emerges is by no means the only pattern possible. The exigencies of filming impose changes, and other advantages occur that you simply discover. By altering a walk from one side of a table to the other, for instance, an additional camera angle and a lighting change can be saved. Such changes at the point of shooting seem like nothing but confusion to the cast, so avoid this disruption by trying to rehearse in the actual location and by involving the camera crew early. But blocking still remains, from first to last, a process of mutual accommodation, and any part may change at a moment's notice. Actors, geared up for a big moment and then put on hold for a lighting change, are apt to become frustrated unless thoroughly forewarned of the changeable and sporadic nature of filmmaking itself.

For this and other reasons it is best to maintain an open attitude about how the scene may eventually be presented. This way you will not forfeit time and morale when shooting begins.

BENEFITS OF REHEARSING AT ACTUAL LOCATION

The script will often specify locations such as a convenience store or a drugstore that can easily be visualized. Everyone knows what a laundromat is like or what it is like to wait in a typical train station, eat at a typical hot dog stand, or cook in a typical suburban kitchen. But wait, all kitchens are not equal! Each location in some way portrays its owners or its patrons, and a messy, greasy, dark kitchen imposes different physical and emotional conditions on the user than a light, airy, modern one.

A scene rehearsed to a hazy, generalized idea of the location and then transplanted into an actual kitchen at the moment of shooting will contain characters who barely connect with their surroundings, a serious deficiency. But actors can interact with their surroundings in a highly specific way when rehearsals take place in the chosen location.

When multiple on-site rehearsals are not practical, take the actors for a research exploration, or at least show them photographs, so they have a distinct mental image. Director and actor alike can benefit from research. Michael Apted regularly sends his cast out ahead of shooting to research their characters. Aidan Quinn, for instance, in *Blink* (1995) spent time with Chicago detectives before playing one himself.

Research you do might include a documentary taping of an actor at work in his or her own kitchen to learn how the character and her mood are subtly reflected in the actor's actions. Notice how often action is focused and purposeful, compared with the vagueness and gesturing of someone who only signifies living in a kitchen. An example of this focus and clarity of action is Peter Falk's performance as an old Polish baker in *Roommates* (1995).

Make each location expressive and integral to the characters, not a mere container for words and action. And make setting a character, worthy in itself of loving portrayal. This way you will set up an environment that makes the spectators imaginatively inhabit the movie, and maybe leaves them haunted by it long after. Any Wim Wenders movie is a lesson in making full use of settings.

HOW MUCH REHEARSAL IS ENOUGH?

Actors often express the fear that a scene will be over-rehearsed. If rehearsal is drilling to a master plan, this is a real threat. But if it means digging into ever deeper layers of meaning within the scene, developing perceptions and restrictions that flow back and forth between the characters, and creating links and resonances with other parts of the script, it can be unendingly productive. Incidentally, Bresson used to rehearse his "models" (as he called the nonprofessionals he always used as actors) for 30 or 40 rehearsals of each scene to get the authentic sleepwalking manner in which people naturally do so many things.

Not all scenes merit intensive work. Some exist merely to supply an uncomplicated story point—that a letter is delivered to the wrong address, for instance. Such scenes may require little or no rehearsal. Others are a gold mine of possibilities that richly repay persistent exploration. Decide which scenes need special work during your preparation, but also be influenced by the ensemble's growing ability to focus on problem areas and discover their own solutions. This aspect, really a consequence of good leadership and good casting, can be the most rewarding aspect of collaborative work.

If an actor becomes convinced that developmental work cannot improve an impromptu performance, you as director may have to prove otherwise. Do not, however, extend rehearsing when you can see no way ahead. When you reach your threshold, switch to another scene. Seldom can you fully develop a scene on its own because of its dramatic dependence on others. Spend time on related scenes in rotation rather than concentrating exhaustively upon one. This keeps actors' energies high and keeps their attention on the piece as a whole.

ONSCREEN LENGTH, REHEARSALS, AND MAINTAINING TIMING

Films intended for commercial showing have an optimum length related to their content. For television, length is determined by the "slot" and must be precise to the second. A 30-minute non-commercial TV slot usually requires a film of 28 minutes, 30 seconds. Anything intended for commercial TV will have to be written with cliffhangers to accommodate commercials. Anyone who doubts the problems this brings should see Jack Gold's production for Hallmark of *The Return of the Native* (1995).

Student films are usually limited by the scope of their ideas and budget rather than by any commercial considerations. The tendency is to shoot overlong scenes with too little coverage and far too much dialogue. It's a common mistake to try for the longest possible film from available resources and story content. In the cutting stage it becomes apparent that the compression missing from the conceptual stages must now somehow be accomplished by the hapless editor. Invariably these problems are worse when rehearsals haven't been taped or timed.

How long, then, should a film be? One way to guess at screen length is to decide on the basis of a bare story outline what the shortest screen time should be and to budget screen time accordingly for each of its parts. This calls in advance for a professional economy in the writing. It also means that adding to one sequence means making savings in another. Lengthening your film beyond the original plan has consequences on stock requirements and scheduling, so keeping an account of final screen time is vital.

At rehearsals someone—the script supervisor or the assistant director—should time each scene with a stopwatch. If you are taping rehearsals, simply time the recording and mark the script accordingly. By adding the latest scene timings together you have an overall timing for the whole movie at any time. In rehearsals scenes inevitably get longer because each gathers *business*. Characters increasingly adopt realistic thinking and authentic behavioral rhythms, so scenes become shorter to watch but longer in real time. Be careful, for collectively they may not hold up! Your piece, a Prince Charming at the scripted 30-minutes, can easily turn into a 47-minute toad.

As work proceeds, check new timings against earlier ones so you can *make necessary decisions about length prior to shooting*. While axing material is difficult or even traumatic with a tightly written piece, only one script in 1000 has been shaved to its working minimum. During rehearsal, always be ready to review, edit, or tighten pacing as you go.

Can't it all be sorted out in the cutting room? Yes, they sometimes do miracles in the cutting room, but don't rely on them for more than minor savings, and certainly not unless you have provided sufficient coverage and cutaways. In fact, carry this written on the back of your hand as you shoot: "I will never end a scene without shooting full coverage, so help me."

MAKING A TRIAL MOVIE

An easy way to know what film you will have is to assemble the best-taped rehearsal versions and watch the whole piece through. Seeing it in entirety, especially if you bring in a small audience of filmmakers unconnected with the project, will give you an invaluable new perspective. True, the film will look awful, but even in this trial form it will alert you to redundancies, slow areas, expository omissions, restrictions, or mannerisms in the performances. These lessons will afford you invaluable guidance over pacing, coverage, and point of view. If the assembly is overlong (and it will be), you should run it several times until the cuts you need to make in the text scream out at you. Because you are working on video, you can even try them.

All this, happening before you have begun shooting, need not extend your schedule by more than a week. By this method you can painlessly make your film twice, with the second version profiting immeasurably from the first.

CHAPTER 26

PRODUCTION DESIGN

The production designer's job is to plan the look of a film and to design what it says visually about its characters and their settings, predicaments, and moods. This involves conceiving a complete world with all its characters, costumes, settings, furniture, properties, and color schemes.

EXAMPLES FOR DISCUSSION

Let's take three very different films for discussion: Stanley Kubrick's *Barry Lyndon* (1975), Sam Mendes' *American Beauty* (1999), and Lasse Hallström's *Chocolat* (2000). Each has a strong design and each represents a very different milieu.

Kubrick's adaptation of William Thackeray's *Barry Lyndon* tells the story of an 18th-century opportunist rake who, believing he has killed a man in his Irish hometown, goes on the run and encounters a lawless world. He becomes a soldier, then robs, cheats, and lies his way up the social ladder until he has established an honorable place for himself as the husband of Lady Lyndon. All of this is accomplished with alluring charm and humor (Figure 26–1).

Kubrick has directed the actors to behave entirely naturally. Remarkably, the film lacks the usual self-consciousness of a period movie, and it feels almost like a visit to the 18th century. Roy Walker and Ken Adam, art director and production designer, did an extraordinary job researching to recreate the feel of the period. Architecture seems authentic inside and out, and costumes and wigs are worn as naturally as today's accessories would be. The whole film feels like a lavishly made documentary captured during a bout of time traveling. A lot of this comes from John Alcott's photography, which pioneered special lenses so he could shoot without artificial light. Night interiors, which have a golden glow, were shot using nothing but candlelight.

Sam Mendes' *American Beauty* is a sardonic fable set in present day suburban America that tells of a marriage gone awry and a husband casting himself loose from keeping up with the Joneses. The film centers on a middle-aged

FIGURE 26–1

Kubrick's *Barry Lyndon* (1975), a meticulously recreated period film about an 18th-century rake's progress [The Kobal Collection/Warner Bros].

American male waking up to realize that the ideas he had starting out in life have foundered, and he feels alone and isolated. Now he reaches for what he once wanted before it is too late. The film is about characters searching for meaning and beauty amid a landscape that is as bright, man-made, and standardized as only the American suburbs can manage. Naomi Shohan and David S. Lazan, the production designer and art director, have made a hilarious study of everything wealthy suburbanites cram into their lives in hope of luxury and distraction. What is typical in dress, cars, domestic objects, and manners is so keenly reflected that it is both funny and ultimately sobering because of the spiritual darkness at the edge of everything. A film in the same spirit, though more surreal in action, is David Lynch's *Blue Velvet* (1986), which uses children's bright, primary, toy colors for its hometown, and dresses its central character entirely in black and white.

In Lasse Hallström's sentimental *Chocolat*, an adaptation from a Joanne Harris novel, a young woman arrives with her illegitimate daughter to set up a chocolate shop in a tightly wound provincial French town. Facing the insularity and disapproval of a sternly church-going population, she wins them one by one with the delicious confections she makes in her store. As she does so, she learns their stories and makes peace with each through her light-hearted acts of kindness. The production design team of John Frankish, Louise Marzaroli, and Lucy Richardson produce a quintessential French ambience of stone buildings, intimate old-fashioned interiors, and tiled floors. The townspeople are types: peasants living 50 years out of date and the small, isolated upper crust bent on keeping up standards. Their small town is a dark, sober world unto itself, an affectionate caricature of French inwardness.

DESIGNING A WORLD

What each of these films—and what all films—take is research into the specifics of a particular way of life. Each expresses a distinct point of view on the enclosed world they present, and this is realized in the overall view as the production designer interprets the script in consultation with the director and producer. The art director's job (along with others on the team) is to realize a whole design in sets, properties, costumes, color juxtaposing, and sequencing.

COSTUMES

When planning costumes, think of what personality and mood each character should project and how the clothing should contrast with that of the other characters. Think also of the overall tone of the costuming and not just color and design. Very light tones may be problematic to light, while dark tones, in night exteriors, may disappear altogether. Clothing can be thought of as a code that projects its owner's self-image and intentions in the world.

DESIGN AND SOUND

Shoes should be chosen for their style (and size!) but shod with rubber so they don't clatter during movements or dialogue. Groceries should be carried in and taken out of a nice quiet plastic bag, if there is concurrent dialogue. A paper bag sounds thunderous, but is manageable if no dialogue accompanies it. Manmade fibers should be avoided because they generate static electricity, which microphones pick up as crackling and popping. Ceilings can be a problem for both lighting and sound, and constructed sets should not include them.

SHOWING IDEAS

The work of the production design team may result in storyboards but is more likely to be sketches and drawings. When sets are built, drawings become as specific as architectural blueprints because sets have to be large and precise enough to accommodate the action, and flexible in construction so that certain walls can be made to break away to allow the camera to enter the set.

THE IMPORTANCE OF THE PALETTE

The production design team puts a large imprint on a film with the choice of colors in their palette. Kubrick's film is rich in golds, browns, and dark reds like an Old Master painting—and paintings evidently played a large part in the design and lighting of the whole film. Mendes (who comes from a theater background) worked with his design team to use the slightly loud, discordant colors that a culturally naive but wealthy population uses in its dress, objects, and interior design. The palette for *Chocolat* seems to have started from the rich browns of Vianne's confections and then matched to it a range of very saturated greens, purples, and reds. The chocolate store seems built out of chocolate and cream (don't go to the cinema hungry!).

MOODS

Every film proceeds in sequences, and if you read a script for the mood in each, you can visualize its content in predominating colors and color combinations. One of the production designer's tasks, then, is to cadence the movie by color, in step with the mood of the story and characters. There will be interiors and exteriors and day and night to give a sense of breathing in and out, each change contributing its own new mode of feeling. Combine these with color designs, and a very large statement lies in the hands of the production designers.

MAKE-UP AND HAIRDRESSING

A further step is to design the make-up and hairdressing. In *Barry Lyndon* some of the most affected characters have a chalk-white make-up, which was fashionable in the 18th century but lends a peculiar falsity and corpse-like atmosphere to their presence. This, too, is part of the design. If it departs from the norm, make-up in particular should be tried out in camera tests. Often skin tone differences from character to character condition our reflexes to each.

WALLS, FURNITURE, PRACTICAL LAMPS

Some common gambits:

- When you put furniture together on a set, raise chairs or tables by putting blocks or boxes under the legs if characters are at wrong or mismatched heights.
- Consider redecorating a room in an apartment that is presently white—an awful proposition for lighting—in a neutral gray or a bamboo color. This allows lighting a foreground without the background burning out. After filming is complete you can paint it white again for the generous owner.
- Plan to move furniture away from walls so any shadows cast from high-key lights are cast low and out of sight. Dropping shadows out of sight becomes impossible if characters are too near walls.

- When using *practicals* (any table or other prop lamp in sight of the camera), have different size bulbs available so you can adjust light output for naturalness. Place a neutral density filter around the inside of the shade to control the lamp's brightness in frame.
- Be ready to use dulling spray on anything shiny in case it sends off blinding highlights or reflections.
- Characters who appear to turn on lights upon entering a room should do so to a countdown so the electrician can fire up the movie lights at the right moment.

PRODUCTION DESIGN QUESTIONNAIRE

To design a film, you should make sketches of each setting and think in terms of its colors. Lighting, of course, will affect very much how sets render on film, and the director of photography (DP) is a major resource during the planning stages. In low-budget filmmaking, you are unlikely to shoot on a stage and will mostly shoot in locations.

- What is the film's theme?
- What is its overall mood?
- What kind of location should each sequence have? (Take photos for discussion.)
- What can you do with each location so it makes an appropriate statement?
- How should each set be lit?
- What kind of props go with the set?
- What kind of belongings do the characters keep around them?
- What kind of clothes do the characters wear?
- How does their wardrobe vary from scene to scene?
- What is the color progression through the film, which accords with its thematic statement?

PROPOSING A DESIGN

Use a digital still camera to record your characters in their costumes against a limbo background or at the proposed locations under varying lighting conditions. Working with Adobe Photoshop™ or other digital imaging programs, make a storyboard of sorts, then experiment with changing the image characteristics. By roughly lighting the set and manipulating the contrast, hue, and brightness of the image in your computer, you can produce a set of pictures that relay what you like and serve as a discussion medium with the cinematographer and production designer.

By working with a good sketch artist and by using people with a flair for finding furniture, clothing, and properties through resale shops and junk stores, you can produce at low cost settings that are eloquent of their characters. This is an important part of an authorial point of view.

BLUE SCREEN OR GREEN SCREEN

With the right software you can use what used to be called *traveling matte* in the film world. By shooting scenes against a special blue or green background, you can later replace any visible blue or green with a background shot that the computer obligingly fills in. Thus your impoverished student couple can stand outside Notre Dame cathedral discussing whether they can afford an inexpensive Paris meal. You will have perfect sound to which you later add street background, and no passerby will rubberneck from the background. If you want to have an apartment with a view over Prague, you only have to put the regulation blue or green in the windows, then matte in the Prague skyline in postproduction. The art department designs this and also finds suitable furniture for a Kafka-period apartment.

MODELS

The art department will also be involved with producing miniatures—an aerial view of a village in the Black Forest or a railway yard at night. This is a fertile area for fantasy or children's films, but miniatures can sometimes look very amateurish. Always try things out before you rely on them.

CHAPTER 27

THE PRODUCTION MEETING

This chapter's title might suggest that one meeting is enough. Typically the production meeting is the culmination of many weekly planning sessions, and the last one exists to sign off on everything important before the unit launches into action. Below are the main areas a production meeting must cover. Everyone heading a department must be present with their respective breakdowns derived from a close reading of the script: producer, production manager (PM), director, script supervisor (also known as continuity supervisor), director of photography (DP), art director, and head of sound. Everyone must have visited locations and accepted them as viable.

TROUBLESHOOTING

Anyone with a problem to be resolved brings it up at this meeting. Now is the time to coordinate everyone's efforts and to make corrections or changes if something has been overlooked or needs a schedule change.

DRAFT SCHEDULE

Preliminary budgeting will be based on the shortest practical schedule. Everyone must check the logistics of travel, time to build and strike sets, and so on. Some time will be built in for contingencies such as bad weather or breakdowns.

DRAFT BUDGET

This is the moment when everything planned must be considered in terms of its cost, so the meeting involves a rough budget based on known schedule, locations, equipment, crew, and artists (Figure 27–1). It is good to consider higher and not just the lowest likely figures because the total for a film in which the

SHORT BUDGET ESTIMATE FORM

1. Production & Personnel Details

Working Title:______________________________Length_____mins_____secs

*Producer*______________________Tel: __________(h)__________(w)
Street Address__________________________ City ______________
State/Postcode________________ Email__________@______________

Director ______________________Tel: __________(h)__________(w)
Street Address__________________________ City ______________
State/Postcode________________ Email__________@______________

*Cinematographer*________________Tel: __________(h)__________(w)
Street Address__________________________ City ______________
State/Postcode________________ Email__________@______________

*Sound*_________________________Tel: __________(h)__________(w)
Street Address__________________________ City ______________
State/Postcode________________ Email__________@______________

*Editor*_________________________Tel: __________(h)__________(w)
Street Address__________________________ City ______________
State/Postcode________________ Email__________@______________

Other___________________________Tel: __________(h)__________(w)
Street Address__________________________ City ______________
State/Postcode________________ Email__________@______________

Project stage is: Preproduction Production Postproduction
Format (circle one): Betacam, Digital Betacam, MiniDV, DVCAM, 16mm, 35mm, Other_______
Premise:____

Thematic focus:____

FIGURE 27–1

Short budget-estimate form. Note high and low estimate figures. A contingency percentage of the below-the-line costs is added to the total to allow for the unforeseeable.

2. Above the Line Costs

	High	Low
Screenplay	$_____	$_____
Story rights	$_____	$_____
Producer's fee	$_____	$_____
Director's fee	$_____	$_____
Principle actors' fees	$_____	$_____
Travel	$_____	$_____
Accommodation	$_____	$_____
Phone	$_____	$_____
Rehearsal	$_____	$_____
Hospitality	$_____	$_____
Other (_____________________________)	$_____	$_____
Other (_____________________________)	$_____	$_____
TOTAL	$_____	$_____

3. Below the Line Costs

	High	Low
Art Dept:		
Salaries _____ days at $_______ per day	$_____	$_____
Sets	$_____	$_____
Props & Costumes	$_____	$_____
Makeup & Hairdresser ____ days at $_______ per day	$_____	$_____
Production Dept:		
Production manager ____ days at $_______ per day	$_____	$_____
Assistant directors ____ days at $_______ per day	$_____	$_____
Camera Dept:		
Director of photography _____ days at $_______ per day	$_____	$_____
Camera assistant 1 _____ days at $_______ per day	$_____	$_____
Camera assistant 2 _____ days at $_______ per day	$_____	$_____
Gaffer _____ days at $_______ per day	$_____	$_____
Electrician _____ days at $_______ per day	$_____	$_____
Other___________ _____ days at $_______ per day	$_____	$_____
Sound Dept:		
Sound recordist _____ days at $_______ per day	$_____	$_____
Boom operator _____ days at $_______ per day	$_____	$_____
Other___________ _____ days at $_______ per day	$_____	$_____
Artistes		
Non principal talent (See 4a below for itemization)	$_____	$_____
Stand-ins ____ for ____ days at $_______ per day	$_____	$_____
Crowd ____ for ____ days at $_______ per day	$_____	$_____
Personnel		
Accommodation	$_____	$_____
Social Security contributions	$_____	$_____
Living expenses ____people for ____days @ $____ per day	$_____	$_____

FIGURE 27–1 (Continued)

Equipment:

	High	Low
Camera equipment (See 5a below for itemization).................................	$_____	$_____
Lighting equipment (See 5b below for itemization).................................	$_____	$_____
Sound equipment (See 5c below for itemization).................................	$_____	$_____
Materials (film & sound stock, cassettes, labs--see 5b itemization below).	$_____	$_____
Power...	$_____	$_____
Studio and location facility rentals..	$_____	$_____
Transport..	$_____	$_____
Catering..	$_____	$_____
Insurances..	$_____	$_____
Other (________________________________).............................	$_____	$_____
Other (________________________________).............................	$_____	$_____
Other (________________________________).............................	$_____	$_____
TOTAL..	$_____	$_____

4. Itemization of Talent and Materials

a) *Talent*

					High	Low
______________________	x ______days at $	______	per day		$_____	$_____
______________________	x ______days at $	______	per day		$_____	$_____
______________________	x ______days at $	______	per day		$_____	$_____
______________________	x ______days at $	______	per day..............		$_____	$_____
______________________	x ______days at $	______	per day		$_____	$_____
______________________	x ______days at $	______	per day		$_____	$_____
______________________	x ______days at $	______	per day..............		$_____	$_____
______________________	x ______days at $	______	per day		$_____	$_____
	TOTAL..				$_____	$_____

b) *Materials*

Film camera raw stock	____ to _____	rolls of type_____	@ $___	per roll	$_____	$_____
Video cassettes	____ to _____	type___________	@ $___	each	$_____	$_____
Video cassettes	____ to _____	type ___________	@ $___	each	$_____	$_____
Sound rec. raw stock	____ to _____	rolls of type_____	@ $___	per roll	$_____	$_____
Develop	____ to _____	rolls of type_____	@ $___	per roll	$_____	$_____
Workprint	____ to _____	rolls of type_____	@ $___	per roll	$_____	$_____
Sound transfer	____ to _____	rolls of type_____	@ $___	per roll	$_____	$_____
Video transfer	____ to _____	type cassettes_____	@ $___	per hr.	$_____	$_____
Lab digitization	____ to _____	cassettes type_____	@ $___	per hr.	$_____	$_____
	TOTAL..				$_____	$_____

FIGURE 27–1 (Continued)

5. Equipment Itemization

		High	Low
a) **Camera** (film or video):			
Lenses	type________for___ days at $____per day	$______	$______
Filters	type________for___ days at $____per day	$______	$______
Tilt head	type________for___ days at $____per day	$______	$______
Tripod/Baby legs, etc.	type________for___ days at $____per day	$______	$______
Dolly & Tracks	type________for___ days at $____per day	$______	$______
Magazines	type________for___ days at $____per day	$______	$______
Changing bag (film)	type________for___ days at $____per day	$______	$______
Clapper board	type________for___ days at $____per day	$______	$______
Light meters	type________for___ days at $____per day	$______	$______
Batteries	type________for___ days at $____per day	$______	$______
Video monitor, etc.	type________for___ days at $____per day	$______	$______
Other__________	type________for___ days at $____per day	$______	$______
Other__________	type________for___ days at $____per day	$______	$______
	TOTAL..	$______	$______
b) **Lighting**:			
Quartz lamps	type________for___ days at $____per day	$______	$______
Softlights	type________for___ days at $____per day	$______	$______
Spots	type________for___ days at $____per day	$______	$______
PARs	type________for___ days at $____per day	$______	$______
HMIs	type________for___ days at $____per day	$______	$______
Sun guns	type________for___ days at $____per day	$______	$______
Stands	type________for___ days at $____per day	$______	$______
Tie-in cables	type________for___ days at $____per day	$______	$______
Clamps	type________for___ days at $____per day	$______	$______
Gaffer equip.	type________for___ days at $____per day	$______	$______
Other__________	type________for___ days at $____per day	$______	$______
Other__________	type________for___ days at $____per day	$______	$______
	TOTAL..	$______	$______
c) **Sound:**			
Sound recorder	type________for___ days at $____per day	$______	$______
Mikes: Gun	type________for___ days at $____per day	$______	$______
Omni type	type________for___ days at $____per day	$______	$______
Cardioid	type________for___ days at $____per day	$______	$______
Lavalier	type________for___ days at $____per day	$______	$______
Radio	type________for___ days at $____per day	$______	$______
Mike cords	type________for___ days at $____per day	$______	$______
Mixer board	type________for___ days at $____per day	$______	$______
Headphones	type________for___ days at $____per day	$______	$______
Mike boom	type________for___ days at $____per day	$______	$______

FIGURE 27–1 (Continued)

Other__________	type________for___ days at $____per day	$______	$______
Other__________	type________for___ days at $____per day	$______	$______
	TOTAL..	$______	$______

6. Postproduction

			High	Low
Editor	______days at $_______	per day	$______	$______
Assistant editor	______days at $_______	per day	$______	$______
Editing equipment	______days at $_______	per day	$______	$______
Foley studio	______days at $_______	per day	$______	$______
Automatic dialogue replacement	______days at $_______	per day	$______	$______
Composer	______days at $_______	per day	$______	$______
Performers ________ for	______days at $_______	per day	$______	$______
Music rights..			$______	$______
Sound editor	______days at $_______	per day	$______	$______
Sound mix	______days at $_______	per day	$______	$______
Titles...			$______	$______
Transfer magnetic master to optical..			$______	$______
Conform camera original..			$______	$______
Make first answer print...			$______	$______
Make first release print..			$______	$______

7. GRAND TOTAL

Above the line (Section 2)..			$______	$______
Below the line (Section 3)..	$______	$______		
Below the line (Section 6)......................................	$______	$______		
Below the line subtotal Section 3 + Section 6..........	$______	$______		
Add 10% of below-the-line costs as **contingency**......	$______	$______		
Subtotal **below-the-line + contingency**..................	$______	$______ →	$______	$______
Legal..			$______	$______
Production office expenses..			$______	$______
Miscellaneous____			$______	$______
Miscellaneous____			$______	$______
Miscellaneous____			$______	$______
Other ____			$______	$______
Other ____			$______	$______
Other ____			$______	$______

GRAND TOTAL...................................... $______ $______

FIGURE 27–1 (Continued)

higher figures prevail can be a shock. It's good to confront this while you can still make adjustments.

There are a number of component calculations leading to the budget, the most significant being the number of locations and days spent shooting at each. Software exists for simple budgeting, but the industry favorite is Movie Magic™, an all-encompassing (though expensive) software package that provides tools to break down the script, turn it into a schedule, and arrive at a budget based on all the variables you enter. The beauty of a relational database of this magnitude is that any change anywhere, such as in script, rates, or scheduling, will immediately be reflected everywhere that it matters. You can also use the software to keep tabs on daily cash flow so there need be no unpleasant surprises hiding in the accounts department. You can see descriptions and reviews of different software for screenwriting, budgeting, and scheduling at *www.writersstore.com,* which also lists tutorials and manuals on how to get the most out of the software. Most people will need something akin to a producer's training to make proper use of the software.

Budget issues divide into *above-the-line* and *below-the-line* costs. The line is the division between preproduction and beginning production. So:

Above-the-Line costs:
- Story rights
- Screenplay
- Producer's fee
- Director's fee
- Principal actors' fees

________________________________ "The Line"

Below-the-Line costs:
- Production unit salaries
- Art department
  - Salaries
  - Sets and models
  - Props and costumes
- Artists (other than those above)
  - Cast, stand-ins, crowd
- Studio or location facility rentals (with location and police permissions)
- Film or video stock
- Laboratories
- Camera, sound, and other equipment
- Power
- Special effects
- Personnel
  - Catering, hotel, and living expenses
  - Social Security
- Transportation
- Insurance
- Miscellaneous expenses
- Music
- Postproduction
- Publicity

Indirect costs include finance and legal overhead costs. The pertinent questions are:

- How much does the production have in the bank?
- What is still to come?
- Using the projected shooting schedule, what will the film cost?
- Are there enough funds to cover projected costs?
- Are more funds needed?
- Can savings be made?
- Can any shooting be delayed until funds have been assembled?

Many factors lie behind arriving at a budget and its attendant cash flow forecast, not the least of which is what medium you are going to originate the film in. This is probably an early decision, but the final word is cast at the production meeting. Be aware that all movie budgets include a *contingency percentage*, usually 4% or more of the budget, which is added on to cover the unexpected, such as equipment failure, reshooting, and so on.

DRAWING UP AN EQUIPMENT WANT LIST

Learn as much as possible about the special technical requirements of the shoot so you, your DP, and your PM can decide what costs are truly justified. Some extra items turn out to be lifesavers; others just cost money and never get used. Keep in mind it's human ingenuity and not just equipment that makes good films.

How the film looks, how it is shot, and how it conveys its content to the audience are decisions that affect your equipment needs, but these decisions are about the form of the film and need to be made organically from the nature of the film's subject. Plan to shoot as simply as possible, choosing straightforward means over elaborate ones. The best solutions to most problems are elegantly simple.

With anything to be shot on film and edited digitally, your camera original must carry Keycode™ or it cannot be conformed at the end to the edit decision list. Two good sources of information at every level are Kodak's student program, reachable through *www.kodak.com/go/student* and DV Magazine at *www.dv.com* for up-to-date information and reviews on everything for digital production and postproduction. Kodak has every reason to want people to continue using film and provides superb guidance in its publications and Web sites, which are prolific and as labyrinthine as you would expect of an organization with so many divisions.

Testing and repair equipment: When the time comes to check out equipment, never leave the checkout point without putting all the equipment together and testing that absolutely everything functions as it should. Make sure you have spare batteries for everything that depends on a battery and extra cables, which have a habit of breaking down where the cable enters the plug body. Carry basic repair equipment, too: screwdrivers, socket sets, pliers, wire, solder and soldering iron, and a test meter for continuity and other testing.

ACQUISITION ON FILM

Major equipment needs hinge on what image format you will use to shoot. Using the traditional film camera means a fairly straightforward (if long and expensive) equipment list. Film captures the best image quality, has a usefully limited depth of field, can be shown in any cinema in the world, and can be transferred to any video format—at a price. It requires heavy funding at the front end when you buy stock and will be expensive to process and make prints. Anybody experienced enough to light and shoot in film will probably know where to get the equipment and how much it will cost to carry what you need for the days that you need it.

16 mm shoot: If you have quiet interiors, be sure to get a quiet camera. Old cameras can sound like coffee grinders, and it's a myth that they have a camera noise filter in postproduction. Be aware that the small formats magnify any weave or jiggle, and this shows up dramatically with titles or overlays.

Super 16 mm shoot: Find someone who has recently and successfully completed the chain of production. Remember that Super 16 camera original has a different aspect ratio and runs on different sprockets in the lab. Not many labs can handle and print it. Are you going to strike workprints or have the camera original transferred to tape? Who's going to do it and for how much?

35 mm shoot: Especially if you shoot in 35 mm Panavision (Figure 27–2) you will need the appropriate camera support, probably a dolly with its own rails. If you want to do any handheld shots, you will need a Steadicam™ and someone very strong who is experienced in using it.

ACQUISITION ON VIDEO

The limitation of inexpensive digital cameras is that they have small imaging chips and a correspondingly large depth of field. This gives a typically flat image in which everything is in the same degree of focus. These cameras are also hard to control and have sloppy lenses. Being miniature, many features, such as white balance or sound recording level, can only be accessed by laboriously tapping your way through a menu. When your work is in NTSC you must make a special choice concerning timecode. NTSC is the American video recording standard, and the acronym stands for the National Television Standards Committee that invented it. PAL (Phase Alternate Line) is the standard common in Europe, and each is formulated to work at a different frame rate that is based on either 60 cycles per second alternating current frequency (NTSC) or 50 cps (PAL). Working in NTSC requires that you choose whether to use *drop frame* or *non-drop frame* timecode. Drop frame removes a digit every so often so the recorded timecode remains in step with real time. It usually isn't important, but you must stay consistent through the production as it affects the editor. Electronic menus have a nasty propensity for somehow getting changed without anyone noticing. A professional camera is large, has external setting knobs and switches instead of menus, and the camera assistant can periodically run an eye over the settings—impossible with internal menus. Professional cameras also have a slot for a

FIGURE 27–2

Samantha Sanders checking the frame while directing her Columbia College thesis film "Gypsy Blood," shot in Panavision 35 mm (photo by Jane Kim).

memory stick, a solid-state memory the size of a credit card that can hold all the camera settings used to get a particular look. This can save a great deal of time.

Digitally recorded sound is most unforgiving if you over-modulate during recording. Another hassle is focusing the camera. Without manual control, you are often reliant on either setting a fixed distance in advance or letting the automatic focus do what it will. This simply focuses whatever is in the center of frame, no matter what your compositional balance or where you want the audience to look. So manual focusing and manual sound level adjustment are at a premium and usually come with the more advanced cameras only.

Medium of origination: Depending on how high you've set your sights, you may shoot with a modest digital video (DV) camera, with Digital Betacam, or in high definition (HD) using the Sony CineAlta system. If you expect to transfer your edited video final to film for theater projection, the cost must be determined. Each stage of the production has its own price. A great advantage of shooting digitally is that you don't have to change film magazines every 10 minutes of shooting, as you do with film. Cassettes last anywhere from 20–60 minutes, and this keeps everyone focused for longer periods. Typically, digital features are shot in the region of 20–30% less scheduled time than film. This is because the camera runs longer, needs less maintenance (there is no film gate to collect dirt), is light and quick to move, and needs less overall light.

FIGURE 27–3

Panasonic AG-DVX100. This manually controllable three-chip camera records at 30 fps or 24 p, the slower frame speed being progressive scan frames that transfer well to film (photo courtesy of Panasonic).

DV origination for eventual film transfer: For this you may use a tried and true Canon or Sony DV camera, or perhaps a switchable camera offering a choice of frame rates like the Mini DV Panasonic AG-DVX100 (Figure 27–3). This manual or automatic control three-chip camera records at either 30 frames per second (fps) or 24 p (which is shorthand indicating 24 fps, *progressive scan* mode) that transfers well to film. To explain this: The video frame is normally made up of two passes or scans, one recording the odd lines, the other interlacing the even ones. A progressive scan records the entire frame in one pass before moving on to the next frame. This is closer to the film process and produces full-definition frames that are simpler to transfer to film. The camera also has two professional Cannon or XLR sound inputs at microphone or line levels, the usual Firewire or IEEE1394 socket for digital transfer to and from a nonlinear (NLE) system, and a special function for shooting that emulates film gamma range. Most valuable are the large color viewfinder; manual controls for audio volume, zoom, iris (aperture), and focus; and the 48-volt phantom power supply needed by some professional microphones.

High definition video: This video standard has twice the picture cells or 'pixels' of American 720 pixel DV and rivals 35 mm film in picture quality. The Sony CineAlta HDW-F900 (see Chapter 1, Figure 1–1) has four digital sound channels, can shoot interlaced or progressive scan, and has a variable frame rate that allows you to shoot fast or slow motion, something normally attainable only in postproduction with video. In common with all professional-level cameras, its features, including follow-focus, are as fully controllable as a 35 mm camera's. George Lucas, after shooting *Star Wars Episode II* using CineAlta cameras, said, "I think I can safely say I'll never shoot another film on film."

Video to film transfers: Be aware that video to film transfers from 30 fps video (NTSC system) are very expensive. A timebase has to combine the interlaced frames, then do a step-printing operation to render 30 fps of video as 24 fps of film. A 24p or PAL 25p video camera neatly obviates this. 24p is the contraction of fps or frames per second, and also implies progressive scan.

PAL system compared with NTSC: By shooting in the European PAL video standard you gain some advantage in acuity because the PAL image has more lines of resolution. PAL also transfers its interlaced (or better, progressive scan) 25 fps more directly to film. However, when 25 fps is projected at 24 fps, the 5% speed change lowers the pitch of everyone's voice marginally and produces a 5% longer film. Why do PAL and NTSC have different frame rates? Most countries have a 220–230 volt with 50-cycle (or Hertz) alternating current. PAL's frame rate of 25 fps is a straight division of 50 Hz. The United States still uses Thomas Edison's legacy of 110 volts at 60 Hz, so NTSC's 30 fps is a division of the United States' 60 Hz.

SOUND

Where will you record sound? In the video camera? In a separate DAT or analog Nagra recorder? If you shoot analog, how will sound be resolved and transferred for syncing later with its video picture? How many channels will you need to record? How will you mike each different situation? If you are using radio mikes, will you carry wired mikes as backup? What kind of clapper board will you use if you are shooting double system? What special thought has been given to sound design that the sound crew should be aware of? What effects or atmospheres are not obvious in the script and must be found or concocted during location shooting?

POSTPRODUCTION

Whatever origination you use will need the appropriate postproduction setup, from a $3,000 Macintosh computer with Final Cut Pro at the low end to a $225,000 Discreet Smoke HD or $300,000 Avid|DS HD postproduction rig at the high end. The length of the movie, the amount of coverage, and whether there are any special effects will have a profound effect on the postproduction schedule. Don't forget the audio stage, when the film is put through a ProTools software suite and the final track is mixed, possibly in a studio with a large theater costing hundreds or thousands of dollars a day.

CAUTION

If a software or camera manufacturer recommends particular associated equipment, follow the recommendation to the letter. There's a good reason. Before you commit to any of the links in a production chain, you must be 100% certain that all the links work together. For instance:

- Digital tapes shot on Sony equipment may not interface properly with other equipment.
- Panasonic may not have identical recording specifications.
- If you shoot in PAL, check that your computer software is not limited to NTSC or vice versa.

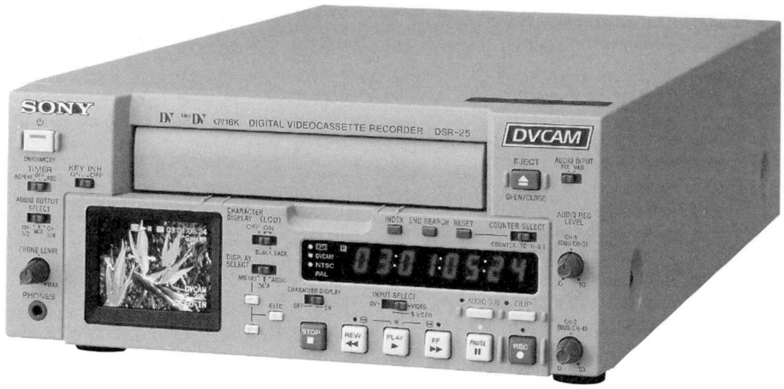

FIGURE 27–4

The Sony DSR-25 can record and playback PAL or NTSC formats using either DV or DVCAM cassettes (photo courtesy of Sony Corp.).

- If you edit in PAL in an NTSC country, you will need a DVCAM multi-standard player and recorder (Figure 27–4).
- Your film lab may not be able to do a 25 fps transfer to film.
- You may have a problem transferring 25 fps sound to your 24 fps editing rig.
- If you mix and match equipment, each manufacturer or supplier will think the other equipment is to blame for the malfunction. Following one manufacturer's recommendations means you can expect to get their ear if anything goes wrong.
- For the same reason, always plan to have your processing lab conform the film prior to answer printing. If you use an outside service and the negative is scratched, the lab will blame the conformer who edits the negative to conform with the workprint or edit decision list (EDL), and the conformer will blame the lab.

Know and understand each stage's process. For any problems you *must have definitive answers* before you commit. When you seek advice, talk with those who have already done what it is you want to do, then use exactly the recommended equipment and procedures.

EQUIPMENT LISTS

At the production meeting, everyone brainstorms about what they need. Make lists and do not forget to include basic repair and maintenance tools. Some piece of equipment is bound to need corrective surgery on location.

Over-elaboration is always a temptation, especially for the insecure technician trying to forestall problems by insisting on the "proper" equipment, which always proves to be the most complicated and expensive. Early in your directing career you will be trying to conquer basic conceptual and control difficulties, so you probably have little use for advanced equipment and cannot afford the time it takes to work out how to best use it. At a more advanced level, sophisticated equipment may actually save time and money. Expect the sound department in particular to ask for a range of equipment so they can quickly adapt to changed lighting or other circumstances. This within reason is legitimate overkill.

If any of your crew are at all inexperienced, ask them to study all equipment manuals beforehand; these contain vital and often overlooked information. Make sure you carry equipment manuals with you on location. At the end of this book is a bibliography with more detailed information on techniques and equipment.

Do not be discouraged if your equipment is not the best. The first chapters of film history, so rich in creative advances, were shot using hand-cranked cameras made of wood and brass.

PRODUCTION STILLS

Someone should be equipped to shoot 35 mm production stills throughout the high points of the shooting. Ideally you would use a good still photographer, but it may have to be someone with intermittent duties, such as a gaffer or electrician, who has an acceptable eye for composition. Stills seem unimportant, but they prove vital when you need to make a publicity package for festivals and prospective distributors. The director should set a policy on shooting stills so everyone knows they are important and will freeze on command while a still is taken. If time permits, the director or DP may be the best person to take the stills because pictures should epitomize the subject matter and approach of the movie, and act as a draw in a poster.

SCHEDULING THE SHOOT

A director needs to be familiar with the details of the organization and scheduling that make filming possible. Scheduling is normally decided by the director and the PM and double-checked by principal crewmembers, in particular the script supervisor and the DP. Excellent scheduling and budgeting software exists so that anyone with a computer can do a thoroughly professional job, as mentioned previously. Movie Magic™ is the film industry's choice of software package that will handle contracts, scheduling, and budgeting (you can see a range of software at *www.filmmakerstools.com* with a range of prices).

Regarding the schedule, you will often have to make educated guesses because no film is ever quite like any other and there are few constants. Because time inevitably means money, your schedule must reflect your resources as well as your needs. Take into account any or all of the following:

- Costs involved at each stage if hiring talent, equipment, crew, or facilities (use Movie Magic or other reputable software, or see basic budget form in Figure 27–1)
- Scenes involving key dramatic elements that may be affected or delayed by weather or other cyclical conditions
- Availability of actors and crew

- Availability of locations
- Relationship of locations and travel exigencies
- Availability and any special conditions attaching to rented equipment, including props
- Complexity of each lighting setup and power requirements
- Time of day, so available light comes from the right direction (take a compass when location-spotting!)

LOCATION ORDER

Normal practice is to shoot in order of convenience for locations, taking into account the availability of cast and crew. During a shoot, lighting setups and changes take the most time, so a compact schedule conserves on lighting changes and avoids relighting the same set. Lighting usually requires that you shoot wide shots (which may take all the light you've got) first and close shots later because these must match their wide-shot counterparts. For these reasons and more, it is highly unusual to shoot in script order.

The character and location breakdown (Figure 17–4) described in Chapter 17 shows which scenes must be shot at each location. It is normal that scenes from the beginning, middle, and end of the film may all be shot in the same location. This makes rehearsal all the more important if actors and director are to move authoritatively between the different emotional levels required. The scene breakdown also displays which characters are needed, and this, in association with the cost and availability of actors, influences scheduling.

SCRIPT ORDER

Some films may need to be shot in script order, particularly if director and cast are inexperienced or poorly rehearsed. Here are some such examples:

- Those depending on a graduated character development—like the king's decline into insanity in Nicholas Hytner's *The Madness of King George* (1995)—that calls for finely controlled changes by actors in the main parts
- Those depending on a high degree of improvisation might need to shoot in script order to maintain control over an evolving story line
- Those taking place entirely in interiors and that have a small, constant cast. Here there is no advantage to shooting out of scene order, so you might as well reap the benefits of sequential shooting

Whenever shooting in script order is impractical, the director, cast, and crew must be thoroughly prepared so that patchwork filming will assemble correctly.

KEY SCENES AND SCHEDULING FOR PERFORMANCES

Some scenes are so dramatically important that there will literally be no film should they fail. Imagine if your whole film hinges on a scene in which your naive heroine falls in love with an emotionally unstable man. It would be folly to shoot everything else trusting that your actors can make a difficult and pivotal scene work.

Key scenes must be filmed neither too early (when the cast is still green), nor too late (when failure might render wasted weeks of work). If the scene works, it will give a lift to everything else you shoot. If the scene bombs, you will want to work out the problems in rehearsal and reshoot in a day or two. You cannot commit to shooting the bulk of the film until this problem is solved.

Problems of performance should show up in rehearsals, but camera nerves may kick in, especially if the scene exposes the actor. Filming is only occasionally better than the best rehearsal, and often it is below it. The cast may feel more deeply during the first takes of a new scene, but strong feeling is no substitute for depth of character development. When cast members realize they must sustain a performance over several takes per angle and several angles per scene, they may also instinctively conserve on their energy level. Knowing this, you should shoot with an editing pattern in mind so you don't yield to the temptation to cover everything. Drawing the line between adequacy and wastefulness is hard for the new director, so it's best to err on the side of safety.

EMOTIONAL DEMAND ORDER

Scheduling should take into account the demands some scenes make upon the actors. A nude love scene, for instance, or a scene in which two characters get violently angry with each other should be delayed until the actors are comfortable with each other and the crew. Such scenes should also be the last of the day because they are so emotionally draining.

WEATHER OR OTHER CONTINGENCY COVERAGE

Schedule exteriors early in case your intentions are defeated by unsuitable weather. By planning interiors as standby alternatives, you need lose no time. Make contingency shooting plans whenever you face major uncertainties.

ALLOCATION OF SHOOTING TIME PER SCENE

Depending on the amount of coverage, the intensity of the scene in question, and the reliability of actors and crew, you might expect to shoot anywhere between 2 and 4 minutes of screen time per 8-hour day. Traveling between locations, elaborate setups, or relighting the same location all greatly slow the pace. Many directors allot setup time for the mornings and rehearse the cast while the crew is busy, but this is unlikely to work as well outside a studio setting.

UNDER- OR OVERSCHEDULING?

A promising film may also be sabotaged by misplaced optimism rather than any inherent need to save money. Consider the following:

- Schedule lightly during the first 3 days of a shoot. Work may be alarmingly slow because the crew is still developing an efficient working relationship with each other.

- You can always shorten a long schedule, but it may be impossible to lengthen one originally too short.
- Most non-professional (and some professional) units try to shoot too much in too little time.
- A cast and crew working 14-hour days become fixed on just surviving the ordeal.
- Artistic intentions go out the window as a dog-tired crew and cast work progressively slower, less efficiently, and less accurately, and as tempers and morale deteriorate.

The first half of the shoot may fall seriously behind if the AD and PM do not apply the screws and keep the unit up to schedule. Not only does an inexperienced crew start slowly and over time get quicker, they also tend to reproduce this pattern during each day unless there is determined progress-chasing by the DP and AD.

AGREEMENT ON BUDGET AND SCHEDULE

By the end of the meeting everyone should have agreed on equipment and schedule. The PM can make a detailed budget and the 1st AD can go to work on preparing the call sheets.

CAVEATS

Make "test and test again" your true religion. Leave nothing to chance. Make lists, and then lists of lists. Pray.

GOLDEN RULE #1: EXPECT THE WORST

Imagination expended darkly, foreseeing the worst, will forestall many potentially crippling problems before they even take shape. That way you equip yourself with particular spares, special tools, emergency information, and first aid kits.

Optimism and filmmaking do not go together. One blithe optimist left the master tapes of a feature film in his car overnight. The car happened to be stolen, and because there were no copies, a vast amount of work was transformed instantly into so much silent footage.

The pessimist, constantly foreseeing the worst and never tempting fate, is tranquilly productive compared with your average optimist.

GOLDEN RULE #2: TEST IT FIRST

Arrive early and test every piece of equipment at its place of origin. Never assume that because you are hiring from a reputable company, everything should be all right. If you do, Murphy's Law will get you. (Murphy's Law: Everything that can go wrong will go wrong.) Be ready for Murphy lurking inside everything that should fit together, slide, turn, lock, roll, light up, make a noise, or work silently. Murphy relatives hide out in every wire, plug, box, lens, battery, and alarm clock. Make no mistake; the whole bloody clan means to ruin you.

COST FLOW AND COST REPORTING

The goal of budgeting is to make a cost flow projection. During production the PM prepares a daily cost report:

1. Cost for period
2. Accumulated cost to date
3. Estimated cost to complete
4. Final cost
5. Over or under budget by how much?

The object is to bring the production in on cost and in the agreed time.

INSURANCES

Depending on the expense and sophistication of a production, it will carry some or all of the insurance. Even film schools, mindful of the litigiousness of John Q. Public, sometimes make their students carry insurance coverage.

Preproduction indemnity: Covers costs if production held up due to accident, sickness, or death during or before production

Film producer's indemnity: Covers extra expense being incurred due to a range of problems beyond the producer's control

Consequential loss: This covers increased production costs due to the loss or damage to any vital equipment, set, or prop

Errors and omissions: Covers claims against intellectual property (copyright, slander, libel, plagiarism, etc.) or other mistakes

Negative insurance: Covers reshooting costs due to loss or any damage to film negative

Employer's liability: Mandatory insurance that may be required for protection of employees

Public or third party liability: Insures against claims for property damage and personal injuries

Third party property damage: Insures against claims brought against film company for damage to property in their care

Equipment insurance: Covers loss or damage to hired equipment

Sets, wardrobe, props: Covers costs resulting from their loss or damage

Vehicles: Coverage for vehicles, particularly specialized vehicles, or those carrying costly equipment

Fidelity guarantee: A financial backer's requirement to guard against infidelity—the budget being embezzled

Union and other insurances: Film workers are often union members, and their union stipulates what coverage is necessary when they are hired. Special insurances are often required when working abroad under unusual health or other conditions.

CREW CONTRACTS

Once all details have been decided, the PM sends out letters of engagement to secure the services of crewmembers. These describe the job, the salary, working hours, and length of contract. There will be a number of clauses stipulating rights and expectations on either side, as in any contract. Any union requirements must be followed scrupulously, if trouble later is to be avoided.

PRODUCTION PARTY

Once the crew is known and actors are cast, it is customary to have a production party. This acts as an ice breaker, bringing everyone together for the first time. One of the pleasant aspects of working in the film business is that over the years you work with the samc people every so often. Because everyone is freelance, everyone is happy to work. Production parties are therefore very pleasant and constructive occasions.

CHECKLIST FOR PART 5: PREPRODUCTION

The points summarized here are only the most salient or those that are commonly overlooked. To find them or anything else, go to the Table of Contents at the beginning of this part, or try the index at the back of the book.

Deciding on Subjects:

- Choose your subject carefully; you are going to live with it for a long time.
- Through your film, be concerned for others.
- Choose a subject and issues you would love to learn more about.

Questions When Assessing a Script:

- How behavioral and visually cinematic is it?
- How well would it play with the sound turned off?
- Whom did you care about and find interesting?
- Is the plot credible, or can it be made so?
- What is the screenplay trying to do, and how is it going about it?
- In each scene decide what each character wants, moment to moment. What do they do to get it?
- What stops the character and how does he or she adapt to each obstacle?
- Are the obstacles intelligently conceived to put the characters to the test?
- Are all characters integrated and multifunctional or are some convenience characters who exist only to solve particular situations?
- Who grows and develops in the script and who remains only "typical?"
- What do you learn from making a step outline?
- What is the screenplay's premise?
- What are the screenplay's thematic concerns, and how effectively does it deal with the main one?
- What does making a flow chart for the final reveal, after you've named the function of each scene?
- What does a scene, character, location breakdown reveal?
- Time the film; does the film's story content merit the time it takes onscreen?
- What problems emerge when you make an oral summary (a *pitch*) to a listener?

Script Editing

Plot and Character:

- Relate story line to basic dramatic situations and the hero's journey archetypes.
- Decide from similar stories whether characters can be made more effective.

Exposition:

- See if vital information comes early enough and whether any reinforcement is needed.
- If it's spoken and too noticeable, hide it within action.

Action:

- How well would the film play if it were silent?
- Try reconfiguring dialogue scenes to play out as behavior instead of dialogue.
- See what actions might better reveal each character's inner life and qualities.

Dialogue:

- Drop lines wherever possible.
- Convert discussion into behavior when possible.
- Tighten, compress, and simplify remaining lines.
- Make sure the dialogue is in the character's own vernacular.

Scenes:

- Mark beats and critically examine the working of each dramatic unit.
- See whether each scene can create more interesting questions in the audience's mind.
- See whether delay before these concerns are answered is too short or too long (often it's counterproductively short).
- Eliminate scenes that repeat information or that fail to advance the story (get this information from your flow chart).

Dramaturgy and Visualization:

- Decide whether convenience characters should be eliminated, amalgamated, or made properly functional.
- From your flow chart assess how well the screenplay "breathes" between different kinds of scenes, and consider transposing to improve variety.
- Consider radical adjustments if parallel works and archetypes promise a better thematic impact.
- Check for evocative imagery that could play a special part (visual leitmotifs, foreshadowing, symbolism, visual analogies, etc.).

Check That the Screenplay's World Is:

- Authentic
- Adequately introduced if it's unfamiliar
- Making full use of its connotations

Organizing the Audition:

- Write brief character descriptions; advertise appropriately.
- Actively search out likely participants for audition.
- Pre-interview on phone before giving an audition slot.
- Thoroughly explain time and energy commitment.
- Ask actor to come with two contrasting monologues learned by heart.

First Audition:

- Receptionist chats with actors and has them fill out information form.
- See actor's monologues and classify his or her self-image.
- Look for acting with whole body, not just face.
- Listen for power and associations of actor's voice.
- Ask yourself, "What kind of character would I get from this actor?"
- Thank actors and give date by which decision will be communicated.

Decisions Before Callback:

- Call each actor and inform whether he or she is wanted for callback.
- When you must reject, tell each actor something positive about his or her performance.
- Avoid casting people for their real-life negative traits.
- Carefully examine videotapes now and later for actor's characteristics relayed from the screen. Your impressions and intuitions here are everything.

Callback:

- Combine promising actors in different permutations.
- Have actors play parts in different ways to assess their capacity for change.
- Test spontaneous creativity with improvisations based on the piece's issues.
- Redirect second version of improv to see how actors handle changes.

Consider Each Actor's:

- Impact
- Rhythm and movements
- Patterns of development
- Quickness of mind
- Compatibility with the other actors
- Ability for mimicry (accents, character specialties, etc.)
- Capacity for holding onto both new and old instructions
- Intelligence
- Temperament

- Type of mind
- Commitment to acting and to this particular project
- Concentration and attention span

Shoot camera test on principals; consider confronting actors with your reservations before casting. Thank all for taking part and arrange date for notification.

Developing the Crew:

- Cast crew carefully because they create the work environment.
- Shoot tests even with experienced members.
- Inquire into crewmembers' interests and values.
- Check reputation in previous collaborations.
- Assess flexibility, dependability, realism, and commitment to project.
- Clearly delineate reporting lines.
- Begin crew relationships formally. You can become more informal later.

Script Interpretation:

- Check all points under "Script Editing" section.
- Determine the givens.
- Convert conversation into action that would relay the story without sound.
- Make sure screenplay establishes facts and necessary values for audience.
- Define point of view, subtexts, and characters' hidden pressures for each scene.
- Graph dramatic pressure changes for each scene, then string them together to graph out dramatic development for the film as a whole.

Rehearsal:

- Actors study the piece and make character biographies, but do not yet learn lines.
- Director and actors break scene into dramatic units, with clear developmental steps within each unit.
- Director encourages the search for action and movement at every stage.
- Director meets principal actors singly to discuss their characters.
- Expect actors to problem-solve.
- Keep notes during each run-through.
- Actors must play the scene, not the lines.

Focusing Thematic Purpose with the Players:

- Discuss backstory and purpose of the piece with cast.
- Discuss subtext for key scenes and what it reveals about each of the characters.
- Develop a hierarchy of themes so you know what is most important.

Rehearsal with the Book:

- Tackle key scenes first.
- Thereafter point out what links these scenes.
- Deal only with top level of a scene's problems at each pass.
- Work on motivations.
- Develop possible actions.
- Find and characterize the beats.
- Develop special actions for the beat points.
- Within each dramatic unit, figure out the stages of escalation that lead to the beat.
- Rehearse on location or thoroughly brief actors on particularities of location.
- Now actors can learn their lines!

Rehearsal without the Book:

- Dialogue should be a verbal action that seeks an effect.
- Film actors have no audience; they should be indistinguishable from real people coping with a real situation.
- When an actor keeps losing focus, figure out the obstacle.
- Staying in character comes from staying appropriately busy in mind and body.
- Focus leads to relaxation.
- Watch your actor's faces and bodies for telltale signs of inappropriate tension.
- Authentic physical action during performance liberates authentic emotion.
- Use improv to set level of focus to be matched when you work with the text.
- Give local, specific, positive goals for actors to reach.
- Characters' actions should generally seek an effect in other characters.

Review the Taped Scene:

- Does it communicate effectively when viewed without sound?
- Is the cast using space effectively?
- Are characters fully using their physical surroundings?
- Can you see the characters' visions, memories, and imaginations at work?
- Does each character constantly pursue his or her own agenda?

Thinking Ahead about Coverage:

- Set a timing limit for the scene and keep tabs on rehearsal timings.
- Prepare cast for blocking changes should exigency so require (it often does).
- Cut dialogue or action to stay within timing goals.
- Note intentions for each scene while your memory is fresh.

Production Design:

- What era and what world do the characters live in?
- What is that world's palette?
- What are their characteristic clothes and colors?
- How do the characters contrast with each other, and how is this reflected in costuming?
- What objects, furniture, and surroundings are peculiar to the characters?
- What is the succession of moods in the film, and how is this reflected in lighting and color schemes?
- What is the color progression through the film?

Production Meetings:

- All locations scouted?
- Shooting schedule contains bad weather coverage?
- Shooting order takes into account key scenes and emotionally demanding ones?
- Budget worked out and contains contingency percentage?
- Equipment want lists prepared and budgeted?
- Production origination and postproduction methods are worked out and budgeted?
- All equipment is justified?
- Arrangements have been made to shoot production publicity stills?
- Cost flow reporting is organized?
- Necessary insurances are arranged?
- Permissions for locations and police permits for exteriors have been obtained?
- Crew contracts are ready to issue?
- Production party has been scheduled?

PART 6

PRODUCTION

Part 6 (Chapters 28 through 37) covers the production period. For anyone using an untried crew, this should involve some trial shooting. The amount and expense of equipment and the degree of technology will vary greatly between those shooting their first works and a more seasoned group making a short or even independent feature, but the basic organization and procedures vary only in scale, not principle. The director should never lose sight of the preeminence of the cast, engage a director of photography (DP) who can effectively lead the crew, and stay free to direct the action.

When you are ready to shoot, use the checklist at the end of this part. It can save you grief and expense and help you make a better film.

CHAPTER 28

DEVELOPING A CREW

ON CREW AND ACTORS

USING PEOPLE WITH EXPERIENCE

Because your crew members will affect your actors, they should be cast for personal as well as technical capabilities. This chapter is titled *developing* rather than *choosing* a crew because even when experienced crew members are available, you will still need to see their work and do some trial shooting with them before the main shoot. Expect to continue developing standards and communication all through the production.

Chapter 23 strongly advised videotaping rehearsals using a documentary style of spontaneous coverage. If you haven't done so yet, reconsider and cover some rehearsals now. There are definite benefits that should be reiterated. You will:

- Find out how well you and your crew understand each other.
- Develop a terse and unambiguous language of communication before you need it.
- Discover what developments (or outright changes) are required in key crew members.
- Confirm that equipment is functioning and determine how expertly the crew handles it.
- Dispense with surprises: one camera operator's close-up is another's medium shot, depending on prior experience.

Filmmaking is relativistic—framing, composition, speed of camera movements, and microphone positioning all arrive through mutual values and adjustment. This happens only when crew members are attuned to each other's reflexes, terminology, and assumptions. From shooting rehearsals and test footage, expect to find wide initial variations in skill levels, interpretations of standard jargon, and assumptions about solving technical problems. The key is a common language and clearly understood lines of communication and responsibility. These must be locked down before shooting, which brings enough problems.

DEVELOPING YOUR OWN CREW

If you are working with colleagues who have already proved themselves in film school, some of what follows may not be relevant, but read it anyway. Let us take the most daunting situation—that you live in a place remote from centers of filmmaking and must start from scratch, work up your own standards, and find and train your own crew. We will assume you have access to an adequate camcorder, a microphone on a short boom, and computerized editing with good sound reproduction. How many and what kind of people will you need? What are their responsibilities?

Commitment: First and foremost, everyone you recruit must understand and accept your commitments to the project and to the importance of drama. Ideally they should share them. Naturally this matters more in a DP than in a grip or assistant editor, but a low-budget enterprise needs optimal unity because much will be done by few. Belief and morale really matter.

Ideas and identity: Before committing to crewmembers, assess not only their technical expertise and experience, but also their ideas and values. Of course you must see (or hear) their work, but ask about favorite films, books, plays, hobbies, and interests. Technical acumen is important, but under stress their maturity and values become more so. Technical deficiencies can be remedied, but someone lacking maturity or positive responses to your work can quickly turn into dead weight.

CREW MEMBERS' TEMPERAMENTS

A low-budget film crew is small, perhaps six to 10 persons, and a good team is immensely supportive not only of the project, but also of the individuals in front of the camera, some of whom may be acting for the first time. The crew's aura of commitment and optimism can easily be undermined by a single misfit with a bad attitude. Such people are like black holes, swallowing up energy, enthusiasm, and morale.

Crew problems can vary. One member may need some pressure to maintain focus on the job at hand, or more seriously, at a location far from home or under pressure someone may become unbalanced and regress into bizarre hostilities. You may even have to deal with someone actively subversive or emotionally out of control. You can seldom foresee such extremes, but they are an appalling liability in something so dependent on good working relationships. Truffaut's *Day for Night* (1973) shows these all-too-human tendencies at work in the cast, but crews are susceptible, too. Under the benign but watchful leadership of the DP, the crew makes a huge contribution to cast morale, for their interest and implied approval is a vital supplement to that of the director. Conversely, any crew member's detachment or disapproval may be taken to heart by actors, whose work naturally makes them hypersensitive to judgments of any kind.

When recruiting, speak with key figures in prior workplaces about their experience with the person you intend to use. Filming is intense and former colleagues will know the person's strengths and weaknesses. If you are unable to verify a potential crew member's teamwork record, you may just have to rely on your intuition about how he or she bears up under stress.

Warning: In all acting or crew positions, beware of people who:

- Have only one working speed (usually slow). Faced with pressure, this temperament can slow up in confusion or even go to pieces.
- Forget or modify verbal commitments.
- Talk too much.
- Fail to deliver on time—or at all.
- Habitually overestimate their abilities.
- Have a short attention span.
- Act as though doing you a favor (in mid production they may use you as a stepping stone to something better).

In addition to relevant experience, look for:

- Sociability and a good sense of humor
- A love of their work
- Enthusiasm for films and an appreciation of how painstaking filmmaking is
- A nurturing temperament
- Low-key realism
- Reliability
- Ability to sustain effort and concentration for long periods

ORGANIZE AREAS OF RESPONSIBILITY CLEARLY

Lines of responsibility: No crew functions well unless roles and responsibilities are clearly defined and a chain of command is established. Contingencies make this all the more important. When the director is occupied with the cast, the DP normally leads the crew and makes necessary decisions. In most cases, crew members should take queries first to the DP and not to the director. The assistant director(s), production manager (PM), and DP are all there to take most burdens from the director, whose entire energies should go into the craft of directing, which includes a heavy responsibility to the cast. The director should not be expected to decide whether someone should put another coin in a parking meter.

Keep it formal: When first working together, and for a long time after, *stick to a formal working structure* (Figure 28–1). Everyone should take care of their own responsibilities and refrain from action or comment in anyone else's area. As people come to know and trust each other, the formality can be relaxed by cautious and mutual consent.

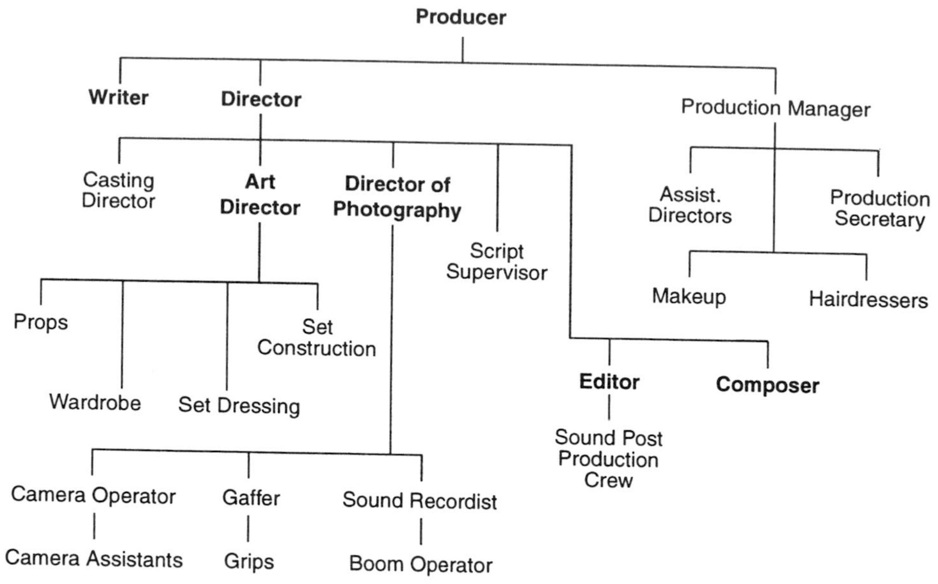

FIGURE 28–1

Lines of responsibility in a small-feature crew. Relationships may vary according to actual unit. Department heads are in bold type.

Other roles: In time, the members of a small film crew fall into additional roles such as prophet, diplomat, visionary, navigator, earth mother, scribe, nurse, and strong man. Someone in every situation always assumes the role of jester or clown, for every crew develops its own special humor and inside jokes.

Synergy: Working effectively as a group can be the most exhilarating and energizing experience imaginable, especially during times of crisis. Careful selection of the right partners makes anything in the world possible. A team of determined friends is unstoppable.

CREW ROLES AND RESPONSIBILITIES

Judging from a feature film's end credits, a unit has a bewildering number of roles and an army of people. Paradoxically, low-budget films often have even more personnel in the titles because many have contributed only a day or two of service. A "genealogical chart" of a small film unit, showing customary lines of responsibility, is Figure 28–1.

The role descriptions that follow are confined to the modest core likely to carry out the low-budget film or video shoot. I have assigned desirable personality types and backgrounds to the different crew positions, but, of course, in real life the best practitioners may always be the exception. This list outlines each crew member's responsibilities and the strengths and weaknesses you can expect to find. To make it complete, I have included a summary of the director's role.

A large feature film unit is made up of departments, and I have organized the job descriptions under these.

DIRECTION

DIRECTOR

Answers to: The producer

Responsible for: Nothing less than the quality and meaning of the final film, which requires:

- Writing or working with writers
- Envisioning the film's scope, purpose, identity, and meaning
- Researching locations
- Auditioning and casting actors
- Assembling a crew (though this may be done by the producer or PM)
- Developing both cast and script through rehearsals
- Directing actors and crew during shooting
- Supervising editing and finalization of the project
- Promoting the production in festivals and other circuits

Personal traits: A good director is:

- Broadly knowledgeable in the arts
- Possessed of a lively, inquiring mind
- Someone who likes delving into people's lives and looking for hypothetical links and explanations
- Methodical and organized even when outwardly informal and easygoing
- Able to scrap prior work if assumptions become obsolete
- Possessed of endless tenacity when searching out good ideas and good performances
- Articulate and succinct
- Able to make instinctive judgments and decisions
- Able to get the best out of people without being dictatorial
- Able to speak on terms of respectful equality with any film specialist
- Able to understand technicians' problems and co-opt their best efforts

If this sounds too idealistic, here are some of the negative traits that make even good directors decidedly human. Many directors:

- Are obstinate, private, even awkward beings who work in idiosyncratic ways

- Find difficulty in giving appropriate time and attention to both crew and actors
- Tend to desert actors for crew, and vice versa
- Sink into acute doubt and anxiety during shooting
- Suffer sensory overload and find choice painful
- Go into depression and/or physical illness at the end of a production

During production, most directors sooner or later show signs of insecurity (depression, manic energy, low flashpoint, panic, irresolution). If that is not enough to puzzle crew members, the director's mental state often generates superhuman energy and endurance that push the crew's patience to the limit. The truth is that directing a reflection of life is a heady business. The person responsible for making this happen is living existentially, that is, fully and completely in the moment and as if it were the last.

The pressures of directing a movie usually make all this happen whether you like it or not. This is especially true after an initial success: Thereafter you face failure and artistic and professional extinction every step of the way. Like stage fright, the dread and exhilaration of the chase may never go away. But the sign of any worthwhile experience is that it both attracts and scares you.

SCRIPT SUPERVISOR

Answers to: The director

Responsible for: Understanding how the film will be edited together and, during shooting, continuously monitoring what words, actions, props, and costumes are in use from shot to shot. The script supervisor, also called *continuity supervisor*, assists the director by ensuring there is adequate coverage of each scene, and when time or resources must be saved, is able to define what can be omitted or shortened. Shooting on video makes checking a shot's contents simple though time-consuming, but shooting on film leaves no such record visible until the rushes have been processed. If one shot is to reliably match another, you need an eagle-eyed observer who keeps a record of every significant variable no matter what acquisition method you use. If a video assist is used with a film camera, it is a simple matter to back up the script supervisor's notes by rolling a consumer VCR as a running record.

Personality traits: The good script supervisor:

- Has formidable powers of observation and memory
- Thoroughly understands editing
- Knows the script and how the film will be constructed inside out
- Has fierce powers of concentration
- Produces continuity reports used extensively in features by the editor
- Is a fast and accurate typist

On student films when directors are unable to find a script supervisor, I have seen the editor do the job. The motivation is certainly there to do it well.

PRODUCTION DEPARTMENT

PRODUCER

Answers to: Investors or studio heads

Responsible for: Assembling and administering the necessary funds, and overseeing the project as a whole. Traditionally, the producer also has ultimate say in an artistic dispute between, for example, a principal actor and the director. Because status is defined by a number of factors, relative influence may be unconventional and the producer must arbitrate such problems. Because the producer's role in the United States is primarily fiscal and logistical, the producer also heads the production department consisting of assistant producer, PM, production secretary, and assistant directors. In Europe, a different tradition places the producer more as an artistic entrepreneur, putting together a triangular creative team of writer, director, and producer around a project. This works well when financing comes piecemeal from TV commissioning editors. European TV corporations, unlike their American counterparts, sometimes develop new talent in fiction.

Producers often have assistants called *Associate, Assistant, or Line Producers*, each of whom has different responsibilities on a larger production.

Personal traits: The ideal producer concentrates on being an enabler, supplier, and rationer of vital resources. To this end, planning, scheduling, and accounting should be a producer's strengths, but producers of experience and taste are also important arbiters of the film's artistic progress, especially because they normally have some distance from day-to-day production. The ideal producer is a cultivated, intelligent, and sensitive businessperson whose goal in life is to nourish good work by unobtrusively supporting the artists and craftspeople hired to produce it.

And here is where it can all go wrong. Because they control money, producers have power, and some, especially the inexperienced, assume that because artists and technicians are subordinates, their work and values are subordinate, too. Experienced filmmakers are wearily familiar with the crass philistine who made his money in insurance and now wants to express what he imagines to be his artistic side by producing a film. This type of person assumes that the creative and organic process of filmmaking can be organized like a property construction project. In the end, much energy is wasted in diplomatically trying to educate this person into trusting the hired experts, and usually the film suffers as well as its makers.

Probably all producers want to control the artistic identity of the work, but the wise ones sublimate their impulses and retain respect for those whose artistry has taken many years to mature. Producers of some experience have a track record like anyone else, and you can find out through the grapevine what their reputations are. Never *ever* believe from the producer's overtures that you will be treated differently or better than your predecessors.

With producers of all degrees of experience, look for these danger signs:

- Visceral distrust of everyone's motives
- A drive to personally control everything (micromanagement)
- Inability to listen to or learn from experts' explanations
- Great interest in money and status, and impatience with the film process

Filmmakers usually lack all flair for venture capitalism and are only too aware of their dependency upon financial operators. It is in their interest to educate a producer, and vice versa, but this is sometimes frustrated by the unscrupulous financial operator's common compulsions:

- Trying to play people against each other
- Solving problems using aggression and fear tactics
- Trying to look competent when the opposite is true
- A willingness to trash anybody or anything that looks as if it can be bettered
- The desire to replace anyone who has seen the producer's ignorance
- Taking credit for other people's work

These strategies may pay dividends in the business jungle, but they alienate film crews in record time. Until recently there has been no schooling for producers, and no induction into the tightly organized, interdependent world of filmmaking for the outsider. Anyone with access to money can call themselves a movie producer and still get away with it. In the last four decades I recall working for producers who were, variously, an insurance man, a real-estate developer, a gentlemanly hood, and a playboy draft-dodger. For one or two of them, hell has room reservations. While the funds assembled by these people made production possible, their congenital distrust, crassness, and megalomania made the crews' lives into a tragicomic rollercoaster ride. Using threats, sudden dismissal, and humiliation, such people survive because filmmakers depend on financing.

I also worked under producers who were principled, educated, restrained, and a source of support and discriminating encouragement to everyone. These men and women were the professionals—true leaders with a long history of deserving survivorship.

PRODUCTION MANAGER

Answers to: The producer

Responsible for: Day-to-day logistics and money disbursement. The PM is a necessity with any size crew. When nobody trained is available, there are many whose business background equips them to do this vital job surpassingly well. Having a PM makes a huge difference to everything and everybody.

The PM is the producer's delegate and is closely concerned with preproduction and production. He or she is a business manager who is based in an office and takes care of all the arrangements for the shoot. These include:

- Being the contact person for the outside world
- Finding overnight accommodations
- Booking rented equipment to the specifications of camera and sound people
- Making up (with the director) a shooting schedule
- Arranging for the rushes to get to and from the laboratory
- Making transport arrangements and negotiating air and other travel
- Locating hotels, restaurants, and toilet facilities near the shoot
- Monitoring cash flow
- Incubating contingency plans in case bad weather stymies exterior shooting
- Hustling and preparing the way ahead

The PM's work lightens the load for the rest of the crew and helps them keep up the pace of shooting without distractions.

Personality traits: The good PM is:

- Organized, methodical, and an able negotiator
- Trained in business practices, as well as computerized scheduling and budgeting
- A compulsive list keeper
- Socially adept and diplomatic
- Able to multitask
- Able to delegate and juggle shifting priorities
- Able to make quick and accurate decisions involving time, effort, and money
- Not intimidated by officialdom

Good PMs often become producers, especially if they have developed the requisite contacts, cultural interests, and knowledge of the film industry.

ASSISTANT DIRECTOR

Answers to: The PM

Responsible for: All the legwork and logistical planning of the production. On a feature shoot there may be first, second, and third ADs. They almost never become directors because their skills are organizational rather than artistic and lean toward production management. Their jobs include:

- Scheduling for shoots
- Arranging locations and permits

- Getting the right people to the right place
- Coordinating props, wardrobe, hairdressing, and make-up personnel
- Contacting
- Reminding
- Acquiring information
- Calling artists
- Herding crowds
- Barking orders in a big voice for the director

Sometimes in a director's absence an AD will rehearse actors, but only if he or she has a strong grasp of the director's intentions. The experienced AD may direct the second unit, but this more often falls to the editor.

Personality traits: The main requirements for an AD are to be organized, have a good business mind, a voice that can wake the dead, and a nature both firm and diplomatic.

CAMERA DEPARTMENT

CAMERA CREW GENERALITIES

Personality traits: Camera crew members should be:

- Image-conscious
- From a background in photography or fine art
- Good at composition and design
- Observant of details found in people's surroundings
- Team players
- Decisive
- Practical
- Inventive
- Methodical
- Dexterous

Depending on the weight of the equipment, camera crew members may also need to be robust. Handholding a 20-lb camera for most of an 8-hour day is not for the delicate, nor is loading equipment boxes in and out of transportation. The job is dirty, grueling, and at times intoxicatingly wonderful. The best camera people seem to be calm individuals who do not ruffle easily in crises. They are knowledgeable and resourceful and take pride in improvising solutions to intransigent technical and logistical problems. What you hope to find is the perfectionist who still aims for the best and simplest solution when time is short.

Rather alarmingly, some quite experienced camera personnel isolate themselves in the mechanics of their craft at the expense of the director's deeper quest for themes and meanings. While it can be disastrous to have a crew of would-be directors, it can be equally frustrating to find isolated operatives in your crew. The best crew members comprehend both the details and the totality of a project and can see how to make the best contribution to it. This is why a narrow technical education is not good enough for anyone in a film crew.

DIRECTOR OF PHOTOGRAPHY

Answers to: The director.

Responsible for: All aspects of cinematography or videography. Also known as lighting camera person, the director of photography (DP) is the most important crew member after the director and is responsible for the look of the film. That is, he or she collaborates closely with the director and makes all decisions about camera, lighting, and equipment that contribute to the camerawork. The DP is also:

- Responsible for specifying the lighting and camera equipment, lenses, filmstock, or their video equivalents
- Leader of the crew's work while the director concentrates on the actors
- Responsible for selection (and on a low-budget film, the testing and adjusting) of the camera and lighting equipment and knowing its working principles
- Responsible when the crew is small for reconnoitering each location in advance with the gaffer to assess electrical supplies and lighting design
- The person who decides and supervises the placement of lighting instruments
- Supervisor of the camera and lighting crews

No important work should ever be done without running tests as early as possible to forestall Murphy's Law, which is inexorable in filmmaking.

CAMERA OPERATOR

Answers to: The DP.

Responsible for: Every aspect of handling the camera, which means deciding on camera positioning (in collaboration with the director) and physically controlling framing and all camera movements such as panning, tilting, zooming in and out, and dollying.

The operator should be someone quick to learn the behavioral nuances that reveal when each actor is going to move. In improvisation work, as in documentary, the camera work is often *grab-shooting*, or shooting on the run, so the operator must decide moment to moment what to shoot in a busy scene. Even in a highly controlled shoot, actors going wide of their marks can pose a compositional conflict that the operator must resolve if the take is not to be wasted.

While the director sees content happening in three dimensions in front of (or sometimes behind) the camera, the operator sees the action in its framed, cinematic form. The director may redirect the camera to a different area, but without a video assist, the operator alone knows exactly what the action will look like on the screen. The director must be able to rely on the operator's discrimination. This is also true for very controlled framing and composition because movement within the frame often requires immediate and spontaneous reframing.

CAMERA ASSISTANTS OR ASSISTANT CINEMATOGRAPHERS

Answers to: The camera operator.

Responsible for: Everything concerning the camera. Assistant cinematographers (ACs) keep the camera optics and film gate clean and manhandle the camera equipment from place to place. Their main requirements are to be highly organized, reliable, and zealous at maintaining the camera in prime condition, whether it is film or videotape. Because their responsibilities are almost wholly technical, it is more important they be good and diligent technicians. A feature film will use several ACs. Division of labor makes one a clapper operator and magazine loader and another the person who follows focus when the distance changes between subject and camera. On a small unit, one AC may do all the ancillary work, though this can lead to costly holdups.

GAFFER AND GRIPS

Answers to: The DP.

Responsible for: The job of the **gaffer** is to rig lighting and to know how to handle anything that needs to be fixed, mounted, moved, pushed, lifted, or lowered. The gaffer must have a good grasp of mechanical and electrical principles to improvise solutions for which there is no available piece of equipment. A good gaffer also understands not only the lighting instruments but the principles and practice of lighting itself, because he or she must be able to quickly grasp the intentions behind the DP's lighting instructions. Under the gaffer is the **best boy electrician.**

The job of the **key grip** is to fetch and carry and to rig lighting according to the gaffer's instructions. He or she also has the highly skilled and coordinated job of moving the camera support (dolly, crane, truck, etc.) from mark to mark as the camera takes mobile shots. Under the key grip is the **best boy grip**. Grips should be strong, practical, organized, and willing. On a minimal crew they may double up to help with sound equipment, camera assisting, turning on and off the videotape deck, and they may leave the crew to fetch or deliver while shooting is in progress. A skilled grip knows something about everyone's job and is capable of standing in for some technicians in an emergency.

Personality traits: Gaffers and grips need patience because their work involves moving and maintaining large varieties of equipment, of which there never seems enough for the job at hand. While they work, production waits; while production is in progress, they wait. When everyone else is finished, they go to work tearing down their masses of equipment and then stow it and haul it away ready to set up again for the next day's shoot. All this must be good for the soul, for they are often highly resourceful and very funny. *Gaffer* is old English for grandfather, singularly appropriate for one who must know every imaginable way to skin the proverbial cat.

SOUND DEPARTMENT

SOUND RECORDIST AND BOOM OPERATOR

Answers to: The DP.

Responsible for: Quality sound, which is the unfailing casualty with an inexperienced crew. Capturing clear, clean, and consistent sound is deceptively difficult, and sound recording lacks the glamour that would cause most people to care about it. Today's camcorders have excellent sound quality if you use the highest sampling rate. It is vital to keep this consistent or the editor may have tracks that cannot be played from a time line.

It is the **sound recordist's** responsibility to check sound and videotape equipment in advance and to solve problems as they arise. The **boom operator's** job is to place the microphone as close to sound sources as possible without getting it in the shot or creating shadows. In a complicated dialogue scene this requires moving the mike around to catch each new speaker. In an interior setup, lighting and camera position are determined first, and the sound recordist is expected to somehow position the mikes without them being seen or causing shadows, and without losing sound quality. A shoot, therefore, turns into a series of aggravating compromises that the recordist is all too inclined to take personally. Exterior location shooting is often the most troublesome because background sound levels are uncontrollable and any hope of getting the best quality is usually compromised by a tight schedule. This generates Foley (voice and sound effects recreation) and other costly post-synchronization work in the postproduction phase.

Personality traits: Sound crew members need patience, a good ear, and the maturity to be low man on the totem pole. An alarming number of professionals turn into frustrated mutterers who feel that standards are routinely trampled. But it's the disconnected craftsman more than the whole filmmaker who fails to see the necessity and priority of compromise. Sound can at least be reconstituted to a degree in the sound studio later, but camerawork and actors' performances are immutable once shot.

The recordist is often kept inactive for long periods and then suddenly expected to "fix up the mike" in short order, so you need a person who habitually thinks ahead. The unsatisfactory recordist is the one who comes to life when the setup time arrives and then asks for a lighting change.

The sound recordist listens not to words but to sound quality, so you need someone able to listen analytically and who hears all the buzz, rumble, or edginess that the novice will unconsciously screen out. The art of recording has very little to do with recorders and everything to do with the selection and placement of mikes—and being able to hear the difference. No independent assessment is possible apart from the discerning ear. Only musical interests and, better still, musical training seem to instill this critical discipline.

Sound recording is often brushed aside as easy and unglamorous among the uninitiated and left uncritically to anyone who says he or she can do it. But poor sound disconnects the audience even more fatally than a poor story. Too many student films sound like studies of characters talking through blankets in a bathroom.

When shooting is done with a Steadicam and sound equipment must be mobile, the sound crew must be ready to work without a conclusive rehearsal. With a cast and camera on the move, it takes skill and agile, quiet footwork to keep the mike close to, but not in the edge of, the camera's field of view. There are always multiple solutions to any sound problem, so knowledge of available equipment and an interest in up-to-date techniques is a great advantage.

ART DEPARTMENT

ART DIRECTOR

Answers to: The director.

Responsible for: Designing everything in the film's environment so it effectively interprets the script. This means overseeing props and costumes, as well as designing all aspects of sets and locations. If the film is a period production, the art director will research the epoch and its social customs to ensure that costumes and decor are accurate and make an impact. On a low-budget movie the art director will do his or her own sketching and set dressing, while on a larger production there are draughtspeople and set dressers.

Personality traits: A good art director has:

- A design, fine arts, or architecture background
- The ability to sketch or paint fluently
- A lively eye for fashion, tastes, and social distinctions
- A strong interest in the social and historical background of these phenomena
- A strong grasp of the emotional potential of color and its combinations
- Ability to translate the script into a series of settings with costumes, all of which heighten and intensify the underlying intentions of the script
- Managerial abilities and good communication skills because the art director works closely with painters, carpenters, props, set dressers, and wardrobe personnel

CONSTRUCTION SPECIALISTS

These include the specialists you would find on a large construction site such as carpenters, plasterers, painters, electricians, and riggers.

Answers to: The art director.

Responsible for: All aspects of constructing sets with removable walls and ceilings or making anything with the inbuilt flexibility required for convenience in shooting. Construction crews must be able to build a convincing nightclub, cave, subway tunnel, airplane hold, jungle camp, or whatever else. It must be modular and moveable and not hurt its users.

Personality traits: Each must be a master craftsperson and good at teamwork.

SPECIAL EFFECTS

Answers to: The art director.

Responsible for: May be required to make explosions, contained fires, bridges that collapse, or windows that a stunt artist can safely jump through. (*Lord of the Rings* (2001) is a veritable dictionary of special effects, from Middle Earth rock kingdoms to creatures that crawl, prowl, and fly.) Providing answers to special script requirements. At one time they provided models for ships sinking or cars blowing up and process shooting in which a live foreground was married to a pre-shot background. With the advent of computers and robotics, and a market for exotic spectacle, the special effects purview has expanded into covering everything from dinosaurian life to space travel. The script says what is wanted, and it's a point of honor for them to make it, using every imaginable principle—electrical, mechanical, computer, robotic, biological—to provide a working answer. They also handle anything that involves danger and stunts.

Personality traits: Tenacious, inventive, resourceful, with a love of impossible challenges. Stunt people have a Houdini relationship with danger: They are attracted to it and get something out of cheating injury and death. They embody survival of the fittest.

WARDROBE AND PROPS

Answers to: The art director.

Responsible for: Locating, storing, and maintaining costumes and properties (objects such as ashtrays, baby toys, or grand pianos that dress the set). Must keep master lists and produce the right thing in good order at the right time. When no wardrobe person is available, each actor becomes responsible for his or her own costumes. The assistant director (AD) should double-check beforehand what clothes each actor must bring for the next scene so today's costume is not still sitting in the actor's laundry basket.

Personality traits: Highly resourceful and able to develop a wealth of contacts among antique, resale, theatrical, and junk shop owners. Very practical because things borrowed or rented must often be carefully operated, maintained, or even first put into working order. Costumes, especially ones that are elaborate or antique, take expertise to keep clean and functional and usually need temporary alterations to fit a particular actor. Props and wardrobe departments must be completely organized: Each scene has its special requirements and the right props and costumes must appear on time and in the right place or shooting becomes a nightmare.

MAKE-UP AND HAIRDRESSING

Answers to: The PM.

Responsible for: The appropriate physical appearance in face and hair, often needing careful attention to period details. A hidden part of the job is catering to actors' insecurities by helping them believe in the way they look. Where the character demands negative traits, the make-up artist may have to work against an actor's resistance. Make-up is particularly tricky; shoot tests to ensure make-up is credible and compatible with color stock and any special lighting.

Personality traits: Diplomacy and endurance. My father was a make-up man and arrived at work before anyone else, preparing actors hours ahead of shooting when elaborate beards and whiskers were required. Apart from character or glamour preparation, his work included the bizarre, such as putting a black patch over the eye of Fagin's dog in David Lean's *Oliver Twist* (1948), applying gold paint to the naked girl in *Goldfinger* (1964), and inventing ghoulish effects for Hammer horror films like flesh melting from a face to leave eyeballs staring out of bony eye-sockets. It helps to be resourceful and to relish the unusual, but he also spoke of the miseries of trying to make up foul-tempered alcoholics in the early morning. After the dawn rush, make-up and hairdressing must often sit idle on the set, keeping a weather eye for when their handiwork needs repair.

POSTPRODUCTION

Descriptions of postproduction personnel and their responsibilities will be found in Chapter 37: Beginning the Editing Stage.

CHAPTER 29

MISE EN SCÈNE

PURPOSE

The French expression *mise en scène* (literally, putting into the scene) is a usefully holistic term for those aspects of directing that take place during shooting. *Mise en scène* has to be decided globally and in broad outline for the whole script, and then each scene can be designed within the intentions of the larger structure. Globally or locally, *mise en scène* includes:

- Blocking, which includes planning positions of:
  Actors in relation to each other
  Action in relation to set or location
  Camera placement in relation to actors and set
- Camera
  Filmstock and processing, or color settings (video)
  Choice of lens
  Composition
  Movements
  Coverage for editing
- Image design
  Use of color
  Depth, perspective, and treatment of space
  Lighting mood, and treatment of time of day and place
  Frame design in terms of the scene's dramatic functions
- Dramatic content
  Rhythms (action rhythms and visual rhythms)
  Point of view (whose consciousness the audience should identify with)
  Motifs or leitmotifs
  Visual or aural metaphors
  Foreshadowing

- Sound Design
  Whether sound is diegetic or non-diegetic
  What part sound plays as a narrative device
  Whether it relays a subjective or objective point of view
  Whose point of view it is

All this must eventually be planned in practical rather than intellectual terms. The director must know what options exist and how to eventually discuss them with the DP, who is undoubtedly the most important collaborator during the shoot. This is also a time when directors can fall completely under the spell of strong-minded DPs. And that would be another invitation to abdicate the director's role.

SURVEYING THE FILM

Translate each scene in your film into a brief content description, then annotate it with how you want the audience to feel about it, and you have a firm beginning. If possible, turn the list into a graph or storyboard showing what the audience must feel from scene to scene, and then you can think about how the Storyteller must tell the tale to make this happen. Once you have an overall strategy, you can move to designing individual scenes.

LONG-TAKE VERSUS SHORT-TAKE COVERAGE

Covering a scene means shooting enough variation of angle and subject so you can show it to advantage on the screen. Depending on the nature of the film this can mean long, intricately choreographed takes lasting an entire scene as used by Hitchcock in *Rope* (1948), or it might call for a flow of rapidly edited images as favored by such disparate filmmakers as Eisenstein in *The Battleship Potemkin* (1925), Nicholas Roeg in *Don't Look Now* (1973), and just about any MTV music video.

The long-take method: generally requires a mobile camera and intricate blocking of both camera and actors to avoid a flat, stagey appearance. Because you cannot cut around anything, it requires virtuoso control by actors and technicians as any errors consign an entire take to the trashcan. There is also a risk that only shows up in the first assembly: Because no control of individual elements is possible within any scene, the editor cannot rebalance the rhythm of the performances or the pacing of the story. For a superb example of fluid camera control and blocking in long takes, see Jacques Demy's masterpiece, *The Umbrellas of Cherbourg* (1964). A story of lovers in a small French town when the upheavals in Algeria took recruits off to war, it is an operetta in which all dialogue is realistic and sung. Surprisingly this works very well. The film is also masterly in its design and use of color. Another that uses movement exceptionally well is Wim Wenders' *Faraway, So Close!* (1993). By this time the Steadicam™ body mount had been invented and DP Jürgen Jürges and Jörg Widmer, his Steadicam operator, took full advantage of the extraordinary handheld liberty afforded the ponderous 35 mm camera.

The short-take method: makes the material more evidently manipulated because it requires frequent cuts. At MTV's frenetic extreme the viewer is bombarded with fragments of action from which to infer the whole. In short-take coverage generally, shots are edited together to create rhythm, juxtaposition, and tension, but for the audience, any cut always takes energy to interpret. Rather than rely on blowhard editing, many directors choreograph their *mise en scène* as individual shots containing complex blocking. Following the example of the wise and the foolish virgins, they also shoot safety coverage in case longish takes are flawed or their inalterable pacing fails.

FIXED VERSUS MOBILE CAMERA

A camera on a tripod is able to zoom in and hold a steady close shot without physically crowding the actor. On the other hand, it cannot dolly or crab to a better vantage point. Mounting the camera on a dolly or crane allows smooth movement through a predetermined cycle but requires great precision from both crew and cast, who must hit predetermined chalk marks on the floor if composition and focus are to hold up. Here the casualty may be spontaneity in the cast. A dolly and its crew are also apt to make some noise, so you may pay with more sound postproduction work and extra takes where floor creaks obscure dialogue.

Intelligent handheld camerawork may be the only solution if you are to shoot a semi-improvised performance under a time constraint. The handheld camera gives great mobility but at the price of a certain unsteadiness. A Steadicam in the right hands can solve all of these problems. In the hands of someone inexperienced, however, you can lose hours.

SUBJECTIVE OR OBJECTIVE CAMERA PRESENCE

The two kinds of camera presence, the one studied, composed, and controlled, and the other mobile, spontaneous, reactive, and adaptive to change, will each give a different sense of an observing presence. Each implies a relatively subjective or objective observation of the action. Camera-handling alone may thus alter the *voice* of the film, making it either more or less personal and vulnerable. Maintaining either mode may become dull, while shifting justifiably between them can be very potent.

RELATEDNESS: SEPARATING OR INTEGRATING BY SHOT

Composition and framing alter a scene's implications drastically. Isolating two people, each in his own close shot, and then intercutting them has a very different feel than intercutting two over-shoulder shots in which the two are always spatially related. Their relationship in space and time appears less manipulated by the filming process than in over-shoulder shots. In the single shots, the observer is always alone with one of the contenders and inferring the unseen participant. In cinema this isolation is the exception, for limitations of frame size usually compel using precious screen space to the utmost by packing the

FIGURE 29–1

Space and distance must be deliberately created on the screen. Still from Zsolt Kézdi Kovács' *Forbidden Relations* (1982, courtesy Spectrafilm).

frame and showing the spatial relationship between everything and everybody (Figure 29–1).

HAVE THE COURAGE TO BE SIMPLE

Viewing heavily edited scenes is hard work, so a strong reason to move the camera (or subjects in relation to camera) is to increase the amount that can happen in a single take, which conserves on the need for associative editing. Other camera movements are necessary to preserve composition and framing when characters are on the move or to reveal something or someone formerly out of frame. The very best lessons in camera positioning and movement lie waiting in the best films in your chosen genre. Study them. You'll be surprised how good simple films look when they rely on a good story, good acting, and inventive blocking rather than swishy camerawork.

THE CAMERA AS OBSERVING CONSCIOUSNESS

Treat the camera as a questing observer and imagine how you want the audience to experience the scene. If you had a scene in a turbulent flea market, it would not make sense to limit the camera to carefully placed tripod shots. Make the camera adopt the point of view of a wandering buyer by going handheld and peering into circles of chattering people, looking closely at the merchandise, and then swinging around when someone calls out.

If, instead, you are shooting a church service, with its elaborate ritualized stages, the placing and amount of coverage should be rock steady because that is our usual experience in such a setting. Ask yourself whose point of view the audience is mostly sharing. Where does the majority of the telling action lie? With the newcomer? The priest? The choir or the congregation?

THE STORYTELLER'S POINT OF VIEW

David Mamet, in his *On Directing Film,* has protested that too much fiction filmmaking consists of *following* the action like a news service. Do you want to document happenings or connect like a Storyteller? The first is passive, value-free surveillance, and the second involves inflection, having an active purpose, raising critical questions, and implying a mind and heart at work. What identity will you give your Storyteller, and what singularity should we notice in your characters and their situations? These are not easy questions, but they will not answer themselves during shooting or editing.

Help is at hand when you call on the connotations of the word *attitude*. The attitude of the storytelling mind, intelligence, and heart is really the lens through which an audience experiences your story. How would you describe this attitude? What will it be like? What are the ironies and humor in its way of seeing? How will you make these show, because that slant must infuse the movie. Your Storyteller's attitude must show throughout, which means implying puzzlement, doubts, enjoyment, censure, opprobrium, delight, distrust, regret, fascination—whatever changing thoughts grip the Storyteller as he or she gives birth to the unfolding tale.

You have definite ideas about this from moving around during rehearsal and watching these newly born characters living the salient pieces of their lives. You watched and identified according to a pattern that's based on the intentions behind the writing and arises now from the chemistry of personalities and situation. You must remain sensitive to this. Is how you notice, what you notice, and what you feel being reflected in the video rehearsal coverage? If not, why not?

By pausing to dig into your impressions you can go further toward understanding their sources and their impact. *You can use your mind to examine the heart, and come away more strongly convinced of who you are and what you have seen*. A friend used to say, "Nothing is real until I have written about it." Make a point of writing the Storyteller's part as the invisible Observer and further developing the symbiotic nature of the tale and the teller. They go together; one depends on the other. To create the Storyteller you have to bring the telling alive as well as the tale, that is, you must give it the integrity of a quirky human mind that sees, weighs, wonders, feels, and supposes as the story unfolds. Do that successfully, and your work will acquire the magical quality of humor and intelligence that characterizes work having soul. Not too many films have soul. It is an attribute to which audiences universally respond.

The encouragement to make films at all always comes from seeing special films. For heart and soul, see Jean-Pierre Jeunet's immensely popular *Amelie* (2001). It is a fable about a lonely Paris waitress who finds a box of old toys hidden behind the floorboards and sets out to return them to their owner. She discovers joy in anonymously contributing to other people's lives from a distance. Of course, if you do good, good eventually comes back to you, and she at last finds love. This funny, quirky film, made intimately around the presence of the enchanting Audrey Tautou, celebrates the Paris of 40 years ago and the extraordinary films that emerged during the era of the French New Wave.

In the struggle for narrative clarity and efficient plotting, the factory-like process of most filmmaking tramples the soul out of most work. Occasionally a film appears whose boldness of conception and execution transcends the process, and *Amelie* is one such work. Of course, there can be no formula for making a film with a soul. It lies in an integrity in your way of seeing. Like everything else in fiction, this can be distilled, heightened, and enjoyed in the making, all to the greater good. But it takes a director with a clear, strong identity—one not overwhelmed by the people and process. You have your work cut out, don't you?

APPROACHING A SINGLE SCENE

SCRIPT, CONCEPT, AND SCENE DESIGN

Although influenced by limitations inherent to the setting or in the cinematographic process, a scene's design is based on its intended function in the script and your gut feelings about the scene. How, for instance, might you show a man who is being watched by the police get into his car and try to start it? Here is a checklist you can apply to any scene:

- What is the scene's special function in the script?
- What does the audience need to know about the scene's setup and spatial content:
  At the outset of the scene?
  Later? (How much later?)
- What perspectives and relationships must be indicated through using space?
- What information can be left to the audience's deduction or imagination?
- What elements should be juxtaposed
  Visually within each shot's framing?
  Conceptually by editing shots together?
- How much are characters aware of their predicament and what are each character's expectations:
  At the start of the scene?
  At its end?
- Who learns and develops?
- Where is the scene's obligatory moment?
- Is there anything the audience but not the characters should learn?
- What is the ruling image or motif here?
- Is any foreshadowing called for?

- What visual design is called for in:
  Amount and distribution of light?
  Tonality?
  Hue?
  Costuming?
  Set design?
  Illusion of space—or lack of it?
- What is the Storyteller's attitude to this scene compared with others?

Should the audience see our man being watched by police from the policeman's point of view or from a more omniscient one (that is, the Storyteller's) in which the audience, but not the man, notices the cop? This will probably be decided on plot grounds, but what the characters experience should influence your coverage, just as characters in real life influence whom you choose to watch in any given situation.

Now imagine a more complex scene in which a child witnesses a sustained argument between his parents. How should point of view be handled there? First, what does the argument represent? Is it "child realizing he is a pawn," or is it "parents are so bitter that they don't care what their child can hear?" Is it what the child sees or how the dispute acts upon him that matters?

Questions like these determine whose scene it really is: the boy's, the father's, or the mother's. The scene can be shot and edited to polarize our sympathetic interest in any of these directions at any given moment in the scene. Remember that making no choice leads to faceless, expressionless filmmaking—technical filmmaking with no heart or soul. This is not what you want.

There remains a detached way of observing events, that of the Omniscient Storyteller. This point of view is useful to relieve pressure on the audience before renewing it again. Sustained and unvarying pressure would be self-defeating because the audience either becomes armed against it or tunes out. Shakespeare in his tragedies intersperses scenes of comic relief to deal with this problem.

To summarize: what is salient will vary with the scene depending on its contents, complexity, and what it contributes to the film as a whole. Defining what the Storyteller notices and feels helps you decide how to reveal what matters and makes everything less arbitrary. Here you've got to develop instincts and really listen to them.

POINT OF VIEW

WHOSE POINT OF VIEW?

Controlling point of view probably remains a baffling notion. As we said, it is not literally "what so-and-so sees," though this may comprise one or two shots. Rather, it attempts to relay to the audience how a character in the film is experiencing particular events. Top priority will always be to ask whose point of view this scene favors. A great many of your decisions about composition, camera placement, and editing will flow from this.

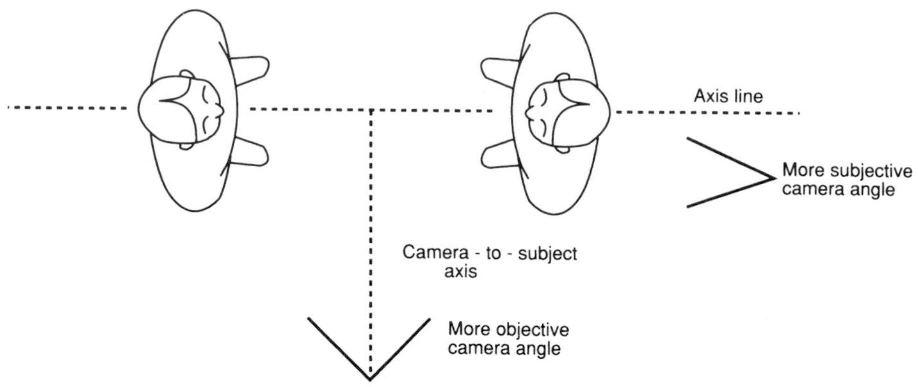

FIGURE 29–2

Camera-to-subject axis can be close or at right angles to the scene axis; this controls how subjective or objective the angle feels to the audience.

POINT OF VIEW CAN CHANGE

Remember, *point of view* (POV) means the way our sympathy and curiosity migrates between patient and doctor, subject and object—even though finally the film is about the patient. To understand and care for the doctor, we need to share those paradoxical moments when he empathizes with our central character, vacating his own protected reality to enter that of the condemned man. A character who never temporarily relinquishes his own identity to something larger would be someone alienated or inhuman.

Decide POV by asking what makes dramatic sense to the Concerned Observer. Answers come from the logic of the script and from your instincts. There may be no overriding determinant, in which case the editor will have to decide later, based on the nuances of the acting *and whether you've shot enough alternative coverage.*

A reminder: Subjective POV shots tend to be close-ups and shots close to the axis or the line of psychic tension between characters. Objective POVs tend to be wider shots and farther from that line (Figure 29–2). These generalizations are no more than a rule of thumb because POV is oblique and impinges on the audience through a subtle combination of action, characters, lighting, mood, events, and context.

COMPROMISES: SPACE, PERCEPTION, AND LENSES

The art of the cinema gets delivered through a series of compromises made to accommodate the fact that the camera sees in two dimensions instead of three, and that its field of view is very limited compared with human visual perception. To compensate for this, we render the spirit of consciousness, not its actuality, by using associative techniques to counterpoint sound and images; we compress more in the frame and accomplish more in space and time than happens in real life.

CAMERA EYE AND HUMAN EYE ARE DIFFERENT

The eye of the beholder during rehearsals is misleading, for the human eye takes in a field of almost 180 degrees (Figure 29–3). Although a 16 mm camera lens of 10 mm focal length is called a wide angle when shooting in TV aspect ratio, it still only takes in 54 degrees horizontally and 40 degrees vertically. This means that a reasonably comprehensive wide-angle lens (before gross fairground distortion sets in) only has *one quarter* of the eye's angle of acceptance. This translates to a very restricted field of view indeed and one with resounding consequences for dramatic composition. Film aspect ratios are described later in this chapter.

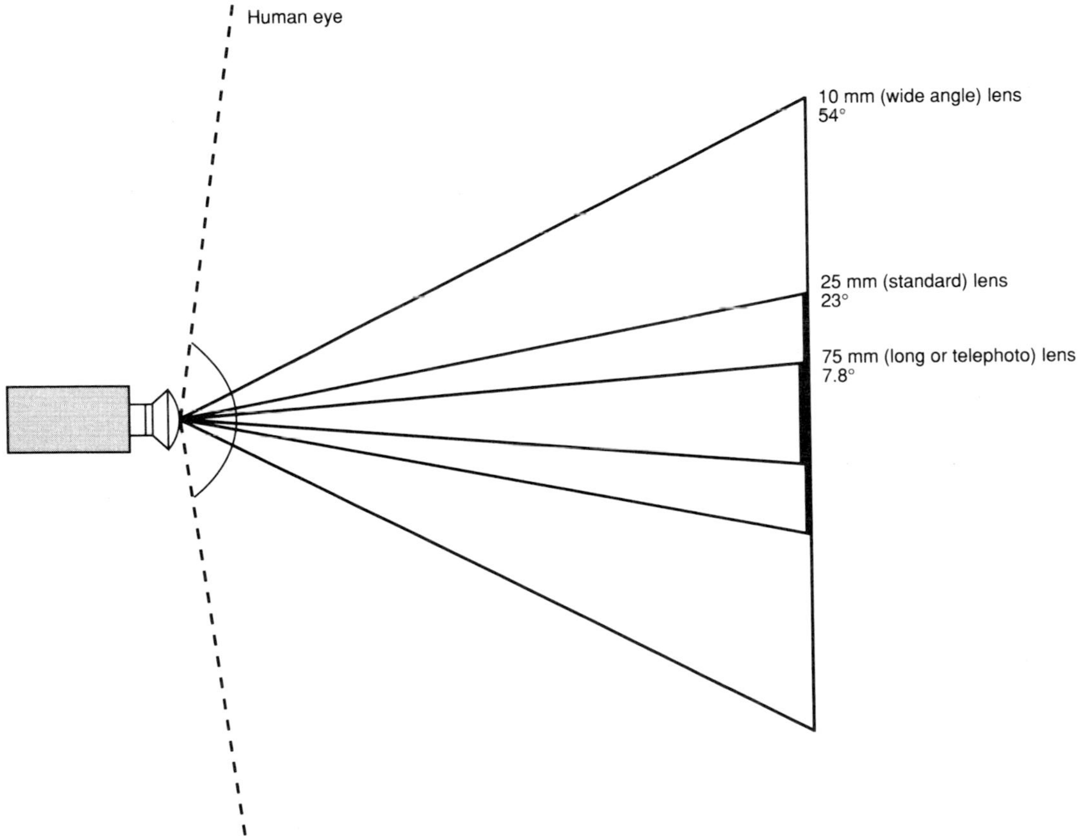

FIGURE 29–3

Human eye's field of vision compared with much more limited angle of acceptance for 16 mm camera lenses. Note that vertical angles of acceptance (not shown) are 25% smaller still.

We compensate for such limitation by rearranging compositions so they trick the spectator into the sensation of normal distances and spatial relationships. Characters holding a conversation may have to stand unnaturally close before the camera, but will look normal onscreen; furniture placement and distances between objects are often *cheated*, that is, they are moved either apart or together to produce the desired appearance onscreen. Ordinary physical movements like walking past the camera or picking up a glass of milk in close-up may require slowing by a third or more to look natural onscreen. Note, however, that comedy dialogue (though not necessarily movement) often needs faster than normal playing if it is to avoid looking slow onscreen. As always, screen testing helps you make all such decisions.

Packing the frame, achieving the illusion of depth, and arranging for balance and thematic significance in each composition can all compensate for the screen's limited size and its tendency to flatten everything. As the Hardy quotation mentioned previously says, "Art is the secret of how to produce by a false thing the effect of a true."

ASPECT RATIO

This refers to the proportions of the image in terms of height versus the width. Early cinema had an aspect ratio of 1.33:1, that is, it was 1.33 units wide to every 1 unit high. Television maintained roughly the same proportions. In the 1950s wide screen aspect ratios came along and today's cinema aspect ratios are 1.66:1 (Europe) and 1.85:1 (United States).

High definition television (HDTV) camcorders are designed to shoot wide screen, but less advanced camcorders, if they shoot in wide screen at all, do so by electronically chopping a band off the top and bottom of the image. This means the recorded image uses fewer pixels (picture cells inherent to the electronic imaging chip) than the standard ratio and is less satisfactory in terms of quality. Television viewers are by now familiar with the result, called letterbox format, in which the image seems to have shrunk, leaving unused black bands at the top and bottom.

The adoption of digital HDTV means that all film and video will in the future be shot wide screen. Cinemas and television sets will have similar aspect ratios, and directors and DPs will in the future compose for wide screen. This means that inherently wide pictorial matter, such as landscape shots and anything making horizontal movement, can take place more satisfactorily on the screen. Virtually everybody feels that wide screen allows for more interesting filming and that 1.33:1 is restrictive compared with the wider formats.

CHOOSING LENS TYPE

This is an area some people find forbidding, but you don't need a physics degree to use lenses intelligently. As the standard reference, we call *normal* those lenses that give the same sense of perspective as the human eye, while the departures to either side of normalcy affect magnification and are called wide and telephoto. Analogies from everyday life show the basic differences:

Wide angle of acceptance	Normal angle of acceptance	Narrow (or telephoto) angle of acceptance
Wide angle analogy = door security spyglass (diminishes sizes, makes foreground seem huge compared with background)	The human eye (gives the sense of perspective we consider normal)	Telephoto analogy = telescope (magnifies, brings everything closer, but compresses foreground and background together)

These familiar optical devices allow us to pursue a range of dramatic possibilities in the camera lens. Compare the telescope image to that of the security spyglass, which allows the cautious householder to see if the visitor on the other side of the door is friend or foe.

The telescope: brings objects close; squashes together foreground, middle ground, and background; and isolates the middle ground object in sharp focus while foreground and background are in soft focus.

The security spyglass: brings in a lot of the hallway outside and keeps all in focus, but it produces a reduced and distorted image. If your visitor is leaning with one hand on the door, you are likely to see a huge arm diminishing to a tiny, distorted figure in the distance.

PERSPECTIVE AND NORMALCY

Our sense of perspective comes from knowing the relative sizes of things and judging how far apart they are in near and far planes. In a photo containing a cat and a German shepherd, we judge how far the dog is behind the cat from experience of their relative sizes. Human eye perspective is normal while other lenses alter this relationship radically. The focal length of a lens rendering perspective as normal onscreen will vary according to what camera format is being used:

Format	Focal length for normal lens
8 mm	12.5 mm
16 mm	25 mm
35 mm	50 mm

There is a constant ratio between the format (width of film in use) and the lens' focal length. The examples that follow discuss only 16 mm-format lenses, the equivalent of which are found (though seldom calibrated) in many small-format video cameras.

Normal perspective (Figure 29–4) means the viewer sees an *as is* size relationship between foreground and background trucks and can accurately judge the distance between them. The same shot taken with a wide-angle lens (Figure

29–5) changes the apparent distance between foreground and background, making it appear greater. A telephoto lens (Figure 29–6) does just the opposite, squeezing foreground and background close together. If someone were to walk from the background truck up to the foreground, the implications of their walk would be dramatically different in the three shots; all would have the same subject but offer a different formal treatment through the choice of lens.

PERSPECTIVE CHANGES ONLY WHEN CAMERA-TO-SUBJECT DISTANCE CHANGES

By repositioning the camera and using different lenses (as in Figures 29–4, 29–5, and 29–6), we can standardize the apparent size of the foreground truck, as shown diagrammatically in Figure 29–7. What this implies is that ultimately *changes of perspective result only from camera-to-subject distance* rather than the lens itself.

Now examine Figures 29–8, 29–9, and 29–10. Each is taken with a different lens but from the same camera position. The proportion of the stop sign in relation to the background portico is identical in all three. Perspective—size proportions between planes—has not changed, although we have three different magnifications. So indeed, perspective is the product of camera-to-subject distance, for when this remains constant, the proportions between foreground and background remain the same although the image was shot through three different lenses, with three different degrees of magnification.

MANIPULATING PERSPECTIVE

Using the magnifying or diminishing capacity of different lenses allows us to place the camera differently, and yet produce three similar shots (see Figures 29–4, 29–5, and 29–6); and when camera-to-subject distance changes, we can manipulate perspective. Wide-angle lenses appear to increase distance while telephoto lenses appear to compress the distance.

ZOOMING VERSUS DOLLYING INTO CLOSE-UP

A zoom is a lens having infinite variability between its extremes (say 10 to 100 mm, which is a zoom with a ratio of 10:1). If you keep the camera static and zoom in on a subject, the image is magnified but perspective does not alter. With a prime (fixed) lens dollying in close, the image is magnified *and* you see a perspective change during the move, just as in life. One is movement, the other magnification.

LENSES AND IMAGE TEXTURE

Examine Figures 29–8 and 29–10. The backgrounds are very different in texture. Although the subject is in focus in both, the telephoto version puts the rest of the image in soft focus, isolating and separating the subject from its foreground and background. This is because the telephoto lens has a very narrow depth of field and only the point of focus is sharp.

FIGURE 29–4

Normal lens.

FIGURE 29–5

Wide-angle lens.

FIGURE 29–6

Telephoto lens. Foreground and background distances appear quite different in Figures 29–4 and 29–5.

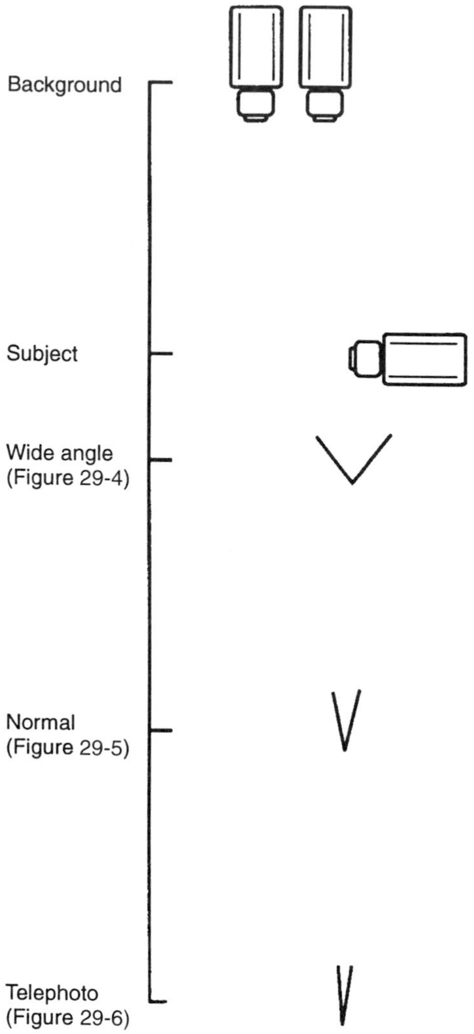

FIGURE 29–7

Perspective changes come from altering the camera-to-subject distance in relation to the subject-to-background distance.

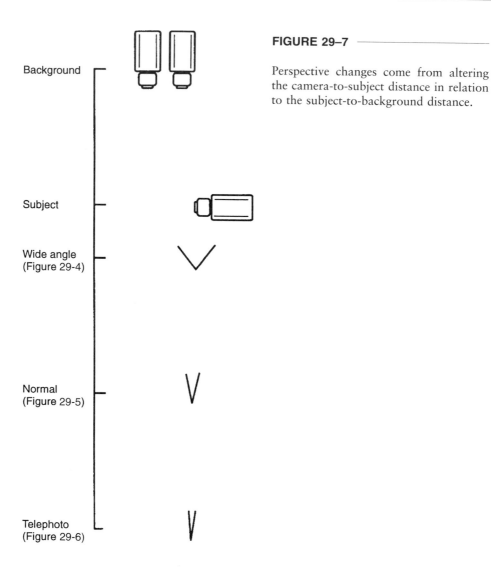

Conversely, a wide-angle lens (Figures 29–5 and 29–8) allows deep focus. This is useful when it allows you to hold focus while someone walks from foreground to background. Deep focus can be a distraction when its image drowns its middle-ground subject with a plethora of irrelevantly sharp background and foreground detail. We say that the telephoto has a *soft* textured background, while the wide angle has one that is *hard*. Lens characteristics can be limiting or have great dramatic utility, depending on what you know and how you use it.

WHY THERE IS A FILM LOOK AND A VIDEO LOOK

There are differences of appearance between film and video that derive from the size of the image-collecting area. A 35 mm-film aperture has many times as much area as a digital video (DV) camera imaging chip. The larger the image size at

FIGURE 29–8

Wide-angle lens.

FIGURE 29–9

Normal lens.

FIGURE 29–10

Telephoto lens. Figures 29–8, 29–9, and 29–10 are taken from a single camera position. Notice that the stop sign remains in the same proportion to its background throughout.

FIGURE 29–11

The P + S Technik Mini35 Adapter, which enables the videographer to realize all the depth of field and other qualities of a 35 mm film lens (courtesy of P + S Technik).

the focal plane, the more refraction it takes and the more critical is the lens's depth of field. If you've ever looked at the image produced by a plate still camera, it is remarkable for two things: the negative (imaging) area is huge, and large parts of the image are soft focus, particularly when using a telephoto lens. The two facts are interdependent. That's why a home 8 mm film camera hardly ever needed focusing. The imaging area was tiny and the angle of refraction between lens and film gate very narrow.

The German optical firm P + S Technik has produced the Mini35 Digital adapter (Figure 29–11). In a two-stage optical operation, the adapter uses interchangeable 35 mm lenses to produce an internal image. This image is then copied and projected into the video camera's imaging path. The result is that the adapter preserves the focal length, depth of field, and angle of view of the 35 mm format. It is available for the Canon XL1, XL1s, and Sony DSR PD150, VX1000, VX2000. You can read about it at *www.pstechnik.de/*. At an (expensive) stroke, it hands the videographer the lens choice and control of the 35 mm cinematographer—and a larger camera that many prefer for handheld shooting.

You may think the Canon XL range of DV cameras is already equipped for 35 mm lenses. It's true they take 35 mm lenses, but the camera's tiny imaging area discards much of the given image. You get manual lens control and superior acuity, but are back in amateur land so far as depth of field and angle of view are concerned.

LENS SPEED

Lens speed is a deceptive term. It has nothing to do with movement and everything to do with how much light a lens needs for minimal operation. A *fast* lens is one in which the iris opens up wide so the lens is good for low-light photography. A *slow* lens is simply one that fails to admit as much light. By their inherent design, wide-angles tend to be fast (say, f1.4) while telephotos tend to be slow (perhaps f2.8). A two-stop difference like this means that the wide-angle is operative at one-quarter the light it takes to use the telephoto. This may be the difference between night shooting being practical or out of the question. Prime (that is, fixed) lenses have few elements so they tend to be faster than zooms, which are multi-element. Primes also tend to have better acuity, or sharpness, because the image passes through fewer optics. Note that zooms have one optimal lens speed over their whole range.

CAMERA HEIGHT

The film-manual adage says that a high camera position suggests domination and a low angle, subjugation. There are other, less colonial-sounding reasons to vary camera height. A high or low camera angle may accommodate objects or persons in either the background or foreground, or accommodate a camera movement. This is covered in the upcoming section, Relatedness: Separating or Integrating by Shot. If you completed Chapter 5, Project 5-1: Picture Composition Analysis, taking as your subject a film as cinematically inventive as Orson Welles' classic *Citizen Kane* (1941), you saw many occasions when the departure from an eye-level camera position simply feels right. Often there is a dramatic rationale behind the choice, but don't turn them into a filmmaking Ten Commandments.

The veteran Hollywood director Edward Dmytryk in his book *On Screen Directing* makes a persuasive case for avoiding shots at characters' eye level simply because they are dull. There may also be a psychological reason to avoid them. At eye level, the audience feels itself intruding upon the action, just as we would feel both threatened and intrusive by standing in the path of a duel. Being above or below eye level positions puts us safely out of the firing line. This is something to remember whenever your camera approaches the axis.

LIMIT CAMERA MOVEMENTS

Most camera movements, apart from zooming, panning, and tilting, spell trouble to your schedule unless you have an expensive dolly and tracks and a highly experienced team to operate them. Understandably, student camera crews love to hire advanced camera support systems because it gives them practice and makes them feel professional. The price of this education may be a production repeatedly paralyzed while someone attempts to perfect a complex move with nothing beyond egocentric virtuosity to offer the story.

ADAPTING TO LOCATION EXIGENCIES

It's hard to recommend rules for camera positioning and movement because every situation has its own nature to be revealed and its own unique limitations. The latter are usually physical: windows or pillars in an interior that restrict shooting in one direction or an incongruity to be avoided in an exterior. A wonderful Victorian house turns out to have a background of power lines strung across the sky and has to be framed low when you wanted to frame high. Even when meticulously planned, filmmaking is always a serendipitous activity and often your vision must be jettisoned and energy redirected to deal with the unforeseen.

For the rigid, linear personality, this constant adaptation is unacceptably frustrating, but for others it represents a challenge to their inventiveness and insight. Nonetheless, you must plan, and sometimes things even go according to intention.

BACKGROUNDS

Deciding what part background must play in relation to foreground is a camera-positioning issue. If a character is depressed and hungry, there is a nice irony in showing that her bus stop is outside a McDonalds and that she is being watched by a huge Ronald McDonald. The composition will unobtrusively highlight her dilemma and suggest that she is tempted to blow her bus money on a large portion of french fries. Sometimes the subject is in the middle ground (a prisoner, bars in foreground, cellmate in background at back of cell, for instance). Foreground compositional elements are an important part of creating depth.

CAMERA AS INSTRUMENT OF REVELATION

Looking down on the subject, looking up at the subject, or looking at it through the treetrunks of a forest all suggest different contexts and different ways of seeing—and therefore of experiencing—the action central to the scene. The camera should be used as an active instrument of revelation. While you can manufacture this sense of revelation through Eisenstein's dialectical cutting, this may be just too intrusive a way to get your point across. More subtle and convincing is to build this multilevel consciousness into the shooting itself. Exploiting the location as a meaningful environment and being responsive to the actions and sightlines of participants in a scene can create a vivid and spontaneous sense of the scene's dynamics unfolding. Why? Because we are sharing the consciousness of someone intelligent and intuitive who picks up all the underlying tensions. Instead we often get the consciousness of someone who merely swivels after whatever moves or makes a noise, as dogs do.

SPEED COMPROMISES FOR THE CAMERA

When shooting action sequences, you may need to ask people to slow their movements because movement within a frame can look 20–30% faster than it does in life. Even the best camera operator cannot keep a profile in tight framing if the actor moves too fast. If the actor strays from the chalk line on the floor, the operator may lose focus. Such compromises on behalf of technology raise interesting questions about how much you should forego in the way of performance spontaneity to achieve a visually and choreographically polished result. Much will depend on the expertise of your actors and crew, but even the time of day you shoot may affect where you compromise because tired actors are more likely to feel they are being treated like glove puppets than fresh ones. Politics and expediency do not end here, for the crew can be disappointed or even resentful if you always forego interesting technical challenges on behalf of the cast.

WORK WITHIN YOUR MEANS

Any departure from the simple in cuts and camera movements must be motivated by the needs of the story if the audience is to feel they are sharing someone's consciousness. Good examples of subjectively motivated technique are Oliver's shock-cut view of the convict in the graveyard scene in *Oliver Twist* (1948) and dollying through the noise and confusion of a newsroom in *All the President's Men* (1976).

Such visual devices are dramatically justified, but dollying, craning, and other big-budget visual treatments are not strictly necessary for the low-budget filmmaker because few impressions cannot be achieved in simpler ways. Whole films have been successfully made with a static camera mainly at eye level or without cuts within a scene. Look at the opposite extreme: heavily scored music, rapid editing, and frenetic camera movement. These are mostly used as nervous stimulation to cover for a lack of content. Just roll around the channels on your TV and visit MTV.

Complex camera movement needs to be justified or it's gratuitous. In a film about dance like Emil Ardolino's *Dirty Dancing* (1987), Jeff Jur's camera cannot remain static on the sidelines. It must enter the lovers' dance and accompany them. Can this ever be done inexpensively? Yes. An experienced camera operator, using a wide-angle lens and taking advantage of a moving subject in the foreground that holds the eye, can handhold the camera and dispense with truckloads of shiny hardware. As mentioned, the Steadicam™ counterweighted body camera support can, in experienced hands, produce wonderfully fluid camerawork. See Mike Figgis' *Leaving Las Vegas* (1995) for good examples by DP Declan Quinn, who was first a documentary cameraman.

STUDY THE MASTERS

To know how best to shoot any particular scene, study the way good directors have shot situations analogous to yours. Learn from them, but do not be ruled by them. In Chapter 5, Project 5-2: Editing Analysis, there is a film study project to help you define a director's specific choices and intentions.

CHAPTER 30

BREAKING DOWN THE SCRIPT

Shooting rehearsals on video should have given you a firm sense of the camera coverage required, but final codification with your director of photography (DP) can only be decided in relation to your authorial intentions and the limitations of the medium itself. While simple poverty may preclude dollying or craning shots, freeze frames, special titling, and optical work, this is, after all, just slick packaging and its absence should never debilitate a worthwhile film.

The responsibility for the graphic aspects of filmmaking lie variously with the director, cinematographer, and art director. Steven Katz's *Film Directing Shot by Shot* (Boston: Michael Wiese Productions in association with Focal Press, 1991) does a fine job explaining the staging options for different kinds of scenes. From its more than 350 pages of storyboards and diagrams you learn how useful drawing skills are when you want to plan coverage on paper of a three-dimensional world. Many of the book's techniques depend on dollies, cranes, and take-apart sets that are common in professional filmmaking but beyond the purse of the low-budget group. Even if you can afford this equipment, to operate it adequately and make all the lighting changes that its use may demand will massively slow the production, especially if its operators are learning on the job. This is very wearing on the cast.

Keep in mind that decades of classic cinema were shot with absurdly limited equipment. You will do your best work using the simplest techniques that serve the film's artistic intentions. Resist your crew's desire to experiment with "better" equipment. The over-elaborate staging you accede to (only because you don't want to disappoint your DP) may fail and may kill a scene that would have worked perfectly well had it been kept simple. Fight for simplicity—simple is strong, less is more. For your level of expertise, stay focused on what you can do and what matters.

With your DP, decide, in the light of what camerawork revealed in rehearsal, what coverage is now desirable for each scene.

DIAGNOSTIC QUESTIONS

Use these questions to help you develop a shooting and editing strategy for a scene:

Geography:

- What must the scene show to establish the environment satisfactorily?
- Does this orientation come early, or is it delayed for dramatic reasons?
- What combination of distance and lens will you need to contain the widest angle, and is the location big enough to allow this?
- Will you have enough lighting to shoot the most comprehensive shot?

Movements by Characters:

- At which points do characters move from one point to another and why?
- How will you show it? (Drop back to a wide angle? Move the camera with a character? Show another character's eyeline changing as he or she hears the moving character's footsteps?)
- What axis does the character move along at each stage of his or her movements?

Point of View:

- At each significant moment, whose point of view (POV) are we sharing?
- Whose global POV predominates in the overall story?
- When and why does POV change?
- Does a particular change move toward the subjective or the objective, and why?
- What emotion, thought, or preoccupation might POV convey?
- How does the Storyteller feel about the events in this scene?

Eyelines:

- What are the significant eyelines in the scene? (These motivate what the audience wants to see and therefore motivate camera placement from shot to shot.)
- Where do eyelines change?
- Where should the camera look along an eyeline?

Camera Movement:

- When and why should the camera move?
- What feeling does its movement create?
- At what speed should the movement be? (Movements must be paced appropriately if they are to integrate with other aural or visual rhythms in a scene. Be careful of strobing when panning over repetitive patterns such as railings. See camerawork manual for further information.)

Compositional Relationship:

- At what significant moments must you show relationship? (You might frame a sleeping character supposed to be catching a plane with a clock in the background—more effective than laboriously intercutting the clock—or you might play a whole mother-daughter argument in tight, single shots to emphasize the adversarial, isolated feel of their relationship.)

Isolation:

- Who or what might legitimately be isolated from surroundings? (A misfit boy might frequently be shown alone, while the gang members who try to recruit him always appear as a pack. A phone silently refusing to ring for someone waiting on tenterhooks for a call might also be shown as a single shot. In each case this isolation complements a dominant perception, either of someone within the film or that of the Storyteller.)

Space:

- What is the significance of space between characters? (Space between people is charged and even political. The changing distance between two characters having a conversation is highly indicative of who is gaining control and who is retreating or hiding. Camera position and the choice of lens can alter the audience's perception of space. For instance, a crowded street is often shot with a telescopic lens to compress cars and people into a bobbing sea, while someone reaching imploringly through prison bars might be shot with a wide-angle lens so his or her hand comes across a void and becomes enormous in the foreground.)

PLANNING COVERAGE

Taking into consideration everything mentioned previously, you must now lock down how you want to cover each scene and provide yourself with graphics and reminders so you don't have to rely on your memory while directing. Once a shoot gets under way, sensory overload will turn your memory into a blank.

COVER IMPORTANT ASPECTS IN MORE THAN ONE WAY

Be prepared to cover vital story points or important emotional transitions more than one way so that later you have a choice and can exercise maximum control over the telling moment. For instance, in a family reunion scene where a glass from an old wedding set gets broken by the mother, your beat may be her moment of realization and grief. The incident can, however, be given additional poignancy by shooting reactions on the part of others present. Her son may show anger at her clumsiness, her daughter may be surprised, her husband may be amused because he thinks it is just a minor accident, and her daughter-in-law may be concerned that she cut herself. You would not use all these reactions, but having them allows you later to choose the right inflection as required by the scene's finished state and context.

Covering these reactions allows for a variable richness in defining the moment. It also follows our often-mentioned principle of abundance in which *you generate more than strictly necessary to permit options, and therefore control, later*. This is not about artistic compromise but survival; only foolish optimists take a 2-day water supply to cross a 2-day desert.

THE FLOOR PLAN AND THE STORYBOARD

Draw a floor plan. It will help you consolidate your intentions for blocking and indicate how to use the fewest and most effective camera angles. On it show the characters' movements and the camera angles necessary for the edited version you want. Figure 30–1 is the bracket scene in a script and Figure 30–2 is its floor plan. This diagram, growing out of the blocking developed during rehearsals and

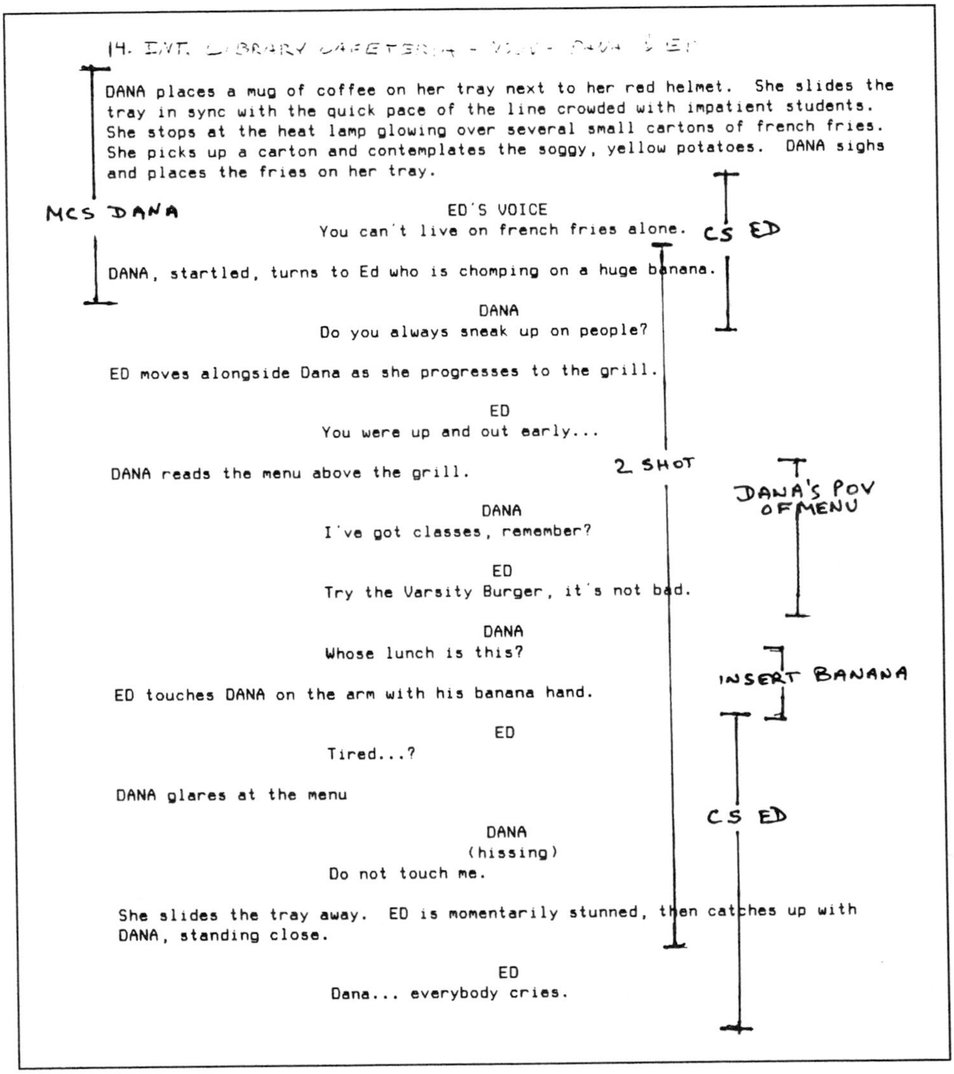
14. INT. LIBRARY CAFETERIA - DAY - DANA & ED

DANA places a mug of coffee on her tray next to her red helmet. She slides the tray in sync with the quick pace of the line crowded with impatient students. She stops at the heat lamp glowing over several small cartons of french fries. She picks up a carton and contemplates the soggy, yellow potatoes. DANA sighs and places the fries on her tray.

MCS DANA

ED'S VOICE
You can't live on french fries alone.

CS ED

DANA, startled, turns to Ed who is chomping on a huge banana.

DANA
Do you always sneak up on people?

ED moves alongside Dana as she progresses to the grill.

ED
You were up and out early...

DANA reads the menu above the grill.

2 SHOT

DANA'S POV OF MENU

DANA
I've got classes, remember?

ED
Try the Varsity Burger, it's not bad.

DANA
Whose lunch is this?

INSERT BANANA

ED touches DANA on the arm with his banana hand.

ED
Tired...?

DANA glares at the menu

CS ED

DANA
(hissing)
Do not touch me.

She slides the tray away. ED is momentarily stunned, then catches up with DANA, standing close.

ED
Dana... everybody cries.

FIGURE 30–1

Script page bracketed with intended shots. Editing options are immediately visible.

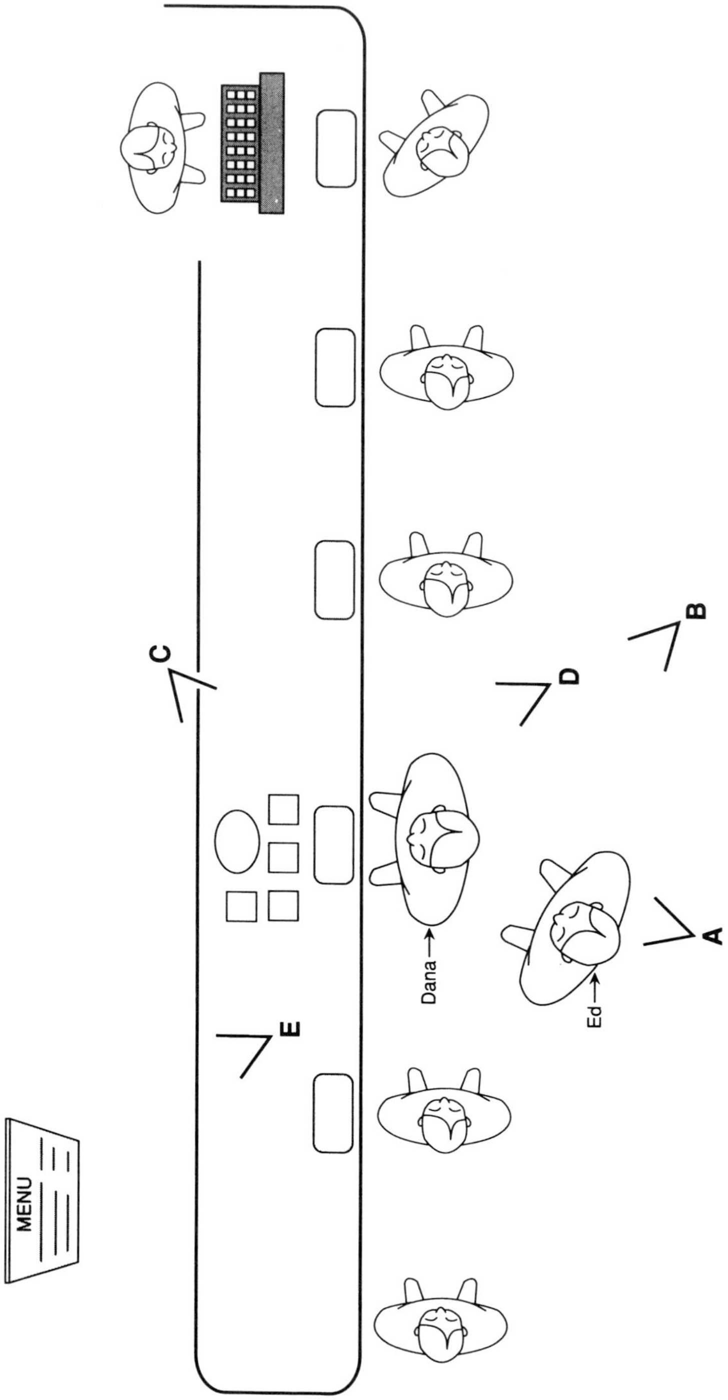

FIGURE 30–2 Floor plan for lunch counter scene scripted in Figure 30–1.

modified by location realities, helps further work out the editing in advance and enables the DP to plan lighting and camera movements.

On a tightly planned production, the art director may make storyboard sketches for each angle, as in Figure 30–3A. These help ensure that the contents of each composition are as interesting and relevant as possible. The suggestions each expert contributes may be so good that the director revises the original conception. As always in a true collaboration, the whole can be greater than the sum of its parts.

Whatever the original intentions, the storyboard plan often goes out the window when you shoot. The particularities of a *lens's* field of view, problems with lighting, the needs of a character's movements, and even the size of the framing can all lead you to recompose the image and block actors quite differently.

SCRIPT BREAKDOWN

Better than a simple list is a graphic representation (as always) to show the intentions and the state of play. A development of the floor plan and bracketed script as described in Chapter 29 will provide you with a thorough and up-to-date version. It works like this:

1. Ground Plan
   a. Make a floor plan of the intended scene showing walls, doors, windows, furniture, etc. and indicating the characters' movements and stopping points, as in Chapter 5, Figure 5–3.
   b. As in Figure 5–3, mark the camera positions, but for clarity designate them A, B, C, etc.

      Position A will be shot first because lighting for the widest or master shot determines all the others. Each tighter shot (positions B, C, etc.) will follow because closer shots usually need individual relighting to match the lighting logic of the master shot.
2. Shooting Script
   a. Bracket each intended shot on the shooting script (see Figure 30–1) using a color to indicate its size. (Cool blue for wide shots, warm yellow for medium shots, and hot red for close ups). Remember to give good overlaps between shots so the editor has a range of options for cutting from one to the next.
   b. Designate each bracket Cam A, Cam B, Cam C, etc. to show where you intend to shoot it from.
   c. Place a brief description of the angle by the head of the bracket to avoid ambiguity (Example: CS hand lighting fire).

Each bracket represents a camera angle with its brief identifying description, as in Figure 30–1. Now the script reveals at a glance how you intend to cover the action and what editing alternatives you have designed. For smooth and seamless editing, *the best place to cut is always on a strong physical movement.* To best understand this, pick a well-made feature film scene like yours and analyze the coverage and cutting points. Remember that you *must* ensure generous overlaps from shot to shot so your editor has a choice of action match cuts.

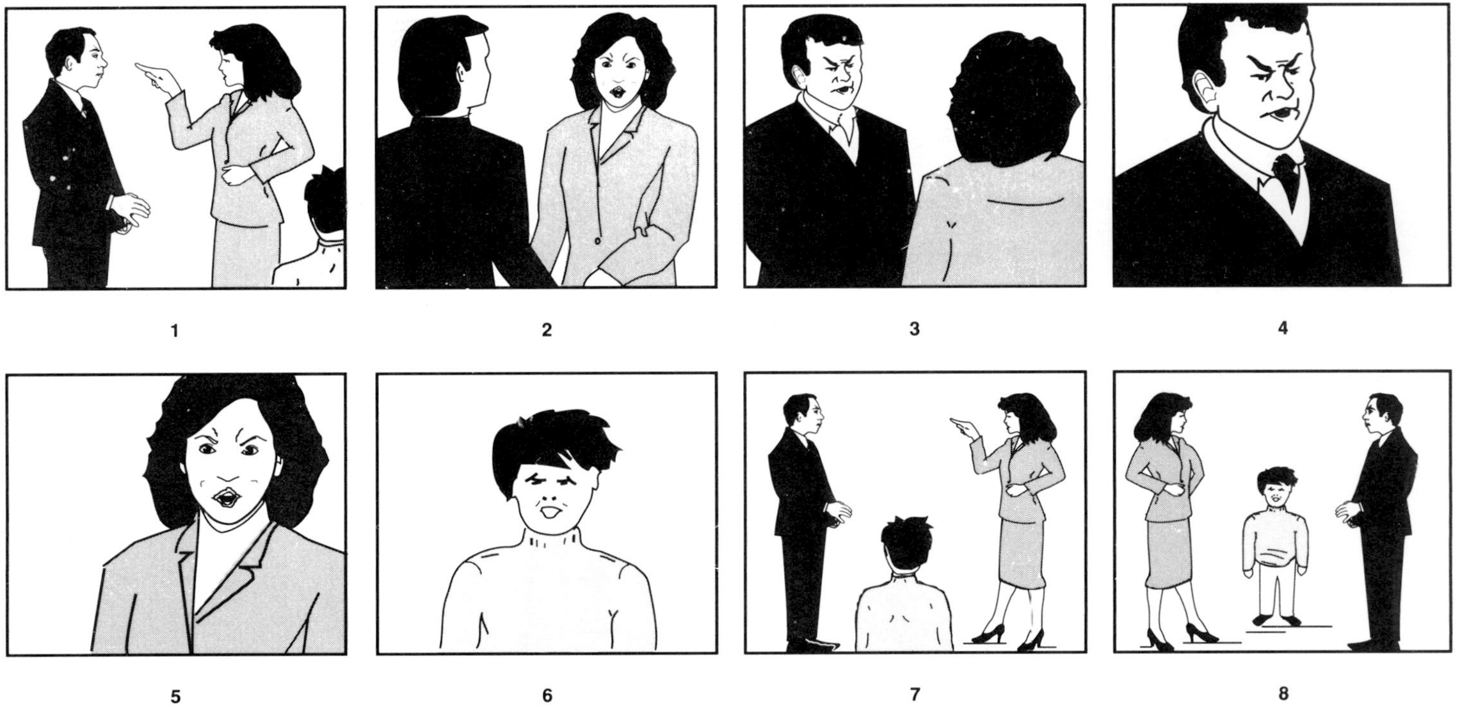

FIGURE 30–3A

Storyboard frames for camera positions 1 through 8. Note that in position 8 the two figures have reversed screen direction because the camera has crossed the major axis line.

CAMERA PLACEMENT

Placing the camera can seem like an industrial decision based on lighting or other technical considerations. But technique must be made to mimic the way human awareness works at an event, or the event will have no soul.

USING LINES OF TENSION

The following are some reminders concerning the camera's relationship to a scene's *axes* or *lines of tension*. These are the invisible lines of strong feeling you would draw between the most important people and objects in a scene. Often they are also *sightlines* and have great dramatic potential (changes of eyeline, for instance), and often they dominate the composition. Lines of tension and sightlines justify particular camera angles and imply the emotional connections (and therefore POVs) associated with particular characters. This is not easy to describe, and you will understand best if you have done the close editing analysis suggested earlier in this book.

SUBJECTIVE AND OBJECTIVE

No matter whose POV your film favors, POV will move. Changes in lines of tension or changes in their intensity are your prime clues. Let's look at the way the consciousness of an onlooker moves around when observing the archetypal scene of two people in conversation.

The concept of there being a Concerned Observer is important. The observation itself is the normal, relatively objective movement of human perception, and we use it as a model for how the camera and editing moves our attention around within a scene. Quite simply, *camerawork and editing together mimic the way any observer's ears, eyes, and psychological focus migrate within an environment,* whether quiet or busy.

Angle and shot changes are motivated by stimuli from the scene, but they also represent a narrative agenda as the Storyteller pursues a line of inquiry. Perception is often shaped noticeably by the predispositions of the Storyteller, once that sensibility has been established. Observation can be by a character within the film or that of a Storyteller from outside, directing our attention. The mood of observation may start relatively detached, and then become involved with the predicaments and personal qualities of the characters, or it can happen in reverse order. Like you or me in any consuming life-situation, a film will "breathe" in and out between these extremes. The difference can be dramatized by returning to the familiar experience of watching a tennis game (see Chapter 4: The Actor and the Acted Upon).

The closer the camera is to a line of tension, the more subjectively involved the audience will feel. When complementary angles are used, the audience is switched rapidly between each protagonist's subjective experience, so the aggregate effect may be to enter the fray without necessarily identifying with one contestant or another. This depends on the balance of editing, as well as, less measurably, the power in each actor's characterization.

We can vary the Observer's relationship to the axes, and vary his or her closeness to what is observed. Close shots are not magnification alone but mimic the psychological *exclusion* of other concurrent events, which may reach us through sound only. Juxtaposing subjects in antithetical relationship can be accomplished either by editing them together or, less obviously, by blocking them together within a single shot.

SIGHTLINES AND LINES OF TENSION

Look at the floor plan for a mother and father argument as observed by the child (see Figure 30–3A). The various psychic connections or possible lines of tension are in fact duplicated by the dotted-in sightlines. The major axis is between the parents, but others exist between each parent and the silent child. Each sightline suggests a camera position. What each camera angle covers is shown in the storyboard sequence (Figure 30–3B). Some angles are close (as in 4, 5, and 6), some in medium two-shot (1, 2, and 3), and there are two master shots—further angles that take in everything (7 and 8). Positions 1, 2, and 3 are all to some degree omniscient because they are an outsider's view of the characters, that is, in pairs and related to each other. Position 7 is even more comprehensive, taking in all three. Positions 4, 5, and 6 are, however, close and subjectively involved, as if viewed by one of the other characters. Position 6 would be useful to show the child's eyeline shifts.

SHOW RELATEDNESS

How are the protagonists to be spatially related? Showing the couple arguing in the same frame but the boy separated in a close-up reinforces his separation from both of them. Relating boy and mother in one frame to father alone in another suggests a different configuration of alliances or antipathies. There could be other factors—using foreground and background, the sides of the frame, different camera heights, and different levels of lighting—any combination of which might predispose the audience toward interpreting the scene in a particular way or from a particular POV. It would be misleading to suggest hard and fast rules here because human judgment is made from a multiplicity of nuances. What matters is the sensibility and rationale by which each shot is composed, lit, and blocked.

THERE ARE NO RULES, ONLY AWARENESS

From the audience perspective, everything on the screen is interactive and interrelated, so there can be few formulae. Compositionally you are always showing the specifics of relationship among subject and object, one object and another, or one person and another and implying the relationship of one idea, principle, or judgment to another. To do this you may also use editing or story construction (parallel storytelling, for instance, where you might intercut a boxing match with a lover's feud). Whatever works does so through suggestion and implied comparison. It is more important to try out an idea and judge from what you see and feel, rather than rely very much on a theory.

AVOID CROSSING THE SCENE AXIS

Because the child in our argument example remains in a fixed position, camera coverage that replicates his vision of his parents must stay to one side of the A

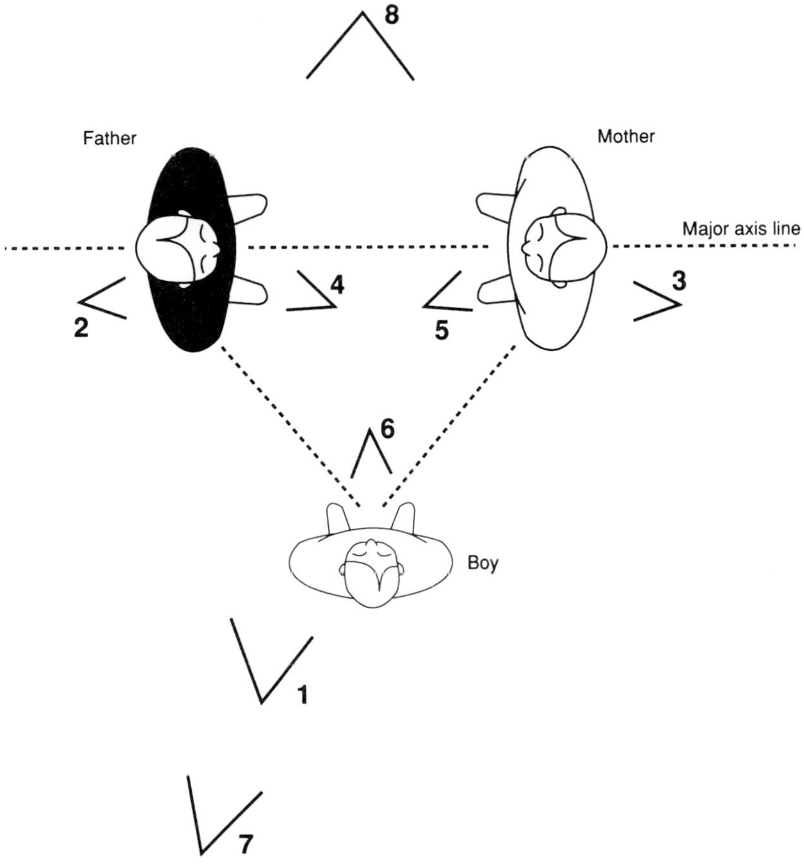

FIGURE 30–3B

Camera positions to cover a child's view of an argument between his parents. Lines of tension are indicated between characters.

to B axis line. If you cross this axis with your camera, as in position 8, your characters begin to look in the wrong screen direction, as you see in the storyboard sequence. In positions 1 through 7, the father always looks screen left to screen right, and the mother right to left. Even in the big close-ups (4 and 5) the character's eyelines maintain the same screen direction. However, in camera position 8 that consistency disappears because the camera has strayed across the scene axis line. Conventionally this is avoided. Try shooting an additional shot after *crossing the line* and intercutting it to see if you really want to break the conventions.

MOVEMENTS THAT LEAD TO REGROUPING MUST BE SHOWN

In scenes where characters move, they usually regroup to face in new screen directions. At the very least this means that early and late reaction shots cannot be interchanged, and the scene cannot easily be restructured in the cutting room if so desired. *Movements that lead to regrouping must be shown onscreen.* Regard them as *reset* transitions that establish new compositional phases of the scene. From a scene design POV, you don't want people milling around but want instead to choreograph movements (and therefore group configurations) strictly for their new importance. Movements should have dramatic significance, and you will want to show them anyway. Plan carefully so the scene will cut together effortlessly on the screen.

PLANNING WHERE TO EDIT

In marking up the script for the scene, you now know what shots you intend to use to cover each part, but you probably feel unsure about how to cut from one angle or one size of shot to another. Here are some guidelines, but remember to leave plenty of overlap between shots so the editor has a choice of cutting place.

EDITING IN MOVEMENT

Plan to *use any pronounced movement in the scene as a convenient cutting point between angles*. These are called *action match cuts* or simply *match cuts*. They are useful as transitions because they take place in movement at a time when the eye is least critical. At the point when the mind decides what is going to happen next, the eye becomes uncritical. The best match cuts are made thus:

> **Outgoing shot:** Initiate just enough of the movement for the audience to recognize what's about to happen.
>
> **Incoming shot:** Complete the bulk of the movement, but on most action add three frames of repeating action to overlap the outgoing shot.

The three or four frames of repeated action on the incoming shot are needed because the eye does not register the first three or four frames of any new image. Make a literal matched action, with no overlap, and the match stutters and fails to look smooth. Try it.

EDITING AS REFRESHMENT

Cutting between different angles can also renew and refresh the spectator's perspective, showing different POVs, and invoking different kinds of experiences. If the angles stay close to the axis, we remain subjectively involved and eventually become desensitized. So for variation, the Storyteller may take us out of the firing line to review the situation from a more detached perspective. In a political meeting this might suggest a stepping away from the intensely personal to take a historical or sociological perspective. This interrupts what has become standard to push us into interpreting from another intellectual or emotional angle. You will, of course, have to foresee this and shoot it.

CONTINGENCY PLANNING

Plan your coverage but ensure against surprises. Foresee weather changes, scheduling difficulties, and though you intend to show only one character onscreen during an intense exchange, shoot both. This allows you abundance—a fallback alternative if your plans are not fulfilled.

CRIB SHEETS

When first directing, work hard to brief yourself by making copious, organized reminder lists on note cards so you forget nothing in the hurly-burly of the set. As fatigue sets in, your memory and imagination will shut down, and those notes (Figure 30–4) will be a lifesaver. Defining the story points you want to make and nailing down what you intend for each sequence means you are directing from a plan instead of waiting to recognize success when it appears.

SCHEDULING THE SHOOT

A glance at the shooting script and the floor plan shows in what order to schedule the shooting. Wide or establishing shots are done first for lighting reasons and because they set the performance levels. Closer shots and over-shoulder shots follow, with reaction shots, inserts, and cutaways done last. If you make changes of approach during the shoot, it may have an impact on scheduling, so make a

```
              Scene 15: TONY RETURNS HOME AFTER 5 YEARS' SILENCE.

Metaphor: Return of the prodigal son

Timing:   2 mins 25 secs

     Tony wants to:  avoid showing the love he feels for his father
                     evade specifics of the past
                     signify apology but evade admissions
                     make his father think he's returned out of duty
                     make contact with his childhood again
                     move his father to affection and thus forgiveness
                     retrieve mother's photo
                     convince Dad he's not a failure
                     ask for forgiveness

     Dad wants to:   keep Tony at an emotional distance
                     deny to himself that he's very moved by the boy's return
                     get him to think he's washed his hands of him
                     let him know the whole family disapproves of him
                     not act in the authoritarian way that alienated the boy
                     not let him know his bedroom has been kept unchanged
                     deny that he used the boy to get at his mother
                     signify that he loves him
                     ask for forgiveness

     Scene must convey that:  Tony has grown in confidence through travel
                              Dad has been ill and sees his own mortality
                              House is still as Mother left it
```

FIGURE 30–4

Example of director's crib notes.

practice of periodically going over the shooting script with the Script Supervisor, DP, and AD to make sure scheduling still reflects the most logical way of organizing the shooting.

KEEPING TRACK

You have the shooting script marked up, and once the shoot is under way, the script supervisor will amend a copy of the shooting script as each setup is completed, checking off what was shot by adding takes and circling those considered best. Bracket lines can be amended or added in purple or some other color so that at any point the director, script supervisor, or DP can see intended and amended coverage at a glance. This can be a lifesaver when shooting departs from the original intentions.

At all times the unit must know unequivocally what it has shot, what it still needs to shoot, and how it will cut together. Unlike lists, which obstinately remain abstract, good graphic representations require no cross-referencing or special knowledge.

During your first projects these records of first intentions and final execution will be valuable when you do post-mortem sessions afterward and compare your planning against the resulting shoot.

CHAPTER 31

BEFORE THE CAMERA ROLLS

Making a dramatic film is an expensive, industrialized process, with stages of manufacture made necessary by the need to work with maximum efficiency. With several well-respected films under his belt, such as *Leaving Las Vegas* (1995), *Miss Julie* (2000), *Timecode* (2000), and *Hotel* (2001), Mike Figgis has greeted the smaller, digital filmmaking process enthusiastically:

> The further that I went into the digital world the more intrigued I became with the possibilities of this new and unexplored technology. What started out as a marriage of convenience turned into a love affair.
>
> My dissatisfaction with the mainstream cinema scene stems from a deep frustration with the stranglehold that technology has in the 35 mm, studio-based film business.
>
> Visit any set and you can observe the bullshit at first hand.
>
> Observe the reverence with which the camera is treated. The iconic status of the crane and the Steadicam; the vast armada of trucks and motor homes; the platoons of young men and women carrying clip boards and wearing status clothing with walkie talkies and hi-tech communication devices; the sense of self importance and Godliness that seems to permeate everyone involved with the process of pretence and fabrication; the deadly trios of execs and agents feeding their faces at the food table whilst talking on their mobiles to other execs on other films at other food tables.
>
> One year later the results of this "holy" labour can be seen in a multiplex anywhere in the world. Another Hollywood film about nothing in particular.
>
> *Unpublished Interview with Mike Figgis at the Dramatic Institute, Sweden (courtesy of Göran Gunér)*

No system or procedure is holy, and yours should be firmly adjusted to the needs and size of your production. Planning how things will be done and by whom has everything to do with how much you shoot per day and whether you come in on budget and within the schedule.

RIGGING THE STAGE

Although you are almost certainly shooting in real locations instead of constructing sets on a stage, we will use the conventional terminology for simplicity. The first shot of any scene will be the wide, establishing, or *master shot*, because:

- Wide shots take most light, and if this is in short supply you want to use your light wisely.
- Closer shots must match the wide shot for lighting and continuity.
- You want to work out blocking problems for the whole first and the parts later.
- All continuity matches must go back to the master shot, which is why it's often called the *establishing shot.*

Rigging the stage therefore involves placing lighting instruments and adjusting furniture and objects for the widest imaginable shot that will contain the expected action. Usually this involves deciding a general direction for the camera and hiding lighting stands and cables out of shot so there is an unobstructed field of view. Often furniture will be moved away from walls, so that anyone using a couch or chair doesn't immediately cast a shadow. By placing people away from reflective surfaces and setting lamps high, shadows are thrown down behind characters and usually out of sight. Because films are constructed from fragments of action, and walls tend to be bland planes, the audience will not notice any unnaturalness in the placing of characters in their surroundings. This is called *cheating* distances, because it doesn't register on film, and you expect to get away with it.

This is also when the sound crew sets up their equipment, in view of the set but out of the camera's field of view.

FIRST SETUP AND LINEUP

After generally rigging up lighting, placing props and furniture, and anticipating the action, the camera crew now asks for the precise setup from the director, who will discuss with the director of photography (DP) what is and isn't in shot and point out what the characters are going to do. The camera is now set in place and the operator can frame what's expected. The actors will probably be asked to do a *walk-through* so the operator can see general framings and report difficulties or make requests.

BLOCKING AND FIRST REHEARSAL

Now the actors speak their lines and move in stages, under the director's instruction, to the points where they will be standing or sitting through the scene. The

DP and operator decide framing and lighting—in particular how to handle the key and fill lighting and what shadows will be cast that indicate the intended light source. This might be a table lamp, a window or skylight, or a candle carried by one of the characters. At this stage the crew is focused on getting the environment ready for a performance, not on any aspect of the performance itself. The sound crew takes a close interest in where the lights are going to be, which direction the characters face as they speak, and thus how they will cover the scene from the sound point of view. They may ask for compromises if sound coverage presents difficulties.

PLACING MARKS

Where a character stops to say something and where they next move and stop will be marked on the floor with tape by the camera assistant, who must follow focus and to whom these distances represent focus points. If the camera has a professional lens, the assistant will put tape on the focus ring and mark on it the salient points of the action denoted by the floor marks, so the camera will be in sharp focus at each important moment. The less light there is on the set, the less the depth of field, so it's important that the actor hits the mark and the camera assistant keeps the lens in focus.

REHEARSAL

The director, cast, and script supervisor now leave the set to rehearse elsewhere and do last-minute work on the scene. If an actor is missing, the script supervisor will read his or her lines or provide action cues so the scene can be worked over. This is called *running lines*. Similarly, for reaction shots, the script supervisor will read whatever lines the character is reacting to, unless the other actor is present. Some directors make it a policy to have all cast present for such scenes.

LIGHTING WITH STAND-INS

Lighting can be a long, slow business, especially if there are two or more characters with elaborate movement paths. This may require multiple key lights and a great deal of careful planning. Any practicals (lights meant to be seen in shot) must be adjusted either in wattage or with scrim or neutral density filter inside the shade so they render as the right intensity and color.

To see the effect of their work, the DP and crew will use stand-ins who move as directed so the DP can see the lighting's effect at each stage of the scene. In a small crew, stand-ins may be the least-busy crewmembers chosen for approximate height and bulk. The first shots of the production always seem to take an eternity to line up, and the AD should be on hand to supply some pressure and report as soon as the set is ready.

FIRST WALK-THROUGH

Actors now take the place of stand-ins and are brought up to speed with any revisions in the path of the action or the marks they must hit. They are first walked through, both for their benefit and for that of the DP and operator. If all is well, they get into their costumes. Their hair and make-up, first attended to in the morning, probably need touching up by make-up artists and hairdressers.

DRESS REHEARSAL

Next comes a *dry run,* which is a full rehearsal in costume and make-up but without running any film through the camera. The cast will do this at low intensity, as they want to conserve their energy and focus until the camera is running. This part of the process helps them internalize what they must think and do to make their lines and action coincide with the precise needs of the camera, its movements, and attendant lighting. At this time, the sound crew are covering sound and rehearsing what they must do to get the best sound without casting shadows or making any noise. If wireless mikes are to be used, they are running at this stage. The script supervisor will take a timing of this scene as a benchmark for other shots to follow.

Everything should now be in order, and everyone is ready to *roll camera.*

CHAPTER 32

ROLL CAMERA

As the time comes to roll camera, the script supervisor makes a last check to see that characters are correctly costumed. The right props must be on the set and at hand, and nothing can be forgotten or misplaced.

The AD's task is to marshal everyone into their starting positions, ensure that doors and windows are closed, and get silence on the set, ready for action. There is a last hair and make-up check, and the director of photography (DP) checks that all lights are switched on. If you are using a film camera, the assistant cinematographer (AC) has checked the film gate for debris, something that must be done regularly.

Distances have been measured out and the focus puller is ready to adjust the lens in perfect synchronization with the actors' movements, all according to a marked piece of tape on the lens focus ring. With 35 mm this becomes vital because the depth of field is selective and focus is critical for viewing on a large screen.

The script supervisor confers with the AC concerning the next slate number, which we will assume is Scene 62 Take 1, and she takes her position next to the camera. Correctly slating every shot is the key to knowing what you have covered and being able to organize it afterward in the cutting room. This information goes into the camera, sound, and continuity logs, which become sources of vital information. So vital, in fact, that we must digress for a moment to establish how marking systems work.

SHOT AND SCENE IDENTIFICATION

Your crew must keep logs of important information when you shoot. These serve the same end for both videotape and film, but record keeping and continuity observation are more stringent for film because it allows no instant replay.

CLAPPER BOARD

There are many fancy, automatic film-marking systems, such as the Smart Slate, but the exquisitely low-tech clapper board, with only a piece of chalk and a hinge to go wrong, is my favorite. The clapper-board ritual has three main functions:

- Visually, the slate identifies the shot number and the production for the film laboratory.
- Aurally, the operator's announcement identifies the track for sound transfer personnel.
- When sound and picture are processed separately and must be synchronized, the closing bar provides an exact picture frame against which to align the bang in the recorded track.

When video recording is single-system (sound and picture on the one piece of tape), sync is not an issue. No clapper board is needed unless you shoot double-system sound (film or video picture and sound recorded separately on a Nagra or DAT machine). For either film or video double-system productions, the clapper board is essential to precision sync.

If you shoot single-system video, you will still need a shot-numbering system to identify setup and take numbers against the script. Then, using high-speed scan and *timecode* (a unique time signature for every frame) recorded in a log, a chosen section can be rapidly located for viewing on the set. This is invaluable on location when time spent reviewing tape is often stolen from much-needed rest.

Clapper or numbering boards carry not only scene and take numbers but a quantity of vital information for the image quality-control experts in film labs or video online studios. These include a gray scale, white and black as a contrast reference, and a standard color chart. In video, a color chart called *color bars* is usually generated electronically by the camera and recorded for reference purposes at the head of every camera original tape.

To summarize:

- For film production, use a clapper board with verbal announcement before filming.
- For single-system (camcorder) video production, use a number board for the camera with announcement only.
- For double-system video or film, treat the operation like film and use an announcement and a clapper board.

SETUP AND TAKE NUMBERS

The *setup* is the apparent position of the camera, which is usually altered by physically moving the camera to a new position. However, a simple lens change also counts as a new setup. There are two philosophies of numbering.

Method 1: The *Scene/Setup/Take* system is favored in the Hollywood fiction film system. Numbering is based on the script scene number. For example: Scene 104A, shot 16, take 3. Translated this means script scene 104A, setup 16, attempt number 3. Hollywood makes big, highly supervised productions, and needs lengthy factory part numbers. For the small, flexible production, this is unnecessary. The more elaborate a system is, the more susceptible it is to error and to breakdown when people get tired or if you depart from the script. Also, by taking longer to announce, it wastes precious filmstock.

Method 2: The *Cumulative Setup/Take* system is used in both documentaries and features in Europe. Shooting simply begins at slate 1 and each setup gets the next number. For example: 142 take 2. This system is preferred for the over-stretched small crew because it requires no liaison to coordinate numbers with the script, and no adaptation when the inevitable script departures come up. The disadvantage is that one more step is necessary for the script supervisor. Every setup number must be recorded against a scene in the master script or kept in a database.

SHOOTING LOGS

A film shoot requires various logs:

A *camera log* (Figure 32–1) kept by the assistant cinematographer (AC) recording each film magazine's contents by slate, take, and footages. Each magazine gets a new camera roll number. This information comes into play during processing and later in editing. A day-for-night scene, for example, would be shot using a blue filter to give it a moonlit look, but if the lab lacked the relevant documentation, it might easily treat the filtering as an error needing color correction in the workprint.

A *sound log* (Figure 32–2) kept by the film sound recordist records slate and take numbers and whether each track is sync or *wild* (non sync voice or effects recording). The latter information is important to whomever does the transfer from DAT or 1/4″ master tape because there may be no pilot tone (electronic sync reference signal).

DOUBLE-SYSTEM RECORDING

Whenever sound is recorded by a mechanically and electrically independent recorder, the film camera rolls and video cassettes do not stay in numerical step with their sound equivalent master roll. This is because stock durations are often different, or because wild track, sound effects, or atmosphere recordings have been added to the sound master rolls as the production progresses, and now there is simply more sound shot than picture.

FILM

Separate sound and camera logs are a necessity as component parts of film dailies travel to their destination in the cutting room by different routes (Figure 32–3).

Film, cutting film: The film laboratory processes the negative and strikes a workprint, which they send to the editor. Meanwhile the 1/4″ magnetic master tape or DAT cassette goes separately to a sound transfer suite, where a copy is made onto sprocketed magnetic stock. This, too, is sent to the editor. Sound and picture are thus reunited for the first time under the editor's hand.

FILM CAMERA LOG Production Title____________________________ Page______

Operator________________ Camera #_____________ Magazine #_____ Cam. Roll #____

Location_______________________ Film Type ________________ Date ___/___/______

Setup	Take	Comments	Footage

Process Normal Yes/ No:____________________________ Total Shot

Notes:

Cam. Assistant:

FIGURE 32–1

Camera log for film production.

SOUND RECORDER LOG Production Title__________ Page______

Mike Op. __________ Recorder_#__________ Tape Type__________ Roll #______

Location__________ Date ___/___/______

Setup	Take	Comments	Mike(s)	Sync?

Notes:

Recordist:

FIGURE 32–2

Sound recorder log for film or video double-system production.

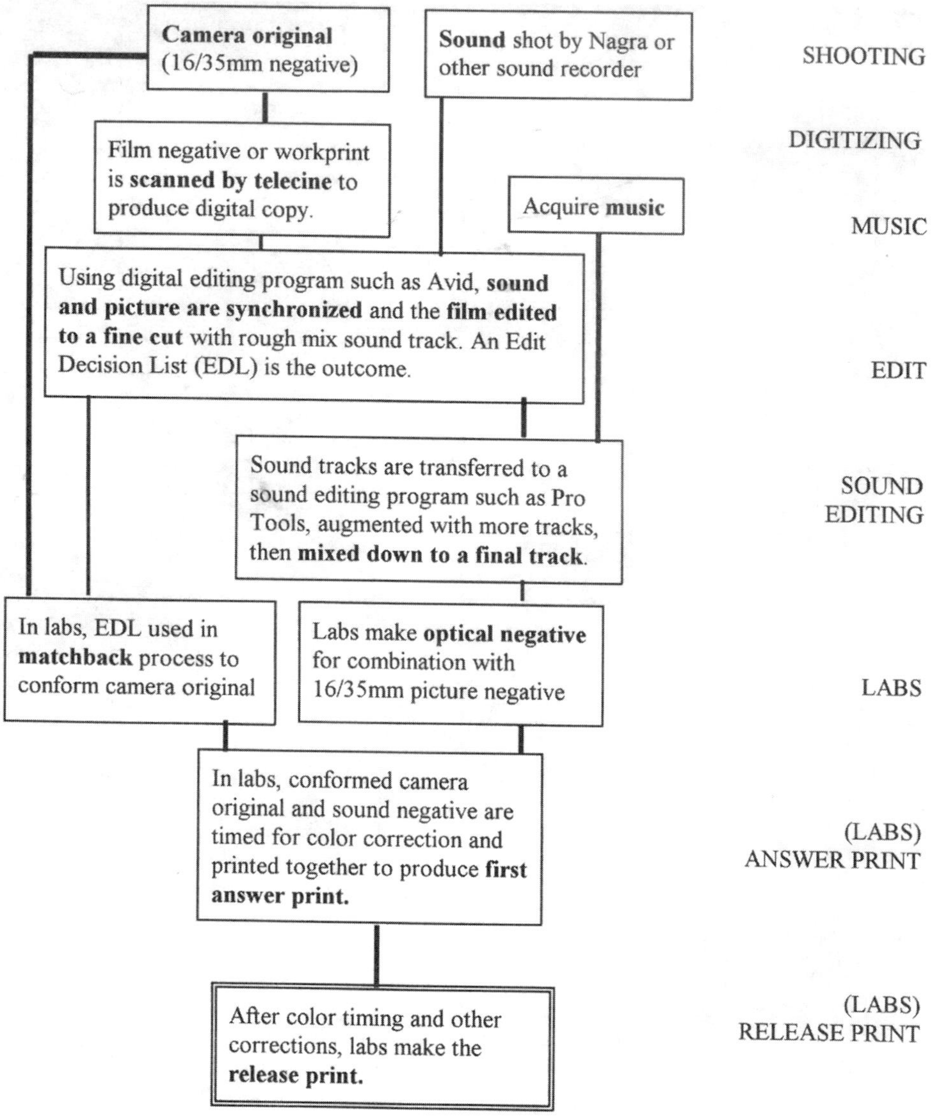

FIGURE 32–3

Flow chart for a production shot on film (double-system).

Film, cutting digitally: For television, the film negative is run through a telecine machine and sound synchronized by the lab to produce a cassette of sync sound takes, which the editor then digitizes into the editing system. Feature films, fearful of any undue negative handling, strike a workprint from the negative, and this is digitized in the labs and sound synchronized. The editor works from digitized cassettes as in the television method.

VIDEO

Single-system: When shooting single-system with a camcorder, logs (Figure 32–4) can be simpler because sound and picture are usually recorded side by side and on the same cassette (Figure 32–5). The AC simply keeps a master log by timecode numbers and makes a record of slate, take, and camera setup information. The recorded cassette, containing both sound and action, goes to the cutting room for digitizing.

Double-system: Sometimes when using video, sound is recorded for quality reasons "double-system" on a separate recorder (see Figure 32–5) as in a film shoot. The sound is synchronized to the picture by the cutting room assistant after the two have been digitized for editing.

LOGS IN ACTION

Logs are going to help the right material go to the right place. The camera log will inform the labs what to expect as they process and print the workprint from the camera original. If a scene looks very blue, they won't try to color-correct the workprint because the camera log says in block capitals: DAY FOR NIGHT. The sound log similarly acts as an inventory of what the sound transcription service, and later the editor, can expect. Much time is saved when syncing up dailies if you know, for instance, that the rest of a cassette contains only wild tracks of trains shunting.

Another less obvious function of logs is to record (by serial number) which piece of equipment made which recording. Should a strange hum appear in the sound or scratching turn up on a film negative, the offending machine must be quickly identifiable so it can be withdrawn for examination.

THE COUNTDOWN TO SHOOTING

The director, satisfied that all is ready for a take, nods to the AD and so begins an unvarying ritual designed to get everything rolling:

AD (*loud voice*): "OK, quiet everybody, we're about to roll."

Silence descends. The clapper operator takes position holding the clapper board or clap-sticks in front of the first actor, at a height where it is clearly visible. On close shots, the operator will sometimes direct its placement to ensure that the all-important number and clapper bar are in shot.

AD: "Roll sound."

The sound mixer turns on the recorder and waits a few moments until able to report that its mechanism has stabilized.

Sound Mixer: "Speed."

The camera operator now turns on the camera, which comes up to speed almost instantaneously.

Camera Operator: "Mark it."

Camera Assistant: "Scene 62 take 1"

VIDEO LOG Production Title__________ Page____

Cam. Operator__________ Camera__________ Date__/__/__

Location__________ Roll # ____

Counter reading	Scene # and take	Description	Remarks

Notes:

Signed:

FIGURE 32–4

Log for video production.

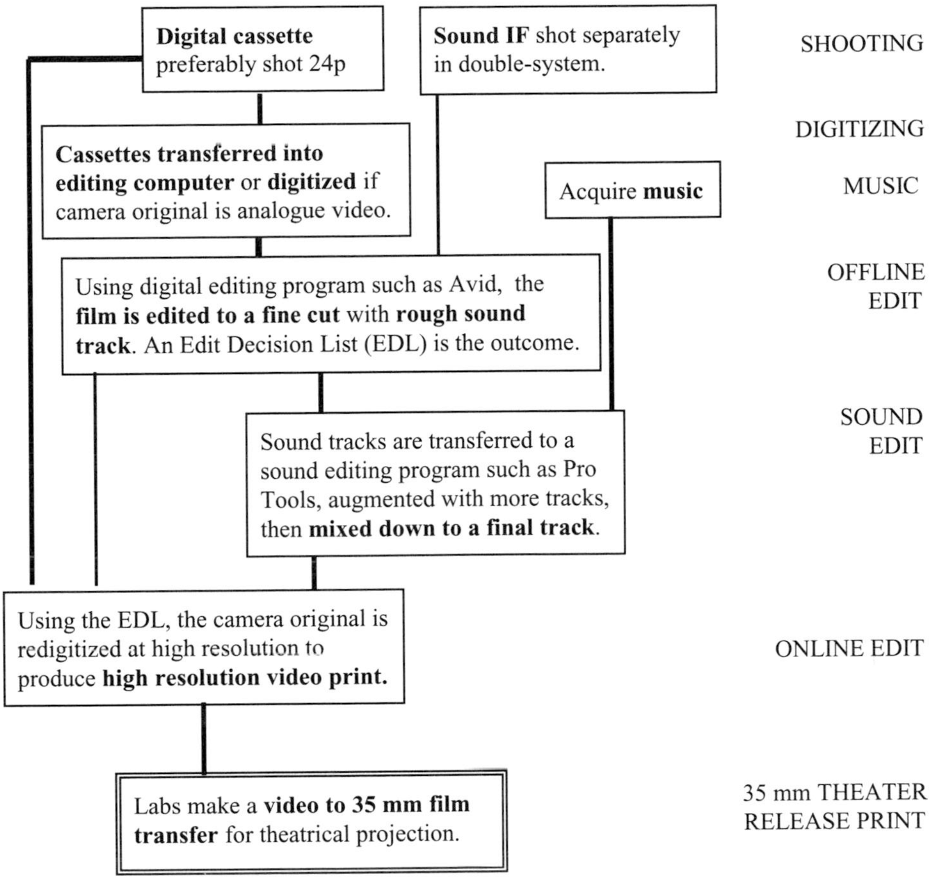

FIGURE 32–5

Flow chart for a production shot on digital video, with single- or double-system sound, resulting in a 35 mm release print for theatrical exhibition.

BANG—*the clapper closes, and the camera operator scuttles out of shot and into position next to the camera.*

Camera Operator: "Rolling."

Director: "Action."

The magic word *action* can be said in a variety of ways, depending on what you want to convey: excitement, mystery, surprise, dread, routine. It's the director's last prod, and as the scene begins, the script supervisor turns on the stopwatch.

If during the scene a car horn is supposed to sound from Johnnie waiting in the road, the script supervisor will call out "Beep, beep" at the right place, and a character will respond with "Aha, there's Johnnie. I gotta go." Any other scripted cues, such as a voice calling from the alley below, or a plane going overhead, will be cued in the same way.

CREW ETIQUETTE

During the scene, crew stand as still as possible and stay out of the actors' eye-lines, so as not to distract them. If the film is a comedy, they remain silent and expressionless, even on the funniest line. It is vital not to behave like an audience, for that would initiate theatrical rather than cinematic performances. In any case, every member of the crew has something to monitor:

- **Camera operator** is watching through the camera viewfinder for focus, composition, framing, movements, and whether the mike is dangling into shot. Film cameras have an oversized viewfinder so the operator sees something encroaching on the frame before it enters the filmed area.
- **Director of photography** is watching the lighting as the actors move from area to area.
- **Script supervisor** is watching to see how each physical movement is accomplished in this take and listening for any variations from the scripted dialogue.
- **Director** is watching the scene for its emotional truth and intensity. What is being expressed? Is the scene focused? Does it deliver what it's meant to deliver?
- **Sound recordist** is listening to dialogue quality, background, any sound intrusions, and whether the voices are on axis and clear of any footsteps or body movements.
- **Assistant director** is watching to see if actors hit their marks and listening that all is quiet on the set.
- **Make-up and hairdressers** are watching to see if their work is wilting under the lights.
- **Electricians** are watching to see that all lights stay on.
- **Grips** are watching to see that the rigging they have done is remaining firm, lights are staying up, and scenery is firmly anchored.

The scene proceeds until the director calls "Cut."

STARTING WITHOUT A CLAPPER

Sometimes when the clapper board could not get into shot, or when you are shooting spontaneous material in the street and not wanting to alert everyone that the camera is rolling, the director will simply signal to start the camera and sound recorder rolling. After the action is complete, the clapper board, (also called *clap-sticks*) is brought in by the AC, but upside down. The AC calls out the scene number and says "Board on end" or "End clap-sticks," then claps the bar, after which the director calls "Cut." In the cutting room the person syncing the material will have a note in the continuity sheets warning of the end-clapped material, which will have to be end-synced, then wound back to the beginning.

WHO CAN CALL "CUT"

There are one or two situations in which someone other than the director calls "Cut." The camera operator may see a hopeless framing mistake or see that an actor went wide of the mark and veered out of frame. The sound mixer may for some reason be getting unusable sound. Either may call "Cut" if their right to do so has been established with the director. The idea is to save the actors' energies and not put them through a wasted performance. A stunt person or the stunt person's supervisor, seeing a situation of danger or a failure about to unfold, may also call for the take to end. Very occasionally an actor may call "Cut," but it depends on the circumstances. An actor doing something difficult and stressful like lifting a barrel would be allowed to abort the take. But directors usually don't want the cast deciding when their work is not useable. A big-name actor might be accorded that privilege, especially if the director is of lesser status. But ordinary mortals are expected to keep the scene going until released by the director. Even though an actor flubs a line, the director may know that this part of the scene is to be covered in another shot, and won't care about a momentary glitch.

PICKUP SHOTS

It sometimes happens that a take is excellent except for a couple of lines or a movement. Then and there, the director will reshoot that section, sometimes by calling out "Go back and do the section about the storm again" without even stopping the camera. The script supervisor will call a beginning cue, and the scene will resume until the director calls "Cut." At that point, director and script supervisor will confer and decide that they must shoot some cutaway shots of listeners so the new section can be edited in. These shots will get appropriate numbers, and their function will be noted in the continuity sheets. Another way to cover the inserted section would be to move the camera and shoot it from another character's angle, and in editing bounce the section off a close shot of this listening character, so it becomes her point of view.

PRINT THAT

In film shooting, the director chooses whether to print the take just shot or go for another take. If the take was good, the director will say "Cut . . . print that one" and will go on, if it's needed, to say what was good about that take. If the director wants another take, it will be: "Cut, let's go for another take." Then the director will have a quiet word with the actors saying what he is looking for, and from whom. Particularly if the scene is longish, there may be two or three takes printed up, with accompanying notes such as "Use the first part of Take 4 and the last part of either Take 6 or 7." With video there is less need to make these choices because everything gets dumped into the editing computer.

COMPLEMENTARY SHOTS

Once the master shot has been achieved, the camera will be moved in to get medium shots, close shots, over-shoulder shots, and so on. Each will be a new setup, and each will get a new number, with each attempt being slated as a new take. Different camera positions may use different lenses or different camera heights to alter the sense of space and perspective. The backgrounds may be cheated to contain enough of something significant in the frame as a juxtapositional comment. Lighting will also be cheated because lighting for a wide shot only sets the general mood of the scene, and individual closer shots must often be adjusted for contrast or to achieve a better effect. The key lighting must still come from the same direction, and the changes cannot so change the shot that it stands apart from the master shot, but within these parameters, there is still plenty of latitude for poetic license.

KEEPING TRACK OF WHAT'S SHOT

The script supervisor has to monitor how each segment of script is being covered, especially when the director departs from the original plan for some reason. In such a case the two of them must confer to make sure there are no ghastly omissions. Usually the script supervisor marks the script in light pencil, then goes over it with a heavy line for everything successfully covered. When changes happen, the light original can be left, and a heavier alternative marked in for the new approach.

BLOCKING CHANGES

Sometimes the blocking is changed. Be very careful that the footage doesn't *cross the line*, which means the camera has somehow crossed the scene axis. This will cause headaches in the cutting room and a scene that looks awful once it is cut. Here's where a ground plan is useful. You can check, when the camera is moved to such and such a position, to see who is supposed to be looking in which direction. Everyone must logically look either camera left or camera right, however slightly, if the scene is to cut together correctly.

DIRECTOR, SCRIPT SUPERVISOR, AND CONTINUITY REPORTS

Directing means being wholly occupied with the actors every moment of the shoot. You have planned your coverage in advance with your script supervisor, and now it would be counterproductive to waste precious energy ensuring that the coverage is being fulfilled. That is your script supervisor's job. He or she must see that the editor is supplied with adequate coverage and ensure that matching shots really match. Which hand a character used to open the suitcase, how long his cigarette was when he stood by the window, and which direction he turned as he left for the door must be consistent in adjacent shots.

In the event of changes or economies, the script supervisor needs to know how the revised footage could be edited together and must at all times guard against omissions.

CONTINUITY SHEETS

For a feature shoot, the script supervisor produces reports that are often masterpieces of observation. Each setup has its own sheet to record the following:

- Production, personnel, and date
- Slate and take number
- Script scene number
- Camera and lens in use

- Action and dialogue variations
- Successes and flaws for each take
- Which takes are to be printed by the lab (big-budget films are able to print selectively)
- Any special instructions from director or script supervisor to the editor

Not surprisingly, a script supervisor needs fierce powers of concentration and the ability to do huge amounts of typing in spare moments. When everyone else has gone to sleep during a location shoot, you will hear the script supervisor still at work. Because you cannot replay an exposed film as you can a recorded video tape, the script supervisor's work is vital in feature filmmaking. Its quality later determines how readily the cutting rooms can locate a given shot in their filing system and how well it fits together with its complementaries.

IT'S A WRAP

When all the materials for a scene have been shot, and everyone is satisfied that the editor has everything needed, it comes time to strike (dismantle) the set. But wait, the sound department must first shoot a presence track. Everyone stand still! In eerie silence everyone stands like statues, uncomfortably aware of their own breathing and of the little sounds in the room. "Cut," calls the sound recordist. "It's a wrap!" yells the AD. Pandemonium breaks out as everyone moves to start their winding-up responsibilities:

- Electricians lower all the lights and roll up cables while hot lighting fixtures cool down.
- Grips strike the set and collect up their clamps, stands, and boxes.
- Props collect all the properties and stow them for safety, marking them off a list.
- Camera people take the camera off its support, start dismantling it, and stow gear in its many travel boxes.
- Stuff accumulates on the floor in family groups: all the C-clamps here, all the sandbags there, all the cables in a grubby pile.
- Sound equipment goes in its boxes.
- Actors clean off make-up and change into their street clothes.
- Wardrobe collects costumes for any cleaning and repairs.
- The AD hands out call sheets for the next day, plus some script revision sheets photocopied on different colored paper. Several people groan at the sight of changes still coming in.
- The director is in close conversation with the actors, then goes around the unit thanking everyone for a good day's work.
- The AD checks that there is no damage to the location and that everything is left clean and tidy.
- The *gopher* (the runner or "go for this, go for that" person) unexpectedly produces coffee and sandwiches for all, and a low sigh of delight goes up.

Doors open and close as weary people schlep the equipment out to the transport, munching as they go. The camera assistant is checking the lens and camera gate or carefully labeling cassettes or film cans while the recordist and continuity supervisor are finishing reports. The latter is filling out a daily progress report for the production manager, who will be anxious to know how many pages of script were covered and how much shooting stock got consumed. Engines start up and the circus moves on its way, to reconvene the next day at the next location.

CHAPTER 33

LOCATION SOUND

Sound recording is the neglected stepsister in low-budget or film school filmmaking. The most common oversight is to record without monitoring through headphones, trusting that all is well. Machines have nasty little black souls all their own, so all is frequently *not* well and you later find there are crackles, dropouts, or no sound at all. Thus, the reward for misplaced optimism . . .

Another costly assumption is that location sound can be skimped because it can be fixed in the cutting room. Though true to a degree, this is damaging when practiced wholesale, for recreating dialogue later in a *looping* or *automatic dialogue replacement* session is damaging to your drama and expensive in time and effort. See following sections for explanations.

Any low-budget film's effectiveness depends absolutely on getting good original dialogue tracks. This takes preparation, skill, and the will to accommodate the needs of those responsible for sound recording. In a fine article full of information and examples from a raft of feature films, sound designer Randy Thom contends that most directors have no sound design consciousness at all. Even the professional film industry relegates location sound recording to lowest priority. You can find his article through at *www.filmsound.org*, an excellent Web site for all sound information.

Following are some basic guidelines for successful sound coverage.

MONITOR ALL RECORDED SOUND

All sound that is recorded must be carefully monitored through high-quality headphones that enclose the ears and isolate the user from external sound. No exceptions, ever.

SOUND THEORY

How sound behaves in different environments is logical enough to anyone who has ever watched kids throwing balls in a small courtyard. Of course, there's a lot more to sound theory than how sound bounces, and you should read up on it. But even a small amount of knowledge will help you choose film sound environments wisely and enable you to understand when your sound recordist explains a problem. Again, *www.filmsound.org/* is a good source for all sound information.

The most potent aspects of sound for film lie not just in faithful recording techniques but also in psychoacoustics, which describe the perception of sound by an audience. The doyen in this area is the French sound expert Michel Chion, whose *Audio-Vision–Sound on Screen* (New York: Columbia University Press, 1994) explains the ideas he has been developing over the last 30 years. Be warned that his ideas are not simple and require learning a specialized vocabulary.

SOUND EXPERTS SHOULD SCOUT EACH LOCATION

During preproduction, when you choose locations, have your sound crew scout the location along with the director of photography (DP) and director. On seeing where you want to shoot, the sound department may argue persuasively for an alternative, and you should take what they tell you seriously.

The first thing a sound specialist does in a new location is to clap her hands, once and loudly. She is listening to what follows the *attack* of the hand clap. Ideally it is an equally rapid *decay*. If the room is *live* (reverberant) there is an appreciable comet's tail of sound being reflected and thrown around the room. This concerns her greatly. The composition of surfaces in a location can make the difference between sound that is usefully *dry* or non-reverberant, and that which is unworkably live and reverberant. Reverberation is multiplication of the original or *source* sound by hard, sound-reflective surfaces. A resonant room is one that has a "note" within the range of speech to which the room resonates. You'll know this phenomenon from singing in your shower, and finding one note (or frequency) at which the room joins in, augmenting your song with a resonance of its own. Resonances are bad news to sound recordists.

If the room is small, they may recommend that you mock up the desired small space within a larger one, to avoid a boxy acoustical quality. How do you know how bad this will be in advance? The best proof is to audition dubious sound locations by shooting tests. Record some sample dialogue from representative microphone positions, then edit the results together. In no time at all, you have the measure of your problem. The sound crew will be concerned with:

- Reflectivity of ceiling, walls, and floor (drapes and carpet greatly reduce this)
- Whether there are, or can be, soft furniture or irregular walls to break up the unwanted movement of sound within the space
- Alignment of surfaces likely to cause standing waves (sound bouncing to and fro between opposing surfaces, augmenting and cross-modulating the source sound)
- Whether the room has intrusive resonances (this happens mainly in rooms with a lot of concrete or tile surfaces)

- Whether actors can walk and cameras can be dollied without the floorboards letting out tortured squeaks
- Ambient sound and sound penetrating from the outside

Typical intermittent sound intrusions from the surroundings occur when you are:

- In an airport flight path.
- Near an expressway, railroad, or subway.
- Near refrigeration, air conditioning, or other sound-generating equipment that runs intermittently and will cause problems unless you can turn it off while shooting.
- Near construction sites. You scouted the location on a weekend, not realizing that come Monday morning, a pile driver and four jackhammers greet the dawn. You have no hope of stopping them.

Dialogue shooting must usually be done with all doors and windows closed. In summer this can be trying, but part of checking a location is to ensure that you can get electric power cables in under the doors so they can be completely closed during takes.

UNWANTED LOCATION AMBIENCE

Locations come with all sorts of problems, with wind and other ambient noise at exterior locations being prominent. Beautiful autumn leaves may introduce the sound of swishing cornflakes as actors walk and talk. Sound from an expressway may be minimal at 2 in the afternoon and rise to a dull roar by 5 o'clock when the rush hour begins. Overhead wires turn into aeolian harps, dogs bark maniacally, garbage trucks mysteriously convene for bottle crushing competitions, and somebody starts practicing scales on the trumpet. Some of these sonic disasters the astute location spotter can anticipate, some not. During the scout you look for clues to Armageddon, then take your chances.

Urban locations spring most of the cruel surprises on the sound recordist, yet it's usually sound that makes a film work dramatically. There is no substitute for experience and a good complement of sound gear to create optional ways of covering the situation.

SOUND EQUIPMENT

As with all equipment, never leave the checkout point without putting all of it together and testing that absolutely everything functions as it should. Make sure you have spare batteries for everything that depends on a battery and extra cables, which have a habit of breaking down where the cable enters the plug body. Carry basic repair equipment, too: screwdrivers, socket sets, pliers, wire, solder and soldering iron, and a test meter for continuity and other testing.

RECORDERS

For highest reliability and highest quality recording in either analog or digital format, the Nagra range of recorders is unparalleled. A digital audio tape (DAT) recorder such as those made by Tascam are often used on lower-budget productions. Some DATs offer up to eight tracks on one machine, which means you can record up to eight monophonic microphones, or four stereo, and worry about mixing a useable master track later. A recent trend is to record into a portable hard drive. The Zaxcom Deva II is a four-channel location mixer and recorder that can pack 60 track hours of uncompressed recording into a tough and hermetically sealed hard disk. It has a 10-second sound buffer that can reclaim the 10 seconds of sound prior to switching on—very useful for spontaneous shooting or the odd missed cue, for you know the previous 10 seconds are included with the recording. The hard drives can be rapidly downloaded in the cutting room or even plugged directly into the computer, and having no moving parts, the machine is immune from grit and dust, as well as temperature and humidity extremes (see *www.zaxcom.com*). The conservative sound engineer may want to simultaneously record on tape, too, "just in case."

MICROPHONES

Film recording is done with a variety of microphones made by Sennheiser, Schoeps, Audio Technica, and other manufacturers. While an *omnidirectional* mike produces the most natural voice recording, it can seldom be used because it picks up sound from *off axis*, such as reverberant or ambient sound. Contrary to legend, there is no such thing as a zoom microphone and no way to cheat a microphone's characteristics to make it sound close when it is distant. A close recording can, however, be made to sound distant in postproduction by adjusting its level and subtracting some of the lower frequencies, which fall off earlier over a distance than upper frequencies.

The counterpart to an omnidirectional mike is a *cardioid* or directional mike, which gets its name from its heart-shaped pick-up pattern. Cardioids are able to discriminate against sound coming from the sides or behind, and by suppressing sound from unwanted directions, their signal-to-noise ratio is enhanced. This means ambient and reflected sound are a little lower in relation to the desired source. The *hypercardioid* or *gun mike* (because of its shape and appearance) does the best job of discrimination, but at some cost to naturalness of reproduction. Other mikes have various advantages and disadvantages, but basically there is no substitute for a quiet background and a good mike close to each speaker.

Another answer to miking actors is the *lavalier* or body mike connected to a personal radio transmitter. Radio mikes are worn on the body and produce a good and constant voice level with a low ratio of ambient sound. They do, however, have one or two little quirks. Unless you obtain top-rate, wireless systems, radio transmission sometimes fails or unexpectedly pulls in taxis and police messages. They are also prone to picking up clothing rustles and body movements, especially if an actor is wearing any clothing made from man-made fibers. These generate static electricity, which is thunder on a small scale.

Lavaliers are without *sound perspective*. This is the aural sensation of distance we get from acoustical changes in a voice as someone moves around. Partly it's due to changes of subject-to-mike distance and partly the voice's changing relationship to its acoustical surroundings. The lavalier, by remaining at a constant distance from the speaker and picking up so little reverberant coloration, removes all sense of the speaker's movement or perspective changes. These must be emulated later in the mix. Live now, pay later.

BOOM

An overhead microphone boom is a large and specialized piece of mike support equipment that needs plenty of space to operate. Low-budget productions generally use a hand boom or *fishpole*, which has the added advantage of being able to place the mike out of sight below the frame instead of above it.

MIXING DESK

Most location recorders are two-track stereo and need a battery-powered mixing desk when several mike inputs must be combined and balanced. Mackie makes ones favored by low-budget productions. Monitor all sound using professional, ear-enclosing headphones that isolate you from the surrounding world.

RECORDING REQUIREMENTS

DIRECT AND REFLECTED SOUND

In dialogue sequences, the sound crew aim to get clean sound that is *on mike*, which means spoken near a microphone and into its most receptive axis. They want sound that is relatively uncolored by sound reflected from walls, ceiling, floor, or other hard surfaces like tables and other furniture. *Reflected sound*, bouncing off surrounding surfaces before finding its way to the mike, travels by a longer route and arrives fractionally after its direct, source sound. If loud, it can appreciably muddy the clarity of the original. You may not realize this until you start editing different mike positions together—position changes mandated by the different camera positions necessary to any well-covered dialogue sequence. In a reverberant location, each mike position has a different sound characteristic determined by the different admixtures of reflected sound and the different distances from the speakers. Editing them together makes all the seams evident in what should sound seamless.

Reflected sound can be greatly reduced by laying felt or other soft, sound-absorbent material on hard floors and hanging blankets in front of any walls out of camera sight. To be fully effective, blankets must be hung about 6 inches away from the wall, not directly on it.

Getting mikes close enough to actors without causing shadows will require planning between sound and camera specialists and the director. Quite often this requires placing more than one mike and feeding their inputs into a mixer. Location sound must be thought out carefully because every mike left open records its own share of ambient, source, and reflected sound, and these joined together can produce a chaotic set of problems. If you can, record each mike into a different sound channel (by using something like an an eight-channel DAT recorder) and keep their contributions discrete. You can audition the various mike outputs later and make a mix of the most successful coverage. If mixing must be done on the spot, the sound mixer really must know what he or she is doing, for once mixed, the omelette cannot be unscrambled. After the first mixed take, listen to the results through the headphones before proceeding.

SOUND SOURCE TO MICROPHONE DISTANCES

Getting microphones close enough to actors on the move so you can record well is a rare skill. The boom operator's main task is to stay just out of frame at all times, but also near the axis of each speaker. Not doing so means that sound levels plummet as the mike-to-subject distance increases. Ambient sound levels, however, remain constant. Thus the ratio of source to ambient sound can vary a lot. Cranking up the playback level afterward in the mix can compensate for the drop in source level and make the speaker's voice consistent from angle to angle, but at the expense of large changes in the ambient levels that were recorded with each angle.

The fundamental problem is that film-shooting procedures are usually optimized for photography. Sound recording must fit around the needs of the camera and at the same time keep its microphones from ever being visible. The director can help by stabilizing speakers during a dialogue sequence, minimizing sound recording problems, or creative set dressing so a nice potted plant on a dining room table conceals a strategically placed microphone.

AMBIENT SOUND AND PRESENCE TRACKS

Ambient sound is sound inherent to the location, whether interior or exterior. A playground may have a distant traffic accompaniment coming from one particular direction. A riverside location may have the hum of a power station a quarter mile off. Every room you record in will have its own ambient sound noticeable only during silences. It may be a faint buzz from fluorescent fixtures, the hum of voices from an adjacent office, or birdsong and trees rustling from outside.

Before calling for a wrap at any location, interior or exterior, the sound department always records an *atmosphere* track (also known as *room tone*, *presence track*, or *buzz track*). The procedure is simple: on the heels of the last scene, nobody leaves the set or changes anything and actors and crew freeze. For a couple of minutes the sound crew makes a recording of the particular quality of silence in the location. This becomes the all-important sound filler for gaps in dialogue tracks. The two minutes can be duplicated to create as much track as needed.

SOUNDS ON THE SET

It's imperative to keep the crew stationary and silent during takes and to make sure that the camera isn't making any sound the mike can pick up. Most film-camera sound comes from the hollow metal magazines, and these can be muffled with a soft, sound-proof casing called a *barney*. When this fails, sound may pass through tripod legs and be amplified by a resonant floor. Placing carpet under the camera support should fix this. Fluorescents like to buzz, filament lamps can hum, and pets come to life at inopportune moments. Sound cables, placed in parallel with power cables, may produce electrical interference through induction, and sometimes, long mike cables pull in cheery DJs via radio frequency (RF) interference. Any large motor or elevator equipment can generate alternating current magnetic fields, and the most mysterious hum sometimes proves to come from something on the floor above or below.

SMART SLATE

A smart slate is a type of clapper board containing a timecode display that comes on when the bar is opened and whose timecode freezes at the point where the clapper bar is closed. This makes synching sound to its timecoded picture easy. However, camera and recorder must be compatible with the smart slate, and the camera department must *jam-synch* (synchronize) the timecode generators every morning because they drift apart over a period of time.

EFFECTS AND WILD TRACKS

A *wild track* is any track shot independent of picture. When an actor flubs a line or some extraneous sound cuts across a line of dialogue, the alert sound recordist asks for a wild voice-only recording immediately after the director calls "Cut." This way the actor repeats the lost line just as he or she spoke it during the take. By recording in exactly the same acoustic situation, the words can usually be seamlessly edited in, and a reshoot avoided.

An *effects track* (FX) or *atmosphere* is a wild recording of sounds that might be useful to augment the sequence's sound track later. The recordist might get a separate track of that barking dog, as well as other sounds to help create a *soundscape*. In a woodland location this might mean getting up early to catch bird calls, river sounds of water gurgling, ducks dabbling, and wind rustling in reeds. A woodpecker echoing evocatively through the trees is probably best found in a wildlife library, as they are hard to get close to. Initiative and imagination are important in the sound recordist, plus a high level of tolerance to frustration.

AUTOMATIC DIALOGUE REPLACEMENT

Automatic dialogue replacement (ADR) in postproduction, sometimes called *looping*, is expensive and time-consuming and mostly kills all dramatic potential. The problem is that actors can never regain the emotional truth of a scene when they record one line at a time in a sound studio. Actors loathe doing it. ADR is misnamed: It is neither automatic nor any real replacement.

ATMOSPHERE LOOPS

Often a short original atmosphere is made long by repeating or *looping* it. This can be perfectly acceptable unless recognizably individual sounds return at set intervals. A bus station with the same sneeze or cackling laugh every 6 seconds makes for a very strange place indeed. When recording atmospheres, the recordist listens intently to make sure an appreciable amount, clear of such noises, has been recorded so an effective loop can be made later. By the way, atmospheres in sound libraries are often loops, and they often have giveaway sounds.

SOUNDSCAPES

While researching for this chapter I discovered that a World Soundscape Project researching the acoustic ecology of six European villages began in 1975. Sponsored by the Tampere Polytechnic Institute in Finland, the goal is to document acoustic environments in change over time (see *www.6villages.tpu.fi/*). The Web site gives an idea of the riches you discover when you set out to explore using your ears, something I learned as a teenager from Brian Neal, a musician and great friend who is blind. Every place has its soundscape, and what makes it individual and special takes listening and analysis. To create with sound is to provoke imagination at a high level, much as music does. Usually the most memorable soundscapes come from simplifying and heightening rather than being literally true to everything in the location. Less is more in sound as in everything else.

CHAPTER 34

CONTINUITY

For this chapter I am indebted to Pat P. Miller's *Script Supervising and Film Continuity*, 3rd edition (Boston: Focal Press, 1999), which is a mine of detailed information on procedures and methods. I strongly recommend studying it in detail. If you have nobody covering continuity on your film, using the editor is a very good fallback. Editors have good reason to want to get things right.

COORDINATING AND REPORTING

The script (or continuity) supervisor works closely with the director and editor and plays a key role in guarding against omissions or mismatches in the production. Continuity work begins as soon as a finished script exists, but it comes into its own during shooting when the script supervisor takes over monitoring continuity of costumes, properties, and characters' words and behavior—something that would otherwise fall haphazardly to the director. The continuity supervisor's note-taking culminates in reports that are used extensively by the editor and may at any time provide guidance during the shoot.

SCRIPT BREAKDOWN

A close reading of the script yields a list of locations and of people in the first breakdown. Very important are their names, characteristics, physical attributes, overt action (as opposed to action that is implied offscreen or in the past), and their entries and exits.

CHRONOLOGY

Next comes a chronology for the story that, at the very least, will have time lapses. If the story is told out of order, or has *flashbacks* or *flashforwards*, this may have profound consequences for the age or condition of the characters and for their make-up and costuming. Continuity must at all times know where the story is, spatially and temporally, as well as what has befallen the characters before we see them and where they go after we see them. Key to keeping track of this is to make a chronology measured off in minutes, hours, days, or years—whatever the story calls for. If the story is set in 4 days, the main unit will be Day 1, Day 2, Day 3, and Day 4, and each scene will be specified by time. Other key temporal and spatial aspects are day or night and interior or exterior.

PLANNING THE SHOOT

The script supervisor, being the clearing house of so many important details, supplies the production manager with details for each scene. The unit *call sheets* include vital detail such as costuming, properties, transport to locations, and other special provisions.

TYPES OF CONTINUITY

You think of continuity as matching details from one scene to the next, but if a chronologically late scene precedes an earlier one, continuity must be *back matched* to preserve the logic of compatibility. There is also *direct* and *indirect* continuity:

> **Direct continuity** is when one scene follows another. The character cannot appear in a different jacket stepping from one room to another, for instance.
>
> **Indirect continuity** is continuity between scenes separated by time or by other scenes. If a man goes out on the town and we see him many hours later much the worse for wear, this is indirect continuity because although he is in the same clothes, they are rumpled and stained, and his face is shadowed with stubble. During parallel storytelling, we might intercut two stories, and there must be indirect continuity in all the A segments and in all the B segments.

Somebody must be alert to everything that an audience will ever notice, and this is the script supervisor's job. Sometimes this takes research, for someone is bound to write in to point out that Slender Willow cigarettes were not produced in China until 5 years after the period of the film.

WARDROBE AND PROPERTIES

Wardrobe from scene to scene, once decided, is something the script supervisor must also know intimately. The script supervisor keeps a hawk-eyed on wardrobe and *props* or properties to make sure the right ones are used from scene to scene and that a cake with two slices taken in one scene does not appear in the next with only one piece gone. There are three classes of property:

- **Hand props**, such as a comb or diary, which the characters handle
- **Breakaway props**, such as a pottery figure, which get broken or used up in some way (and for which replacements must be on hand for subsequent takes)

- **Stage props**, such as a lava lamp or princess bed, which are part of an environment and may be related to one of the characters.

BREAKDOWN OR CROSSPLOT

The script supervisor must read, analyze, break down, read, and reread the script until its every need is committed to memory in its every aspect. The script supervisor makes a *crossplot* as in Chapter 17, Figure 17–4 to lay out the scenes in order, each with their:

- Location
- Time of day
- Chronological data
- Characters
- Pages in script
- Length

TIMING

Scene length is calculated to the nearest eighth of a page, with a normal page expected to last one minute of screen time. Naturally, a scene description saying only "A montage of shots shows the transition from fall through winter and spring" will have to be separately assessed for its content.

The careful page count is part of tracking how long each scene should last. While shooting, the script supervisor is responsible for timing with a stopwatch every scene and every take of every shot in a scene. Master scenes, usually shot first for lighting purposes, are the large unit into which others scenes fit, and these yield the first overall timing. Keeping track of screen time and edited screen time shot per day is how the unit knows whether the film is going to come in at its intended length and be shot in the time allotted.

MONITORING DIALOGUE

The script supervisor's job is to watch what dialogue actors actually use from take to take and to record any variations in what they say or do because variations can create huge problems in editing. When the plot depends on particular information emerging through dialogue, for instance, it will be disastrous if the director settles for a take that happens to omit a vital reference.

PHYSICAL CONTINUITY

If a character picks up a glass of wine with her right hand in the master shot and her left in closer shots, the editor has a big problem. Similarly, if a character rises during a line in one shot, and after the line in another, the editor is in trouble.

Continuity's job is to alert the director to any of these variations, as well as inconsistencies in camera movements or timing, and to know immediately what options exist as alternatives. This means being very prepared and very observant, all the time.

Taking Polaroid or digital snaps of characters or sets just before a scene begins or after it ends is a way to log what people wore, how they wore it, and how their hair looked. Shooting on video makes this degree of caution less necessary, but it's vital if you are shooting on film. It's amazing how certain an actor can be that he had his jacket buttoned, when video proves otherwise.

COVERAGE

The script supervisor knows from discussions with the director not only how a scene *should* be covered, but how it actually did get covered and how, subsequently, it can be edited together. A good knowledge of editing is therefore essential, as is a good sense of dramaturgical structure because the script supervisor must keep all these aspects under constant review.

BRACKETING THE SCRIPT

The basic principle of bracketing a script lightly in pencil (see Chapter 24, Figure 24–1) is the means of knowing how the scene is to be covered, and penciling it heavily in the end makes a record of how it was actually covered. Color codings for particular characters, or for their entries and exits, may be helpful, but like any system, they must be used consistently if the system is to work.

SCRIPT SUPERVISOR'S POSITIONING

The script supervisor normally sits close to the camera to know what it is seeing, but he or she can watch a monitor if one exists. However, often the acuity of a monitor simply isn't good enough, so script supervisors usually watch from beside the camera.

CHAPTER 35

DIRECTING THE ACTORS

Directing a film means carrying a detailed movie in your head that you have broken into component parts, and then manipulating cast and crew until you get the parts you want. Crew and cast know this, and when they turn to you expectantly, they are asking, "Did you get what you wanted?" You have to know, one way or the other. Naturally, along the way, other possibilities intrude, so the movie you are assembling in your head is constantly evolving and adjusting to opportunities and disappointments.

During shooting, a supportive, enthusiastic cast and crew will endure and triumph together, but under the best of conditions this will be a stressful time for everyone. It's a period of high concentration for the crew, all of them trying to do their best work, and for you it is a time of occasional euphoria or despair. Unlike anyone else, the director must simultaneously scan many people's work. Hardest to fulfill is your actors' need for your feedback while you are also directing the crew.

SENSORY OVERLOAD

The director's occupational hazard is sensory overload. In a typical take, while you watch the actors keenly, you will also hear a lamp filament humming and a plane flying nearby. Can the sound recordist hear them? Insulated inside her headphones, she only returns your look questioningly with a silently mouthed, "Huh?" Next you see a doubtful camera movement, and wonder if the operator will call, "Cut!" Your heroine turned the wrong way when leaving the table, and your mind races as you figure out whether it can possibly cut with the longer shot. Now, to further boggle your mind, the camera assistant holds up two fingers, signifying only two minutes of film left. At the end of the take your cast looks at you expectantly. How was it? Of course you hardly know. If you are working on tape or have a video assist, you could replay their work, but doing that too often would double the shooting schedule.

More practical is to be ruthless about how you will use your energy. A competent crew will catch all the sound, camera, and action problems and report anything you need to rectify. If you have a union crew, who come from a system that produces highly reliable workers, you can delegate without fear. But if you draw from a casual labor system, you are probably using freelancers who generally lack experience. A film school produces some quite brilliant people, but their lack of practice results in a higher number of mistakes and omissions. No way around it: You get what you pay for, and when you can't pay, you have to work twice as hard.

ACTORS NEED FEEDBACK

From experience in school and theaters, actors come to depend on audience signals. Filming is without such signals, for the director is the sole audience and cannot give feedback during a take. Afterward you must try to give each actor the sense of closure normally acquired from an audience.

Actors are not fooled by empty gestures. Your brain has been running out of control trying to factor in all the editing possibilities that make the last performance even usable, and now you must say something intelligent to your trusting players, each of whom is (and must be) self-absorbed and self-aware. You manage something and the cast nods intently.

Now your crew needs you, and the actors are already asking, "What are we doing next?" The production manager is at your elbow demanding confirmation for the shooting at the warehouse next week. The warehouse people are on the phone, and they sound testy.

So there you have it: The true glamour of directing is walking around faint from lack of sleep, feeling that your head is about to explode.

DELEGATE

The solution lies in setting priorities and delegating as much as possible of the actual shooting to the director of photography (DP), who directs the crew. Your assistant director (AD) and production manager (PM) should also take much of the logistical work off your shoulders.

ACTORS' ANXIETIES AT THE BEGINNING

PREPRODUCTION PARTY

Bring cast and crew together for a picnic or potluck party before production begins to break the ice.

WARN ACTORS THAT SHOOTING IS SLOW

Thoroughly warn actors *that all filming is slow*. Even a professional feature unit may only shoot 1–4 minutes of screen time per 8-hour day. Tell them to bring good books to fill the inevitable periods of waiting.

BEFORE SHOOTING

The time of maximum jitters and minimum confidence for the actors is just before first shooting. Take each aside and tell him or her something special and private. It should be something sincere and personally supportive. Thereafter that actor has a special understanding to maintain with you. Its substance and development will reach out by way of the film to the audience, for whom you are presently the surrogate.

TENSION AND ITS CONSEQUENCES

Whatever level of performance was reached in rehearsal now comes to the test when shooting begins. Actors will feel they are going over Niagara Falls in a barrel. Wise scheduling puts the least demanding material early as a warm-up. In the first day or two there will be a lot of tension, either frankly admitted or displaced into one of the many behaviors that mask it (see Chapter 20: Actors' Problems). Try not to be wounded or angered; if someone is deeply afraid of failing a task, it is forgivably human to demote the work's importance. It does not mean actors are deficient as a breed (the belief of many film technicians) but rather that they are normal people temporarily succumbing to vulnerability and self-doubt. Having no equipment to hide behind like the crew, actors can easily feel exposed and humiliated. Filming is incomprehensibly slow, and the crew, enviably busy with their gadgets, seem removed and uncaring. Your appreciation and public recognition given for even small achievements, and your crew's astute catering work, will work wonders for morale.

GETTING INTO STRIDE

As the process settles into a familiar routine, anxieties subside, and actors fall in with the pace and demand of the shooting, arriving eventually at pride in being a member of the team. Performances improve so much that you wonder about the usability of the earlier material.

DIRECTING

While actors are visibly working their way through a labyrinth of strong feelings, the director must suffer any similar crises in silent isolation. Because cast members invest such trust in their director, you must play the role of the all-caring, supportive, and supremely confident parental figure.

The poor novice is racked with uncertainty about whether he or she even has the authority to do the job. How do you wield authority when you feel like a fraud? The secret to success involves acting, so you play at being confident—a role the whole film unit wants to believe. Help yourself by limiting the area you oversee, by being better prepared than anyone, and by keeping everyone busy. Your major responsibility is to the cast, and your authority with them rests on how well you can tell each what they have just given and then point the way forward. This is your central function, so *divest yourself of anything impeding it.*

Both cast and crew are apt to try your patience and judgment. It is the fate of leaders to have their powers challenged, yet behind what seems like a sparring and antagonistic attitude may lurk a growing respect and affection. The unaccustomed parental role—supporting, questioning, challenging—may leave you feeling thoroughly alone and unappreciated. You are Authority, and many creative people have their most ambivalent relationships with such figures.

For your cast, "my director" and the other actors may be the most important people in their lives, allies with whom to play out complex and personal issues that involve love and hate and everything else between. This is just as legitimate a path of exploration for an actor as it is for any other artist. Finding a productive working relationship with the subtle personalities of your actors is really discovering how best to use your own temperament. There are no rules because the chemistry is always different and changing. Always aim to be respected rather than liked. Liking comes later if things go well. Never confuse the roles of friend and director. A director directs and stands implacably at the crossroads to all the important relationships that go into the film's making. You must do whatever it takes to keep everyone focused on the common enterprise. There is no set way to handle this except to demand implicitly that everyone remain more loyal to the project than anything else in the world. Professionals understand this—the rest do not.

DIVIDING YOURSELF BETWEEN CREW AND CAST

The director of a student production is usually using an untried crew and feels justifiably that every phase of the production must be personally monitored. But to adequately direct the human presence on the screen, you must entrust directing the crew to the DP and the AD. You cannot afford not to know how the material will work on the screen, and this will take all of your attention.

Directing is easier (though hardly less stressful) for those arriving via professional work in one of the allied crafts because long years of industry apprenticeship teach people how to work in a highly disciplined team. Without this conditioning, the student director and crew are in a precarious position, but if Truffaut's *Day for Night* (1973) is as representative as I think, a lowering of ideals during shooting is a common experience.

DAILY ORGANIZATION

Be sure everyone is well prepared. A smoothly running organization signals professionalism to cast and crew and is vital if low-paid (or unpaid) people are to maintain confidence in your leadership. This means preparing the following:

- Printed call sheets for cast and crew well in advance
- A map of how to get to the location
- A list with everyone's cell phone contact numbers in case of emergency
- Floor plans for camera crew
- A pre-established lighting design
- Tricky camera setups rehearsed in advance

- Correct props and costumes ready to go
- Scene coverage thoroughly worked out with DP and script supervisor
- AD has lists of everything so you carry nothing in your head and nothing gets forgotten

RUN-THROUGH

You will have to run through the action of the shot for the camera crew, who are interested at this stage in resolving framing and lighting problems. The DP may borrow crew members as stand-ins for lighting and movement checks so cast members aren't unnecessarily fatigued by the time the unit is ready to shoot.

BEFORE THE TAKE

As the crew finalizes the setup, take your cast aside and rehearse them intensively. *Remind each actor of his or her character's recent past and emotional state on entering the scene.* This is vital both as information and as implied support and may need to be repeated in a few words before every take. With you alone rests the knowledge of the prior scene's emotional level, and whether the new scene grafts naturally on to the old.

Your AD will quietly tell you when the setup is ready so actors can start with the minimum of waiting. Actors take their positions. The DP makes a last check that all lights are on and everything is ready.

AFTER THE TAKE

Immediately after calling "Cut!":

- Tell the crew whether you are going for another take or a new setup.
- Go up to the actors and confidentially tell them how they did. This may simply be "Fine, everyone" or it may be more analytical. Any specific differences you note will reassure them that you are aware of what they are giving.
- If going for another take, brief each actor on what to aim for (whether the same or something new).
- Shoot before the collective intensity dissipates.

Sometimes a further take is necessary because of a technical flaw in sound or in camera coverage, but usually you want better or different performances. This may affect each actor in a group scene differently. From one you want the same good level of performance, from another a different emotional shading or energy level. *Each actor needs to know what you expect.*

Actors themselves will sometimes feel they can do better and will ask for another take. You must instantly decide whether that's necessary. If you think it is, you call, "We're going for another take. Roll camera as soon as possible." While cast should always be allowed to improve, asking for just one more take can become a fetish or a manipulation of directorial decisions. Sometimes you must insist that the last take was fine and that you must move on. Actors' insecurity has a thousand faces.

FOR THE NEW SHOT

As soon as you have an acceptable take, brief the DP what the next shot is to be, and turn to the cast to explain what you need next. Give positive feedback about the last shot and provide preparation for the next. The AD may decide to take the actors aside to rest them as the crew roars into action changing the camera, set, lights, everything. Previously the cast had control—now they slip into obscurity as the crew collaborates in setting up a new shot.

DEMAND MORE OF ACTORS

The enemy in directing is your passive and gullible tendency to accept what actors gave as the best they could do. There is a lot of guilt at first when you are an audience of one. All these people are doing all this . . . for little old you! You want to please them, to thank them, to be liked by them. And you can't even react while they perform, to tell them how grateful you feel. You echo their need for approval with your need to be liked . . . It's an uncomfortable experience.

Try to instill in yourself the artist's creative dissatisfaction with every first appearance. Treat what you see as the deceptive surface of a deep pool, a reflective façade covering a teeming life underneath whose complexity will only be found by diving deeper. Treat each scene as a *seeming* beneath which hide layers of significance that only skill and aspiration can lay bare.

Rather than give your players different pass levels, concentrate on what they communicated. This will vary from take to take. You can say what you would like to try for next time and give additional input to individual players.

Always pushing for depth means expecting to be moved by the players, and sometimes it will happen strongly. You are tempted to *make* yourself be moved. This happens because you feel guilty that the cast is trying so hard and your own role is that of hard-to-please pasha. This is not the point; you must resist onlooker's guilt and allow yourself to be acted upon. If it works, it works; if it doesn't, ask why. Report to your cast what you felt and to what degree. When your players deliver real intensity, you are creating as you go, not simply placing a rehearsal on record.

Because you are working in a highly allusive medium, your audience expects metaphorical and metaphysical overtones. To draw us beneath the surface of normalcy, to get beyond externals and surface banality, and to make us see poetry and conflict beneath the surface, you will have to challenge your actors in a hundred interesting ways. These demands keep the cast and crew on their toes and make the work challenging and fascinating. *You represent the audience, and actors work to please you.* They want your approval because your demands personify their own gnawing sense of always somehow being capable of better. This dissatisfaction is as it should be. It may be accompanied on some people's part by an undertow of complaining. Emphasize the positive and think of the grumbling as the noise of the rigging in a ship pushed to capacity. Or think of dancers, so often in bodily pain. That pain comes from pushing themselves to the limit to make dance look effortless and wonderful. Your cast is in pain, too, so take it for what it is, and don't think you have to make anyone feel better.

WHEN THE SCENE SAGS

To put tension in a scene that threatens to subside into comfortable middle age, take one or more actors aside and privately suggest to each some small but significant changes that will impact other cast members. By building in little stresses and incompatibilities, by making sure cast members are working off each other, you can restore any tautness that has languished.

SIDE COACHING WHEN A SCENE IS BECALMED

When a scene goes static and sinks to a premeditated appearance, try *side coaching* to inject tension. This means you interpolate at a quiet moment in the scene a verbal suggestion or instruction, such as, "Terry, she's beginning to make you angry—she's asking the impossible." Your voice injects a new interior process in the character addressed, but it will not work if your actors are caught by surprise. If they are unfamiliar with side coaching, warn them not to break character should you use it.

REACTION SHOTS

Side coaching is most useful when directing simple reaction shots. The director provides a verbal image for the character to spontaneously see or react to, or an idea to consider, and gets an immediacy of reaction by challenging the actor to visualize something new and face the unexpected.

Usually the best reactions are to the actual. If a character must go through a complex series of emotions while overhearing a whispered conversation, make it a rule that the other characters do a full version of their scene even though it is off camera. If, however, your character must only look through a window and react to an approaching visitor, her imagination will probably provide all that is necessary.

One way during casting to test an actor's imaginative resources is to give him or her a phone in order to improvise a conversation with another (imagined) person whom you specify. You should be unable to tell whether an actual person is on the other end or not.

Reaction shots are enormously important, as they lead the audience to infer (that is, create) a character's private, inner life. They also provide vital, legitimate cutaways and allow you, in editing, to combine the best of available takes. Never dismiss cast and crew from a set without covering the reactions, cutaways, and inserts for each scene. And always make certain the sound recordist has shot some presence track.

CRITICISM AND FEEDBACK

Be prepared for personality problems and other friction during shooting. Actors' preferences and criticisms that were expressed during rehearsal often surface more vehemently under duress. There will be favorite scenes and scenes the actors hate, scenes that involve portraying negative characteristics and even certain lines upon which an actor becomes irrationally fixated. One palliative in serious cases is to allow a take using the actor's alternative wording. Don't offer this until all

FIGURE 35–1

A student unit at work. The director must oversee many interlocking operations and never lose track of the actors' needs (photo by Nancy Platt).

other remedies have been exhausted, and do it as a one-time-only concession, or your cast may all want to start writing alternatives.

As knowledge of each other's limitations grows, actors can become critical or even hostile to each other. Occasionally two actors who are supposed to be lovers take a visceral aversion to each other. Here, loyalty to the project and commitment to their profession can save the project from utter disaster. Filming makes intense demands on people, and a director must be ready to cope with everything human. You will learn hugely about the human psyche under duress, and this will make you a better director—and also a better human being! If this sounds scary, take heart. The chances are good that you and your cast will like each other and that none of these horror stories will happen to you—yet.

FROM THE CAST

Creative initiative cannot be limited to the director if the cast is to become a company. The cast may have criticism or suggestions in relation to the script, the crew, or yourself, the director. Acknowledge the criticism and if it is justified and constructive, act upon it diplomatically and without guilt. A wise director stimulates and utilizes the creativity of all the major figures in the team, aware that organic development and change will always be something of a threat to everyone's security, including his or her own.

When critical suggestions are incompatible with the body of work already accumulated, say so as objectively as you can. Remaining open-minded does not mean swinging like a weather vane. The best way to deflect impractical suggestions is to be so prepared and so full of interesting demands that everyone is too busy to reflect. This won't deter genuinely thoughtful and constructive ideas.

FROM THE CREW

Actors find the spectacle of dissent among the crew disturbing, so criticism by them should be discreet and kept completely from public view. Student crew members are sometimes unwise enough to imply how much better they could direct than the director and to publicly voice their improvements. This is an intolerable situation that must be immediately corrected. Nothing diminishes your authority faster than actors feeling they are being directed by a warring committee.

Guard against this situation by making sure that territories are clearly demarcated before the shooting starts. Anyone who now strays should be told privately and very firmly to tend his own area and no-one else's. When a crew member thinks he or she has a legitimate complaint, it should be routed through the DP.

There will be occasions when you have to take a necessary but unpopular decision. Take it, bite the bullet, and do not apologize. Like much else, it is a test of your resolve, and the unpopular decision will probably be the one everyone knows is right.

MORALE, FATIGUE, AND INTENSITY

Morale in both crew and cast tends to be interlocked. Giving appropriate credit and attention to each member of the team is the best way to create loyalty to the project and to each other. Everyone works for recognition, and good leadership trickles down. Even so, immature personalities will fracture as fatigue sets in or when territory is threatened. Severe fatigue is dangerous because people lose their cool and work becomes sloppy. Essentials can easily get overlooked, but careful and conservative scheduling can guard against this.

One simple insurance against failing morale is to take special care of creature comforts. Your production department should make sure that people are warm, dry, have bathrooms to go to, somewhere to sit down between takes, and food and drink. Avoid working longer than 4 hours without a break, even if it's only a 10-minute coffee break. From these primal attentions cast and crew infer that "the production" cares about them. Most will go to the ends of the earth for you when they feel valued.

PROTECT THE CAST

Everything that can weigh unnecessarily on the actors should be kept from them. Disputes or bad feeling among the crew should be scrupulously kept confidential. Actors are vulnerable to emotional currents, and their attention should remain with their work.

YOU AS ROLE MODEL

You are the director. Your seriousness and intensity set the tone for the whole shoot. If you are sloppy and laid back, others will outdo you, and no film may get made. If you demand a lot of yourself and others but are appreciative and encourage appropriate humor, you will probably run a tight ship. Your vision and how you share it will evoke respect in the entire team. People will follow an organized visionary anywhere.

Present any negative criticism you have as a request for a positive alternative.

USING SOCIAL TIMES AND BREAKS

During the shooting period, spend time (outside the actual shooting) with your cast. However exhausted you become, it is a mistake to retreat from the neuroses of your actors to the camaraderie of the crew. Instead, try to keep cast and crew together during meals or at rest periods. Frequently, while lunching or downing a beer after work, you will learn something that significantly complements or changes your ideas. Under good conditions, the process of filmmaking shakes out many new ideas and perceptions and generates a shared sense of discovery that binds crew and participants together in an intoxicating feeling of adventure. Conserved and encouraged, this sense of excitement can so awaken everyone's awareness that a profound fellowship and communication develop. Work becomes a joy.

AT DAY'S END

Thank people formally and individually at the end of each day's work. Respectful appreciation affirms that you take nobody for granted. By implication you are demanding that respect in return. Under these conditions, people will gladly cede you the authority to do your job.

WHEN NOT TO LET THE CAST SEE DAILIES

Under the usual pressured shooting schedule, show dailies only to make a point that can be made no other way. I once convinced a player that he was acting instead of simply *being* by showing him some surreptitiously shot footage of himself in spontaneous conversation. The contrast between this and him performing a scripted conversation was so striking that he abandoned his resistance to my judgment. This kind of revelation takes a negative approach and can easily backfire. Show footage cautiously and supportively only if you can get results no other way. The same procedure can be used with the actor of fragile ego who insists on projecting a rich and unnatural acting voice instead of his or her natural range. The worst consequence of showing dailies is that you end up with five cast members and six directors. At any time, actors may shift feelings of humiliation on to other cast members or the director and, in their anguish, seek control.

With familiarity, actors seeing themselves on the screen come to more or less accept how they appear, but the journey to equanimity can be long and rough. If you must go that route, get it over during the rehearsal period while they are learning to trust you, their director. Nobody will seek control if your cast trusts what you communicate. Most actors will say that their greatest pleasure comes from working with a strong director who demands much of them and is appreciative.

It is quite normal to show dailies only to the crew, and you should make no bones about doing this if you suspect that anyone in the cast will be undermined by it. Promise the cast a viewing of the first cut, if you like, to assuage their natural curiosity. By then they have given their performances, and however their image influences them will not jeopardize your film.

CHAPTER 36

DIRECTING THE CREW

Look in a film school's movie credits for a particular period, and you will find the same few names in different capacities for different films. These are the people in their cadre who loved the process of filmmaking and would direct one month and be a friend's gaffer or production manager the next. This is whom you should aim to become and whom you hope to find in your crew.

LIMIT YOUR RESPONSIBILITIES

Beginning directors often try to oversee the whole crew's work. In search of perfection you will have the urge to set the lights, operate the camera, and control a hundred other small details. Too often neglected is the human presence on the screen, the one aspect the audience really notices. A check of composition, as we shall see, is absolutely necessary, but the director must be willing to give technicians and production personnel control of their areas. For their part, those people must be fully responsible and aware at all times and take the appropriate initiative without waiting for explicit instructions.

INITIATIVE

Finding crew members who take initiative yet work as a team is not easy. Some are too passive to act without instructions. Some in a student shoot, regimented by family and schooling, can only produce from within a punitive, monitoring structure and cannot act when something in their area needs doing. Others take initiative to exert control for its own sake. Status and control issues absorb too much of some people's energy to make them suited for the give-and-take of film teamwork.

COMMUNICATING

Before shooting begins, each crew member should have read and questioned the script and contributed ideas about his or her own area of specialty. A director should, in turn, understand the rudiments of each technician's craft and be able to communicate in the craft's special terms. That's why this book contains so much about the whole production process.

From you or your delegates, *the crew needs positive, concise directions* with as much advance warning as possible. The crew will not rise to genuine crises if things that could have been foreseen go unattended. Avoid thinking out loud, especially when the pace heats up. Try instead to arrive at your conclusions and produce brief, practical instructions worded so they cannot be misinterpreted. Without being condescending, get people to repeat instructions of any complexity so you know they understand. Anything that can be put in writing should be.

Wherever possible during shooting, the assistant director (AD) and director of photography (DP) should deal with all production and technical questions. This releases you to do your job properly, which is to *answer the needs of the actors* and to concentrate on building the film's dramatic content. Your script supervisor will be an important ally, although this person is unable to judge performance quality as the job requires a fierce concentration on words, actions, and materials. Do, however, confer over coverage, especially if you make changes.

RELATIONS WITH CAST AND THE PUBLIC

Warn crew members that actors may privately seek their opinions on the quality of the work. This is treacherous ground, and the crew member must react with extreme diplomacy. However flattering this may be, it is probably neurosis and can, if wrongly handled, become dangerously divisive. To avoid such pitfalls, crew members should only be supportive, which is mainly what actors seek. When actors solicit support for negative attitudes or communicate something the director should know about, the crew member should remain neutral and afterward discreetly report the situation up the chain of command. Warn crew never to voice criticism that can weaken anyone else's authority, either on the set or off of it. This preserves the all-important working morale.

Everyone should exercise the same caution when conversing with bystanders on location, who may take it upon themselves to cause trouble or attract unwelcome publicity. Any purposeful questions should be referred to the AD or other crew member delegated to deal with public relations.

LOOK THROUGH THE CAMERA

When a new shot has been set up *you must look through the viewfinder* to ensure that framing at the start and other key compositions are as you expect. You may need to do the same at the take's end to check the camera's finishing composition. When there is a lot of moving camera coverage, you will need to agree with your operator on compositions, angle, size of the image, and so on (see Figure 36–1). Walk the actors (or stand-ins) through the take, freezing them at salient points to agree with the operator on what should appear in the frame. To stabilize these decisions, your crew will need to make chalk marks on the floor for both actors and the camera dolly. Everyone may have to hit particular marks at particular moments in the scene.

Precision of this kind separates the experienced from the inexperienced. Trying to impose this degree of control on an inexperienced ensemble may be an exercise in futility that wastes time and wrecks cast morale. Because framing,

FIGURE 36–1

When shooting a dynamic scene on film, the director must place trust in the camera operator's sense of framing and composition (photo by author).

composition, lighting, and sound coverage are the formal structuring that translate a live world into cinema, the director must keep the strongest possible contact with the outcome on the screen. When shooting video or film with a video assist, you can watch the whole take on the monitor during recording and know immediately what you have. With film and no video assist, the results remain in doubt until the rushes return from the laboratory. This is why *rushes* or *dailies* are rushed back to the unit—so reshooting can take place if it's ever needed.

On a film shoot, all you can do to ensure your vision is being recorded is to clearly brief the technical crew through the DP and to stand close to the camera so you can monitor what it is doing. With a little practice you can see from the operator's movements if he or she is in sync with the action. Not doing these things invariably leads to rude shock at the dailies viewing, when it's usually too late to make changes.

If you can watch the action on a video monitor because you are shooting film with a video assist or shooting video, the actors may feel abandoned if you are not beside the camera and physically present for them.

MAKING PROGRESS

Shooting is stop-start work, with many holdups for lighting or camera setups. A crew can easily slow down while everyone waits for A. N. Other. Nobody quite knows who they are waiting for, but everyone knows that *somebody* is not ready.

Eventually it becomes apparent that everyone is waiting for the notorious and elusive A. N. Other. This character hounds the disorganized and the tired. The good AD is, among other things, a sheepdog who constantly monitors bottlenecks and who barks everyone into action the moment that shooting can continue.

WHEN YOU AND YOUR CREW ARE ALONE

If you have a fairly small and intimate crew, encourage them, when you are alone, to discuss their impressions of the shoot. Some members such as grips, electricians, and ADs do their work before shooting and stand observing during the actual take. What they notice may usefully complement your sense of what is really happening. You, after all, have goals from rehearsal to fulfill while they may be seeing the action for the first time and have an audience-like reaction.

The work of other crew members such as the camera operator, DP, and sound recordist demands such localized attention to quality that they cannot reliably register the dramatic. You will therefore get a very mixed bag of observations, some of them way off track. Hear and encourage all views, but do not feel you must act upon or rebuff ideas that imply criticism of your work. If, however, most of the crew, including the female members, were to find the main female character abrasive, you should take serious notice.

WRAPPING FOR THE DAY

At the end of a working day, thank each actor and crew member personally and make sure that everything in a borrowed location has been replaced exactly as found. This attention to someone else's property signifies your concern and appreciation. It also helps ensure a welcome should you want to return. Initial reluctance to accept a film crew's presence often arises because people have heard horror stories about a boorish crew's treatment of property.

On a small crew, those with little equipment should help those with much (lighting for instance). Like most human organizations, a film crew can personify divisions of rank. As their general you must be concerned for the whole army's welfare. You need your foot-soldiers' affection and loyalty. If it seems appropriate, pitch in and help with the donkey work.

No wrap is complete without a careful reiteration of the following day's arrangements with the AD and production manager (PM). If you are shooting exteriors, someone must check the latest weather report and have contingency shooting ready if bad weather threatens. Call sheets should be issued to cast and crew, and rented equipment should be returned, batteries charged, and film dailies delivered to wherever they must go.

DAILIES

If you can watch a video version of the day's work, now is the time—before dinner is better than after—to see it. You are interested in every aspect: the performances, camerawork, lighting, sets, and support organization. This is when trends—good or not so good—can be spotted and congratulations or corrections can be diplomatically handed out.

CHAPTER 37

MONITORING PROGRESS

A director's recurring nightmare is to discover that a vital angle or shot has been overlooked, and it is impossible to reconvene the crew and cast. Such catastrophes are more likely in low-budget filmmaking, where too few people cover too many tasks. Working fast and hand-to-mouth, intentions must often be modified, and crossing intended shots off a list can easily go awry. The list may be so rife with changes that the list itself becomes a hazard.

When a film's story proceeds by a series of images or when the narrative is carried by nonverbal actions, directing and keeping track of what you have covered is relatively simple. The mistakes and omissions begin to appear when scenes involve several simultaneous actions, such as crowd or fight scenes that involve a lot of people in frame whose relativity must match from shot to shot. Even complex dialogue scenes, especially if characters are moving around, can spring unpleasant surprises when shooting crosses the axis or reaction shots get forgotten. Fatigue and last-minute changes increase the odds of error in all situations.

If the script supervisor and cinematographer really understand editing, their attention or that of the editor (standing in for script supervisor) can provide vital checks and balances as shooting progresses.

CUT TO SEAGULLS

You should, in any case, provide every sequence you shoot with safety coverage such as reaction shots, cutaways, or insert shots that can be used to bridge shots that don't match. The saying in the industry used to be, "When in doubt, cut to seagulls."

MONITORING YOUR RESOURCES

Many inexperienced shoots are liberally covered in the first stages and stretched thin toward the end. The resulting coverage often can be edited only one way, if at all. Your production must budget and monitor its resources as they are expended or your shoot will be like an expedition that eats steak upon leaving home and then has to boil its shoes in the wilderness to stay alive.

No matter what order you shoot in, your production manager (PM) should be able to compute from day to day whether the production is over or under its projected budget. Knowing early that a complicated sequence has consumed more resources than intended will signal that you must either raise more money, economize to get back on track, or be ready to drop the least vital scenes.

DRAMATIC AND TECHNICAL QUALITY

There are various levels of oversight to monitor dramatic quality, which is top of the list so far as your future audience is concerned.

Film without Video Feed: To see no dailies until the final *wrap* (end of shooting) means relying on limited and subjective impressions as you shoot. For a low-budget film unit away on location, this may seem the only practical solution, but the risks are manifold. Without dailies you have little or no check on the following possible faults:

- Camerawork (inaccurate viewfinder, focus problems, negative scratching, unsteady image or inaccurate camera movements, exposure inequities)
- Lighting (inadequacy or mismatches)
- Sound (quality, consistency)
- Action (continuity)
- Performances (level, credibility, consistency, relativity)

Running dailies silent on a projector is better than nothing, but you should see them with sound synced up. A cassette copy of the dailies made via telecine at home base and viewed on a videocassette player at the location is best when no portable double-system projector is available on location. Both camera and sound crews will take a dim view of this representation of their work, but it will provide you with essential feedback on acting, coverage, continuity, camera handling, composition, and so forth. Lighting and sound quality will be harder to judge.

Digital Video or Film with Video Feed: A feature unit should see its dailies every day (hence the term *dailies* for dailies) so that any reshooting can be done before the set is struck or lighting becomes difficult to reconstruct. Even a dog-tired unit can summon enthusiasm for seeing its own work. You must, however, politely but firmly exclude the actors. They will almost certainly be thrown by seeing their own performances. Tell them it's a technical check for the unit only.

Quality of the Edited Piece: Truly significant quality-monitoring is now available to low-budget independents. Because computerized editing is now possible anywhere, the editor can accompany a location unit and digitize taped dailies as they become available. Once all the material is captured, a day's work can be cut together in an hour or two. The unit then sees its latest work in rough outline, at least before the set is struck. Many additional aspects show up in edited form, such as inconsistencies in acting, lighting, framing, sound, or continuity—all of which may be improved on or even corrected in subsequent shooting. Most importantly, the director can see whether performances are consistent and pitched right and whether stylistic intentions are working out. Because the editor can be continuously assembling and revising the whole film as its parts become available, a rough assembly should be available within days of the end of shooting. This avoids what used to be a delay of weeks or months as the production scraped together money for a *workprint* (single light-positive print used as the working copy by the editor). The camera crew alone will lack final proof of their work until the camerawork has been viewed in film form.

FULFILLING YOUR AUTHORSHIP INTENTIONS

Some big questions in your mind during shooting are: Am I fulfilling my authorial intentions and, Do I have a film? (see Figure 37–1) Success is hard to measure except in unreassuringly subjective terms. One way to make this easier is to break your intentions into specific goals.

FIGURE 37–1

From one's first film onward, the director is haunted by the question "Do I have a film?" (photo by author).

Dramatic Clarity: Earlier I recommended graphing a scene to clarify the intended changes of intensity and to specify where each beat begins and ends (see Graphics to Help Reveal Dramatic Dynamics section in Chapter 17). Doing this effectively is the only guarantee that the audience will experience the film's dramatic elements, and nobody else but the director can make this happen.

Success as a director of film actors lies in insisting on clear detail in the performances. Of course you must pre-establish what the intended detail is going to be, and ensure it happens each moment of the performances, or your direction will be rudderless. That means watching like a hawk so that detail and clarity of performance are sustained in every take. Never forget that *effective performances make you feel, every time you stand by the camera, what the audience will feel.* It is something that strongly overtakes you. If you have to search for the feelings you expect, then something important is missing and you must dig into the players' psyches to set feeling in motion. In the end, an effective human presence on the screen is frighteningly simple: When actors truly feel what their character is feeling, you and the audience will feel, too. If they fail or fake it, you must take them to a place where they *do* experience their characters' emotions.

Professional directors imbibe so much experience with actors that their reflexes become as idiosyncratic and intuitive as a slalom skier's. This is why you cannot learn much about how *you* should handle directing from observing someone else at work, no matter how good he or she is. Directing is like swimming or dancing. It's something you learn from doing—and doing over and over again. You will find your own true path in rehearsals or from directing a theater play if you can get the experience.

Subtext: After material from a scene has been played, there should be an elusive imprint left on the observer concerning subtext. This, especially if it's a long scene with several angles, can subtly metamorphose from take to take into something different and can compromise the scene's integrity once it's cut together. The enlightened director acts as an extremely aware, uncluttered, and articulate audience member who can give immediate feedback on what he or she just saw and felt. The subtext that actors generate is vital, and your cast will not always know what they communicated. You cannot rely on their sense of it and must extract reliable, coherent impressions from yourself. Sometimes the unexpected can work, sometimes not. To keep yourself focused when you're exhausted, use your crib cards to check the expectations against which to question yourself. Did he convince me he's lost? Is she fooling when she says she will walk out?

To show how self-interrogation works, I have applied some typical questions to two takes of a hypothetical scene set in a bus station. Late at night, two stranded passengers start a desultory conversation. Action and dialogue of each take is identical, yet each elicits different responses from anyone alert who is watching:

Q: What life-roles did the characters adopt?

Take 1: Two of life's losers unenthusiastically size each other up.

Take 2: Two depressed, disgruntled people decide whether they can be bothered with company at this time.

Q: What truth was played out here?

Take 1: One instinctively despises someone else with the same shortcomings.

Take 2: Alienated people tend to isolate themselves further.

Q: What analogy sums up how the scene emerged?

Take 1: Two neutered cats circle round each other.

Take 2: Two exhausted convicts decide it is not worth cooperating to break rocks.

Facing questions that are fundamental to your story forces not just a candid examination of what was planned and expected, but takes you beyond. The answers they elicit are quite typical and reveal subtle differences between the two takes. Quite spontaneously, a slightly different subtext is emerging from the playing in each take. The difference shows how wrong is the notion of a *finished performance* that some actors confer on themselves. Relationship, both on or off camera, is always alive and in flux. To catch it you must be alert to the nuance of the moment, which is always actual, never theoretical.

Because *all* takes on *all* angles of *all* learned scenes remain unpredictable in terms of outcome, you need a high degree of concentration and sensitivity if you are to interpret nuances accurately. Any director who operates largely from expectations or allows his or her attention to ever leave the players' process will miss the boat. Needless to say, the concentration all this demands is enormous, which makes directing intense and draining work.

Scene Dialectics: Make sure the dialectics in each scene are well evidenced. By this I mean the opposing polarities of will and opinion that set person against person, movement against movement, idea against idea, and the parts of a person against himself or herself. These are the insoluble and irresolvable pressures and the tensions that stand out like spars in a majestic bridge construction.

Interrogating your psyche is the only way to break into that sealed room where your consciousness lives, your intuitive self that already knows and recognizes the scene's underlying qualities and meaning. It will resist unless you are merciless. Once you access it, you can set about remedying any shortfall between intention and execution. Your cast will also know instinctively when you are right, and their respect for you will rise.

MEASURING PROGRESS

Keep nothing in your head that can be dumped onto paper as a checklist. Lists save your life when you become too tired to think—that fatal fog that descends during sustained shooting. Keep your intentions for each scene handy on an index card small enough to fit in your shirt pocket (see Crib Sheets section in Chapter 30). Check the scene list so you waste no energy searching in memory to call up your goals. Check them at the start of the scene, and check them again at its conclusion. Did you cover them all? Are there fresh consequences for scenes that follow?

At each juncture, assess whether you have won or lost each of the individual battles. This is hard and lonely work because you are often underwhelmed by what you see taking place before the camera. During the shoot, just when you expect to feel creative, you often suffer a gnawing doubt, an emotion you cannot share with anybody. But the dailies generally reveal a lot more present on film than you were able to realize at the time. There is a negative aspect to this: A bravura performance seen live comes across as hamming it up on the screen. Should you suspect this while shooting, call for more takes and direct the actors to seek more contained and sincere emotion. The less confidence you have in your judgment, the more you should provide yourself with alternatives for editing later.

MOVING BEYOND REALISM

When film moves beyond the literalness of recorded realism, cinema begins linking up with forms pioneered in its sister arts, such as music, dance, theater, and literature. There is no set formula for achieving this and you cannot know if your design, worked out in writing, rehearsal, and preproduction, is succeeding until the film is on its way to being fully edited. Your film's inner life ultimately comes from the life and spirit of the players, from the mood of the company's chemistry together, from the juxtaposition of materials, and from assembling them into a provocative antiphony. It also emerges through expressive lighting or settings, sound composition, music, or by other approaches germane to your piece. This complex identity the production somehow achieves for itself is something you hope for, but never something you can control or feel coming into being during shooting.

If complete control is what you want, become an animator. But if you are ready to gamble with metaphysics and accommodate the unexpected, you'll like making fiction films. If you really love the idea of serendipity and improvisation as ingredients in storymaking, do some *cinéma vérité* documentary in preparation for a more improvisational approach to fiction (see my book, *Directing the Documentary*, 2nd ed., London and Boston: Focal Press, 1992). Giving priority to your actors and to chance will put you in very distinguished company.

CEDING CONTROL

Artistic control is a paradoxical notion because it requires that somewhere during the postproduction process, or even earlier, you find yourself yielding control to some higher truth that the film begins to emanate. It works like this: Your assembled piece will begin to make its own insistent demands, dictating to you and your editor what it wants its final form to be. Like a growing child, it begins to assert its own nature, to have its own imperfections and integrity, and even to start asserting its own autonomous decisions. With shock and delight you find you are assisting your film to make itself.

Similar capitulation may be required during shooting. A typical situation is an actor producing an unexpected and arresting quality that affects the character's potential or skews a certain situation you are shooting. You must decide whether to rein it in or to acknowledge the new direction and let the consequences luxuriate. Whatever you decide will have an impact on the other players and may put your authority on the line if they don't like what is happening. Yet to deny these emerging, elusive truths would be to choose security over the living, breathing quality of true drama. Directing is never free of moral and ethical dilemmas, or of compromise.

KEEP THE STORYTELLER ALIVE

The elements of authorship are analyzed in some depth in Part 4: Aesthetics and Authorship. When you author a movie, you are probably using it to recreate some aspect of your own inmost experience and vicariously to extend and further that experience. My friend Lois Deacon once said, "Nothing is real until I have written about it." Had she been a filmmaker she would have said, "Nothing is real until I have made a film about it." Whatever our medium, we use it to extend the boundaries of our own experience and make that earlier journey real—first for ourselves, then for others. Perhaps it only becomes real when others see and believe. Group psychotherapy certainly works that way. Because others are moved, they confer recognition on some aspect of our inmost selves that we could hardly believe in until we could share it with others.

Thus, when you direct a story with special meaning, you carry responsibility for the voice of the film; that is, your final responsibility is to keep vividly alive the observing witness who rises up to become the proactive Storyteller. The Storyteller, in his or her humanity and intelligence, is the crucial guide who mediates between the surface reality of the fiction and its underlying significances. Your poetic intelligence, feeling its way, often in doubt, seeks to fit the *seemings* of the film together into a humane statement about the human condition and to move the audience, with whose hearts and minds you are playing in the most purposeful way. A story exists to make a point, or maybe several points. Will yours?

As director, you covertly play the most important role: that of the unseen but ever present Storyteller. If you lose your vision of why the story exists, of what the film could be and should be, you lose your storytelling identity, and the film loses its way. This is why it matters intensely to have a clear idea of this functional hierarchy: the Storyteller's point of view, then the main character or characters' points of view of the story's purpose and its premise. Whom should we see into and whom should we see through at every stage of the movie? Who should make our heart bleed, and at what points in particular? What must the audience know and feel at the end?

Dialogue sequences are the quicksand where this identity most easily sinks from sight, which is why so much of this book concentrates on handling the interaction between characters. If you fear this is happening, make sure you shoot enough to allow shaping options in the cutting room. Single-setup coverage for any part of a scene means that no changes in point of view, pacing, or reaction are possible. Always provide yourself with alternatives in case your plans don't work out.

COST REPORTS

As the director you handle the human, the spiritual, and the ineffable, but there are always bills, costs, rates, schedules, and business matters to bring you down to earth. Every day during production, your PM will want bills to keep track of costs. Is the production under or over budget? If you've overspent, what will you do? Maybe you can shoot the last scene without the crane. . . .

AT THE END OF THE PRODUCTION

Just as it's nice to have an icebreaker party before shooting begins, you should have a get-together at the end of shooting to thank and congratulate everybody. If money's low, have a potluck in which everyone makes their favorite dish or brings drinks or desserts. Someone should coordinate this, so you don't get five pasta salads and no dessert.

CHECKLIST FOR PART 6: PRODUCTION

The points summarized here are only those most salient. Some are commonly overlooked. To find them or anything else relating to the production phase, go to the Table of Contents at the beginning of this part.

Planning on Paper:

- With the script supervisor, turn the screenplay into a final shooting script.
- With your director of photography (DP), draw a floor plan for each sequence showing characters' movements.
- Mark in the scene's axis (or axes) and camera positions.
- Mark up the script to show coverage from each camera position.
- Plan an establishing shot to clarify scene geography and character placement.
- Use movement to link angles at action match cutting points.
- Make sure there will be plenty of overlap between angles so you will have adequate choice of cutting points.
- Use characters' eyeline shifts. Follow them with a camera movement or with a point of view shot.
- Decide where the scene will profit from changes between subjective (near axis) and objective (far from axis) camera angles.
- Cover any regrouping of characters in a comprehensive shot so that spatial changes can be made evident.
- Show relatedness through composition wherever possible so you do not have to manufacture juxtaposition through editing.
- Sketch a storyboard frame for each camera setup to make sure screen direction is maintained.
- Make up crib sheets for each scene with "must not forget" points listed.
- Cover important moments of the scene from more than one angle.

Scheduling and Reconnaissance:

- Be pessimistic when scheduling; you will never have too much time to shoot.
- Schedule the early shooting for a slower pace.
- Arrange contingency alternatives (in case of bad weather, etc.).
- Crews need a typewritten schedule with map details and contact phone numbers.
- PM should double-check lodging and dining arrangements for locations.
- To conserve time, bring food to the unit, not the unit to the food.
- Check location with a compass to assess available light's direction.
- When everyone is in transit, make sure there is a central phone contact.
- Map out electrical supplies, permissible loadings, circuits, and their fuses.

Getting Ready to Shoot:

- Remember to include tools and spares.
- For locations, bring first aid and basic medicine kit.
- Locate nearest toilets and emergency medical facilities if on location.
- Research nearest point for repairs, spares, and dealers.
- PM should prepare daily cost projection.
- Make sure everyone knows his or her responsibilities. Every area of the undertaking should fall within someone's responsibility.
- Establish crew protocols for dealing with actors or the public.
- Hold a potluck party before shooting so you start out with good morale.
- Warn actors that shooting is slow, and they should bring books, chess, a yoga mat, whatever.

Shooting:

- Check scene's important points on your crib card.
- Have your act together. Your leadership and leadership style set the tone for the shoot.
- Delegate directing the crew to your DP.
- Make the decision for a further take quickly so everyone stays focused.
- Make allowances for extreme tension in everyone at the beginning.
- Cater to creature comforts to keep up morale.
- Give credit publicly to anyone who deserves it.
- Use breaks for mending fences and picking up loose ends of information.
- Have personal exchange with all crew members so you are seen as a personal friend.
- Script supervisor keeps strict watch over coverage and matching.
- Sound recordist listens for any inadequate lines and shoots a wild track.
- Sound recordist can ask for silence to pick up any atmosphere or sound effects on location.
- Keep dissent away from ears of actors.
- Ask your crew when you need advice or help.
- Do not wrap without shooting reactions, cutaways, and location presence track.
- Replace locations exactly as you found them.
- Thank everyone personally at the end of each day.
- Director and key personnel should confer at day's end to plan next day.

***Mise en Scène*:**

- Know whose point of view audience should sympathize with moment to moment.

- Use camera for storytelling, not just as a passive observer.
- Decide with DP or camera operator the size and framing of each shot.
- Look through camera often to check framing, composition, and image size.
- During shot, stand close to camera so you see more or less what it is seeing.
- Make the location a character, not a mere container for action.
- Try wherever possible to create a sense of depth in the frame.
- Use characters' eyelines as guides for shooting safety cutaways.
- Use a particular lens for its dramatic revelation potential as well as to cope with limitations imposed by the shooting environment.
- Decide whether there is a simpler technical means to achieve the same effect.
- Consider varying camera height from shot to shot.
- Decide what the camera can legitimately look through to create foreground and background planes.
- Slow down or simplify character movements if the camera is to follow them.
- Decide whether the necessary geographic revelation of a scene is early or delayed.
- Try to tie spatial elements together in same frame rather than manufacture relationship through cutting.
- How is space being used between characters?
- Cover anything important more than one way so you have a choice.
- Leave hefty overlaps between matching shots so editor has choice of cutting points.

Directing Actors:

- Give actors private, personal feedback and encouragement from time to time.
- Be careful to be egalitarian toward actors and not to let your preferences or antipathies show.
- Make each character active in his or her surroundings.
- Each situation must reveal something about the characters through behavior.
- Make sure each character has plenty to do, externally or internally, to avoid self-consciousness.
- Remind actors often where, emotionally and physically, their character is coming from.
- Be relaxed so you do not signal to actors that it is a tense situation.
- Support, question, and challenge. Make lots of interesting demands.
- Feed in the unexpected and side-coach when a scene needs refreshing.
- Be ready to attenuate the speed of action covered in close-up to accommodate the camera.

Location Sound:

- Monitor all recorded sound.

- Try to always get useable location sound even if it takes longer to set up.
- Make room tone and atmosphere recordings to suit sound-design plans.

Script Supervision:

- Make story chronology so material shot out of continuity will match when cut together.
- Make prop and costume list for each scene and liaise with assistant director (AD), property, and costume people to ensure right materials are on hand for each sequence.
- Script supervisor should observe action from beside camera.
- Maintain close watch on what is and isn't yet shot.
- Note all dialogue variations in case they lead to matching problems.
- Watch where actions take place and how they are done so there will be no matching problems.
- Watch handling and placement of props and other objects, so shots will match.

Authorship and Monitoring Progress:

- Try to hear and see the scene's actual subtext, not just what you want it to say.
- Make sure each beat is clear so the dialectics of the scene become evident.
- Cover exposition and other vital points more than one way.
- Examine the imprint a take has left on you: What life-roles were played out? What came from the characters this particular time? What truths emerged?
- Check your crib card to see what is being gained and what needs bolstering.
- Be sensitive to the scene's hidden meaning and energy, and allow it to exert the appropriate control.
- Expect always to have missed something good. What have you missed this time?
- Make sure you have on film the necessary confrontations inherent in your movie's system of issues.
- See rushes as soon as possible and more than once. Let them act on you.
- Make sure cost flow is being monitored and that you are keeping up to schedule.

PART 7

POSTPRODUCTION

Part 7 (Chapters 38 through 44) covers the vital postproduction phase of filmmaking, when raw materials are fashioned into a seamless tale. Because of digital editing and the experimenting it encourages, and because today's editors are so familiar with screen techniques, this is a stage that is usually done rather well even by novices. Anyone who loves film can tell from the screen what needs doing next, and digital editing makes the doing easy.

My purpose in these chapters is not to discuss the merits of the different software programs because the outlook changes almost monthly. Rather, I will lay out procedural steps and discuss what to expect conceptually in terms of your work's evolution. This is an extremely important and exciting phase of the creative process. In documentary, the editor is looked on as the second director, and the fiction editor, provided there is adequate coverage, can have almost as much creative input. Film is an unbelievably malleable medium, and though a poor individual performance is hard to mask, editors regularly perform miracles at the narrative level, where sheer momentum may cover local woes.

The cutting room is the crucible of filmmaking. The experience of being present while your work is edited will teach you more about your directing than any other exposure possibly could. Many directors in the professional world were once editors, and editing is a superb launch pad if you want to eventually direct feature films.

Be sure to look periodically at the checklist at the end of this part. Just before the heat of battle, it can save you wasted time and energy.

CHAPTER 39
Editing the First Assembly 508

CHAPTER 40
Editing Principles 519

CHAPTER 41
Using Analysis and Feedback 533

CHAPTER 42
Working with a Composer 539

CHAPTER 38

PREPARING TO EDIT

Most of the operations described in this chapter are the editor's responsibility, but a director must know postproduction procedures to get the best film from the editing stage. Editing is not just assembly, as the Hitchcock mythology suggests, but more like coaxing a successful performance from an imperfect and incomplete composer's score. This operation requires you to see, listen, adapt, think, and imagine as you try to fulfill something to the best of its emerging potential.

POSTPRODUCTION PERSONNEL

The people who complete the postproduction of a film are the editor and his or her assistants, the composer, the sound editor, and the sound mix engineer.

THE EDITOR'S ROLE AND RESPONSIBILITIES

From the number and complexity of the postproduction processes below, it's evident how important the editor and editing assistants are, both technically and creatively. For this reason, and because editors deal with the structure and flow of narrative, being an editor is the most common professional path to directing.

DIPLOMACY

If the editing staff are not hired until after shooting, they receive the director when he or she may be in a state of considerable anxiety and uncertainty. For the film, though shot, has yet to prove itself. Many directors suffer a sort of postnatal depression in the trough following the sustained impetus of shooting, and most, however confident they may appear, are morbidly aware of their material's failures. If the editor and director do not know each other well, both will usually be formal and cautious. The editor is taking over the director's baby, and the director often carries mixed and potentially explosive emotions.

PERSONALITY

The good editor is patient, highly organized, willing to experiment endlessly, and diplomatic about trying to get his or her own way. Assistant editors mirror these qualities.

CREATIVE CONTRIBUTION

The editor's job goes far beyond the physical task of assembly, and the good editor—really someone of author caliber working from given materials—is highly aware of the material's possibilities. Directors are handicapped in this area by over-familiarity with their own intentions. The editor, not being present at shooting, comes on the scene with an unobligated and unprejudiced eye and is ideally placed to reveal to the director what possibilities or problems lie dormant within the material.

On a documentary or improvised fiction film, the editor is really the second director because the materials may be inherently entertaining, but they lack design and so are capable of broad possibilities of interpretation. The editor must often make responsible subjective judgments. Even in a tightly scripted fiction film, the editor needs the insight and confidence to know when to bend the original intentions to better serve the film's underlying needs. Editing is thus always far more than following a script, just as music is much more than playing notes in the right order. Composing is in fact the closest analogy to the editor's work, and many editors have music among their deepest interests.

DAILIES

Feature films normally employ the editor from the start of shooting, so the unit's output can be assembled as fast as it is shot. With low-budget films, however, economics may prevent cutting until everything is shot. This, as we have said, is risky because errors and omissions surface when it may be too late to rectify them. The editor should see dailies so that any necessary reshooting can be scheduled before quitting the location. Many 35 mm feature film cameras generate a video feed and enable a simultaneous video recording. This allows instant replay and mitigates the unit's absolute dependency on the script supervisor's powers of observation. The low-budget film shoot will probably have no such luxury, but if dailies can be synchronized at home base they can be transferred from the editing machine screen to videotape at minimal cost and seen at the location on a VCR.

PARTNERSHIP

Relationships between directors and editors vary greatly according to the chemistry of status and temperaments, but the director will initially discuss the intentions behind each scene and give any necessary special directions. The editor then sets to work making the *assembly*, which is a first raw version of the film. Wise directors leave the cutting room so they can return with a usefully fresh eye. The obsessive director sits in the cutting room night and day watching the editor's every action. Whether this is at all an amenable arrangement depends on the editor. Some enjoy debating their way through the cutting procedure, but most prefer being left alone to work out the film's initial problems in bouts of intense concentration over their logs and equipment.

In the end, very little escapes discussion; every shot and every cut is scrutinized, questioned, weighed, and balanced. The creative relationship is intense, and often draws in all the cutting room staff and the producer. The editor must often use delicate but sustained leverage against the irrational prejudices and fixations that occasionally close like a trap around the heart of virtually every director. Ralph Rosenblum's book *When the Shooting Stops . . . the Cutting Begins* (New York: Viking Press, 1979) demonstrates just how varied and even crazed editor/director relationships can be.

DIRECTOR-EDITORS

In low-budget movies, the director often becomes the editor under the rubric of economics. This is a false economy, with the real reason often being an unwillingness to share control under the mistaken belief that no unified artistic identity for the film will otherwise be possible. Such a person often has great difficulty absorbing criticism, seeing it as an attack on his or her right to individuality and autonomy. Editing your own work, unless it is a limited or exercise film, is always a mistake, particularly for the inexperienced. Even among famous feature directors, some of the slackest films come from people wearing too many hats. See *Dances with Wolves* (1990) at 183 minutes, then bear in mind that Kevin Costner—star, director, and producer—issued a director's cut of *224* minutes.

Every film is created for an audience, so every film needs the steadying and detached point of view of an editor as a proxy for the audience. A good mind in creative tension with the director is also an inestimable asset. Not only does it ensure against tumbling into the abyss of subjectivity, but it will advance alternatives and help to question every assumption. Lacking this partnership tension, the director never gets the necessary distance from the material, and falls prey to subjective familiarity with it. Either the director-editor cannot bear to cut anything, or the cuts will get shorter and shorter, and the movie will be intercut to the point where only the film's progenitor can still understand it. This is less an indulgent love relationship than a self-flagellating dislike in which the director-editor puts the film through contortions in the attempt to cure all its imagined deformities.

In truth, the scrutiny of the emerging work by an equal, the editor's advocacy of alternative views, and collaboration all on its own produce a tougher and better balanced film than any one person can generate alone. You are the exception? Please, please think again.

EDITING: FILM OR VIDEO?

With film and video nonlinear editing (NLE), any part of an edited version can be substituted, transposed, or adjusted for length. This was emphatically not so with earlier linear video editing systems, which some people may still have to use. In linear systems the edit is compiled by making a series of transfers from a source machine to a recorder. Subsequent work on the edited version is hampered because changing the length of a shot means either altering a following shot by the added or deleted amount or retransferring absolutely everything subsequent to the change. Using some workaround techniques, you can do perfectly sophisticated editing, but it is deathly slow and labor-intensive.

Nonlinear editing using NLE systems such as Adobe Premiere, Avid, Final Cut Pro, Lightworks, Media 100, or other software has become almost ubiquitous. From video original or film camera original material scanned by a telecine machine, the material is digitally recorded in the editing computer's hard drive. Edits are compiled as a series of clips arranged on a timeline. As in computerized word processing, you may enter at any point and transpose, lengthen, or contract what is there. With film editing you carry out a similar operation but use a splicer to cut and join the workprint and a synchronizer to keep picture and sound in synchronization. Using a table editing-machine such as a Steenbeck or Moviola, you are really using a motorized synchronizer with sound and viewing capability.

The early established Avid system (Figure 38–1) remains the front-runner in performance and user-friendliness but has been legendarily expensive to maintain. Avid has been losing ground among independents to the Apple computer company's Final Cut Pro (Figure 38–2), which is stable, modestly priced, and so flexible and capable that Avid has been forced to compete in the lower-end market. An advantage of Avid's low-end product is that the interface you learn is the same throughout Avid's range and will stand you in good stead if good fortune takes you up-market. If you want to buy the industry leader, be warned that Avid gained a reputation for arrogance toward smaller users and has a long history of frequent and costly upgrades. For Hollywood this is small potatoes, but small potatoes are usually the independent filmmaker's only potatoes.

Adobe Premiere and Final Cut Pro are both backed by large companies dedicated to serving large consumer markets, and their pricing and general

FIGURE 38–1

Avid Media Composer, the film industry's preferred editing software (photo courtesy of Avid).

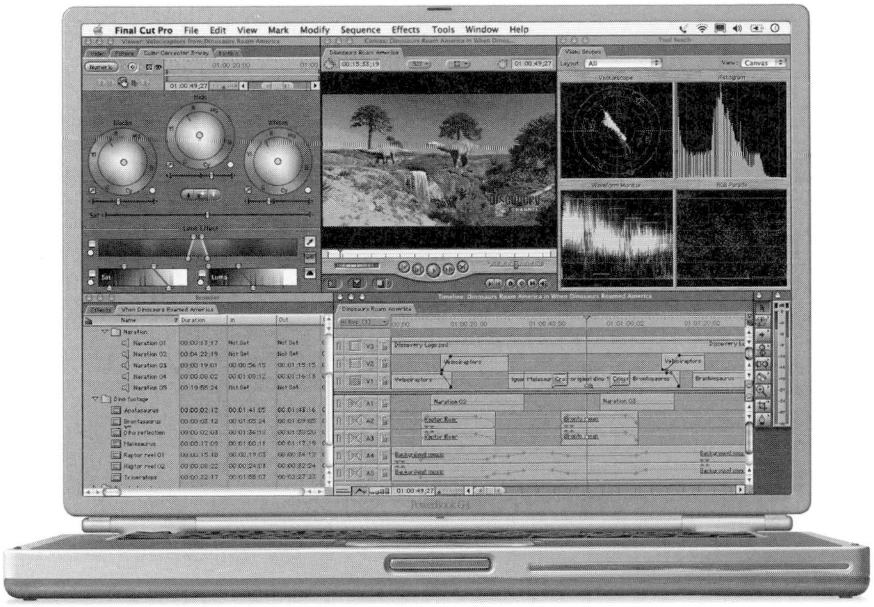

FIGURE 38–2

Apple Final Cut Pro editing software on a Powerbook portable computer (photo courtesy of Apple).

reliability reflect a respect for the discriminating low-end user who wants professional features. There are a host of other NLE systems, but as always, when you contemplate uniting your destiny with equipment, look long and hard before you leap, and do so only after checking out a variety of comparable users' experiences via professional journals and user groups on the Internet.

A POSTPRODUCTION OVERVIEW

Postproduction is that phase of filmmaking when sound and picture dailies are transformed into the film seen by the audience. Supervised by the editor, both film and video postproduction include the following:

1. For film or double-system video recording, synchronizing sound with action
2. Screening dailies for the director's and producer's choices and comments
3. Marking up the editing script strictly according to what was shot
4. Logging material in preparation for editing
5. Making a first assembly
6. Making the rough cut
7. Evolving the rough cut into a fine cut
8. Supervising narration or looping (post-synchronized voice recording)

9. Preparing for and supervising original music recording
10. Finding, recording, and laying component parts of multi-track sound such as atmospheres, backgrounds, and sync effects
11. Supervising mix-down of these tracks into one smooth final track
12. Supervising shooting of titles and necessary graphics
13. Supervising the film lab or video postproduction finalization processes

In *film*, the process subsequent to shooting also involves the following film laboratory processes:

1. Developing the camera original, and for larger-budget films, making a workprint to protect the negative from unnecessary further handling
2. Delivering to the cutting room either a film workprint or a tape for digitization made from a telecine scan of the negative
3. Once editing arrives at a fine cut and sound mix, the lab uses either the edited workprint or the edit decision list (EDL) to do the following:
    a. Make film *opticals* (optical effects such as dissolves, fades, freeze frames, titling) that cannot be done during the final printing. This is an expensive, highly specialized, and fallible process that nobody should undertake lightly.
    b. *Conforming* (or *negative cutting*), in which the original negative is cut to match the workprint so that fresh prints may be struck for release. Conforming includes instructing the printing machine to produce fades, superimpositions, and dissolves.
        i. Conforming the traditional film-editing method is simply matching negative to workprint in a synchronizer.
        ii. *Matchback conforming* follows a digitally edited film. An EDL of Key Code™ numbers compiled during digital editing is the sole guide to cutting the negative. This is risky business—see Digital Editing from Film Dailies section later in this chapter.
    c. Making a sound optical negative from:
        i. The sound magnetic master in the case of traditional mixing
        ii. The sound program output in the case of a digitally edited film
    d. Timing (or color grading) the picture negative by the lab in association with the director of photography (DP)
    e. Combining sound negative with timed picture print to produce a composite or "married" print to produce the first *answer print* (or *trial print*)
    f. Making *release prints* after achieving a satisfactory answer print
    g. Making *dupe* (duplicate) *negatives* via a fine grain *interpositive* process. For films with a large release, too many copies would subject the original negative to too much wear and tear, so dupe negs are made.

In *nonlinear video* postproduction, the camera original material has been digitized, stored in a computer hard drive, and assembled as segments laid along a timeline. Multiple sound tracks are laid and levels predetermined so you can listen to a layered and sophisticated track even while editing. Many systems are now so fast and have such large storage that you can edit on a laptop computer at full resolution. This abolishes the need for the two-pass offline and online processes with their extra time and expense. High definition video may force the use of editing at *lo-res* (low resolution) until it's once again cost-effective to use high-speed, high-capacity computing at the editing stage. This retrograde step will surely be only temporary. Depending on the features of the NLE system you use, postproduction will involve:

1. Digitizing a low-resolution, (inferior-grade) image so that much material can be stored in a hard drive of limited capacity
2. Finalizing sound in the *audio-sweetening* process using sophisticated sound processing software such as DigiDesign's ProTools. Beyond simple level setting, such programs enable:
    a. Dynamics. Control over sound dynamics such as:
        i. Limiting (sound dynamics remain linear until a pre-set ceiling, when they are held to that ceiling level).
        ii. Compression (all sound dynamics are compressed into a narrower range but remain proportionate to each other)
    b. Equalization control (sound frequency components within top, middle, and bottom of sound range can be individually adjusted, or preset programs applied)
    c. Filtering. For speech with prominent sibilants, for instance, you can use a de-essing program.
    d. Pitch changes or *pitch bending*. This betrays ProTools' musical roots, and it can be very useful for surreal sound effects or creating naturalistic variations from a single source.
    e. Musical Instrument Digital Interface (MIDI) integration. This allows you to integrate a keyboard-operated sampler or music setup.
    f. The EDL of the final edit is used to re-digitize only the selected material.
3. The edit is reassembled by the computer at high resolution (*hi-res*).
4. The hi-res version is output to tape and becomes the master copy for future duplication.

The facility of NLE for finding everything you want in a flash obviates the old necessity to search through out-takes and other material. Editors report that because they are no longer forced to contemplate unused material in their daily work, it is fatally easy to miss diamonds in the rough. Editing schedules have also gotten shorter, so the editor must fight these pressures and make sure nothing useful has been overlooked by the fine-cut stage.

Online Edit: If offline editing has produced a low-grade picture and an EDL, the production is ready for online editing. A computer-controlled rig uses the EDL to assemble a high-quality version of the film from re-digitized camera original cassettes. This process is the video equivalent of the film process's conforming or negative cutting. Producing a video final print includes:

1. Timebase correction (electronic processing to ensure the resulting tape conforms to broadcasting standards)
2. Color correction
3. Audio sweetening as described previously
4. Copy duplication for release prints

Two good sources of information at every level are Kodak's student program, reachable through *www.kodak.com/go/student*, and *DV Magazine* at *www.dv.com* for up-to-date information and reviews on everything for digital production and postproduction. Kodak has every reason to want people to continue using film and provides superb guidance in its publications and Web sites, which are prolific and as labyrinthine as you would expect from an organization with so many divisions.

SYNCING DAILIES

It is beyond the scope of this book to describe the procedure of film dailies syncing, other than to say that the picture marked at the point where the clapper board bar has just closed and the sound track marked at the clapper bar's impact are aligned in a synchronizer or table editor so that discrete takes can be cumulatively assembled for a sync viewing. Every respectable filmmaking manual covers this process (see this text's bibliography).

KEEPING A DAILIES BOOK

When assembling dailies for either a film or video viewing, make a dailies record book or use the NLE database. A simple old-fashioned book is a preparatory log of slate and take numbers in a sturdy notebook, divided by sequences and using one line per take. Take scene, slate, and take numbers from the camera log and leave columns for film edge numbers (or video timecode numbers) and blank space for cryptic notes during the dailies viewing. Figure 38–3 shows a completed section of the dailies book. An NLE program will outline its database functions in the manual, and this should allow you to display your material by different

```
                 LAUNDRY SEQUENCE
1-1  NVG
 -2  End good for David
 -3  Best, but focus change NG (slow)
2-1  Safety cutaway only
3-1  NG
 -2  Fair (Liz has interesting dreamy reaction to bad news)
  3  Liz angriest - try to use
  4  Best for consistency - David's reaction best in T2
```

FIGURE 38–3

Typical dailies book notes.

priorities such as ID number, date, description, and so on. Date is useful because sequences are usually shot contiguously.

CREW'S DAILIES VIEWING SESSION

At the completion of shooting, even though dailies have been viewed piecemeal, have the crew see all their work in its entirety. This lets everyone learn from their mistakes as well as from the successes that will make it to the final edit. Screening may have to be broken up into more than one session because 4 hours or so of unedited footage is about the longest even the most dedicated can maintain concentration. The editor may be present at this viewing, but discussion is likely to be a crew-centered postmortem rather than one useful to the editor.

EDITOR'S AND DIRECTOR'S VIEWING SESSION

If by the end of shooting nothing has been cut, editor and director should see the dailies together. A marathon dailies viewing highlights the relativity of the material and the problems you face for the piece as a whole. You might discover that certain mannerisms are used repeatedly by one actor and must be cut around during editing if he or she is not to appear phony. Or you might discover that one of your two principals is often more interesting to watch and threatens to unbalance the film.

Next, view the material a scene at a time. With some labor, film dailies can be reassembled in scene order, and if dailies have been digitized, they can easily be called up in scene order. Run one sequence at a time and stop to discuss its problems and possibilities. The editor will need the dailies book (see previous discussion) to record the director's choices and note any special cutting information.

GUT FEELINGS MATTER

Note any unexpected mood or feeling. If, during the dailies viewing, you find yourself reacting to a particular character with, "She seems unusually sincere here," write it down. Many gut feelings seem logically unfounded, and you are tempted to ignore or forget them. However, these are seldom isolated personal reactions and what triggered them is almost certainly embedded in the material for any first-time audience to experience.

Any spontaneous perceptions you note will be useful when inspiration lags later from over-familiarity with the material. If you fail to commit them to paper, they are likely to share the same fate as those important dreams that evaporate because you did not write them down.

TAKING NOTES

It is useful to have someone present who can take these dictated notes. If you write during a viewing, try never to let your attention leave the screen, as you can easily miss important moments and nuances. This means making large, scribbled notes on many pages of paper whenever you make notes yourself.

REACTIONS

When the crew or other people see dailies, there will probably be debates over the effectiveness, meaning, or importance of different aspects of the movie, and different crew members may have opposing feelings about the credibility and motivation of the characters. Listen rather than argue, for some of these reactions may be those of a future audience. Keep in mind that crew members are far from objective. They are disproportionately critical of their own discipline and may overvalue its positive or negative effect. They also have their own relationships with the actors and the filming situations.

THE ONLY FILM IS IN THE DAILIES

The sum of the dailies viewing is a notebook full of choices and observations (both the director's and those of the editor) and fragmentary impressions of the movie's potential and deficiencies. Absolutely *nothing beyond what can be seen and felt from the dailies is any longer relevant* to the film you are making. The script is a historic relic, like an old map to a rebuilt city. Stow it in the attic for your biographer. The film must be discovered in the dailies.

Now you confront the dailies; you change hats. You are no longer the instigator of the material, but with your editor you are a surrogate for the audience. Empty yourself of prior knowledge and intentions; your understanding and emotions must come wholly from the screen. Nobody in the cutting room wants to hear about what you intended or what you meant to produce. Keep it for your grandchildren.

SYNC CODING (FILM)

Film coding (also known as *edge numbering* or *Dupont numbering*) enables the editor to keep sound and picture in lip sync during the complicated operations involved in editing. It happens like this: After the dailies have been viewed (to ensure that they are indeed in sync), a film laboratory prints consecutive, yellow-ink numbers every foot or half-foot. Every new roll starts from where the last roll ended. Sync code numbers, printed in parallel on both sound and picture, function as unique, unambiguous sync marks, allowing original sync to be restored at any time. Recorded in a log, they also allow almost any length of anonymous-looking film to be reunited with its parent trims or off-cuts.

POOR MAN'S SYNC CODING (FILM)

Because edge coding is expensive, subsistence-level filmmakers handwrite numbers on the workprint dailies, sound and picture, every 3 feet or so. Use a 3-foot loop in the synchronizer as an interval guide.

TIMECODING AND WINDOW DUB (LINEAR VIDEO)

When using linear videotape editing, you will need a timecoded camera original and a window-dubbed copy if you are to later use online (computerized)

FIGURE 38–4

Timecoded video frame.

postproduction editing. *Timecode* means frame identification numbers generated at the time of recording and electronically interwoven with the video signal. Wherever possible, start each new cassette from a unique hour number, rather than always starting from zero, so that no two timecodes in your dailies are the same.

Next make a *window dub* or *window burn-in*. This is a copy cassette made from its original tape with the timecode displayed visually at the bottom of the frame in a window as cassette number, hours, minutes, seconds, and frames (Figure 38–4). Every frame in your production now has an individual identifying set of numbers, necessary for online editing.

DIGITAL EDITING FROM FILM DAILIES

It is almost universal to digitize film dailies and edit on NLE software. This requires that every negative image has its own timecode (called KeyCode™) because the resulting EDL will be used to conform, or *match-edit*, the camera original. There is no margin for error here; once the original is physically cut, there is no going back.

There is one tricky aspect. With a system that transfers 24 frames per second (fps) film to 30 fps or 60 fields per second of video, you end up with four film frames being represented by five video frames. The process may be complicated by PAL and NTSC equipment that runs at different frame rates and film cameras that run at either 24 fps or 25 fps according to whether the material was generated for either American or other TV systems. If you edit on a phantom frame, it can only be approximated at the conforming stage. This means that if your sound track has been completely prepared in the digital mode, a succession of phantom frames over a succession of cuts may lead to cumulatively gaining or losing time. Put bluntly, your track may drift out of sync with the conformed film.

Make sure the person coordinating the process is thoroughly aware of the need for clarity about the ratio of film frames to video frames, known as *pull-down mode* in digitization, and knows definitively how to avoid unwanted consequences. There is a good description of all this in Thomas Ohanian's *Digital Nonlinear Editing*, 2nd ed. (Boston and London: Focal Press, 1998) in the chapter "The Film Transfer Process." If you think it looks like video's resurrection of the "how many angels can dance on the point of a pin" debate, remember that ignoring the problem will be very, very costly.

LOGGING THE DAILIES

Because scenes will be shot, and therefore logged, out of order, it is a good idea to start each new sequence on a fresh page so the pages can eventually be re-filed in script order. If you type your log into a computer database, the computer will do the shuffle for you in a trice and print in scene order.

In film, every new camera start receives a new clapper-board number (see Chapter 32's Shot and Scene Identification section for a fuller explanation of different marking systems). The clapper exists so the editor can easily synchronize the separately recorded picture and sound. In the United States the board usually includes a script scene number, camera setup, and take numbers, while the European system often consists of just a consecutive setup and take number that must be reconciled with the shooting script or continuity sheets, if you have them.

In video, because picture and sound are usually recorded alongside each other on the same tape, no syncing up is necessary and a simpler marking system can be employed. Scene numbers (and clapper boards) are not even strictly necessary because videotape-editing methods do not permit working materials to be physically dismantled. While film beginnings and ends are defined by edge or KeyCode™ numbers, video is defined by timecode. Logging by timecode permits you to trace any piece of action back to its parent take.

The film-editing log may have to facilitate easy access to perhaps thousands of small rolls of film. The filing system and log format will depend on the editing equipment in use. If an upright Moviola—still the fearsome workhorse in the occasional cutting room—is used, the workprint will be broken down into individual takes and filed numerically in cans or drawers. If a table editor such as Steenbeck, Kem, or flatbed Moviola is used, the editor is more likely to withdraw selected sections from large rolls, each containing materials for a single scene. Even then, practice will depend on the work preferences of the editor. If large rolls are used, film logs may be organized like videocassette logs to reflect what is to be found cumulatively in that particular dailies roll.

Film, using separate sound and picture in the cutting room, requires that you log photographic edge numbers and the inked-on sync code numbers (or hand-applied sync code numbers) for the beginning and end of each take. Figure 38–5 is a typical film log entry for script scene 29. A log like this is a mine of useful information. We can see how many takes were attempted, how long (and therefore complete) each scene and each take were, where to find particular takes in camera original rolls if you need to make reprints, and even at what points the camera magazine was changed and which magazines were in use at the start of a new day.

Scene	Edge #	Sync Code #	Cam Roll	Sound Roll	Date
29-1-1	29J6 434114- 158	000 - 018	14	6	13 Aug 87
2	434159- 207	019 - 038	"	"	"
3	434208- 222	039 - 050	"	"	"
29-2-1	34Z7 945781- 879	051 - 099	15	"	"
2	945880- 904	100 - 151	"	"	"
29-3-1	945905- 965	153 - 186	"	7	"
2	945966- 971	187 - 193	"	"	"
3	945972-6034	194 - 224	"	"	"
29-4-1	21X3 100676- 771	225 - 277	9	MOS	14 Aug 87

FIGURE 38–5

Typical film log entries.

Cassette 12 SCENE 15: HOTEL LOBBY (NIGHT)

00:00	43-1	WS Henry entering hotel lobby.
00:31	2	
00:59	3	
01:41	44-1	MS Henry seen through palm tree.
01:51	2	
02:24	3	
03:02	4	
03:35	5	(uses whip pan)
03:54	45-1	CS clerk's hands writing.
04:17	46-1	MCS clerk's face as he works. Stops, smelling smoke.
04:46	2	
05:11	47-1	Phone grabbed (4 rounds)

FIGURE 38–6

Typical videocassette log entries.

The video-editing log is a set of cumulative timecode numbers that allow the editor to quickly locate the right piece of action in a cassette that may hold from 20 to 120 minutes of action. It gives the starting point for each new scene and take. Descriptions should be brief and serve only to remind someone who knows the material what to expect. Note that the log (Figure 38–6) records function, not quality; there is no attempt to add the qualitative notes from the dailies book. To do so would overload the page and make it hard to use.

The figures at the left (see Figure 38–6) are minutes and seconds, but they might be cumulative numbers from the digital counter on your player deck. When materials are timecoded, log by the code displayed in the electronic window.

In the log examples there are a number of standard abbreviations for shot terminology that are listed in the glossary. Make a dividing line between sequences and give the sequence a heading in bold writing. Because the log exists to help quickly locate material, any divisions, indexes, or color codes you can devise to assist the eye in making selections will ultimately save time. This is especially true for a production with many hours of dailies.

MARKING UP THE SCRIPT

When logging is complete, the editor is ready to prepare the editor's script, each page of which should end up looking like Figure 38–7. Although the editor's markings appear to duplicate the shooting script (see Chapter 30, Figure 30–1), they are made in the peace of the cutting room and reflect actual footage and the

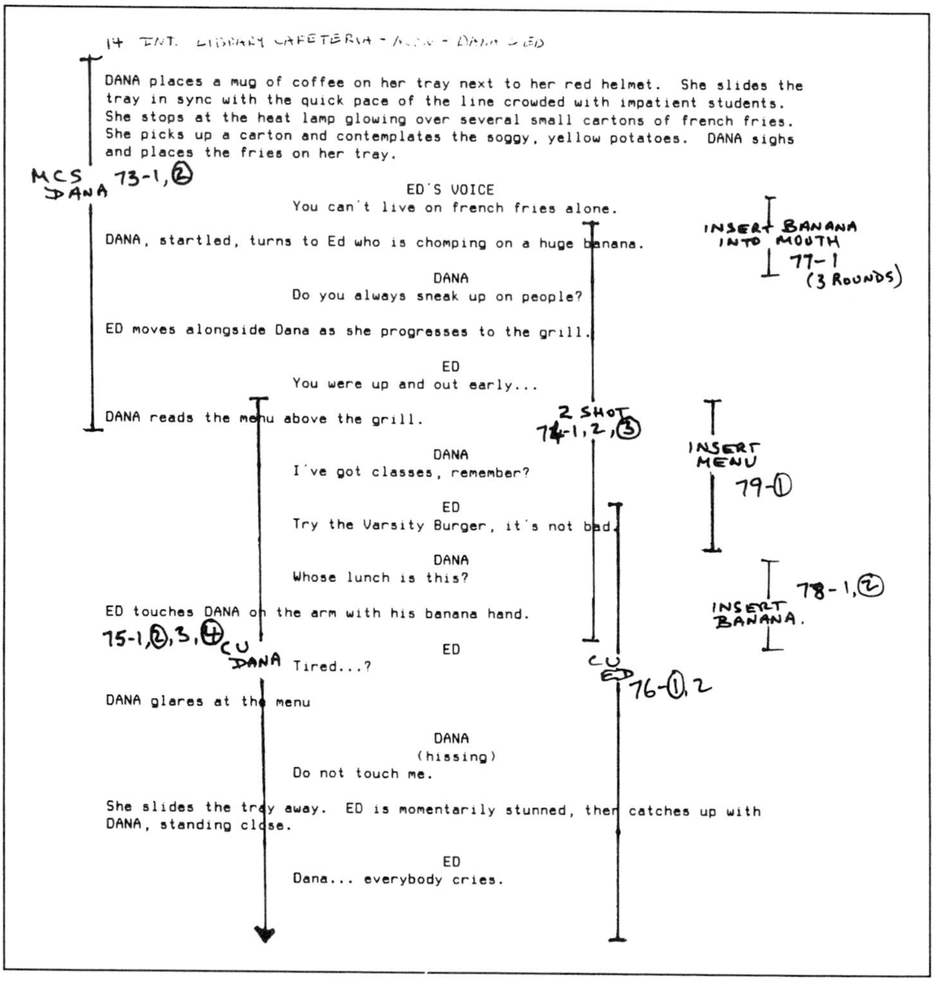

DANA places a mug of coffee on her tray next to her red helmet. She slides the tray in sync with the quick pace of the line crowded with impatient students. She stops at the heat lamp glowing over several small cartons of french fries. She picks up a carton and contemplates the soggy, yellow potatoes. DANA sighs and places the fries on her tray.

ED'S VOICE
You can't live on french fries alone.

DANA, startled, turns to Ed who is chomping on a huge banana.

DANA
Do you always sneak up on people?

ED moves alongside Dana as she progresses to the grill.

ED
You were up and out early...

DANA reads the menu above the grill.

DANA
I've got classes, remember?

ED
Try the Varsity Burger, it's not bad.

DANA
Whose lunch is this?

ED touches DANA on the arm with his banana hand.

ED
Tired...?

DANA glares at the menu

DANA
(hissing)
Do not touch me.

She slides the tray away. ED is momentarily stunned, then catches up with DANA, standing close.

ED
Dana... everybody cries.

FIGURE 38–7

Editor's script marked up with dailies coverage.

chosen takes—footage that finally and definitively exists in the cutting room. At a glance the editor can see from the bracketing and notations what angles exist for every moment of the scene and which takes seem best. This greatly speeds up assessing alternative cover during the lengthy period of refining the cut. When you must problem-solve, having graphic representation like this rather than thickets of verbiage saves untold time and energy.

To mark up the script, view material for one scene looking at one camera setup at a time. Note that a change of lens is treated as a new setup, for although the camera may not have physically moved, the framing and composition will be different. Each setup is represented as a line bracketing what the angle covers. Shots that continue over the page end in an arrow to indicate that the shot continues on the next page. Leave a space in the line and neatly write in the scene number, all its printed takes (circling those chosen), and the briefest possible shot description. More detailed information can now be quickly found in the continuity reports or dailies book.

CHAPTER 39

EDITING THE FIRST ASSEMBLY

THE PHYSICAL PROCESS FOR FILM

MACHINERY

For those unused to handling film, the best type of editing machine is undoubtedly a flatbed table editor such as the Steenbeck (Figure 39–1). Easy to thread, it keeps sound and picture in constant sync but allows either to be moved in relation to the other. Sound and picture are simply spliced into the left side of the film's passage through the machine.

SOUND TRACK EVOLUTION

Until the fine-cut stage, the sound track is dialogue only and is assembled into a single track. This is a compromise, for within a single sequence several mike positions may be cut together, and the sound may vary in level and acoustical quality. Because the priority at this stage is to achieve a correct dramatic balance, the simplest assembly method is used to allow rapid editing changes during the lengthy and experimental business of achieving a fine cut. Many table editors permit two or more sound tracks, but editorial changes become slower when you have to adjust more than one sound track every time you shorten a cut or transpose two sequences.

Once a fine cut is achieved, dialogue tracks are split apart into separate tracks to allow the appropriate control in the sound mixing stage over each mike position in dialogue. Sound effects (FX), music, and atmosphere tracks will be laid as appropriate. Some sequences may need *post-synchronizing* (also known as *looping* or *automatic dialogue replacement* [ADR]). Original dialogue tracks recorded near an old house next to a noisy expressway, for instance, may not be very intelligible and will have different amounts of traffic noise on each camera angle.

FIGURE 39–1

Steenbeck flatbed table editing machine.

A mix chart is made of all tracks laid, especially because the sound editor will probably have laid extra tracks to allow for experimental alternatives. Editor, chart, and tracks then go to a sound studio where specialists make the final mix under the director's and editor's guidance. The final mix, which does so much to condition where spectators direct their imagination, determines much of the film's force with an audience.

PICTURE EVOLUTION

The final-cut workprint picture will eventually go to a conformer, who very carefully cuts the camera original negative to exactly match what is by now a very tired and beaten up workprint. The conformed negative sections are joined by cement splices, each of which requires an overlap. While the workprint was simply cut and butt-spliced with an adhesive tape splicer, cement splicers need a portion of overlap and therefore lose part of the next frame of camera original wherever a splice is made. And so, when editing film workprint, you must *never use adjacent sections of film without dropping out three frames between them*. These unused workprint frames will ensure that an allowance of frames exists in the camera original to effect cement splices with their overlap requirements. Keep the three frames from the workprint (in a "cutlet" can) in case during editing you later decide to reconstitute the two workprint shots back into one.

> CAUTION: Forgetting this means certain disaster. When cutting workprint, never use adjacent footage without a minimum of three frames separation. This allows a conformer to overlap-splice the camera original to match the butt-spliced workprint. Nothing else will work.

In the lab, the negative is conformed to the workprint not as a single strand of spliced negative, but as two *checkerboard* rolls, each containing every other shot, with black spacing between shots that produces a checkerboard appearance in the synchronizer. The procedure, also called the *A/B roll printing process*, uses at least two rolls called Roll A and Roll B, with possibly a C Roll if titles or other matter are to be superimposed. Checkerboarding allows:

- Resetting the printer light and color filtering during the black spacing ready for the next shot instead of these changes taking place during the first frames of the shot
- Black spacing that hides the unsightly overlap portion of 16 mm cement splices, which once used to appear in the first frame of every new shot
- Picture overlaps so that *cross fades,* or *dissolves,* can be made during printing

A photographic sound negative is prepared from the magnetic master mix, ready to combine with the picture. Next, the A and B rolls of negative are *timed* or *graded* (color- and exposure-graded), then passed through a contact printer where negative and positive stock are passed under a light during emulsion-to-emulsion contact with each other to make a contact positive print. Occasionally there will be additional picture rolls, should titling or subtitling require it. The A/B roll printing process allows a print with no splice marks showing and low-cost dissolves and fades. In fact, the print stock always passes at least three times through the contact printer as follows:

First pass:	Roll A picture
Second pass:	Roll B picture (alternate shots printed in Roll A's spaces left by its black spacing)
Third pass:	Sound negative (sound photographically printed on the edge of the film).

During the multiple passes, the machine can be programmed to make fade-ins and fade-outs. In the overlap portion one pass fades out, then at the next pass the other scene fades in, producing an inexpensive and reliable cross fade, otherwise known as a dissolve.

COMPOSITE PRINTS

The resulting *composite print* (sound and action married together on one print) shows the result of adjustments made for inequities in color or exposure of the original negative. This first print is called the *answer print* because it demonstrates the viability of these changes. If perfectly acceptable, it becomes the first release print. Usually further changes are required, and these are incorporated in the next answer print. The first acceptable print becomes the first release print.

THE PHYSICAL PROCESS FOR VIDEO

HARDWARE AND SOFTWARE

Linear Editing: This method, and the large tape players and recorder that it requires, have practically vanished, but for anyone still using the method, a rundown follows. The most common format for offline video editing machines was 3/4″ U-Matic, but 1/2″ VHS editing and later Hi8 became standard. When you shoot in one format and want to edit in another, you simply *dub* (electronically transfer) from one to the other before editing. Though there is some quality loss, especially in picture from one generation to the next, this is a minor consideration because offline editing leads eventually to final *conforming* by way of an online postproduction edit.

Nonlinear Editing: The professional standard is presently the Avid company's software, which uses a Macintosh computer, digitizing and other hardware, and a large hard drive as the center of its operations (see *www.avid.com*). The Avid Film Composer edits digitally from a 24 fps original (meaning 24 frames per second) and will minimize pull-down problems. Video acquisition is moving to 24P (which is 24 fps high definition video) in progressive scan format because it allows a simple transfer to film. This frame rate, originally chosen for being fairly low and flicker-free, is likely to remain standard for future theater projection systems because it constitutes the entire history of film to date.

Many excellent competitors to Avid exist, such as Media 100 (see *www.media100.com*) and Final Cut Pro for Macintosh computers (see *www.apple.com/finalcutpro/*), which handles Digital Video (DV) at normal or high definition for a fraction of the cost of Avid. For IBM PC there is the superbly ergonomic Lightworks and its sister Heavyworks (see *www.lwks.com*), which were designed by film editors instead of computer people, Adobe Premiere (see *www.adobe/motion/main*) and a host of other systems.

Because everything in picture and sound is retrieved by timecode numbers, you will need a good logging system to keep track of your materials. This may be a separate logging database, or it may be incorporated into your editing software. Once clips have been arranged on the timeline and all the minute decisions made to produce a fully effective film, the system will list what you have done as an EDL, ready to program the online machine. The most advanced systems can edit at broadcast quality, but usually editing is carried out at a lower resolution so a large body of dailies can initially be stored on the hard drive. As high definition television (HDTV) takes over, all existing video equipment will become obsolete.

EDITING MECHANICS

Linear or cassette-to-cassette editing is quite simple in principle, and the mechanics do not take long to master. Essentially you pick sections from cassettes played by the source machine and transfer each chosen section to the record machine. This involves picking an out-point to material already cut, and then determining in- and out-points for the new section to be added on. When you press the record button, you see it all on the monitor: the last seconds of previously compiled material and then the new segment cut onto the old.

Timecode-driven machines give frame-accurate editing, and each preview is the same. With control-track editing (where the machine syncs to a count of the sine wave control track), editing decisions are plus or minus a few frames. Worse, as you preview, the decision point may drift even further.

Nonlinear or digital editing (NLE) offers great advantages in speed of execution and in sound quality. Virtually any imaginable experiment with your footage can be tried in seconds once you know how to use the program. The best editors are said to be those who learned their aesthetics from film, but film editors seem to unanimously approve of nonlinear's advantages. Optical effects, such as slow or fast motion, freeze frames, titling, fades, or dissolves are easy to specify in video form, but they become very expensive and difficult to specify when you execute them in film.

SOUND CONSIDERATIONS

NLE programs of any sophistication have multiple sound tracks so you can split them and lay them in parallel according to their origin and purpose in the movie. Movie sound postproduction has always included provisions for mixing multiple tracks together, but until recently they were rolls of film. Now they are tracks originating from a diagram on the monitor screen. Sound should mostly be seamless, even when recording conditions produce components that do not cut together seamlessly at all. In a dialogue scene, for instance, there may be four different microphone positions, each having a slightly different level, coloration, and resonance. Played without any adjustments they sound truly awful and fragment the scene for the audience. Plainly they must all come to sound like one track. This is done by placing all the close shots on one track in the sound timeline, all the two-shots on another, all the long shots on a third, and so on. Then you can set levels and tone equalizations for each mike position to make all the tracks sound acceptably similar. You will, of course, have to allow for sound perspective because we expect sound to vary in quality according to how close or distant we are from the sound source, such as people speaking.

Now you can view the film under optimal sound conditions during the edit and make dramatic and other decisions based on a close knowledge of their potential. Having multiple tracks available also allows you to lay in *wild* (that is, non-sync) sound like doorbells, car horns, or various atmospheres, exactly where they belong. They, too, can now play their part. Often a sound effect helps to narrate the story, and editing pace will be affected by its presence.

You can also lay in specially recorded presence track when you background from one angle to another. There may be a match in the foreground voice recording but a mismatch in amounts of *ambient sound* (background noise inherent to the location). Remember that you can always add presence to quieter tracks, but cannot subtract it from the louder ones.

If you have the right music at hand while editing, this too can be laid in. Now you can make compositional decisions concerning scene rhythm and duration that would be quite uncertain if taken on a theoretical basis. This so often happens with feature films, which record their music last.

MINIMIZING GENERATIONAL LOSSES

Copying Limitations: In analog sound, repeated copies and premixes in analog recording (that is, non-digital audio and video) led to deterioration from generation to generation that was audible as an increased hiss level and diminished fidelity. Likewise, between generations of analog picture, losses were also disturbingly evident as increasing picture noise (picture break-up particularly in the color red), color shift (in which red in particular moves across the screen, like bad newspaper printing), and an overall deterioration in color fidelity and acuity (sharpness of detail). Anyone who has ever copied a VHS tape knows this kind of image degradation intimately.

Digital copying, however, can run to 30 or 40 generations before any discernible deterioration shows. This is because waveform information is recorded as a stream of on/off or binary pulses that are very robust compared with the fine gradations of voltage that determine analog recording. With re-recording, these quickly lose their integrity, while the same waveform made up in graph fashion by the binary zeroes and ones of digital recording is very enduring.

Digital Copying: In practice, most consumer and *prosumer* (high-end consumer) camcorders now employ Firewire technology. This ingeniously uses a single cable, called an i.LINK 1394 DV in/out cable, to link together camcorders, recorders, or computers, much as USB cables do with computer peripherals and MIDI cables do with computerized music. A Firewire link not only sends picture, sound, and timecode information in either direction, it can also transmit deck control information from your computer to your camcorder or record/replay deck. The ability to copy back and forth, virtually free of generational loss, is a quantum leap for digital technology.

Compression: All is not roses, however, because digital recording usually involves different types and degrees of compression, which involves discarding some original data. This is done by a timebase that compares each new frame, be it picture or sound, and records the difference rather than all the information in the whole frame all over again, as analog recording does. Compression is accomplished by using one of the industry-determined compression algorithms called *codecs*. Those that involve more loss than others are called *lossy* codecs. Lossless recording and re-recording is (like most things in the electronic world) just around the corner and promises ever better quality, provided the computer industry can produce ever faster and more capacious computers at a price mere mortals can afford. Under optimal conditions, projected HDTV is difficult to distinguish from 35 mm projection and will obviously just keep getting better.

TIMECODE: NTSC DROP FRAME AND NON-DROP FRAME

Timecoding provides every frame of picture and sound with its own elapsed time identity in hours, minutes, seconds, and frames, and every kind of video editing operation utterly depends on it. However, because of the primeval nature of American 525-line television running on a 60 Hz electrical supply, although

NTSC (National Television Standards Committee) appears to have a 30 frames per second (fps) rate, it really runs at 29.97. This becomes cumulatively significant over time, so an electronic band-aid solution was devised called *drop frame timecode*. This arrangement drops a frame every so often to keep the displayed timecode in sync with actual time. For this reason camcorders and editing software offer the (initially bewildering) choice between *drop frame* and *non-drop frame* recording. Just remember to stay consistent and know which one you chose. The irreverent will tell you that NTSC really means Never The Same Color.

LINEAR ONLINE AND OFFLINE EDITING

The *window dub* is a copy of the camera original with its timecode *burned in* as a window (see Chapter 38, Figure 38–4). The window dub is edited in place of the precious camera original to preserve it from undue handling. The timecode window copies through to subsequent editing generations and is sometimes the last recognizable detail. Most importantly, it lets you dub from one generation to another, knowing that when cutting is complete you can transcribe an edit decision list (EDL) from the screen and then use it to drive a computerized (online) editing setup to reconstruct a pristine copy from the camera original tapes.

EDITING CONCEPTS

Basic editing can be self-taught using common sense, but both basics and the further reaches of sophistication can be best learned after some detailed analysis of finished films (see Chapter 5, Project 5-2: Editing Analysis). Most editing programs come with an instructional project of some kind, but invariably they exist not to teach you editing but to teach you how to use the software. Most young people, having ingested an average of 18,000 hours of television while growing up, take to editing like ducks to water. If you carry out the hands-on shooting and editing projects (Chapter 6: Shooting Fundamentals) and edit your results, you will learn a huge amount both about editing and shooting. Much film education is *Yow* learning, as in "Yow! Why didn't I shoot a [fill in the blank] shot?" During editing the chickens come home to roost.

What follows is an overview of the conceptual process of editing, with particular attention to what you can expect to find as you move stage by stage through editing a project.

THE FIRST ASSEMBLY

Putting the material together for the first time is the most exciting part of editing. Don't worry about length or balance at this stage. Adapting experimentally to the problems you encounter is everything. To make a first assembly, work on one scene at a time and put the film together in whatever order is convenient, as follows:

- Run all the material for the scene to refresh your memory. Sit through outtakes, false starts, aborted takes, everything because there may always be something in there that you'll need.

- Referring to the editor's marked-up script, figure out how the coverage might best be assembled. At this stage, use a lot of the master shot and leave aside close ups or double-cutting (repeatedly cutting between, say, two speakers when a single angle would adequately relay the action). Nor at this stage should you use any overlap cutting (where a speaker's outgoing dialogue, for instance, overlaps a shot of the listener before the listener replies).
- Assemble the simplest version that is faithful to the script without trying to cure any questionable changes in the actors' pacing.
- If you have two versions of something and both seem equally viable, include both so you can choose later in the widest possible context.

See the whole film as soon as possible in a long, loose form before doing detailed work on any sections. Of course, you will be longing to go to work on a favorite sequence, but to fix nagging details would be to avoid confronting the film's overall identity and purpose.

FIRST ASSEMBLY VIEWING

NO INTERRUPTIONS

Run the first assembly without stopping and without interruption of any kind. Make no notes because this will take your attention from the screen. You want to take in the film as an audience would.

WHAT DO YOU HAVE?

The assembly viewing will yield some important realizations about the character, dramatic shape, and best length of the film. You will also have a handle on all the performances and know what kind of overall control you may have to exert. Fundamental issues are now out of the closet. You will sense an overall slowness, that some scenes include unnecessary exposition, or hang on beyond a good ending point. You may find you have two endings, one false and one intended, or that one character is unexpectedly stronger than another. A sequence you shot in miserably cold conditions by a river at night turns out to stall the story's advance and must be dropped.

The first assembly is the departure point for the denser and more complex film to come. As a show it is long and crude, yet despite its artlessness, it can be affecting and exciting.

RUN THE FILM A SECOND TIME

Now run the film again to see how your original impressions stand up. Following further discussion with your editor, make a list together of major aims for each sequence, arranging them strictly by priority.

DIAGNOSTIC QUESTIONING

To question the imprint the film has made and predict a likely audience response, you must view the film as if seeing it for the first time. At this point you are dealing with the film in its crudest form, so the aim is to elicit your dominant reactions.

After seeing an assembly, rapidly list the memorable material. Refer to the script and make a second list of whatever left no particular memory. Why does this other material not deliver? The human memory discards quite purposefully what it does not find meaningful. All that good stuff you could not recall was forgotten because it simply did not work. This does not mean it can never work, only that it is not doing so at present. Here are some possible reasons, each suggesting a different solution.

Problem	Possible Solutions
The writing is poor in comparison with other sequences.	Cut the whole scene? Shorten? Rewrite and reshoot?
Acting is at fault. Dramatic rhythms are too predictable or actors are not in character or in focus.	Help, but not a cure, is available in further editing. Very often reaction times are wrong and convey the wrong (or no) subtext. Rebalancing these can help.
Scene outcome is predictable.	Scene structure is at fault? Too long or too slow? Maybe the scene is in the wrong place?
Two or more sequences make a similar point.	Repetition does not advance a film's argument unless there is escalation in dramatic pressure, so make choices and ditch the redundant.
Dramatic intensity plummets. A useful analogy is the idea of a rising or falling emotional temperature. To see material in its context is to see correct relative temperatures more clearly.	If your film is raising the temperature, then inadvertently lowering it before the intended peak, the viewer's response is seriously impaired. The transposition of one or two sequences will sometimes work wonders. Naturally, this can only be done if the scenes are not locked into a fixed time development.
The viewer is somehow set up by the preceding material to expect something different.	We read film by its context; if the context gives misleading signals or fails to focus awareness in the right area, the material itself will fall flat.

These suggested areas of examination are just a few involved in the kind of dramatic analysis that a playwright or theater producer uses when rehearsing a new work. Just as a playwright routinely rewrites and adjusts a work based on audience feedback, so the filmmaker makes a vast number of adjustments, large and small, before admitting that a work is finished. First you dig for your own instincts by feeling the dramatic outcome of your material. Later, when you have a fine cut and the material becomes showable, you will call in a few people whose reactions and tastes you respect. You will probably find quite a bit of unanimity in what they tell you. Because a filmmaker has only trial audiences until the work is finished, assessments are hard to make and are certainly not objective.

While still in this assembly stage you and your editor begin asking basic questions:

- Does the film feel dramatically balanced? If you have a very moving and exciting sequence in the middle of the film, the rest of the film may seem anticlimactic.
- Does the film seem to circle around for a long while before you feel it start to move?
- When is there a definite feeling of a story unfolding, and when not? Asking this will help you locate impediments in the film's development.
- Which parts of the film seem to work?
- Which parts drag, and why? Some of the acting may be better than others. Sometimes the problem is that a scene is wrongly placed or repeats the dramatic contours of a previous one.
- Which of the characters held your attention most, and which the least?
- Was there a satisfying alternation of types of material, or was similar material indigestibly clumped together?
- Which were the effective contrasts and juxtapositions? Are there more to be made?
- Sometimes a sequence does not work because the ground has not been properly prepared, or because there is insufficient contrast in mood with the previous sequence. Variety is as important in storytelling as it is in dining.
- What metaphorical allusions did you notice your material making? Could it make them more strongly? That your tale carries a metaphorical charge is as important to your audience as a water table is to pasture.

RESOLUTIONS AFTER SEEING THE FIRST ASSEMBLY

Once you have seen and discussed the whole ungainly epic, you and your editor can make notes of far-reaching resolutions about its future development. These may involve performances, pacing, parallel storytelling, structure, or overall meaning. Remember that your editor is massively uninterested in whatever you originally intended. That is now irrelevant, and you must come to terms with it, consigning all other intentions to history.

PRIORITIZE

When you tackle the problems that inevitably show up in any cut, arrange them by hierarchy and, as in building a scene during rehearsal, deal only with the largest faults. If the film's structure is awry, reorder the scenes and run the film again without making any refinement to individual scenes. If there is a serious problem of imbalance between two characters who are both major parts, go to work on bringing forward the character presently deficient. Correct only the major problems after each running.

LENGTH

Look to the content of your film itself for guidance over length and pacing. Films have a natural span according to the richness and significance of their content, but the hardest achievement in any art form is having the confidence and ability to say a lot through a little. Most beginners' films are agonizingly long and slow, and the advice of professionals on a film's proper length is usually painful but valuable. If you can recognize early that your film should be, say, 20 minutes long at the very most, you can get tough with that 40-minute assembly and make some basic decisions.

Remember that nonlinear editing (NLE), unlike other editing forms, can preserve every one of your cuts. You can always look back at earlier versions to decide whether there is anything you still like about the film's earlier incarnation.

STRUCTURE

Most of all, you need to find the best dramatic structure to make the movie into a well-told tale. A good screenplay does not guarantee the best experience for an audience because during production and editing other criteria come into play. These result from the emotional changes and development brought by the cast and the filming itself. These are what an audience will experience, and to these you must address yourself as they become apparent. The director is always the one most encumbered by the film's history.

LEAVE THE EDITOR TO EDIT

Having decided what the next round of changes should be, leave the cutting room until summoned back. Not all editors or directors can work this way but it is important to try. The reason is simple: The editor loses objectivity while correcting the many problems, and so will any director who remains present. But a director returning with a fresh eye to see a new cut can tell the editor, whose eye is now conditioned by the work, which changes are actually working. The director is always a surrogate audience whose keenest tastes must be satisfied.

CHAPTER 40

EDITING PRINCIPLES

THE ROUGH CUT VIEWING

The cut following the first assembly is called the *rough cut*. Here the full range of material is deployed toward goals decided from seeing the assembly. No sequence is yet fine-tuned, but the editor tries to make each sequence occupy its right place and be dramatically successful.

The scrutiny you give this new cut is similar to the previous versions, and it remains important to deal with the large-scale dimensions first:

- Is there adequate, too little, or too much expository detail?
- Is exposition integrated with the action or does the film pause to inform the audience?
- What exposition, if excised, could the audience still infer?
- What exposition could be delayed (always better to make the audience wonder and wait if you can)?
- Does the film keep momentum throughout?
- Where does the momentum falter and why?
- Does the film breathe so that, like music, each movement feels balanced and inevitable, or is there a misshapen, unbalanced feel to some parts?
- What sequences feel long and what material feels redundant?
- How logical and satisfying is the development of each major character?
- Is anything misleading or alienating about the characters?
- Is there a satisfying balance between interiors and exteriors? (This often means dealing with claustrophobia the film generates. Well-constructed films alternate between intensity and release, much as a person must alternate intimacy with solitude, indoors with outdoors, family with work, day with night, and so on.)
- What is the film's present thematic impact?

After seeing the rough cut a second or third time you might ask more localized questions, such as:

- Which sequences would benefit from later in-points and/or earlier out-points? (Most scenes are better entered or left in action rather than opened and closed).
- What needs to be done for each character to exert maximum impact, and in which sequences?
- Which sequences cry out for special attention to rhythm and pacing?
- How effective is the ending?
- Are there still false endings before (or worse, after) the true one?

Again, ask the editor to fix only the glaring faults before having another showing.

SEE THE WHOLE FILM

Even if work has been done on only two sequences, make a practice of running the whole film. A film is like a tent: Change one pole height or guy-rope length and stresses alter the entire tent's structure. Never go long without examining changes in the context of the whole work, and never undertake major changes without a fresh viewing of the whole film.

EDITING MIMICS AN OBSERVING CONSCIOUSNESS

We have said that how and why we cut between speakers in a dialogue scene is based upon whatever it is that makes us shift our attention in ordinary life. This is best seen by observing how eye contact and eyeline shifts function in real life, for these are the outward signs of shifting attention. The practiced editor builds on eyeline changes extensively, but it is important to work from human behavior rather than disembodied theory.

Counterpointing visual and aural impressions is only an extension of what was called *montage* early in film's history. Because film was silent, film grammar developed the juxtaposition of two shots to imply contrast, relatedness, or continuity. But it is the audience's imagination that supplies the relational links between shots or scenes. I contend that the audience's enjoyment comes not from what they see and hear, but from what they imagine or project as they pursue the narrative and its ambiguous subtexts. Few filmmakers seem consciously aware of this. If you grasp this principle and find effective ways to put it into effect, your work will immediately bear the marks of sophistication.

The use of contrapuntal sound came relatively late and was, I believe, developed by documentary editors in search of narrative compression for lengthy materials drawn directly from life. In fiction filmmaking, Robert Altman's films—beginning with *M*A*S*H* (1970) and continuing to *Gosford Park* (2002)—show great faith in the audience's readiness to interpret densely layered sound tracks. Altman's pioneer sound recordist even built a 16-track location sound recorder capable of recording from multiple radio microphones to eliminate the whole problem of miking individuals during shooting. Today you can use two little eight-track DAT machines slaved together and a lot of radio mikes if you want to do the same thing.

EYE CONTACT

Take the common situation in student projects where two diners have an intimate conversation across a restaurant table. Inexperienced actors play it by gazing soulfully into each other's eyes as they speak. But this is an *idea* of how people converse, not what happens in life, so it gives phony results, either in acting or used as a guiding principle for editing. Go to a restaurant and do some people watching. What really happens, as always, is far more subtle and interesting. It may be unusual for either person to make eye contact more than fleetingly. The situation varies with the individual and with the situation, but generally we reserve the intensity of eye contact for special moments. Normally we use eye contact to:

- Determine information from the other person's expression so we know how next to act on him or her
- Check what effect we have just had
- Put additional pressure on the other person as we act on him or her
- See from the person's body language or expression what is meant when he or she is acting on us

In each case we glance only momentarily at the other person's face to rapidly gather information. In subtle ways, each speaker is either pressing or being pressed. Only at crucial moments does one search the other for facial or behavioral enlightenment. Much of the time the listener's gaze rests on isolated or neutral objects while he or she mentally focuses on what the other person means or how the other person means to act. Hearing may be totally focused on the other person for the duration of the conversation. Or, it, too, may wander. Eyes and ears move their attention independently but are always working in tandem, feeding information into the overworked brain.

APPLYING THE ANALOGY TO FILM

Film, unlike literature, is handicapped because it has difficulty in portraying interior life. But where people look and what they see always indicates (even when they try to hide it) what they feel, so we can and do show these shifts through editing. This can imply a special significance to each moment of change. Through editing choices, we do have a powerful tool to *imply* inner life and *suggest* character contours.

While observing a couple in conversation, consciously play the Concerned Observer role and be highly aware of how and why your eyeline shifts between the speakers. Notice how:

- You often followed the shifts in their eyelines, wanting to see what they were looking at, and involuntarily switching your gaze from subject to object
- How your mind hypothesized a new motivation after each eyeline change

- How there is a rhythm to your eyeline changes (controlled by the shifting contours of the conversation itself)
- How your eyes made their own judgment about who and what to look at, often on the basis of something on the periphery that demanded a closer look

Independently, your center of attention switches back and forth, often following the conversing pair's action and reaction, their changes of eyeline, and their physical action, but also making choices based on your own evolving thoughts and hypothesis, not just on outside stimulation alone.

Notice that *your eyes often leave someone speaking to examine his effect on the listener even while he still speaks.* Unconsciously, the Observer "edits" according to his own developing insight, looking for the most telling information. Making a hypothesis is like shining a light ahead in the dark.

To reproduce on film what you have been observing, you would need to cover each speaker from the viewpoint of the other, and add a third viewpoint to encompass them both as you, the Observer, see them. This last point of view is outside the enclosed consciousness of the two speakers, and because it shows them in a more detached, observational way, it *implies a third, outside point of view.* Add two complementary over-shoulder shots, and you have completed the basic movie coverage.

Flexibility of viewpoint allows the director not only to structure what the spectator sees, but to suggest whose point of view and whose state of mind the spectator shares at any particular moment. *This probing, cinematic way of seeing is modeled on the way we unconsciously delve, visually and imaginatively, into any event that interests us.* The film narrative process is thus never objective, but instead it reproduces the moving, selective consciousness of a particular observer.

According to choices made in editing, the audience can now either identify with one or another of the characters inside the story or with the more detached perspective of the invisible Storyteller/Observer. While character A talks, the film might allow the audience to look detachedly at either A or B, to share the perspective of either one upon the other, or to look at both of them in long shot. The Observer turns into the Storyteller when the Observer's faithful, thoughtful watching (such as you might see in a documentary) becomes a more active, identifying involvement with its own distinct attitudes and expectations of the characters and its own ideas about the underlying meaning and truth.

Though observation is often routed through an involved character in the film, it can also come powerfully from outside the characters and imply that the Storyteller is struggling to understand the characters by trying out different ways of seeing them.

INFLUENCING SUBTEXTS

ALTERING PERFORMANCE RHYTHMS

A very significant dramatic control now rests in the cutting room for any scene adequately covered. This concerns not only who or what is shown at any particular moment, but *how much time each character takes to process what he sees or hears*. Though this timing originates with the actors, it is finally controlled by the editor whenever there is sufficient coverage. Reaction time—which is the inner action that occurs before outward action—contributes hugely to the power and consistency of a scene's subtext.

THE POWER OF SUBTEXT

Inexperienced film actors, learning lines and repeating them in numerous takes and angles, tend to drop into a set rhythm and level the characters' inner lives into a shared average. If this shows up in the first cuts, it is deadly and must be reconfigured in editing to recover some of the changeableness and unpredictability of spontaneous action. Imagine a two-person, interior scene where a man asks a simple question of a woman who is visiting his apartment for dinner: "Do you think it's cold outside?" Depending on the context and on her nonverbal reaction, this could imply several subtexts. He could be saying:

- "Because we're about to leave, do you think I need warmer clothes?"
- "Let's not go to the party after all."
- "Do you want to stay the night with me?"

What makes the audience choose the most likely subtext? How the lines are said and how the listener reacts to the speaker tell you a lot. An easy and unreflecting "No" is very different from one delivered after a momentary silence or one that is long delayed by apparent internal struggle. Not only do such timing differences and behavioral nuances direct what we imagine, but prior events (if the man visited the doctor) also condition the subtext we supply. Thus, the order of material in a film and the amount of apparent thought each character devotes to each part of their interaction will imply quite different subtexts and lead the audience to generate a whole set of open questions. This is highly desirable because it keeps up dramatic tension.

RESCUING SUBTEXT IN EDITING

When performances are not stellar, and particularly if they are uneven, sensitive editing can drive up the stakes in a scene so it acquires more intensity and a more defined point of view. By exerting fine control over the original rhythms of reply, eyeline changes, actions, and reactions, the scene can become a unified entity that nobody could quite foresee.

Of course, no editor can change a character's rate of speech or reaction times in a single, unbroken take. But much potential opens up when the scene is covered from more than one angle or image size. Look at Figure 40–1. Diagram A is a representation of the master take, a timing that the actors reproduced in all subsequent takes. The diagram shows picture and sound as separate strands, much as you see them while cutting film.

In Diagram B, the cut to close-up simply preserves the actors' original timing, though merely by using it the audience begins to expect a greater significance in her reply. Diagram C uses overlap cutting (see following section for extended

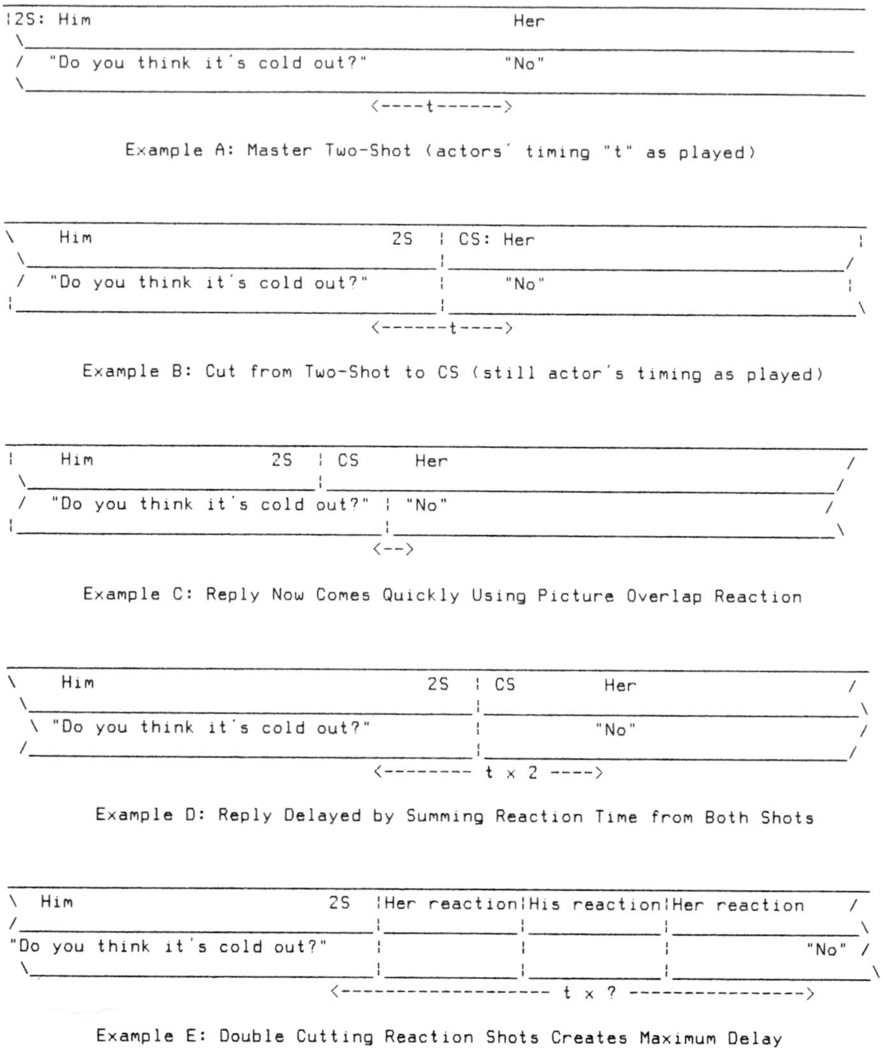

FIGURE 40–1

How the original timing of a pause (t) between lines can be removed or augmented to alter the rhythm of dialogue responses.

explanation) to make her reply come as quickly as possible. Diagram D, however, doubles her reaction time by adding together the pauses from both takes. Diagram E goes still further by double-cutting her thinking and his waiting reaction before cutting back to her in thought before she replies. To create this degree of delay you will need a complementary close-up reaction shot on him and a second take on her from which to steal the extra close-shot reaction.

Intelligent choices of reaction and rebalancing of performance reaction times can add massively to the credibility of the characters' inner lives, and thus to the apparent choices and reactions that compel each into action or speech. This contributes greatly to the overall impact of the film by aiding and abetting performances and creating the grounds for us to infer thought, feeling, and reaction.

VISUAL AND AURAL EDITING RHYTHMS: AN ANALOGY IN MUSIC

The interplay of editing's rhythmic elements needs further explanation if the possibilities are to be visible. Though everything in editing takes place in minutes, seconds, and frames, dramatic decisions can no more be made from script measurements or calculations with a stopwatch than music can be composed using a metronome.

RHYTHMIC INTERPLAY

Music offers a useful analogy here if we examine an edited version of a conversation between two people. We have two different but interlocked rhythms going. First there is the rhythmic pattern of their voices in a series of sentences that ebb and flow, speed up, slow down, halt, restart, and continue. Set against this, and often taking a rhythmic cue from the sound rhythms, is the visual tempo set up by the complex shifts of visual choice, outlined previously and evoked in the interplay of cutting, camera composition, and movement. The visual and aural streams proceed independently yet are rhythmically related, like the relation between music and the physical movements of two dancers.

HARMONY

When you hear a speaker and see his face as he talks, sound and vision are allied like a melody with its harmony. We could, however, break the literalness of always hearing and seeing the same thing (harmony) by making the transition from scene to scene into a temporary puzzle.

COUNTERPOINT

We are going to cut from a woman talking about her vanished husband to a shot panning across a view of tawdry seashore hotels. We start with the speaker in picture and sound and then cut to the panning shot while she is still speaking, letting her remaining words play out over the hotels. The effect is this: While our subject is talking about her now fatherless children and the bitterness she feels toward the absent husband, we glance away and in our mind's eye imagine where he might now be. The film version of this scene can suggest the mental (or even physical) imagery of someone present and listening. The speaker's words are powerfully counterpointed by the image, and the image lets loose our imagination, so we ponder what he is doing and what is going on behind the crumbling façades of the hotels.

Counterpointing one kind of sound against another kind of image has its variations. One usage is simply to illustrate. We see taking place what the woman's words begin to describe: "... and the last I heard, he was in Florida...."

Many an elegant contrapuntal sequence in a feature film is the work of an editor trained in documentary who is trying to raise the movie above a pedestrian script, as Ralph Rosenblum relates in *When the Shooting Stops ... the Cutting Begins* (New York: Viking Press, 1979). Directing and editing documentaries has contributed importantly to the screen fluency of Robert Altman, Lindsay Anderson, Carroll Ballard, Werner Herzog, Louis Malle, Alain Resnais, Alain Tanner, and Haskell Wexler, to name but a few of the better-known fiction directors.

DISSONANCE

Another editing approach exploits discrepancies. For instance, while we hear a salesman telling his new assistant his theory of dynamic customer persuasion, we see the same man listing the virtues of a hideaway bed in a monotone so dreary that his customer is bored into a trance. This discrepancy, if we pursue the musical allusion, is a dissonance. It spurs the viewer to create a resolution. Comparing the man's beliefs (heard) with his practice (seen), the viewer is driven to conclude, "Here is someone who does not know himself." This technique of ambiguous revelation is equally viable in documentary film, where it may have originated. Documentary has a big problem getting the audience to look critically at reality. People think documentary is just a record when, in fact, it, too, is a construct like fiction and must use all the devices at its disposal to alert the audience to critical subtexts and hidden dimensions.

THE PROBLEM OF ACHIEVING A FLOW

After you run your evolving cut a few times, it will strike you more and more as a series of clunky blocks of material, with a distressing lack of flow. Dialogue scenes in particular seem to bog down, being centered as they probably are upon showing each speaker. First there is a block of this speaker, then a block of that speaker, then a block of both, and so on. Even sequences seem to change from one to the next in a blocky way, like watching train boxcars pass, each discrete and hitched to its fellows with a plain link device. I think of this kind of editing as *boxcar cutting*.

How to achieve the effortless flow seen in the cinema? To move in this direction we must recall our Concerned Observer principle and reflect on how human perception functions.

COUNTERPOINT IN PRACTICE: UNIFYING MATERIAL INTO A FLOW

Once you have improved on the script's order for the material, you will want to combine sound and action in a form that takes advantage of counterpoint techniques.

In practice this means bringing together the sound from one shot with the image from another, as we have said. To return to my example of a salesman

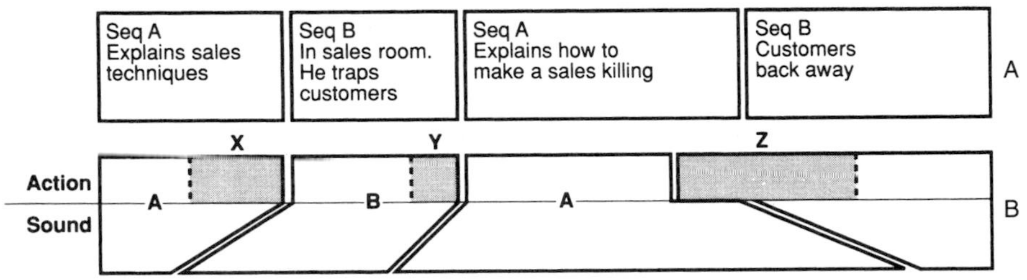

FIGURE 40–2

Counterpointing the content of one sequence against another. Sequence A assembles material in blocks with straight cut sound, while sequence B takes advantage of overlap editing and counterpoint.

with a great self-image who proved to have a poor performance, you could show this on the screen by merging two sets of materials, one of him talking to his assistant over a coffee break (sequence A) and the other of him in the salesroom making a pitch to clients (sequence B).

We can edit the materials into juxtaposition. The conservative, first-assembly method would alternate segments as in Figure 40–2A, a block of explanation, then a block of sales talk, then another block of explanation and another of sales, and so on until the point had been made. This is a common, though clumsy, way to accomplish the objective, and after a few cuts, both the technique and the message become as predictable as a boxer slugging a punching bag.

Instead of crudely alternating the sequences, let's integrate the two sets of materials as in Figure 40–2B. Start Harold explaining his sales philosophy (sequence A) during the salesmen's coffee break. While he's showing off to the younger men, we begin fading up the sound from the salesroom (sequence B) in which we hear Harold's aggressive greetings. As he reaches full volume we cut to the salesroom picture (sequence B) to see he has trapped a reluctant customer and is launching into his sales pitch. After this is established we fade up the coffee break conversation again (sequence A). We hear the salesman say how he first fascinates the customer. We cut to sequence A's picture and see Harold has moved uncomfortably close to his juniors. He tells them how you must now make the customers admit they like the merchandise. While the voices continue we cut back to the salesroom (sequence B) picture only to see the customer backing away angrily. We bring up sequence B's sound as the customer says she only came to buy a pillow.

Notice that in the overlap areas (x, y, and z) of Figure 40–2B, picture from one sequence is being counterpointed against sound from another. Instead of having description and practice separated as discrete blocks of material, description is now laid against practice, and ideas against reality in a much harder-hitting counterpoint.

The benefits are multiple. The total of the two sequences is shorter and more sprightly. Conversation is kept to an interesting minimum while the behavioral material—the salesroom evidence against which we measure his ideas—is now in the majority. The counterpointing of essentials allows the combination of materials to be pared down to essentials, giving what is presented a muscular, spare quality usually lacking when film writing is theatrically conceived. There is a much closer and more telling juxtaposition between vocalized theory and actual performance, and the audience is challenged to reconcile the gap between the man's ideas and what he is actually doing.

Counterpoint editing cannot really be worked out in scripting, because entry and exit points depend on the nuances of playing or camerawork. But if both scenes are shot in their entirety, one becomes a parallel action to the other. The resulting sequence can be worked out from the materials themselves, and will reliably and effectively compress the two.

There is a shooting/editing project to practice these skills in Chapter 6: Shooting Projects. Look for Project 6-2C, Vocal Counterpoint and Point of View. This adds a vocal counterpoint to action, but you might want to try improvising the salesman scene used as an example earlier, using one scene as parallel action to the other and fusing the two in counterpoint.

THE AUDIENCE

DRAMA TAKES PLACE IN THE AUDIENCE'S IMAGINATION

By creating a texture of sound and picture that requires an interpretation, a film can juxtapose the antithetical with great economy and kindle the audience's involvement in developing ideas to resolve the story's dialectical tensions. Now the audience is no longer passively identifying and submitting to the controlling will of the movie, but rather it is stimulated to live an imaginative, critical inner life in response to the film. Critical awareness like this is what Berthold Brecht, striving to arrest the audience habit of identifying, set out to accomplish in the theater.

THE AUDIENCE AS ACTIVE RATHER THAN PASSIVE PARTICIPANTS

This more demanding texture of word and image thrusts the spectator into a critical relationship with the action presented and encourages active rather than passive participation in watching. The Storyteller has developed a contract with the audience that promises not just diversion but a challenge to interpret, a chance to weigh what is seen against what is heard and to balance an idea against its contrary. The film will now sometimes confirm and other times contradict what had seemed true. As in life, the viewer must use critical judgment when, as in our example, a man's self-image turns out to be unreliable.

More interesting ways to use juxtaposition and counterpoint emerge when the basic coupling of sound and picture is broken. For instance, you might show an interior with a bored teenage girl looking out a store window at people in the street. A radio somewhere offscreen is broadcasting the report of a dog show as she watches a boy and his mother having a violent argument outside. The girl is too abstracted to notice the counterpoint. Though we see the mother and child, we hear the commentator detailing the breeds and their traits. There is an ironic contrast between all the different planes of consciousness: an argument is raised to the level of a public spectacle, yet our main character is too naive or too inward-looking to notice. Very succinctly and with not a little humor, both her unconsciousness and a satirical view of mother and child relationships have been compressed into a 30-second shot. Now *that's* economy!

THE OVERLAP CUT

DIALOGUE SEQUENCES

The overlap cut is another contrapuntal editing device useful for blurring the unnatural seams between shots. It works by bringing a speaker's voice in before his picture, or vice versa, and this removes the level cuts that produce boxcar cutting.

Figure 40–3 is a straight-cut, boxcar version of a conversation between A and B. Whoever speaks is shown on the screen, and before long this becomes predictable and boring. You could alleviate this by slugging in some reaction shots (not shown).

Now look at the same conversation using overlap cuts (also called *lap cuts* or *L cuts*). Person A starts speaking, but then we hear B's voice (during overlap x). We wait a sentence before cutting to him. B is interrupted by A (during overlap y), and this time we hold on B's frustrated expression before cutting to A driving his point home. Before A has finished, because we are now interested in B's rising anger, we cut back to him shaking his head (during overlap z). When A has finished, B, whom we have seen waiting, caps the discussion, and this ends the sequence.

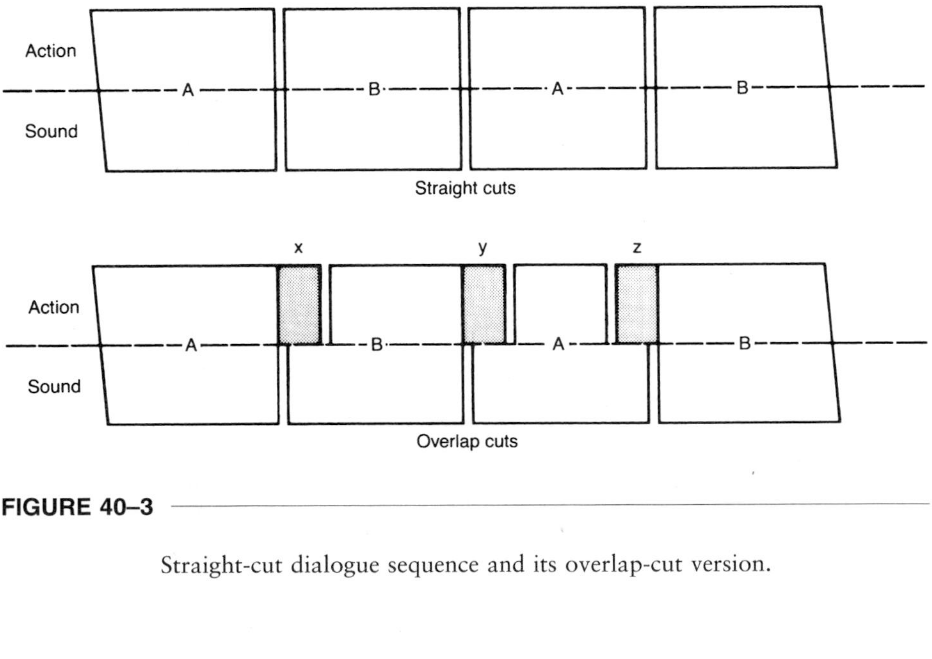

FIGURE 40–3

Straight-cut dialogue sequence and its overlap-cut version.

How do you decide when you should make overlap cuts? Let's return to our trusty guide to editing: human consciousness at work. Imagine you are witnessing a conversation between two people; you have to turn your head from one to the other. Seldom will you turn at the right moment to catch the next speaker beginning; only a suspiciously omniscient intelligence could be so accurate. Such omniscience in a movie destroys the illusion of watching something spontaneous. Inexperienced or downright bad editors often make neat, level cuts between speakers, and the results give a prepackaged, premeditated effect.

Because in real life you can seldom predict who will speak next, it is hearing a new voice that tells you where to look. If a film or video editor is to convince us that a dialogue sequence comes spontaneously from real life, he or she must replicate the disjunctive shifts we unconsciously make as our eyes follow our hearing or when our hearing (that is, concentration) catches up late with something we have just seen.

The guideline to effective cutting is always to be found from building the unfolding consciousness of the story's point of view. This is modeled on the motives and intelligence of what I have called the concerned and observant Storyteller. This spectator and guide is engaged not just in hearing and seeing each speaker as he speaks (which would be boring) but also in interpreting what is going on inside each protagonist through clues embedded in moments of action, reaction, or hypothesis developed by the observer. Through what the Concerned Observer notices from the evidence shown on the screen, the Storyteller's consciousness of the events is subtly established in addition to that of point-of-view characters—and sometimes in contradiction to theirs.

For filmmaking, the message is clear. For a film to be true to life and to implant in the audience the developing subjectivity of the critical observer, the editor must make sound and picture changeover points as staggered cuts much more often than level ones.

SEQUENCE TRANSITIONS

In the worst and most uncinematic scene transition, a character exits the frame leaving an empty set, and the film cuts to another empty set in anticipation of his arrival. This is really proscenium arch theater, a kind of clumsy scene shifting that puts a huge hiccup in a film's momentum. Inexperienced directors often engineer scenes to start and stop this way, but a good editor quickly looks for ways to axe the dead footage.

Just as there are dialogue overlap cuts, so are there live transitions from one sequence to another by using the lap cut. Imagine a scene with a boy and girl talking about going out together. The boy says he thinks her mother will try and stop them. The girl says, "Oh don't worry about her; I can talk her round." Cut to the next scene where the girl asks the question of her mother, who closes the refrigerator with a bang and says firmly, "Absolutely not!"

First, it is redundant to restate the girl's situation in this way. A level cut would take us instantly from the boy/girl sequence to the mother/girl scene where the mother answers, "Absolutely not!" A more interesting way of leaving the boy/girl scene would be to cut to the mother at the refrigerator while the girl is still saying ". . . I can talk her round." As she finishes, the mother slams the fridge door and says "Absolutely not!" as the camera pans to show the girl already in the scene.

Another way to create an elision instead of a creaky scene change would be to hold on the boy and girl and have the mother's angry voice say "Absolutely not!" over the tail end of their shot. You would use the surprise of the new voice to motivate lap cutting to the mother in picture as the new scene continues.

Either of these devices (sound trailing or sound leading picture) serves to make less noticeable the coupling of one sequence and the next. Though you sometimes want to bring a scene to a slow closure, perhaps with a fade out, more often you want to keep up momentum. Though filmmakers choose dissolves because a level cut jerks the viewer too rudely into a new place and time, the dissolve also inserts a rest period between scenes and may dissipate your valuable forward momentum.

SOUND EFFECTS AS SCENE ELISION

You have seen this overlap technique done with sound effects. It might look like this: The schoolteacher rolls reluctantly out of her bed, and as she ties up her hair we hear the increasingly loud sound of a playground until we cut to her on duty at the school door. Because our curiosity demands an answer to the riddle of children's voices in a woman's bedroom, we do not find the location switch arbitrary or theatrical. Anticipatory sound dragged our attention forward to the next sequence.

Another type of overlap cut makes sound work another way; we cut from the teacher leading kids chanting their multiplication tables to her getting food out of her refrigerator at home. The dreary class sound subsides slowly while she exhaustedly eats some leftovers.

In the first example, anticipatory sound draws her forward out of her bedroom, while in the second, holdover sound persists even after she gets home. Because the Storyteller shows how the din exists in her mind, the implication in both cases is that she finds her workplace unpleasant. So overlap cutting does more than soften transitions between scenes; it here implies what dominates our schoolteacher's inner consciousness. We could suggest something quite different by playing it another way and letting the silence of her home trail out into the workplace. In this scenario she is seen at work with her bedroom radio still playing softly before its sound is swamped by the rising uproar of feet echoing in a corridor. At the end of the day, her TV sitcom could displace her voice giving out the dictation, and we cut to her relaxing at home.

By using sound and picture transitions creatively, we can transport the viewer forward without cumbersome (and in film, expensive) optical effects like dissolves, fades, or (God help us) wipes. We are also able to scatter important clues about the characters' subjective lives and inner imaginings, something film cannot otherwise easily do.

SUMMARY

In the previous examples, we have established that our consciousness can probe our surroundings, either:

- Monodirectionally (eyes and ears on the same information source)
- Bidirectionally (eyes and ears on different sources)
- Ears pull eyes forward to seeing a new setting
- Eyes pull ears forward to hearing a new setting

Film suggests these aspects of consciousness by making the audience share the sensations of a character's shifting planes of consciousness and association. A welcome and money-saving result from creative overlap cutting is that you can completely dispense with the fade or dissolve.

HELP, I CAN'T UNDERSTAND!

These cutting techniques are hard to grasp from a book, even though, as I have said, they mimic the way human awareness shifts. If this is getting beyond you, do not worry. The best way to understand editing is to take a complex and interesting sequence in a feature film and, by running a shot or two at a time on a VCR, make a precise log of the relationship between the track elements and the visuals. Chapter 5: Seeing with a Moviemaker's Eye, Project 5-2: Editing Analysis is an editing self-education program with a list of editing techniques for you to find and analyze. Try shooting and editing your own sequences from the directions in Chapter 6: Shooting Projects, Projects 6-5 through 6-10. After some hands-on experience, return to this section and it should be much clearer.

CHAPTER 41

USING ANALYSIS AND FEEDBACK

After perhaps months of sustained editing work on a film, a debilitating familiarity sets in. As you lose objectivity, your ability to make judgments on behalf of an audience departs. Every version begins to look the same, and all of them seem too long. You become obsessed with particular faults in your footage and curing them seems an overwhelming task. Not unusually, you want to hang on to a sequence or a minor character that the editor and others think is redundant. These aspects of the film are your *darlings*, and the director must kill the darlings if the film is to be consistent and work well.

This disabling condition is particularly likely to overwhelm the *hyphenation*, the director-editor, who has lived closely with the intentions and the footage since their inception. But it also afflicts whole editing crews at this stage and is why you should now prepare to call on outsiders' reactions to the piece.

DIAGRAMMING YOUR FILM

After you have already altered, abbreviated, or transposed so much of the original, you usually feel you cannot possibly need any further analysis, but this is wrong. Before you show the cut to outsiders, make an abstract of your film in the form of a block diagram so you can spot anomalies. Some you will easily fix because diagramming alone brings revelations and new ideas.

MAKING A DIAGNOSTIC FLOW CHART

As we have said before, to better understand something, translate it into another form. Statisticians, for instance, know that the full implications of their figures are not evident to the great, unwashed public until expressed as a graph, pie chart, or other proportional image. In our case, we are dealing with a slippery, deceptive medium whose mesmerizing present-tense detail inhibits much sense of overview. But by using a flow chart you can take control and find a fresh and objective perspective on your work.

A useful dual-purpose form that speeds up the job of analysis can be photocopied from Chapter 17, Figure 17–1. Run your film a sequence at a time and:

1. Make a brief note of each new sequence's content in a box (characters and main action).
2. Next to the box, write what the sequence contributes to the development of the film as a whole. This might be factual information; it might introduce a setting, a character, or a relationship to be developed later in the film; or it might exist to create a special mood or feeling.
3. Now look at the flow chart for your film. Like any representation, it has limitations because film sequences are not like a succession of soloists, each singing a self-contained song, but more like the delayed entry of several parts in a choral work. Each entering voice joins and cross-modulates with those preceding. Some foreshadow or make references that will only make sense later.
4. Draw and annotate lines indicating any special relationship existing between each new sequence and those preceding. This might show that in parallel storytelling, for instance, one sequence is too far away from its counterpart.
5. Examine how much time each sequence takes and give each an impact rating so you can assess how the film's dramatic pressures evolve.

Analyzing your work in this way forces you to conceptualize what actually comes from the screen and to translate what are conveniently inchoate sensations into hard-edged statements. It is vital, therefore, to do this work from the life on the screen and not from memory or the script. Articulating what each sequence contributes will help you to see dispassionately and functionally what is truly there for an audience.

What does the progression of contributions in your film add up to? As with the first assembly, you will again find some of the following:

- The film lacks early impact or has an unnecessarily pedestrian opening that makes it a late developer (fine for 19th-century Russian novels but fatal for a film that may depend on TV showings).
- The main issues are unclear or take too long to emerge (writing problem, but you may be able to reposition a scene earlier, even ahead of titles, to commit the film to an interesting line of development).
- The type and frequency of impact is poorly distributed over the film's length (feast or famine in dramatic development and progression).
- There is a nonlinear development of basic, necessary information about characters, backstory, and environment, including

  Omissions

  Duplication

  Backdoubles (going back to something that should have been dealt with earlier)

Redundancy

Expository information positioned too early so audience forgets it

Insufficient expository information or it's placed too late

- The film makes the same dramatic contribution in several ways (three consecutive scenes reveal only that the hero has a low flashpoint; choose the best and reposition or dump the others).
- A favorite sequence or character does not contribute to the thrust of the film. (This is one of your darlings. Close your eyes and swing the ax.)
- The film's resolution emerges early, leaving the remainder of the film tediously inevitable (rebalance or withdraw indicators in the film to keep resolution in doubt, so audience stays interested and working).
- The film appears to end before it actually does (false or multiple endings are a common problem).

Naming each ailment leads to its cure. When you have put these remedies into effect, you will sense the improvement rather than see it. It is like resetting a sail; the boat looks the same but surges under new power.

DIAGNOSIS: USING THE FLOW CHART AGAIN

I cannot overstress the deceit film practices upon its makers. After several rounds of alterations, make a new flow chart to ensure that housecleaning has not introduced new problems. Even when it seems utterly unnecessary, you will almost certainly find another round of anomalies sitting there like time bombs. Filmmakers of long standing know this and subject their work to intensive formal scrutiny. Most of the discussion during the cutting of a feature film is during the last phases and centers on the film's dramatic shape and effectiveness.

A TRIAL SHOWING

Preparing flow charts brings one more benefit. Knowing now what every brick in your movie's edifice is supposed to accomplish, you are excellently prepared to test the film's intentions during a trial show for a small audience.

AUDIENCE

Your audience should be half a dozen or so people whose tastes and interests you respect. The less they know about your aims the better, so tell them as little as possible.

PREPARATION

Check sound levels and adjust them in your software, or you will get misleadingly negative responses. Even film professionals can drastically misjudge a film whose sound elements are inaudible or overbearing.

Once you have your audience members in their seats, warn them that the film is a work in progress and still technically raw. Also warn them if any music, sound effects, or titles are missing. Incidentally, it helps to give the film a working title because a title signals a film's purpose and identity to its audience and forms part of the viewer's "contract" with the film. You may also want to call out, while the film is running, a brief description of any vital sound component that is missing.

SURVIVING YOUR CRITICS AND MAKING USE OF WHAT THEY SAY

LISTEN, DO NOT EXPLAIN

Asking for critical feedback must be handled carefully, or it can be a pointless exercise. After the viewing:

- Ask for impressions of the film as a whole.
- Say little, listen much, and retain your fundamental bearings toward the piece.
- Focus and direct your viewers' attention or you may find the discussion quite peripheral to your needs.
- Avoid the temptation to explain the film in any way. Explanations at this stage are not only irrelevant, they confuse and compromise the audience's own perceptions. Among strangers, your film must soon stand or fall on its merits, so concentrate on hearing what your audience may be telling you.

Taking in reactions and criticism is an emotionally draining experience. It is quite usual to feel threatened, slighted, misunderstood, and unappreciated and to come away with a raging headache. You need all the self-discipline you can muster to sit immobile, say little, and listen. Take notes or make an audio recording of the proceedings so you can go over what the audience said in peace.

LINES OF INQUIRY

Because you usually need to guide the inquiry into useful channels, here are some open-ended questions that move from the large issues toward the component parts.

- What is the film really about?
- What are the major issues in the film?
- Did the film feel the right length or was it too long?
- Were there any parts that were unclear or puzzling? (You can itemize those you suspect fit the description because audiences often forget anything that passed over their heads.)
- Which parts felt slow?
- Which parts were moving or otherwise successful?
- What did you feel about ___ (name of character)?
- What did you end up knowing about ___ (situation or issue)?

With these questions, you are beginning to test the effectiveness of the function you assigned each sequence. Depending on your trial audience's patience, you may be able to survey only dubious areas or you may get feedback on most of your film's parts and intentions.

BALANCING CRITICS' VIEWPOINTS

Dealing with criticism really means absorbing multiple views and then, after the dust settles, reviewing the film to see how audience members could get such varying impressions. In the cutting room, you and your editor now see the film with the eyes of those who never understood that the messenger was the work-mate seen in an earlier scene. You find a way to put in an extra line where the woman asks if Don is still at work and, without compromising the film in any way, the problem is solved.

Before rushing to fix anything, you must, of course, take into account the number of people reporting any particular difficulty. Where comments from different audience members cancel each other out, there may be no action called for. Make allowance for the subjectivity and acuity of your individual critics.

THE EGOCENTRIC CRITIC

An irritation you must often suffer, especially among those with a little knowledge to flourish, is the person who insists on talking about the film he would have made rather than the film you have just shown. Diplomatically redirect the discussion.

MAKE CHANGES CAUTIOUSLY

Make no changes without careful reflection. Remember that when people are asked to give criticism, they want to leave a contributory mark on your work. You will never be able to please everyone, nor should you try.

HOLD ON TO YOUR CENTRAL INTENTIONS

Never let your central intentions get lost and never revise them unless there are overwhelmingly positive reasons to do so. Act only on suggestions that support and further your central intentions. This is a dangerous phase for the filmmaker, indeed for any artist. If you let go of your work's underlying identity, you will lose your direction. If in doubt, keep listening and think deeply about what you hear. Do not be tempted by strong emotions to carve into your film precipitously. You may need to wait a week for your contradictory passions to settle.

MEA CULPA

It is quite normal by now to feel that you have failed, that you have a piece of junk on your hands, that all is vanity. If this happens, take heart. You might have felt this during shooting, which would have been a lot worse. Actually, things are never so awful as they seem after the first showings. Keep in mind that the conditions of viewing themselves invite mainly negative feedback. Lay audiences (and even professionals) are often disproportionately affected by a wrong sound balance here, a missed sound dissolve there, a shot or two that needs clipping, or a sequence that belongs earlier. These imbalances and rhythmic ineptitudes massively downgrade a film's impact. The glossy finish you have yet to apply will greatly improve the film's reception.

THE USES OF PROCRASTINATION

Whether you are pleased or depressed by your film, it is always good to stop working on it for a few weeks and do something else. If this degree of anxiety and depression is new to you, take comfort; you are deep in the throes of the artistic experience. It is the long and painful labor before birth. When you pick up the film again after a lapse, its problems and their solutions will no longer seem overwhelming.

TRY, TRY AGAIN

A film of any substance usually demands a long evolution in the editing room, so expect to make several rounds of alterations and to try the film on several new audiences. You may want to show the last cut to the original trial audience to see what changes they report. Sometimes you can get a real sense of progress made during editing and sometimes not.

As a director with a lot of editing in my background, I know that a film truly emerges in the editing process. Magic and miracles appear from the footage, yet even film crews seldom have much idea about what really happens. It is a process unknown to those who have not lived through it, and for the beginner it will seem extremely slow. Putting a year of part-time work into a 30-minute film is not unusual for a new director who wants to make the work live up to its potential. To abridge this work is like pulling a car chassis off the assembly line and driving it away because the engine is already connected to the wheels.

KNOWING WHEN TO STOP

Never set a deadline for the end of editing. Instead, be aware of when the learning curve begins to flatten. Some directors will go on fidgeting and fiddling with the cut ad infinitum. This is the fear of letting go. Ending editing is like giving up being the shepherd to your children. There comes a point where they are as grown up as they are going to be, and you must let them go forward alone, to win friends as they may.

CHAPTER 42

WORKING WITH A COMPOSER

Composers are the last in the creative chain to be hired, and in film they generally have to work under pressured circumstances. The more time you can give them, the better. For most of what follows I am indebted to my son Paul Rabiger, who lives and works in Cologne, Germany, where he makes music for television and film. Like many involved in producing music these days, he works largely with synthesizers, using live instruments as and when the budget allows. Software favored by composers includes Steinberg Cubase and Emagic Logic Audio. Programs like these permit many tracks, integrate Musical Instrument Digital Interface (MIDI) with live recording, and support video in QuickTime format so the composer can build music to an accurate video version of the film.

COPYRIGHT

Never assume that recorded music you would like to use will be available when you get around to inquiring. The worst time to negotiate with composers, performers, publishers, and performing rights societies is when your film has come to depend on a particular recording. You are now in the weakest position, and lawyers with a nose for such things will capitalize on this. Commissioning original music obviates the difficulty of getting (and paying for) copyright clearance on music already recorded.

WHEN THE COMPOSER COMES ON BOARD

If the composer comes on board early, he or she will probably read the screenplay and see the first available version of the edited film. An experienced composer will probably avoid coming in with preconceived ideas and will inquire what the director wants the music to contribute. The composer can then mull over the characters, the settings, and overall content of a film, taking time to develop basic melodic themes and deciding within the budget what instrumental texture works best. Particular characters or situations often evoke their own musical treatment or leitmotif (recurring theme), and this is always best worked out with some time on hand, especially if research is necessary because music must reflect a particular era or ethnicity.

WHEN THERE'S A GUIDE TRACK

Sometimes while editing, the editor may drop in sample music that nobody expects to keep but which helps assess the movie's potential. At the screening the composer may be confronted with a Beatles song or a stirring passage from Shostakovich's Leningrad Symphony. This certainly shows what a certain kind of music does for the scene and indicates a texture or tempo that editor and director think works, but it also raises a barrier because the composer must extract whatever the makers find valuable (say in rhythm, orchestration, texture, or mood) and then try to reach beyond the examples with his or her own musical solutions.

DEVELOPING A MUSIC CUE LIST

Once the content of the film is more or less locked down, it is screened in video form with composer, director, editor, and producer. The tape version has timecode burned into the lower part of the screen, which displays a cumulative timing for the whole film. The group will break the film down into acts and note where these occur on the film's timeline. They will discuss where music seems desirable and what kind seems most appropriate. Typical questions will center on how time is supposed to pass and whether music is meant to shore up a weak scene. The composer finds out (or suggests) where each music section starts and stops and aims to depart with a music cue list in hand and full notes as to function, with beginnings and endings defined as timecode. Start points may begin with visual clues (car door slams, car drives away) or dialogue clues ("If you think I'm happy about this, you've got another think coming.").

If the editor generates the music cues, sections should be logged in minutes and seconds down to the nearest half second. Figure 42–1 shows what a composer's cue sheet looks like. Like other addictive substances, music is easy to start but difficult to finish. You'll have no difficulty starting a music segment, but ending one so the audience does not feel deprived will take careful planning. A rule of thumb is to conclude or fade out music under cover of something more commanding. You might take music out during the first seconds of a noisy street scene or just before the dialogue in a new scene. The best study of practice is to view films that successfully integrate music with the kind of action you have in your film.

The computer-savvy composer then gets a tape copy to compose to. He or she will either first create a traditional score to be performed and recorded or will work with computers and MIDI-controlled synthesizers to make music sections directly. In the course of hands-on composing, music cues are occasionally

"THE WATER-PEOPLE" MUSIC SECTION 4

00:00.0	Music segment begins as Robert jumps in car
00:03.5	Engine starts
00:05.0	Car lurches forward
00:10.5	Cut to Robert checking fuel gauge
00:14.5	Looks in rearview mirror
00:19.0	Frowns, realizing that a motorcycle is behind
00:27.5	Cut to Carl gunning his Harley-Davidson
00:38.0	Cut to Robert staring in mirror, car going off track
00:46.0	Shriek of tyres for 3 seconds as Robert drags car back on to road
00:58.5	Cut to Carl lying forward on motorcycle tank
01:06.5	Cut to BCU Robert's face realizing it's Carl behind
01:08.5	Begin Robert's line: "So you want trouble. I can give you trouble"
01:12.0	End of line.
01:14.5	Cut to BCU hand opens glove pocket, takes out revolver
01:16.0	Revolver visible
01:17.5	Cut to flashing ambulance light, zoom back and siren drowns out music fades to silence and...
01:29.0	music ends here.

FIGURE 42–1

Typical scene measurements for a music cue segment.

added, dropped, or renegotiated when initial ideas meet actuality. Poorly placed or unjustified music may be worse than no music at all.

Sometimes a courageous composer will work backward from a musical destination. In Joseph Losey's *The Go-Between* (1971) Michel Legrand's superb score starts in the main character's boyhood with a simple, though slightly ominous theme taken from Mozart. As the boy's trauma over conflicting loyalties unfolds and more of the older man's present-day inquiry intrudes, the theme is developed into a fuller and more tragic voice for its elderly subject—whose outward life, ironically enough, is utterly atrophied.

WHEN TO USE MUSIC, AND WHEN NOT

Though music is most commonly used as a transitional device, filler, or to set a mood, there are other ways to use it. Try never to use it to enhance what can already be seen on the screen. Better is to use it to suggest what cannot be seen, such as a character's expectations, interior mood, or feelings he withholds. The classic example is Bernard Herrmann's unforgettable all-violin score for Hitchcock's *Pyscho* (1960), with its jabbing violin screams as the pressure within Norman Bates becomes intolerable. Music, so natural an element to melodrama, is perhaps hardest to conceive for comedy.

Music is often used to foreshadow events and build tension, but it should never give the story away. Nor should it ever "picture point" the story by commenting too closely. Walt Disney was infamous for *Mickey Mousing* his films—an industry term for fitting scores like aural straitjackets around the minutia of action. The first of his true-life adventures, *The Living Desert* (1953), was full of extraordinary documentary footage but marred by scorpions made to square dance and music that supplied a different note, trill, or percussion roll for everything that dared move. Used like this, music becomes controlling and smothering.

A related mistake is to use too much music, burdening the film with a musical interpretation that disallows making your own emotional judgments. Hitchock's *Suspicion* (1941) and many a film of its vintage is marred this way. Far from heightening a film, the score flattens it by maintaining an exhausting aura of perpetual melodrama. The ubiquitous TV westerns of the 1950s and 1960s served up unending music punctuated by gunshots, horse whinnies, and snatches of snarling dialogue. Luckily, fashions change, and today less is considered more. A rhythm alone, without melody or harmony, can often supply the uncluttered accompaniment a sequence needs.

When its job is to set a mood, the music should do its work and then get out of the way to return and comment later. Sometimes a composer will point out during the screening just how effective, even loaded, a silence is at a particular point. The rhythms of action, camera movement, montage, and dialogue are themselves a kind of music, and you need not paint the lily.

Better than using music to illustrate (which merely duplicates the visual message) is to counterpoint the visible with music that provides an unexpected emotional shading. An indifferently acted and shot sequence may suddenly come to life because music gives it a subtext that boosts the forward movement of the story. In a story with fine shading, a good score can supply the sense of integrity or melancholy in one character and the interior impulse directing the actions of another. Music can also enhance not just the givens of a character, but it can indicate the interior development leading to an action and imply motives not otherwise visible. Music can supply needed phrasing to a scene or help create structural demarcations by bracketing transitions in scenes or between acts. Short stings or fragments of melody are good if they belong to a larger musical picture.

Given that an intelligent film is a weave of scenes whose longitudinal relationships can often stand strengthening, a composer may color-code his cues to group scenes, characters, situations, and the like longitudinally into musically related families. In a 40-minute film there may be 30 music cues, from a *sting*, or short punctuation, to a passage that is extended and more elaborate. He (or she, of course) may want to develop music for a main plot, but have musical identities for two subplots. Keeping these separate and not clashing during cross cutting can be problematic, so their relationship is important, particularly in key. Using a coding system keeps the composer aware of the logical connections and continuity the music must underpin.

Because there are many factors involved in producing an integrated score, it is important that music cues, once decided, should not be changed later without compelling reason.

KEYS, AND DIEGETIC AND NON-DIEGETIC MUSIC

An initial planning stage for the composer is deciding what progression of keys to use through the film, based on the emotional logic of the story itself.

Especially when one kind of music takes over as a commentary upon another, the key of the latter must be related so the transition is not jarring. This is true for all adjacent music sections, not just original scoring. A film may contain popular songs the characters listen to in their car, and related scored music must be appropriate in key.

Any sound that is a part of the characters' world is called *diegetic* sound. Following it may be a very different kind of music, perhaps a score of massed cellos. Of course the characters do not hear or react to this, for it is part of the film's authorial commentary and is addressed to the audience. This is called *non-diegetic* sound.

CONFLICTS AND COMPOSING TO SYNC POINTS

An experienced musician composing for a recording session will write to very precise timings, paying attention to track features such as the tire screech and dialogue lines. The choice of instrumentation must not fight dialogue, nor can the arrangement be too busy at points where music might compete with dialogue or effects. Music can, however, take over the function of a diegetic sound track that otherwise would be too loaded. Musical punctuation, rather than a welter of naturalistic sound effects, saves time and labor and can produce something more impressionistic and effective. It's worth noting that an overloaded, over-detailed sound track takes energy on the part of the audience to interpret and is not well reproduced by the television speakers through which many people may hear your work.

If the composer is to work around dialogue and spot effects, he or she should have an advanced version of the sound track rather than the simple dialogue one used during editing. This is particularly true in any track that will be heard in a cinema setting. The sound system is likely to be powerful and sophisticated, and the film's track will come under greater artistic scrutiny.

When a written score is recorded to picture, it is marked with the cumulative timing so that as the music is recorded (normally to picture as a safeguard), the conductor can make a running check that the sync points line up. The composer might put a dramatic sting on the first appearance of the pursuing motorcycle at 27.5 seconds and on the appearance of the revolver at 01:16, for instance.

Low-budget film scores aren't usually live recordings but instead make use of MIDI computerized composing techniques. The composer builds the music to a QuickTime scratch version of the film, digitized from a cassette, so music fitting is done at the source.

HOW LONG DOES IT TAKE?

An experienced composer likes to take more than 6 weeks to compose about 15 minutes of music for a 90-minute feature film, but she may have to do it in 3, with a flurry of music copyist work at the end, to be ready for the recording session.

THE LIVE MUSIC SESSION

The editor makes the preparations to record music and attends the recording session because only the editor can say whether a particular shot can be lengthened or shortened to accommodate the slight timing inaccuracies that always appear during recording. Adjusting the film is easier and more economical than paying musicians to pursue perfect musical synchronicity.

FITTING MUSIC

After the recording session, the editor fits each music section and makes the necessary shot adjustments. If the music is appropriate, the film takes a quantum leap forward in effectiveness. Some editors specialize in cutting and fitting music. Their expertise is important to a musical, in which much of the film is shot to playback on the set.

THE MIX

The composer will want to be present at all mix sessions affecting the functionality of the music he or she has composed. When music has been composed on MIDI, it is only a matter of a small delay to return to the musical elements and produce a new version with changes incorporated.

CHAPTER 43

EDITING FROM FINE CUT TO SOUND MIX

Sound is an incomparable stimulant to the audience's imagination and only rarely gets its due. Ideally everyone is alert to sound-composition possibilities from the moment the script begins to be written and keeps building on these concepts until postproduction ends. Opportunities and special moments arise in addition to those programmed in from the beginning, and this is part of a work asserting its identity. It's important to keep track of every idea for sound that anyone has along the way, and not leave it all to an *audio-sweetening* session. That, by the way, is an expression I detest. It suggests that sound is sour and needs sugaring. *Sound design*, *sound editing*, and *sound mix* are more direct and respectful terms. Especially if you have monitored and directed the sound treatment throughout, the sound mix will be a special and even exhilarating occasion.

What happens when sound is left to fend for itself? Poor handling of dialogue tracks alone will disrupt the dreamlike quality that a good film attains, so it's worth learning a lot about the handling of sound. Sound specialists will be the first to say they work most creatively with good groundwork from the director and script.

Finalizing sound is another computer operation, usually using ProTools and a first-rate amplifier and speaker system to replicate a hypothetical cinema's sound environment. I say *hypothetical* because few cinemas approach the state of the art. Yet good sound, as Dolby cinemas have discovered, is good business, so sound may yet get its day.

THE FINE CUT

With typical caution, filmmakers call the result of the evolutionary editing process the *fine*, not final, cut for there may still be minor changes and accommodations. Some of these arise from laying further sound tracks in preparation to produce a master mixed track.

MAKE A FINAL CHECK OF ALL SOURCE MATERIAL

As mentioned previously, the editor must, as a last act, view all shot material to make sure nothing useful has been overlooked. At this point in editing, and especially if there is a lot of coverage, this demand is skull-crackingly tedious and time-consuming, but almost invariably there will be some "Eureka!" discoveries in compensation. If there aren't, you can rest easy that night.

SOUND

SOUND DESIGN DISCUSSIONS

How and why music gets used needs careful discussion, as described in the previous chapter: Working with a Composer. Although sound is made of different elements—music, dialogue, atmospheres, effects—it is a mistake to put them in a hierarchy and think of them separately at this, the ultimate compositional stage.

Before the sound editor goes to work splitting dialogue tracks and laying sound effects, there should be a detailed discussion with the director about the sound identity of the whole film and how each sequence should be treated within this identity from the sound point of view. You should agree on the known sound problems and on a strategy to handle them. This should be a priority because dialogue reconstruction—if it's needed—is an expensive, specialized, and time-consuming business, and no film of any worth can survive the impact of having it done poorly.

Walter Murch, the doyen of editors and sound designers, makes a practice of watching a film he is editing without the sound turned on, so he imagines what the sound might properly be. Among the less-usual functions of sound, among many listed in Randy Thom's "Designing a Movie for Sound" (*www.filmsound.org/articles/designing_for_sound.htm*), are to:

- Indicate a historical period
- Indicate changes in time or geographical locale
- Connect otherwise unconnected ideas, characters, places, images, or moments
- Heighten ambiguity or diminish it
- Startle or soothe

That Web site, *www.filmsound.org*, is an excellent source of information for all aspects of sound in film, by the way.

Any good sound editor will tell you it's not quantities of sound or complexity that make a good sound track, but rather the psychological journey sound leads you on while you watch. This is the art of *psychoacoustics*, and usually sound is most effective when it is simple rather than complex, and highly specific and special rather than generic.

POST-SYNCHRONIZING DIALOGUE

Post-synchronizing dialogue means each actor creating new speech tracks in lip sync with an existing picture, and the laborious operation is variously called *dubbing*, *looping*, or *automatic dialogue replacement* (ADR). This is done in a studio with the actor or actors watching a screen or monitor and rehearsing with the picture before they get the OK to record. A long dialogue exchange will be done perhaps 30 seconds at a time.

The process is ardently to be avoided because newly recorded tracks invariably sound flat and dead in contrast to live location recordings. This is not because they lack background presence, which can always be added, or even because sound perspective and location acoustics are missing. What kills ADR is the artificial situation. The actor finds himself flying blind to reconstitute every few seconds of dialogue and completely in the hands of whomever is directing each few sentences. However good the whole, it invariably drags down the impression of their performances, and actors hate ADR with excellent reason.

THE FOLEY STAGE AND RECREATING SYNC SOUND EFFECTS

Many sound effects shot wild, on location, or in a Foley studio can be fitted afterward and will work just fine. The Foley studio was named after its intrepid inventor, Jack Foley, who realized back in the 1940s that you could mime all the right sounds to picture if you had a sound studio with different surfaces, materials, and props. As everyone now knows, it takes invention to create a sound that is right for the picture. Baking powder under compression in a sturdy plastic bag, for instance, makes the right scrunching sound of footsteps in snow, and a punched cabbage can sound most like someone being struck over the head.

A Foley studio has a variety of surfaces (concrete, heavy wood, light wood, carpet, linoleum, gravel, and so on. The Foley artists may add sand or paper to modify the sound of footsteps to suit what's on the screen. In the most forgettable Jayne Mansfield comedy, *The Sheriff of Fractured Jaw* (1959), directed by Raoul Walsh, my job was to make horse footsteps with coconuts and steam engine noises with a modified motorcycle engine. It was fun.

Repetitive sounds that must fit an action (knocking on a door, shoveling snow, or footsteps) can usually be recreated by recording the actions a little slower and then cutting out the requisite frames before each impact's attack. This is easy with a computer. More complex sync effects (two people walking through a quadrangle) will have to be post-synced just like dialogue, paying attention to the different surfaces the feet pass over (grass, gravel, concrete, etc.). Surviving a grueling series of post-sync sessions makes you truly understand two things: one, that it is vital for the location recordist to procure good original recordings if at all possible, and two, how good top-notch location film sound and editing crews really are at their jobs.

On a complex production with a big budget, the cost is economically justified. For the low-budget filmmaker, some improvisation can cut costs enormously. What matters is that sound effects are appropriate (always difficult to arrange) and that they are in sync with the action onscreen. Where and how you record them is not important provided they work well. Sometimes you can find appropriate sound effects in sound libraries, but *never* assume a sound effect listed in a library will work with your particular sequence until you have tried it against picture. By entering *sound effects library* in a search engine, you will turn up many sources of sound libraries. Some let you listen or even download effects. Try Sound Ideas at *www.sound-ideas.com/bbc.html.*

A caution: Most sound libraries are top heavy with garbage shot eons ago. Many effects tracks are not clean, that is, they come with a heavy ambient background or ineradicable system hiss. The exotic sounds such as helicopters, Bofors guns, and elephants rampaging through a Malaysian jungle are easy to use. It's the nitty-gritty sounds such as footsteps, door slams, dog growling, and so on that are so hard to find. At one time there were only six different gunshots used throughout the industry. I heard attempts at recording new ones. They were awful and sounded nothing like you would expect. Expectation is the key to getting it right. Authentic sounds are nowhere next to those you imagine and accept as the Real Thing.

SOUND CLICHÉS

Providing sounds for what is on the screen can easily be overdone. Because a cat walks across a kitchen is not an excuse for a cat meow, unless the cat is seen to be demanding its breakfast in a coming shot. Do look up this Web site for a hilarious list of sound clichés: *www.filmsound.org/cliche/.* In it all bicycles have bells; car tires must always squeal when the car turns, pulls away, or stops; storms start instantaneously; whistling types of wind are always used; doors always squeak; and much, much more.

WHAT THE SOUND MIX CAN DO

After the film has reached a fine cut, the culmination of the editing process is to prepare and mix the component sound tracks. A whole book could be written on this preeminent subject alone. What follows is a list of essentials along with some tips.

You are ready to mix tracks into one master track when you have:

- Finalized content of your film
- Fitted music
- Split dialogue tracks, grouping them by their equalization (EQ) needs and level commonality:
  - A separate track for each mike position in dialogue tracks
  - Sometimes a different track for each speaker, depending on how much EQ is necessary for each mike position on each character
- Filled-in backgrounds (missing sections of background ambience, so there are no dead spaces or abrupt background changes)
- Recorded and laid narration (if there is any)
- Recorded and laid sound effects and mood-setting atmospheres
- Finalized ProTools timeline contents

The mix procedure determines the following:

- Sound levels (such as between a dialogue foreground voice track and a background of a noisy factory scene if, and only if, they are on separate tracks)
- Equalization (the filtering and profiling of individual tracks either to match others or to create maximum intelligibility, listener appeal, or ear comfort; a voice track with a rumbly traffic background can, for instance, be much improved by *rolling off* the lower frequencies, leaving the voice range intact)
- Consistent quality (for example, two tracks from two angles on the same speaker will need careful equalization and level adjustments if they are not to sound dissimilar)
- Level changes (fade up, fade down, sound dissolves, and level adjustments to accommodate sound perspective and such new track elements as narration, music, or interior monologue)
- Sound processing (adding echo, reverberation, telephone effect, etc.)
- Dynamic range (a compressor squeezes the broad dynamic range of a movie into the narrow range favored in TV transmission; a limiter leaves the main range alone but limits peaks to a preset level)
- Perspective (to some degree, equalization and level manipulation can mimic perspective changes, thus helping create a sense of space and dimensionality through sound)
- Multi-channel sound distribution (if a stereo track or surround sound treatment is being developed, different elements go to each sound channel to create a sense of horizontal spread and sound space)
- Noise reduction (Dolby and other noise-reduction systems help minimize the system hiss that would intrude on quiet passages)

Be aware that when old technology must be used, changes on a manually operated mixing board cannot be done instantaneously on a cut from one sequence to the next. Tracks must be *checkerboarded* (meaning they alternate from track to track) so that a channel's equalization and level adjustments can be set up in the section of silent sound spacing prior to the track's arrival. This is most critical when balancing dialogue tracks, as explained in the following section.

SOUND MIX PREPARATION

Track elements are presented here in the conventional hierarchy of importance, although the order may vary; music, for instance, might be faded up to the foreground and dialogue played almost inaudibly low. When cutting and laying sound tracks, be careful not to cut off the barely audible tail of a decaying sound or to clip the attack. Sound editing should be done at high volume so you hear everything that is there or isn't there when it should be.

Laying nonlinear digital tracks is much easier than in the old manual days because you follow a logic that is visible to the eye and can hear your work immediately. Fine control is quick and easy with a sound-editing program such as

ProTools because you can edit with surgical precision, even within a syllable. The equivalent operation in manual film is not difficult but you cannot properly hear the results until mix time. Traditional mix theaters are nowadays about as common as steam trains, and there is not much weeping over their loss. Getting dozens of tracks laid for a mix was a monumental task, and watching them churn to and fro in 30 dubbing players slaved to a film projector was stressful (my first job was cement splicing in a feature film studio). Twelve people worked a day or more to mix 10 minutes of film track. For battle sequences or other complex situations, you could multiply that period several times. Some battles did not stay on the screen, either.

NARRATION OR VOICE-OVER

Getting actors to make a written narration sound spontaneous is next to impossible, so consider using the improv method in which actors, given a list of particular points to be made, improvise dialogue in character. By judicious side coaching, or even interviewing, the actor produces a quantity of entirely spontaneous material in a number of passes that can be edited down. Though labor-intensive, the result will be more spontaneous and natural than anything read from a script.

If you lay narration or interior monologue you will need to fill gaps between narration sections with room tone so the track remains live, particularly during a quiet sequence.

DIALOGUE TRACKS AND THE PROBLEM OF INCONSISTENCIES

You will have to split dialogue tracks in preparation for the mix. Because different camera positions occasion different mike positioning, a sequence's dialogue tracks played *as is* will change in level and room acoustics from shot to shot. The result is ragged and distracting when you need quite the contrary effect—the seamless continuity familiar from feature films. This result is achieved by painstaking and labor-intensive sound editing work in the following order:

1. Split dialogue tracks (lay them by grouping on separate tracks) according to the needs imposed by the coverage's mike positioning.
   a. In a scene shot from two angles and having two mike positions, all the close-shot sound goes on one track, and all the medium-shot sound goes on the other. With four or five mike positions, you would need to lay at least four or five tracks.
   b. Sometimes tracks must additionally be split by character, especially if one of them is under- or over-modulated in the recording.
2. Equalization (EQ) settings can be roughly determined during track laying, but final settings must be determined in the mix. The aim is to bring all tracks into acceptable compatibility, given that the viewer can expect a different sound perspective to match the different camera distances. These settings may now apply to multiple sound sections as they have been grouped according to EQ needs.
3. Give special attention to cleaning up background tracks of extraneous noises, creaks, mike handling sounds—anything that doesn't overlap dialogue and

can therefore be removed. Any gaps will sound like drop out unless filled with the correct room tone.

4. If you have to join dissimilar room tones, do it as a quick dissolve behind a commanding foreground sound so the audience's attention is distracted from the change. The worst place to make an illogical sound change is in the clear.

Although manual and nonlinear sound mixing can handle many tracks, it is usual to premix groups of tracks and leave final control of the most important to the last stage.

Inconsistent Backgrounds: The ragged, truncated background is the badge of the poorly edited film in which inadequate technique steals attention from the film's content. Frequently, when you cut between two speakers in the same location, the background of each is different either in level or quality because the mike was angled differently or background traffic or other activities had changed over time. Now is the time to use those presence tracks you shot on location so you can add to and augment the lighter track to match its heavier counterpart. If an intrusive background sound, such as a high-pitched band saw, occupies a narrow band of frequency, you can sometimes effectively lower it using a graphic equalizer. This lets you tune out the offending frequency. But with it goes all sounds in that band, including that part of your character's voices.

Inconsistent Voice Qualities: A variety of location acoustical environments, different mikes, and different mike working distances all play havoc with the consistency of location voice recordings. Intelligent adjusting with sound equalization (EQ) at the mix stage can massively decrease the sense of strain and irritation arising from having to make constant adjustment to unmotivated and therefore irrational changes.

LAYING MUSIC TRACKS

It is not difficult to lay music, but remember to cut in just before the first sound attack so its arrival isn't heralded by studio atmosphere or record surface hiss prior to the first chords. Arrow A in Figure 43–1 represents the ideal cut-in point; to its left is unwanted presence or hiss. To the right of A are three attacks in succession leading to a decay to silence at arrow B. A similar attack-sustain-decay profile is found for many sound effects (footsteps, for instance) so you can often use the same editing strategy. By removing sound between x and y, we could reduce three footfalls here to two.

SPOT SOUND EFFECTS

These sync to something onscreen, like a door closing, a coin placed on a table, or a phone being picked up. They need to be appropriate, in the right perspective, and carefully synchronized. Sound effects, especially tape library or disk effects, often bring problematic backgrounds of their own. You can reduce this by cutting into the effect immediately before a sound's *attack* (see Figure 43–1, arrow A) and immediately after its decay (arrow B), thus minimizing the

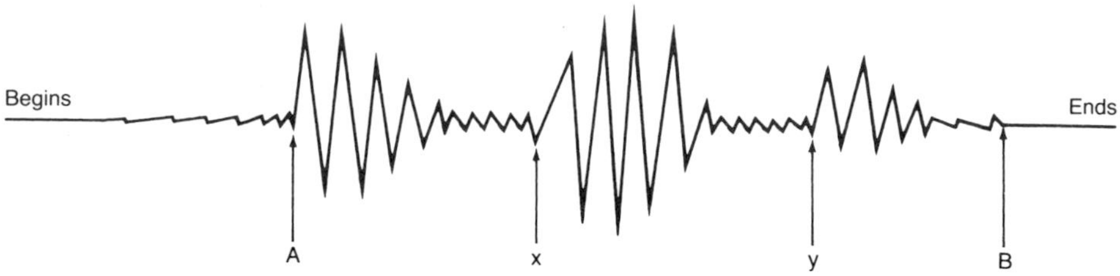

FIGURE 43–1

Sound modulations: attack, three bursts, and decay. Arrows x and y indicate the best cutting points.

unwanted background's intrusiveness. Mask unwanted sound changes by placing them behind another sound. An unavoidable atmosphere change could be masked by a doorbell ringing, for example. You can bring an alien background unobtrusively in and out by fading it up and down rather than letting it thump in and out as cuts.

Bear in mind that *the ear registers a sound cut in or a cut out much more acutely than a graduated change.*

ATMOSPHERES AND BACKGROUND SOUND

Atmospheres are laid either to create a mood (birdsong over a morning shot of a wood or wood saw effects over the exterior of a carpenter's shop) or to mask inconsistencies by using something relevant but distracting. Always obey screen logic by laying atmospheres to cover the entire sequence, not just a part of it. Remember that if a door opens, the exterior atmosphere (children's playground, for instance) will rise for the duration that the door is open. If you want to create a sound dissolve, remember to lay the requisite amounts to allow for the necessary overlap and listen for any inequities in each overlap, such as the recordist quietly calling "Cut."

TRADITIONAL MIX CHART

For traditional film mixes, you will need to fill in a mix chart blank (Figure 43–2), which reads from top to bottom, unlike a computer timeline, which reads horizontally from left to right. In the completed sample (Figure 43–3), each column represents an individual track. By reading down the chart you see that:

- Individual tracks play against each other, like instruments in a vertically organized music score.
- The sync pip or "BEEP" at 00:30 is a single frame of tone on all tracks to serve as an aural sync check when the tracks begin running.
- Segment starts and finishes may be marked with footages or cumulative timings.
- A straight line at the start or finish represents a sound cut (as at 04:09 and 04:27).

S O U N D M I X L O G Production____________________

Date__/__/____ Reel #____ Page # ____ Premix #____ Editor____________

Action cues	Track 1	Track 2	Track 3	Track 4	Cassette/Disc

FIGURE 43–2

Traditional film sound mix blank form.

- An opening chevron represents a fade in (Track 4 at 04:10).
- A closing chevron represents a fade out (Track 2 at 02:09).
- Timings at fades refer to the beginning of a fade in or the end of a fade out.
- A dissolve is two overlapping chevrons (as at 02:04 to 02:09). There is a fade out on Track 4 overlapping a fade in for the cassette machine. This is called a *cross fade* or *sound dissolve*.

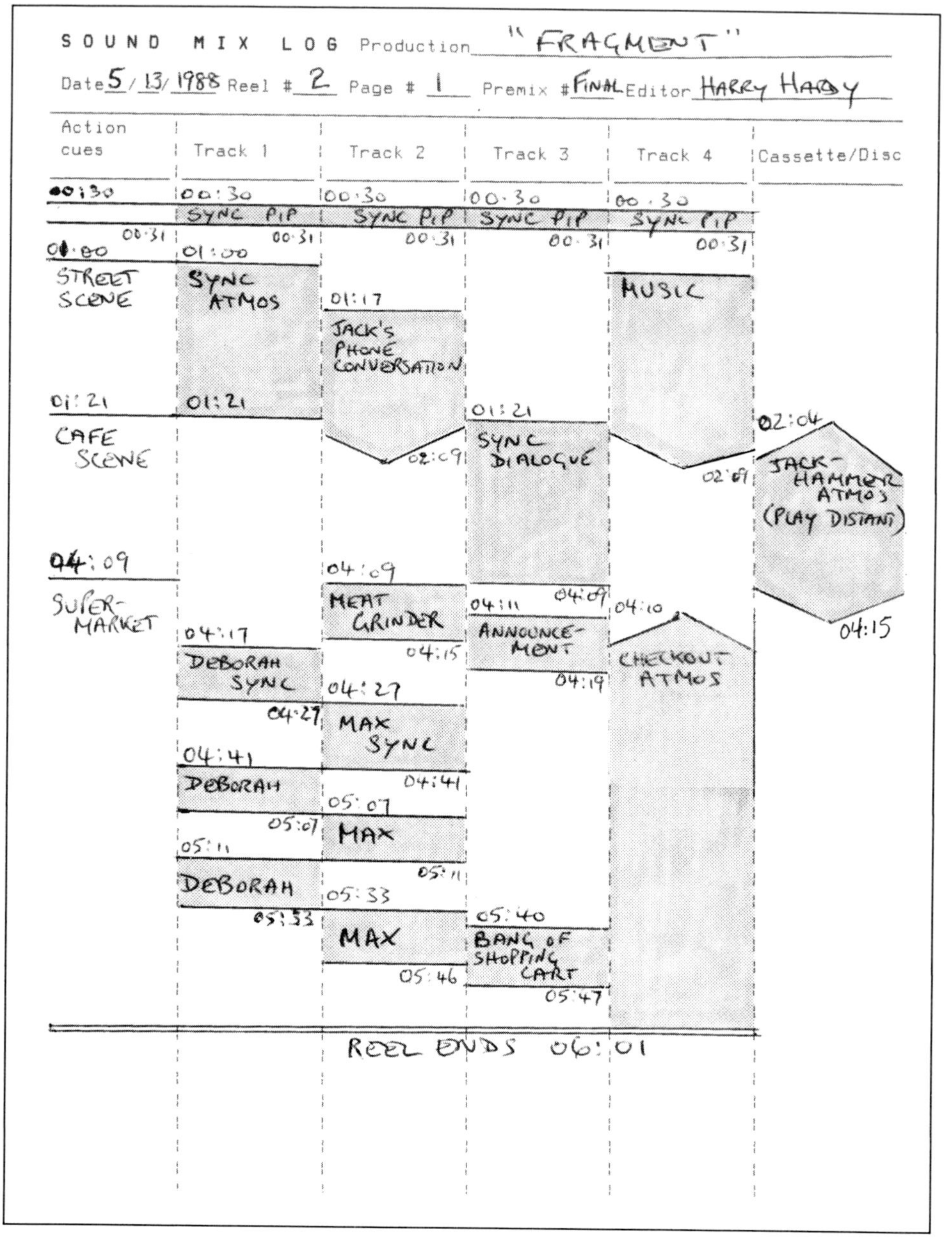

FIGURE 43–3

Sample sound mix log for traditional film mix.

- Timings indicate length of cross fade (sound dissolve), ours being a 5-second cross fade.
- It is always prudent to lay both tracks longer in case you decide during the mix session that you would like a longer dissolve.
- You can lay up alternative approaches to a sound treatment, then choose the most successful by audition during the mix.

Vertical space on the mix chart is seldom a linear representation of time. You might have 7 minutes of talk with a very simple chart, then 30 seconds of railroad station montage with a profusion of individual tracks for each shot. To avoid unwieldy or overcrowded mix charts, use no more vertical space than is necessary for clarity to the eye. To help the sound mix engineer, who works under great pressure in the half-dark, shade the track boxes with a highlight marker.

SOUND MIX STRATEGY

PREMIXING

One reel of a feature film may comprise 40 or more sound tracks. Because only one to four sound engineers operate a traditional mix board, it requires a sequence of premixes, and the same principle holds for computerized mixes. *It is vital to premix in an order that reserves until last your control over the most important elements.* If you were to premix dialogue and effects right away, a subsequent addition of more effects or music would uncontrollably augment and compete with the dialogue. Because intelligibility depends on audible dialogue, you must retain control over the dialogue-to-background level until the very last stage of mixing. This is particularly true for location sound, which is often near the margin of intelligibility to start with.

Note that each generation of analog (as opposed to digital) sound transfer introduces additional noise (system hiss). This is most audible in quiet tracks such as a slow speaking voice in a silent room or a very spare music track. Analog video sound is the worst offender because sound on VHS cassettes is in narrow tracks recorded at low tape speed, which is the worst of all worlds. The order of premixes may thus be influenced by which tracks should most be protected from repeated re-transfer. Happily, digital sound copies virtually without degradation.

TAILORING

Many tracks, if played as laid, will enter and exit abruptly, giving an unpleasantly jagged impression to the listener's ear. This negatively affects how people respond to your subject matter, so it is important to achieve a seamless effect whenever you are not deliberately disrupting attention. The trouble comes when you cut from a quiet to a noisy track, or vice versa, and this can be greatly minimized by tailoring—that is, making a very quick fade-up or fade-down of the noisy track to meet the quiet track on its own terms. The effect onscreen is still that of a cut, but one that no longer assaults the ear (Figure 43–4).

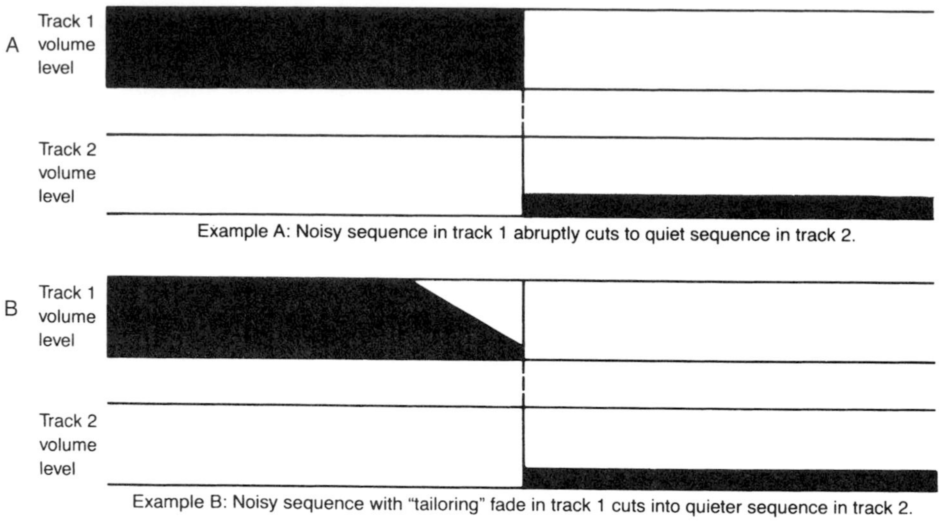
A
Track 1
volume
level
Track 2
volume
level
Example A: Noisy sequence in track 1 abruptly cuts to quiet sequence in track 2.
B
Track 1
volume
level
Track 2
volume
level
Example B: Noisy sequence with "tailoring" fade in track 1 cuts into quieter sequence in track 2.

FIGURE 43–4

Abrupt sound cut tailored by quick fade of outgoing track so it matches level of the incoming track.

COMPARATIVE LEVELS: ERR ON THE SIDE OF CAUTION

Mix studios sport excellent and expensive speakers. Especially for video work, the results can be misleading because low-budget filmmakers must expect their work to be seen on domestic TV sets, which have miserably small, cheap speakers. Not only do luckless consumers lose frequency and dynamic ranges, they lose the dynamic separation between loud and soft, so foregrounds nicely separated in the mix studio become swamped by backgrounds. If you are mixing a dialogue scene with a traffic background atmosphere, err on the conservative side and make a deliberately high separation, keeping traffic low and voices high. A mix suite will obligingly play your track through a TV set so you can be reassured of what the home viewer will actually hear.

REHEARSE, THEN RECORD

If you mix in a studio, you, as the director, approve each stage of the mix. This does not mean you have to know how to do things, only that you and your editor have ideas about how each sequence should sound. To your requests, and according to what the editor has laid in the sound tracks, the mix engineer will offer alternatives from which to choose. Mixing is best accomplished by familiarizing yourself with the problems of one short section at a time and building sequence by sequence from convenient stopping points. At the end, it is very important to listen to the whole mix without stopping, as the audience will do. Usually your time will be rewarded by finding an anomaly or two.

FILM MIXES AND TV TRANSMISSION

The film medium is *sprocketed* (has sprocket holes to ensure synchronization) so tracks or a premix are easily synced up to a start mark in the picture reel leader. The final mix, whether it is made traditionally or digitally, will be transferred by a film laboratory to a sprocketed optical (that is, photographic) track and then photographically combined with the picture to produce a composite projection print. Television used to transmit films from double-system; that is, picture and the magnetic mix were loaded on a telecine machine with separate but interlocked sound. The track was taken from the high-quality magnetic original instead of from the much lower-quality photographic track. Today television transmission is from the highest quality digital tape cassettes, which are simpler, easier, and more reliable in use.

MAKE SAFETY COPIES AND STORE THEM IN DIFFERENT LOCATIONS

Because a sound mix requires a long and painstaking process, it is professional practice to immediately make safety or backup copies. These are stored safely in multiple buildings in case of loss or theft. Copies are usually made from the master mix so that should its damage or loss occur, there are backups.

The same principle should be followed for film picture or video original cassettes; keep masters, safety copies, negatives, and internegatives (copy negatives) in different places so you don't lose everything should fire, flood, revolution, or act of God destroy what you might otherwise keep under your bed.

MUSIC AND EFFECTS TRACKS

If there is the remotest chance that your film will make international sales, you will need to make a music and effects mix, often referred to as an *M & E track*. This is so a foreign language crew can dub the speakers and mix the new voices in with the atmosphere, effects, and music tracks.

CHAPTER 44

TITLES AND ACKNOWLEDGMENTS

TITLES

Although every film acquires a working title, its final title is often plucked late from an agony of indecision because it must be short, special, and epitomize the final version's identity. Remember that your film's title may be the only advertising copy your audience ever sees, so it should be informative and alluring. TV listings and festival programs rarely have space to describe their offerings, so the title you choose may be your sole means of drawing a potential audience.

Titles, especially when film rather than video is involved, are a minefield of trouble. Here's a short guide to avoid blowing yourself up.

Style: Form follows function. Emulate by finding models among films of a length and budget commensurate with your own film and see which approach to titling you like. There are plenty of examples available on TV or for rent in the video store. Some of the most artistically ambitious films use brief and classically simple white-on-black titles. You could do a lot worse.

Over-laden titles: A sure sign of amateurism is a film loaded with an ego-centric welter of credits. The same name should not crop up in multiple key capacities, and acknowledgments should be kept eloquently brief. An actor unknown to the general public should never be introduced with "Starring Sherry Mudge."

Contractual or other obligations: If you have used union actors, they have assuredly come with contractual specifications that may affect the size and wording of title credits. Obey these scrupulously or live to regret you were ever born. Because many favors are granted filmmakers in return for an acknowledgment in the titles, be sure you honor your debts to the letter. Funding or college degrees also may have a contractual obligation that you acknowledge them in prescribed wording, so this and all such agreements should be carefully checked and double-checked before titles are locked down.

Font, layout, and size: Choose a font for clarity and size, and avoid small lettering. Anything too small or too fancy disappears on the television screen, where so much work is first seen. When spacing adhesive letters, note that some letters can be put close to each other, while others need some space for the word to look balanced. There are plenty of manuals to help you.

Spelling: Spelling in titles and subtitles should be checked scrupulously by at least two highly literate and eagle-eyed checkers. The spelling of people's names should receive special care because a misspelling indicates for all time that you care too little about them or their work to give their correct names.

Title lengths: Decide the right duration for a title to remain onscreen by reading the contents of each card (which represents one screen of titling) *one and a half times, out loud.* If you are shooting titles for film, be sure to shoot at least three times as much as you need. This allows for a title to be extended if needed. Crawl titles, if long, are run fast, or TV just chops them off.

Titles for film: If your film is to compete in festivals, reserve some of the budget to shoot the best titles you can afford because professional-looking titles signal a high-quality film. Here is the procedure:

1. Make up title cards ready for shooting. You will need to get adhesive letters and lay them out scrupulously on black card. This must be done meticulously because even small inequities of proportion and straightness show up badly and make titles look amateurish.
2. Title cards are best shot on an animation stand with a known field of view.
3. If you shoot your titles using a regular camera:
   a. First, do a viewfinder field test using a grid to check that what you see is what you are putting on film. If titles come up misaligned, suspect your camera's viewfinder. Judging alignment through a film viewfinder is hard anyway because the image is so small.
   b. Shoot using high-contrast film or else black won't be true black but gray. Run tests with standard lighting to determine the best exposure. Light titles on black are easy to overexpose, leading to a puzzling loss of definition that gives your lettering an out-of-focus look.
4. A/B roll titling—that is, shooting complete titles on film then fading them in and out before the film begins—is low-cost and very serviceable. However:
   a. If you want lettering conventionally superimposed on an image for background, you can only superimpose black titles on that image if you use a negative-to-positive printing process. This is because black lettering produces white lettering on the negative, which lets through a fully exposing light that prints black on a positive print. Few topics benefit from black titles unless you specialize in graveyard comedy.

b. If you try to superimpose white titles using the negative-to-positive process, white lettering renders as black in a clear negative. Light then passes all *around* the titling, burning out the image meant to be the background.
c. For white titles on a moving background, the printing elements must first be converted into positive form, then contact printed to a new negative, which is then cut into the appropriate place in the film printing negative.
d. If you are making composite prints (one shot superimposed on another) be aware that registration in 16 mm is none too steady, and expect some jiggle between lettering and background. Do a camera *steady test* first (shoot a grid, rewind the film, move the camera slightly and shoot the grid again, then process and project to see how much movement is apparent between the two passes).
e. Colored or fancy titles probably have to be shot using an optical printer. First-rate opticals are done in 35 mm, at astronomical cost.

For elaborate film titling, you will have to talk with the customer representative at one of the few surviving film labs to see who specializes in making up and shooting titles. They may use either the traditional, optical-printer process or one that is computer-generated. Because the bulk of such work is for feature films, check prices very carefully, preferably when sitting down in case you faint. If you go ahead, meet with the person who will be making them and get all prices and everything else you discuss in writing. Be sure that any further charges for reshooting are fully defined.

Never leave film titles until late in the process and assume that all will be right on the night. They are tricky to get right, especially if you are at all ambitious and want fancy effects. Titles, like troubles, are sent to try us, so give yourself plenty of time in case you must reshoot.

Titles for video: Most editing software comes with excellent titling capability that includes a large array of typefaces, drop shadow, movement, crawl, and other exotic behaviors. Resist the temptation to exult in your new freedom; keep titling classically simple—unless, of course, your film's topic and treatment call for something more. The blessing with video is that you see immediately what you are getting and can make changes until everything looks right. Superimposed lettering, whether colored or white, is more legible with a black outline.

SUBTITLES

Often when you submit your film to a foreign competition, the festival asks for a subtitled print in a particular language. This is now easy (if time-consuming) to do using video. Here are some guidelines:

1. Pick a clear typeface in yellow with black edging. You want your subtitles to be visible no matter how light or dark the background. Use a size of font that can easily be read on a TV screen and place subtitles well into the TV safe area, so nothing gets lost on a poorly adjusted set.

2. Make an *abbreviated* transcription of dialogue that you want to appear as a subtitle. You don't want the audience to be too busy reading to see your film, so abbreviate words to absolute essentials.
3. Get the text translated by a literate, native speaker (not that friend who took several Spanish classes) and have it typed up with all the appropriate accents.
4. Make video subtitles using yellow lettering with black edging superimposed, and place them in the lower part of frame. Many TV sets cut off the sides of the image, so do not place your titles too low. The software may already indicate the *TV safe area*, as do many film camera viewfinders.
5. Place every sentence within a continuous shot because we read the title all over again if it hangs over the following cut. This is very irritating and unnecessary.
6. Break any long sentences into short sections, indicating anything that is run-on with triple periods (. . .) as in this example, spread out over four shots:

"How are you?"	Shot 1
"I am feeling all right . . .	Shot 2
. . . but am hoping that you can . . .	Shot 3
. . . give me some advice."	Shot 4

Copyright: At the very end of the titles, remember to include your name and the © symbol, with the year as a claim to the copyright of the material. To file for copyright in the United States, write to the Registrar of Copyrights, Library of Congress, Washington, D.C. 20450, and ask for current information on copyrighting. If you reside in another country, be sure to check the correct copyright procedure with professionals. If and when you come to sell your film, any legal omissions can be costly or even paralyzing.

Once your film is completed, you can enter it in festivals. To give yourself the best chance, you will need to prepare a publicity package to help you market your work. At last you get to experience the ultimate rite of passage: seeing your film in the company of your true masters—a paying audience. This can be a thrilling or a chastening experience. Whichever comes your way, it's the final reckoning and represents closure for the filmmaker.

Now, what film will you make next?

CHECKLIST FOR PART 7: POSTPRODUCTION

The points summarized here are only those most salient from the previous part. Some are commonly overlooked. To find them or anything else relating to post-production, go to the Table of Contents at the beginning of this part.

Editing in General:

- Interesting discrepancies of information drive the audience into an active, problem-solving relationship with the film, instead of the usual passive one.
- Every call you make to their imagination or judgment is an acknowledgment of the audience as equals and an invitation to participate in discovery.
- Are there dramatic advantages to be gained from disrupting the subject's natural advance in time?
- Cross cutting between two stories allows time to be telescoped or stretched and heightens comparison and irony.
- The operative word of dialogue falling on each new shot helps us interpret the image's meaning.
- Changing the juxtaposition of words and shots can imply different meanings.
- It is easier to shorten a film than to pump substance back into one prematurely tightened.
- If an edited version is different from what you expected, see it again before commenting.
- Stay away from the cutting room and preserve your objectivity.

Viewing Dailies:

- Avoid taking your attention away from the screen.
- In the dailies book, note chosen takes, special comments, and any ideas and transient impressions; they will be an important resource later.
- Note moods and feelings evoked by scenes or individuals.
- Nothing outside the dailies is relevant to the film you can make.
- The director should discuss intentions for each sequence with the editor and encourage an early, loose assembly of the whole film.

Preparing to Start Editing:

- Time spent making a consistent, intelligent log is time liberated for creativity later.
- From dailies, mark up script to show actual coverage and number of takes for each angle.

Editing Procedure:

- When cutting film, *never* forget to put aside three frames minimum between adjacent lengths of film to allow for cement splices in conforming.

- Assemble film workprint sound as one track containing main dramatic elements (dialogue, atmosphere, or music). Later you will split these tracks apart.
- Assemble video tracks, especially dialogue, in checkerboard fashion to allow early premix with equalization.
- Leave spaces in dialogue for featured sound effects.

First Assembly:

- Make first assembly long, loose, and simple using master shots and a minimum of intercutting so you get an early view of the whole film.
- See first assembly without interruption and make a quick list of what was memorable.
- See first assembly a second time and see if your impressions are confirmed.

Rough Cut:

- Work on each sequence to make use of all material, but still keep pace slow and cutting simple.
- View the whole film and pay attention to material that is not working.
- Tackle only the top level of problems in each pass and see new version before addressing a further level of problems.

Diagnostic Methods:

- Make a flow chart of the whole movie to spot invisible anomalies.
- After re-cutting and viewing, check results by making a revised block diagram of the film.

Fine Cut:

- Where necessary, alter performance rhythms of action and reaction to allow the appropriate time characters need to process particular information.
- Use eyeline changes and reactions to alert us to those moments of special awareness that yield access to a character's inner life.
- Where you have multiple-angle coverage, experimentally rebalance subjective and objective angles so the sequence feels right.
- Try counterpointing visuals against speech to suggest a person's subjective vision.
- In dialogue sequences, examine coverage for its balance—showing either the actor or the acted upon. Frequently the character acted upon adds more dimension to the exchange.
- Introduce overlap cutting to set up a visual cutting rhythm that is separate and meaningful in contrast with speech and sound effect rhythms.
- Tighten transition cuts where action flows from one composition to another.
- Examine sequence transitions for sound-overlap or sound-dissolve possibilities.

- Put the film aside for a week or two, and see it again before deciding the fine cut is final.

Evoking a Trial Audience Response:

- You can't please everyone.
- Tell your audience the film's title and warn them of what is missing (music, sound effects, atmospheres, etc.).
- In a trial showing, exert maximum control over sound.
- Direct audience attention to issues for which you need information, but ask nondirective questions and listen carefully for what is really being said.
- Do not abandon any central intention without long, hard thought.
- Do not rush into changes of any kind.
- Expect to feel depressed about the film: that it's failing, etc.

Sound Effects and Music:

- Choice of music should give access to the interior of character or subject.
- Music can signal the emotional level at which audience should approach the scene.
- You cannot know that music works until you try it against the picture.
- Decide what, if anything, needs post-synchronizing.
- Start looking for sound effects early; they are part of your orchestra.
- Plan featured sound effects to go in dialogue gaps (or vice versa).

Working with a Composer:

- Develop music cue list.
- Show film to composer.
- Discuss why music is desirable and what sort of music you'd like.
- Be open to suggestions from the composer.
- Leave open framework for music to work; don't tighten the film around dialogue so there's no space for the score.
- Be ready after music is fitted to move cuts and extend or shorten to fit music.
- When cuts must appear to happen on the beat, they must come three frames *before* the beat to look right on the screen.

Sound Mix:

- Premix and retain control over balance of important elements until last.
- Soften ragged sound cuts by tailoring the louder to the quieter.
- When mixing foreground speech with background (music, sound effect (FX), atmosphere, etc.), err on the side of caution and separate foreground widely from background.
- Check completed mix against picture at end without stopping.
- Make at least one sound mix safety copy and store it separately.

Titles:

- Keep credits short and few.
- Each title card should be on the screen long enough to be read aloud one and a half times.
- Choose a legible, clean typeface that goes with the period and style of your film.
- Double-check all spelling, especially people's names.
- Don't straddle subtitles across cuts.
- Use legible, yellow print with black edging for subtitles.
- Contract text when you subtitle or you'll exhaust your audience.
- Include acknowledgments, funding sources, dedications, etc. exactly according to contractual obligations.
- Copyright your film with the Library of Congress or appropriate national authority and put © sign and year at end.

PART 8

CAREER TRACK

Part 8 (Chapters 45 through 47) is concerned with setting your sights on a career. This involves making a self-assessment for film school and beyond, choosing a place of study, and initiating the planning and self-directedness that begins in film school if you want to launch yourself into making films for a living. It also deals with getting recognition in festivals for your film work and how to use this to leverage a job.

Do use the checklist at the end when you want to refresh your memory of this part.

CHAPTER 45

PLANNING A CAREER

All careers in filmmaking are much sought after, so you should decide how ready you are to sink your fortunes and identity in a whole way of life. There is always a gamble, of course, when you start something. Will you like it? Will you be good enough? The only way to know this is to do it. The competition will be stiff, but even if finally you go from film school into Web design, theater, or radio, for instance, there isn't another liberal education like it. A preparation in film, depending on what you absorb, is an education in photography, light, electricity, drama, writing, narrative construction, design, sound, composition, acting, and organization. Your time won't be wasted, no matter what you end up doing.

PERSONALITY TYPES

The film industry, unlike engineering or real estate management, lacks a career ladder with predictable steps for promotion. It's a branch of show business, and how far you get and how long you take to get there depends on your ability, tenacity, and to a lesser degree on your luck. Sustaining a commitment to filmmaking may be impractical if your primary loyalties are to family, community, and material well-being because the industry is informally structured, unpredictable, and assumes initiative and a total commitment in the individual. Actors, dancers, and anyone in the arts who doesn't have a private income will face the same conditions.

OPPORTUNITIES

Film and video are now inseparable and should be regarded as one multifaceted industry. At the local end are Web site development, wedding videos, advertising, corporate and educational films, and up in the stratosphere are the national or international high-budget feature films. Indie shorts and features are somewhere in the impoverished middle. At the local level, the adroit and those with good connections can sometimes set their own terms and over time develop a comfortable income. In the upper-level industry where budgets are high, the stakes are high, too, and so the demand on the young entrant for reliability and appropriate behavior is roughly the same as working in mine clearance. Those who march to a different drummer can cost themselves and their supervisors their professional lives.

THE IMPORTANCE OF PASSION

A truism: People only become good at what they are passionate about. If you are passionate about the cinema, you may be equally passionate about making movies, even though it is hard, slow, and unglamorous work. Yes, unglamorous. If you really love it, you can make your way in that world. This, however, is true for anything at all, anywhere, that takes strong personal initiative. A lot of people go to film school to see whether they "have it" and whether they like production—and not all do.

How can you tell who has it? After decades of teaching in an open-admissions film school, my colleagues and I still cannot accurately predict who will thrive, although who *won't* is a lot more evident. Most film schools are strictly selective, and each faculty tends to believe the self-fulfilling prophecy that their selection methods work. If a film school rejects you, consider yourself in some good company and find another way to go forward—as Mike Figgis did, for example.

Below are descriptions of the three major personality types that tend to succeed in film school and the film industry. You should know the stakes before you decide to head to film school.

WHO SUCCEEDS IN FILM SCHOOLS AND THE FILM INDUSTRY

Filmmaking flies in the face of many romantic cultural beliefs. It is not glamorous and not an individualist's medium, for you can't be the isolated, suffering artist among a dozen or more hard-pressed collaborators. It is unsuitable for those who are undisciplined, unreliable, and non-perfectionist. Equally unsuitable are those whose egos, hostilities, and insecurities prevent them from working with (or especially under) other people. Film schools therefore receive people with many illusions culled from publicity and wishful thinking. Such students either adapt or let the dream go. But many people discover the impediments in themselves in film school and move successfully to change them, which is a large part of a film school's job.

There are places in the industry for three kinds of persons:

1. **The meticulous, committed craftsperson.** This person gives his or her all to the work taken on and practices the highest standards in work, commitment, and diplomacy. Most find huge satisfaction in crafts other than directing. This is not a tragedy because most really grow to love what they do and find it very fulfilling.

2. **The craftsperson with an author inside struggling to get out.** This person learns to become successful in his or her area—usually editing, cinematography, acting, and occasionally screenwriting—until someone influential recognizes that he or she has sufficient experience and a special authorial reach and is ready to direct.
3. **The craftsperson who is a fully realized visionary.** This person is to film schools what Mozart was to music. He or she emerges from film school with a film that everyone recognizes as masterly.

Anyone lacking #1's discipline, commitment, and low ego is unsuited to the collaborative nature of filmmaking. This category is by far the most numerous, although most younger people in the industry think of themselves as #2 material. Only #3 directs straight out of film school, and the likelihood that you are naturally this kind of person is roughly equal to your chances of winning the lottery. Most progress, in film as in everything else, is won by hard work and application, not talent or brilliance. Sometimes this person takes a comet's path: a successful student film leading straight into a disastrous experience in the film industry. A productive director's first experience can prove fatal through a too-rapid promotion. Better to move slowly and carefully.

GETTING STARTED

How to get started? Old timers used to scorn any form of schooling, but that has changed now that virtually every new film director is a film school alumnus (see Figure 45–1). A good school, of which there are now many, can cut years out of the learning curve, but even here there are drawbacks. Formal schooling is and must be geared to the common denominator; so it will be frustrating for those who learn slowly, rapidly, or who are more motivated than the average. In short, there are no sure routes, only intelligent traveling. If film school is out of the question, this book shows a way to prepare yourself outside the available educational structures. In any case, the best education will always be that you give yourself.

APPRENTICESHIP AS A BEGINNING

Older people in the film and TV industries may tell you that only on-the-job experience counts. Many of them received no college-level education and believe it fills young people's heads with idealistic dreams unrelated to the business. Because they tend to value procedural knowledge and professionalism (often deficiencies in recent graduates), they assume schooling fails.

Certainly school cannot teach the consistency, tact, and reliability that are the hallmarks of professionalism, nor should it drill students in industrial procedures at the expense of a conceptual education, which is the job of a college. Some students eagerly drop their schooling when an industry opening comes their way. It seems like a dream come true, but it is almost always a terrible mistake. They should know that their progress will be slow and their self-esteem eroded by the self-serving mystiques propagated by their seniors.

FIGURE 45–1

Film students shooting an early project at Columbia College Chicago. Film schools are now the accepted cradle of the film industry (photo by author).

I am myself a scarred survivor of industry apprenticeship, so I want to stress the benefits of a purposeful education. During my teaching career I saw students in a 15-week editing class mastering techniques and using insights that took me 10 years on the job to invent for myself. That I learned slowly and in isolation isn't unusual: in the freelance world, know-how and experience are earning power, so workers systemically avoid enlightening their juniors. Most are not secure enough to share their knowledge, or they live highly pressured lives and consider it no part of their job to prepare "the kid" for more responsibility. You have to steal knowledge while serving as the company peon. How much easier it is when prior schooling has made you ready and eager to assume more complex duties as they arise.

WHAT FILM SCHOOL CAN DO

A good film/video education imparts:

- A broad cultural and intellectual perspective on your chosen medium
- The history from which your role grows
- The opportunity to relive that history by starting with simple and primal techniques

- Some marketable skills
- A lot of hands-on experience
- Experience of working as part of a team, sometimes in a senior and sometimes in a junior capacity
- A can-do attitude that isn't fazed by equipment and technical obstacles
- Aspirations to use your professional life for the widest good
- A community of peers with whom you will probably work for much of your life

By encouraging collaboration and unbridled individual vision, the educational process:

- Helps you determine early where your talents, skills, and energies truly lie
- Just as helpfully shows you where you do not belong
- Exposes you to a holistic experience of filmmaking, so you are not overawed by other people's knowledge and jobs
- Lets you learn through experiment and by overreaching yourself, something risky in the professional world until you are at the top of your craft
- Allows you to form realistic long-range ambitions
- Equips you to recognize appropriate opportunities when they arise, something the under-prepared worker is mortally afraid to do

Almost every entering film student wants to be a director. The true visionaries (they are very rare) direct all through film school and go straight into directing when they leave. Others of promise graduate with a useful technical skill and with the beginnings of an artistic identity. Most, on leaving school, will be neither ready nor wanting to direct for a number of years.

How do you find out which kind of person you are? Only by going through all the stages of making a film—no matter how badly. Here you will truly see the strengths and weaknesses of your own (and other people's) work. Film is such a dense and allusive language that a director must develop two separate kinds of skills, only one of which can be taught. The first is the slew of human and technical skills needed to put a well-conceived, well-composed series of shots on the screen and make them tell a story. The other is the skill of knowing yourself, of knowing what you can contribute to the world, and the capacity to remain true to yourself even when your work comes under attack. This has nothing to do with self-promotion and manipulating a gullible world into accepting your genius, as some people think.

The beginning filmmaker relives and reinvents the history of film and is surprised to discover how much about personal identity and perception he or she has taken for granted, and how meager and precarious this identity feels when placed in film form before an audience. This is the beginning of the humility and aspiration that fuels the artistic process. A good film school is the place to have this experience, for learning is structured and executed in the company of contemporaries. There should be enough technical facilities and enthusiastic expertise available. Here you can experiment and afford failures, whereas in the professional arena, unwise experiment is professional suicide.

In summary, film/video school is the place to:

- Learn crafts in a structured way that includes both theory and practice.
- Acquire an overview of the whole production process.
- Learn to use technical facilities.
- Learn professionalism (Be nice to people on your way up because you're going to meet them on your way down.).
- Learn how to use mentors and how to be one yourself.
- Experiment with roles, techniques, topics, and crafts.
- Put work before an audience.
- Become familiar with every aspect of your medium, including its history and aesthetics.
- Fly high on exhilarating philosophies of filmmaking and of living life.
- Continue to grow up (hard, lifelong work for us all).
- Develop a network of contacts, each tending to aid the others after graduation.
- Make the films that will show what you can do; you are what you put on the screen.

FINDING THE RIGHT SCHOOL

Many schools, colleges, and universities now have film courses. Although no serious study of film is ever wasted, be careful and critical before committing yourself to an extended course of study. Many film departments are under-equipped and under-budgeted. Sometimes film studies are an offshoot of the English department, perhaps originally created to bolster sagging enrollment. Avoid departments whose course structure shows a lack of commitment to field production. Film studies are necessary to a liberal education and for sharpening the perceptions, but divorced from film production, they become criticism, not creation. The measure of a film school is what the students and faculty produce. Quite simply, you must study with active filmmakers.

Be cautious about film departments in fine arts schools, especially if they undervalue a craftsperson's control of the medium and overvalue exotic form presented as personal vision. Fine art film students are sometimes encouraged to see themselves as reclusive soloists, like the painters and sculptors around them. This encourages gimmicky, egocentric production lacking the control over the medium that you can only get from a team. Graduates who leave school with no work under their arm find developing a career next to impossible.

At another extreme is the trade school, technically disciplined but infinitely less therapeutic. The atmosphere is commercial and industry-oriented, concerned with drilling students to carry out narrowly defined technical duties for a standardized industrial product. Union and Academy apprenticeship schemes tend to follow these lines; they are technically superb but often intellectually arid. They do lead to jobs, unlike the hastily assembled school of communications, which offers the illusion of a quick route to a TV station job. For every occupation there is always a diploma mill. In the TV version, expect to find a private, unaffiliated facility with a primitive studio where students are run through the rudiments of equipment operation. Needless to say, nobody but the much vaunted few ever find the career they hope for.

A good school balances sound technical education with a strong counterpart of conceptual, aesthetic, and historical coursework. In a large school like my own (Columbia College Chicago, see *www.filmatcolumbia.com*), a core of foundation courses leads to specialization tracks in screenwriting, camera, sound, editing, directing, producing, documentary, animation, and critical studies. Only a large school can offer a multiplicity of career tracks with a wide spectrum of types of filmmaking. My school has a unit located on a Hollywood studio lot so that our writers and producers can study with practitioners. Many go directly into internships, as you can find out from the Web site. Live action filmmakers sometimes feel as if they should also know about animation. To know it is an advantage, but it is an utterly separate discipline and closer to the graphic arts in its training.

There should be a respectable contingent of professional-level equipment as well as enough basic cameras and editing equipment to support the beginning levels. Students tend to rate schools by equipment, but this is shortsighted. More important is that a school be the center of an enthusiastic film-producing community, where students routinely support and crew for each other. The school's attitude toward students and how they fit into the film industry is the key. A school that rewards individualist stars or one isolated from working professionals can only partly prepare its student body for reality. A school too much in awe of Hollywood will probably promote pernicious ideas about success that destroy valuable potential. Be warned that some of the most reputable schools use a competitive system to decide whose work is produced. You may enter wanting to study directing but find your work doesn't get the votes and end up recording sound for a winner's project.

If the film school of your choice has been in existence for a while, successful former students may give visiting lectures and return as teachers. They often employ or give vital references to the most promising students. Through this networking process, the lines separating many schools from professional filmmaking are being crossed in both directions. The school filmmaking community tapers off into the young (and not so young) professional community to mutual advantage. In the reverse flow, mentors not only give advice and steer projects but exemplify the way of life the students are trying to make their own. Even in the largest cities, the film and video community operates like a village where personal recommendation is everything.

Although there is Garth Gardner's *Gardner's Guide to Colleges for Multimedia and Animation, Third Edition* (Fairfax, Virginia: Garth Gardner Publishing, 2002), there is nothing current that does the same for live action filmmaking. Some practical information, if you want to study film at graduate level, can be gained from Karin Kelly and Tom Edgar's *Film School Confidential: The Insider's Guide to Film Schools* (New York: Perigee, 1997), but currently it is 5 years out of date. Its opinions are formed on very small samples and should be taken with a pinch of salt. Kelly and Edgar have a Web site for *Film School Confidential* at *www.lather.com/fsc/* where you can find comments, updates, and other information. There is no substitute for doing your own research, for which the Internet is now quite helpful. The main thing is to make comparisons and decide on a department's emphasis. A rousing statement of philosophy may be undercut when you scan equipment holdings and the program structure. Sometimes a department has evolved under the chairmanship of a journalist or radio specialist, so film and television production may be public relations orphans within an all-purpose communications department.

You can do a top-down study by reading Nicholas Jarecki's *Breaking In: How 20 Movie Directors Got Their First Start* (New York: Broadway Books, 2001), which contains interviews with directors on how they broke into the business. This is valuable for the reiteration of common values that go with making a film career, but it won't show you where the rungs of the ladder are. The fact is that you make them for yourself. The first attribute of a director is the ability to research a situation and to put together a picture from multiple sources of information. As you decide whether a particular film school fulfills your expectations, here are some considerations:

- How extensive is the department and what does its structure reveal?
  - Number of courses? (More is better)
  - Number of students? (More may not be better, but does enable variety of courses)
  - Subjects taught by senior and most influential faculty?
  - Average class size?
  - Ratio of full-time to part-time faculty?
- How long is the program? (see model syllabus; less than 2 years is suspiciously short)
- How much specialization is possible, and do upper-level courses approach a professional level or specialization?
- How much equipment is there, what kind, and who gets to use it? (This is a real giveaway)
- How wide is the introduction to different technologies?
  - At what level and by whom is film used?
  - Has the school adapted to digital video? (Faculties are sometimes dominated by film diehards)
  - How evenhanded is the use of technologies?
- What kind of backgrounds do the faculty members have?
  - What have they produced?
  - Are they still producing or do they rest on past laurels?
- How experienced are those teaching beginning classes? (Many schools have to use their graduate students.)
- Consider tuition and class fees:
  - How much equipment and materials are supplied?
  - How much is the student expected to supply along the way?
  - Does the school have competitive funds or scholarships to assist in production costs?
  - Who owns the copyright to student work? (Many schools retain their students' copyrights)

- What proportion of those wanting to direct actually do so? (Some schools make students compete for top artistic roles and sideline the losers)
- What does the department say about its attitudes and philosophy?
- What does the place feel like? (Try to visit the facilities)
- How do the students regard the place? (Speak to senior students)
- How much are your particular interests treated as a specialty?
- What kind of graduate program do they offer?
  If you have a BA, an MFA is a good qualification for production and teaching.
  A Ph.D. signifies a scholarly emphasis that generally precludes production.
- If the degree conferred is a BA or BFA, how many hours of general studies are you expected to complete, and how germane are they to your focus in film or video?

The very best way to locate good teaching is to attend student film festivals and note where the best films are being made. A sure sign of energetic and productive teaching, even in a small facility, is when student work is receiving recognition in competitions.

Some of the larger and well-recognized film/video schools in the United States are listed in the next chapter. Also listed are the major film schools around the world because many of this book's users will live in other parts of the globe. Most of these schools only take advanced or specially qualified students. A hard-to-get-into, expensive school is not necessarily a good school or the one that fits your profile. An inexpensive school that is easier to get into at the undergraduate level (like mine) may, in fact, fit you and your purse very well.

Americans sometimes assume that work and study abroad is easily arranged and will be an extension of conditions in the United States. Be warned that most foreign film schools, especially national film schools, have very competitive entry requirements, and that self-support through part-time work in foreign countries is usually illegal. As in the United States, immigration policies exclude foreign workers when natives are underemployed. That situation changes only when you have special, unusual, and accredited skills to offer. Check local conditions with the school's admissions officer and with the country's consulate before committing yourself. Also check the length of the visa granted and the average time it takes students to graduate—sometimes these durations are incompatible.

SELF-HELP AS A REALISTIC ALTERNATIVE

Perhaps you can afford neither the time nor money to go to school and must find other means to acquire the necessary knowledge and experience. Werner Herzog has said that anyone wanting to make films should waste no more than a week learning film techniques. Even with his flair for overstatement this period would appear a little short, but fundamentally I share his attitude. Film and video is a practical subject and can be tackled by a group of motivated do-it-yourselfers. This book is intended to encourage such people to learn from making films, to learn through doing, and, if absolutely necessary, through doing in relative isolation.

Self-education in the arts, however, is different from self-education in a technology because the arts are not finite and calculable. They are based on shared tastes and perceptions that at an early stage call for the criticism and participation of others. Even painters, novelists, poets, photographers, or animators—artists who normally create alone—are incomplete until they engage with society and experience its reaction. Nowhere is public acceptance more important than with film, the preeminent audience medium.

PROS AND CONS OF COLLABORATION

If you use this book to begin active filmmaking or videomaking, you will recognize that filmmaking is a social art, one stillborn without a keen spirit of collaboration. You will need other people as technicians and artistic collaborators if you are to do any sophisticated shooting, and you will need to earn the interest of other people in your end product. If you are unused to working collaboratively—and sadly, conventional education teaches students to compete for honors instead of gaining them cooperatively—you have an inspirational experience ahead. Filmmaking is an intense, shared experience that leaves few aspects of relationship untouched. Lifelong friendships and partnerships develop out of it, but not without flaws emerging in your own and other people's characters as the pressure mounts. With determination you can change your habits, and many people do.

Somewhere along the way you will need a mentor, someone to give knowledgeable and objective criticism of your work and to help solve the problems that arise. Do not worry if none is in the offing right now, for the beginner has far to go. It is a law of nature in any case that you find the right people when you truly need them.

PLANNING A CAREER TRACK DURING YOUR EDUCATION

Whether you are self-educated or whether you pursue a formal education at school, the way people receive your finished work will confirm which filmmaker category is yours and whether you are a visionary and can realistically try to enter the industry as a director. Chances are you belong with the vast majority for whom directing professionally is still very far off. In this case *you must develop a craft specialty to make yourself marketable and gain a foothold in the industry*. This is the subject of Chapter 47: Breaking into the Industry.

CHAPTER 46

MAJOR NATIONAL AND INTERNATIONAL FILM AND VIDEO SCHOOLS

There is no special accreditation for film schools and none even for teachers. So it's *caveat emptor*, as warned in Chapter 45. The schools listed in this chapter are affiliated with professional bodies, but you should use all your research powers to determine a school's reputation and what you can expect to get from its education.

The first list is schools affiliated with the University Film and Video Association (UFVA), an up-to-date version of which can be seen on the Internet via *www.ufva.org/* under "About UFVA." A way to find out more is to look at the UFVA Job Listings, which often describe the facilities at an institution seeking teachers.

Another way to check reputations is the Web site *www.filmmaker.com*, which includes some lengthy and often sulphurous film school reviews. These are by students, and you should read them gingerly for tendencies and peripheral information, generally discounting anything written by those who can't spell or punctuate. Being free and anonymous, it is a great place for malcontents to unload spleen, but common denominators among the reviews may help you avoid a costly mistake. Avoid trade schools and anything that offers to give you the complete, no-nonsense lowdown in a weekend. Film school is like medical school. It takes several years of hard learning to come out with something useful.

UFVA-AFFILIATED FILM SCHOOLS

These mainly North American schools will have Web sites you can find by entering the school name in an Internet search engine. Their facilities and expertise will vary hugely.

Curtin University of Technology
Doane College
Duke University
Eastern Michigan University
Emerson College
Florida Metropolitan University, Melbourne
Florida State University
Gallaudet University
Georgia State University
Grand Valley State University
Hellenic Cinema/TV School
Houston Community College Southwest
Ithaca College
Lane Community College
La Salle University
Los Angeles Film Studies Center
Mills College
Montana State University
Montclair State University
New York Film Academy Ltd.
New York University
North Carolina School of the Arts
Northeastern University
Ohio University
Piedmont Community College
Rochester Institute of Technology
Rowan University
Ryerson Polytechnical Institute
San Antonio College
San Diego State University
San Francisco State University
School of Visual Arts, Inc.
Smith College
Southern Illinois University
Stanford University
Suffolk University
Syracuse University
Texas A&M University, Corpus Christi
UNIACC—La Universidad de las Comunicaciones (Santiago, Chile)
Unitec Institute of Technology
University of Arizona
University of Central Florida
University of Florida Foundation, Inc.
University of Hartford
University of Kansas
University of Nevada, Las Vegas
University of New Orleans, Lakefront
University of North Carolina
University of South Carolina
University of Southern California
University of Toledo
University of Toronto
University of Washington, Educational Outreach
University of Windsor
Valencia Community College
Vanderbilt University
Vassar College
Villanova University
Watkins Film School
William Patterson University
York University

SCHOOLS AFFILIATED WITH THE INTERNATIONAL FILM SCHOOLS ASSOCIATION

This list of schools affiliated with the international film schools association, Centre Internationale de Liaison des Ecoles de Cinéma et de Télélvision (CILECT) can be found in its latest version on CILECT's Web site (*www.cilect.org/*), organized by country. Clicking on a film school either gives you a form that lists standard information or links you directly to the school's own Web site. The + sign before a phone or fax number indicates the overseas telephone code that you must first dial in your own country to make any international call. The numbers that follow are the country code, the area or city code, and finally the school's phone number.

ARGENTINA

Carrera de Diseño de Imagen y Sonido
Facultad de Arquitectura, Diseño y Urbanismo
Universidad de Buenos Aires
Pabellón 3
Cuidad Universitaria
1248 Buenos Aires
Tel: +54 11 4789 6279
Fax: +54 11 4576 3205

Escuela de Experimentación y de Realización Cinematográfica
Moreno 1199
1191 Buenos Aires
Tel/Fax: +54 11 43 84 67 04

Universidad del Cine
Pasaje Giuffra 330
1064 Buenos Aires
Tel: +54 11 4300 1407
Fax: +54 11 4300 0674

AUSTRALIA

Australian Film and Television School (AFTRS)
Corner Balaclava Road & Epping Highway
Box 126, North Ryde
N.S.W. 2113
Tel: +61 2 9805 6401
Fax: +61 29805 6563

Victorian College of the Arts
School of Film & Television
234 St. Kilda Road
Melbourne, Victoria 3004
Tel: +61 3 9685 9000
Fax: +61 3 9685 9001

AUSTRIA

Universität für Musik und Darstellende Kunst Wien
Abteilung "Film und Fernsehen"
Metternichgasse 12
1030 Wien
Tel: +43 171155 2902
Fax: +43 171155 2999

BELGIUM

Erasmus Hogeschool Brussel
Departement RITS
Moutstraat 15
1000 Brussel
Tel: +32 2 507 14 11
Fax: +32 2 507 14 56

Hogeschool Sint-Lukas Brussel
Paleizenstraat 70
1030 Brussel
Tel: +32 2 250 11 00
Fax: +32 2 250 11 11

Institut des Arts de Diffusion (IAD)
Rue des Wallons, 77
1348 Louvain-la-Neuve
Tel: +32 10 47 80 20
Fax: +31 10 45 11 74

Institut National Supérieur des Arts du Spectacle (INSAS)
Rue Thérésienne 8
1000 Bruxelles
Tel: +32 2 511 9286
Fax: +32 2 511 0279

BRAZIL

Escola de Comunicações e Artes
Universidad de São Paulo
Av. Prof. Lucio Martins Rodrigues, 443
Cidade Universitaria CEP 05508-900
São Paulo
Tel: +55 11 818 4020
Fax: +55 11 211 2752

Universidade Estadual de Campinas (UNICAMP)
Programa de Pós-Graduação em Multimeios
Instituto de Artes
CP6159
13083-970 Campinas/SP
Tel: See CILECT Web site
Fax: See CILECT Web site

BULGARIA

Nacionalna Academia za Teatralno i Folmovo Izkoustvo (NATFIZ)
"Krustyo Sarafov"-Sofia
Rakovski Street 108a
Sofia 1000
Tel: +359 2 87 98 66
Fax: +359 2 89 98 66

New Bulgarian University
Dept of Mass Communications
21 Montevideo Str.
1635 Sofia
Tel: +359 2 9571629
Tel/Fax: +359 2 955 5291

BURKINA FASO

Programme de Formation à l'Image et au Son (PROFIS)
Direction de la Cinématographie Nationale
01 BP 647 Ouagadougou 01
Tel: +226 30 17 85
Fax: +226 30 17 84

CANADA

The School of Image Arts
Ryerson Polytechnic University
350 Victoria Street
Toronto, Ontario M5B 2K3
Tel: +1 416 979 5167
Fax: +1 416 979 5139

Université du Québec à Montréal (UQAM)
Module de communications
Case Postale 8888, succursale A
Montréal (Québec) H3C 3P8
Tel: +1 514 987 3759
Fax: +1 514 987 4650

York University
Faculty of Fine Arts
Dept of Film & Video
4700 Keele Street
North York, Ontario M3J 1P3
Tel: +1 416 736 5149
Fax: +1 416 736 5710

Institut National de l'Image et du Son (INIS)
301 Boulevard De Maisonneuve, Est
Montréal (Québec) H2X 1K1
Tel: +1 514 285 1840
Fax: +1 514 285 1953

CHILE

Universidad de Artes, Ciencias y Comunicación (UNIACC)
School of Audiovisual Communications
Avenida. Salvador 1200
Providencia, Santiago
Tel: +56 2 640 6000
Fax: +56 2 640 6200

CHINA

Beijing Broadcasting Institute
No. 1 Ding Fu Zhang Dong Jie
Chao Yang District
Beijing 100024
Tel: +86 10 6577 9359
Fax: +86 10 6577 9138

Beijing Film Academy (BFA)
Xi Tu Cheng Lu 4
Haidian District
Beijing 100088
Tel: +86 10 8204 8899-295
Fax: +86 10 8204 2132

The Hong Kong School for Performing Arts
School of Film and Television
1 Gloucester Road
GPO Box 12288
Wanchai, Hong Kong
Tel: +852 2584 8679
Fax: +852 2802 4372

Hong Kong Baptist University
School of Communication
Dept of Cinema & Television
Kowloon Tong, Hong Kong
Tel: +852 2339 7395
Fax: +852 2339 7821

Zhejiang Radio and Television College
22 East Zhoushan Road
Hangzhou 310015
Tel: +86 571 8801 0127
Fax: +86 571 8801

CROATIA

Akedemija Dramske Umjetnosti (ADU)
Trg Marsala Tita 5
10 000 Zagreb
Tel: +385 1 482 85 06
Fax: +385 1 482 85 08

CUBA

Escuela Internacional de Cine y TV (EICTV)
Ap. Aéreo 40/41
San Antonio de los Baños
Tel: +53 7 335 196
Fax: +53 7 335 341

CZECH REPUBLIC

Akedemie Múzickych Umeni Filmová a Televisni Fakulta
Filmová a televisni fakulta, (FAMU)
Smetanovo Nábr. 2
116 65 Prague 1
Tel: +420 2 24 22 91 76
Fax: +420 2 24 23 02 85

DENMARK

Den Danske Filmskole
Theodor Christensens Plads 1
DK 1437 Copenhagen K
Tel: +45 32 68 64 00
Fax: +45 32 68 64 10

The European Film College
Carl Theodore Dreyersvej 1
8400 Ebeltoft
Tel: +45 86 34 08 55
Fax: +45 86 34 05 35

EGYPT

Academy of Arts
High Cinema Institute
Pyramids Road
Gamal El Din El Afghany Str.
Giza
Tel: +202 58 68 203
Fax: +202 561 1034

FINLAND

Arcada Nylands Svenska Yrkeshögskola
Institutionen för Media
Skogsmansgränden 3,
02130 Esbo
Tel: +358 9 52 53 21
Fax: +358 9 52 53 2333

Lahti Polytechnic
Institute of Design—Department of Film and TV
Pl 92 Saimaankatu 11
15141 Lahti
Tel: +358 3 82 82 855
Fax: +358 3 82 82 854

University of Art and Design Helsinki (UIAH)
Media Centre LUME
Department of Film and TV
Hämeentie 135 C
00560 Helsinki
Tel: +358 9 756 30111
Fax: +358 9 634 303

Turku Polytechnic, Arts Academy
Turun ammattikorkeakoulu, Taideakatemia
Linnankatu 54
20100 Turku
Tel: +358 1055350
Fax: +358 105535202

FRANCE

Ecole Nationale Supérieure Louis Lumière
7 Allée de Promontoire
B.P. 22
Marne-la-Vallée
93161 Noisy-le-Grand Cédex
Tel: +33 1 48 15 40 10
Fax: +33 1 43 05 63 44

Ecole Nationale Supérieure des Métiers de l'Image et du Son (FEMIS)
6 rue Francoeur
75018 Paris
Tel: +33 1 53 41 21 00
Fax: +33 1 53 41 02 80

Institut Internationale de l'Image et du Son (IIIS)
Parc de Pissaloup
F-78190 Trappes
Tel: +33 1 30 69 00 17
Fax: +33 1 30 50 43 63

Atelier de Réalisation Cinématographique (VARAN)
6 Impasse Mont-Louis
75011 Paris
Tel: +33 1 43 56 64 04
Fax: +33 1 43 56 2902

Ecole Supérieure d'Audiovisuel (ESAV)
Université Toulouse Le Mirail
5 Allées Antonio Machado
31058 Toulouse Cédex
Tel: +33 5 61 50 44 46
Fax: +33 5 61 50 49 34

GEORGIA

The Georgian State Institute of Theatre and Film
Film and TV Department
Rustaveli Avenue 19
380008 Tbilisi
Tel/Fax: + 995 32 99 73 88

GERMANY

Filmstudium Universität Hamburg
Institut für Theater, Musiktheater und Film
Friedensallee 9
22765 Hamburg
Tel: +49 40 42838 4143
Fax: +49 40 42838 4168

Deutsche Film-und Fernsehakademie Berlin (DFFB)
Potsdamer Strasse 2
10785 Berlin
Tel: +49 30 25759 0
Fax: +49 30 25759 161

Filmakademie Baden-Württemberg
Mathildenstraβe 20
71638 Ludwigsburg
Tel: +49 (0)7141 969 0
Fax: +49 (0)7141 969 299

Hochschule für Fernsehen und Film
Frankenthalerstrasse 23
D-81539 München
Tel: +49 89 689 57 0
Fax: +49 89 689 57 339

Hochschule für Fernsehen und Film "Konrad Wolf"
Marlene-Dietrich Allee 11
14482 Potsdam-Babelsberg
Tel: +49 331 6202 0
Fax: +49 331 6202 199

Kunsthochschule für Medien Köln
Television and Film Dept
Peter-Weller Platz 2
D-50676 Köln
Tel: +49 221 201 890
Fax: +49 221 201 89124 {

GHANA

National Film & Television Institute (NAFTI)
Private Mail Bag - GPO
Accra
Tel: +233 21 71 76 10
Fax: +233 21 77 71 59

GREECE

Hellenic Cinema and Television School Stavrakos
65 Patission Str.
104 33 Athens
Tel: +30 1 8230 124
Fax: +30 1 8211 651

HUNGARY

Szinház - es Filmmüvészeti Egyetem
Szentkirályi U. 32/a
1088 Budapest
Tel/Fax: +36 1 318 5533

INDIA

Film and Television Institute of India (FTII)
Law College Road
Pune 411 004
Tel: +91 20 543 10 10
Fax: +91 20 543 04 16

INDONESIA

Institut Kesenian Jakarta Fakultas Film dan Televisi (IKJ)
Jl. Cikini Raya No. 73
Jakarta 10330
PO Box 4014
Jakarta 10001
Tel: +62 21 324 807
Fax: +62 21 323 603

IRELAND

DunLaoghaire Institute of Art, Design & Technology
Kill Avenue
DunLaoghaire
Co. Dublin
Tel: +353 1 214 4655Fax: +353 1 280 3345

ISRAEL

Camera Obscura
School of Art
5 Rival Street
Tel Aviv 67778
Tel: +972 6368430
Fax: +972 3 688 1025

Ma'ale School of Television, Film and the Arts
20 Shivtey Israel St.
Jerusalem 95105
Tel: +972 2 6277366
Fax: +972 2 6277331

The Sam Spiegel Film & Television School
4 Yad Harutzim St.
Talpiot Industrial Zone
Jerusalem 91103
Tel: +972 2 6731950
Fax: +972 2 6731949

Tel Aviv University
Film and Television Department
The Yolanda and David Katz Faculty of the Arts
Ramat-Aviv – Tel Aviv 69978
Tel: +972 3 640 9483
Fax: +972 3 640 9935

ITALY

Scuolo del Cinema e di Televisione
Via Ariberto 14
20123 Milano
Tel: +39 02 89408858
Fax: +39 02 89408857

Nuova Università del Cinema e della Televisione
Via Tiburtina 521
00159 Rome
Tel: +39 06 43599892
Fax: +39 06 43599859

Scuola Nazionale di Cinema
Via Tuscolana 1524
00173 Rome
Tel: +39 06 722 94247
Fax: +39 06 72 11 619

Zelig
School of Documentary, Television and New Media
Via Carducci, 15a
I - 39 100 Bolzano
Tel: +39 0471 977930
Fax: +39 0471 977931

JAPAN

Japan Academy of Moving Images
1-16-30 Manpukuji
Kawasaki-shi
Kanagawa 245
Tel: +81 44 951 2511
Fax: +81 44 951 2681

Nihon University
College of Art
Department of Cinema
2-42-1 Asahigaoka
Nerima-Ku
Tokyo 176-8525
Tel: +81 3 5995 8220
Fax: +81 3 5995 8229

KENYA

Kenya Institute of Mass Communication (KIMC)
Film Production Training Department
PO Box 42422
Nairobi
Tel: +254 2 540 820
Fax: +254 2 554 566

LEBANON

Université St. Joseph
Institut d'Etudes Scéniques, Audiovisuelles et Cinématographiques
Damascus Road
Beyrouth
Tel: +961 1 611456
Fax: +961 1 611362

MEXICO

Centro de Capacitación Cinematográfica (CCC)
Czda. de Tlalpan 1670 Esq Rio Churubusco
México 21, D.F. 04220
Tel: +52 5 420 44 90
Fax: +52 5 420 44 92

Centro Universitario de Estudios Cinematográficos (CUEC)
Universidad Nacional Autónoma de México
Adolfo Prieto 721 (Colonia del Valle)
México D. F. 03100
Tel: +52 5 687 3862 / 5288
Fax: +52 5 536 1799

NETHERLANDS

Nederlandse Film en Televisie Academie
Markenplein 1
1011 MV Amsterdam
Tel: +31 20 527 73 33
Fax: +31 20 527 73 55

NIGERIA

The National Film Institute
7 Gbadamosi Close,
P.O. Box 693
Jos, Plateau State
Tel: +234 73 463 625
Fax: +234 73 561 233

NORWAY

Den Norske Filmskolen
Pb. 1004
2626 Lillehammer
Tel: +47 61 28 80 00 (Switchboard)
Fax: +47 61 28 81 10

PHILIPPINES

University of the Philippines
Film Center (UP Film Center)
Magsaysay Avenue
P.O. Box 214
Diliman
Quezon City 1101
Tel: +63 2 92 63640/50286
Fax: +63 2 92 62722

POLAND

Państwowa Wyźsza Szkola Filmova i Teatralna (PWSFTviT)
Targowa 61/63
90-323 lódź
Tel: +48 42 674 39 43
Fax: +48 42 674 81 39

PORTUGAL

Escola Superior de Teatro e Cinema
Departamento de Cinema
Av. Marquês de Pombal 22-B
2700-571 Armadora
Tel: +351 21 498 94 00
Fax: +351 21 493 76 20

Universidade Católica Portuguesa
Departamento de Som e Imagem
Rua Diego Botelho 1327
4150 Porto
Tel: +351 22 619 62 95 or 351 22 619 62 00
Fax: +351 22 619 62 91

ROMANIA

Universitatea de Arta Teatrala si Cinematografica "I.L. Caragiale" (UATC)
Facultatea de Film si TV
Str. Matei Voievod 75-77
73224 Bucuresti
Tel/Fax: +40 1 252 58 81

RUSSIA

Russian State Institute of Cinematography (VGIK)
Wilhelm Pieck Str. 3
Moscow 129226
Tel: +7 095 181 3868
Fax: +7 095 187 7174

St. Petersburg Institute of Cinema and Television (SPIC&T)
Pravda Str. 13
191126 St. Petersburg
Tel: +7 812 315 72 85
Fax: +7 812 315 01 72

SINGAPORE

Ngee Ann Polytechnic
School of Film and Media Studies
535 Clementi Road
Singapore 599489
Tel: +65 460 6992
Fax: +65 462 5617

SLOVAKIA

Vysoka Škola Muzických Umeni (VŠMU)
Filmová a televisna fakulta
Ventúrska 3
813 01 Bratislava
Tel: +421 2 59 301 461
Fax: +421 2 544 321 82

SLOVENIA

Akademija za Glendalisce Radio Film in Televizijo (AGRFT)
University of Ljubljana
Nazorjeva 3
1000 Ljubljana
Tel: +386 1 2510 412
Fax: +386 1 2510 450

SPAIN

Escuela des Artes Visuales
Fuencarral 45, 4
28004 Madrid
Tel: +34 91 523 17 01
Fax: +34 91 523 17 63

Escuela de Cinematografía y del Audiovisual de la Comunidad de Madrid (ECAM)
Juan de Orduña 3
Ciudad de la Imagen
Pozuelo de Alarcón
28223 Madrid
Tel: +34 915 12 10 60
Fax: +34 915 12 10 70

Escola Superior de Cinema i Audiovisuals de Catalunya (ESCAC)
Immaculada 25-35
08017 Barcelona
Tel: +34 3 212 15 62
Fax: +34 3 417 26 01

Escuela de Cine y Video (ESKIVI)
Avda. Ama Kandida s/n.
20140 Andoain (Guipúzcoa)
Tel: +34 943 59 41 90
Fax: +34 943 59 15 62

SWEDEN

Dramatiska Intitutet (DI)
University College of Film, Radio, Television, and Theatre
Borgvägen 5
Box 27090,
102-51 Stockholm
Tel: +46 8 665 13 00
Fax: +46 8 662 14 84

Göteborg University
School of Photography and Film
Konstepidemins Väg 2A
Box 540
SE 40530 Göteborg
Tel: +46 31 773 43 44
Fax: +46 31 773 18 37

SWITZERLAND

Ecole Cantonale d'Art de Lausanne
Département Audiovisuel
46 rue de l'Industrie
1030 Bussigny
Tel: +41 21 702 92 15/01
Fax: +41 21 702 92 09

Ecole Supérieure des Beaux Arts
Section Cinéma/Vidéo
2 rue Général Dufour
Genève 1204
Tel: +41 22 311 05 10
Fax: +41 22 310 46 36

Hochschule für Gestaltung und Kunst Zürich
Studienbereich Film/Video
Limmatstrasse 65
8005 Zürich
Post address: P.O. Box 8031 Zurich
Tel: +41 1 446 23 57
Fax: +41 1 446 23 55

TAIWAN (CHINA)

National Taiwan University of Arts
No. 59 Section 1 Da-Kuan Rd.
Pan-Chiao
Taipei, Taiwan 220
Tel: +886 2 2272 2181 x354
Fax: +886 2 2968 7563

UNITED KINGDOM

National Film and Television School (NFTS)
Beaconsfield Film Studios
Station Road,
Beaconsfield, Bucks HP9 1LG
Tel: +44 1494 731472
Fax: +44 1494 671213

The Leeds School of Art, Architecture and Design
Film and Moving Image Production
Leeds Metropolitan University
2 Queen Square
Leeds LS2 8AF
Tel: +44113 283 1900
Fax: +44 113 283 1901

London Film School (LFS)
24 Shelton Street
London WC2H 9UB
Tel: +44 207 836 9642
Fax: +44 207 497 3718

National Association for Higher Education in the Moving Image (NAHEMI)
London Guildhall University
Dept of Communications
31 Jewry Street
London EC3N 2EY
Tel: +44 208 566 5673
Fax: +44 208 320 3009

University of Westminster
School of Communication, Design and Media
Harrow Campus Studios
Northwick Park
Harrow HA 1 3TP
Tel: +44 207 911 5000
Fax: +44 207 911 5943

UNITED STATES

American Film Institute (AFI)
PO Box 27999
2021 North Western Avenue
Los Angeles, CA 90027
Tel: +1 323 856 7711
Fax: +1 323 856 7884

Chapman University
School of Film & TV
One University Drive
Orange, CA 92866
Tel: +1 714 997 6715
Fax: +1 714 997 6572

California Institute of the Arts (CALARTS)
24700 McBean Parkway
Valencia, CA 91355
Tel: +1 661 253 7825
Fax: +1 661 253 7824

Columbia College Chicago
Film/Video Department, Columbia College
600 S. Michigan Avenue
Chicago, Illinois 60605-1996
Tel: +1 312 344 6701
Fax: +1 312 344 8044

Columbia University
Film Division
513 Dodge Hall, School of the Arts
116th Street and Broadway
New York, NY 10027
Tel: +1 212 854 2815
Fax: +1 212 854 7702

Florida State University
School of Motion Picture, Television and Recording Arts
A3102 University Center
Tallahassee, FL 32306-2350
Tel: +1 850 644 8968
Fax: +1 850 644 2626

Loyola Marymount University
School of Film and Television
7900 Loyola Blvd
Los Angeles, CA 90045-8230
Tel: +1 310 338 7532
Fax: +1 310 546 2363

New York University (NYU)
Tisch School of the Arts
Maurice Kanbar Institute of Film and Television
721 Broadway
New York, NY 10003 6807
Tel: +1 212 998 1800
Fax: +1 212 995 4040

North Carolina School of the Arts
School of Filmmaking
1533 S. Main Street
Winston-Salem, NC 27117
Tel: +1 336 770 1330
Fax: +1 336 770 1339

Stanford University [documentary program only]
Dept of Communication
McClatchy Hall
Stanford, CA 94305-2050
Tel: +1 650 723 4700
Fax: +1 650 725 2472

University of California, Los Angeles (UCLA)
School of Theater, Film and Television
Dept of Film & Television
East Melnitz
405 Hilgard Avenue
Los Angeles, CA 90095
Tel: +1 310 825 7741
Fax: +1 310 206 1686

University of Southern California (USC)
School of Cinema and Television
University Park Campus
850 West 34th Street, Lucas 209
Los Angeles CA 90089-2211
Tel: +1 213 743 2804
Fax: +1 213 740 7682

VIETNAM

The Hanoi Academy of Theatre and Cinema
Truong Dai Hoc San Khau Va Dien Anh
Mai Dich
Caugiay
Hanoi
Tel: +84 4 764 33 97
Fax: +84 4 834 87 32

YUGOSLAVIA (SERBIA, MONTENEGRO)

Fakultet Dramskih Umetnosti (FDU)
Bulevar Umentnosti 20
11070 Beograd
Tel: +381 11 140 419
Fax: +381 11 130 862

CHAPTER 47

BREAKING INTO THE INDUSTRY

You have finished your training period and must now make the transition from student or learning filmmaker to freelance crew person. Raising yourself by your own bootstraps requires that you publicly establish your skills, first of all, by making films and showing them at festivals or conferences. Getting work won't be easy or fast, and it may depend on the luck of your cohort. Many people leaving school remain in contact with each other, and the good luck of a cameraperson means the good luck of several more unit members whom he or she can recommend.

YOUR LOCATION MATTERS

You must live in a film-producing area to find employment. Either go to film school in or near a film-producing area, or be ready to move to one after you graduate. Many people dream of going home after film school and starting a film or video company there, but it seldom works, and if it does, there is a glass ceiling that keeps you perennially making commercials for Joe's Used Cars (Walk In, Drive Out).

FESTIVALS, CONFERENCES, AND EARNING RECOGNITION

During your learning period in film school (or out of it), you have made short works of 5–15 minutes, and now you should enter them in as many competitions and festivals as you can afford. Carefully check the entry conditions, maximum length specification, fee, and other expectations such as student status, or you will waste your time and money. If a festival only accepts film, it's pointless sending a digital film, but you'd be surprised how many people do so. If your digital film is in NTSC, be certain that a festival in Germany will accept anything that is not PAL. Pay particular attention to language or translation requirements. You may need to subtitle your film or supply a transcript to enter foreign competitions.

The best place to find out about festivals is the Internet. By entering "short film festival" in a search engine, I brought up around 100 Web sites. With another choice of search words, you would find even more. Beginning guidance on festivals is available through these Web sites:

1. *www.film.queensu.ca/Links/Festivals.html* This is a full list of festivals and their deadlines.
2. *www.ufva.org/index.php* This is the University Film & Video Association for North America's Web site, and it is a good site to check periodically.
3. *www.filmfestivals.com/index.shtml* This is a Web site devoted to festivals. It lists them by country and month, as well as by other criteria.
4. *www.variety.com/* This is *Variety* magazine's Web site. Look up "Festivals."
5. *www.cilect.org* This is the Web site for the international film schools association, and there are many Web links to databases, scholarly articles, and information of all kinds.
6. *www.cyberfilmschool.com/links/festivals.htm* This is a Canadian site that has much information for the independent filmmaker, including a full festival guide.
7. *dir.yahoo.com/Entertainment/Movies and Film/Film Festivals/* This site is run by Yahoo, and it breaks festivals down by genres.

Films meant to compete in festivals should be short and snappy and avoid a welter of titles. The cassette should be cued up for viewing and should be professionally packaged. Festivals are so numerous and the entries so dismal that a competent piece will pick up an award or two without difficulty. If your work is really special, you may well pick up a number of awards, and the existence of these—more than your work itself—will recommend you to potential employers as someone out of the ordinary. Curiously, few people have the time or inclination to make judgments by actually seeing a film, but everyone is impressed by prizes.

Go to as many festivals and conferences as you can. They are great places to meet people of similar backgrounds and interests, and it's amazing how many ideas and possibilities emerge from informal social situations. You will get encouragement and stimulation from these festival gatherings, and who knows, maybe some partnerships or notoriety, too.

PERSONAL QUALITIES YOU NEED TO SHOW

Breaking into the film industry begins with building a good social and educational track record and having competent work to show. Whether you accomplish this in film school or outside it is immaterial, but it's always easier to learn from teachers than to learn without them. To make lateral career moves later in life, you will doubtless need the educational degree, but a degree does not impress media employers. Only awards, an attested good reputation, and demonstrably good work will get you taken seriously. How fast you advance in the film industry after you get a toehold, and what responsibilities people care to give you, depends on your contacts, luck, and maturity. Almost certainly you will start as a freelancer, dependent on your contacts and on how much work is available.

In the industry, just as in film school, you become established by maintaining positive and constructive relationships with others, and by doing good work that is completed on time and within the agreed parameters. Sustain this over a period of time and under grueling conditions, and your good reputation will slowly spread through the grapevine so you become a preferred crewmember. However, make a costly mistake and this will circulate to your detriment. Most of the splenetic Web site commentary you see about film schools (see *www.filmmaker.com/loafs*) comes from those who alienated partners by bucking the written and unwritten rules of conduct. A dead giveaway is poor writing discipline and a self-serving plethora of blaming.

COMPROMISE

Becoming known and fitting into a commercial system may seem like the slipway to compromising your artistic values, but it does not have to be. After all, the films on which we were raised were produced for profit, and many were good art by any standard. Almost the entire history of the cinema has its roots in commerce, with each new work predicated upon the ticket sales of the last. If cinema and capitalism go hand in hand, this marriage has a certain cantankerous democracy. Tickets are votes from the wallet that prevent the cinema from becoming irrelevant or straying too far from the sensibilities of the common man. Shakespeare and his Globe Theatre Company flourished under similar conditions. Then as now, purists got themselves to a monastery.

To acquire a cautionary sense of the market forces at work, grit your teeth and regularly read the cinema trade journal *Variety* (*www.variety.com*). Read everything you can about recent low-budget productions and their tortuous relationship to distribution by following the *The Independent,* which is published by the Association of Independent Video and Filmmakers (*www.aivf.com*). Work your way through the independent filmmaking Web sites for a sense of international trends, beginning with *www.cyberfilmschool.com.* Go to genre festivals and see examples of your preferred kind of work so you know in what area and at what level you are competing.

PATHS TO THE DIRECTOR'S CHAIR

Of those successfully completing film school, the majority who get jobs in the industry go into the ancillary crafts. This is both a realistic and honorable decision. To employers *you are what you have done before and can show on the screen.* To become a director, then, you must continue making exceptional short films, and you will need more than one excellent script. I mentioned in Chapter 46 three types of candidates for professional work in film or video:

1. The crew craftsperson
2. The crew craftsperson with directing potential
3. The craftsperson who is a fully realized visionary and ready to direct professionally

All film work requires craft meticulousness all the time—in every area, and at every stage. Let us suppose that you have gone through 3–4 years of film school and have acquired a fundamental knowledge and experience in at least one of the fields of film- or videomaking. To make the transition from student to paid worker in the medium, look honestly at your track record and decide which of the previously mentioned categories is yours.

CRAFTSPERSON

Virtually everyone begins in the film industry as a humble craft worker assisting in the camera, sound, editing, production, or writing departments. Straight out of school, plenty of people get work as a grip, assistant editor, camera assistant, or assistant director, but this happens *only if you have developed industry contacts and have proven skills, professional discipline, and great references from film professionals* to prove it. If you are given work, you will be initially given very limited responsibilities and watched closely to see how you fulfill them.

If you left school with an excellent body of work that won national or international awards, you may be able to make your way by talking people into letting you direct either local commercials, or educational or industrial work. This can get you valuable experience with actors. A good resource for self-starters is *DV Magazine* (*www.dv.com/magazine/*). But more likely you will enter the field in a humbler position, so you must develop expertise in school in at least one craft specialty and use your school and its teachers to make the appropriate industry contacts. An important facet of choosing a film school is whether it has an industry internship program in which to prove yourself and get a foot on the first rung of the ladder.

INTERNSHIPS

Well-established film schools have internship programs that allow you to work unpaid as a professional and prove yourself. When choosing a school, then, it's smart to choose one with a thriving internship program. My own institution, Columbia College Chicago, has a program called "A Semester in LA" where producing and screenwriting students round out their knowledge in Hollywood. My school also places selected students who are near graduation at professional companies in an (unpaid) study-on-the-job program. Go to *www.filmatcolumbia.com* and under Special Interest look up Semester in LA Program, which lists Hollywood internships. Other major American film schools have similar programs, and foreign national film schools quite often have a symbiotic relationship with their own industry and use leading production figures as part-time teachers and mentors.

CRAFTSMAN WORKER WITH A DIRECTOR STRUGGLING TO GET OUT

Your bread and butter work will be entry-level craft work, but if you are ambitious to direct, continue developing your directing skills after you graduate. Keep social and professional contact with those ex-students whose values you share because getting established is long and lonely, and it is best done through networking with friends.

Film and video production has always been an area for the self-starter, so unless you are accepted as a full-time employee, you and your friends must make independent and cooperative efforts to get established. Form an entrepreneurial film unit around a likely script and shoot and edit sample sections digitally. Make sure you are working with a finished, professional, and commercially viable script from the outset. *Commercial* doesn't mean crass, it means that somebody somewhere would pay actual money to see it.

At the outset of your career, the best you can do is to keep the faith, work hard to keep body and soul together, and become acclimatized to the self that emerges under duress. Fire, said Seneca, is the test of gold, and adversity is the test of strong people. Developing an artistic identity rests now on your ability to live life courageously and fully, and this, all by itself, will lead to a fulfilling and meaningful life no matter where it takes you.

A decided point of view on the human condition emerges gradually during much active study of, and experience in, living. The operation is one of maturing—a tempering process that happens as you withstand the pressures and discoveries associated with work, intimate relationships, marriage, parenthood, and other crucial responsibilities.

Most barriers to your directing may seem to lie with those higher up—in your film school or in the film and television industry—but really they lie mostly within yourself. If you are normal, your early professional life is centered on mundane fundamentals that do not equip you with much to say that is out of the ordinary. If and when you have worked beyond this, you will eventually want to express it. That identity will be sensed as an aura of authority and will be implicitly recognized by others around you. When you have it, you'll know it. Until then, keep working.

THE VISIONARY: DIRECTING STRAIGHT OUT OF SCHOOL

As I have said, it is a rare and remarkable human being who moves straight from school into directing, and a distinctly endangered one if success comes too quickly. Directing this early usually comes only to people whose early work gains them immediate recognition. Roman Polansky's earliest films, *Two Men and a Wardrobe* (1958) and *The Fat and the Lean* (1960), forcefully express a skeptical view of the human condition through surreal allegory. Profound suffering as a child in central Europe during WWII lies behind these convictions—experiences that nobody would ever choose or want. Some have vision thrust upon them; some find it over time.

To be a first-rate director or a screenwriter is really to have learned something about life that you must give to others as a compelling story. For those deeply marked and deeply ambitious, the time may be now, and their ambition and persistence will overcome most obstacles. Film school is the best, though not the only, place to find out whether you have the vision, leadership, and sheer drive to put together outstanding films. Such films win festival prizes, which in turn provide professional openings and momentum.

Filmmaking is essentially a capitalist endeavor, so you must also be an entrepreneur who can assemble *packages*, about which much has been written to help the novice (see this text's bibliography). If you are to be paid for your work, you will need to have tastes shared by a sizeable chunk of the paying public, something you cannot control. You can no more decide to become a popular director than you can decide to become Shakespeare or Elvis Presley.

EXPERIENCED INDUSTRY WORKER WANTING TO DIRECT

If you are in the film industry and have a frustrated director inside, consider setting up a unit of your peers to cooperatively produce independent work that will benefit all of you. Shoot some scenes of a script on speculation, knowing that everyone's skills will be appreciably improved. If you shoot a complete feature film, make absolutely certain you have a viable script in the first place, because this is a murderously expensive way of discovering a script's weaknesses. Keep in mind that film labs are full of abandoned feature film negatives, and these represent a graveyard of poor scripts, inept production, and of money wasted by people who trusted in luck more than researching good advice.

If your piece is commercially viable, decently acted, and wins a festival or two, you have a chance of getting it distributed and recouping your costs. The main thing is to get experience and encouragement to go on to something bigger and better.

Do *not* listen to the greybeards who say, "Never make films with your own money." That's another way to say you should never invest in yourself. The world doesn't work that way. Who will believe in your talent if you aren't willing to take any risks to prove it? Make several short films, and the odds keep improving. People only accomplish what really matters to them.

FREELANCING TO GAIN EXPERIENCE

The aspiring director will for a long time have to use his or her craft skills (camera, editing, sound, production management, or writing) to fulfill quite humdrum commercial needs. You may find yourself expending lots of imagination and effort crewing for educational, industrial, training, or medical films, and occasionally even shooting conferences and weddings. Doing this reliably and to high standards will teach you a great deal. A training in industrials and documentaries served Robert Altman and many other directors well. Commercials, too, are a good training ground because incredible expense and effort are focused on highly specific ends. The superb technical and production knowledge you gain can later be transferred to the features setting—if you can let go of the good living that commercials can provide.

Most crew work is freelance, which means feast or (mostly) famine living conditions until demand for your services exceeds supply. As an aspiring director, you must aim to be in the right place at the right time, taking other craft work until, in Mr. Micawber's immortal words, *something turns up*. While making a precarious living as a freelance technician, try to continue making your own films with contemporaries who are also struggling to gain experience and recognition. By investing in your own talent and developing it to the point where you have concrete, visible results, you then have something to offer an employer or a sponsor. Once you get a little paid directing work, you start building up a track record and a reputation. It is this and festival recognition that recommend you for more interesting and demanding work.

TELEVISION AS A ROUTE

American television produces very little drama outside the soaps and sitcoms made in Hollywood, but these, if you can get work there, represent exceptional experience in fast, professional-level production. European television, in particular French, British, Dutch, German, Scandinavian, and Italian, has nurtured many fine directors and actors, and some of these countries, in self-defense against the rapacious attractions of the Hollywood product, have schemes to help developing local product get off the ground.

In Amsterdam, the Maurits Binger Film Institute (*www.binger.ahk.nl/*) teaches in English and accepts graduated students on a competitive basis who have promising script ideas. The aim is to help them develop their scripts to a professional level and then link them with an appropriate European production company. The best way to find out what your own country offers is to use the Internet to trawl for information, beginning with independent filmmaker Web sites. One site leads by links to another, but keep a log as you go to serve as the metaphorical ball of string so you can find your way back.

There is a crying need in the United States and elsewhere for first-rate regional production such as the Amber Group in the north of England (see *www.amber-online.com/*) or the Dogme Group in Denmark. The Dogme people have individually moved on to other things, but they still can be read about in the Internet. These collectives have pioneered filmmaking that challenges the formulaic vision of the mainstream production centers. The problem remains in convincing money sources that *regional* can mean something other than second-rate. Mostly such prejudices are far from misplaced.

CRAFTS THAT LEAD TO DIRECTING

Some craft areas lead to directing much more readily than others. Editing is a common route because the editor orchestrates acting, directing, camerawork, sound, music, and everything else. Writers and directors of photography also make the transition, and occasionally so do actor-writers, comedians, and even the visionary choreographer or painter. Assistant directors, producers, and production managers seldom if ever become directors because they handle logistics and organizational details rather than creative ones.

If you really want to become a feature film director, you should perhaps make a choice between editing and camerawork, with a strong emphasis on screenwriting because you'll only get anywhere as a director by constantly winnowing and propagating film ideas.

If you can contrive to have both spare time and spare cash (usually mutually exclusive for freelancers) you should try to work with a theater group to gain experience with actors, and maybe emulate Fassbinder by making a short dramatic film every few weekends. If you are an actor or you already work in the theater, getting experience in filmmaking can be a prelude to working with your company as film actors.

DIRECTING DOCUMENTARIES STRAIGHT OUT OF SCHOOL

If you have studied documentary form and production, you may prefer to enter the film industry through nonfiction filmmaking (documentary, educational, travelogue, industrials, corporate, or promotional films). It will get you out in the world, and through working with a small crew you will immediately have that high degree of control and responsibility by which people grow. You should be warned that making a living in documentary is very difficult unless you have a nose for finding sensational subjects.

If you liked this book and want to try documentary work, its sister volume *Directing the Documentary, 3rd Edition* (Boston: Focal Press, 1998) will tell you how. Look first at the career section. As I have implied all along, documentary and fiction are allied genres, and experience in documentary has been a wonderful preparation for many a feature film director. Don't take any notice of the patronizing attitude many in features take toward *docs*. Becoming a big fish in a small pool is good for many who are highly motivated but lack the connections or confidence to break into the big feature league. There is plenty of nonfiction peripheral work if you are resourceful. It pays a slender living, but you will be working for yourself, and in the process you will self-administer a terrific further education. Many people with long-term fiction goals start in nonfiction work or in commercials (if their technical control is good enough) and then try later for fiction work.

IMPORTANCE OF THE SAMPLE REEL

Because you are what you can show, you need more than anything *a sample reel of work that demonstrates your capabilities* to prospective employers or financial backers. If you have some original directing work, this may help you get interviews for feature crew work. If you have good screen work, you must have a script or two in case somebody is impressed enough to ask what you would direct if you could. It should be a superb script, and you should be able to pitch it like a practiced impresario.

DEVELOPING NEW PROJECTS

FINDING FICTION SUBJECTS

Re-read Chapters 2 and 3 of this book for a full treatment of sources for stories. What follows here places that information in a more commercial perspective.

People who invest in films do so to make money, not films. If they could make $50 million in 2 weeks by backing horses or making potato chips, horses or potato chips is where they would put their money. Any feature film you propose must have wide audience appeal, so you must be equipped and ready to argue that you have the goods to hit the jackpot.

The search for subjects is really a search for those issues and situations that stir you at the deepest levels. Most of the population has opted to live in pursuit of comfort and happiness and will never unlock the rooms in which those shadowy parts are stored. Maybe because sustained comfort brings a sense of deprivation ("The unexamined life isn't worth living," Plato c.428–348 B.C.) they need you and your films to live vicariously by watching other lives unfold on a screen—lives that are akin to their own.

When you search for subjects that will move a wide audience, you are in reality searching for the ways you can connect with and represent a sector of contemporary humanity. You will do this by plunging into the mainstream of modern awareness. This requires a keen curiosity about the ebb and flow of currents in contemporary society, not just those egocentric concerns circulating in restricted areas.

For this you will need to read books, newspapers, and journals omnivorously; to feel that political and international affairs are your responsibility; and to assume that poets, novelists, and songwriters are your equals because you share in a common consciousness-raising endeavor. It means striving to discover the humanity you share with writers, painters, poets, and philosophers of the present and the past and finding your own story in tales, myths, and legends. You will need a deep curiosity about the suffering and dreams of other people, and other peoples.

During this quest you will find fellow spirits. Some will be on the other side of the grave, their voices still urgent and speaking personally to you through their works. Some will be very much alive, struggling to make sense and give utterance. Some will become your friends and collaborators, allies with whom you face the world and tell what it's like to be alive at this moment and in this particular century.

You have probably noticed a strange omission from my list of recommended sources—other films. Of course you will be seeing films and will be influenced by them. But film subjects and film approaches should ideally be developed from life, not from other films; that road leads to derivative and imitative work having no authentic voice.

If there is a writer whose tastes and interests you share and with whom you can collaborate, you should jointly explore subjects and make a commitment to meet regularly even if he or she is not currently writing. Truly creative partnerships are tougher, more resilient, and more likely to lead to a strong, marketable story idea than trying to be a one-person band.

FINDING AN AGENT

No commercial film company will read unsolicited scripts. It is too wasteful of their time and too risky. Reputable film companies only read scripts forwarded by reputable agents, so your scripts (if you write them) must first find favor with an agent. This person's job is to advise you and represent your work wherever he or she thinks it will find favor. A good way to find an agent is to win a screenwriting competition, but Web sites for screenwriters are full of up-to-date advice on how to work your way up the ladder. The Writers Guild of America's Web site (*www.wga.org/*) lists agents of different degrees of accessibility. Some accept only a letter of inquiry, some accept new writers, and some accept new writers only with a reference from someone known to them. One thing the whole film industry agrees upon is that there are too few original scripts, so it follows that there are channels open to new product.

FORM AND MARKETABILITY

More than just content, a film is also *a way of seeing*. The implication is important: How a film shows its world may be more important than its plot or subject. There are only a limited number of plots, but infinite ways of seeing—as many as there are original characters. The special subjectivity of characters and of the teller of the tale means that *creativity in developing form is equally important as ingenuity in finding content.*

So building an artistic identity means not only finding a subject of general interest to an audience, but also a stimulating way of seeing it. Part 4: Aesthetics and Authorship dealt with the many issues that affect form.

CONTINUING TO LEARN FROM OTHER PEOPLE'S WORK

It is possible to see other people's films and learn very little. The problem is that good films tend to fascinate us to the exclusion of our critical (and thus learning) abilities. You can overcome this by methodically analyzing with a VCR or DVD player whatever film speaks strongly to you. A basic study method is suggested in Chapter 3, Project 3-3: A Scripted Scene Compared with the Filmed Outcome, which you might modify as follows:

- See the whole film as an audience does, without stopping and without allowing your expertise to make you reflect on technique.
- Write down dominant impressions, especially what the film conveys thematically. Most importantly, what does it leave you feeling?
- Run the film one sequence at a time, making a block diagram of the movie as a whole.
- Analyze each sequence for its contribution to the whole.
- Analyze any special technique each sequence uses to achieve its ends, and assess the language or form chosen. Was it appropriate? Could you see a better way of reaching the same communicative ends?
- Keep a journal of thoughts, ideas, techniques, and approaches, and add to it regularly.

From this exercise you will learn an immense amount about the way movies affect you, and how film art is used to create certain kinds of persuasion. Another priceless outcome is that you can now intelligently question the makers of the film if they happen to appear in your area. Nobody who labors to create something as complex as a film, no matter how famous, is indifferent to truly informed questions and comments. Out of such conversations, links are formed. Informal though they are, contacts of this nature frequently lead to work of some sort.

If you knowledgeably admire someone's work, he or she will take very seriously your desire to work and learn. Film work is irregular and unpredictable; film crews may suddenly need a gopher or will find room for an observer. If your dedication shows you value that position, you become someone special—someone everyone will remember. Film people seldom forget how hard it was to get started; work most often goes to those who earn a warm spot in everyone's heart.

PRESENTING YOURSELF FOR EMPLOYMENT

Following are some pointers to help you find employment. Employers look for a knowledge of what they do and for strong signs that you would fit well into their environment. This depends on how you handle yourself, how specific your knowledge and experience are, and how committed you are to the kind of work they do.

1. **Resumé.** A good resumé is vital when you seek work. It should be professionally laid out (get a book on resumé writing or take a workshop) and should present what you have done in the best light. Show evidence of pertinent employment, dependability, good character, and (only where relevant) initiative. A range of different employment is good, and you should have letters of recommendation available from past employers ready for inspection. Include any work you did for good causes because selfless commitment to a community will impress.
2. **Awards.** The most persuasive recommendation will be awards won at festivals. The Web site *www.studentfilms.com/* shows student films on the Internet and, like many sites, has links to other organizations. Awards are inordinately persuasive in swinging votes during a funding application or in securing an employment interview. Nothing, they say, succeeds like success, and people with judgmental responsibilities often seem most impressed by prizes and honors. Make sure you get yours.
3. **Your reel.** With your resumé enclose a 3–5 minute sample VHS cassette that shows *brief* highlights of your work. The items should be numbered and titled, and the clips should be itemized on a separate list. Collectively they should show your range of work and professionalism. The aim is to make yourself look as capable, flexible, and interesting as possible. The work on your reel should be keyed to your resumé and to the kind of work you are seeking. Some people put together a different sample tape according to the type of job or company they are approaching. A home computer able to assemble custom reels is a great asset.

4. **Knowledge of your potential employer's business.** Whenever you make a job application, use your research skills to learn everything possible about the business or organization. Write to the appropriate individual by name in the company or group. With your resumé send a brief, carefully composed, *individual* cover letter that shows how your work goals might best contribute to what the company does.
5. **Follow-up call.** After a week, follow up with a phone call. You will probably be told the company has no positions open. Ask if you might stop by for a brief chat in case a position opens up in the future.
6. **Interview.** If you are granted an interview, dress conservatively, be punctual, and have all relevant information at hand. How professionally you conduct yourself is the key to whether the interviewer decides to take matters further.
7. **Leave your resumé and reel.** Bring further copies of your resumé and reel to leave with the interviewer in case he or she, or anyone you meet, is interested in your capabilities.
8. **Let the interviewer ask the questions** and be brief and to the point when you reply.
   a. Don't take up more time than you sense is appropriate.
   b. Be ready to open up if invited to do so.
   c. Say concisely what skills and qualities you have to offer. Don't try to hoodwink or manipulate the interviewer. Be neither grandiose nor groveling but modest, realistic, and optimistic. Energy, realism, and a great desire to learn are attractive qualities.
   d. Say what you want to do, and show you are willing to do any kind of work to get there.
   e. Use the interview to demonstrate your knowledge of (and therefore commitment to) the interviewer's business.
9. **Be ready to work *gratis*.** If necessary and if you can afford to do so, volunteer to work without pay for a set period. It will give you experience, a reference, and possibly a paying job after you've proved yourself.
10. **Have questions ready.** Interviewers often finish by asking if you have any questions, and you should have two or three good questions ready. This is an opportunity to engage your interviewer in discussion about the company's work. Most people in a position to hire are proud of what their company does, and through conversation you may learn something useful.
11. **Extend the contact.** When the interview is over, ask politely if you can keep in touch in case something turns up. Polite persistence over time often makes the deepest impression because it marks you as someone who really wants to join them.

People accustomed to dealing with a volume of job seekers can rapidly distinguish the determined realist from naively hopeful souls who are adrift on alien seas. The *judgment is made not on who you are, but on how you present yourself*—on paper, on the screen, and in person. You'll only do this well if you do your homework through resourceful reading and networking on the phone. You don't know the right people? Write this on your cuff: *Anyone can get to anyone else in the world in five or fewer phone calls.* This means that anyone can find out a lot before an important meeting.

If you know that shyness is holding you back, don't wait around for a benefactor to recognize you. Be proactive and do something about it. Do it now. If you need assertiveness training, get it. If none is available, join a theater group and force yourself to act, preferably in improvisational material. It will be an impressive addition to your resumé and will do wonders for what you project about yourself. Your fingerprints prove you're different, but they won't get you employed. You've got to *actively demonstrate* your worth to the world. You alone can take action to start believing in yourself, and only you can make yourself stand out from the herd.

Thank you for using this book. If our paths cross, don't hesitate to tell me whether it helped and how I can make it better.

My very best wishes go with you.

CHECKLIST FOR PART 8: CAREER TRACK

The recommendations and points summarized here are only those most salient or the most commonly overlooked from the previous part. To find more about them or anything else, go to the Table of Contents at the beginning of this part or try the index at the back of the book.

To get on target for becoming a director:

- Get hands-on knowledge of all the production processes you are most likely to oversee.
- Accept that you'll need to know writing, acting, camerawork, sound, and editing.
- Look to your temperament and track record for clues about which specialty to take as your craft stepping-stone toward eventual directing.
- Resolve to make lots and lots of short films.

As a director you'll need to:

- Become a tough-minded leader who leads by example
- Be able to function even when feeling isolated
- Be passionately interested in other art forms
- Have original, informed, and avidly critical ideas about your times

To make educational progress:

- Use good short works to argue for your competency at directing longer ones.
- Be ready to adapt and improvise when working low-budget (people and imagination make films rather than equipment).
- Use trial and error in a long developmental process prior to production to arrive at professional-level results.

To entertain your audience means:

- Giving the audience mental, emotional, and imaginative work, not just moving pictures of externals
- Using myth and archetype to underpin anything you want to be powerful
- Using screen language that suggests a lot more than it shows, so your audience can imagine

Authorship essentials require:

- Using your work to search for your artistic identity, not illustrating what you know
- Knowing what is average, normal, usual, and clichéd, and doing something fresh and original instead
- Picking a form after you've found a story—remembering that form follows function

- Knowing what marks your life has left on you and being ready to make art from them
- Knowing the unfinished business in your life and using your art to go into dangerous waters; only what's scary is really worth doing

Film school:

- A good one will massively accelerate your career, *if* you get established after school.
- No school can give you the energy, persistence, intelligence, and drive to succeed. These are hard choices that you make daily.
- You can't avoid technical stuff, writing, or bouts of drudgery in filmmaking.
- Leave your ego at the door.
- A filmmaking community, finding your equals, and the immersion of film school are what come first, not the equipment. The most famous and productive film school was once Lodz in Poland at a time when it had almost no equipment or funds.
- Check out a school's production facilities, its support for production, morale, and attitude toward non-star students (the majority).
- Check the production activity of senior faculty and the experience of those teaching beginner classes (often they are graduate students recycling knowledge only recently acquired).
- Only self-starters succeed in freelance arts, so use the school and don't hang about waiting to be recognized. You have to create an identity for yourself and create a visibility through energy and excellence.
- Plan your life, break tasks down into stages, and set goals and deadlines for yourself. Confusion and inertia overtake many people when control of their lives passes into their own hands. Don't be one of them, and don't depend on anyone showing you the ropes.
- Make friends by seeking and using good advice, especially from active faculty.
- Take little notice of conventional wisdom among students, it's always full of negativity and doom.
- Don't kid yourself that you're keeping your options open by avoiding craft specialization. Decide what you're suited to do and pursue it—it will be your bread and butter.
- Learn to be creative from those with a positive attitude toward work, authority, and other students.
- Do not under any circumstances leave film school without saleable skills in something other than directing—that is, production, camera, sound, editing, production design, special effects, etc.
- Make sure you have a reel of good and varied work as evidence of your competency.

- Your parents, not the film industry, care that you got a degree; it won't get you film work.
- Get all the internship experience you can and all the references from film and video employers that are possible so you can pump up your resumé.
- Excellent directing work, prizes to prove it, and a great script may get you into directing straightaway, but it's unwise to expect it and foolish not to prepare for a less dazzling destiny.

After film school when you're looking for work, remember:

- Reaching the top rung of film school prepares you to apply for the bottom rung of work in the film industry.
- Send out a professional looking resumé and a 5-minute VHS or DVD reel of clips from your best and most varied work. Follow up with a politely insistent call asking for a chat.
- Know where you want to work, know who's there, what they do, and keep trying.
- Don't embarrass employers by overestimating your abilities, importance, or potential.
- You are what you have done.
- One or two whiz kids make it big, the rest move *s-l-o-w-l-y* up through the freelance ranks and usually take several years to achieve regular employment.
- Film or video is always a small professional community, even in Hollywood. Everyone watches everyone else. Good people get known the way they do in a village. If you work well and are always a good trooper, you'll come to be valued.
- Think of starting in nonfiction to gain experience and worldly immersion.
- Your capital is your reliability, resourcefulness, and capacity for originality. Work night and day at expanding your mind in all the arts.
- Don't believe in talent; believe in persistent self-development.
- Learn from others, especially from their mistakes (we all make them).
- Learn how the funding circus works.
- Plug into all the information sources and follow all the trade information.
- Don't listen to cynics. They'll tell you the world is going to the dogs and that you will never succeed.
- Know what you want. People accomplish what matters to them and not much else.
- Things happen because of personal connections and friendship, not merit alone.
- Get proficient at networking. Anyone can get to anyone else in the world by personal connection in five or fewer phone calls.

- There are a lot of highly intelligent, kind, and responsible people in the film and video industry. They all work on junk a lot of the time, and you will, too, until someone genetically re-engineers mass taste.
- You can win the pro's respect, affection, and help if you earn it.
- Keep on writing, keep on making short projects, keep on entering them in competitions and festivals.
- Expect the freelance life in a collaborative medium to take a toll on your personal life.
- Believe in yourself and work with others who do so, too.
- Keep the faith.

APPENDIX 1

OUTCOMES ASSESSMENT FORMS

Outcomes assessment is a recent development in education that looks in detail at what students can do, rather than what they know. Outcomes assessment lets teachers state a full range of criteria for a given piece of work, and teacher and student subsequently have a broad ground for discussion. For each project, a list of desired positive outcomes shows the student what aspects of his or her work are important and to what group each belongs. The criteria should be a balance of the conceptual, creative, and technical, or students will concentrate on smooth technique rather than trying to say something—which should always be the object of every piece of work.

Given that a term's work will have several projects, students see their cumulative development from the first project onward, and because scores take the form of a bar graph, they can recognize and correct their persistent weaknesses, and of course rejoice in their accomplishments. Many teachers will want their students to score their own and other students' work as practice in evaluating screen work.

SCORING METHOD

After each project is a list of desirable facets for you or your group to assess according to agreement. Numbers aren't in themselves useful but having to make decisions about relative quality is. The five-point scale of agreement is:

Not true or not applicable	0
Only minimally true	1
Somewhat so	2
Average and acceptably so	3
Considerably so	4
Unusually and strikingly so	5

ASSESSMENT 6-1A, B (EDITING)

Editing	Action match cuts are smooth and natural-looking	0 1 2 3 4 5
	Uses match cuts on major moments of action to bridge shots wherever possible	0 1 2 3 4 5
	Match cuts between two sizes of same action use an image size change large enough to make a natural-looking cut (If size change is too small it looks like a messy jump cut.)	0 1 2 3 4 5
	Rhythm of footsteps is perfectly matched	0 1 2 3 4 5
	Cutting from angle to angle feels natural and motivated	0 1 2 3 4 5
	Overall editing rhythm feels natural	0 1 2 3 4 5
Camera operating	Camera movements are so smooth they seem entirely motivated by the subject's movements	0 1 2 3 4 5
	Pans and tilts sync with motivating action, neither ahead nor behind	0 1 2 3 4 5
Composition	Camera height is varied to create interesting angles	0 1 2 3 4 5
	Framing and composition on static shots is excellent	0 1 2 3 4 5
	Compositions create maximum perspective and depth	0 1 2 3 4 5
	Lead space ahead of subject is well judged	0 1 2 3 4 5
	Compositional proportions around subject are maintained between images of different sizes	0 1 2 3 4 5
Blocking	Screen direction of subject remains logical	0 1 2 3 4 5
	Does not *cross the line.*	0 1 2 3 4 5
Human presence and continuity	Actor looks so unself-conscious that footage could pass for documentary	0 1 2 3 4 5
	Nature and speed of actions is consistent from angle to angle	0 1 2 3 4 5
	Mood changes and development make a character of compelling interest	0 1 2 3 4 5
	Where actors come from and where they are going is suggested interestingly by acting, props, costuming, etc.	0 1 2 3 4 5
Dramaturgy	Sequence has a natural and satisfying arc of development and conclusion	0 1 2 3 4 5
	TOTAL	

ASSESSMENT 6-1C (MUSIC)

Music use	The music made a valid, not facile contribution	0 1 2 3 4 5
	Music was chosen that didn't drown particular sound effects (SFX). Places were left in sound mix for natural effects to *bleed through*	0 1 2 3 4 5
	Particular cuts or sections of movement were effectively repositioned to fit the rhythmic dictates of the music	0 1 2 3 4 5
	Music started at a natural point in the sequence	0 1 2 3 4 5
	Music ended naturally	0 1 2 3 4 5
	Using music added new layers of meaning and impact	0 1 2 3 4 5
	TOTAL	

ASSESSMENT 6-2A (BLOCKING, ACTING, AND CAMERAWORK)

Blocking and use of location	The setting is used throughout to great advantage (Often settings get used as a generalized "container" instead of as an active component in the story)	0 1 2 3 4 5
	The essential action is always visible	0 1 2 3 4 5
	The action is in wide shot whenever necessary	0 1 2 3 4 5
	The action is in close shot whenever necessary	0 1 2 3 4 5
	Main character's movements are predominantly contrived to happen down the depth of the frame and create depth	0 1 2 3 4 5
	No actions came out of nowhere—you always saw a transitionary movement or action when it was needed	0 1 2 3 4 5
Acting	You learn something about the main character(s) from everything they do	0 1 2 3 4 5
	They look naturally occupied throughout	0 1 2 3 4 5
	You get a good sense of how they spent time previous to this scene	0 1 2 3 4 5
	You can guess something about the day they anticipate	0 1 2 3 4 5
	There is considerable variation of mood and rhythm in what they do	0 1 2 3 4 5
	Main character is natural and there are no dips in credibility	0 1 2 3 4 5

	You get the sense of a whole character with some issues bearing on him or her	0 1 2 3 4 5
Dramaturgy	The piece is consistently interesting to watch	0 1 2 3 4 5
	The piece has an overall sense of development	0 1 2 3 4 5
	We see a whole, complex character emerge	0 1 2 3 4 5
	There is evidence of personality conflicts and unfinished business	0 1 2 3 4 5
	The pace of the development does not lag or get stuck	0 1 2 3 4 5
	The piece feels resolved and finishes satisfyingly	0 1 2 3 4 5
	The high spot in the piece occurs where it should, not late or early	0 1 2 3 4 5
	The piece accomplishes its mission within the 4-minute time requirement	0 1 2 3 4 5
Camerawork	The camerawork feels natural and unobtrusive	0 1 2 3 4 5
	There are changes in camera height and all are motivated	0 1 2 3 4 5
	The camera seeks to relate main characters to everything they are doing (for instance, shoot over the toaster at main character's face waiting for toast to pop up, rather than show toaster, then pan to main character waiting)	0 1 2 3 4 5
	Composition is always in control (action isn't held safely wide so you feel you are watching a stage performance)	0 1 2 3 4 5
	Main character's movements onscreen are always at the right distance, never so close that the audience feels seasick	0 1 2 3 4 5
	The camera was never taken by surprise	0 1 2 3 4 5
	The camera never illegitimately anticipated what was going to happen next	0 1 2 3 4 5
	TOTAL	

ASSESSMENT 6-2B, C (INTERIOR MONOLOGUE)

Interaction between voice over (VO) and picture	VO doesn't over-inform and suffocate audience	0 1 2 3 4 5
	VO doesn't under-inform and leave the audience guessing for too long	0 1 2 3 4 5
	The order of showing and telling is always intelligent	0 1 2 3 4 5

	No duplication between what we see and what we hear	0 1 2 3 4 5
	There are ample *breathing spaces* in the VO during which audience can examine central character's actions and make their interpretations as perceptions arise	0 1 2 3 4 5
	Thoughts seem to arise out of what character does, as he or she does it	0 1 2 3 4 5
	Nicely ironic juxtapositions exist between words and actions	0 1 2 3 4 5
Acting	Voice sounds completely spontaneous, not reading	0 1 2 3 4 5
	Voice is naturally paced for the content	0 1 2 3 4 5
	Voice mood and mood changes are all believable	0 1 2 3 4 5
	Central character, both in voice and in action, emerges as interesting and credible	0 1 2 3 4 5
Recording	Well recorded, intimate on-mike voice quality	0 1 2 3 4 5
Editing and Mix	Ratio of VO to action is nicely judged, and action can breathe	0 1 2 3 4 5
	In the movement back and forth between VO and diegetic tracks, the level changes are well judged and sound natural	0 1 2 3 4 5
Dramaturgy	Audience is encouraged to observe and make its own judgments	0 1 2 3 4 5
	Sometimes the juxtapositions provocatively contradict what audience sees (and keep it guessing and therefore actively involved in decision-making)	0 1 2 3 4 5
	Central character fully developed with agenda, obstacles, and something to overcome	0 1 2 3 4 5
	There is a resolution	0 1 2 3 4 5
	The character develops	0 1 2 3 4 5
	Using VO is motivated and justified	0 1 2 3 4 5
	VO contributes to the sense of a completed dramatic arc in the piece	0 1 2 3 4 5
	TOTAL	

ASSESSMENT 6-3A (DRAMATIZING AN ENVIRONMENT)

Structure	There are clear developmental phases in the sequence like acts in a play	0 1 2 3 4 5
	The sequence has an overall rhythmic development that is satisfying and *right*	0 1 2 3 4 5
	There is a clear peak and *turning point*	0 1 2 3 4 5
	The sequence is neither too short nor too long	0 1 2 3 4 5
Form	The sequence flows and does not seem fragmented (if it did, this would point to a lack of sub-sequences, each with its own beginning, middle, and end)	0 1 2 3 4 5
Content	A strong mood is established	0 1 2 3 4 5
	The piece deals with what you expect of that setting	0 1 2 3 4 5
	The piece shows some of the unexpected	0 1 2 3 4 5
Point of view	There is a strongly defined observing consciousness at work (anger, fear, lethargy, hedonism, etc.)	0 1 2 3 4 5
	The point of view develops and changes	0 1 2 3 4 5
Use of sound	Natural sound plays a narrative part in the sequence	0 1 2 3 4 5
	Natural sound supplies an emotionally laden atmosphere	0 1 2 3 4 5
Impact	The sequence has a strongly sensual impact and mood	0 1 2 3 4 5
	TOTAL	

ASSESSMENT 6-4A, B (DIALOGUE SCENE)

Editing	Action match cuts flow smoothly	0 1 2 3 4 5
	Screen directions are correctly maintained	0 1 2 3 4 5
	Room geography is revealed as necessary, and not confusingly for a first-time viewer	0 1 2 3 4 5
	Convincing dialogue rhythms are maintained even when a picture cut happens in mid-sentence	0 1 2 3 4 5
	Moments of significant action and charged silence have been fully exploited	0 1 2 3 4 5
	Changes of scene rhythm occur convincingly with changes in the characters' moods, perceptions, thought patterns, and actions	0 1 2 3 4 5

	Eyeline shifts have been fully exploited as cutting points	0 1 2 3 4 5
	No character makes a major change of position offscreen (A screen convention, not always obeyed, is that when cutting back to a character, we find him or her as last seen. Transitional movements are often shown, rather than heard or implied.)	0 1 2 3 4 5
	Editing appropriately and consistently shows characters as either the actor or the acted upon	0 1 2 3 4 5
Point of view	The scene is shot and cut to convey a discernible point of view (that is, it effectively reveals the state of mind of the main character or of the Storyteller)	0 1 2 3 4 5
	The scene makes psychological sense by *breathing*, that is, it moves us close or far from the action in answer to our needs as audience members	0 1 2 3 4 5
	The game (or other shared activity) is used to effectively reveal psychological changes in the characters	0 1 2 3 4 5
Dramaturgy	The game develops convincingly	0 1 2 3 4 5
	The environment is fully utilized by the characters and made into an active component in the drama	0 1 2 3 4 5
	There are no redundancies of dialogue, action, or angle, etc.	0 1 2 3 4 5
	The scene feels right in length (better to feel a little short than too long)	0 1 2 3 4 5
	The scene implies backstory and what might come after	0 1 2 3 4 5
Impact	The piece holds your interest throughout	0 1 2 3 4 5
	The actors are engaging and natural throughout	0 1 2 3 4 5
	Significant subtexts are implied	0 1 2 3 4 5
	TOTAL	

ASSESSMENT 6-5A, B, C (IMPROVISED SCENE)

Authorship and directing	Situation included all necessary expository detail	0 1 2 3 4 5
	Exposition was artfully concealed in the action	0 1 2 3 4 5
	A definite point of view emerged	0 1 2 3 4 5
	The piece was revealing of the characters' relationships	0 1 2 3 4 5
	There was a definite premise and the piece delivered on it	0 1 2 3 4 5
	Pacing was excellent throughout	0 1 2 3 4 5
	There was a clear structure to each dramatic unit	0 1 2 3 4 5
	The beats were clear and effective	0 1 2 3 4 5
Acting	All actors were at ease	0 1 2 3 4 5
	Actors were equally active; nobody took passive position	0 1 2 3 4 5
	Actors were listening and in communion with each other	0 1 2 3 4 5
	Each character was sharply drawn and credible	0 1 2 3 4 5
	Each character's agenda was evident	0 1 2 3 4 5
Camerawork	Mobile, handheld coverage was well-framed throughout	0 1 2 3 4 5
	Camera was where it needed to be at all times	0 1 2 3 4 5
	Camera was never caught by surprise	0 1 2 3 4 5
	Mobile coverage motivated by characters' movements worked well throughout	0 1 2 3 4 5
	Close detail and close-ups always came when the audience needed them	0 1 2 3 4 5
	Camera coverage managed to juxtapose crucial elements in the frame whenever it was important	0 1 2 3 4 5
Sound	Sound coverage was consistently good	0 1 2 3 4 5
	Sound edited seamlessly together	0 1 2 3 4 5
	The mike was never in frame	0 1 2 3 4 5
Editing	Any action match cuts flowed smoothly	0 1 2 3 4 5
	Screen directions are correctly maintained	0 1 2 3 4 5
	Room geography is revealed as necessary, and not confusingly for a first-time viewer	0 1 2 3 4 5
	Convincing dialogue rhythms are maintained even when a picture cut happens in mid-sentence	0 1 2 3 4 5
	Moments of significant action and charged silence have been fully exploited	0 1 2 3 4 5

	Changes of scene rhythm occur convincingly with changes in the characters' moods, perceptions, thought patterns, and actions	0 1 2 3 4 5
	Eyeline shifts have been fully exploited	0 1 2 3 4 5
	No character makes a major change of position offscreen	0 1 2 3 4 5
	Editing appropriately and consistently shows characters as either the actor or the acted upon	0 1 2 3 4 5
Point of view	The scene is shot and cut to effectively reveal the state of mind of the main character or of the Storyteller	0 1 2 3 4 5
	The scene makes psychological sense by breathing, that is, it moves us close or far from the action in answer to our needs as audience members	0 1 2 3 4 5
	The action effectively reveals psychological and emotional changes in the characters	0 1 2 3 4 5
Dramaturgy	The piece develops convincingly	0 1 2 3 4 5
	The environment is fully utilized by the characters and made into an active component in the drama	0 1 2 3 4 5
	There are no redundancies of dialogue, action, or angle, etc.	0 1 2 3 4 5
	The scene feels right in length (better to feel a little short than too long)	0 1 2 3 4 5
	The scene implies backstory and what might come after	0 1 2 3 4 5
Impact	The piece holds your interest throughout	0 1 2 3 4 5
	Significant subtexts are implied	0 1 2 3 4 5
	The piece makes a real and moving statement	0 1 2 3 4 5
	TOTAL	

ASSESSMENT 6-6A, B, C, D (PARALLEL STORYTELLING)

Authorship and directing	Each situation included all necessary expository detail	0 1 2 3 4 5
	Exposition was artfully concealed in the action	0 1 2 3 4 5
	A definite point of view emerged	0 1 2 3 4 5
	Each piece was revealing of the character	0 1 2 3 4 5
	There was a definite premise and each piece delivered on it	0 1 2 3 4 5

	Pacing was excellent throughout	0 1 2 3 4 5
	There was a clear structure to each dramatic unit	0 1 2 3 4 5
	The beats were clear and effective	0 1 2 3 4 5
Acting	Actors were at ease	0 1 2 3 4 5
	Each character was sharply drawn and credible	0 1 2 3 4 5
	Each character's agenda was evident	0 1 2 3 4 5
Camerawork	Mobile, handheld coverage was well-framed throughout	0 1 2 3 4 5
	Camera was where it needed to be at all times	0 1 2 3 4 5
	Camera was never caught by surprise	0 1 2 3 4 5
	Mobile coverage motivated by characters' movements worked well throughout	0 1 2 3 4 5
	Close detail and close-ups always came when the audience needed them	0 1 2 3 4 5
	Camera coverage managed to juxtapose crucial elements in the frame whenever it was important	0 1 2 3 4 5
Sound	Sound coverage was consistently good	0 1 2 3 4 5
	Sound edited seamlessly together	0 1 2 3 4 5
	The mike was never in frame	0 1 2 3 4 5
Editing	Any action match cuts flowed smoothly	0 1 2 3 4 5
	Screen directions are correctly maintained	0 1 2 3 4 5
	Room geography is revealed as necessary, and not confusingly for a first-time viewer	0 1 2 3 4 5
	Moments of significant action and charged silence have been fully exploited	0 1 2 3 4 5
	Changes of scene rhythm occur convincingly with changes in the characters' moods, perceptions, thought patterns, and actions	0 1 2 3 4 5
	Eyeline shifts have been fully exploited	0 1 2 3 4 5
	No character makes a major change of position offscreen	0 1 2 3 4 5
	Editing appropriately and consistently shows characters as either the actor or the acted-upon	0 1 2 3 4 5
Point of view	The scene is shot and cut to effectively reveal the state of mind of the main character or of the Storyteller	0 1 2 3 4 5
	The scene makes psychological sense by breathing, that is, it moves us close or far from the action in answer to our needs as audience members	0 1 2 3 4 5

	The action effectively reveals psychological changes in the characters	0 1 2 3 4 5
Dramaturgy	The piece develops convincingly	0 1 2 3 4 5
	The environment is fully utilized by the characters and made into an active component in the drama	0 1 2 3 4 5
	There are no redundancies of dialogue, action, or angle, etc.	0 1 2 3 4 5
	The scene feels right in length	0 1 2 3 4 5
	The scene implies backstory and what might come after	0 1 2 3 4 5
Impact	The piece holds your interest throughout	0 1 2 3 4 5
	Significant subtexts are implied	0 1 2 3 4 5
	The piece makes a real and moving statement	0 1 2 3 4 5
	TOTAL	

ASSESSMENT 6-6A, B, C, D (SUPPLEMENT—PARALLEL STORYTELLING)

Parallel stories	Each portion of each story consistently contributes to its counterpart	0 1 2 3 4 5
	The rhythms of cross-cutting seem balanced	0 1 2 3 4 5
	There are a number of interesting counterpoint moments	0 1 2 3 4 5
	Movement is sometimes used as a cutting point between stories	0 1 2 3 4 5
	Dialogue is sometimes used as a cutting point between stories	0 1 2 3 4 5
	The frames of each story *design* well with each other	0 1 2 3 4 5
	The whole is greater than the sum of its parts	0 1 2 3 4 5
	TOTAL	

ASSESSMENT 11-1 (SCENE WRITING)

Characters	Gender identity of POV character is very convincing	0 1 2 3 4 5
	Each character pursues his or her own agenda through action	0 1 2 3 4 5
	The POV character's internal issues come across well	0 1 2 3 4 5

	What the POV character(s) try to do or get really allows us to understand them	0 1 2 3 4 5
	The central characters are *round*, that is, fully realized rather than *flat* support characters	0 1 2 3 4 5
	POV character's age is convincing in its concerns and characteristics	0 1 2 3 4 5
	All the characters have a dramatic function in the piece	0 1 2 3 4 5
	The characters each have different and characteristic actions	0 1 2 3 4 5
	There is really someone to like and care about	0 1 2 3 4 5
Situation	The situation(s) developed from the scene title are original and compelling	0 1 2 3 4 5
Genre	The piece has a decided genre identity	0 1 2 3 4 5
	The character types really belong in this genre	0 1 2 3 4 5
	The story and the genre really complement each other	0 1 2 3 4 5
	The genre is fully utilized and explored	0 1 2 3 4 5
	The writer has imposed his or her own stamp on the norms	0 1 2 3 4 5
	The genre has been extended but not disabled by the writer's individual handling	0 1 2 3 4 5
Screen time	The piece feels neither too long nor too short	0 1 2 3 4 5
	The piece comes in at its specified screen time	0 1 2 3 4 5
	It covers considerable ground for its screen time	0 1 2 3 4 5
Scene crisis placement	The high or turning point of the scene came where it was supposed to come	0 1 2 3 4 5
	The lead up to it was wholly credible and well paced	0 1 2 3 4 5
	The lead up built tension	0 1 2 3 4 5
	The resolution after the scene crisis was convincing and well paced	0 1 2 3 4 5
Number of beats	The writer built in the required number	0 1 2 3 4 5
	Each beat was earned and effective	0 1 2 3 4 5
	There was a developing pressure leading up to the beat	0 1 2 3 4 5

	The beat caused changed consciousness (measurable in behavior) by at least one character	0 1 2 3 4 5
Setting(s)	The settings are interesting and organic to the characters' situations	0 1 2 3 4 5
	Time and environment are evident and necessary	0 1 2 3 4 5
	The settings are used by the characters, not just included as backdrop	0 1 2 3 4 5
	The settings feel authentic	0 1 2 3 4 5
Conflict	Major issue or conflict is evident	0 1 2 3 4 5
	Conflict is organic to characters and their situation, not contrived	0 1 2 3 4 5
	Forces in opposition come to a point of confrontation	0 1 2 3 4 5
	Conflict results in material issues and changes	0 1 2 3 4 5
Plot	Necessary factual information is implied or evident	0 1 2 3 4 5
	Exposition is artfully disguised, not verbalized	0 1 2 3 4 5
	Events generate a forward movement	0 1 2 3 4 5
	Story logic and character motivation is impeccable	0 1 2 3 4 5
	Scene has energy and tension throughout	0 1 2 3 4 5
Structure	Time progression is well handled	0 1 2 3 4 5
	Events happen in their most effective order	0 1 2 3 4 5
	There is a clear sense of developmental phases through the scene	0 1 2 3 4 5
Theme	Thematic concerns develop naturally out of events we see	0 1 2 3 4 5
	The piece implies a substantial comment on the piece's thematic concerns	0 1 2 3 4 5
Dialogue	The dialogue rings true	0 1 2 3 4 5
	Each character speaks with his or her own voice and vocabulary	0 1 2 3 4 5
	There isn't a redundant word or syllable	0 1 2 3 4 5
Voice	The piece comes from the heart as well as the head	0 1 2 3 4 5
	The piece feels individual, not derivative or imitative	0 1 2 3 4 5

	You can feel an individual and critical human spirit behind the conception of this scene	0 1 2 3 4 5
Impact	Conflict is credible enough to have moral dimension	0 1 2 3 4 5
	Someone, however minimally, changes and grows	0 1 2 3 4 5
	You really want to know what happens next	0 1 2 3 4 5
	TOTAL	

APPENDIX 2

FORM AND AESTHETICS QUESTIONNAIRE

Name ____

Film Working Title _________________________________

Phone # ____________________ Email ____________________

Fill out this form to see how much you know about your film. Take the time to refine your answers and fill out all the spaces. Notice how the questionnaire encapsulates the artistic process by starting with your major belief, then moving through information about your film and its characters, and ending with how you want to act on your audience.

1. Statistics

My film will be _____ minutes long, will be shot on (format) _____, is expected to take _____ shooting days, and to cost $ _____. So far I have (check what applies):

A rough idea, incomplete __	A thematic statement __	All cast __
Complete but rough idea __	A treatment __	Principal cast __
A beginning __	Screenplay __	Production manager __
A middle __	Shooting script __	All funds __
An end __	Producer __	____% funds raised __
A step outline __	Director of photography __	____$ still to raise __

2. Personal philosophy behind the making of this film

In life I believe that ______________________________

____

____

3. Premise

The film explores my convictions by showing (here briefly write your film's premise): ______________________________

____

____

4. Genre

The genre (type or family) of this film is ____________, and my film only departs from this genre in that it ______________________________

____

____

5. Main characters, their wants, dominant traits, and major conflict for each (most important first)

Character A ____________ mainly wants ______________________________

____

Dominant traits ______________________________

____

Major conflict ______________________________

____

Character B ____________ mainly wants ______________________________

Dominant traits ______________________________

____

Major conflict ______________________________

____

Character C ____________ mainly wants ______________________________

Dominant traits ______________________________

____

Major conflict ______________________________

____

Character D ____________ mainly wants ______________

Dominant traits ______________________________

____

Major conflict ______________________________

____

Character E ____________ mainly wants ______________

Dominant traits ______________________________

____

Major conflict ______________________________

____

Character F ____________ mainly wants ______________

Dominant traits ______________________________

____

Major conflict ______________________________

____

More characters? Add on separate sheet.

6. Major situation affecting the main characters

The major situation in which the characters find themselves is ____________

____

____

____

7. Point of view

(a) The point-of-view character is ______________ and his/her biased way of seeing means that ______________________________

____

____

____

(b) Subsidiary characters are ______________________________ and their way of seeing, by contrast, means that ______________________________

____

____

____

(c) The Storyteller's characteristics are ______________________________

____

and this makes him/her see in a particular way that is ______________________________

____

____

8. The film's main conflict

The major forces at conflict in this film are between ______________________________ and ______________________________

9. The confrontation

The story's main conflict is finally played out between ____________________ and ____________________ in ______________________________ scene.

10. Story resolution

The resolution to the characters' struggle is ______________________________

____

____

11. Intended impact

After they have seen my film, I want my audience members to:

(a) Feel ______________________________

____

(b) Think ______________________________

____

(c) Tell all their friends to go and see the film because ______________________________

____

____

12. Other

Anything important not included above:

____

____

____

____

____

____

GLOSSARY

A & B rolls Two or more rolls of film camera original from which release prints are struck.
acetate sheet Clear plastic sheet used as base for titles or animation "cel" frames. In traditional animation, each frame is painted onto cellulose acetate sheet.
action match cut Cut made between two different angles of the same action using the subject's movement as the transition.
AD Assistant director.
adaptation The unique way characters adjust to the changing obstacles that prevent them from gaining their ends and a prime component in externalizing their conflicts.
ADR Automatic dialogue replacement. *See* post-synchronization.
aerial shot Shot taken from the air.
AFI American Film Institute.
ambient sound Sound naturally occurring in any location. Even an empty, quiet room has its own special atmosphere because no space is truly silent.
analog recording Any sound or picture that records its waveforms in a proportional representation, rather than digitally in which the waveform is registered by digital numbers as in the coordinates for a graph.
angle of acceptance The height and width of the subject filmed by a particular lens at a given distance expressed in a lens table, either in degrees or as measurements. Photographed image also depends on aspect ratio of the format in use. Wide-screen format will have longer horizontal measurement.
anticipating Term used to describe when an actor speaks or acts in advance of the appropriate moment.
anticipatory sound Sound brought in ahead of its accompanying picture.
artistic process The manner in which a human being goes about making an artwork. This has common elements of discovery and experiment no matter what art form is in use.

aspect ratio The size of a screen format expressed as the ratio of the width to the height. Films made for television are photographed at a ratio of 1.33 : 1. *See also* angle of acceptance.
atmosphere track Sound track providing a particular environment (cafe, railroad, beach, rain, etc.).
attack (sound) The beginning portion of any sound.
audio-sweetening The level and equalization adjustment process that accompanies sound mixing.
***auteur* theory** The concept that one mind controls the creative identity of a film.
axis *See* scene axis, sound axis.

baby legs A miniature tripod for low-angle shots.
back lighting Lighting from behind the subject.
backstory The events stated or implied to have happened prior to the period covered in the screenplay.
barney A soft camera cover designed to muffle camera noise.
bars Standard color bars generated in video systems, usually by the camera.
BCU Big close-up.
beat Point in a scene where a buildup of dramatic pressure effects a noticeable change in one or more characters' consciousness.
best boy Assistant to the gaffer.
BFI British Film Institute.
BG Background.
blocking Choreographic arrangement of movements by actors and camera in relation to the set.
body copy Non-dialogue descriptive portion of screenplay, usually consisting of stage directions and physical description.
book, the Actors' name for the script.
boom Support pole suspending the microphone close to the speakers but just out of shot.
boxcar cutting Crude method of assembling sound and action as level-cut segments for speed and convenience.
breakaway properties Those properties that are broken in the course of a scene and for which replacements must be on hand for multiple takes.
broad lighting Lighting that produces a broad band of highlight on a face or other three-dimensional object.
business The in-character activity generated by actors to fill out their characters' behavior.
butt splice Taped film splice made without the overlap necessary for cement splicing.
buzz track *See* presence.

callback Second round of auditioning for actors who have successfully passed the first round.
call sheet Document issued by production office detailing what is being shot on a certain day, and who and what are required at the shoot.
camera left, camera right Method of specifying movement or the placement of objects in relation to the camera: "Davy turns away from camera and walks off camera left." Also expressed as screen right or left.

camera motivation A shot or a camera movement must be motivated within the terms of the scene or story if it is not to look alien and imposed. Camera motivation is often answered by asking, "What is the point of view here?"
camera-to-subject axis The invisible line drawn between the camera and the subject in the composition. *See also* scene axis.
capturing *See* digitizing
cardioid microphone A directional microphone with a heart-shaped pickup pattern.
cattle call The call for a number of actors or dancers to try out, often simultaneously, for parts.
cel The clear cellulose acetate sheet used as a base for title lettering or for the painted frame of an animation sequence. The cel is clear so it can be laid as a foreground over a background.
cement splice A film splice made by cementing two overlapping portions of film together.
chalk marks Temporary marks made on the floor to ensure that the actor or camera stops at a precise place.
character biography The biographical portrait an actor invents as background to the character he or she is to play.
character generator An electronic device for producing video titles.
checkerboarding The practice, during conforming, of alternating film scenes with black leader in each A & B roll of camera original. Sound tracks prior to mixing are likewise alternated between two channels, with silence separating sound segments. Both black frame and silence allow the operator a grace period in which to adjust printer or sound channel settings before the arrival of the next segment.
chippy Carpenter.
cinéma vérité Documentary shooting method in which the camera is subservient to an actuality that is sometimes instigated by the director.
clapper board Marker board used at the beginning of takes whose bar closing permits separate sound to be synchronized. Also called the slate.
climax The dramatic apex of a scene.
coincidence Dramatists in a tight spot make things happen or people meet "by coincidence," a crutch overused at the dramatist's peril.
color bars Standard electronic video color test, usually generated by the camera.
color chart Chart attached to film slate board as color reference for laboratory processing technicians.
color temperature Light color quality is measured in degrees Kelvin (°K). Common light sources in moviemaking contain a different mix of colors. The eye compensates effortlessly, but film and video cameras (or lighting itself) must be adjusted to prevailing color temperature if white objects are to be rendered as white onscreen. Mixing daylight (around 5,400 °K) and studio lights (3,200 °K) in the same scene leads to an unnatural lighting effect. One source must be filtered to make its output match the other, and the camera must likewise be filtered or electronically color balanced for all scene colors to be rendered faithfully.
comm Commentary.
communion The principle by which actors react to the unforeseeable nuances in each other's performances to regain the spontaneity of real life during a rehearsed performance.

complementary shot A shot compositionally designed to intercut with another.
composite print A film print combining sound and picture.
compression Sound with a wide dynamic range can be proportionately compressed so that loudest and softest sounds are closer in volume. All TV transmissions and most radio transmissions, with the exception of high-fidelity music stations, are compressed. Cinemas usually give you the authentic range between whispers and the roar of battle.
concept The dramatic *raison d'être* underlying the whole screenplay.
conforming The process by which the film camera original is edited in conformity with the fine-cut workprint prior to making release prints.
confrontation Bringing into final collision those people or forces representing the dramatic piece's main conflict.
contingency percentage A percentage added to a budget to provide for the unforeseeable.
contingency planning Scheduling alternative shooting for any scenes that could be threatened by weather or other imponderables.
continuity Consistency of physical detail between shots intended to match.
continuity script Script made after postproduction as record of film contents. Useful in proving piracy or censorship.
continuity supervisor *See* script supervisor.
contrast Difference in brightness between highlight and deep shadow areas in an image.
contrast ratio Ratio of lightest to darkest areas in an image.
controlling point of view The psychological perspective (a character's or the Storyteller's) from which a particular scene is shown.
counterpoint The juxtaposing of antithetical elements, perhaps between sound and picture, to create a conflict of impressions for the audience to resolve.
coverage The different angles from which a given scene is covered to allow variations of viewpoint in editing.
crab dolly Wheeled camera support platform that can roll in any direction.
crane A boom supporting the camera that can be raised or lowered during the shot.
crash zoom Very fast zoom in or zoom out.
crib notes Director's notes listing intentions and *don't forgets* for a scene.
crossing the line Moving the camera across the scene axis. Can be problematic.
crossplot (or scene breakdown) A chart displaying the locations, characters, and script pages necessary to each scene.
CS Close shot.
CU Close-up.
cutaway A shot, often from a character's physical point of view, that allows us to cut away momentarily from the main action.

dailies The film unit's daily output, processed and ready to be viewed. Also called rushes because of the rush involved in readying them.
DAT recorder Digital audio tape recorder.
day for night Special photography that allows a sunlit day shot to pass as moonlit night.
decay The tapering away of a concluding sound.

deep focus Photography that holds objects both near and far in sharp focus.
degradation Deterioration of a picture, either video or photo, when it passes through several generations of copying.
depth of field The depth of the picture that is in acceptably sharp focus. Varies widely according to lens and f-stop in use.
deus ex machina The improbable event imported into a story to make it turn out right.
diegetic sound Sound that characters can hear and which belongs naturally with what we can see in picture.
diffused light Light composed of disorganized rays that casts an indistinct shadow.
digitizing (or capturing) The process of turning an analog signal, whether audio or video, into a digital record. This usually involves using an algorithmic formulation to compress the information to avoid wasteful recording of similarities in one frame to the next.
direct cinema A low-profile documentary style of shooting that disallows any directorial intrusion to shape or instigate incidents.
discontinuity Form of storytelling in which time progression is deliberately confused or abridged.
dissolve Transitional device in which one image cross fades into another. Also called a lap dissolve. One sound can dissolve into another.
DOF Depth of field.
Dolby A proprietary electronic recording system that produces low-noise sound recording, that is, having a lowered systemic hiss.
dolly shot Any shot from a wheeled camera support.
double-system recording Camera and sound recorder are separate instruments.
DP Director of photography.
dramatic dynamics The ebb and flow of dramatic pressure through the length of a scene or of a whole piece.
dramatic interpretation The selection of a dominant meaning for a particular text.
drop frame An adjustment, which involves periodically dropping a frame, made in NTSC timecode to make it correspond with clock time. Non-drop frame is unadjusted NTSC code.
dry run A rehearsal for the camera that is not filmed.
dry sound One that is clean and not augmented by reverberant additions.
dub To copy from one electronic medium to another. Can be sound or video picture.
dupe Duplicate negative.
dutch angle Shot made with camera deliberately tilted out of horizontal.
dynamic character definition Defining a dramatic character by what he or she wants and is trying to accomplish.
dynamic composition Pictorial composition as it changes within a moving shot.

echo Sound reflections that return after a constant delay time.
edge numbers Code numbers imprinted on the edge of camera original film and printing through to the workprint.
edit decision list (EDL) Sound and picture edit decisions in a movie defined as a list of timecode or Keycode™ numbers. Taking camera originals and a

standard EDL to a postproduction facility allows them to make a perfect facsimile of the workprint.

effects Sounds specially laid to augment the sound track of a film. Abbreviated as FX.

elision Omission of unnecessary elements in editing, usually to make a long process acceptably short.

emotional memory Actors who carefully devise specific actions to fit a particular character mood find, when they perform, that they spontaneously experience the characters' emotions.

emotional transition Emotional change during a scene. Scripts often challenge actors by calling for leaps from one mood to another in a shorter time than is normal in life.

energy level Both scenes and performances have their own energy levels. A director will often call for a change in energy level when a scene is not working or when actors are getting tired.

epic hero Larger than life main character with superhuman attributes.

equalizing (EQ) Using sound filters to reduce the discrepancy between sound tracks that are supposed to match and sound seamless.

establishing shot A shot that establishes a scene's geographical and human contents. *See* also master shot.

exposition The part of a scene or a story in which basic information is relayed to the audience. Good exposition is buried within action and goes unnoticed.

expressionism A mode in art in which verisimilitude is laid aside in favor of techniques that evoke the subjective vision of a character or the Storyteller.

ext Exterior.

external composition The compositional relationship between two images at the point of cutting between them.

eye light Low-wattage light mounted on camera to put a liquid sparkle in actors' eyes.

eyeline The visual trajectory of a character in a scene.

fade down To lower sound level.

fade to white To fade an image to white instead of black.

fade up To raise sound level.

falling action *See* resolution.

FG Foreground.

FI Fade in.

fill light Diffused light used to raise light level in shadows cast by key light.

fishpole A handheld microphone boom.

flash forward Moving temporarily forward in time, the cinematic equivalent of the future tense. This quickly becomes a new form of present.

flashback Moving temporarily backward in time; a cinematic past tense that soon becomes an ongoing present.

floor plan *See* ground plan.

FO Fade out.

focal distance Distance between camera and subject.

focus (acting) Seeing, hearing, thinking in character. When an actor loses focus, he or she becomes self-conscious and aware of participating in a make-believe world.

Foley Generic name for a stage where sound is re-created to picture.
foreshadowing A somewhat fatalistic narrative technique by which an outcome is hinted at in advance. Helps to raise expectant tension in the audience.
form The means and arrangement chosen to present a story's content.
freeze frame A single frame arrested and held as a still picture.
frontal lighting Key light coming from the direction of the camera and showing the subject virtually without shadows.
FTs Footsteps. Often must be recreated.
FX Sound effects.

gaffer Works closely with the director of photography. Sets lights and ensures their power.
generation Camera original (in film or video) is the first generation, and copies become subsequent numbered generations, each showing increased degradation of the original's fidelity.
genre A kind or type of film (horror, sitcom, cowboy, domestic drama, etc.).
givens Whatever is non-negotiably specified in a text.
gopher Junior production team member who has to go for this and go for that. Known as *runner* or *dogsbody* in England.
grading *See* timing.
graduated tonality An image composed of midtones and having neither very bright nor very dark areas.
gray scale Test chart useful to camera and lab technicians that shows the range of gray tones and includes absolute black and white.
grip Location technician expert in handling lighting and set construction equipment.
ground plan Diagram showing placement of objects and movements of actors on a floor plan. Also called *floor plan*.
gun/rifle mike Ultra-directional microphone useful for minimizing the intrusiveness of ambient noise.

hand properties Those props an actor handles.
hard light *See* specular light.
headroom Compositional space left above heads.
high angle Camera mounted high, looking down.
high contrast Image with large range of brightnesses.
high down Camera mounted high, looking down.
high-key picture Image that is overall bright with few areas of shadow.
highlight Brightest areas in picture.
hi-hat Ultra-low camera support resembling a metal top hat.
hypercardioid microphone One that is super-directional in its pickup pattern.
hyphenation Anyone who combines crafts, such as an actor-director.

improv Improvisation. A dramatic interaction that deliberately permits an outcome to emerge spontaneously. Improvs can involve different degrees of structure or may set a goal to be reached by an undetermined path.
insert A close shot of detail to be inserted in a shot containing more comprehensive action.
int Interior.

interior monologue The interior *thoughts voice* an actor will sustain to help stay in character and in focus.
internal composition Composition internal to the frame as opposed to the compositional relationship existing between adjacent shots, called *external composition.*
irony The revelation of a reality different from that initially apparent.

juicer Electrician.
jump cut Transitional device in which two similar images taken at different times are cut together so the elision of intervening time is apparent. From this the audience infers that time has passed.
juxtaposition The placing together of different pictorial or sound elements to invite comparison, inference, and heightened thematic awareness on the part of the audience.

Keycode™ Kodak's proprietary system for bar coding each camera original film frame. This facilitates digitizing by assigning each frame its own timecode. Later, after digital editing, the coding permits negative cutting (conforming) from a digitally produced edit decision list (EDL).
key light A scene's apparent source of illumination and the one creating the intended shadow pattern.
key numbers *See* edge numbers.
keystone distortion The distortion of parallel lines that results from photographing an object from an off-axis position.
knowing narrator Literary term for a narrator who is of superior knowledge and intelligence.

LA Low angle.
L Cut *See* overlap cut.
lap cut *See* overlap cut.
lap dissolve *See* dissolve.
lavalier mike Any neck or chest microphone.
lead space The additional compositional space allowed in front of a figure or moving object photographed in profile.
legal release A legally binding release form signed by a participant in a film that gives permission to use footage taken.
leitmotif Intentionally repeated element (sound, shot, dialogue, music, etc.) that helps unify a film by reminding the viewer of its earlier appearance. May represent a particular character or event.
lens speed How *fast* a lens is depends on how much light it transmits at its maximum aperture.
level Sound volume.
lighting ratio The ratio of highlight brightness to shadow illumination.
limiter Electronically applied upper sound limit, useful for preventing momentary transient sounds like a door slamming from distortion through over-recording.
line of tension Invisible dramatic axis, or line of awareness, that can be drawn between protagonists and important elements in a scene.

lip sync Re-created speech that is in complete sync with the speaker. Singers often lip sync to their recordings and fake a singing performance on television.
looping *See* post-synchonization.
lose focus *See* focus.
low angle Camera looking up at subject.
low-contrast image Small differences of brightness between highlight areas and shadow.
low-key picture A scene that may have high contrast but which is predominantly dark.
LS Long shot.

M and E track *See* music and effects track.
magazine Removable light-proof film container for a film camera.
mannerisms An actor's idiosyncratic and repeated details of behavior. Very hard to change or suppress.
master mix Final mixed sound, first generation.
master shot Shot that shows most or all of the scene and most or all of the characters.
matchback The process of conforming a film negative from numbers generated by a nonlinear video editing process.
match cut *See* action match cut.
MCS Medium close shot.
memory stick A solid state memory carrying setup information that can be plugged into a digital video camera. Useful for standardizing setup parameters from certain kinds of shots.
metaphor A verbal or visually implied analogy that ascribes to one thing the qualities associated with another.
MIDI Musical Instrument Digital Interface, a connection system that enables computers to control musical instruments.
midtones The intermediate shades of gray lying between the extremes of black and white.
mimesis Action that imitates the actuality of life.
mise en scène The totality of lighting, blocking, camera use, and composition that produces the dramatic image on film.
mix The combining together of sound tracks.
mix chart Cue chart that functions like a musician's score to assist in the sound mix.
MLS Medium long shot.
montage Originally meant editing in general, but now refers to the kind of sequence that shows a process or the passage of time.
montage sequence *See* montage.
MOS Short for *Mit out sound*, which is what the German directors in Hollywood called for when they intended to shoot silently. In Britain this shot is called *mute*.
motif Any formal element repeated from film history or from the film itself whose repetition draws attention to an unfolding thematic statement. *See also* leitmotif.
motivation Whatever plot logic impels a character to act or react in a particular way, usually a combination of psychological make-up and external events.

MS Medium shot.
Murphy's law Whatever can go wrong will go wrong. Applies also to people.
mus Music.
music and effects track A mix of non-dialogue tracks to provide all background sound for a foreign version dub. Often called an *M and E track*.
music sync points Places in a film's action where music must exactly fit. Also called picture pointing and can be overdone.
mute shot *See* MOS.

naive narrator Literary term for a character, like Forrest Gump, whom the audience knows is less knowledgeable than they are.
narr Narration.
narrating point of view A literary term for the first person point of view telling the story.
narrow lighting Lighting in portraiture that produces a narrow band of highlight on a face.
negative cutting *See* conforming.
NLE Nonlinear editing.
noise Noise inherent in a sound recording system.
noise reduction Recording and playback technique that minimizes system noise. *See also* Dolby.
normal lens A lens of a focal length that, in the format being used, renders distances between foreground and background as recognizably normal.
NTSC (National Television Standards Commission) video The signal standard used in American broadcasting. Also known as composite video or RS-170A.

obligatory moment The moment of maximum dramatic intensity in a scene and for which the whole scene exists.
offline edit Manual, non-computerized video editing. *See also* online edit.
omnidirectional microphone One whose pickup pattern favors all directions equally.
omniscient point of view A storytelling mode in which the audience is exposed to the author's capacity to see or know anything going on in the story, to move at will in time and space, and to freely comment upon meanings or themes.
online edit Completion process that uses the offline edit's EDL to make a final computerized version at the highest possible resolution complete with opticals and titles.
on the nose Writing that is literal and overly explicit.
optical Any visual device, including a fade, dissolve, wipe, iris wipe, ripple dissolve, matte, superimposition, etc.
optical house A company specializing in visual special effects.
optical track A sound track photographically recorded.
OS Can mean offscreen, or overshoulder, depending on context.
over the top Expression signifying a performance carried out with a surfeit of emotion.
overlap cut Any cut in which picture and sound transitions are staggered instead of level-cut.

parallel storytelling The intercutting of two separate stories proceeding through time in parallel. Useful for abridging each and for making ironic contrasts.
pan Short for panoramic. Horizontal camera movement.
perspective The size differential between foreground and background objects that causes us to infer receding space. Obviously distorted perspective makes us attribute subjective distortion in the point of view being expressed.
picture pointing Making music fit picture events. Walt Disney films used the device so much that its overuse is called *Mickey Mousing*.
picture texture This can be hard or soft. A hard image has large areas in sharp focus and tends to be high contrast, while a soft image has areas out of focus and lacks contrast.
playwriting One actor's tendency to take control of a scene, particularly in improv work, and manipulate other actors into a passive relationship.
plot The arrangement of incidents and the logic of causality in a story. Plot should create a sense of momentum and credibility and act as a vehicle for the thematic intention of the piece.
plot-driven narrative Story strategy that may depart from chronology to reveal the events according to the story's type and plot strategy. Plot-driven narrative sets out to entertain by generating tension.
PM Production manager.
point of view Sometimes literally what a character sees (a clock approaching midnight, for instance) but more usually signifies the outlook and sensations of a character within a particular environment. This can be the momentary consciousness of an unimportant character or that of a main character (*see* controlling point of view). It can also be the Storyteller's point of view (*see* omniscient point of view).
post-synchronization Dialogue or effects shot in sync with existing action.
POV Point of view. When abbreviated thus in a screenplay it nearly always means a shot reproducing a character's eyeline view.
practical Any light source visible in the frame as part of the set.
premise *See* concept.
premix A preliminary pass in which subsidiary sound elements are mixed together in preparation for the final mix.
preroll The amount of time a video-editing rig needs to get up to speed before it can safely make a cut.
presence Specially recorded location atmosphere to authentically augment "silent" portions of track. Every space has its own unique presence.
progressive scan The drawing of a complete video frame from top to bottom in one scan instead of the conventional interlace method in which odd lines and even lines are drawn in two separate passes.
prop Property or object used for set dressing or by actors. *See also* hand, stage, and breakaway properties.
property Physical object handled by actors or present for authenticity in a set. A term also used for a script to which someone has secured the rights.
psychoacoustics Human perception and evaluation of sounds in contrast to their scientific evaluation.

rack focus Altering focus between foreground and background during a shot. Prompts or accommodates an attention shift (a figure enters a door at the back of the room, for instance).
radio frequency interference Sound system intrusions that have their origins in radio transmissions. Also called RF.
radio microphone A microphone system that transmits its signal by radio to the recorder and is therefore wireless. Famous for picking up taxis and CB enthusiasts at inopportune moments.
reader's script Transcript of a finished film presented in a publisher's format that makes maximum use of the page.
recall The faculty of selective memory that is useful to writers because memory tends to drop what is unnecessary or uninteresting.
reconnaissance Careful examination of locations prior to shooting. *See also* scouting.
reflected sound Sound thrown back by sound-reflective surfaces.
release print Final print destined for audience consumption.
research Library work and observation of real life in search of authentic detail to fill out fictional characters and situations.
resistance Human evasion mechanisms that show up in actors under different kinds of stress.
resolution The wind-down events following the plot's climax that form the final phase of the plot's development. Also called *falling action.*
reverberation Sound reflections returning in a disorganized pattern of delay.
RF *See* radio frequency interference.
rising action The plot developments, including complication and conflict, that lead to a plot's climax.
room tone *See* presence.
running lines The action of actors rehearsing lines before a take, usually done with the script supervisor.
rushes Unedited raw footage as it appears after shooting. Also called *dailies.*
rushes book Log of important first reactions to performances in rushes footage.

scene axis The invisible line in a scene representing the scene's dramatic polarization. In a labor dispute scene this might be drawn between the main protagonists, the plant manager and the union negotiator. Coverage is shot from one side of this line to preserve consistent screen directions for all participants. Complex scenes involving multiple characters and physical regrouping may have more than one axis. *See also* crossing the line.
scene breakdown (or crossplot) A chart displaying the locations, characters, and script pages necessary for each scene.
scene dialectics The forces in opposition in a scene that usually require externalizing through acting, blocking, composition, visual and aural metaphors, etc.
scene geography The physical layout of the location and the placing of the characters when they are first encountered. *See also* master shot.
scouting Careful examination of locations prior to shooting. Also called *reconnaissance.*
screen direction The orientation or movement of characters and objects relative to the screen (screen left, screen right, upscreen, downscreen).

screen left, screen right Movement or direction specifications. *See* screen direction.
screenplay Standard script format showing dialogue and stage direction but no camera or editing instructions.
script supervisor Also called *continuity supervisor*, this person notes the physical details of each scene and the actual dialogue used so that complementary shots, designed to cut together, will match.
segue (pronounced *seg-way*) Sound transition, often a dissolve.
set light A light whose function is to illuminate the set.
setup The combination of particular lens, camera placement, and composition to produce a particular shot.
SFX Sound effects.
shooting ratio The ratio of material shot in relation to its eventual edited screen time. 8 : 1 or higher is usual for dramatic film.
shooting script Screenplay with scenes numbered and amended to show intended camera coverage and editing.
side coaching During breaks in a scene's dialogue, the director can quietly feed directions to the actors who incorporate these instructions without breaking character. Most often used when shooting reaction shots.
sightlines Lines that can be drawn along each character's main lines of vision and influence the pattern of coverage in order to reproduce the feeling of each main character's consciousness.
silhouette lighting Lighting in which the subject is a dark outline against a light background.
simple narrative Primarily functional and supplies an exposition of events, usually in chronological order. Simple narrative exists to inform.
single shot A shot containing only one character.
single-system recording Sound recording made on film or video that also carries the picture. *See* double-system recording.
slate *See* clapper board.
slate number Setup and take number shown on the slate, or clapper, which identifies a particular take.
soft light Light that does not produce hard-edged shadows.
sound axis The direct line between the microphone and the source of sound such as speech. Directional microphones favor sounds *on axis* and discriminate against sound that is *off axis.*
sound dissolve One sound track dissolving into another.
sound effects Non-dialogue recordings of sounds intended either to intensify a scene's realism or to give it a subjective heightening.
sound mix The mixing together of sound elements into a sound composition that becomes the film's sound track.
sound perspective Apparent distance of sound source from the microphone. Lavalier mikes, for instance, give no change of perspective when characters move or turn because they remain in a fixed relationship to the wearer.
soundscape The aural picture built in the audience's imagination by skillfully deployed sound tracks.
sparks Electrician.

specular light Light composed of parallel rays that casts a comparatively hard-edged shadow.
split-page format A script format that places action on the left side of the page and its accompanying sound on the right.
stage directions Non-dialogue screenplay instructions, also known as *body copy*.
stage properties Those properties that are used to dress the stage but are not handled by characters.
stand-in Someone who takes the place of an actor during setup time or for shots that involve special skills, such as horseriding, fights, etc.
static character definition Giving a character static attributes instead of defining him in terms of dynamic volition.
static composition The composition elements in a static image.
Steadicam Proprietary body-brace camera support that uses counterbalance and gimbal technology so the camera can float while the operator walks.
step outline Synopsis of a screenplay expressed as a series of numbered steps, preferably including a definition of each step's function in the whole.
sting Musical accent to heighten a dramatic moment.
storyboard Series of key images sketched to suggest what a series of shots will look like.
strobing The unnatural result onscreen resulting from the interaction of camera shutter speed with a patterned subject such as the rotating spokes of a wheel or panning across a picket fence.
structure The formal organization of the elements of a story, principally the handling of time, and their arrangement into a dramatically satisfying development that includes a climax and resolution.
style An individual stamp on a film; the elements in a film that issue from its makers' own artistic identity.
subjective camera angle An angle that implies the physical point of view of one of the characters.
subtext The hidden, underlying meaning to the text. It is supremely important and actors and director must often search for it.
superobjective The overarching thematic purpose of the director's dramatic interpretation.
surrealism Also a movement in art and literature. Concerned with the free movement of the imagination particularly as expressed in dreams, where the dreamer has no conscious control over events. Often associated with helplessness.
sweetening *See* audio-sweetening.
sync coding Code marks to help an editor keep sound and action in sync.
synecdoche A literary figure of speech in which a part stands for a whole. In film, you might use a revolving blue light to stand for the police.

tag An irreducibly brief description useful for its focus upon essentials.
take One filmed attempt from one setup. Each setup may have several takes.
telephoto lens Long or telescopic lens that foreshortens the apparent distance between foreground and background objects.

tense, change of Temporary change from present to either past, future, or conditional tenses in a film's narrative flow. Whatever tense a film invokes speedily becomes a new, ongoing present. For this reason screenwriting is always in the present tense.
thematic purpose The overall interpretation of a complete work that is ultimately decided by the director. *See* superobjective.
theme A dominant idea made concrete through its representation by the characters, action, and imagery of the film.
three-shot (3S) Shot containing three people.
thumbnail character sketch Brief character description useful either in screen writing or in recruiting actors.
tilt Camera swiveling in a vertical arc, tilting up and down to show the height of a flagpole, for instance.
timebase correction Electronic stabilization of the video image, particularly necessary to make it compatible with the sensitive circuitry used in transmission over the air.
timecode Electronic code number unique to each video frame.
timing The process of examining and grading a negative for color quality and exposure prior to printing. Also called *grading*.
tracking shot Moving camera shot in which the camera dolly often runs on tracks like a miniature railroad.
transitional device Any visual, sound, or dramatic screen element that signals a jump to another time or place.
treatment Usually a synopsis in present-tense, short-story form of a screenplay that summarizes dialogue and describes only what an audience would see and hear. Can also be used to refer to a puff piece designed to sell the script rather than give comprehensive information about content.
trucking shot Moving camera shot that was originally shot from a truck. The term is used interchangeably with *tracking*.
two-shot (2S) Shot containing two people.

ultra-directional microphone *See* hypercardioid microphone.
unit The whole group of people shooting a film.

VCR Videocassette recorder.
verbal action Words conceived and delivered so as to act upon the listener and instigate a result.
video assist or video feed Video taken from the film camera's viewfinder and displayed on a monitor, usually for the director to watch during film shooting.
visual rhythm Each image according to its action and compositional complexity requires a different duration onscreen to look right and to occupy the same audience concentration as its predecessor. A succession of images, when sensitively edited, exhibits a rhythmic constancy that can be slowed or accelerated like any other kind of rhythm.
VO Voice-over.

volition The will of a character to accomplish something. This leads to constant struggle of one form or another, a concept vital in making dramatic characters come to life.
VCR Videocassette recorder.
VT Videotape.
VTR Videotape recorder.

WA Wide angle.
walk-through The stage during lighting setup when actors or stand-ins are asked to walk through their physical movements.
whip pan Very fast panning movement.
white balance Video camera setup procedure in which circuitry is adjusted to the color temperature of the lighting source so a white object is rendered as white onscreen.
wide-angle lens A lens with a wide angle of acceptance. Its effect is to increase the apparent distance between foreground and background objects.
wild Not in sync.
wild track A sound track shot alone and with no synchronous picture.
window dub A transfer made from a timecoded, video camera original that displays each frame's timecode number in a window near the bottom of frame.
wipe Optical transition between two scenes that appears onscreen as a line moving across the screen. An iris wipe makes the new scene appear as a dot that enlarges to fill the screen. These effects are overused on the TV screen.
wireless mike *See* radio microphone.
workprint A film print made for the express purpose of editing.
wrap End of shooting.
WS Wide shot.
WT Wild track.

XLS Extra long shot.

zoom lens A lens whose focal length is infinitely variable between two extremes.
zoom ratio The ratio of the longest to the widest focal lengths. A 10 to 100 mm zoom would have a 10:1 zoom ratio.

BIBLIOGRAPHY AND USEFUL WEB SITES

ACTING

Barr, Tony & Eric Stephan Kline. *Acting for the Camera.* New York: Harper-Collins, 1997.

Caine, Michael. *Acting in Film: An Actor's Take on Moviemaking* (Videocassette). NY: Applause Theatre Book Publishers, 1997.

Hagen, Uta and Haskel Frankel. *Respect for Acting.* New York: Wiley, 1973.

Hodgson, John and Ernest Richards. *Improvisation.* New York: Grove Press, 1974.

Marowitz, Charles. *The Art of Being: Towards a Theory of Acting.* New York: Taplinger, 1978.

Moore, Sonia. *The Stanislavski System.* New York: Viking Press, 1965.

Moore, Sonia. *Stanislavski Revealed.* New York: Applause Theatre Books, 1991

Morris, Eric with Joan Hotchkis. *No Acting Please.* Los Angeles: Ermor Enterprises, 1995.

Spolin, Viola. *Improvisation for the Theatre.* Evanston, Illinois: Northwestern University Press, 1990.

SCREENWRITING

Bergman, Ingmar. *Four Stories by Ingmar Bergman.* New York: Boulevard Books, 1976.

Biro, Yvette and Marie-Geneviéve Ripeau. *To Dress a Nude: Exercises in Imagination.* Dubuque, Iowa: Kendall/Hunt, 1998.

Blacker, Irwin R. *The Elements of Screenwriting.* Indianapolis, Indiana: Hungry Minds, Inc., 1996.

Blum, Richard A. *Television and Screen Writing From Concept to Contract 4th Ed.* Boston: Focal Press, 2000.

Cooper, Pat & Ken Dancyger. *Writing the Short Film 2nd Ed.* Boston: Focal Press, 1999.

Dancyger, Ken. *Global Scriptwriting.* Boston: Focal Press, 2001.

Dancyger, Ken and Jeff Rush. *Alternative Scriptwriting: Writing Beyond the Rules 2nd Ed.* Boston: Focal Press, 1995.

Field, Syd. *Screenplay: The Foundations of Screenwriting*. New York: Dell, 1984.

Field, Syd. *The Screenwriter's Workbook*. New York: Dell, 1984.

Horton, Andrew. *Writing the Character-Centered Screenplay.* Berkeley, California: University of California Press, 1999.

Howard, David. *The Tools of Screenwriting*. New York: St. Martin's Press, 1995.

Rosenthal, Alan. *Writing Docudrama: Dramatizing Reality for Film and Television*. Boston: Focal Press, 1995.

Vale, Eugene. *Vale's Technique of Screen and TV Writing*. Boston: Focal Press, 1998.

Vogler, Christopher. *The Screenwriter's Journey: Mythic Structures*. Studio City, California: Michael Wiese Productions, 1998.

ADAPTATION

Bluestone, George. *Novels into Film*. Berkeley, California: University of California Press, 1957.

Boyum, Joy Gould. *Double Exposure: Fiction into Film*. New York: Universe Books, 1985.

Brady, Ben. *Principles of Adaptation for Film and Television*. Austin, Texas: University of Texas Press, 1994.

Halperin, Michael. *Writing for the Second Act: Building Conflict and Tension*. Studio City, California: Michael Wiese Productions, 2000.

Horton, Andrew. *Writing the Character Centered Screenplay 2nd Ed.* Berkeley, California: University of California Press, 1999.

McDougal, Stuart Y. *Made into Movies: From Literature to Film*. New York: Harcourt, Brace and Jovanovich, 1997.

Portnoy, Kenneth. *Screen Adaptation: A Scriptwriting Handbook 2nd Ed.* Boston: Focal Press, 1998.

Richardson, Robert. *Literature and Film*. New York: Garland, 1985.

Seger, Linda. *The Art of Adaptation: Turning Fact and Fiction into Film*. New York: Henry Holt, 1992.

DIRECTING

Bresson, Robert. *Notes on the Cinematographer.* Los Angeles: Green Integer Books, 1997.

Crisp, Mike. *The Practical Director 2nd Ed.* Boston: Focal Press, 1996.

Crisp, Mike. *Directing Single Camera Drama*. Boston: Focal Press, 1997.

Katz, Steven D. *Film Directing Shot by Shot*. Boston: Focal Press in association with Michael Wiese Production, 1991.

Lumet, Sidney. *Making Movies*. New York: Knopf/Random House, 1996.

Mamet, David. *On Directing Film*. New York: Penguin, 1991.

Rabiger, Michael. *Directing the Documentary 3rd Ed.* Boston: Focal Press, 1998.

Rea, Peter and David Irving. *Producing and Directing the Short Film and Video 2nd Ed.* Boston: Focal Press, 2001.

Sherman, Eric. *Directing the Film: Film Directors on Their Art*. Los Angeles: Acrobat Books, 1988.

CONTINUITY

Miller, Pat P. *Script Supervising and Film Continuity 3rd Ed.* Boston: Focal Press, 1999.

Rowlands, Avril. *The Continuity Supervisor 4th Ed.* Boston: Focal Press, 2000.

LIGHTING

Box, Harry. *The Set Lighting Technician's Handbook: Film Lighting Equipment, Practice, and Electrical Distribution 2nd Ed.* Boston: Focal Press, 1997.

Carlson, Verne and Sylvia Carlson. *Professional Lighting Handbook 2nd Ed.* Boston: Focal Press, 1991.

Ferncase, Richard K. *Film and Video Lighting Terms and Concepts.* Boston: Focal Press, 1995.

Ferncase, Richard K. *Basic Lighting Worktext for Film and Video.* Boston: Focal Press, 1992.

Fitt, Brian. *A–Z of Lighting Terms.* Boston: Focal Press, 1998.

Gloman, Chuck and Tom LeTourneau. *Placing Shadows: Lighting Techniques of Video Production 2nd Ed.* Boston: Focal Press, 2000.

Millerson, Gerald. *Lighting for TV and Film 3rd Ed.* Boston: Focal Press, 1999.

Samuelson, David W. *Motion Picture Camera and Lighting Equipment: Choice and Technique.* Boston: Focal Press, 1986.

Uva, Michael G. and Sabrina Uva. *The Grip Book.* Boston: Focal Press, 1997.

Viera, John David and Dave Viera. *Lighting for Film and Electronic Cinematography.* Belmont, California: Wadsworth, 1992.

CINEMATOGRAPHY AND MOTION PICTURE TECHNIQUES

Arijon, Daniel. *Grammar of the Film Language.* Los Angeles: Silman-James, 1991.

Ascher, Steven and Edward Pincus. *The Filmmaker's Handbook.* New York: Plume, 1999.

Beacham, Frank, ed. *American Cinematographers Video Manual.* Hollywood, California: American Society of Cinematographers, 1994.

Carlson, Sylvia and Verne Carlson. *Professional Cameraman's Handbook 4th Ed.* Boston: Focal Press, 1994.

Detmers, Fred, ed. *American Cinematographer's Handbook.* Hollywood, California: American Society of Cinematographers, 1990.

Ettedgui, Peter. *Cinematography.* Boston: Focal Press, 1999.

Hines, William E. *Operating Cinematography for Film and Video: A Professional and Practical Guide.* Los Angeles: Ed-Venture Films/Books, 1997.

Hirschfeld, Gerald and Julia Tucker. *Image Control: Motion Picture and Video Camera Filters and Lab Techniques.* Boston: Focal Press, 1993.

Laszlo, Andrew and Andrew Quicke. *Every Frame a Rembrandt: Art and Practice of Cinematography.* Boston: Focal Press, 2000.

Lobrutto, Vincent. *Principal Photography: Interviews with Feature Film Cinematographers.* Westport, Connecticut: Greenwood, 1999.

Malkiewicz, J. Kris and Jim Fletcher. *Cinematography: A Guide for Film Makers and Film Teachers 2nd Ed.* New York: Simon & Schuster, 1992.

Malkiewicz, J. Kris, Leonard Konopelski, and Barbara Gryboski. *Film Lighting: Talks With Hollywood's Cinematographers and Gaffers*. New York: Simon & Schuster, 1986.

Mascelli, Joseph. *The Five C's of Cinematography: Motion Picture Filming Technique*. Los Angeles: Silman-James Press, 1998.

ART DIRECTION

Affron, Charles and Mirella Affron. *Sets in Motion*. New Brunswick, New Jersey: Rutgers University Press, 1995.

Ettedgui, Peter. *Production Design and Art Direction*. Boston: Focal Press, 2000.

Olson, Robert. *Art Direction for Film and Video 2nd Ed*. Boston: Focal Press, 1998.

Preston, Ward. *What an Art Director Does*. Los Angeles: Silman-James, 1994.

Sennett, Richard S. *Setting the Scene: The Great Hollywood Art Directors*. New York: Harry N. Abrams, Inc, 1994.

COSTUMING AND MAKEUP

Delamar, Penny. *The Complete Makeup Artist: Working in Film, Television, and Theatre*. Evanston, Illinois: Northwestern University Press, 2002.

Ingham, Rosemary, Liz Covey, and Elizabeth Covey. *The Costume Designer's Handbook: A Complete Guide for Amateur and Professional Costume Designers 2nd Ed*. Portsmouth, New Hampshire: Heinemann, 1992.

Timpone, Anthony. *Men, Makeup, and Monsters: Hollywood's Masters of Illusion and FX*. New York: St. Martin's Press, 1996.

PRODUCTION MANAGEMENT

Cleve, Bastian. *Film Production Management 2nd Ed*. Boston: Focal Press, 1999.

Gates, Richard. *Production Management for Film and Video 3rd Ed*. Boston: Focal Press, 1999.

Maier, Robert G. *Location Scouting and Management Handbook*. Boston: Focal Press, 1994.

Patz, Deborah S. *Surviving Production: The Art of Production Management for Film and Video*. Studio City, California: Michael Wiese Productions, 1997.

Silver, Alain and Elizabeth Ward. *The Film Director's Team*. Los Angeles: Silman-James, 1992.

MICROPHONES, RECORDING, AND SOUND

Bartlett, Bruce and Jenny Bartlett. *Practical Recording Techniques 2nd Ed*. Boston: Focal Press, 1998.

Bartlett, Bruce and Jenny Bartlett. *On Location Recording Techniques*. Boston: Focal Press, 1999.

Borwick, John. *Sound Recording Practice 4th Ed*. Oxford & New York: Oxford University Press, 1994.

Huber, David Miles. *Modern Recording Techniques 5th Ed*. Boston: Focal Press, 2001.

Lyver, Des and Graham Swainson. *Basics of Video Sound 2nd Ed.* Boston: Focal Press, 1999.

Nisbett, Alec. *The Sound Studio 6th Ed.* Boston: Focal Press, 1994.

Pendergast, Roy M. *Film Music: A Neglected Art 2nd Ed.* New York: W. W. Norton, 1992.

Rumsey, Francis. *The Audio Station Handbook.* Boston: Focal Press, 1996.

Rumsey, Francis. *Sound and Sound Recording: An Introduction 3rd Ed.* Boston: Focal Press, 1997.

Watkinson, John. *The Art of Digital Recording 2nd Ed.* Oxford & Boston: Focal Press, 1993.

Watkinson, John. *An Introduction to Digital Audio.* Boston: Focal Press, 2001.

White, Glenn D. *The Audio Dictionary.* Seattle: University of Washington Press, 1991.

EDITING

Anderson, Gary H. *Video Editing and Post Production: A Professional Guide 4th Ed.* Boston: Focal Press, 1998.

Bayes, Steve. *The Avid Handbook: Techniques for the Avid Media Composer and Avid Express 3rd Ed.* Boston: Focal Press, 2000.

Browne, Steven E. *Nonlinear Editing Basics: Electronic Film and Video Editing.* Boston: Focal Press, 2001.

Burder, John. *The Technique of Editing 16mm Films.* Boston: Focal Press, 1990.

Collins, Mike. *ProTools: Practical Recording, Editing, and Mixing for Music Production.* Boston: Focal Press, 2001.

Dancyger, Ken. *The Technique of Film and Video Editing: Theory and Practice 3rd Ed.* Boston: Focal Press, 2001.

Murch, Walter. *In the Blink of an Eye: A Perspective on Film Editing.* Los Angeles: Silman-James, 2001.

Ohanian, Thomas A. *Digital Nonlinear Editing: Editing Film and Video on the Desktop 2nd Ed.* Boston: Focal Press, 1998.

Oldham, Gabriella. *First Cut: Conversations with Film Editors.* Berkeley, California: University of California Press, 1995.

Reisz, Karel and Gavin Millar. *The Technique of Film Editing 2nd Ed.* Boston: Focal Press, 1995.

Rosenblum, Ralph. *When the Shooting Stops, the Cutting Begins.* New York: Penguin, 1981.

Rubin, Michael. *Nonlinear: A Guide to Digital Film and Video Editing 4th Ed.* Gainesville, Florida: Triad Publications, 2000.

Solomons, Tony. *The Avid Digital Editing Room Handbook.* Los Angeles: Silman-James, 1999.

MUSIC

Russell, Mark and James Young. *Film Music.* Boston: Focal Press, 2000.

FINANCE, PRODUCTION, AND DISTRIBUTION

Cones, John W. *Film Finance and Distribution: A Dictionary of Terms.* Los Angeles, Silman-James, 1992.

Gates, Richard. *Production Management for Film and Video 2nd Ed.* Boston: Focal Press, 1995.

Houghton, Buck. *What a Producer Does: The Art of Moviemaking (Not the Business).* Los Angeles: Silman-James, 1991.

Koster, Robert J. *The On Production Budget Book.* Boston: Focal Press, 1997.

Lazarus, Paul N. III. *The Film Producer.* New York: St. Martin's Press, 1992.

Levison, Louise. *Filmmakers and Financing: Business Plans for Independents 3rd Ed.* Boston: Focal Press, 2001.

Litwak, Mark. *Dealmaking in the Film and Television Industry from Negotiations to Final Contracts 2nd Ed.* Los Angeles: Silman-James, 2002.

Ohanian, Thomas A. and Michael E. Phillips. *Digital Filmmaking: The Changing Art and Craft of Making Motion Pictures 2nd Ed.* Boston: Focal Press, 2000.

Rosen, David. *Off-Hollywood: The Making and Marketing of Independent Films.* New York: Grove/Atlantic, 1990.

Russo, John. *How to Make and Market Your Own Feature Movie for $10,000 or Less.* New York: Barclay House, 1994.

Singleton, Ralph. *Film Budgeting.* Los Angeles: Lone Eagle, 1994.

Wiese, Michael. *Film and Video Financing.* Boston: Focal Press, 1992.

Wiese, Michael. *Film and Video Marketing.* Studio City, California: Michael Wiese Productions, 1989.

Wiese, Michael. *The Independent Filmmakers' Guide 2nd Ed.* Studio City, California: Michael Wiese Productions, 1997.

Wiese, Michael and Deke Simon. *Film and Video Budgets 3rd Ed.* Studio City, California: Michael Wiese Productions, 2001.

EDUCATION AND CAREER POSSIBILITIES

Bayer, William. *Breaking Through, Selling Out, Dropping Dead.* New York: Limelight Editions, 1989.

Bone, Jan and Kathy Siebel. *Film Careers.* Lincolnwood, Illinois: NTC Publications, 1998.

Bone, Jan and Julie Rigby. *Opportunities in Film Careers.* Lincolnwood, Illinois: NTC Publications, 1999.

Horwin, Michael. *Careers in Film and Video Production.* Boston: Focal Press, 1990.

Kelly, Karen and Tom Edgar. *Film School Confidential: The Insider's Guide to Film Schools.* New York: Berkley Publishing Group, 1997.

Laskin, Emily, ed. *Getting Started in Film.* New York: Prentice-Hall, 1992.

Lazarus, Paul. *Working in Film.* New York: St. Martin's Press, 1993.

O'Donnell, Gail & Michele Travolta, eds. *Making It in Hollywood.* Naperville, Illinois: Sourcebooks, 1994.

Peterson's *Guides to Graduate Programs in the Humanities.* Stamford, Connecticut: Petersons (a division of Thomson Corporation), 2002.

USEFUL WEB SITES

Organizations

www.aivf.org	Association of Independent Video and Film Makers. Great information source for the low budget independent filmmaker.
www.afionline.org	American Film Institute, a center for archives, film studies, and film education.
www.bfi.org.uk	British Film Institute. Archives, publications and screenings.
www.cilect.org	CILECT (Centre International de Liaison des Ecoles de Cinéma et de Télévision) is the Brussels-based organization of international film schools, and it always has an interesting range of special projects going.
www.cinematography.com	Professional motion picture camera people, news, and resources.
www.facets.org	Facets Cinémathèque has 35,000 films of every kind for sale on tape or DVD. A helpful and knowledgeable organization with a passion for international and minority interest movies. Be sure to check that they have the tape you want in the format you can play. Consider banishing compatibility problems by getting a VHS international player, such as the AIWA HV MX-100, which will play any VHS PAL, SECAM, or NTSC format through any television set. When you want to record it will also convert NTSC to PAL or vice versa.
www.focalpress.com	Focal Press Web site for the newest books on media.
www.lcweb.loc.gov	Library of Congress.
www.soc.org	Society of Camera Operators site, information, booklists and links to other professional societies around the world.
www.ufva.org	University Film and Video Association, an organization for North American screen educators.
www.wga.org	Writers Guild of America site.

Informational Databases

www.allmovie.com	Another large movie database.
www.boxofficeguru.com	Box office and other statistics.

www.cineweb.com	Cineweb is a film production resource.
www.megahitmovies.com	Analysis of hits, scene by scene script analyses, agents, contests, magazines, resources.
www.us.imdb.com	Gargantuan movie database that enables every imaginable kind of production research, down to the careers of obscure technicians.

Screenwriting Resources

www.cinestory.com	Screenwriters' resource.
www.newcenturywriter.org	New Century writer awards.
www.screenplay.com	Screenwriting software download site.
www.screenstyle.com	Screenplay software center.
www.screenwriting.com	Screenwriters' resource with many links.
www.screenwritingexpo.com	Annual screenwriting exposition.
www.scriptsales.com	Columns, books, advice, contests, examples, agencies, links.
www.writersstore.com	Everything for writers including software.

Periodicals

www.backstage.com	Backstage magazine.
www.dv.com	Digital Video magazine. Excellent for software and equipment reviews and for keeping up to date with developments in the digital world.
www.filmlinc.com	Film Comment magazine.
www.theasc.com/magazine	American Cinematographer.
www.variety.com	Variety, the show business oracle. Get ready to learn a whole new vocabulary.
www.videomaker.com	Videomaker Magazine. Lots of good basic information.

INDEX